State and Tribe in Nineteenth-Century Afghanistan

HYDER KHAN, GOVERNOR OF GHUZNEE.
DOST MAHOMED KHAN.
MAHOMED AKRAM KHAN.

State and Tribe in Nineteenth-Century Afghanistan

The Reign of Amir Dost Muhammad Khan (1826–1863)

Christine Noelle

CURZON

First published in 1997
by Curzon Press
15 The Quadrant, Richmond
Surrey, TW9 1BP

Typeset in Sabon by LaserScript, Mitcham, Surrey

Printed in Great Britain by
TJ Press International, Padstow, Cornwall

British Library Cataloguing in Publication Data
A catalogue record for this book is available from the British Library

Library of Congress in Publication Data
A catalogue record for this book has been requested

ISBN 0–7007–0629–1

Frontispiece (from upper left to lower right):
Ghulam Haidar Khan, Amir Dost Muhammad Khan, Muhammad Akram Khan and 'Abd al-Ghani b. Nawwab 'Abd al-Jabbar Khan, sketched by Emily Eden in 1841

CONTENTS

ACKNOWLEDGEMENTS

The present work has grown out of a PhD dissertation submitted at U. C. Berkeley in 1995. My endeavor to gain a better understanding of the political setting in nineteenth-century Afghanistan has not only taken me across continents but has in many ways constituted a journey into the past for me. I would like to take this opportunity to thank all those who undertook to be my travelling companions in this process. I am grateful to my supervisors at U. C. Berkeley, Professors Hamid Algar, Ravan A. G. Farhadi and Ira Lapidus for their willingness to follow the circuitous route my project often took, in particular during its early stages. Professors Ludwig Adamec, Ashraf Ghani, Hasan Kakar, Sayed Qassem Reshtia, Anuradha Sareen, Tilak Raj Sareen, Nazif Shahrani, Kulbhushan Warikoo and Malcolm Yapp gave me valuable guidance in the formulation of my research topic and directed me to relevant source materials. Ivan Midgley's constructive criticism helped me to keep my bearings throughout the writing process. I also wish to thank my family and my friends for their encouragement and confidence in my work, and for keeping me in touch with the present as well.

My research in London and Delhi was made possible by a Fulbright-Hays DDRA grant in 1989-90. I am indebted to Professor Bert G. Fragner and the Otto Friedrich Universität of Bamberg for supporting the latest phase of my research and writing. Special thanks go to the personnel of the India Office Library in London, the National Archives of India at Delhi and the Bayerische Staatsbibliothek in Munich. The frontispiece of this book was reproduced with the permission of the Bibliotheca Afghanica in Liestal, Switzerland. I am grateful to Malcolm Yapp, Jonathan Lee, E. J. Brill and the Nordic Institute of Asian Studies for the permission to reproduce maps and charts.

Finally, I would like to thank Malcolm Campbell of Curzon Press and LaserScript for their attentiveness and patience in seeing the publication of this work through.

PREFACE

Afghanistan – Land of Legends! Legends of the Afghans' unquenchable spirit of freedom; legends of the Pashtuns' proud customary law unbroken by the precepts of orthodox Islam; legends of 'Afghanistan' a historical entity, which can be traced to antiquity by a variety of other names: Ariana, subjugated by the Achaemenids; Bactria, the glorious empire of the Kushans; Khurasan, oppressed by the Sasanians, unconquered by the Arabs; the mighty and glorious empire of Mahmud of Ghazna; periods of oppression by the Mongols, Turkmens and Safavids; the foundation of Afghanistan by Ahmad Shah Durrani in the mid-eighteenth century; later, freedom struggles against the British; and, finally, resistance to the Soviet Union. The Afghans: a people often oppressed and tormented, but ultimately invincible!

So much for the legends. The author of the present work has employed the tools, knowledge and ardour of an academic historian to retrieve historical fact from the twilight of legends. The political entity founded as Afghanistan in 1747 – formally a royal dominion based on tribal affiliation with the other Pashtun tribes – was in fact one of many political formations which were based on the military clout of tribal confederacies and afflicted by an inherent instability. The military prowess of these confederacies was constantly on the verge of being paralysed by political altercations breaking out among the component tribes.

By the beginning of the nineteenth century it seemed as though Afghanistan had already reached the end of its history. Internal discord had rendered the empire powerless, the rich Indian provinces had been lost. Then in 1826 a ruler came to power who did not rest his attempt at state building solely on the question, 'State or tribe?', but rather sought to extend his base of power beyond tribal allegiances. Dost Muhammad Knan, a Pashtun from the Muhammadzai lineage, proclaimed himself *amir al-muʾmenin*, 'commander of (all) the faithful', staged *jihad* (against the heathen Sikhs) and set out to undermine the monopoly that the tribal warriors held over military affairs. Attempts at structural modernization and the first major confrontation with the British colonial empire were soon to follow.

The creation and maintenance of a precarious balance between honouring Pashtun tribal loyalties and transforming the non-Pashtun population into obedient subjects – this was the task Dost Muhammad Khan's political establishment recognized and tried to implement. In these policies we may discern the political beginnings of modern Afghanistan, for Dost Muhammad Khan's dynasty lasted one and a half centuries, twice as long as the once so powerful Soviet Union. The dichotomy between the martial power of Pashtun tribes and the endeavour of the non-Pashtun ethnic groups to be placed on an equal footing has not been solved to the present day. In Dost Muhammad Khan's time this problem was first understood.

Christine Noelle has successfully probed this decisive period of Afghan history. The resulting book is the first systematic analysis of the beginnings of a state system that since the 1930s has been seeking to realise itself as a modern nation-state, fluctuating between tribalism and ethnic pluralistic participation. This book teaches us much more about Afghanistan than the existing wealth of romanticising descriptions, all of which fail to appreciate the salience of politics in society and thus continue to give sustenance to the legends. I consider this book an auspicious step towards the unveiling of the history of Afghanistan.

Professor Dr Bert Georg Fragner
Department of Iranian Studies
Otto Friedrich University at Bamberg
1997

ABBREVIATIONS

1. PRINTED BOOKS

EI (1,2, G, S)	1: *Encyclopaedia of Islam.* 1st ed. 2: *Encyclopaedia of Islam.* New ed. G: German Edition S: *Shorter Encyclopaedia of Islam.* Leiden: E. J. Brill
EIr	*Encyclopaedia Iranica.* Edited by Ehsan Yarshater. London: Routledge and Kegan Paul
Gaz I-VI	Adamec, Ludwig (1972–1985), *Historical and Political Gazetteer of Afghanistan.* 6 vols. Graz: Akademische Verlags- und Druckanstalt.
SM	Sultan Muhammad (ed.) (1980), *The Life of Abdur Rahman, Amir of Afghanistan.* 2 vols. Karachi: Oxford University Press.
ST	Faiż Muḥammad (1912), *Sirāj al-tawārīkh.* Kabul: Government Press.
TB	Badakhshī, Mīrzā Sang Muḥammad and Mīrzā Afżal ᶜAlī Beg Surkh Afsar (n.d.), *Tārīkh-i Badakhshān*, edited by Manūchihr Sutūda.
TSu	Sulṭān Muḥammad Khān b. Musā Durrānī (1881), *Tārīkh-i sulṭānī.* Bombay: Kārkhāna-yi Muḥammadī.
TT	ᶜAbd al-Raḥman Khan (n. d.), *Tāj al-tawārīkh, yaᶜnī sawāniḥ-i ᶜumrī-yi aᶜlāḥażrat Amīr ᶜAbd al-Raḥmān Khān.* Kabul.

2. ARCHIVAL RECORDS

ABC	Afghan Boundary Commission (1885–1886)
AJN	Abstract of Jalalabad News
AKN	Abstract of Kabul News
EJN	Extracts from Jalalabad News

EKN	Extracts from Kabul News
EQN	Extracts from Qandahar News
JI	Jalalabad Intelligence
JN	Jalalabad News
KD	Kabul Diary
KI	Kabul Intelligence
KN	Kabul News
QM	Qandahar Mission
QN	Qandahar News

3. PERIODICALS

Afghanistan J.	*Afghanistan Journal*
AQR	*Asiatic Quarterly Review*
BSOAS	*Bulletin of the School of Oriental and African Studies*
HJ	*Historical Journal*
JASB	*Journal of the Asiatic Society of Bengal*
JRAS	*Journal of the Royal Asiatic Society*
JRGS	*Journal of the Royal Geographical Society London*
RGS	*Royal Geographical Society London*

INTRODUCTION

This study aims at reconstructing the political setting in Afghanistan during the reign of the first Muhammadzai ruler, Amir Dost Muhammad Khan (r. 1826–1863). Apart from establishing a chronological framework for the period in question, it explores the relationship between the Amir and the groups he sought to control both from the perspectives of the center and the periphery. By taking a detailed look at the workings of the Muhammadzai system of government and the ways in which it affected the local leadership, I hope to create an understanding of the configurations of power prevailing in nineteenth-century Afghanistan.

In the previous century, the term 'Afghan' was reserved for the large ethnic group generally known as 'Pashtun' today, of which the Abdali/Durrani and Ghilzai confederacies formed two major components. The other Pashtun groups to be discussed are the so-called eastern or border tribes located on the fringe of the territories claimed by the Sikhs and, after 1849, by the British. Apart from its crystallization as an ethnic term, the designation 'Afghan' had also gained a political connotation with the rise of the Sadozai empire in the middle of the eighteenth century. In 1747 Ahmad Khan, a member of the Sadozai subdivision of the Abdali/Durrani confederacy, used the disintegration of Nadir Shah's empire to lay claim to the lands east of Nishapur, in the conquest of which he had assisted the Iranian king less than a decade earlier. While the Durrani empire originated with the ascendance of Ahmad Khan, later Ahmad Shah, the political role of the Sadozais and other influential Durrani and Ghilzai tribes can be traced to the late sixteenth and early seventeenth centuries, when their chiefs acted as intermediaries for Mughal and Safawid interests. Like Ahmad Shah, the leaders of these groups had played a prominent role in Nadir Shah's army, and the Sadozai king could only maintain his claims to supremacy over them by making them privileged partners of his expansionist policies.

During the period which forms the focus of this study, the ruling Sadozai family was deposed by another influential Durrani subdivision, the Muhammadzai Barakzais. This transition of power was accompanied by a prolonged period of civil war which not only weakened the state-supporting Durrani elite but also left the new ruler of Kabul, Amir Dost Muhammad Khan, with considerably fewer resources than his Sadozai predecessors. In his endeavor to consolidate his authority, the Amir alternately resorted to strategies of conciliation and confrontation. The first group affected by his policies were his half brothers and nephews holding Peshawar, Jalalabad, Ghazni and Qandahar. In the second place, the Amir's increasing reach into the rural areas located between these urban seats of power brought him into closer contact with the tribal groups controlling the approaches to Kabul. For this reason, the analysis of the political circumstances characterizing Dost Muhammad Khan's reign requires an understanding of the position and strength of the groups he was interacting with. Wherever a sufficient density of data has allowed me to do so, I have attempted to shed light on their internal organization, the contours of the local leadership and its attitudes towards the central rulers.

Not all the groups Dost Muhammad Khan interacted with may be termed 'tribal'. Yet, given the British preoccupation with the Pashtuns, there is a greater amount information available on these groups, considered 'tribes' par excellence, than the 'peasantized' Tajiks, Farsiwans and Hazaras inhabiting the core region of the Muhammadzai kingdom.[1] North of the Hindu Kush, in the area known as Lesser Turkistan, the Amir encountered ethnic groups of Turkic origin, such as the Uzbeks and Turkmens. In the twentieth century, only certain Uzbek groups, such as the Qataghan of the Qunduz region, have been classified as 'tribal'. During the period prior to the Muhammadzai invasion of 1849 the Uzbeks of Lesser Turkistan derived their political identity from their affiliation with one or the other of a number of independent or semi-independent khanates which had sprung up with the decline of Bukharan authority from the late seventeenth century on.

Dost Muhammad Khan seems to have considered the petty Uzbek principalities in the north less formidable adversaries than the powerful Pashtun groups controlling the southern trade route with Qandahar. At any rate, his military campaigns against Balkh from 1845 on preceded his attempts to enforce his authority among the Hotak and Tokhi Ghilzais by several years. Beyond this, however, there is no evidence that the Amir's military progress and the local responses it elicited took a radically different form in Lesser Turkistan than in the Pashtun areas experiencing royal pressure for revenues. In other words, local reactions to Dost Muhammad Khan's presence were apparently less affected by 'ethnic' factors than the wider political setting which determined the strength of the government presence and the range of strategies open to those resisting it. For the Uzbeks of Lesser Turkistan, Bukhara in the north and Herat and Iran in the west represented alternative centers of power, particularly during the first half of the nineteenth century. South of Kabul, the Hotak and Tokhi

Ghilzais profited from the rivalry between the Amir and his half brothers at Qandahar, who in turned received backing from the Qajar rulers of Iran. With the incorporation of Qandahar into Dost Muhammad Khan's realm, the region bordering on Herat became the scene of shifting allegiances.

Located along the fringes of British control, the Pashtuns in particular held the colonial imagination. While offering valuable insights into Pashtun history and organization, travelogues and political reports from the nineteenth and early twentieth centuries have also had the effect of creating some of the most enduring stereotypes. The notions of the greater group of Pashtuns as 'republican', 'turbulent' and 'hungry' hillmen still influence some of the modern historiography, which continues to play on the fascination the 'Khyber' exercises on western minds to the present day. In this body of literature, all of Afghanistan is incorporated into the local perspective of British frontier officials and is thus viewed as an extension of the circumstances prevailing in the region immediately west of Peshawar. Waller, for example, holds the 'crazy-quilt tribal structure' of Afghanistan responsible for the frustrated British efforts to reestablish the Sadozai ruler Shah Shuja' during the First Anglo-Afghan War of 1839–1842.[2] In the same vein, Singer characterizes Dost Muhammad Khan's reign subsequent to this war as 'devoted to the traditional Pushtun pastime of family and tribal feuding'.[3] The idea of Afghan invincibility is reinforced by modern Afghan and Soviet historians, who, rather than emphasizing the unpredictability of tribal politics, view the determined resistance of the Afghan 'masses' to colonialization as epitomized by the First and Second Anglo-Afghan Wars of 1839–1842 and 1878–1880 in the light of nascent Afghan nationalism and patriotism. The premises of both approaches certainly contain a grain of truth. The creation of the Afghan state in its present outlines was brought about in great part by the difficulty the Afghan terrain presented, both geographically and politically speaking, in the face of foreign intervention. Even more so, however, Dost Muhammad Khan owed his success in consolidating his authority to a switch in British outlook from a program of 'forward policy' to one of 'masterly inactivity'.

This study is less concerned with the factors determining British policy towards Afghanistan than the internal circumstances prevailing within the country. Even so, the formative role the British played in shaping the political landscape in the wider region and the resulting historical narrative cannot be ignored. In Afghanistan, we encounter a curious deficit in this respect. Just as this country was never properly incorporated into the British empire, it remained in many ways veiled to the penetrating colonial eye. While the Indian historian constantly encounters the colonial heritage in the form of a well established discourse, the student of Afghan history is largely preoccupied with the elementary task of reconstructing the bare bones of the historical narrative on the basis of thin and often contradictory data. This holds particularly true for the period prior to the reign of Amir

'Abd al-Rahman Khan (1880–1901), which has so far only been dealt with in the course of general historical overviews or in the light of the two focal points of British interest, the First and Second Anglo-Afghan Wars. Another general shortcoming of the existing historiography on Afghanistan is that it mostly takes the viewpoint of the center. From this perspective, the 'tribes' generally assume phantom-like characteristics, appearing on the horizon of the narrative seemingly only when it is their business to 'vex' the government, subsequently withdrawing to some elusive 'island of disaffection'[4] again.

There are a number of notable exceptions to this rule. Apart from his research concerning British policymaking, Yapp has devoted several detailed studies to the local responses the British presence elicited during the First Anglo-Afghan War. For the region north of the Hindu Kush, Holzwarth's and Grevemeyer's works on the historical developments in Badakhshan need to be mentioned. The political setting of Lesser Turkistan has recently been analyzed by Lee and McChesney. The goal of my work is to provide a fuller picture concerning the relationships of power prevailing in all the provinces making up Dost Muhammad Khan's realm. For this purpose, I have attempted to elucidate both the perspectives of the government and the groups it was interacting with. The contact between these two entities being mediated by the local leadership, I have paid special attention to its historical origins and the ways its position and outlook were affected by Dost Muhammad Khan's expansion of authority. In the study of Lesser Turkistan, I have combined the information available from the published histories with my own data gleaned from British documents and Persian sources. My analysis of the Amir's relationship with the Pashtuns rests in great part on hitherto unpublished materials and thus sheds light on a domain that has largely been uncharted so far. My aim in presenting these materials is to place the discussion concerning the interaction between state and tribe in nineteenth-century Afghanistan on a firmer footing, to furnish background information for the developments during the present century, and, finally, to allow comparisons with tribalism in other Middle Eastern countries.

Throughout my research I have been intensely aware of the problems besetting any endeavor to establish a 'grip' over or to impose 'order' on a setting as large and variable as that of Afghanistan. In the chapter concerning the position of the Pashtuns my approach has been guided in great part by Janata's warning against an uncritical generalization of locally observed phenomena, which ignores differences inherent in the political organization of sedentary and nomadic groups, the uneven impact of colonialization, as well as historical developments which tend to give each region its unique 'stamp'.[5] The historical case materials I have put together corroborate Janata's statement. Labels like 'segmentary' and 'acephalous', as generally applied to the Pashtuns, only assume meaning if linked to a careful analysis of the socioeconomic and political circumstances that produce a specific tribal texture. While all Pashtun tribes formally adhered to the genealogical principles typical of the segmentary lineage organization, only the groups located at a certain, and, at Dost Muhammad Khan's time, 'safe' distance from the seats of government approximated the ideal of balanced opposition closely. Among the Pashtun tribes maintaining a greater degree of interaction with the Amir, by contrast, the factors shaping the nature of leadership and tribal identity tended to be of a political origin. Thus the powerful Pashtun tribes, which were arranged along the major trade routes like 'pearls on a string', were characterized by a much greater amount of internal stratification than their counterparts in the more inaccessible regions. While genealogical reasoning continued to inform the tribal world view of the prominent sections of the Mohmand, Ghilzai and Durrani Pashtuns, it served primarily to bolster the hereditary prerogatives of entrenched leading lineages. Though subject to constant competition, positions of paramount leadership were only accessible for members of the local elite. This is not to say that contenders for power could not rely on segmentary processes of fission and fusion to work in their favor. In addition to proving their qualities as leaders, however, they had to be able to point to a suitable pedigree and to demonstrate their ability to garner external support, e.g. through connections with the royal court. The last element added importance to matrilateral ties, the significance of which is generally obscured by the emphasis segmentary ideology places on patrilineal descent.

Therefore, tribalism in nineteenth-century Afghanistan may be looked at from different angles. On the one hand, the lack of political centralization prevailing in Dost Muhammad Khan's kingdom lends itself to interpretations in the light of the theory of segmentary lineage organization and the related concept of 'political segmentation'. Unable to enforce a steady government presence 'on the ground', the Amir had to rely on the assistance of local middlemen to give substance to his claims to authority. This web of personal loyalties could only be maintained by the distribution of privileges, and its stability was a function of the king's ability to obtain and dispense wealth.[6] On the other hand, this royal largesse fostered inequalities on the tribal level, as the recipients of such government favors acquired a social standing far above that of their fellow tribesmen. Government patronage thus had a fundamental impact on the local configurations of power, bringing forth an entrenched and hereditary leadership.

While I have attempted to weave the available data into a narrative from the local point of view, I have consciously abstained from 'streamlining' them to fit one theory or another. Rather, it is my object to convey a sense of the cumulative processes at work in Dost Muhammad Khan's kingdom by depicting a whole range of tribal settings. This conceptual framework has to be reconciled with the need to keep track of the impulses emanating from the royal capital. Accordingly, I have attempted to link the description of the sociopolitical circumstances in the periphery with a chronological account of the Amir's consolidation of power, the milestones of which were the conquests of Balkh, Qandahar and Herat in 1849, 1855 and 1863 respectively.

Chapter 1 depicts the political setting in Afghanistan at the time of Dost Muhammad Khan's rise to power, tracing the origins of the prominent Durrani and Qizilbash leadership and investigating its position up to the conclusion of the First Anglo-Afghan War. Furthermore, the data collected by the British observer Masson allow a fairly detailed description of the Hazara region of Bihsud at the time of Dost Muhammad Khan's first reign.

Chapter 2 begins with a description of the origins of the Uzbek elite of Lesser Turkistan and discusses its changing status under Muhammadzai rule.

Chapter 3 analyzes the internal organization of a number of Pashtun groups and sheds light on their position during the reigns of Dost Muhammad Khan and his successor Sher 'Ali Khan.

Chapter 4 discusses the fortunes of the Durrani leadership of Qandahar and, returning to the viewpoint of the center, explores the nature of Dost Muhammad Khan's administration.

This narrative does not include a detailed description of the situation of Herat, which was incorporated into the Muhammadzai domain only thirteen days prior to Dost Muhammad Khan's death. The political events which befell this city between 1796 and 1863 have been treated in a detailed fashion by Champagne. From the viewpoint of the Muhammadzais, Herat only assumed critical importance during the era of Amir Sher 'Ali Khan (1863–1878), the analysis of which will be reserved for a future date.

A NOTE ON THE SOURCES

Given the fragmentary and often contradictory nature of the available sources concerning Dost Muhammad Khan's reign, this study represents an attempt at describing the political setting in nineteenth-century Afghanistan as closely as possible on the basis of a variety of materials. The sources I have consulted fall into four major categories: works produced by Afghan authors, mostly unpublished British documents, reports published by British officials and other European observers, and modern ethnographic studies.

In 1864–65 Sultan Muhammad b. Musa Barakzai wrote *Tarikh-i sultani* (TSu) concerning the history of the Pashtuns from their genealogical beginnings to the First Anglo-Afghan War. The most valuable Afghan source is *Siraj al-tawarikh* (ST), a chronicle of Afghan history beginning with the ascendancy of Ahmad Shah Sadozai, which was compiled by Faiz

Muhammad b. Sa'id Muhammad Mughul, a scholar in the service of Amir Habibullah Khan, in the early twentieth century. Dost Muhammad Khan's period is also discussed in the introductory chapters of a number of other histories produced by Afghan authors. The *Tarikh-i padshahan-i muta'akhir* was written roughly at the same time as *Siraj al-tawarikh* by Mirza Ya'qub 'Ali Khafi (b. 1850), a former official of Amir Sher 'Ali Khan, who had to flee to Samarqand following Sardar Muhammad Ishaq Khan's unsuccessful rebellion in 1888. Nur Muhammad Nuri of Qandahar devoted a biography entitled *Gulshan-i imarat* to his contemporary Sher 'Ali Khan, which spans the period from the birth of the future Amir in 1823 to the first two years of his second reign beginning in 1868. Muhammad Yusuf Riyazi Harawi (1873–1911) described the events unfolding in the region of Herat between 1792 and 1906 in a work entitled *'Ain al-waqayi'*. The events accompanying the decline of Sadozai power and the rise of the Muhammadzais in the early nineteenth century have been described by one of the central historical figures, Shah Shuja' Sadozai.[7] Also noteworthy are two epics commemorating the events of the First Anglo-Afghan War, the *Akbarnama* by Hamid Kashmiri and the *Jangnama* by Muhammad Ghulam Kohistani Ghulami. *Taj al-tawarikh* (TT), the autobiography of Amir 'Abd al-Rahman Khan, provides some insights into the early policies of the Muhammadzai Sardars in Lesser Turkistan. In the 1920s Burhan al-Din Kushkaki, an official at Amir Amanullah Khan's court, produced the *Rahnama-yi Qataghan wa Badakhshan*, a gazetteer containing useful information concerning the political history and administration of this region. The historical events of Badakhshan in the seventeenth and eighteenth centuries are described in Mirza Sang Muhammad Badakhshi's *Tarikh-i Badakhshan*. The data available from the older Afghan sources has been rounded off and commented upon by modern Afghan historians, such as Farhang, Ghubar, Habibi, Kakar, Kohzad and Reshtia. Fofalzai's detailed studies of the reigns of Timur Shah and Shah Zaman provide a useful basis for understanding the Sadozai state system. Unfortunately, the present political situation in Afghanistan has made it impossible for me to gain access to Afghan archival sources. Another set of Persian sources, the works by nineteenth-century Iranian authors dealing with the events in western Afghanistan and Lesser Turkistan, has not been utilized to the extent it deserves.

The greater part of my data concerning the political setting in Afghanistan has been derived from sources of European, mostly British provenance. My access to Russian works has been restricted to works available in English translation. In the course of my research at the India Office Library (IOL) in London and the National Archives of India (NAI) in Delhi I had the opportunity to study mostly unpublished British records. The respective holdings of of IOL and NAI have been discussed in a detailed fashion by Hall (1981) and Kakar (1979). At the IOL I studied the

Elphinstone Collection, i. e. the materials gathered by the Elphinstone Mission to Shah Shuja''s court in 1808–9, and the Masson Papers named after the British national who first visited Afghanistan in the late 1820s, resided in Kabul from 1832 to 1838, and became a British newswriter in 1835. At the IOL, the unpublished newsletters and diaries produced by British agents with increasing frequency and detail from the 1830s on are contained in large volumes entitled 'Secret Letters and Enclosures from India' and are coded as L/P&S/5. The political and secret correspondence conducted with India after 1875 forms the L/P&S/7 series. The official memoranda are included in L/P&S/18. At the National Archives of India, the proceedings of the Foreign and Political Department of the Government of India contain all the correspondence of Britain, India and Afghanistan. They are primarily organized under the headings For. Sec., For. S. I., For. Pol. A and are indexed according to topic.

The third category of my sources is made up by works mostly published in the British Empire in the course of the nineteenth and early twentieth centuries. Among these, three kinds may be distinguished:

a) the narratives produced by members of official missions to Afghanistan, such as the ones headed by Elphinstone in 1808–9, Burnes in 1832–33 and 1837–38, and Lumsden in 1857–58;
b) the reports by British officials either stationed inside Afghanistan during the first two Anglo-Afghan wars or, during more peaceful periods, assigned to posts along the British frontier;
c) travelogues written by private visitors to the region, such as Vambéry, Ferrier etc.

Another invaluable published source is Adamec's *Historical and Political Gazetteer of Afghanistan*, in which a great part of the information available from the above three sources is incorporated.

While there is thus no lack of contemporary materials, they tend to be of varying usefulness. Many of the observations, mostly made in the course of journeys or based on second-hand information, lack depth and accuracy. In order to gain a better understanding of the factors shaping tribal organization I have turned to a fourth category of source materials, recent ethnographic studies. Apart from providing insights into present-day styles of leadership and their origins, the works of Centlivres, Centlivres-Demont and Rasuly-Paleczek on the Uzbeks, and Ahmed, Anderson, Barth, Christensen, Glatzer and Lindholm on the Pashtuns also contain useful information concerning the historical events of given regions. The materials compiled by Rasuly-Paleczek on the basis of interviews with the leadership of the Chechka Uzbeks, for example, provide a glimpse of the historical developments of the Qataghan region otherwise not available from written sources. Tapping the tribal perspective in this manner provides an alternative narrative to the one presented by the court historians, who, relating history from the viewpoint of the government, project the idea of the Muhammadzai state as a unified system. The tribal perspective, on the other hand, is strongly informed by the way a given group perceives its position in the world. Accordingly, historical events tend to be ordered to conform with tribal ideals of self-determination. While providing insights into local politics, the resulting narrative hardly reflects larger political processes at work.

This brings up the question of the relationship between 'oral' and 'written' information in the sources consulted. The court historian Faiz Muhammad is a case in point. Describing the political setting of Afghanistan from the goverment perspective, he relied on written sources like the Imam al-Din Husaini's *Tarikh-i husain shahi,* Muhammad Hayat Khan's *Hayat-i afghani*, and *Tarikh-i sultani*, as well as court documents. His information concerning Herat was derived in part from Iranian sources, such as Riza Quli Khan's *Rauzat al-safa-yi nasiri* and Muhammad Taqi Sipihr Lisan al-Mulk's *Nasikh al-tawarikh*. At the same time, there are indications that Faiz Muhammad also had access to oral information. He was personally acquainted with some of the younger members of the Muhammadzai family, such as Sardars Muhammad Yusuf Khan b. Amir Dost Muhammad Khan (b. 1845) and Nur 'Ali Khan b. Sher 'Ali Qandahari. Their reminiscences, as well the oral accounts of earlier events current in their families, were incorporated into *Siraj al-tawarikh*. This might help to explain why many of the dates given are inaccurate.

Among the British authors, Faiz Muhammad's counterpart is Raverty (1888), who attempted to reconstruct local Pashtun history on the basis of Persian sources partly dating back to Mughal times. Court documents obtained by the British during the First and Second Anglo-Afghan Wars also belong to the category of written information. With most of the British literature, however, one cannot help being struck by the 'oral' nature of the information collected. Apart from repeating the correspondence read at the Amir's court, the reports submitted by British and Indian officials ring with gossip and rumors and often echo the particular biases of their informants. As a rule the written sources the British observers came across were few and far between. Lord, a member of Burnes's mission of 1837–38 summed up his efforts to reconstruct the political career of the Uzbek ruler Mir Murad Beg in the early nineteenth century in the following manner:

> My materials ... have been altogether traditionary, and have been derived from some of the principal actors in the latter scenes described, of whom I may particularize the Meer himself, his brother Mahomed Beg, and his former rival but present subject Meer Walee. For documentary evidence I made every search but totally without success, unless indeed we except an old deed of the sale of land which I got from the Meer himself, and a list of the Oorooghs into which the tribe was divided...[8]

During the period prior to the First Anglo-Afghan War, British intelligence concerning the internal political developments of Afghanistan was generally poor. The occupation of Afghanistan in 1839 and the missions preceding it, by contrast, furnished the Indian government with a unique opportunity to gather information. With the withdrawal of the British troops in 1842 the flow of political news all but dried up again. This situation improved somewhat in 1849, when the annexation of Punjab brought the British into immediate contact with the Afghan frontier. From this point on, the political diaries compiled at Peshawar and the reports submitted by newswriters based in Kabul, Jalalabad and Qandahar began to furnish a greater variety of news. Another source of information were a number of informants, including members of the royal family, who corresponded with the British representatives stationed on the frontier. Even so, the British authorities were far from satisfied with the kind of intelligence they received. On the occasion of the conclusion of the Anglo-Afghan Treaty of 1855, Governor General Dalhousie expressed the hope that the improved relations with the Afghan government also offered brighter prospects for the British endeavor to gain more accurate information on Afghanistan and Central Asia, as, in his opinion, the reports submitted by the newswriter stationed in Kabul had been 'of very little authority or value' so far.[9] Indeed the ratification of this treaty in 1856 gave the British representative Khan Bahadur Fatih Khan Khatak and other members of his mission the opportunity to visit Qandahar and to gather information concerning Dost Muhammad Khan's government.[10] The Anglo-Afghan Treaty of Friendship concluded in 1857 stipulated that a British mission was to monitor the expenditure of British subsidies for the modernization of the Afghan army. This led to the Qandahar Mission under Lumsden in the spring of 1857, which, owing to the Indian Mutiny breaking out shortly afterwards, was to remain in Qandahar for a little over a year. The treaty of 1857 also provided for the exchange of representatives (*wakils*) between Kabul and Peshawar. The *wakils* deputed to Kabul during Dost Muhammad Khan's time were Faujdar Khan (1857–1860) and Bahadur Ghulam Hasan Khan 'Alizai (1860–1865), who allegedly were Pashtuns from Multan.[11] The presence of these *wakils* at Kabul had the effect that the ordinary newsletters were complemented by the so-called Kabul Diary.

While the quantity of information available to the British authorities thus increased significantly, the general problems besetting their efforts to gain reliable intelligence remained much the same. For one thing, the British observers found themselves closely monitored by the Afghan government, which also determined the flow of news. In Qandahar, the Lumsden Mission was housed within the citadel and was 'completely shut in from access to, or communication with, the city, except through the heir-apparent's guards... '[12] Pointing to the necessity to protect the members of the mission from an allegedly hostile, truculent and fanatic population, the heir apparent Sardar Ghulam Haidar Khan effectively controlled all their outside contacts:

> we can only derive information from such men as the it may suit the Sirdar's views to allow to come to me [Lumsden], and the greatest caution is necessary to avoid raising suspicion. For although we are at liberty to run about the country as much as we please, still there is no disguising the fact that all who approach us are watched with extreme jealousy.[13]

The local newswriters and the *wakil* at Kabul faced similar restrictions. Up to the time of Dost Muhammad Khan's successor Sher 'Ali Khan it was generally understood that any British Indian agent 'who took a perfectly independent tone at Cabul and made no secret of reporting regularly to his Government without reference to the wishes of the Ameer all information that he believed to be correct would very shortly find his position unbearable.'[14] Acutely aware of their precarious position, the British agents mostly relied on the news fed to them by the royal court and did not dare to cultivate alternative sources of information openly.

The second problem the British faced was that the information obtained did not cover all regions of Afghanistan in an even manner. Thus the intelligence gathered from court proceedings and bazaar rumors at Kabul, backed up by news from Jalalabad and Peshawar, generally proved to be fairly reliable for the areas bordering on British India. With increasing distance from the British seats of administration, however, the available information became more sketchy. Just as the Amir or his representatives determined what kinds of news were communicated to the *wakil* or local newswriter, his provincial governors, such as Sardar Muhammad Afzal Khan in Turkistan, controlled the flow of information to the capital. As Turkistan was separated from Kabul by difficult communications, occasional reports by the merchants plying the trade route to Bukhara provided the only alternative source of information. Another difficulty in the study of British documents is the lack of homogeneity. The primary concern of the newswriters was to depict the crises besetting Dost Muhammad Khan's administration. Routine aspects of government, by contrast, seem to have appeared less noteworthy to them. As a result, rural settings only entered the narrative when their inhabitants attracted royal attention by rebellious behavior. Once the crisis was resolved from the government point of view, the circumstances in the area in question also ceased to be a newsworthy item. For this reason, conclusions concerning the nature of Dost Muhammad Khan's government have to be based at least in part on negative inferences. For example, if there was no news on Ghazni, it is likely that the routine administrative procedures were taking their ordinary course.

Because of the dependance of the British newswriters on information made available to them by the royal or provincial governments, their reports do not display a strikingly different perspective from native court historians like Faiz Muhammad. Like *Siraj al-tawarikh* the British documents chronicle events and shifts in power without yielding much information on the underlying processes which gave rise to these developments. However, their preoccupation with crises sets the British sources apart from the native chronicles. While the British reports emphasize moments of instability both in the center and the periphery, Faiz Muhammad rarely casts doubt on Dost Muhammad Khan's scope of authority. From his point of view, even nominal pledges of allegiance to the Amir are equated with 'obedience', and uprisings are categorized as instances of 'treason' deserving the royal punishment which inevitably follows. The British documents also differ from Faiz Muhammad's narrative in that–within the limitations described above–they pay greater attention to local affairs.

Most of my information concerning individual tribal groups has been gleaned from published and unpublished British sources. Thus we come up against the phenomenon that, although Afghanistan was never 'swallowed up' by the British Empire or incorporated as fully into the colonialist discourse as neighboring India, most of the data available concerning its history in the nineteenth century have been processed and passed along by British observers. The relative weight of the existing British narrative is also reflected in the histories produced by modern Afghan authors. My work is innovative in that it uses hitherto largely unstudied documents to investigate the local responses Dost Muhammad Khan's policies elicited. At the same time, my reliance on British sources places this study firmly within the context of the existing historiography on Afghanistan. Given the nature of my sources, it is evident that the political landscape as I have reconstructed it is profoundly influenced by the perspective of British colonialists, whose perceptions were shaped in great part by their cultural background and the political imperatives of their time. Following Lindholm's dictum that colonial ethnography is not merely to be seen as 'commentary upon itself',[15] I have endeavored to strip away this layer of colonial biases and to sift out the information relevant for my project of mapping the relationships of power in nineteenth century Afghanistan.

Chapter 1

DOST MUHAMMAD KHAN'S FIRST REIGN AND THE FIRST ANGLO-AFGHAN WAR

THE POLITICAL SETTING IN THE EARLY NINETEENTH CENTURY

Dost Muhammad Khan was formally proclaimed ruler of Kabul in 1834–5. But his reign unofficially began in 1826, when he was able to gain control of this city after a prolonged civil war. The first part of this chapter is concerned with the circumstances accompanying his rise to power, which marked the end of Sadozai supremacy and the beginning of the Muhammadzai era. In the second part, I will discuss the unsuccessful attempt of the British to reestablish the Sadozai ruler Shah Shuja' in the course of the First Anglo-Afghan War. The legitimacy of Dost Muhammad Khan's claims to kingship was not only challenged by his half brothers but was also called into question by the remaining Durrani elite, which had entertained close links with the Sadozai dynasty. This is not to say that Dost Muhammad Khan and his relatives were newcomers to the political arena in Afghanistan. As will be seen from my introductory discussion concerning the prominent subdivisions of the Durrani confederacy, the claims of the Muhammadzai Barakzais to leadership among the Durranis were as old as those of the Sadozais.

Shah Mahmud, the last sovereign Sadozai ruler of Kabul, was deposed in 1818, but the crumbling of Sadozai power had already begun in the final decade of the eighteenth century at a time when the Sadozai empire was barely fifty years old. Its founder, Ahmad Shah Sadozai had gainded ascendancy in Afghanistan in 1747, at a period when the equilibrium of power which had previously existed between the Safawids of Iran, the Mughals of India and the Uzbek khanate of Transoxania had dissolved. In the political vacuum resulting from the demise of the Safawid dynasty and the abrupt end of Nadir Shah's efforts at empire building, Ahmad Shah assumed leadership over the Pashtun contingents which had formerly served in the Nadirid army and made them privileged partners of his expansionist policies. While deriving a great part of his strength from his close linkage with the chiefs of the Durrani and Ghilzai confederacies, Ahmad Shah sought to balance their influence by forming a personal bodyguard of tribal outsiders, the Qizilbash of Iran. His son Timur Shah (1772–1793) continued this policy, extending the Qizilbash force in his service and primarily relying on this group in administrative matters.

In 1762, at the height of Ahmad Shah's power, the Afghan empire included Kashmir, Punjab, Sind, Baluchistan, and part of Khurasan. Controlling the trade routes linking Iran, Central Asia and Eastern Turkistan with India, it was, next to the Ottoman empire, the largest state in the Middle East. Yet by the 1820s the core regions of the Sadozai empire had broken up into several independent principalities. While Kabul and Qandahar were held by two competing sets of Muhammadzai brothers, Herat had become the last bastion of Sadozai authority. North of the Hindu Kush, a number of Uzbek khanates had reasserted their independence. In the west, parts of Khurasan had fallen to the Qajar dynasty of Iran.[1] East of the Khyber Pass, the Sikh ruler Ranjit Singh (r. 1801–1839) had gained control of the revenue-rich Indian provinces.[2] What were the causes of this dramatic disintegration? To begin with, the Sadozai empire had been built on Ahmad Shah's ability to garner tribal support by offering the prospect of profitable military campaigns to India. Securing these conquests was a more difficult matter, and the allegiance of the provincial governors tended to waver with each indication of weakness at the center. Thus the maintenance of this sphere of influence required constant efforts. Already in 1767 the Sikhs were able to wrest Lahore from Afghan control.[3] Ahmad Shah's successor Timur had to contend with resistance in Khurasan, Turkistan, Kashmir, Baluchistan, and Sind throughout his reign. This situation was exacerbated with the power struggles breaking out after Timur Shah's death. While his successor Shah Zaman was able to establish his claims to kingship over the opposition of his elder half brother Humayun, he continued to face the rivalry of another influential set of half brothers, Shah Mahmud and Haji Feroz al-Din. In the course of the ensuing conflicts, Shah Zaman relied on the assistance of Dost Muhammad Khan's father, Payinda Khan Muhammadzai. Ironically, his reign came to an end in 1799 when, fearing the immense influence of Payinda Khan, he executed the man who had protected his claims to kingship in the first place. This process was to repeat itself under Shah Zaman's successor Shah Mahmud, who gained royal authority twice with the support of Payinda Khan Muhammadzai's eldest son Fatih Khan. His reign, and Sadozai supremacy over Afghanistan, dissolved after he ordered Fatih Khan to be blinded and killed in 1818.

Between 1800 and 1818, Afghanistan was the scene of the rivalry between Shah Zaman's full brother Shah Shuja' on the one hand and Shah Mahmud and his son Kamran on the other. Another contender for power was Shah Zaman's eldest son Qaisar Mirza. In the unfolding game of constantly shifting coalitions, Fatih Khan Muhammadzai assumed a central position. Fatih Khan's growing political influence was in turn resented by certain powerful Durrani and Ghilzai leaders, who, fearing the loss of their traditional privileges, espoused the cause of Shah Shuja'. In revenge for the death of his father at the hands of Shah Zaman, Fatih Khan brought Shah Mahmud to power for the first time in 1800. Shah Mahmud's first reign lasted only until June 1803, when a Sunni-Shi'a riot encouraged by members of the Durrani leadership allowed Shah Shuja' to gain control of the capital. In 1809 Kabul passed to Shah Mahmud's possession again, who strongly relied on the political acumen of his *wazir* Fatih Khan for the administration of his realm. Throughout these events, Shah Mahmud's full brother Haji Feroz al-Din had been able to hold on to the government of Herat, maintaining a precarious independence between the interests of the rulers of Kabul and Teheran. But in 1817 Haji Feroz al-Din, seeking to develop a counterpoise to the increasing pressure exerted on his dominion by the Qajar ruler Fath 'Ali Shah, turned to Shah Mahmud for assistance. This gave Fatih Khan Muhammadzai and his youngest brother Dost Muhammad Khan the opportunity to gain control of Herat and to engage in a battle with the Iranian army under the Qajar governor of Mashhad, Hasan 'Ali Mirza Shuja' al-Saltana.[4] Fatih Khan's political and military success notwithstanding, Shah Mahmud gave in to the resentment harbored by his son Kamran and other members of the Durrani elite and ordered Kamran to remove Fatih Khan from power. Fatih Khan's blinding and execution in 1818 triggered a rebellion by the remaining Muhammadzai brothers, which eventually led to Dost Muhammad Khan's proclamation as Amir.

In the following, I will take a more detailed look at the events summarized above, shifting the focus of my discussion from the ruling Sadozai family to the most prominent sections of the state-supporting elite. Among the Abdalis/Durranis, the Alikozai, Popalzai and Barakzai subdivisions were most closely associated with Nadir Shah Afshar and the early Sadozai kings and were able to gain privileges disproportionate to their numerical strength. I will outline the careers of some of the most prominent members of these subdivisions in order to introduce the reader to some of the influential contemporaries and rivals of the Muhammadzai family. As will be seen below, the Alikozais were to retain an influential position in Herat, acting as ministers and eventually seizing the authority there for themselves. In Kabul, the interests of the Bamizai Popalzais were pitted against those of Fatih Khan's family. The historical narrative touched upon in the sections concerning the Alikozais and Popalzais will be expanded upon in the description of the Muhammadzai rise to power. In order to provide a frame of reference for the events to be discussed below, I would like to begin by recapitulating the milestones of Afghan history in the eighteenth and early nineteenth centuries:

1708/9	Qandahar breaks away from Safawid rule
1716/17	Herat asserts its independence from the Safawids[5]
1722–1729	Hotak rule at Isfahan
February 1732	Nadir Shah Afshar occupies Herat
March 1738	Nadir Shah Afshar conquers Qandahar
1747–1772	Ahmad Shah Sadozai
1772–1793	Timur Shah Sadozai
1793–1800	Shah Zaman Sadozai
1800–1803	Shah Mahmud Sadozai
1803–1809	Shah Shuja' Sadozai
1809–1818	Shah Mahmud Sadozai's second reign

The Alikozais

In the early nineteenth century, the Alikozais were estimtated at 10,000 families.[6] The most prominent families among them played an important role in Durrani politics even before Nadir Shah's assumption of power. In the early 1720s, 'Abd al-Ghani Khan Alikozai (the maternal uncle of Ahmad Shah) was instrumental in promoting Zulfaqar Khan (Ahmad Shah's elder brother) to a leading position among the Abdalis. During Nadir Shah's reign 'Abd al-Ghani Khan became the governor of Qandahar province. At the beginning of the Sadozai era he refused to relinquish control of the city of Qandahar to the newly proclaimed king, Ahmad Shah, and was killed. When Ahmad Shah set out to erect a new capital in the vicinity of Qandahar in the early 1760s, 'Abd al-Ghani's descendants forced him to postpone his plans by refusing to let him build on their land.[7] In 1799 two Alikozai leaders were part of an unsuccessful plot hedged in Qandahar by Payinda Khan Muhammadzai and a number of Durrani and Qizilbash nobles, which aimed at deposing Shah Zaman and killing his minister Wafadar Khan but resulted in the execution of the noblemen involved instead.[8]

In the 1820s the Alikozais moved to center stage in the politics of Herat. 'Ata Muhammad Khan, a member of the Naso section of the Alikozais and descendant of Sardar 'Abd al-Ghani Khan, had been influential during Shah Mahmud's second reign in Kabul.[9] In late 1818 Shah Mahmud lost control of Kabul and Qandahar and was forced to settle in Herat, 'Ata Muhammad Khan served him as minister until his death in 1828/9.[10] 'Ata Muhammad Khan was succeeded by his nephew Yar Muhammad Khan (d. 1851) whose father 'Abdullah Khan had been governor of Kashmir at the time of Shah Zaman and during Shah Mahmud's last reign. Yar Muhammad Khan, who was to become known as an able and ruthless administrator, assisted Shah Mahmud's son Kamran in removing his father from power. Once Kamran was installed as ruler of Herat, Yar Muhammad virtually controlled all sectors of the government. In early 1842 he had Kamran killed and assumed full authority. The ministership of 'Ata Muhammad Khan and Yar Muhammad Khan not only furthered the interests of those linked immediately to their family interests but also brought many members of the greater group of Alikozais to Herat.[11]

The Popalzais

In the early nineteenth century, the Popalzais were thought to number 12,000 families. Among them the Sadozai and Bamizai subdivisions, being closely related to Ahmad Shah by genealogical links, occupied a prominent position at the Sadozai court.[12] Officially known as 'Khan-i Khanan', Jahan Khan Popalzai acted as Ahmad Shah's war minister and commander in chief of the army. Fatihullah Khan Kamran Khel Sadozai held the title 'Wafadar Khan' and was highly influential at the courts of Ahmad Shah and Timur Shah. His son Rahmatullah Khan was closely connected with Shah Zaman and, depriving Payinda Khan Muhammadzai of his ministership in 1799, prepared the ground for his rebellion and subsequent execution. Rahmatullah Khan was executed in 1801 at the beginning of Shah Mahmud's first reign. His son Nawwab Muhammad 'Usman was influential during Shah Shuja''s first reign from 1803 to 1809 and was awarded the title 'Nizam al-Daula'. During the First Anglo-Afghan War, his ill-fated policies as Shah Shuja''s minister were to trigger the great uprising which put an end to the British presence in Afghanistan.[13] Among the Bamizais, the person of 'Abdullah Khan Ayubzai Bamizai needs to be mentioned. During Ahmad Shah's and Timur Shah's time he held a number of positions, among them those of *ishik aqasi* (chief master of ceremonies) and *diwanbegi* (highest civil magistrate). In 1785 'Abdullah Khan was succeeded by his son 'Alam Khan, who was active in the politics of the Sadozai empire until the early part of Shah Mahmud's second reign.[14]

The most influential and, in many ways, controversial figure in the politics of early nineteenth-century Afghanistan was Sher Muhammad Khan, the third son of Bagi Khan Salihzai Bamizai. Between 1738 and 1747 Bagi Khan acted as a military commander in Nadir Shah's army. At the time of Ahmad Shah's rise to power Bagi Khan was the first Durrani noble to pledge allegiance and was appointed as prime minister with the title 'Ashraf al-Wuzara'. Henceforth known as Shah Wali Khan, Bagi Khan was instrumental in establishing Ahmad Shah's authority in Afghan Turkistan and Bamiyan in 1751. In return, he received rich tracts of land in Gulbahar. At the beginning of Timur Shah's reign, Shah Wali Khan was executed because he had supported Sulaiman Mirza, his son-in-law and Timur's elder brother, as rival contender for the throne.[15]

After Shah Wali Khan's death, Sher Muhammad resided in Baluchistan. In 1773 he interfered in favor of Timur Shah during a rebellion by Sardar 'Abd al-Khaliq Khan Sadozai and his brother at Qandahar and was restored to his father's possessions. Even so, he received no office or title from Timur Shah and played no political role. Sher Muhammad Khan's situation improved significantly when Shah Zaman came to power in 1793. From this point on he was allowed to assume the title of his father, Ashraf al-Wuzara, and acted as commander-in-chief of the army. Furthermore, Shah Zaman gave him the title Mukhtar al-Daula and recognized him as leader of the Bamizais.[16]

During Shah Mahmud's first reign, Sher Muhammad Khan retained his titles, position, and salary. Although he played a great role in subduing the Ghilzai rebellion in 1801, he found his position at court increasingly eclipsed by Fatih Khan Muhammadzai, who usurped his title as Shah Mahmud's minister. Closely linked to the Sunni faction of Kabul, he was instrumental in inciting the Sunni-Shi'a riots of 1803 that led to the downfall of Shah Mahmud. Having thus elevated Shah Shuja' to the throne, he was again appointed to the positions he held under Shah Zaman.[17] Moreover, he controlled the revenues of Sind.[18] In 1807 Shah Shuja' deputed Sher Muhammad Khan Bamizai to Kashmir to deprive Shah Mahmud's appointee 'Abdullah Khan Alikozai of the governorship of that province. Subsequently, Sher Muhammad Khan's son 'Ata Muhammad Khan was made governor of Kashmir. Sher Muhammad Khan's career ended when he was killed in battle after an unsuccessful attempt to depose Shah Shuja' by proclaiming Shah Zaman's eldest son Qaisar Mirza king in 1807/8.[19]

Despite his father's defeat and death 'Ata Muhammad Khan Bamizai continued to hold the government of Kashmir for the first few years of Shah Mahmud's second reign. Around the year 1813 he was defeated by an alliance between Fatih Khan Muhammadzai and Ranjit Singh and had to give up the government of the province to Fatih Khan's brother Muhammad 'Azim Khan.[20] Nevertheless, he was able to assume an important position among Shah Mahmud's courtiers after his return from Kashmir. Having had the hereditary title of his father, Mukhtar al-Daula, bestowed on him, he was put in charge of the affairs at Kabul. Together with his namesake 'Ata Muhammad Khan Alikozai, he became a formidable antagonist of Fatih Khan Muhammadzai, playing an instrumental role in his eventual removal from power. After the blinding and death of Fatih Khan in 1818 'Ata Muhammad Khan Bamizai retained his influence in Kabul as the advisor of Shahzada Jahangir, Shah Mahmud's grandson. Given his strong links with the Sunnis of Kabul, he became an important mediator in the ensuing power struggle between the Muhammadzais and Sadozais. Aiming to carve out independent authority over Kabul for himself, he attempted to play off the ruling family against the brothers of Fatih Khan by pretending to hold Kabul in favor of the former while entering secret negotiations with the latter. Rather than attaining his goal, however, he was blinded by Fatih Khan's brother Pir Muhammad Khan Muhammadzai in revenge for his role in the blinding of Fatih Khan.[21] 'Ata Muhammad Khan thus lost his political clout and the remaining brothers of Fatih Khan became the strongest political force in Kabul. During the final phase of the First Anglo-Afghan War another member of Sher Muhammad Khan Bamizai's family was to assume an influential position. 'Ata Muhammad Khan's brother Ghulam Muhammad was one of the main participants of the uprising of November 1841 and its aftermath.

The Barakzais

The most influential section of the Barakzais were the Muhammadzais. If contemporary sources are to be trusted, the population of this group increased significantly between the eighteenth century and the second half of the nineteenth century. According to these estimates, the Muhammadzais had numbered only four to five thousand families in the eighteenth century, but amounted to 30,000 families during Amir Dost Muhammad Khan's second reign.[22] In great part, this population growth may be attributed to the patronage the greater group of Muhammadzais enjoyed under the leadership of the descendants of Payinda Khan. After Nadir Shah's death, Payinda Khan's father Haji Jamal Khan had been the most powerful contender for leadership among the Abdalis. However, he had to relinquish his claims to authority in view of the religious legitimization given to Sadozai rule. Another argument in Ahmad Khan's favor was that his ancestors had occupied a more prominent position among the Abdalis during Safawid times. Haji Jamal Khan accepted the selection of Ahmad Khan as king and under his leadership the Barakzais played an important role in the military, holding the hereditary position of *topchibashi* (commander of artillery).[23]

At the time of Haji Jamal Khan's death in 1770/71, Ahmad Shah bestowed the leadership of the Barakzais on Haji Jamal's eldest son Rahimdad Khan and assigned a generous allowance to him. When Timur Shah became king he initially confirmed Rahimdad Khan in this position. In 1774, however, Rahimdad Khan was divested of his position, title and *jagir*. In his stead, Timur Shah appointed Payinda Khan, Haji Jamal's fourth son and Rahimdad Khan's half brother, to the leadership of the Barakzais and awarded the title 'Sarafraz Khan' to him in 1775.[24] Payinda Khan soon assumed an active role in government matters. After he had successfully contained a rebellion in Kashmir and collected the revenues of Quetta and Sialkot, he was awarded the leadership (*sardari*) of the Ghilzais.[25] He also was instrumental in quelling a rebellion by Timur Shah's son 'Abbas. Payinda Khan's role in securing the throne for Timur Shah's son Shah Zaman has been mentioned above. During Shah Zaman's reign, Payinda Khan's salary was the highest in the country. Furthermore, he was awarded the sardarship over all tribal groups in addition to the Ghilzais and Durranis, that is, the Tajiks, Uzbeks, Hazaras, etc.[26]

Despite his powerful position at Shah Zaman's court, Payinda Khan viewed himself first and foremost as a tribal leader who derived his strength from his standing among his own kinsmen. For this reason, he opposed Shah Zaman's unprecedented efforts to weaken the influential Durrani leaders by taking away their hereditary government posts. Payinda Khan's resistance to these measures caused Shah Zaman to make Rahmatullah Khan Kamran Khel Sadozai ('Wafadar Khan') his new chief minister. In 1799 Payinda Khan, stripped of all his offices, joined other disenchanted chiefs in a plot aiming at replacing Shah Zaman with his brother Shahzada Shuja'. In an attempt to revitalize the claims of the Durrani leadership to equal standing with the kings, the conspiracy also aimed at making the assumption of royal power contingent on the confirmation by the tribal nobility.[27] The revelation of this plan by the *munshi bashi* Muhammad Sharif Khan Qizilbash to Wafadar Khan gave Shah Zaman a welcome pretext to execute Payinda Khan and his fellow conspirators, thus doing away with a number of influential nobles at court. If Shah Zaman aimed at curtailing Muhammadzai power by executing Payinda Khan, he failed miserably. Rather than disappearing from the political arena, Payinda Khan's sons increasingly dominated the politics of Afghanistan from the turn of the nineteenth century on.

On his death, Payinda Khan left behind twenty-one sons and several daughters. As many of them figure largely in the following narrative, it will be worthwhile giving a complete listing of their names, dates, and their maternal descent here:

1) Fatih Khan	(1778–1818)	mother Muhammadzai
2) Timur Quli Khan	(1780–1822)	
3) Muhammad 'Azim Khan ('Sardar-i Kalan')	(1785–1823)	mother Nusratkhel
4) Nawwab Asad Khan	(1778– ?)	
5) Nawwab 'Abd al-Samad Khan	(1785–1828)	mother Barakzai
6) Tura Baz Khan	(1795– ?)	
7) Nawwab 'Abd al-Jabbar Khan	(1782–1854)	mother Kohistani
8) Purdil Khan	(1785–1830)	
9) Sherdil Khan	(1786–1826)	
10) Kuhandil Khan	(1793–1855)	mother Idukhel Hotak
11) Rahmdil Khan	(1796–1859)	
12) Mihrdil Khan	(1797–1855)	
13) 'Ata Muhammad Khan	(1786–1824)	
14) Yar Muhammad Khan	(1790–1828)	
15) Sultan Muhammad Khan	(1795–1861)	mother Alikozai
16) Sa'id Muhammad Khan	(1797–1860)	
17) Pir Muhammad Khan	(1800–1871)	

18) Dost Muhammad Khan	(1792–1863)	mother Jawansher
19) Amir Muhammad Khan	(1794–1834)	Qizilbash
20) Jum'a Khan	(1800–1871)	mother Tajik
21) Islam Khan	(? – ?)	mother Siyahposh Kafir[28]

Although Shah Zaman had given orders for the arrest of all Barakzai leaders, Payinda Khan's eldest son Fatih Khan, along with his brothers Asad Khan, Purdil Khan, and Sherdil Khan, as well as approximately 85 Barakzai and 'Alizai followers, was able to escape to Iran.[29] In the following years, he not only revenged his father's death by having Shah Zaman blinded but succeeded in bringing Shah Mahmud to the throne twice. Popularly known as 'Tajbakhsh', he received the title of 'Shahdost' from Shah Mahmud and served as *wazir* during both of his reigns.[30] Particularly during Shah Mahmud's second reign, Sardar Fatih Khan' s power increased considerably. Because of Shah Mahmud's lack of interest in government matters he became the virtual ruler of the country, to the chagrin of Shah Mahmud's son Shahzada Kamran.

Fatih Khan's rising fortune also benefitted his relatives, whom he appointed as governors in various important provinces. Muhammad 'Azim Khan became governor of Peshawar in 1809. After Fatih Khan's conquest of Kashmir and the deposal of 'Ata Muhammad Khan Bamizai, Muhammad 'Azim Khan gained the governorship there. Derajat and Sind were governed by Nawwab Asad Khan and Nawwab Samad Khan respectively. Sardar Rahmdil Khan was entrusted with the government of Baluchistan and resided at Shikarpur. Sardar Purdil Khan received control of Qandahar. Their full brothers Sherdil and Kuhandil governed Ghazni and Bamiyan. Nawwab Asad Khan's son Nawwab Muhammad Zaman Khan was in charge of Jalalabad.[31] During Shah Mahmud's second reign, Dost Muhammad Khan, who had been only seven years old when his father was executed by Shah Zaman, began to assume political functions. Thanks to Fatih Khan's influence at court, the young Dost Muhammad received the title 'Sardar' from Shah Mahmud and was made *na'ib* (deputy) of Kabul. Sometime in 1813 he added the governorship of Kohistan to his duties.[32] Although Fatih Khan frequently changed appointments in order to prevent his brothers from concentrating too much power in their hands, they were able to carve out important bases and grouped themselves on the basis of maternal descent.[33] Purdil Khan and his younger brothers, for example, were to become increasingly powerful in the Qandahar region. Sardar 'Ata Muhammad Khan and his younger brothers were centered in Peshawar. Dost Muhammad Khan was to receive a large measure of support from Kohistan and the city of Kabul in his quest for power.

Like his father, Fatih Khan was to become the victim of his own success. The main factor leading to his downfall 1818 was the resentment Shah

Mahmud's son Kamran and other Durrani nobles harbored against the Muhammadzai leader. Kamran, who had been deprived by Fatih Khan of all access to government offices, seized upon the news of Dost Muhammad Khan's misbehavior in the harem of Haji Feroz al-Din and his son Malik Qasim to weaken Shah Mahmud's trust in Fatih Khan. Hearing that Dost Muhammad Khan had insulted Malik Qasim's wife, who was Kamran's sister, Shah Mahmud agreed to have Fatih Khan removed from power.[34] Kamran went to Herat and addressed a letter to Hasan 'Ali Mirza, the Qajar governor of Khurasan, apologizing for Fatih Khan's aggressive behavior and alleging that the minister had acted without the consent of the Sadozai government. Fath 'Ali Shah, who had recently arrived in Mashhad responded by asking Kamran to demonstrate the seriousness of his accusations against Fatih Khan either by handing him over as a prisoner or by blinding him. Kamran took the letter from the Qajar king as a further pretext to execute his designs against Fatih Khan, in effect bringing about the demise of the Sadozai empire.[35]

DOST MUHAMMAD KHAN'S ASSUMPTION OF POWER

The blinding and subsequent execution of Fatih Khan in 1818 led to, as Reshtia has characterized it, a period of 'civil war' (*khana jangi*) among the Muhammadzais and the break up of Afghanistan into 'tribal principalities' (*muluk al-tawa'ifi*). Immediately after Fatih Khan's imprisonment at Herat, the energies of his remaining brothers were primarily directed against Shah Mahmud and Kamran. Sherdil Khan and Kuhandil Khan fled from Herat to Fatih Khan's mother Bibi Ade residing in the fort of Nad 'Ali near Seistan and began to gather followers. From Kashmir, the eldest remaining brother, Sardar 'Azim Khan coordinated the activities of his brothers Dost Muhammad Khan, Yar Muhammad Khan and Nawwab 'Abd al-Jabbar Khan. For a while, he even considered cooperating with Shah Shuja'.[36] Once Shah Mahmud and Kamran had been forced to withdraw to Herat, the Muhammadzai brothers began to compete with each other for the possession of Kabul.

The Power Struggle among the Muhammadzais (1818–1826)

While Shah Mahmud had effectively lost control over Kabul in 1818, the Muhammadzai parties contending for power there formally continued to adhere to the notion of Sadozai supremacy by making a number of Sadozai princes figureheads for their political ambitions. As it is beyond the scope of this work to give a detailed account of the frequent shifts of authority which befell Kabul between 1818 and 1826, I will restrict my discussion to some of the milestones in this period of seemingly unceasing conflict. Let us start with a chronological overview of the lords of Kabul:

1818: 'Ata Muhammad Khan Bamizai holds Kabul in the name of Shahzada Jahangir b. Kamran b. Shah Mahmud;

1818: Dost Muhammad Khan occupies Kabul, sets up Sultan 'Ali b. Timur Shah

late 1818 – early 1823: Muhammad 'Azim Khan rules in the name of Shahzada Ayub b. Timur Shah.

1823: Muhammad 'Azim is succeeded by his son Habibullah Khan; end of Sadozai rule: Shahzada Ayub is imprisoned and his son Shahzada Isma'il is killed;

1823/24 Habibullah is deposed by Sherdil Khan;[37]

1824: Yar Muhammad Khan;

1824–1826: Sultan Muhammad Khan.

Although Muhammad 'Azim Khan's claims to leadership were generally disputed by his brothers, his four-year reign in Kabul was a period of comparative stability. From 1819 until 1823 the remaining Muhammadzai Sardars had to content themselves with the bases of power they had carved out for themselves during Shah Mahmud's second reign. The 'Dil' brothers, for example, had been able to regain control over Qandahar with Barakzai support in 1818. With the exception of the First Anglo-Afghan War (1839–1842), they were to control Qandahar and its surroundings well into Dost Muhammad Khan's second reign (1843–1863). In the 1820s and 1830s they governed not only the fertile districts in the immediate vicinity of the city but also Deh Raud, Zamindawar, and the Hazara territories north of Qandahar. The districts under their authority in the south included Garmser, Shorabak, Pishin, and Sibi. Sind was able to break away from their control with Sherdil Khan's death in August 1826. The two eldest of the Qandahar Sardars, Purdil Khan and Sherdil Khan, were serious contenders for authority in Kabul. After Muhammad 'Azim's death in 1823, Sherdil Khan intervened in Kabul successfully to prevent Dost Muhammad Khan from taking control there. While he thus asserted the superiority of the Qandahar Sardars' claims to authority and was instrumental in redistributing the power among the other brothers of Fatih Khan, he was unable to gain a permanent foothold in Kabul. Nevertheless it was only after his death in 1826 that Dost Muhammad Khan could make a more successful bid for power in the former capital. After Purdil Khan's death in 1830, Sardars Kuhandil Khan, Rahmdil Khan, and Mihrdil Khan became the leading figures of Qandahar.[38]

Peshawar continued to be held by 'Ata Muhammad Khan and his full brothers. At the time of 'Ata Muhammad Khan's death in 1824, his younger brother Yar Muhammad Khan became a tributary of Ranjit Singh, undertaking to pay a yearly tribute of 110,000 rupees. After his death in 1828, his full brother Sultan Muhammad Khan formally continued as governor of Peshawar, sending one of his sons as hostage to Lahore. In

1834 Ranjit Singh assumed direct control of Peshawar.[39] The Afghan governors displaced by Ranjit Singh returned to Kabul. Nawwab 'Abd al-Jabbar Khan, who had succeeded Muhammad 'Azim Khan as governor of Kashmir, received the government of 'Ghilzai', i.e, Laghman, from Muhammad 'Azim Khan after losing Kashmir to Ranjit Singh in 1819. Nawwab Muhammad Zaman Khan was expelled from Dera Ghazi Khan and Dera Isma'il Khan in 1819 and 1821 respectively and assumed his former position as governor of Jalalabad. Nawwab Asad Khan and Nawwab 'Abd al-Samad Khan resided in Kabul with Muhammad 'Azim Khan.[40]

In comparison with his brothers, Dost Muhammad Khan operated from a relatively disadvantaged position. He had lost the protection of Fatih Khan and had only one full brother supporting him. In addition, he was generally looked down upon by his other brothers because of his relative youth and the inferiority of his maternal descent.[41] But in the long run, this apparent weakness was to become a source of strength for Dost Muhammad Khan. In the struggle for the possession of Kabul, his links with his maternal relatives, the Qizilbash of Kabul, and the central role he had played in Fatih Khan's administration were eventually to give him an edge over his rivals. Another factor working in Dost Muhammad Khan's favor was his restless political ambition. Rather than contenting himself with the possession of Ghazni, which Muhammad 'Azim had assigned to him in 1819, Dost Muhammad Khan seized every opportunity to make his influence felt in the changing coalitions among his brothers, all the while skillfully evading all their efforts to eliminate him from the political arena.

In 1819, shortly after Muhammad 'Azim's assumption of power in Kabul, Dost Muhammad, along with Sherdil Khan and Pir Muhammad Khan, undermined his revenue collection in Sind by making a separate agreement with the local Mirs. After a vain attempt to garner further support from the Qandahar Sardars in his rebellion against Muhammad 'Azim Khan, Dost Muhammad Khan went on to Kohistan to seek assistance there. Owing to the mediation of Nawwab 'Abd al-Samad, however, he was prevailed upon to give up this effort and to leave for Peshawar. Shortly afterwards, Dost Muhammad Khan was able to regain Ghazni. He made his brother Amir Muhammad Khan governor there and remained a thorn in Muhammad 'Azim Khan's side until the latter's unsuccessful campaign against the Sikhs and subsequent death in 1823.[42]

With Muhammad 'Azim Khan's death the precarious equilibrium that had prevailed among the various sets of Muhammadzai brothers was upset and the struggle for Kabul resumed with increased intensity. Fearing the rivalry of the Sadozai prince Isma'il (the son of Ayub Shah), Muhammad 'Azim Khan's son and successor, Habibullah Khan, called the Qandahar Sardars for help. Motivated by the desire to assert their leading position among the other brothers of Fatih Khan and to possess themselves of the remaining 900,000 rupees of the treasure Muhammad 'Azim had amassed in Kashmir, Purdil Khan and Sherdil Khan were quick to react. Purdil Khan went to Kabul and removed the last vestiges of Sadozai rule by imprisoning Ayub Shah and killing Shahzada Isma'il. Nevertheless, he hesitated to assume full authority and, having confirmed Habibullah Khan as ruler of Kabul, returned to Qandahar.

Less than six months later, Habibullah again requested the assistance of the Qandahar Sardars, this time to curb the growing influence of Dost Muhammad Khan. The available information concerning the political maneuvering and intrigues which followed during the next few months is contradictory. All sources agree, however, that Habibullah Khan, rather than being strengthened by Sherdil Khan, was imprisoned and removed to Logar. At the same time, Sherdil Khan's foothold in Kabul remained precarious, and he found himself locked into a lengthy military confrontation with the Peshawar Sardars, Dost Muhammad Khan and the Qizilbash. Finally, Nawwab Jabbar Khan and Nawwab Samad Khan were able to negotiate an agreement whereby the remaining Muhammadzai brothers accepted Sherdil Khan's claims to leadership. Despite this political success Sherdil Khan contented himself with the possession of the treasure left by Muhammad 'Azim Khan and handed over the control of Kabul to the Peshawar Sardars Yar Muhammad Khan and Sultan Muhammad Khan. According to Faiz Muhammad Khan, Sherdil Khan's decision to leave Kabul had to be attributed in great part to the fact that the extortionate policies of his maternal uncle, Khuda Nazar Khan Ghilzai, had turned public opinion against the Qandahar Sardars. Under the pretext of recovering Muhammad 'Azim Khan's possessions, Khuda Nazar Khan had deprived a great part of the citizens of Kabul of their movable property.[43]

With Sherdil Khan's return to Qandahar, the distribution of territories among the Muhammadzai brothers appeared to be unchanged. At the same time, Dost Muhammad Khan's had consistently widened his political base in and around Kabul since Muhammad 'Azim's death. During the latest struggles for control over Kabul both Habibullah and Sherdil Khan had come to consider him so dangerous that two plots were hatched to have him blinded. Rather than being removed from the political scene, however, Dost Muhammad Khan had been able to expand his sphere of influence from Ghazni to the immediate vicinity of Kabul by gaining control of Kohistan. Another crucial factor adding to his political stature was his intimate link with the Qizilbash of Kabul through his mother's relations. This connection had become even stronger with his wedding to the Qizilbash widow of Muhammad 'Azim Khan, the daughter of Sadiq Khan Jawansher, during the early phase of his confrontation with Sherdil Khan. As seen above, Dost Muhammad Khan had been able to rely on Qizilbash support during his military contest with Sherdil Khan.

Sardar Yar Muhammad Khan's reign in Kabul was of brief duration. He was summoned to Peshawar by his fatally ill brother 'Ata Muhammad Khan in 1824 and relinquished the government of Kabul in favor of his younger brother Sultan Muhammad Khan. With the death of Sherdil Khan in 1826, Dost Muhammad Khan began to interfere with the affairs of Kabul once again, playing on ethnic divisions among the population of Kabul. While Sultan Muhammad Khan emphasized his links with the Sunni population of the city, Dost Muhammad Khan again brought his Qizilbash allies into the field. In particular, the support rendered by his maternal uncle Mahmud Khan Bayat tipped the scales in favor of Dost Muhammad Khan. Finding himself besieged in the Bala Hisar, Sultan Muhammad Khan agreed to hand over the reins of the government of Kabul to Dost Muhammad Khan in exchange for receiving 100,000 rupees a year of its revenues. Shortly afterwards a cholera epidemic cut short Purdil Khan's renewed attempt to interfere militarily. Thus Dost Muhammad Khan was able to assume control of Kabul in 1826.[44]

The Beginnings of Muhammadzai Rule

In the course of the shifting configurations of power between 1818 and 1826, Dost Muhammad Khan had gradually been able to tighten his grip over Kabul. His base in Kohistan, his temporary alliance with Aminullah Khan Logari, and his connection with the Qizilbash of Kabul had cleared the way for his assumption of power at the former Sadozai capital. Even so, his position remained insecure. It was disputed not only by his Muhammadzai half brothers but also the greater group of Durranis. While the Qizilbash had played a crucial role in bringing Dost Muhammad Khan to power, their support for him was far from unequivocal. In 1827 Husain Quli Khan Jawansher was sent to the court of Fath 'Ali Shah bearing a message from the Qizilbash offering their assistance in case of a Qajar attack on Kabul.[45] When Shah Shuja' attempted to regain power by attacking Qandahar in June 1834, a sizeable section among the Qizilbash military leaders considered taking over Kabul in his name.[46] On the eve of the First Anglo-Afghan War, the Jawansher chief Khan Shirin Khan (d. 1859) intimated his pro-British sentiments both to Alexander Burnes and Shah Shuja'.[47]

But Muhammadzai claims to authority were not only disputed by outsiders. The Muhammadzai Sardars themselves were reluctant to portray themselves as successors to the Sadozai monarchy and avoided the question of their legitimacy as rulers. Despite his influential position under Shah Mahmud, Fatih Khan had made no attempt to assume kingship for himself. Although his death brought about an open confrontation between the Sadozais and the Muhammadzais, none of his brothers dared to disassemble Sadozai authority openly. Immediately after Fatih Khan's death Muhammad 'Azim Khan and Dost Muhammad Khan sided with Shah Shuja'. But this coalition came to an end because of Shah Shuja''s absolute claims to power.[48] During the early phase of the struggle for Kabul, Dost Muhammad Khan and Muhammad 'Azim Khan propped up Shahzada Sultan 'Ali and Shahzada Ayub respectively as figureheads. In 1823 the Muhammadzai brothers finally gave up the pretense of acting in the name of a Sadozai ruler. Even so, they were strongly aware that they lacked the legitimacy Ahmad Shah's descendants had enjoyed.

In the late 1820s Masson reported that the Durranis in Qandahar attributed Purdil Khan's extortionist government practices to the fact that he considered himself an usurper and therefore attempted to amass as much wealth as possible before being deprived of his ill-gotten government by a more legitimate ruler. Meanwhile, in Kabul, Dost Muhammad Khan studiously avoided using or maintaining edifices reminiscent of Sadozai rule. Some buildings, including the former *daftar khana* (record office), were even ordered to be torn down.[49] When Dost Muhammad Khan assumed control of Kabul in 1826 he made no claims to formal kingship. Only in 1834 or early 1835 his avowed plan to engage in jihad against the Sikhs offered the opportunity to seek religious sanction for his rule and to widen his fiscal base. On the basis of the notion that martyrdom and its heavenly rewards could only be attained if jihad was fought under the leadership of a lawful king, Dost Muhammad assumed the title *amir al-mu'minin*, 'commander of the faithful.'

Given the political climate of Kabul in the 1830s, two features of Dost Muhammad Khan's coronation stand out, both of which reflect his attempt to gain legitimacy without evoking the all too recent fall of Sadozai rule. First, the choice of the title 'Amir' is noteworthy. Conferred by the eldest son of Sayyid Ahmad Mir Aqa, who was the *mir wa'iz* (headpreacher) of Kabul, this title gave royal authority and religious legitimacy to Dost Muhammad Khan's reign. His coronation was followed by the typical expressions of royal authority, the striking of coins and the reading of the *khutba* in his name.[50] While Dost Muhammad Khan was thus able to portray himself as a lawful ruler, his selection of the title 'Amir' also avoided any association with the previous Sadozai rulers, all of whom had carried the title 'Shah'.

The second interesting element of Dost Muhammad Khan's coronation is that it was closely modeled on the nomination of Ahmad Shah, the founder of the Sadozai dynasty. After Nadir Shah's death in 1747 his principal Afghan officers had formed a *jirga* (council) in the tomb of Shaikh Surkh at Kushk-i Nakhud, located thirty-five miles from Qandahar, in order to elect a new leader. As no consensus could be reached for nine days, the deadlock was finally resolved by a well-known *darwesh* called Muhammad Sabir Shah, who pointed out Ahmad Khan Sadozai's superior qualities and caused him to be nominated as leader of the Pashtuns. When Ahmad Khan showed reluctance to accept this position Sabir Shah raised a small platform of earth, seated him on it, tucked a few barley shoots from an adjoining field into his turban, and proclaimed him *padshah durr-i dauran*, 'pearl of the age'.[51] While Ahmad Shah's nomination was followed by a pompous coronation after his conquest of Qandahar, Dost Muhammad Khan chose to emulate the earlier, highly evocative nomination event for his coronation. Departing from the Sadozai custom of grandiose coronation processions, his proclamation of kingship appeared muted and was devoid of all 'expressions of joy,' such as discharges of artillery. Towards the evening, Dost Muhammad proceeded to the 'Idgah at Siyahsang (located approximately three miles from Kabul), where the presence of a number of relatives and tribal chiefs recreated the setting of the original council that had nominated Ahmad Shah. The son of Mir Wa'iz placed two or three blades of grass in his turban, proclaimed him *padshah* with the title Amir al-Muminin, and exhorted those present to contribute to the planned jihad against the Sikhs.[52]

By modeling his coronation on Ahmad Shah's nomination Dost Muhammad attempted to refocus public attention from the recent demise of Sadozai rule to the beginnings of Afghan statehood when all Pashtun leaders had operated on an equal footing. This point was also made by those in favor of Dost Muhammad Khan's kingship, who emphasized the fact that his paternal grandfather Haji Jamal Khan had been the strongest candidate for leadership among the Pashtuns prior to the intervention by Sabir Shah. Rather than contending with his public image as usurper, Dost Muhammad Khan could thus bypass recent events in favor of historical Muhammadzai claims to power.[53] Despite his attempt to hark back to the beginnings of Afghan statehood, Dost Muhammad Khan departed from Ahmad Shah's example in choosing the title Amir al-Muminin. His allegiance to Sabir Shah notwithstanding, Ahmad Shah was given the title *durr-i dauran*, 'pearl of the age'. Rather than giving religious legitimacy, this title reflected his claims to royal leadership among his fellow tribesmen, who, henceforth assuming the name 'Durrani', were transformed into a state supporting elite. Dost Muhammad Khan, on the other hand, desperately needed the support of the ulama of Kabul in his attempt to secure his rule and to widen his material base of support. Although he had begun to show a more keen interest in religion after becoming ruler of Kabul, it seems probable that exigencies of his time, including the projected jihad against the Sikhs, played a greater role in the assumption of the title of Amir al-Muminin.

In part, the simplicity of Dost Muhammad's coronation ceremony may be attributed to the fact that he lacked the economic resources for a more grandiose celebration. More likely, however, he limited the scale of his celebration voluntarily in order to avoid an open confrontation with the still powerful Qandahar Sardars. Others of his relatives chose to withhold even their nominal support by staying away from the ceremony. This was the case with Sultan Muhammad Khan, who had resided in Kabul since his expulsion from Peshawar in 1834. While Dost Muhammad was thus able to assume kingship without great celebration or encountering significant opposition, the stability of his reign seemed little improved. Attempts to raise greater government revenues in the name of jihad met with little success and a great part of his war chest of nearly 500,000 rupees had to be collected by extorting compulsory loans from merchants, both Muslim and Hindu, and levying two years' *jizya*, or capitation tax, on all of the Hindus in Kabul, Ghazni, and Jalalabad. Likewise, the number of *ghazis* (religious warriors) raised in the name of jihad was much smaller than Dost Muhammad Khan had anticipated. After the failure of the first military campaign against the Sikhs in 1835 Dost Muhammad Khan still found himself in enormous economic difficulties, facing the necessity of reducing his army while having to provide financial support for recently arrived members of the former Peshawar *darbar*.[54]

Apart from economic considerations, it is not clear whether Dost Muhammad Khan's stature had become enhanced in public opinion as a result of his formal assumption of kingship. Josiah Harlan, who became the general of the regular Afghan troops in the late 1830s, documents that Dost Muhammad was haunted by the spectre of Sadozai superiority even in his own harem. Agha Taj, daughter of Shahzada ʿAbbas and granddaughter of Timur Shah, had been forcefully married by Dost Muhammad Khan on the occasion of her father's flight to Lahore. Although she gave birth to several children, she never ceased to remind her husband of his inferior origin by calling him her 'slave' and addressing him by the diminutive nickname 'Dosto.'[55] It is also questionable whether Dost Muhammad Khan perceived himself as a lawful ruler. In 1839, when the British advanced on Kabul to reinstate Shah Shujaʿ, Dost Muhammad Khan readily offered to surrender to Shah Shujaʿs authority in exchange for receiving Fatih Khan's title of *wazir*.[56]

Dost Muhammad Khan's Person

Born on 8 Jumada I 1207/23 December 1792, Dost Muhammad Khan was only seven years old when his family was dispersed in the aftermath of Payinda Khan's execution. Because of the unsettled circumstances of his early years, Dost Muhammad Khan, unlike his elder brothers, received no formal education. After Fatih Khan's and Shahzada Mahmud's conquest of Qandahar in 1800, he became his eldest brother's personal attendant and close companion. In the course of the intrigues surrounding Shah Shujaʿ's reign from 1803–1809, he began to play an active role alongside Fatih Khan. During Shah Mahmud's second reign he became a prominent military leader and gained important political offices, such as the deputyship of Kabul and the governorship of Kohistan.[57]

The most detailed descriptions of Dost Muhammad Khan's appearance and comportment were given by foreign vistors who came to Kabul in the 1830s. Mohan Lal noted Dost Muhammad Khan's 'tall stature and haughty countenance,' as well as his 'proud tone of speech.'[58] Alexander Burnes was impressed with his accomplished manners and address.[59] The American mercenary Josiah Harlan, on the other hand, observed his 'boisterous and energetic' temperament in conversation and his susceptibility to flattery. Harlan, who claims to have been assigned a seat of honor next to the Amir, apparently had ample opportunity to observe his features and clothing in minute detail. He furnishes us with an account which displays an interesting mixture of western prejudice and medical precision:

> The Ameer is... in vigorous health. When he stands erect his height is six feet, but there is a slight stoop in the neck arising from a rounded contour of the shoulders, characteristic of his family, which militates against the commanding appearance his person is otherwise formed to impress when animated by conversation or excited by passion. He has large features and a muscular frame; a heavy tread in his walk, placing the sole of his foot all at once flat upon the ground, which indicates that the instep is not well arched... The nose is aquiline, high, and rather long, and finished with beautiful delicacy; the brow open, arched and pencilled; the eyes are hazel-gray, not large, and of an elephantine expression; the mouth large and vulgar and full of bad teeth; the lips moderately thick; ears large. The shape of the face is oval, rather broad across the cheeks , and the chin covered with a full strong beard, originally black, now mixed with gray hairs.[60]

Probably the most favorable description of the Amir was given by Wood, who accompanied Burnes to Kabul in 1837. He was particularly impressed with Dost Muhammad Khan's intelligence and his ability to engage his guests in conversation:

> Dost Mohamed Khan is about forty-five years of age, and looks worn out and aged before his time. His frame is large and bony, and all his features strongly marked. There is a sternness in the general expression of his features, which is increased by his flowing, jet-black beard, but his countenance is lighted up by eyes of peculiar brilliancy and intelligence: when he fixes them upon those by whom he is addressed, they actually seem to flash with approbation or dissent... the various subjects on which he spoke, the good sense of his remarks, and the readiness of his replies, proved that his conversational talents were of no mean order. When any of us addressed him, he sat with his eyes rivetted upon the speaker, and his whole soul appeared absorbed by the subject: when he himself spoke, though he did not resort to Persian gesture, nor assume the solemnity

> of a Hindu rajah, there was that in his manner and tone of voice which enforced attention.[61]

All visitors to Dost Muhammad Khan's court concurred with Harlan's observation that the Amir's dress was 'unaffected and plain.'[62] Masson noted the simplicity of Dost Muhammad Khan's attire of white linen, contrasting it favorably with the 'gay dresses' of the chiefs surrounding him, in particular Muhammad 'Azim's son Habibullah Khan. According to Masson, Dost Muhammad Khan made every effort to portray himself as a sober and just ruler. After his assumption of power at Kabul, he 'abjured wine and other unlawful pleasures' and dedicated himself fully to government measures. The choice of his plain dress may have been another expression of his newly found sobriety and a means to set himself apart from the bad reputation that clung to some of his brothers. He clearly disassociated himself from his brother Sultan Muhammad Khan, who was infamous for his poor government of Peshawar and environs. Alluding to Sultan Muhammad's love of fine robes, which had earned him the popular nickname 'Telai' ('golden'), Dost Muhammad Khan derisively called him 'Sultan Bibi' ('lady').[63]

In the early years of his reign Dost Muhammad Khan also made up for his lack of education. Tutored by Naib Muhammad Akhundzada, the Amir read a section of the Koran every day after the morning prayer. This was followed by lessons in history and poetry. Due to his long military career, Dost Muhammad Khan not only spoke Persian and Pashtu but also Punjabi and Turkish. Mohan Lal even credits him with knowledge of the Kashmiri language.[64] This, in addition to his literary studies, allowed him to attend to important government matters independent of his Qizilbash *mirzas* (secretaries), who otherwise controlled all the home and foreign correspondence.[65] Masson notes that important government functionaries, such as Mirza 'Abd al-Sami' and Haji Khan Kakar had pushed for Dost Muhammad Khan's coronation in part because they hoped that his more formal position would divert his attention from the business of government and would give them greater freedom in decision making. Rather than becoming a 'slave to etiquette,' however, Dost Muhammad Khan devoted himself with even greater ardor to the administration of his realm after assuming kingship.[66]

Another aspect in Dost Muhammad Khan's demeanor which did not change with his coronation was his accessibility both to common man and noble. Immediately after having been proclaimed Amir, he

> protested to his friends, that he would not become a king after the manner of the Suddoo Zyes, to be secluded in his haram and to take no cognizance of public affairs – that he should take the same concern in the affairs of the country as formerly, and that all classes of people should have access to him.[67]

Harlan reported that the Amir understood the needs of all classes of the population, as the tumultuous years of his youth had brought him into contact with people from all backgrounds. On Fridays a general court (*bar-i 'amm*) was held during which 'the gateway... was thrown wide open and the doorkeeper withdrawn. Every one who had a cause to urge or curiosity to gratify might come into the presence without impediment. The Ameer heard all complaints in person, attended by the Cauzee.'[68] In his evaluation of Dost Muhammad Khan's reign, Faiz Muhammad even claims that the Amir did not designate a certain day as *bar-i 'amm* but was always available to his subjects, be it in court, in his private quarters, or in the street.[69] While this statement may be exaggerated, it underlines Dost Muhammad Khan's general reputation for tolerance and patience, which allowed even Hindus to approach him in the street 'with the certainty of being attended to.'[70] Lal furnishes another example of the Amir's accessibility: 'any man seeking for justice may stop him on the road by holding his hand and garment, once his beard, may abuse him for not relieving his grievances, and the Amir will continue to listen to him without disturbance or anger.'[71]

Although Dost Muhammad Khan's popularity was more or less limited to the general populace, he was able to placate members of the nobility to a certain degree by treating them as equals at court. Departing from Sadozai customs, the Amir did away with elaborate ceremonial. Seated on a felt rug, he would rise fully to greet his brothers and his nephew Muhammad Zaman Khan. On the entrance of other dignitaries he would come up on his knees or incline his body slightly in a mock attempt to do so. The chiefs composing his court, on their part, entered freely with a bow and uttered the usual salutation of *salam 'alaikum* while touching their forehead with the fingers of the right hand. Then they were conducted by the master of ceremonies to their seats to the left or right of the Amir.[72] The informal character of court proceedings during Dost Muhammad Khan's early rule is also reflected by the events following his coronation. According to Masson, the *darbar* was 'the scene of much mirth, if not buffoonery' for some days afterwards. Apparently the only change in ceremonial instituted was that Dost Muhammad Khan was henceforth to be addressed as 'Amir Sahib' instead of 'Sardar.' In a playful attempt to enforce this new rule it was decided that chiefs who lapsed into the old form of address were to be fined one rupee.[73]

Although most of the tribal leaders were not entirely won over by Dost Muhammad Khan's emphasis on his role as *primus inter pares*, they could not help but note a stark contrast between his easy manners and the strict ceremonial instituted by Shah Shuja' during his reign with British backing from 1839–1842. Possibly in an attempt to hark back to past Sadozai splendor, Shah Shuja' was as remote from his subjects as Dost Muhammad Khan had been accessible to them. Even the nobility had difficulty gaining admittance to the royal court and had to stand for hours at a respectful distance before Shah Shuja' with their hands folded. Often they had to retire from the *darbar* without being allowed to address the king. This had the effect that the Durrani and Qizilbash leaders who had been in favor of Shah Shuja' at the beginning of the British invasion were offended within one month after his arrival in Kabul.[74]

Harlan, Lal, and Masson note with abhorrence the cruel strategies Dost Muhammad Khan employed against his enemies and rivals but readily allow for the possibility that the circumstances of his time did not leave any other course of action open to him. Pointing to Dost Muhammad Khan's military abilities and his 'calm, prudent and wise' manner in cabinet, Lal grudgingly admits that he may be the only person of his time fit to rule the 'vagabond Afghans.'[75] While refusing to see any greatness in Dost Muhammad Khan, Masson also concedes that he 'is... well skilled in stratagem and polity, and only employs the sword when other means fail.'[76] The Amir had the reputation of being 'fair and impartial' in questions where his political interests did not interfere. In the late 1820s his reputation for justice had already become so proverbial that the rhetorical question, 'Is Dost Muhammad dead, that there is no justice?' had become a common phrase among the inhabitants of Kabul. He was also praised for having reestablished relative political stability at Kabul and allowing the city to resume its commercial activities. Travellers Masson met on the way from Qandahar to Kabul generally described the state of Kabul as *abad wa fariman*, 'flourishing and plentiful.'[77]

Nevertheless, the frequent acts of treachery and cruelty the Amir had committed in the course of his rise to power, along with his reputation for avarice, had earned him the permanent distrust of the tribal leaders around him by the 1830s. In their opinion, his display of moderation and love of justice only served as a veneer for his ambitious political aims. On his part, Dost Muhammad Khan also seems to have eyed his courtiers with constant suspicion. Unable to trust his companions, he viewed them as temporary accomplices at best and dangerous enemies at worst. As a possible exception to this rule, he greatly valued the advice of his elder brother Nawwab 'Abd al-Jabbar Khan and his nephew Nawwab Muhammad Zaman Khan. Despite the fact that he forcefully deprived these two nobles of their governorships of Laghman and Jalalabad in 1831 and 1834 respectively they continued to play a steady role in his administration.[78] In general, however, Dost Muhammad Khan's relationships with his courtiers were characterized by constant vigilance and poorly concealed tension. While he needed to garner support for his fledgling government by an outward show of affability and accessibility, the Amir also had to make sure that his political allies did not pose a threat to his authority by rising to all too powerful positions.

DOST MUHAMMAD KHAN'S SPHERE OF INFLUENCE 1826–1839

After his assumption of power at Kabul Dost Muhammad Khan directed most of his efforts to the establishment of a regular army. By 1832 his army consisted of 9,000 cavalry and 2,000 infantry and was considered the strongest military force within Afghanistan.[79] While Dost Muhammad Khan's relative military strength discouraged further attempts by his brothers to take over Kabul, his own sphere of influence remained limited to the vicinity of the former Sadozai capital during the early years of his reign. In the late 1820s his authority ended twenty miles south of Kabul. The base of the Hindu Kush formed the northern boundary of his realm. Until 1826 Parwan was held by his rebellious nephew, Habibullah, whose force included Uzbeks and Hazaras.[80] Although Dost Muhammad Khan controlled Bamiyan, the routes leading there were in Hazara hands. In the east, his supremacy ended at the Jagdalak Pass. Jalalabad and Laghman remained under the authority of Nawwab Muhammad Zaman Khan and Nawwab 'Abd al-Jabbar Khan. The revenues of Balabagh were collected by Nawwab 'Abd al-Samad Khan's son Muhammad 'Usman Khan. Governed by Dost Muhammad Khan's full brother Amir Muhammad Khan, Ghazni formally belonged to the Amir's sphere of influence. Nonetheless, Amir Muhammad Khan exercised 'absolute power' at Ghazni and it is doubtful whether he submitted revenue payments to Dost Muhammad Khan.[81] Apart from formalities, such as the striking of coins and the reading of the *khutba* in the Amir's name, the early Muhammadzai kingdom thus only had 'miniature' resemblance with the empire it had replaced.[82] In the course of the 1830s Dost Muhammad Khan was able to gain direct control over Jalalabad and Ghazni. While tracing the events accompanying his consolidation of power, this section will focus on the political setting in the regions forming the core of this possession, that is, Kabul, Kohistan and Bamiyan.

Kabul in the Early Nineteenth Century

The changing political constellations in the early nineteenth century coincided with a sharpening sense of ethnic/religious divisions among the various segments of the population in and around Kabul. Cultivating links with one or the other of the local groups, the contestants for power played on, and in effect enhanced, existing rivalries. This brought about an increasing polarization along confessional lines, pitting the Shi'i Qizilbash and Hazaras against the Sunni inhabitants of Kabul and Kohistan. The divisions between the various ethnic groups were also reflected by spatial boundaries. Therefore, I will begin with a description of Kabul and its population before moving on to the narrative of the political developments of the early Muhammadzai period.

Located at an elevation of 6,500 feet, Kabul city is 'seated at the western extremity of a spacious plain, in an angle formed by the approach of two inferior hill ridges' (Koh-i Asmai and Koh-i'Sher Darwaza). Because of its proximity to the passes leading accross the Hindu Kush and the Sulaiman mountains, the city of Kabul had traditionally enjoyed a central position in the trade with Central Asia and India. Despite the political unrest it had endured since the turn of the century it was still noted as a lively commercial city in the 1830s, and was able to maintain its position as a trading center even after the destruction of its bazaar by the British in 1842.[83]

In the early nineteenth century Kabul consisted of three geographically and administratively distinct centers, the citadel (*bala hisar*), the city of Kabul, and Chindawul. Similar to Peshawar, but unlike Ghazni, Qandahar, and Herat, the citadel of Kabul was located separately, on the eastern spurs of the Koh-e Sher Darwaza. In the 1820s the citadel inhabited by the Muhammadzai Sardars was generally referred to as *bala hisar-i payin*, the 'lower citadel,' pointing to the fact that there had been an 'upper' one (*bala hisar-i bala*) on the mountain ridge to the south of the city. Timur Shah erected the lower citadel between 1775 and 1779, reserving the upper one for state prisoners. In Dost Muhammad Khan's time, only the Bala Hisar-i Payin was in use, the upper citadel having fallen into ruins. The Bala Hisar-i Payin consisted not only of the citadel but contained nearly 1,000 houses, as well as its own bazaar, police, and judicial court within its walls.[84]

The city of Kabul was estimated to consist of 5,000 houses and 2,000 shops.[85] While most of the houses were 'indifferently built, especially of mud and unburnt bricks,'[86] all travellers who visited Kabul during Dost Muhammad Khan's first reign were favorably impressed with its bazaars. In May 1832 Mohan Lal almost grew lyrical in his description of the Chaharsu bazaar:

> The shops displayed a profusion of those fruits which I used to esteem costly luxuries. The parts of the bazar which are arched over exceed anything the imagination can picture. The shops rise over each other, in steps glittering in tinsel splendour, till, from the effect of elevation, the whole fades into a confused and twinkling mass, like stars shining through clouds.[87]

Like other Muslim cities, the city of Kabul displayed two major organizing principles. Firstly, the principal markets formed the main axes. Extending along straight lines from east to west, they formed conduits of traffic and linked the individual living quarters of the city with each other. The second component, the quarters (*maḥallas*), on the other hand, consisted of small, winding dead-end alleys (*kuchas*) which gave access to the individual houses. The houses were built like small fortresses, allowing access only at one guarded point. The walls adjoining the streets were usually bare and all activity was directed to an inner courtyard.[88] The contrast between the wide open bazaar streets and the secluded living quarters reflects the two different foci of Muslim social life, the 'public' sphere and the more inaccessible 'private' sphere. The thoroughfares, markets, mosques, baths, wells, etc were open to everybody, including strangers. The private household, on the other hand, was solely reserved for family members. Apart from servants, the employment of outsiders was restricted to 'public' locations, which led to the separation of living and working quarters, which in Europe only became the rule with the industrial revolution.

The *kucha* not only assumed an intermediary position between the public throroughfares and the family living quarters but also afforded physical protection in times of crises. Again Kabul shares with other Muslim cities the characteristic that it displayed an 'inner' rather than an 'outer' fortification.[89] Surrounded by a weak mud wall, the city had only two gates on its seven entrances.[90] The *kuchas*, on the other hand, were individually fortified and formed the basic unit of organization:

> [The kuchas] are enclosed and entered by small gates. In occasions of war or tumult the entrance gates are built up, and the city contains as many different fortresses as there are kuchas in it. This means of defence is called kucha-bandi (closing up the kuchas). It must be obvious, that an insecure state of society has induced this precautionary mode of arrangement in the building of the city.[91]

The total population of Kabul and its immediate environs was estimated at 9,000 families or 50,000 to 60,000 souls. Among these, approximately 4500 families were furnished by the Qizilbash, who, along with the Hazaras, were set apart from the other Kabulis by their Shi'i beliefs.[92] While the majority of the Sunnis and approximately 2,000 Hindus dwelled in the city of Kabul, the Qizilbash had separate bases at a distance from the city, as, for instance, in Chindawul. Located to the southwest of the city of Kabul, Chindawul was the stronghold of the Jawansher Qizilbash. In the 1820s it contained about 1,500 to 2,000 houses. Surrounded by 'lofty walls,' it functioned as an autonomous unit, with its own mosques, markets, police, and judicial courts. Another Qizilbash base had developed during Timur Shah's time at Muradkhani near the Lahore gate. In 1772–73, when Timur Shah transferred his capital from Qandahar to Kabul, this region was apportioned to the Popalzai Sardar Murad Khan Qalandarzai, who not only settled his own relatives there but also allotted lands to the Qizilbash soldiers serving in his military contingent. In the early nineteenth century the Qizilbash population of Muradkhani amounted to 1,500 families and was made up of Khafis, Kirmanis, Simnanis, Shirazis and Jalairs under six chiefs. Mahmud Khan, the chief of the Bayats, resided with 700 families in a separate fort. Approximately 300 Afshar families lived in forts at a distance from the city, one of them being Nanakchi north of Kabul.[93]

The Qizilbash

The 'Khurasani' or 'Persian' groups settled in the vicinity of Kabul included some Sunni groups, such as the Rikas, who were of Kurdish origin. The majority of the Iranian groups residing near Kabul, however, were furnished by the Qizilbash, the Jawanshers forming their principal division. Coined in the late fifteenth century, the term *qizilbash* ('red head') referred to the red headgear worn by the members of the Turkoman tribes supporting Shaikh Haidar (d. 1488), the father of the founder of the Safawid dynasty. During the Safawid era, the Qizilbash enjoyed an influential position as administrators and provincial governors. Holding many governorships as *tiyul*, they furnished the Safawid kings with up to 70,000 horsemen in return. As western Afghanistan formed part of the Safawid empire, small numbers of Qizilbash began to move to Herat and Qandahar during this period.[94]

The presence of the greater group of Qizilbash in Afghanistan is generally traced to the garrisons created by Nadir Shah in Qandahar and Kabul during his Indian campaign in 1738–9. The garrison in Kabul, for example, is said to have consisted of 12,000 families.[95] According to this point of view, Ahmad Shah incorporated Qizilbash already present in the area into the administration of his nascent state. Prior to his conquest of Qandahar in the summer of 1747 he was able to confiscate a convoy with revenues from Punjab and Sind intended for Nadir Shah and convinced one of its leaders to enter his service. Muhammad Taqi Khan Shirazi, who had been Nadir Shah's *beglarbegi* (military governor-general) of Sind and Punjab, in turn induced a large number of Qizilbash stationed in Kabul and Punjab to join Ahmad Shah's ranks.[96] Most Afghan historians, by contrast, emphasize that the Sadozai kings played a more crucial role than Nadir Shah in settling the Qizilbash in Afghanistan. Fofalzai points out that Nadir Shah withdrew most of his troops to western Afghanistan in 1740, only leaving one army contingent (*dasta*) each in Kabul and Qandahar. Furthermore, he doubts that Nadir Shah added any permanent settlements to Kabul. In his opinion, major groups of 'new and old Khurasanis' were brought to Kabul and given lands on the basis of their tribal allegiances in the vicinity of the city by Ahmad Shah in 1748 and 1755. One of the settlements erected during this time was the 'Chindawul,' given to the commander of the rearguard of Ahmad Shah's army, Wali Muhammad Khan Jawansher. The Rikas and further Qizilbash groups were settled in Kabul during the reign of Timur Shah.[97]

Shah Zaman's historian Husaini holds that Ahmad Shah brought the Qizilbash from Iran to form his personal bodyguard, the *ghulam khana*.[98] Consisting of cavalry and artillery, this division was made up in great part of Qizilbash but also contained other non-Durrani troops, such as Tajiks, Hazaras, Ferozkohis, Jamshedis, Taimanis, Qalmaqs and Habashis.[99] There is some difference of opinion concerning the exact proportion of the Qizilbash in the *ghulam khana*. According to Singh, the Qizilbash made up one third of this body at Ahmad Shah's time.[100] Timur Shah relied heavily on the Qizilbash as administrators and mercenaries in local expeditions. During his time the *ghulam khana* was expanded to 12,000 men as a counterpoise to the Durrani cavalry.[101] According to Husaini, the *ghulam khana* furnished 15,000 out of Shah Zaman's total cavalry of 100,000 and consisted mostly of Qizilbash. Burnes reports that the Qizilbash retained a great degree of their autonomous organization and only pledged direct allegiance to their individual *khans*, who were in turn answerable to the king. This statement is borne out by the fact that the command of the entire bodyguard rested with the Qizilbash leader Mahmud Khan Bayat during Timur Shah's time. Up to Shah Zaman's reign the Khurasani contingents were listed according to tribal allegiance. The prestigious palace guard of *kashikchis* was under the command of the Jawansher chiefs Ja'far Khan and Khan Shirin Khan. Nevertheless Shah Zaman also entrusted the command of certain *ghulam* contingents to outsiders such as his Pashtun father-in-law, Nur Muhammad Babar Amin al-Mulk and the treasurer Iltifat Khan.[102]

A petition written by Ja'far Khan Jawansher shortly before Shah Zaman's coronation insists on the necessity of maintaining tribal distinctions within the army and may reflect a reaction to an attempt by the Sadozai rulers to override the autonomous organization of the Qizilbash cavalry. Ja'far Khan's and Arsalan Khan's participation in Payinda Khan's plot to depose Shah Zaman was possibly prompted by similar fears of the king's planned centralization of government offices.[103] The death of these two Qizilbash leaders caused the Qizilbash of Kabul and Qandahar to lend Fatih Khan crucial support in bringing Shah Mahmud to power.[104] Despite Fatih Khan's and Shah Mahmud's great dependence on the Qizilbash, the political role of this group began to decline along with the disintegration of Sadozai rule and their role in the military began to dwindle. As the organization of the bodyguards vanished with the Sadozais, only certain *ghulam khana* divisions were able to gain a foothold in Dost Muhammad Khan's new army. In the late 1830s most of their employment had shifted from military offices to administrative services as secretaries (*mirzas*) and stewards (*nazirs*) for individual chiefs. Only one thousand of them served in the Amir's cavalry of 12,000.[105]

Sunni-Shi'a Frictions

In the 1830s Masson described the Qizilbash as the 'most powerful and influential body' in the city of Kabul.[106] At the same time, their continuous efforts to heighten and improve the walls enclosing Chindawul indicated that they felt far from secure.[107] These walls had provided vital protection for the Qizilbash in June 1803, when they found themselves besieged by thousands of irate Sunnis from Kabul, Logar and Kohistan. At first sight a confrontation between the Sunni and Shi'i population of the region, this first 'religious war' of Afghanistan, as Ghubar has called it,[108] represented in many ways a political conflict in which the Qizilbash were identified with the party of Shah Mahmud and Fatih Khan Muhammadzai. The men upholding 'Sunni' interests were Sher Muhammad Khan Bamizai and Mir Wa'iz, the imam of the Jami' Masjid of Pul-i Khishti, who enjoyed a wide following among the Sunnis of Kabul and Kohistan. While little is known about Mir Wa'iz's previous interaction with the court, Ferrier reports that his hostility to Shah Mahmud was well known. Sher Muhammad Khan clearly used this riot as a means to weaken his rival Fatih Khan and to strengthen the cause of Shah Shuja'.[109]

There exist two main versions of the events that led to this outbreak of violence. According to Elphinstone, the resentment was triggered when a young Sunni of Kabul was executed for having killed a Qizilbash during a quarrel. When the enraged populace tried to hold a funeral for the corpse of the executed man, they found themselves fired on by the Qizilbash and had to retire to the house of Mir Wa'iz with the corpse.[110] The author of *Siraj al-tawarikh* and Ferrier, on the other hand, point to the lewd behavior of several Qizilbash men toward a Sunni youth as external cause for the riot. Seeking justice, the father of the abused boy complained to the king. In an attempt to avoid alienating the Qizilbash, Shah Mahmud referred the matter to the *shari'at* court. Apparently equally reluctant to pursue the issue, the Qazi Mulla Muhammad Sa'id Khan Barakzai refused to accept the claims of the father unless he could furnish clear proof of or witnesses to the crime. Unable to obtain redress for their claims, the family of the victim proceeded barefoot and bareheaded to the Jami' Masjid of Pul-i Khishti on the following Friday, placed the boy under the pulpit, and implored Mir Wa'iz for help. Mir Wa'iz reacted promptly by issuing a *fatwa* ordering the assassination and plunder of the Qizilbash.[111] The people of Kabul city (*shahr o bazar*) immediately besieged Chindawul and set fire to the Qizilbash houses located outside its walls. After a few days 20,000 Kohistanis and people from Logar joined the siege. At this point Shah Mahmud appointed Sher Muhammad Khan Bamizai and Sardar Ahmad Khan Nurzai to quell the riot. Rather than following the king's order, however, these two men did their best to fan the flames of the uproar against the Shi'as. Fatih Khan assumed a neutral position during the first four days of fighting. But as Mir Wa'iz's inflammatory preachings continued and the conflict showed no sign of abatement, Fatih Khan and his brothers intervened in favor of the Qizilbash and dispersed the rioters. After a total loss of four hundred lives or more on both sides peace was restored to Kabul.[112]

After the riot had subsided Mir Wa'iz, Sher Muhammad Khan Bamizai, and Sardar Ahmad Khan Nurzai agreed to continue to cooperate in the attempt to remove Shah Mahmud and Fatih Khan from power. The opportunity to do so arose when Fatih Khan had to leave Kabul in order to collect the revenues of Bamiyan and the Hazara territories tributary to Shah Mahmud. The three conspirators invited Shah Shuja' to assume control of Kabul and besieged Shah Mahmud in the Bala Hisar with the support of their followers. Shortly afterwards Shah Shuja' approached Kabul with an army of 150,000 men and encouraged the siege. In the meantime, Fatih Khan returned with a strong army enforced by 10,000 troops from Hazara and Bamiyan but was defeated by Shah Shuja' and had to flee to Qandahar.[113] During Shah Shuja''s reign, Sher Muhammad Khan Bamizai and Mir Wa'iz continued to play an important role in the politics of Kabul. In 1807–8, however, their combined effort to further their political clout by placing Qaisar Mirza on the throne put an end to their careers. Sher Muhammad Khan died in battle and Mir Wa'iz was executed after Shah Shuja''s return to Kabul. After the deaths of these two dignitaries, their sons Hafiz Ji and 'Ata Muhammad Khan maintained close links with the Sunni population of Kabul.

When Shah Mahmud regained power in 1809 the Qizilbash continued to play a prominent role as supporters of the king. At the same time, they remained the main target of political unrest in Kabul. Particularly at times when Fatih Khan and his army had to leave the capital for prolonged military campaigns, the Qizilbash quarters in Kabul became vulnerable to Sunni attacks. In 1811 Fatih Khan and Dost Muhammad Khan had to cut short their attempt to collect the revenues of Kashmir because of political turmoil in Kabul. Two ulama, Sayyid Ashraf from Kohistan and Sayyid 'Ata, had used the Sardars' absence to place Shah Mahmud's half brother 'Abbas on the throne and to incite their Sunni followers to attack the Qizilbash quarters in Kabul. This led the Qizilbash members of Fatih Khan's army to depart precipitately for Kabul, forcing him to retreat to Peshawar. Sardar Dost Muhammad Khan decided to lead the Qizilbash division to Kabul. After a battle of ten days, he was able to take Shahzada 'Abbas prisoner and to have Sayyid Ashraf and Sayyid 'Ata executed.[114]

The crucial role of Qizilbash support for Dost Muhammad Khan in his effort to gain control of Kabul in the years between 1823 and 1826 has already been mentioned. While Dost Muhammad Khan primarily relied on his double link with the Qizilbash by maternal descent and marriage alliance, his opponents cultivated the Sunni leaders of Kabul. Habibullah Khan made Hafiz Ji his main advisor. In his vain attempt to ward off his brother's quest for power, Sultan Muhammad Khan exclusively united with Sunni leaders.[115] With Dost Muhammad Khan's assumption of power, the Qizilbash were soon disappointed in their hopes for greater patronage. Due to his limited resources, the Amir relied on armed personal servants rather than the *ghulam khana* as bodyguards. Along with the other troops the Qizilbash suffered a cut in their pay after the first campaign against the Sikhs in 1835. Dost Muhammad Khan's lack of support for the Qizilbash may also be attributed to the need to conciliate other tribal leaders. His proclamation as Amir al-Muminin was an attempt to gain legitimacy in the eyes of the wider population. Furthermore, he was eager to disassociate himself from the Qizilbash by ridiculing their supposed lack of courage in combat and by showing contempt for Shi'a doctrines.[116] When a conflict broke out between the Jawanshers and the Achakzais during the Muharram celebration in 1832, Dost Muhammad Khan assumed a neutral position, appointing Haji Khan Kakar and Nawwab 'Abd al-Jabbar Khan respectively as the agents of the Shi'as and Sunnis.[117]

At the onset of the First Anglo-Afghan War (1839–1842) the Qizilbash readily joined Shah Shuja''s administration, serving as tax collectors, clerks, and commissary suppliers for the British. Khan Shirin Khan entered Shah Shuja''s service at the head of a contingent of Qizilbash cavalry. This preferential treatment notwithstanding, the Jawansher chief had not become entirely alienated from Dost Muhammad Khan and was heard to complain that Shah Shuja' treated him less respectfully than the Muhammadzai ruler.[118] During Dost Muhammad Khan's second reign (1843–1863), Khan Shirin Khan played a steady role at the court of the Amir. Nonetheless Sunni-Shi'a unrest continued to flare up now and then. Early in 1852, for instance, a 'serious disturbance' broke out in Kabul after Sher Muhammad Khan b. Pir Muhammad Khan attempted to force his way into a bath occupied by the females of a Qizilbash family. In the ensuing quarrel Sher Muhammad Khan was killed and the Qizilbash surrounded his father's house. Dost Muhammad Khan put an end to the unrest by sending troops to Chindawul.[119] Almost two years later an indecent remark made by a Kabuli towards the women of Khan Shirin Khan's family embroiled about two hundred people in a fight, leaving one Sunni dead. Again Dost Muhammad Khan openly took the side of the Sunnis and placed four Jawanshers under surveillance, ordering Khan Shirin Khan to hand over the murderers. In response, Khan Shirin Khan, along with fifty other Jawanshers and Muradkhanis, handed in a petition accusing Dost Muhammad Khan of ignoring their plight as a minority in Kabul and asking him to relieve them of their service. In the negotiations that followed Sultan Muhammad Khan again aligned himself with the Sunni faction, while his younger brother Pir Muhammad Khan acted as a liaison with the Jawanshers. Under the mediation of Hafiz Ji it was finally decided that the Jawanshers were to pay a fine of 1,000 rupees in exchange for the release of the four men seized by Dost Muhammad Khan.[120] During the power struggles surrounding the reign of Dost Muhammad Khan's successor Sher 'Ali Khan, the Qizilbash of Chindawul assumed an important role as they made up the bulk of the troops of the new Amir's nephew, Sardar

Muhammad Isma'il b. Muhammad Amin Khan. Initially Isma'il Khan aligned himself with the faction of Sher 'Ali Khan's rivals. In August 1868, however, he secured Sher 'Ali Khan's reentry into the city and citadel of Kabul with the support of his Qizilbash followers. In June 1869, when his hopes for the governorship of the western districts of Turkistan failed to materialize, he rebelled and occupied Chindawul. Sher 'Ali Khan assembled forces on the Koh-i Sher Darwaza overlooking Chindawul and threatened to destroy the Qizilbash quarters if the inhabitants sided with Muhammad Isma'il Khan. After a stalemate of three weeks the conflict was brought to an end by the meditation of the Qizilbash leadership. Muhammad Isma'il Khan was exiled to India. While concluded peacefully, Sardar Muhammad Isma'il Khan's rebellion once again highlighted the exposed position of the Qizilbash in the politics of Kabul.[121]

Kohistan

There is little information on the exact composition of the Sunni population of Kabul. The only group mentioned in the confrontations with the Qizilbash are the Achakzais, who had been settled in Kabul by Timur Shah in 1773 and lived close to Chindawul.[122] In their attacks on the Qizilbash, the Sunnis of Kabul were often supported by the Kohistanis, who, as mentioned above, had a close connection with Mir Wa'iz and his sons Mir Haji and Hafiz Ji. In this section, I will discuss the position of the Kohistani leadership within the nascent Muhammadzai state.

Adjoining Kabul to the north, Kohistan includes the basins of Kohdaman and Charikar and leads to the valleys of Ghorband, Panjsher, Nijrau, and Tagau. Bounded on the east, west and north by high mountains, it was characterized by Masson as a 'punch bowl,'.[123] Despite its proximity to Kabul, its overwhelmingly Tajik population had successfully evaded government control until the beginning of the nineteenth century. While some parts of Kohistan were held as *jagir* by individuals favored by the royal court, the remaining districts yielded no revenue to speak of to the Sadozais.[124] The general strategy of the Kohistanis was to withdraw to the higher mountain tracts whenever punitive expeditions were sent against them. During Shah Mahmud's second reign, for example, Fatih Khan had to content himself with destroying the fields and orchards of some chiefs based in Istalif because he was unable to force them to engage in an open military confrontation. In retaliation, the Kohistani chiefs in question descended on the Wazir's garden and ploughed up his entire plantation as soon as he left Kabul on some other campaign.[125]

The relative freedom of the Kohistanis came to an end when Fatih Khan appointed Dost Muhammad Khan governor to the region in 1813. Masson, who travelled to the area in the 1830s, noted that 'it is scarcely possible to visit any place in the Koh Daman or Kohistan without learning some proof of the justice or severity of Dost Muhammad Khan.'[126] Within two months after his appointment to Kohistan, Dost Muhammad Khan had 'pacified' the region by killing many of the influential leaders, including Baqa Khan of Parwan, Khwaja Khanji of Karzai, and Saqi Khan of Sheshburja, as well as Agha Jan and Malikji Khan of Istarghij. Another prominent victim of Dost Muhammad Khan was Sayyid Ashrat (Ashraf?), an influential *'alim* of Opian. The robber chiefs of Kohdaman were offered the choice between serving the Sardar or being blown from the mouth of a cannon. Dost Muhammad Khan's reign of terror had the effect that three or four thousand families left Kohistan for Balkh.[127]

Parts of Kohistan, in particular Istalif, formed an important basis of support for Dost Muhammad Khan during his conflicts with Sardars Muhammad 'Azim Khan, Habibullah Khan, and Sherdil Khan. However, the region as a whole became independent during the power struggle among the Muhammadzai Sardars. When Dost Muhammad Khan assumed control of Kabul in 1826 his authority in Kohistan was extremely limited and his tax collectors operated under the constant threat of death. But the loss of the revenue-rich provinces of Kashmir, Multan, Derajat and Peshawar forced the Sardar to assert his authority over Kohistan. Another series of executions of 'ringleaders,' such as Nurak Shakardarrai, Sayyid Baba Qushqari, and Zaman Khan Istalifi followed. In 1831 a rebellion by the inhabitants of Tagau under their chief Mazu (Ma'azullah) Tagawi and their defeat of Nawwab 'Abd al-Jabbar Khan gave Dost Muhammad Khan the opportunity to start a massive military campaign eastward. Mazu Tagawi was taken prisoner and consented to pay revenue. Subsequently the Sardar used Nawwab Muhammad Zaman Khan's failure to assist him in the Tagau expedition as pretext for threatening his authority in Jalalabad. After mediation by Nawwab 'Abd al-Jabbar Khan, Dost Muhammad Khan decided not to attack Jalalabad and contented himself with Muhammad Zaman Khan's offer to pay an annual tribute of 40,000 rupees. Shortly afterwards Nawwab 'Abd al-Jabbar Khan himself was deprived of the government of Laghman.[128]

At the beginning of the First Anglo-Afghan War Dost Muhammad Khan's decision to flee Kabul was caused not only by the approach of two hostile armies from Jalalabad and Qandahar but also by a widespread uprising in Kohistan. Under the leadership of Malik Shahdad Khan ('Bacha-yi Mazu') of Tagau numerous Kohistani chiefs, including those of Nijrau, Panjsher, Ghorband, and Kohdaman displaced the Amir's son Sher 'Ali Khan from the government of Charikar and occupied Kabul in favor of Shah Shuja' immediately prior to his arrival on August 7, 1839.[129] In great measure the Kohistani rebellion was brought about by British intrigues in the region. The link between the British and the Kohistanis was provided by Ghulam Khan Popalzai,[130] who had been a close associate of Dost Muhammad Khan during his early career. Failing to receive adequate compensation for his services after the Sardar's rise to power, he turned to Shah Shuja'. One of the main recipients of bribes given by Ghulam Khan in the name of the British was Dost Muhammad Khan's son-in-law Hafiz Ji b. Mir Wa'iz. Hafiz Ji's pro-British stance encouraged the Kohistani rebellion against Dost Muhammad Khan. According to *Siraj al-tawarikh*, he even led the siege on Charikar.[131] Only a year later, however, Hafiz Ji played a crucial role in galvanizing Kohistani resistance to the increasingly intrusive British administration, while there still was little active opposition to Shah Shuja' on the part of the Qizilbash and Durrani leadership.[132] The strategies of the Kohistani leaders and their allies were thus not solely determined by enmity towards Dost Muhammad Khan but rather aimed at curtailing *all* government interference emanating from Kabul.

Bamiyan and Bihsud

The events from the turn of the century up to the first Anglo-Afghan War display two broad tendencies in Afghan politics. On the one hand, many activities took the form of personal vendettas. Fatih Khan's attempt to subdue the Kohistanis during Shah Mahmud's second reign, for example, did not provoke a reaction against government lands in general. Rather, the people of Istalif chose to direct their retaliation against the property of the man they held immediately responsible for the devastation of their lands. Another instance of the personal nature of politics is furnished by the indecision of the Qizilbash in the 1830s. While the majority was dissatisfied with Dost Muhammad Khan's policies, they were unable to take a unified position against him because of his connection with two influential families among them.

At the same time a broader identification along ethnic/religious lines in the wider population is to be observed. While the political activities of the Kohistanis can in great measure be attributed to their personal allegiance to Mir Wa'iz and his sons, their attacks on the Qizilbash brought them into alignment with other Sunnis, such as the Achakzais of Kabul and the people of Logar. On the other hand, these conflicts brought about a greater sense of common identity among the Shi'as in general. This is reflected by the fact that the Hazaras assisted Fatih Khan in great numbers when he attempted to repel Shah Shuja' after the great riot instigated by Mir Wa'iz. Aware of their vulnerable position in Kabul, the Qizilbash sought to acquire a foothold in the Hazara territory of Bihsud by acquiring property and entering marriage alliances there. Furthermore, they acted as mediators between the local *mirs* and the government of Kabul.[133]

This section concerns the policies of Dost Muhammad Khan's representative Taj Muhammad Khan, popularly known as Haji Khan Kakar, in the Hazara region of Bihsud. Because of its location on the trade route to Bamiyan and its proximity to Kabul, Bihsud was the only region in

Hazarajat exposed to regular government interference during Dost Muhammad Khan's first reign. From the 1820s on the most powerful figure in Bihsud was Mir Yazdanbakhsh of Kharzar, who controlled the main approaches to Bamiyan via the 'Iraq and Hajigak Passes and was linked by marriage alliances to the chiefs of the Shaikh 'Ali and Dai Zangi Hazaras located to the northeast and northwest. Dost Muhammad Khan feared Mir Yazdanbakhsh's increasing influence and attempted to do away with the chief of Bihsud. Using the offices of the Qizilbash of Kabul, he induced the Mir to visit Kabul and promptly imprisoned him. After saving his life by offering to pay 50,000 rupees, Mir Yazdanbakhsh was able to flee to Bihsud. Despite Dost Muhammad Khan's hostile behavior he continued to submit revenues and allowed caravans bound for Turkistan to pass along the Hajigak route.[134]

In the 1820s the revenue collection in Bihsud was carried out by Amir Muhammad Khan, the governor of Ghazni. While Bihsud had only yielded 17,000 rupees in kind under the Sadozais, Amir Muhammad Khan was able to raise the revenue to 40,000 rupees. But often the collection remained incomplete due to the onset of winter and loss by plunder.[135] In 1832 Haji Khan Kakar, the governor of Bamiyan, gained a two-year contract to collect the revenues of Bihsud. The events which followed shed light on the nature of Dost Muhammad Khan's 'administration' during the early phase of his government at Kabul. Unable to establish direct control over Bamiyan and Bihsud, he relied on the services of a Pashtun mercenary, who used this opportunity to carve out an independent base of power for himself. Claiming to work in the interest of the Amir, Haji Khan Kakar inserted himself into the existing tensions between the leader of Bihsud and the ruler of the petty khanate of Saighan north of Bamiyan and eventually brought about the demise of Mir Yazadanbakhsh.

A chief of the independent southeastern Pashtun tribe of the Kakars, Haji Khan had entered Fatih Khan's service during Shah Mahmud's second reign as a 'soldier of fortune.' During the political maneuvering following Sardar Muhammad 'Azim's death in 1823 he saved Dost Muhammad Khan twice from being blinded.[136] After his assumption of power Dost Muhammad Khan rewarded him for this service by appointing him governor to Bamiyan. Although he was a relative newcomer to the political scene, Haji Khan Kakar controlled a vast fortune in the early 1830s. Apart from his *jagir* in Bamiyan assessed at 72,000 rupees, he held the Kohistani town of Robat and villages at Sar-i Chashma and in Logar. Furthermore, he farmed the collection of transit dues for the trans-Hindu Kush trade passing through Charikar for 10,000 rupees. After payment of his government dues he was estimated to have a yearly income of 150,000 rupees. While he was supposed to maintain a cavalry of 350 men, it was thought that he had 1,000 soldiers in his service, 700 of them being horsemen.[137]

The Sunni-Shi'a conflict of June 1832 gave Haji Khan Kakar the opportunity to portray himself as an advocate of Shi'i interests and to further his political ambitions in Bihsud. Initially his contract to collect the revenues in this region seemed to herald an improvement of his relationship with Mir Yazdanbakhsh. In the late 1820s the leader of Bihsud had allowed Haji Khan Kakar to station his soldiers at certain forts between Sar-i Chashma and Kalu in return for one hundred *kharwars* of wheat from the revenues of Bamiyan. Yet the amicable relationship between Haji Khan Kakar and Mir Yazdanbakhsh deteriorated in 1830 when Haji Khan's deputy at Bamiyan entered a treaty with the Tajik ruler of Saighan, Mir Muhammad 'Ali Beg. Controlling the Aqrubat route connecting Bamiyan with Turkistan, the ruler of Saighan was infamous among the Hazaras for his slave raids into the region by which he raised the revenue required by Mir Murad Beg, the Uzbek ruler of Qunduz. In response to the action of Haji Khan's deputy, Mir Yazdanbaksh ejected all the soldiers the Kakar leader had stationed in Bihsud. Assisted by Mir Zafar of Kalu and Allahdad Khan Mughal of Sayyidabad, he occupied all of Bamiyan proper with the exception of the governor's seat at the town of Bamiyan. Nevertheless, Haji Khan Kakar was able to mend his relationship with Mir Yazdanbakhsh. Claiming that his deputy had acted without his orders, he used the influence of the Kabuli Shi'as, and particularly the offices of Khan Shirin Khan, to induce the Mir of Bihsud to evacuate Bamiyan.[138]

The relationship between Haji Khan Kakar and Mir Yazdanbakhsh seemed to take a more positive turn in the summer of 1832. At a meeting in Gardan Diwal in Bihsud the two leaders reached an agreement whereby Mir Yazdanbakhsh was to assist Haji Khan Kakar in the revenue collection of Bihsud in exchange for Haji Khan's promise to engage in a military expedition against Saighan. Although he was accompanied by fewer troops than Amir Muhammad Khan during his revenue collection campaigns to Hazara,[139] Haji Khan's revenue collection in the Bihsud was uniquely successful. With the support of Mir Yazdanbakhsh he was able to raise full revenues in the areas immediately south of the Helmand river which had never paid more than fifty percent of the assessed revenue to Sardar Amir Muhammad Khan. Furthermore, he succeeded in extending his authority to areas which had completely evaded revenue payments so far.[140] While he had farmed the revenue collection of Hazara for 40,000 rupees, Haji Khan Kakar was thus able to gather 60,000 rupees in addition to numerous gifts presented by the Hazara chiefs. Futhermore, the proposed expedition against Saighan had earned him the cautious support of the chiefs of Dai Zangi. Accompanied by 2,500 Hazara troops, Haji Khan Kakar was well in the position to reduce the fortress of Saighan. To the distress of his allies, however, he reneged on his promise to engage in a military confrontation with Muhammad 'Ali Beg and negotiated a treaty with him, apparently as part of an attempt to further his influence northwards to Kahmard and Ajar.

Shortly afterwards he had Mir Yazdanbakhsh seized and returned to Bamiyan with him as a prisoner. On 8 Rajab 1248/ 2 December 1832 the Mir of Bihsud was killed at Sayyidabad.[141]

Haji Khan Kakar attempted to justify his behavior by accusing Mir Yazdanbakhsh of having willingly foiled his military campaign. Furthermore, he claimed to have acted according to the orders of Dost Muhammad Khan. Neither excuse found much credence with his Kakar official Sa'd al-Din and the chiefs of the *ghulam khana* in his service. It is in fact doubtful whether any of Haji Khan Kakar's actions would have met with Dost Muhammad Khan's approval or active encouragement. Even prior to Haji Khan's departure for Hazarajat, Dost Muhammad Khan had felt so threatened by the increasing influence of the Kakar chief that he had reduced his military force for service in Bihsud from 1,500 to 300. Haji Khan Kakar's pact with Mir Yazdanbakhsh and his successful revenue collection can only have added to Dost Muhammad Khan's apprehensions. Masson, who accompanied the campaign to Bihsud and Saighan, formed the impression that Haji Khan Kakar was toying with the idea of assuming independent authority at Bamiyan with the support of Mir Yazdanbakhsh. He even proposed that Masson become his *wazir.* The reasons for the arrest and assassination of Mir Yazdanbakhsh are less clear. Characterized by one of the leaders of the *ghulam khana* as typically 'Afghan', Haji Khan's actions were possibly guided by short-term economic considerations. Having expended the revenues of Bamiyan in the attempt to extend his influence northward, the Kakar chief faced the difficult task of providing for his troops during the harsh winter in his province. The arrest of Mir Yazdanbakhsh allowed him to ask for a ransom of 20,000 rupees, the castle of Kharzar, and some forts along the Hajigak route. The other Hazara chiefs present in Bamiyan at the time of Mir Yazdanbakhsh's arrest were 'fined' 30,000 rupees. When the Mir's deputy at Kharzar resisted complying with Haji Khan Kakar's demands he allowed the sons of Mir Yazdanbakhsh's enemy Wakil Saifullah to do away with his most formidable rival in the area.[142]

Still unable to support his troops in Bamiyan, Haji Khan Kakar again turned northwards and proceeded to Qunduz. Cordially received by Mir Murad Beg, he negotiated a treaty according to which Kahmard, Saighan, and Ajar were to be incorporated into the government of Bamiyan. On his return to Kabul in the following spring, he was accompanied by envoys from Bukhara, Khulm, Shibarghan and Qunduz, as well as the chief of Ajar and the sons of Rahmatullah Beg of Kahmard and Mir Muhammad 'Ali Beg of Saighan. The end of Haji Khan's career was as typical of the circumstances prevailing in Dost Muhammad Khan's realm as his rise. Dost Muhammad Khan simply refused to accept his agreement with Mir Murad Beg and scarcely acknowledged the presence of the representatives he had brought along. Although the Amir himself had earlier resorted to similar tactics, he used Haji Khan's reprehensible conduct towards Mir Yazdanbakhsh as a welcome pretext to deprive the Kakar chief of the government of Bamiyan and to appoint his own son Ghulam Haidar in his stead.[143] Haji Khan Kakar's policies in Bihsud and Bamiyan thus turned out to be as short-lived as they were disastrous. While more or less independent of Kabul, he found himself unable to command the resources necessary for maintaining a strong standing army, which in turn would have enabled him to affect the balance of power between periphery and center in a lasting manner.

Dost Muhammad Khan's Consolidation of Power

Dost Muhammad Khan's relative powerlessness during the early years of his reign is amply demonstrated by the narrative of Haji Khan Kakar's machinations in Bihsud and Turkistan. Apart from Kohistan, which was governed by Dost Muhammad Khan's son Muhammad Akbar Khan, few local areas were touched directly by the Kabul administration. In the course of the 1830s, however, the ruler of Kabul was gradually able to extend his authority. The appointment of Ghulam Haidar Khan as governor of Bamiyan was one step. In the following years, Dost Muhammad Khan was to reach for the governments of Jalalabad and Ghazni, thus entering an open confrontation with his nephews Muhammad 'Usman b. Nawwab 'Abd al Samad Khan, Nawwab Muhammad Zaman b. Nawwab Asad Khan, and Sardar Shams al-Din b. Amir Muhammad Khan Khan.

The opportunity to extend his authority eastwards arose in early 1834 when Shah Shuja''s approach on Qandahar caused the 'Dil' brothers to ask Dost Muhammad Khan for military assistance. Rather than proceeding directly to Qandahar, however, the ruler of Kabul diverted his troops eastward towards Siyahsang. His sons Muhammad Akram Khan and Muhammad Akbar Khan were sent towards Jalalabad where they scattered the army of Nawwab Muhammad Zaman Khan by taking horses and equipment under the pretext of raising an army for the war against Shah Shuja'. In the meantime, Dost Muhammad Khan moved to Jagdalak, the border of the province of Jalalabad. Here Muhammad 'Usman Khan, who held the government of Balabagh by appointment from Muhammad Zaman Khan, submitted to the authority of the Kabul government under the provision that his town would be spared a military attack.[144]

After Dost Muhammad Khan's first attempt to gain control of Jalalabad, Nawwab Muhammad Zaman Khan had entered negotiations with the Peshawar Sardars to garner assistance in case of a renewed attack. At the time of Shah Shuja''s preparations for his campaign to southern Afghanistan, however, Sultan Muhammad Khan himself was threatened by the advance of the Sikh army on Peshawar and was unable to offer any help to the ruler of Jalalabad. Only supported by local chiefs, such as Sayyid

Faqir of Kunar and Sa'adat Khan Mohmand of La'lpura, Nawwab Muhammad Zaman Khan found himself unable to hold Jalalabad against Dost Muhammad Khan's forces.

Dost Muhammad Khan compensated Nawwab Muhammad Zaman Khan with a *jagir* worth 150,000 rupees per year and appointed first Amir Muhammad Khan and subsequently Muhammad Akbar Khan governors of Jalalabad.[145] Extending from the Jagdalak Pass in the west to the town of Dakka in the Mohmand territory, the province of Jalalabad, including the Tajik villages of Laghman, yielded a revenue of 400,000 rupees. After the takeover by Dost Muhammad Khan the revenue was raised to 465,000 rupees.[146] Moreover, new regions became tributary to the Muhammadzai governors. The valley of Kunar, for example, had been more or less independent under the leadership of Sayyid Faqir. After the conquest of Jalalabad, Sayyid Faqir's rival Sayyid Baha al-Din was installed as chief in exchange for a yearly revenue of 19,000 rupees. Sa'adat Khan Mohmand, by contrast, was able to maintain his independence and became one of Dost Muhammad Khan's strongest allies in the region east of Jalalabad.

Shortly after Dost Muhammad Khan's successful battle against Shah Shuja' at Qandahar in July 1834, his full brother Amir Muhammad Khan died and his son Shams al-Din succeeded to the government of Ghazni. Including the districts of Nani, Oba, Qarabagh and Muqur, this province had yielded 200,000 rupees under the Sadozais. Amir Muhammad Khan had been able to extend his authority to the provinces of Wardak and Logar, thus adding 120,000 rupees to his income. A ruthless but able administrator, he also extracted greater revenues within the district of Ghazni. For example, the revenues of the Muhammad Khwaja Hazaras were raised from 25,000 to 35,000 rupees. Including town duties and transit fees on caravans, his revenues amounted to 404,000 rupees.[147]

After the death of Amir Muhammad Khan, Ghazni formally maintained its independence. Naib Amir Akhundzada and Zarin Khan Barakzai, who had played a leading role in Amir Muhammad Khan's government, remained in office under Shams al-Din Khan. But in 1837 Dost Muhammad Khan began to take active steps to assume direct authority over Ghazni. Although both Naib Amir Akhundzada and Zarin Khan Barakzai had successfully participated as military leaders in the battle against the Sikhs at Jamrud in April 1837, the Amir now began to evince signs of displeasure with them. He questioned the trustworthiness of Naib Amir by starting an inquiry into his accounts and confiscated the *jagirs* of both officials. Following this prelude, Dost Muhammad Khan unceremoniously removed Shams al-Din Khan and his family from Ghazni and appointed his own son Ghulam Haidar governor.[148]

Once the take over of Ghazni was completed, the Amir 'publicly avowed his exultation, and remarked that now he felt secure, and convinced that his government had firmly taken root.'[149] Indeed, Dost Muhammad Khan's fortunes had risen considerably. The revenues of Kabul and Kohistan had only provided an income of 500,000 rupees for his early government. In 1837, however, he had been able to assume control over much of eastern Afghanistan and to distribute most governorships among his sons. His eldest son, Muhammad Afzal Khan, held Zurmat, a district east of Ghazni. Muhammad Akbar Khan was governor of Jalalabad and Laghman. A'zam Khan was in charge of Bamiyan and Bihsud, which now yielded 80,000 rupees per year.[150] Ghulam Haidar Khan governed Ghazni. Shams al-Din Khan was appointed governor of Kohistan. It was generally estimated that Dost Muhammad Khan's revenues had increased to 2,400,000–2,600,000 rupees in the late 1830s. This increase was not only due to the acquisition of new territories but the successful collection of higher rates of revenue.[151] Despite this dramatic increase of power Dost Muhammad Khan controlled only a fraction of the former Sadozai empire. His feelings of security were mostly based on the fact that he need not fear his immediate relatives as rivals to the authority of Kabul any more. Yet within two years after his annexation of Ghazni, the British were to invade Afghanistan and to depose Dost Muhammad Khan in favor of Shah Shuja'. Thus the Amir first became a refugee in Bukhara and then a prisoner of the British, and his efforts at statebuilding seemed to have come to naught.

THE FIRST ANGLO-AFGHAN WAR (1839–1842) AND AMIR DOST MUHAMMAD KHAN'S RESUMPTION OF POWER

The First Anglo-Afghan War forms an important theme both for Afghan historians and British scholars, if for different reasons. The traumatic defeat inflicted on a numerous British army by a seemingly unpredictable 'tribal' uprising in the winter of 1841–42 has led many British scholars to deal with the events that led to this rebellion. In most cases, the underlying, nagging question seems to be how this severe blow to the British self-esteem as the major colonial power in the region might have been averted. The resultant argument is that the socio-political structure of Afghanistan in itself did not preclude a successful conquest. Had only the proper strategic and administrative principles been adopted, Afghanistan would have been British. Therefore, the British defeat was not caused by the invincibility of the Afghans but has to be attributed to a number of theoretically reversible political and administrational blunders. Afghanistan's continued independence after 1842 is primarily seen as the result of British disinterest in gaining a permanent foothold in the region.

On the Afghan side, the First Anglo-Afghan war became an important theme for modern historians who used the Afghan struggle for liberation from a colonial power as an image for the Afghan quest for self-determination. This presentation of the war draws in great part on the characteristics of courage and independence as 'national' Afghan traits, a notion that not only served to set the Afghans apart from the neighboring people who had accepted the yoke of foreign rule but has influenced political action in Afghanistan up to the very recent past. The discussion of the First Anglo-Afghan War also feeds into the twentieth-century attempt to foster nationalism. From this point of view, the expulsion of the British becomes the result of the joint effort of the Afghan 'masses' (*tudaha*) or the members of the Afghan 'nation' (*millat*). Given the idea of a general cooperation among the Afghan people, the political and economic problems forming obstacles to the agenda of creating an Afghan nation are attributed to the colonial intervention of the Great Powers combined with the irresolute or self-serving policies of the Afghan rulers. Likewise, Russian authors hold the 'heroic struggle of the Afghan peoples ... well experienced in guerilla warfare' responsible for the inability of the British to gain a permanent foothold in Afghanistan.[152] In the following chapter I will draw on sources from both schools of thought, bearing in mind the divergent concepts which inform them. With the help of these sources, I will attempt to trace the reasons that led to the British invasion, the effects it had on the power structure in Kabul, and the circumstances Dost Muhammad Khan found when he returned to his former seat of power after an exile of two and a half years.

The Events Leading up to the British Invasion

On October 1, 1838, Lord Auckland, the Governor General of India, issued a declaration which was to become known as the Simla Manifesto. Pointing to Dost Muhammad Khan's pro-Persian sentiments and his hostile attitude towards the British ally Ranjit Singh, as well as his general unpopularity, the Governor General reasoned that it was necessary to depose the Amir in favor of a more reliable ally, namely, Dost Muhammad Khan's old rival Shah Shuja'.[153] Accordingly, the 'Army of the Indus', consisting of 15,000 Indian soldiers and 6,000 men hired by Shah Shuja', assembled in Ferozepore in November 1838 and began the conquest of Afghanistan by occupying Qandahar on April 23, 1839. Another force of 4,800–5,000 men led by Colonel Wade and Shah Shuja''s eldest son, Muhammad Timur, entered the Khyber region in July 1839.[154] Less than three years later, this venture, generally to become known as 'Auckland's folly', ended disastrously with the retreat and destruction of the entire Kabul force of 4,500 fighting men along with many of the 12,000 camp followers.[155]

Why did the British invade Afghanistan? Why did they leave it so precipitately after investing £8 million in propping up Shah Shuja' for three years? For the Afghan historians, the British intervention in Afghanistan was the natural outcome of British imperialism (*hirs-i 'azim-i jahangiri*) and its strategical implementation under the banner of the Forward Policy (*siyasat-i ta'arruzi*). According to the court historian Faiz Muhammad and his modern colleagues Ghubar and Reshtia, the British decided to take a more active stand in Afghanistan with the onset of the Persian siege of Herat in November 1837. The presence of Russian soldiers and advisors with the army of Muhammad Shah Qajar (r. 1834–1848), triggered British fears that with the fall of Herat all of western Afghanistan, including Qandahar, would come under Russian influence. This in turn would cause disturbances in India either due to the presence of Russian agents in areas bordering on British possessions or, according to the more extreme scenario painted by the British minister to Iran, McNeill, a joint attack by Iran and Afghanistan on India.[156] The Forward Policy formulated by Malcolm (d. 1833) in the early nineteenth century indeed aimed at extending British influence into the areas lying between the dominions of Britain and Russia in order to create buffer zones between the spheres of interest of the two imperial powers.[157] Assuming a linear development of British strategy, the Persian siege of Herat might be seen as the ideal pretext for advancing British claims in the area. The fact that Auckland stuck to his plan of invading Afghanistan despite the Persian withdrawal in September 1838 (one month before the issue of the Simla manifesto) would only serve to reinforce the notion that the invasion of Afghanistan fitted into a consistent British plan of expanding its influence in Central Asia. In Ghubar's opinion British policy on the eve of the British invasion of Afghanistan was dictated by a clear chain of command reaching from London to Calcutta. He views the First Anglo-Afghan War as part of Britain's ongoing attempts to dismember Afghanistan by various means, be they military or political measures, propaganda, or secret activities. From this point of view, the apparent 'ups and downs' in the implementation of British policies only tend to obscure the underlying unchanging agenda.[158]

While greater themes like 'imperialism' and 'forward policy' point to the origin of British action, they fail to account for the manner in which the British attempted to extend their influence in Afghanistan. Why did they use military means rather than commercial activities? Why did they decide to import Shah Shuja' rather than co-opt Dost Muhammad Khan? British historians, among them Kaye (1857), Durand (1879) and Yapp (1980), have focussed on the process of British decision making, in which the preparation for the First Anglo-Afghan War emerges less as a master plan directed from London but as the result of inconsistencies, lone action, and inaction. Among other factors, biased reports by political agents (e.g. Wade at Ludhiana), Auckland's 'uncertainty of judgement at moments of crisis',[159] and the influence of his immediate advisors (e.g. Macnaghten, the future envoy to Afghanistan), played an important role in determining the direction of British action on the eve of the First Anglo-Afghan War.[160]

After twenty years of relatively little concern with the threat posed to India from the north-west, the early 1830s had witnessed a renewed interest in the protection of the Indian frontier. Alleged Russian designs on the

Khanates of Khiva and Bukhara evoked calls for a greater British involvement in Central Asia. While the then Governor General Bentinck (1828–1835) opposed any active policy in Afghanistan, he supported the plan to develop trade relations with Bukhara in order to challenge the commercial dominance of Russia in that region. To this end, Alexander Burnes was assigned the task of exploring the suitability of the Indus for navigation in 1831. A year later, Burnes was sent on a journey to Kabul and Bukhara.[161] When Auckland became Governor General in March 1836, his approach to Afghanistan was initially characterized by similar caution. He continued Bentinck's policy of gradual commercial penetration and accepted the notion that a unified Afghanistan would form an effective barrier to Russian interests. In August 1836, he decided to send Burnes on a purely commercial mission to Dost Muhammad Khan. But during the year which elapsed between Burnes's assignment to the mission and his arrival in Kabul on September 20, 1837 Auckland's attitude underwent a critical change.

This change of opinion manifested itself first of all in his increasing preference for an alliance with Ranjit Singh rather than with Dost Muhammad Khan. Auckland's bias in favor of the Sikhs apparently developed in great part along with the change of tone in the reports submitted by his agent Wade from Ludhiana. While Wade had supported the idea of an alliance with Afghanistan in 1835 and assumed a neutral position during the Afghan-Sikh battles of 1835 and 1837, his attitude towards Amir Dost Muhammad Khan increasingly hardened from early 1837 onwards. Although he had initially been in favor of Sikh concessions to the Afghans, specifically the return of Peshawar to Sultan Muhammad Khan, he advised in September 1837 that no such demands should be made of the Sikh government. Once committed to an alliance with the Sikhs, Auckland was further hampered by the mistaken notion that they genuinely intended to invade Afghanistan and would turn hostile if restrained from doing so. Auckland's decision not to opt for greater cooperation with Dost Muhammad Khan was also influenced by Wade's argument that the Muhammadzais were not capable of unifying Afghanistan and could thus not become strong allies for the British. His subsequent plan to install Shah Shuja' instead of Dost Muhammad Khan as ruler of Kabul was apparently also guided by mistaken reports of Shuja''s popularity versus Dost Muhammad Khan's unpopularity.[162]

Although Burnes had been merely instructed to act as a channel for possible demands by Dost Muhammad Khan, he rather ambitiously expanded his role to that of an arbitrator between Sikhs and Afghans and also planned to interfere in the negotiations taking place between Iran and Qandahar. Accordingly, he proceeded from commercial negotiations to political ones shortly after his arrival in Kabul. All evidence suggests that Dost Muhammad Khan did not entertain any active hope of gaining direct control over Peshawar in 1837. Burnes's encouraging manner induced the Amir to raise his stakes and to demand possession of the former dominions of his brother Sultan Muhammad.[163] Burnes's offer of support for the Qandahar Sardars was mostly generated by the military successes of the Persian army at Ghuriyan and the beginning of the siege of Herat in November 1837, as well as the arrival of the Russian agent Vitkevich in Kabul a month later. Auckland rejected Burnes's unauthorized actions in toto and refused to make concessions to Dost Muhammad Khan in the Peshawar issue or to support his negotiations with the Qandahar Sardars. When Burnes had to retreat from his earlier promises and could not offer British protection against Iran to Dost Muhammad Khan or his brothers at Qandahar, the Amir began to engage in official talks with the Russian agent on 21 April 1838.

Auckland's rigid attitude towards Dost Muhammad Khan in the winter of 1837–1838 stemmed less from outright hostility than a lack of desire to assume a more active role in this region. Dismissing the danger of Russian designs on Afghanistan, he argued that no British interference in Herat was possible because the treaty concluded with Iran in 1814 did not allow such intervention. Yet, between May 1838 and the conclusion of the Tripartite treaty between the British, Ranjit Singh, and Shah Shuja‘ on 23 June 1838 the Governor General changed his mind and moved from his preference for inaction to reluctant action in Iran (the occupation of Kharg) and the plan to invade Afghanistan.[164] According to Norris, this 'gradual shift from extreme caution to measured counter-action' has to be attributed to the growth of Russian interference in Afghanistan.[165] The Iranian siege of Herat and the concomitant Russian activities in Afghanistan undeniably began to assume threatening dimensions in Auckland's opinion. Norris's rather generous view of the Governor General's policies, however, does not take into account the fact that the threat emanating from Russia had not increased significantly since the onset of the siege of Herat. It was rather Auckland's perception of this danger which had changed. As Yapp puts it, he moved rapidly from underestimating the threat from the west to overestimating it. This was partly due to the perceived danger of internal unrest in India. The possibility of war with Ava and Nepal, as well as reported disturbances in Baroda, Sattara, Indore, Jaipur, and Jodhpur seemed to necessitate a more active policy on India's western frontier in the summer of 1838.

The decision to go to war with Dost Muhammad Khan also stemmed from Auckland's inability to withstand the counsel of the 'hawks' on his staff, in particular Macnaghten. Contrary to the Afghan historians, Yapp is of the opinion that Auckland acted without having received directives from London. Nevertheless, the Governor General's policies were bound by the prerogatives of British interests in Europe, and Yapp raises the possibility that Auckland was indirectly forced to invade Afghanistan because London's slow reaction to Persian actions precluded a timely agreement with Dost Muhammad Khan and his brothers. The plan to put Shah Shuja' on the throne evolved partly due to Auckland's perception that 'he had burned his boats with the Barakzays.'[166] Moreover, Shah Shuja' had traditionally enjoyed fairly close contacts with the British government. He had received Elphinstone's mission of 1809 at Peshawar. While the British had assumed a position of neutrality during Dost Muhammad Khan's early rule, they had supported Shah Shuja' financially when he planned a military campaign against the Muhammadzais in December 1832.[167]

Amir Dost Muhammad Khan's Perspective

On his part, Amir Dost Muhammad Khan had made every attempt to gain British support in his confrontation with the Sikhs. When his appeals of 1834 and 1835 were rejected he turned temporarily to Iran and Russia. These contacts notwithstanding, he sent a congratulatory note to Auckland on his appointment as Governeror General, in which he expressed pro-British sentiments and again solicited British assistance in the Peshawar issue. Burnes's mission was received with great honor at Kabul, and when the Russian agent Vitkevich was approaching Kabul the Amir let Burnes know that he preferred an alliance with the British. Even at the time the negotiations with Burnes began to turn sour Dost Muhammad Khan resisted the pressure of the Qizilbash faction to join ranks with the Qandahar Sardars. When it became clear that the British would not even make a formal offer of support in the Amir's relations with the Sikhs, he opened official negotiations with Vitkevich but, unlike his brothers at Qandahar, did not enter into an agreement with him.[168]

On the eve of the British invasion the Amir sought to gain popular support by discrediting the British protégé Shah Shuja' on religious grounds. To this end, he portrayed his rival as a puppet of unbelievers and extricated a *fatwa* from the ulama of Kabul which denied the legitimacy of Shah Shuja''s claims to power. His son Muhammad Akbar Khan likewise cast his effort to protect the Khyber area from the forces collected by Wade and Shahzada Timur in religious terms. As the British forces lingered in Qandahar for nearly two months after taking the city in late April 1839, the Amir's military preparations initially concentrated on the eastern territories. In their activities at the Khyber Pass, Muhammad Akbar Khan and his brother Muhammad Sharif Khan were assisted by a number of prominent Pashtun leaders, such as Sa'adat Khan Mohmand, Muhammad 'Alam Khan Orakzai and Muhammad Shah Khan Babakr Khel Ghilzai. On July 7, 1839 'Ali Masjid was lost to the forces under Wade and Shahzada Timur. The Amir summoned Muhammad Akbar Khan to Kabul, and the defence of the eastern territories crumbled.

When the Army of the Indus left Qandahar in late June, Dost Muhammad Khan concentrated his military preparations on Ghazni. Strategically the most important station on the way to Kabul, this city was held by the Amir's son Ghulam Haidar Khan. Planning to surround the British forces in case their siege of Ghazni failed, Dost Muhammad Khan deputed another force under the command of his son Muhammad Afzal Khan there and he himself took position at Arghanda, approximately 18 miles southwest of Kabul. But the Amir's hopes to withstand the British invasion were shattered when the fall of Ghazni on July 23, 1839 further encouraged a rebellion in Kohistan which had been fostered by British money and intrigue. Threatened from three directions, Dost Muhammad Khan decided to flee from Arghanda on the eve of August 2, leaving all his artillery with Khan Shirin Khan. The Qizilbash leader set the arsenal on fire, allowed his followers to plunder the Amir's luggage and subsequently joined the British.[169]

Followed by Nawwab 'Abd al-Jabbar Khan and his family, Dost Muhammad Khan moved via Bamiyan to Tashqurghan, where he found refuge with the Uzbek chief Mir Muhammad Amin Beg Khan, generally known as Mir Wali. Mir Wali allowed him to continue to levy the transit duties on the traffic between Turkistan and Kabul in order to maintain his numerous following. Nevertheless, Dost Muhammad Khan left his wives and small children in the care of Nawwab Jabbar Khan and his son Muhammad Akram Khan along with 1,500 followers in Tashqurghan and proceeded to Bukhara accompanied by his sons and nephews, together with 2,000 further followers. Here, he became a virtual prisoner of Nasrullah Khan, the Amir of Bukhara (r. 1827–1860). Having negotiated the release of his younger sons, he sent them back to Tashqurghan with an order to submit to Shah Shuja'. Under the care of Nawwab Jabbar Khan, Dost Muhammad Khan's family arrived in Kabul on July 15, 1840. Shortly afterwards, Dost Muhammad Khan himself was able to flee from Bukhara first to Shahr-i Sabz and then to Qunduz, leaving Muhammad Akbar Khan behind.[170]

With his arrival in the territories south of the Oxus, Dost Muhammad Khan reentered the political scene. According to *Siraj al-tawarikh*, the ex-Amir received liberal support from the Uzbek rulers of Qunduz and Tashqurghan, each of whom furnished him with 5,000 horsemen. Yapp's detailed description of the events of 1840, however, depicts Dost Muhammad Khan's situation as less ideal. In this account, Mir Murad Beg, the ruler of Qunduz, only supplied him with a nominal force of 150–300 men. Mir Wali joined Dost Muhammad Khan's military expedition to Bajgah and Bamiyan mainly out of the desire to enhance his own position among the other small principalities north of the Hindu Kush. After the defeat of the combined forces of Dost Muhammad Khan and Mir Wali at Bamiyan on September 18, 1840, the Wali of Tashqurghan separated from the ex-Amir and rejected all requests for further aid.

Failing to gain any assistance in Turkistan and Hazarajat in October 1840, Dost Muhammad Khan proceeded to Gulbahar in Kohistan, where more fertile ground awaited him. In July 1840, many major chiefs of Kohistan, most prominent among them 'Ali Khan of Tutam Darra, Mir Masjidi Khan of Julgah, Sultan Muhammad Khan of Nijrau[171], Malik Saif al-Din of Kala Darra, Mir Darwesh Khan of Baba Qushqar, Khwaja 'Abd al-Khaliq, and Khwaja Khanji[172] had openly defied government orders for the muster of levies and the payment of revenues.[173] Fearing that Dost Muhammad Khan might join forces with the rebels, the British sent an army consisting of British and Durrani contingents to the area. Under the leadership of General Sale and Shahzada Timur, this army engaged in a series of attacks on the forts of the rebellious Kohistani chiefs in late September and early October. In the early stages of their rebellion, 'Ali Khan, Mir Masjidi Khan and Sultan Muhammad Khan had addressed letters to Dost Muhammad Khan, inviting him to assume the leadership of their operations. Hearing of his arrival in Kohistan, Mir Masjidi Khan and Sultan Muhammad Khan joined forces with his and engaged in a major battle with the British troops in Parwan on November 2, 1840. In the aftermath of the battle Dost Muhammad Khan was separated from the other commanders and proceeded to Nijrau, where he is said to have rejected Mir Masjidi Khan's proposal to prepare further military actions against the British. On November 4, while his Kohistani allies continued operations against the British, he surrendered to Macnaghten at Kabul and was exiled to India a week later.

The event of Dost Muhammad Khan's sudden surrender has preoccupied many historians of the First Anglo-Afghan War. Most of the British authors attribute the ex-Amir's decision to the fact that he was aware of the military superiority of the British and that he did not trust the sincerity and steadfastness of Kohistani support. With the exception of Kaye, they doubt that Dost Muhammad Khan's military success was as decisive as the Afghan sources would have it.[174] From these accounts the battle of Parwan emerges as one last courageous stand by Dost Muhammad Khan which allowed him to prove his valor before accepting the political reality and surrendering to the Britsh. While holding that Dost Muhammad Khan had been victorious in the battle of Parwan, the court historian Faiz Muhammad approximates the British view that Dost Muhammad Khan did not feel he had sufficient support to offer a prolonged resistance. But this sentiment stemmed less from distrust of the Kohistanis than the reluctance to spill further Muslim blood in a fight that might be in vain. Furthermore, he thought that the tribal organization of his former subjects would not allow them to unite beyond links of kinship and to present a widespread and sustained resistance strong enough to remove the British and Shah Shuja' from power.[175] Faiz Muhammad's modern colleagues Ghubar and Reshtia, on the other hand, view the battle of Parwan as a potential stepping stone for a general rebellion. Reshtia attributes Dost Muhammad Khan's failure to make use of the favorable situation created by his success in great part to his ignorance of the great extent of British losses at Parwan and the general state of panic the news of his victory had created among British officials in Kohistan and Kabul alike. He also allows for the possibility that the activities of British spies had created an atmosphere of insecurity in the ex-Amir's camp.[176] But the most important reason for Dost Muhammad Khan's surrender lay with his wrong assessment of the steadfastness of his allies: 'He was unaware that the power of a nation (*millat*), even if it has no means, is superior to that of the biggest regular armies of the world.'[177] Ghubar's criticism of Dost Muhammad Khan's failure to continue the struggle against the British after the battle of Parwan is the most scathing. From his account Dost Muhammad Khan emerges as a coward who fails to accept the role as a national leader proffered to him by history at this juncture. After describing General Sale's forced retreat to Charikar and Macnaghten's willingness to open negotiations with the rebels, Ghubar poses the rhetorical question,

> But what did Amir Dost Muhammad Khan do? After the strength of the people had beaten the enemy at Parwan and [when] the national fighters were advancing [further], the Amir suddenly disappeared from under the blue banner [carried by his troops]. No matter how much they searched they could not find him. Meanwhile, the Amir along with three of his close companions was hurrying away along byways, leaving for an unknown destination in the south. This mad escape of the Amir took place so secretly that he even left his son Sardar Muhammad Afzal Khan unaware of his departure in the battlefield.

In the end, however, Dost Muhammad Khan's behavior was to be irrelevant for the ultimate outcome of the struggle against the British:

> When, at the very moment of their victory over the enemy, the fighters of Kapisa and Parwan heard of Amir Dost Muhammad Khan's disappearance and voluntary surrender to the British they, like all of the people of Afghanistan, were bewildered. But they did not give up the struggle (*dil wa dast-i khesh nashikastand*) and continued to sweep away the enemy.[178]

From the British sources, Dost Muhammad Khan emerges as an isolated ex-ruler who realizes that his struggle against the British is in vain. The Afghan historians, on the other hand, are of the opinion that the Amir would have enjoyed the support of the Afghan masses had he only cared to join forces with them. The different perspectives informing both groups are clear. While the Afghan historians are preoccupied with the question what Dost Muhammad Khan *should* have done in order to foster the national struggle of the Afghan people, the British sources emphasize that no such communality of purpose existed among the various groups forming Afghan society.

The British Occupation of Afghanistan

After the British had occupied the dominions of Dost Muhammad Khan and his brothers with considerable facility, they were confronted with the more complex task of instituting a new administration under the leadership of Shah Shuja'. The desertion of influential leaders to Shah Shuja' shortly before the British conquest of Qandahar and the ready allegiance of many Durrani chiefs at the beginning of Shah Shuja''s reign initially seemed to confirm the British impression of his popularity and the righteousness of their invasion.[179] According to Reshtia, the British planned to establish themselves firmly in Afghanistan once they decided to depose Amir Dost Muhammad Khan. Yet the official British reasoning at least does not reveal that such a complete takeover was envisioned from the beginning. The Simla Manifesto promised that the British forces would be withdrawn as soon as Shah Shuja' was firmly established on the throne. Subsequently the British involvement in Afghanistan gradually assumed greater proportions. The agreement signed with Shah Shuja' on May 7, 1839 provided for the permanent appointment of a British Resident to the court of the king and the creation of a military contingent under the command of British officers. It had been envisaged that Shah Shuja' was to be formally independent in the internal administration of his realm. Although Auckland had initially been extremely optimistic about the prospects of his protégé, he soon had to admit that Shah Shuja' was unable to stand alone. Hampered by lack of revenues and reliable military forces, he was only able to maintain his authority with the assistance of at least part of the troops brought along from India.[180]

While Shah Shuja' required British backing to remain on the throne, it was precisely this association with them which weakened his position. Contrary to the impression the British had formed directly after the occupation of Qandahar, Shah Shuja' found it difficult to assume Dost Muhammad Khan's position. Although he had been praised by some as the rightful successor of the Sadozai kings on the occasion of his entrance at Qandahar,[181] his reception at Kabul on August 7, 1839 was less than enthusiastic.[182] In part, his lack of popularity was due to his ostentatious and autocratic style of government, which formed a curious contrast with his increasingly evident dependence on the British.[183] A token of the public disgust with Shah Shuja''s subservient position was the popular version of the verse engraved in the coins struck in his name, which depicted him as 'the apple of the eye of the British.'[184] During the ministership of Shah Shuja''s appointee Mulla 'Abd al-Shakur Ishaqzai, every effort was made to obscure Shah Shuja''s powerlessness.[185] As the British opposed many of Mulla Shakur's policies, they forced Shah Shuja' to appoint 'Usman Khan b. Rahmatullah Khan Sadozai ('Nizam al-Daula') in his stead in late 1840.[186] According to *Siraj al-tawarikh*, Nizam al-Daula's blatantly pro-British policies were a major reason for Shah Shuja''s downfall. Another major factor for discontent listed by *Siraj al-tawarikh* was the steady stream of prostitutes invited to the British cantonments, which, 'rending the veil of religious honor' (*daridan-i parda-yi namus-i dindari*), was seen as an insult to the public sense of honor and, by association, brought disgrace upon Shah Shuja''s government.[187]

Many of the British policies alienated Shah Shuja''s 'natural' allies, the old state supporting elite. On the economic level, the real income of the chiefs and ulama was negatively affected by the inflation caused by the presence of a large number of British and Indian troops and camp followers. The maintenance of the Shah's troops by assignments on the revenue of certain districts meant a greater tax burden for many local chiefs.[188] Whereas the Durrani chiefs had traditionally been in charge of maintaining their own troops in exchange for remission in crown revenues, this right increasingly passed to the British. In exchange, the chiefs received a compensation in cash which was more vulnerable to inflationary pressures. The privileged position of the Durrani leaders in particular was undermined by the formation of two new forces of cavalry, the Janbaz and the Hazirbash. According to Lal, the raising of 'low and petty persons', particularly Kohistanis and Khyberis, into the ranks of the Hazirbash provided further insult to the Durrani chiefs.[189] In 1840 the imprisonment of prominent men, such as Haji Khan Kakar, Mahmud Khan Bayat and Hafiz Ji, caused many chiefs to waver in their allegiance to Shah Shuja'.[190] The appointment of Nizam al-Daula as minister entailed further attacks on the position of the state supporting elite. Encouraged by British plans to diminish the cost of the occupation of Afghanistan, he set out to reduce the allowances of the Durrani and Ghilzai chiefs by 200,000 rupees.[191] The attempt to save money also included the confiscation of religious endowments, such as the famous shrine of 'Ashiqan and 'Arifan south of Kabul, which was devoted to two grandsons of Khwaja 'Abdullah Ansari.[192]

Prior to the 'great outbreak' at Kabul in November 1841, the British were confronted by a number of rebellions confined to areas at a distance from the centers of power. As early as 1839 the Hotak and Tokhi Ghilzais situated along the route between Kabul and Qandahar began to resist British attempts at administration. Similarly, Sayyid Hashim of Kunar in eastern Afghanistan declared his independence. Apart from the rebellion in Kohistan already discussed above, the following year witnessed unrest in Bajaur and disturbances among the Khugiani Pashtuns near Jalalabad. From December 1840 until August 1841, a large part of Qandahar's resources had to be devoted to curbing the rebellion led by Akhtar Khan ʻAlizai among the Durranis. In Yapp's opinion, these uprisings were caused in great part by the intrusion of British administration at the local level. They 'originated in local disputes and factional rivalries, which were often exacerbated by changes in local authority and in the balance of local power which followed the Sadozay restoration.' While challenging British claims of sovereignty in the areas in question, these rebellions were of a purely localized character and were not coordinated with movements in other regions.[193]

The reaction of the British envoy to the resistance encountered alternated between panic and unfounded optimism. During the Kohistan rebellion of the summer of 1840, Macnaghten and his agents were ready to detect a general conspiracy against British rule.[194] The following year, however, as he attempted to decrease the cost of the British occupation by cutting 200,000 rupees of the subsidies paid to the Durranis, Ghilzais, and ulama, the envoy seemed to be oblivious to the widespread unrest these measures provoked. He shrugged off the uprisings of the eastern Ghilzais in September and October 1841 and the tensions reported from Kohistan as isolated events which had no bearing on the general peace prevailing in the country.[195] With the assassination of the envoy's deputy Burnes on November 2, 1841 (17 Ramazan 1257)[196], however, the focus of the rebellion soon moved to Kabul and the British found themselves besieged in the Bala Hisar and cantonments by Kabuli, Kohistani and Ghilzai forces. On December 23, 1841, Macnaghten lost his life in a failed attempt to sow dissension among the leaders of the rebellion. On January 6, 1842 the British and Indian forces, with the exception of a number of hostages taken by the Afghans, started their retreat to Jalalabad, only to be utterly destroyed by the eastern Ghilzais controlling the passes between Kabul and Gandamak.[197]

The Principal Participants in the Uprising of 1841–1842

The departure of the British in January 1842 did not entail the immediate end of Shah Shujaʻ. Based in the Bala Hisar, he retained a measure of influence during the following three months, and his support was sought by the groups contending for the control of Kabul. This section will deal with the leadership which emerged in Kabul after the end of British rule, i.e. the Durrani nobility, the relatives of Dost Muhammad Khan, and the ulama. Many of these leaders derived their political power in Kabul from the standing they enjoyed among the population in the adjacent areas. The descendants of Mir Waʻiz, for example, were closely linked with the Kohistanis. Dost Muhammad Khan's son Muhammad Akbar Khan, on the other hand, gave substance to his claims to power by calling in the eastern Ghilzais. The uprisings of the Kohistanis and eastern Ghilzais in the fall of 1841 not only formed a preface to the ensuing rebellion in Kabul. Even after the removal of the British both groups continued to play an important role in the coalition making and breaking which determined the politics of Kabul until the return of Dost Muhammad Khan in 1843.

Among the foremost leaders in the uprising of the eastern Ghilzais were Muhammad Akbar Khan's father-in-law, Muhammad Shah Khan Babakr Khel of Badi'abad in Laghman, and the Amir's brother-in-law, 'Abd al-'Aziz Khan Jabbar Khel. Unable to dissuade Nizam al-Daula from reclaiming half of the allowance of 80,000 rupees traditionally paid to the Eastern Ghilzais, these chiefs began to plunder caravans and proclaimed jihad against the British. In the course of their activities they were joined by Hamza Khan Ghilzai, who had lost the governorship of Jalalabad due to his refusal to cooperate with Nizam al-Daula's attempts at increasing the revenue.[198] The extent and the immediate causes of the Kohistani revolt under the leadership of Mir Masjidi are less clear. Possibly the local chiefs had been deprived of subsidies initially granted by Shah Shuja' on the occasion of his accession.[199] Immediately before the Kabul uprising Major Pottinger reported signs of a 'coming tempest' in Kohistan to the British envoy. Mir Masjidi Khan of Julgah, who had refused to submit to Shah Shuja''s authority since General Sale's military campaign a year before, had 'openly put himself at the head of a powerful and well-organized party, with the avowed intention of expelling the Firingis and overturning the existing government.' Including the most influential chiefs of Kohistan and Nijrau, this coalition forced Pottinger to retreat first to Charikar and then to Kabul during the days following November 3rd.[200]

In the very beginning, the revolt of Kabul had no connection with the Ghilzai and Kohistani uprisings. The decision to attack Burnes's residence was taken rather spontaneously by a number of Durrani nobles resident in Kabul and a few Qizilbash and Sunni ulama. Eyre characterizes the early stage of the rebellion as an 'insignificant ebullition of discontent on the part of a few desperate and restless men.'[201] It is interesting to note that the initial impulse for the attack was not given by the adherents of Dost Muhammad Khan but in great part by other Durrani chiefs who had formed the major base of support for Shah Shuja' up to that point. Apart from 'Abdullah Khan Achakzai, the most prominent members of this group were Popalzai *khans*, in particular Ghulam Muhammad Khan Bamizai b. Sher Muhammad Khan Mukhtar al-Daula and 'Abd al-Salam Khan Bamizai b. Muhammad Akram Khan Amin al-Mulk and their relatives. These nobles became finally alienated on September 1, 1841 when Nizam al-Daula attempted to force them to sign a bond according to which they were to agree to reductions in their allowances and to formally pledge allegiance to the government of Shah Shuja'. Upon their refusal to do so, they were threatened with exile. Another important actor in the rebellion was Aminullah Khan Logari who had lost control over his district after failing to submit greater revenues.[202]

The Kabul rebellion was only supported by a part of the Qizilbash. Khan Shirin Khan Jawansher, for instance, retained a cautious pro-British stand. Aqa Husain Topchibashi, Muhammad Husain Khan 'Arzbegi of Chindawul and Mahmud Khan Bayat, on the other hand, participated in the meeting which resulted in the attack on Burnes's residence. Another important figure in the resistance to the British was Dost Muhammad Khan's former official Mirza Imamwerdi Qizilbash, who had accompanied the ex-Amir to Bukhara. After his return to Kabul in 1840, he had continuously attempted to weaken Shah Shuja''s government by pointing out his dependence on the British. Immediately prior to the attack of November 2, he coauthored a circulatory letter warning the Durrani and Qizilbash chiefs of impending exile, thus galvanizing support for the plan to rebel.[203] Among the ulama, Hafiz Ji's brother Mir Haji, and his relative Mir Aftab played a crucial role in inciting the Kohistanis and the wider population of Kabul to join the fight against the British.[204]

Only when the fighting around the British cantonments was in full swing was Dost Muhammad Khan's nephew Nawwab Muhammad Zaman Khan elected leader of the insurrection, with Aminullah Khan Logari as his *wazir* and 'Abdullah Khan Achakzai as his commander-in-chief.[205] With the arrival of Muhammad Akbar Khan and his cousin Sultan Ahmad Khan b. Muhammad 'Azim Khan from Bukhara on November 25, 1841, the focus of the rebellion shifted to the Muhammadzais. Muhammad Akbar Khan derived his powerful position not only from his privileged position within the Amir's family as Dost Muhammad Khan's favorite son. He also enjoyed the support of the ex-officials of his father, including Mirza Imamwerdi. Furthermore, his marriage alliance with Muhammad Shah Khan secured the military assistance of approximately 2,000 eastern Ghilzais under the leadership of that chief. The Durrani nobility and the eastern Ghilzais under the leadership of Hamza Khan Ghilzai, on the other hand, were less interested in the restoration of Muhammadzai supremacy. After initial negotiations between Muhammad Akbar Khan and Macnaghten on December 11, this group let the British know that they did not favor the proposed abdication of Shah Shuja'.[206]

As Muhammad Akbar Khan left Kabul along with the British forces in early January, Muhammadzai influence began to dwindle in the capital and Aminullah Khan Logari became the dominant figure. Under his leadership the Durrani and Qizilbash chiefs increasingly cast their lot with Shah Shuja'. Despite his own claims to kingship Nawwab Muhammad Zaman Khan reluctantly agreed to cooperate with the Sadozai king and accepted a more or less nominal position as his minister. Meanwhile Muhammad Akbar Khan, who was busy besieging the British garrison at Jalalabad, sought to reenter center stage by bringing pressure on Shah Shuja' to declare jihad against the British. To this end, he successfully mobilized the support of the ulama in the countryside. The Kabul ulama, foremost among them Mir Haji, joined the Muhammadzai propaganda in favor of war against the British. After temporizing for two months, Shah Shuja' finally gave in and joined the troops assembled in the vicinity of Kabul on April 4. On the following day he was assassinated by Nawwab Muhammad Zaman Khan's son Shuja' al-Daula Khan.[207]

While the murder of Shah Shuja' did not evoke any public expressions of grief, it did not improve the prospects of the Muhammadzai faction either. Mir Haji and his followers abandoned the plan to join Muhammad Akbar Khan's forces at Jalalabad and returned to Kabul for the time being. Shortly afterwards the news of Muhammad Akbar Khan's defeat at the hands of the British on April 7 reached the city. Shah Shuja''s son Fatih Jang was declared king by an assembly consisting of Aminullah Khan Logari, Mir Haji and the Popalzai, Kohistani and Qizilbash leadership. After this phase of political isolation Nawwab Muhammad Zaman Khan's fortunes began to improve in early May 1842 when Aminullah Khan Logari alienated Mir Haji by abusing him on account of his attempts to mediate between the court faction and the Muhammadzais. Mir Haji's declaration in favor of the Muhammadzais won crucial Kabuli and Kohistani support for Nawwab Muhammad Zaman Khan. During the subsequent siege of Fatih Jang and Aminullah Khan Logari in the Bala Hisar, Nawwab Muhammad Zaman Khan's cause was further strengthened by the desertion of 'Abd al-Salam Bamizai, Mir Afzal Bamizai, and Sikandar Khan Bamizai to his side. Popalzai support for Fatih Jang dwindled to the persons of Muhammad 'Umar Khan Bamizai and Samad Khan Popalzai. Among the ulama, Mir Aftab and Khwaja Khanji of 'Ashiqan and 'Arifan encouraged Fatih Jang to hold out against Muhammadzai pressure.[208]

With the entrance of Muhammad Akbar Khan in Kabul between May 6 and May 9, 1842, Nawwab Muhammad Zaman Khan's position was again weakened, this time in favor of his illustrious cousin. On May 17 Aminullah Khan abandoned Fatih Jang and entered an alliance with Muhammad Akbar Khan. On June 7 Fatih Jang gave in to their combined siege and admitted Muhammad Akbar Khan into the Bala Hisar. On June 29, Muhammad Akbar Khan was formally appointed as Fatih Jang's *wazir*. He assumed full control of government measures, leaving only a nominal role to Fatih Jang, and finally imprisoning him. Despite his claims to the contrary Muhammad Akbar Khan's rise to power was not uncontested and was resented most by his close relatives and the Qizilbash leaders. After his conquest of the Bala Hisar he had secured his position primarily by garrisoning it with the Ghilzai troops of Muhammad Shah Khan and the followers of Aminullah Khan Logari. Neither his cousins Nawwab Muhammad Zaman Khan and 'Usman Khan b. Nawwab Samad Khan nor the Qizilbash were allowed into the citadel. In the ensuing power struggle Muhammad Akbar Khan was able to assert his position over Nawwab Muhammad Zaman Khan with the help of royal funds, which enabled him to buy the support of Mir Haji, the Kohistanis, and the Muradkhani Qizilbash.[209]

Muhammad Akbar Khan retained his powerful position in Kabul until early September 1842 when two British armies approached Kabul from the south and east in an endeavor to recover the British hostages in the hands of Muhammad Akbar Khan and to reestablish the shaken prestige of the British military. On September 13, Muhammad Akbar Khan was defeated by Pollock's army advancing from Jalalabad and fled to Kohistan. Leaving Aminullah Khan and his followers in Istalif, he then continued on his way to Tashqurghan. Until their final departure on October 12, British activities focussed on taking revenge for perceived Afghan atrocities and halfhearted attempts to reestablish Sadozai authority. To the the first end, the great bazaar of Kabul, which had been erected by the Mughal official 'Ali Mardan Khan in the early seventeenth century, was blown up. The destruction of the Kohistani towns of Istalif and Charikar, which formed Aminullah Khan's stronghold, not only served as an act of retribution but was intended to counteract possible opposition to the plan to reinstall Fatih Jang as ruler of Afghanistan. Fatih Jang refused to accept the kingship when it became apparent that the British troops were about to leave Kabul and opted to accompany them to India. In his stead, his younger brother Shahpur was appointed king with Ghulam Muhammad Khan Bamizai and Khan Shirin Khan Jawansher as ministers, the latter having been a steadfast opponent of Muhammad Akbar Khan during his power struggle with Nawwab Muhammad Zaman Khan. As the British failed to supply Shahpur with any financial or military assistance, the semblance of Sadozai power crumbled shortly after their departure. Accepting the counsel of all major Qizilbash leaders, Khan Shirin Khan and Ghulam Muhammad Khan decided to summon Muhammad Akbar Khan to Kabul and Shahpur was forced to flee to Peshawar.[210]

The departure of the British army from Kabul marked, for the next thirty years at least, the end of direct British intervention in Afghanistan. Having announced the abandonment of the buffer state policy in March 1842, the new Governor General Ellenborough (1842–1844) decided in October that he would not interfere with the creation of a new government in Afghanistan. In October, while Shahpur still was the formal ruler of Kabul, Dost Muhammad Khan was permitted to return to his old dominions. Moving via Shikarpur and Lahore, the Amir entered Afghanistan by the Khyber and resumed his government of Kabul in spring 1843.[211]

Again two broad interpretations can be discerned in the analysis of the events that led to the expulsion of the British from Afghanistan. The modern Afghan historians view the events of 1839 to 1842 primarily as a national and popular movement against foreign domination. Ghubar in particular portrays the resistance offered to the British from the point of their entrance into Afghanistan to their withdrawal as a linear development. From this point of view, the early uprisings of the 'Afghan masses' (*tudaha-yi Afghanistan*) from 1839 to 1841 emerge as preparatory stages in a national struggle which culminated in a general revolution (*inqilab-i 'umumi*) coordinated by the central command of a council (*shura*) located in the Shor Bazar of Kabul. While Ghubar cursorily mentions the ulama as participants in the great national uprising, the main focus of his work is the military success of the united Afghan people over a mighty colonial power. The theme of national resistance to foreign usurpers also pervades the work of Ghubar's younger colleague Reshtia. Nevertheless, he does paint a more detailed picture of the events leading up to the rebellion. While concurring with Ghubar that the leadership of the rebellion was well in place before the attack of November 2, he allows for a greater degree of spontaneity in the resistance to the British and compares the rebellion at Kabul to an 'explosion of national tension'. Unlike Ghubar, he attributes the uprising in greater part to religious sentiments. In his opinion, the foreign domination did not only constitute an assault on national sentiments but was synonymous with an attack on Islam per se. The 'national leaders' (Aminullah Khan Logari, 'Abdullah Khan Achakzai et. al.) were motivated to rebel against the British first of all by the need to remove the stain of their presence from the 'skirt of the holy Muslim country' (*daman-i mamlakat-i muqaddas-i islami*). The national struggle is thus seen foremost as the defence of Islam.[212]

The second historiographical concept of the First Anglo-Afghan War was developed by British historians, most prominently Yapp. Unlike Ghubar, Yapp adduces evidence that there was no concept of a national rising in the rebellion against the British. In his opinion, the initial rebellion at Kabul was not the outcome of systematic planning but 'a sudden hasty decision of frightened men.' After its initial success, the movement assumed a greater scope due to the assistance of the Kohistanis and eastern Ghilzais. Contrary to Ghubar, Yapp is of the opinion that links between the rebellion of Kabul and other areas were not well developed. The uprising of the Sulaiman Khel, Andari, and Taraki divisions in November 1841 and their subsequent attacks on Ghazni may have been inspired by the events at Kabul but did not receive any direct guidance from there. The unsuccessful resistance of the Alikozais and Popalzais to the British at Qandahar only developed significant dimensions in Januray 1842 and apparently took place independently of the rebellion at Kabul despite kinship links between the Durranis at both centers of power. Even so, certain parallels between the developments in Kabul and Qandahar can be discerned. In both places the rebellion was carried out by forces who had hitherto been loyal to Shah Shuja'. In both places the revolt was justified in religious rather than national terms. Despite the localized nature of the revolts at Kabul, Ghazni, and Qandahar they have one unifying feature, that is, they were overwhelmingly carried out by Sunni Pashtuns, whereas the Shi'i Qizilbash and Hazaras retained a pro-British stance and the Baluchis, Brahuis and Turkish groups remained neutral.[213]

The Afghan view of the First Anglo-Afghan War as a 'national' struggle is acceptable from the point of view that it aimed at ridding Afghanistan from foreign domination. But Yapp's analysis accurately points out that there was practically no linkage between the activities of the main centers of revolt located in Kabul, Qandahar, Ghazni, and Jalalabad. In the Kabul region, the involvement of the wider population was limited to the Kohistanis and eastern Ghilzais. The above account shows that the members of each group were linked to particular local leaders whose ambitions clashed with those of other prominent men. The ever changing coalitions among the different leaders in Kabul indicate that there was little, if any, concept of working for a common cause once the British invaders were removed.

While rejecting the notion that the resistance offered to the British amounted to a national rising, Yapp points out that the British presence did bring about conditions in Afghanistan which facilitated Dost Muhammad Khan's subsequent attempts to consolidate his power:

> first, by the lasting damage which it did to the power of the chiefs, whom Dost Muhammad could thereafter bring more easily under control; second, by the education which it provided in the creation of stronger systems of government, and particularly by the example of the use of disciplined forces and the training of Afghan troops, which paved the way for the subsequent creation of a powerful standing army by Dost Muhammad with which he could extend his power over the rest of Afghanistan; third, by the jolt which it gave to the whole economy by the import of bullion and the creation of new demands.[214]

The first item in this list of effects is particularly important for the understanding of the political situation in Kabul in 1841–1842. Ironically, the administrative measures adopted by the British first of all affected the groups that had been most inclined to accept Shah Shuja''s return to Kabul. The Durrani nobility, foremost among them the Bamizai Popalzais, had played a preponderant role in the politics of the early nineteenth century and were increasingly eclipsed with the advent of the Muhammadzais. Rather than reversing the policies of Dost Muhammad Khan, the British attempted to weaken this group further by discontinuing the system of military tenure carried over from Sadozai times and forming centrally organized cavalry contingents. While it is not clear how lasting a damage the British policies inflicted on the position of the Durrani nobility, the leading role assumed by the Bamizais in the Kabul uprising shows that they had given up hope of regaining the influential position they had enjoyed during the Sadozai era. In this light, their maneuvering in 1841–42 may be seen as a last attempt to enter center stage in the politics of Kabul.

The same can be said for the ulama under the leadership of the family of Mir Wa'iz, who had closely cooperated with the Bamizai leadership prior to Dost Muhammad Khan's assumption of power. Aware of the political clout of this family of ulama, the Amir attempted to coopt Mir Wa'iz's son Hafiz Ji by entering a marriage alliance with him. Notwithstanding this linkage with Dost Muhammad Khan, Hafiz Ji reverted to the old political alliances of his family with the onset of the First Anglo-Afghan War. By inciting a revolt among the Kohistanis, he facilitated the entrance of Shah Shuja' in Kabul. Hafiz Ji's disappointment with the British policies is reflected in his role in the Kohistani rebellion against the British in summer 1840. With his imprisonment by the British, the leadership of the ulama passed to his brother Mir Haji, who, along with the Bamizai leaders was a 'man of the first hour' in the uprising of Kabul. Like the Bamizais, Mir Haji did not direct his activities primarily against Shah Shuja' but against the British presence. But in the power struggle subsequent to the departure of the British he played a crucial role in finally tipping the scales in favor of the Muhammadzai faction. After the return of Dost Muhammad Khan in 1843, Hafiz Ji and his family were able to retain a measure of influence in the political affairs of Kabul, now and then assuming a public role as mediators between the Qizilbash and the Sunni population of Kabul. Hafiz Ji played a steady role in Dost Muhammad Khan's council. In 1857 he assumed the leadership of a movement pressurizing the Amir to declare jihad against the British. His son Mir Ali also continued to figure in Kabul politics.[215] Among the Bamizais, by contrast, only Ghulam Muhammad Khan was able to retain a prominent position at Dost Muhammad Khan's court. In the following section I will discuss how the Amir set out to concentrate all important positions in the hands of his immediate family during the early years of his second reign.

Administrative Measures Taken by Amir Dost Muhammad Khan after his Resumption of Power

According to *Siraj al-tawarikh*, Dost Muhammad Khan was paid homage by all the tribal leaders far and wide, be they Afghan, Hazara, Qizilbash, Turk, or Tajik, on the assumption of the throne of Kabul. In reality, however, his sphere of influence was even smaller than during his final days of authority prior to the British invasion. Apart from Kabul, he could lay claim to Jalalabad and Ghazni. Immediately prior to the Kabul uprising the chiefs of Kohistan had assumed an increasingly powerful position and were collecting revenue on their own behalf. The Bihsud region of Hazarajat had likewise become independent during this period. The British occupation had done little to change the power structure in the wider region. The areas north of the Hindu Kush remained independent. Herat was firmly in the possession of Kamran's minister Yar Muhammad Khan. After an interregnum by Shah Shuja''s sons Muhammad Timur and Safdar Jang in 1842–1843 the control of Qandahar passed to its former rulers, the Amir's half brothers Kuhandil Khan, Rahmdil Khan, and Mihrdil Khan.[216]

Operating from a relatively weak position, Dost Muhammad Khan did not attempt to indulge in reprisals against chiefs who had cooperated with the British. In his endeavor to consolidate power, however, he had to contend with the men who had assumed a leading position during the rebellion of November 1841 and its aftermath. Among these, 'Abdullah Khan Achakzai, who had died during a military operation against the British on 29 November 1841, posed no further threat.[217] Aminullah Khan Logari was imprisoned for life by the Amir because of, as the author of *Siraj al-tawarikh* puts it, his predilection for 'inciting peaceful people to engage in mischief.'[218] Sardar Sultan Ahmad b. Muhammad 'Azim Khan, who had shared Muhammad Akbar Khan's exile in Bukhara and had played a significant role during the siege of Jalalabad, challenged Muhammad Akbar Khan's authority in Kabul after the final departure of the British in October 1842. Along with Nawwab Muhammad Zaman Khan, he was placated by the promise of a large share in Dost Muhammad Khan's government at that point. Soon after the arrival of the Amir however, he found his hopes for increased powers shattered, declined to accept the allowance assigned to him, left for Qandahar, and encouraged Kuhandil Khan to engage in a short-lived military campaign against Dost Muhammad Khan. Nawwab Muhammad Zaman Khan also failed to receive any influential government post.[219]

Among the Amir's sons, Muhammad Akbar Khan initially retained his position as heir apparent. After the conquest of Bihsud, Dai Zangi, Dai Kundi, and Bamiyan in 1843–44, he was made governor of Hazarajat. Having also been vested with the control of Jalalabad and Laghman, he continued to reside in Kabul and to assist his father in his attempts to gain control of Bajaur, Tagau and Nijrau in Kohistan, and among the Mamakhel Khugianis near Jalalabad. Nevertheless his relationship with the Amir was far from untroubled, and he continued to challenge his father's hesitant policies vis-à-vis the Sikhs and the Qandahar Sardars. As he even questioned Dost Muhammad Khan's right to rule, his death in February 1847 has been viewed by some as the result of the machinations of the Amir.[220] Muhammad Akbar Khan's death was followed by the rebellion of his father-in-law Muhammad Shah Khan Babakr Khel, who resented the fact that Dost Muhammad Khan had ignored him in the distribution of positions in his new government and opposed the Amir's efforts to deprive him of the treasure his son-in-law had deposited with him.[221]

In the administration of his realm, Dost Muhammad Khan relied heavily on the support of his sons. Among his numerous progeny, the sons of his favorite wife Khadija (from an important Popalzai lineage) enjoyed a particularly privileged position. As mentioned above, Muhammad Akbar Khan became governor of Jalalabad, Laghman, and Hazarajat. After his death, his brother Ghulam Haidar Khan was appointed heir apparent and assumed his governorship of Laghman and Jalalabad and control over his military regiments. Next in line, his younger brothers Muhammad Sharif Khan, Sher 'Ali Khan and Muhammad Amin Khan acted as governors of Bamiyan, Ghazni, and Kohistan respectively. While playing a substantial role in the government, the Amir's eldest son Muhammad Afzal Khan could not rival the position of Ghulam Haidar Khan, owing to the Bangash origin of his mother. During the early years of Dost Muhammad Khan's second reign Muhammad Afzal was put in control of Zurmat and Katawaz. His full brother Muhammad A'zam initially received Logar as a *jagir* and later assumed control of Kurram, Khost and Zurmat. Muhammad Akram Khan, whose mother was Kohistani, became governor of Hazarajat. While most power was thus concentrated in the hands of his immediate family, the Amir himself had little direct control in these areas. The provinces were not so much seen as the lower rungs of an administrational hierarchy but rather as *jagirs* awarded to the governors in question. Maintaining their own troops and being in charge of the revenue collection, they enjoyed considerable freedom in the administration of their dominions.[222] Instead of seeking greater control in the inner affairs of the provinces Dost Muhammad Khan attempted to garner the support of his sons in the endeavor to incorporate new regions into his kingdom. In 1845 he began to lay claim to the areas north of the Hindu Kush.

SUMMARY

In this chapter I have discussed the changing political landscape in Afghanistan at the beginning of the nineteenth century. This period witnessed the transformation of the Sadozai empire founded by Ahmad Shah Durrani in 1747 into a small regional state. The state supporting Durrani elite was affected by these developments in different ways. The Muhammadzai Barakzais who had furnished the Sadozais with ministers since the reign of Shah Zaman (r. 1793–1800) were able to expand their involvement in government affairs during the final phase of Sadozai supremacy, finally seizing full control for themselves. In the course of a prolonged civil war Dost Muhammad Khan and his half brothers were able to develop competing strongholds at Kabul and Qandahar, while Herat became the last bastion of Sadozai authority. In this process the other leading Durrani families, particularly the Popalzais, were pushed to the sidelines of the political arena. In favor of Sadozai supremacy, they sympathized with British efforts to reimpose the last Sadozai king Shah Shuja'. During the First Anglo-Afghan War, however, this group found its privileges curtailed even further and played a significant role in the rebellion against the British in 1841–42. The political turmoil accompanying the transition of power from the Sadozais to the Muhammadzais and the British occupation also brought ethnic boundaries more strongly into profile. While Dost Muhammad Khan's familly cultivated close links with the Shi'i Qizilbash of Kabul, their opponents relied on the ability of the headpreacher, Mir Wa'iz Sayyid Ahmad Mir Aqa, and his sons to galvanize the Sunni population of Kabul and Kohistan into action.

Chapter 2

AMIR DOST MUHAMMAD KHAN'S POLICIES IN TURKISTAN

Separated from Kabul by the Hindu Kush and the plateau of Bamiyan, Afghan Turkistan formed a separate geographic and ethnic unit. Although it was formally incorporated into the Afghan empire during the early years of Ahmad Shah's reign, this region remained more or less autonomous until Amir Dost Muhammad Khan's invasion in 1845. In this chapter, I will describe the geographic and historical setting in Turkistan in an attempt to shed light on the circumstances the Amir's officials encountered on their arrival in this region. The discussion of the Afghan activities in Turkistan will show that Dost Muhammad Khan's officials were primarily preoccupied with expanding and securing their authority. By 1863 Tashqurghan, Balkh, Shibarghan, Sar-i Pul and Qunduz were part of the Muhammadzai state. Nonetheless the local leadership had not been displaced entirely and either remained in place or resumed their accustomed positions during the power struggles breaking out after Dost Muhammad Khan's death. Because of the incomplete nature of the conquest of Turkistan, the Amir's officials focussed on their role as military commanders rather than as administrators. Still, their acitivities laid the foundation for the consolidation of Afghan authority in the region during the reign of Dost Muhammad Khan's successor Sher 'Ali Khan.

AFGHAN TURKISTAN – THE GEOGRAPHICAL AND ETHNOGRAPHICAL SETTING

Physical Features

The term 'Afghan Turkistan' or 'Lesser Turkistan' (*turkistan-i saghir*) is generally applied to the region located south of the Oxus (Amu Darya), with the exception of Badakhshan. Its southern portion is defined, from east to west, by the Hindu Kush, a plateau stretching westward from Koh-i Changar to the Balkhab (also known as Rud-i Band-i Amir), and the spurs of the Band-i Turkistan (a mountain range extending northwest from the Koh-i Baba). The topography of Turkistan is thus characterized by two main features, namely the hilly regions in the south and the adjoining plain stretching northward to the Oxus:

> There is a well-marked, and even for the most part an abrupt, transition from the hill country to the plain. The breadth of the latter is somewhat variable, owing to the curves of the Oxus and its northward trend, but the average is between 40 and 50 miles. All along the river is a narrow arable strip.... South of this strip is a band of sandy desert. Its breadth varies from 10 to 20 miles....[1]

The elevation of the plateau west of Koh-i Changar varies between 7,000 and 10,000 feet. Extending from east to west, the valleys of Bamiyan, Saighan, and Kahmard cut into the southeastern portion of this plateau. These valleys, resembling 'gashes rather than ordinary hollows or depressions,' send forth three streams which combine to form the Qunduz river. Travelling in northerly direction, this river passes the towns Baghlan and Qunduz and forms a great marsh before it joins the Oxus. The other rivers of Turkistan are used for irrigating the plain and never reach the Oxus. Issuing from the northern portion of the plateau, the Tashqurghan river, for example, enters the valley of Aibak (Samangan) and then ends in an irrigation system watering the town of Tashqurghan (Khulm) located west of Qunduz. Wood, who visited the area in 1837–38, gives the following description of the country between Tashqurghan and Qunduz:

> West of Khulm, the valley of the Oxus, except on the immediate banks of the stream, appears to be a desert; but in an opposite direction, eastward to the rocky barriers of Darwaz, all the high-lying portion of the valley is at this season [April] a wild prairie of sweets, a verdant carpet enamelled with flowers. Were I asked to state in what respects Kabul and Kunduz most differ from each other, I should say in their mountain scenery. Throughout Kabul the hills are bold and repulsive, naked and bleak, while the low swelling outlines of Kunduz are as soft to the eye as the verdant sod which carpets them is to the foot.[2]

West of Tashqurghan, the Balkhab is diverted into a far-reaching irrigation system known as the Hijdah Nahr ('Eighteen Canals') which waters the town of Balkh and its environs. Located along the silk route linking India, China, and Iran, Balkh was a city of central commercial and cultural importance until the eighteenth century. While this city depended on irrigation for its economic development, its relative wealth also encouraged the maintenance of the canals feeding its lands.[3] With the subsequent decline of the overland trade the fortunes of Balkh were increasingly eclipsed and its population decreased. In the late eighteenth and early nineteenth centuries neighboring principalities, such as Maimana in the west and Tashqurghan and Qunduz in the east, had become regional centers of power.

Located in the westernmost part of Turkistan, the towns of Maimana and Sar-i Pul are situated in the hilly tract of the country, where the spurs of Band-i Turkistan 'sink into grassy down-like ridges and undulations, the glens becoming fertile and well populated valleys.' The areas east and west of the Maimana river, however, are arid, and the towns of Andkhui and Shibarghan located to the north and northeast of Maimana are located in the plain. In the eighteenth and nineteenth centuries, these four towns were the centers of independent Uzbek principalities generally known as the 'Chahar Wilayat'.

The region of Badakhshan adjoins Afghan Turkistan in the east. Dominated in the south by the eastern Hindu Kush, in the east by the Pamir mountains, and in the north by the Darwaz range, it forms a separate geographic unit, only opening in the west to the plains of Taliqan, Khanabad, and Qunduz:

> In the northeast the country is for the most part a waste of sterile, rocky, snow-capped mountains, divided in the east by the shallow, flat, alluvial depressions known as Pamirs. The main feature in this mountainous land is the Oxus with its numerous affluents... The mountain ranges for the most part vary from 10,000 to 20,000 feet... [4]

Prior to the 1870s, when its borders began to be defined by treaties between Russia and England, Badakhshan also included areas located on the right side of the upper reaches of the Amu Darya (Ab-i Panj).[5] The Hindu Kush and the Pamirs form great watersheds of continental dimensions which served to separate the historical empires of Central, South, and East Asia. Because of its position between these empires Badakhshan was traversed by various trade routes, one of them linking Balkh with Central Asia.[6] In medieval times this region was famous for its precious stones and horses throughout the Persian speaking world.[7] Despite these contacts with the outer world Badakhshan remained relatively isolated. The trade passing through its regions seems to have had little, if any, impact on the economic development.[8] Because of its inaccessibility the area was able to retain a great degree of autonomy until the late nineteenth century:

> The political history of Badakhshan is dictated by its geographically central, though politically peripheral position in Central Asia. Seen from the point of view of the emperors, Badakhshan was subordinate to their sovereignty, but in the eyes of the provincial historians (and their mentors, the rulers), an independent nation, the lineage of whose traditional rulers could be traced back to Alexander the Great.[9]

In the course of history, Badakhshan's local centers of power shifted from Kishim (Qal'a-yi Zafar) in the sixteenth century, to Faizabad (Jauzun) in the seventeenth and eighteenth centuries, and to Jurm in the nineteenth century.

At times the sphere of influence of the Badakhshani rulers extended to the adjoining regions of Wakhan, Shighnan, and Roshan.[10] Because of its relative remoteness, Badakhshan was able to evade in great measure Amir Dost Muhammad Khan's attempts to extend his authority northward. For the purposes of this chapter, this region will be treated in connection with the events of the wider region, i.e. Turkistan.

The Inhabitants

The accounts given by travellers who visited Turkistan in the course of the nineteenth century reveal the following ethnic composition of the region: The Chahar Wilayat of Maimana, Sar-i Pul, Shibarghan and Andkhui were clearly dominated by Uzbeks. In addition, there was a minority of Turkmen pastoralists and agriculturists inhabiting the rural areas between the Kushk river in the west and Balkh in the east.

East of Balkh, the Uzbek population thinned out. Though politically dominant, the Uzbeks formed 'a minority in a sea of Tajiks' in Tashqurghan, Qunduz, and western Badakhshan.[11] The overwhelming majority of the subjects of the Uzbek ruler of Tashqurghan, for example, were Tajiks.[12] The Tajiks also seem to have made up the sedentary population of Qunduz, Taliqan, and Saighan.[13] The population of Kahmard, Khost, and Andarab was almost entirely Tajik.[14] Centlivres explains the ethnic composition of Qataghan (the present provinces of Takhar, Qunduz, and Baghlan) on the basis of successive waves of immigration. Accordingly, he distinguishes three ethnically distinct regions. In the middle of the nineteenth century, lower Qataghan was inhabited by Uzbeks. These had displaced Turko-Mongol groups,[15] some of which had settled in the region as early as the eighth century, and caused them to migrate to upper Qataghan and southwestern Badakhshan. The mountainous regions between Andarab, Khost and Ursaj served as refuge for the ancient autochthonous population, the Tajiks.[16]

Tajiks also formed the majority of the population of Badakhshan. The central region, consisting of the valley of the Kokcha and its tributaries, is relatively accessible and fertile.[17] According to most sources, the districts of Faizabad, Kishim, Jurm, and Baharak were inhabited by Tajiks and Uzbeks adhering to Sunni Islam.[18] A group of Shia Tajiks lived in the upper reaches of these river valleys. Ranging in elevation from 8,000 to 11,500 feet, the peripheral districts of Zebak, Ishkashim, Shighnan, and Wakhan were inhabited by the so-called 'Mountain Tajiks' of Isma'ili affiliation. The high Pamir valleys in the Wakhan corridor were home to approximately 1,000 Kirghiz.[19]

While the majority of the Uzbeks were semi-nomads, the Tajiks were mostly known as agriculturists and artisans.[20] Along with Hindus, Jews, and 'Kabulis,'[21] they dominated the commercial life of the towns of

Faizabad, Taliqan, Khanabad, and Tashqurghan.[22] The important role of the Tajiks in the towns east of Balkh is also reflected by the fact that Tajiki remained the bazaar language despite the political dominance of the Uzbeks in this region.[23] Even the various Uzbek groups who settled in and around Tashqurghan became 'tajikized'. In the towns of western Turkistan, by contrast, Uzbek continued to serve as the lingua franca of the artisans and merchants of various backgrounds.[24]

HISTORICAL OVERVIEW

According to McChesney, Dost Muhammad Khan's efforts to establish his authority in Turkistan entailed the imposition of an alien political structure in the area.[25] In order to come to a clearer understanding of the nature of this conflict, it will be useful to trace the origin of the Uzbeks, their political organization under the Chingizid system during the sixteenth and seventeenth centuries, and the subsequent rise of the amirid states in Qunduz and Maimana.

The Origin of the Uzbeks

While there is considerable controversy about the exact origin of the Tajiks, most scholars agree that this group formed the ancient population of the region known as Afghanistan today and the area north of the Oxus, and that it was gradually displaced by, or mixed with, foreign invaders.[26] With the Mongol invasion and the subsequent rule of the Chaghatai *khans*, Turkish groups became the dominant element in Lesser Turkistan and Transoxania (*Mawara al-nahr*) during the thirteenth and fourteenth centuries. Arriving in the early sixteenth century, the Uzbeks were, comparatively speaking, latecomers to the region. They formed the main contingent of Muhammad Shibani's (d. 1510) military forces and migrated south from the lower Syr Darya at the turn from the fifteenth to the sixteenth century. With their assistance, Muhammad Shibani defeated Babur and conquered Bukhara, Qarshi, Samarqand, Balkh, Qunduz, the Ferghana valley, Tashkent, Khwarazm, and Herat between 1500 and 1507. After forcing Babur into Afghanistan and bringing Timurid rule in Transoxania, Balkh and Khurasan to an end, he was able to establish the Chingizid dynasty of the Shaibanids.[27] Lasting from 1500 to 1599, this empire had its centers of power in Farghana, Bukhara, and Samarqand. South of the Oxus, Balkh became the capital of the provinces Andkhui, Balkh, Qunduz, and Badakhshan. Chingizid/Uzbek rule in Bukhara lasted until the early twentieth century and formally came to an end with the incorporation of Bukhara into the Soviet Union in 1924. The Shaibanids were followed by the Chingizid dynasty of the Tuqai-Timurids (also known as Astrakhanids or Janids,1598–1740/1785) and the Uzbek dynasty of the

Manghits (1740/1785–1920). Khiva was ruled by Qunghrat Uzbeks from the end of the eighteenth century on. At the same time a new khanate was formed in Khoqand to the east of Bukhara by the Ming Uzbeks, who had assumed a leading role there for the previous hundred years.[28]

Reflecting the Uzbek ideal of self-determination, a popular etymology breaks up the term 'Uzbek' into the components *uz* ('essence') and *beg* ('chief', 'ruler') and understands the word to mean 'true ruler' or 'self ruler'.[29] More generally, however, the ethnogenesis of the Uzbeks is traced to the western successor states of the Chingizid empire which formed following the death of Chingiz Khan's eldest son Jochi (d. 1227) in the area around the Caspian and the Aral sea. In the course of the thirteenth century this region broke away from the Mongol empire and was organized into the 'Golden Horde' under Jochi's sons Batu and Berke and the 'White Horde' under Jochi's sons Orda and Shiban.[30] The name 'Uzbek' is commonly derived from Uzbek Khan, a descendant of Batu, who ruled the Golden Horde from 1313 to 1341. While his predecessor Berke (r. 1257–1266) had been the first ruler to convert to Islam, it was only during Uzbek Khan's reign that Islam took a firm hold in the Golden Horde.[31] In the historiography of the sixteenth century this process came to be identified with the ethnogenesis of the Uzbeks, Uzbek Khan being viewed both as religious and ethnic or national founder.[32] Those segments of the Golden Horde which followed Uzbek Khan's example in embracing Islam are said to have adopted the name of their leader, thus acquiring a new political identity as 'Muslim Turks'.[33] The notion of an immediate link between Uzbek Khan's conversion and the emergence of the Uzbeks is, however, not documented in earlier sources produced during the fourteenth and fifteenth centuries.[34]

By the fifteenth century, the descendants of Jochi's youngest son Shiban had come to control the entire White Horde. Their adherents were also referred to as 'Uzbeks'. The Shibanid nomads emerged as a political force for the first time when Muhammad Shibani's grandfather Abu al-Khair (r. 1428–1468) began to make inroads into Timurid dominions and established himself in the Syr Darya region. After the death of Abu al-Khair two lines of descent from Shiban split and subsequently formed the twin Uzbek states of Mawara al-Nahr and Khwarazm. The Shaibanid dynasty thus was not named after Abu al-Khair's grandson Muhammad Shibani but his ancestor Shiban.[35]

The Uzbek groups which accompanied Muhammad Shibani's attack on the Timurid principalities in Transoxania mixed with the Turkic groups already present in the area. Their migration to this region seems to have been a gradual process. Apparently the first groups settled in Transoxania at the beginning of the sixteenth century. A century later, during the Tuqai-Timurid era, they reached the left bank of the Oxus. Unlike the Turkmens, Kazakhs, Karakalpaks, and Kirghiz, many of the Uzbeks of Transoxania began to abandon their nomadic lifestyle in favor of agricultural and commercial pursuits in the early seventeenth century. By contrast, a great number of the Uzbeks located on the left bank of the Oxus remained nomads. Soldiers were mainly furnished by the sedentary groups.[36] It is not clear whether the military units of the Uzbeks were organized along tribal lines. According to Vambéry, the tribal names listed in the *Shaibaninama* as Muhammad Shibani's troops cannot be identified as specifically Uzbek but were also common among the Kirghiz, Karakalpaks, and Turkmens. He reaches the conclusion that the term 'Uzbek' was primarily a political designation which subsequently assumed an ethnic dimension. While McChesney rejects the definition of the Uzbeks as a political entity as too vague, he agrees that the Uzbeks displayed little tribal solidarity prior to the late seventeenth and early eighteenth centuries. During the Shaibanid era the name 'Uzbek' was primarily used to distinguish non-Chingizid Turko-Mongol tribal groupings serving military and administrative functions from the agnatic descendants of Chingiz Khan. The most famous among these groups were the Ming, Yuz, Alchin, Jalair, Naiman, Durman, Qunghrat, Qataghan, and Manghit.[37]

The Chingizid System of Government

Muhammad Shibani was set apart from his Uzbek followers by the fact that he was a descendant of Chingiz Khan's eldest son Jochi. This allowed him to portray himself as a legitimate heir to the Mongol empire. The Shaibanid state adopted many features of Chingizid organization, albeit with some modifications. A brief comparison between the main elements of Chingizid and Shaibanid institutions will give some insight into the characteristics of the political organization of the Shaibanids and the dynasties that followed them.

The main organizing principles of the Chingizid system of government were a) that rulers had to be agnatic descendants of Chingiz Khan and b) that sovereignty was corporate within the royal clan. Among the Mongols, succession was determined according to several guiding rules, the most important being that the aspirant to leadership had to be an agnatic descendant of Chingiz Khan, that is, claim a clear line of descent from one of Chingiz Khan's four sons by his principal wife. While this stipulation in theory allowed for a great pool of pretenders, the actual choice of a leader was often determined by other factors. For one thing, rulers often attempted to limit succession to their linear descendants. Furthermore, the contender's proximity to the capital and the support he enjoyed there, as well as his degree of control of the military and economic resources had a great impact on his chances of success. Finally, the winner of the contest for power had to be confirmed by the unanimous decision of a *quriltai*, an assembly of all the tribal leaders of the empire.[38] The concept of corporate sovereignty allowed for a great degree of decentralization. Each of Chingiz Khan's descendants received personal territories (*ulus*). Yet, this distribution of land was not intended as a division of the khanate. The *ulus* apportioned to Chingiz Khan's sons and grandsons were primarily set apart as pastoral lands and did not take up the empire's entire territory. The rich sedentary regions remained under the control of the Great Khan.[39]

While the Chingizid system had become weakened by the fifteenth century, it was infused with new life by the arrival of Muhammad Shibani. During the sixteenth and seventeenth centuries, sovereignty continued to be corporate, but the royal clan was limited to the agnates of Shiban, son of Jochi. Within this lineage, the system of succession was based on seniority. Rather than from father to son, power was handed from elder brother to younger brother before passing to the next generation. As this lateral system of succession engendered a great degree of unpredictability, there were attempts to mitigate the arising level of conflict among the eligibles by designating heir apparents.[40]

Following the Chingizid precedent, only members of the royal clan, known as *sultans*, were eligible to hold the highest offices. The chosen Shaibanid ruler carried the title *khan*. Meaning 'lord' or 'chief', this term served to designate the sovereign in the Mongol-Turkic context until the eighteenth century. In the Durrani kingdom, by contrast, the kings were addressed with the Iranian title 'Shah' until the accession of the Muhammadzais. They used the term *khan* for Pashtun leaders who represented tribal interests vis-à-vis the court.[41] As in the Iranian system, the reigning *khan* enjoyed the right of '*sikka* and *khutba*,' that is, having coins struck and having the Friday sermon read in his name. Moreover, he was in charge of convening and presiding over *quriltais* and conducting military and fiscal audits in the appanages. Compared to the Chingizids the relationship of the Shaibanid *khan* with the other members of the royal clan was much more tenuous. Apart from the 'special mystique and prestige arising from his position as dynastic elder,' the *khan* was basically treated as a *primus inter pares*.[42] Having been assigned hereditary appanages, the *sultans* were in the position to veto decisions in the *quriltais* and to conduct their own foreign affairs. No doubt the control of the capital with its productive resources gave the *khan* a certain economic and political edge over the rival cousin clans from other appanages. Still, the fact remains that the khanate became much more decentralized during the Shaibanid era, which had the effect that the reigning khan tended to find his power restricted to his own appanage. Elected solely on the basis of seniority, he often found he had limited opportunities to wield real political power within his own appanage, too. As his age prevented him from participating actively in military campaigns, he had to rely on the assistance of a younger, more energetic *sultan* for the execution of military and political tasks. This 'acting khan', as opposed to the regnant khan was known as *ratiq wa fatiq*, the 'one who mends and rends' or *khan-i ma'nawi*, the 'real khan'.[43]

The appanages were ruled by other members of the royal clan and were part of a loose confederation united by 'adherence to the Chingizid constitution and acceptance of the legitimacy of a particular royal clan and its right to the khanate.'[44] Otherwise, they enjoyed a great degree of autonomy. The appanage holders were independent in military and diplomatic affairs, as well as the distribution of power among their relatives and the appointment of officials. The independent position of the appanages under Shaibanid rule has caused Dickson to characterize them as 'appanage-states.' The individual *sultan* occupied an intermediary position between his appanage and the reigning *khan*. He was not only bound to the *khan* by loyalty to the royal clan but possibly also by the hope of becoming a *khan* himself one day. His immediate interests more likely focussed on the needs of his own affiliated cousin clan. The appanage being a hereditary possession, it tended to become closely identified with the descendants of the founding *sultan*. These, becoming further removed from the family of the *khan* with each generation, tended to form a 'derivatory or subsidiary' cousin clan. The concept of corporate sovereignty caused an ongoing contest between the cousin clans of the individual appanages, particularly at times when the state had ceased to make new conquests. While the royal clan continued to expand with each generation, the lands available for distribution did not necessarily increase at the same rate. According to Dickson, this led to the periodic rise of 'neo-eponymous' cousin clans:

> the major political fact was the inter-cousin-clan wars of elimination carried on to the point where only one victorious cousin-clan survived. When this occurred, the one surviving clan reappanaged the entire reconquered realm among its own members and became in effect a new neo-eponymous dynastic-clan.[45]

Within the appanages, the Uzbek officials serving the royal clan assumed influential positions and generally provided the military power. Known as *amirs*, 'commanders,' they were rewarded with grants of land (*iqta'*) and financial support for their services, which in turn enhanced their claims to authority among their own groups. The *amirs* also held a number of other offices, the most influential among them being those of *ataliq* and *diwanbegi*. In the sixteenth and seventeenth centuries, the *ataliq* was appointed by the reigning *khan* or appanage-holding *sultan* as a counselor and supervisor of the administration and the military. Often he also functioned as the guardian of a younger member of the royal clan. Thus he was in the position to encourage policies that favored Uzbek interests. The *diwanbegi* had both military and administrative duties and may have played a role in the supervision of appanage finances.[46]

During the Shaibanid and Tuqai-Timurid eras, Balkh formed one of four major appanages, the others being Bukhara, Samarqand, and Tashkent. In the seventeenth century, its borders were formed by the Murghab river in the west and Ishkashim, the entrance of the Wakhan valley, in the east. Kahmard was considered the southernmost point of Uzbek authority. In the north, it included areas located on the right bank of the Oxus, such as Tirmiz, Kulab, and Qubadian.[47] The internal organization of the appanage resembled that of the appanages within the empire. McChesney gives the following description of the distribution of power within the appanage of Balkh:

> Appanage structure in the first half of the [seventeenth] century was typically made up of an appanage center, including an urban site and its immediate environs. In the case of Balkh, the center was Balkh City and its immediate environs, which were defined by the Hazhdah Nahr irrigation system. The appanage center was flanked to the east, west, and south by amirid iqta'-grants: Shibarghan and Maymanah in the west, Kahmard to the south, and Qunduz in the east.[48]

The western *iqta's*, including those of Andkhui, Chichaktu, Jarzuwan, Darzab, Gharjistan, and Jozjan were given to Uzbek leaders in order to protect Balkh against Safawid and Qizilbash expansion. The distribution of *iqta's* was tied to the recognition of Chingizid sovereignty and was subject to appointment by the appanage holder. But on the administrative level the *iqta's* enjoyed a great degree of autonomy. With the exception of a certain percentage of all booty submitted to Balkh, they were fiscally independent and thus gave the Uzbek *amirs* and their followers an economic base. The longer an *amir* looked after a particular grant the more likely he also was to consider it his possession.[49]

The Rise of Amirid States

As seen above, the Chingizid system of government was characterized by a great degree of decentralization on all levels. In the course of the seventeenth century the distribution of power within the appanages shifted further in favor the Uzbek *amirs*. This development may in great part be attributed to the internal weakness of the ruling Chingizid line. The relative smallness of the royal Tuqai-Timurid clan and the formal partition of the empire into the major appanages of Balkh and Bukhara from 1620 to 1642 and 1651 to 1681 enhanced the position of the Uzbeks in the service of the Chingizid clan. The Mughal invasion of Balkh in 1646–1647 and the Nadirid occupation almost a century later not only revealed the weakness of the Tuqai-Timurids but also fostered the rise of independent amirid states. The main beneficiaries of this shift in power constellations were the Qataghan Uzbeks based in Qunduz and the Ming Uzbeks of Maimana.

The rise of the Qataghan Uzbeks began under the leadership of the Kessemir leader Mahmud Bi (d. 1714). While Mahmud Bi accepted the sovereignty of Subhanquli Khan, the Tuqai-Timurid ruler at Balkh (1651–1681) and later Bukhara (1681–1702), he was able to further his sphere of influence eastward from 1658 on by repeated attacks on Badakhshan. In 1685 he was appointed *ataliq* by Subhanquli Khan and functioned as his governor of Balkh and Badakhshan for a decade. Mahmud Bi's position at Balkh was further strengthened in the course of the rivalries following the death of Subhanquli Khan in 1702. Encouraged by Subhanquli's grandson Muqim Khan, he challenged the authority of the Bukharan ruler 'Ubaidullah Khan b. Subhanquli (r. 1702–1711) by extending his influence to areas on the right bank of the Oxus, including Tirmiz and Shahr-i Sabz. After the murder of Muqim Khan in early 1707 he seized absolute power in Balkh and openly defied 'Ubaidullah Khan's sovereignty. While 'Ubaidullah was able to remove Mahmud Bi from Balkh by force in May of the same year, the strength of the Qataghan *amir* remained unbroken in the Qunduz region.[50]

In his conquest of Balkh, 'Ubaidullah was assisted by the Ming leader 'Adil Bi Ming (d. ca. 1772), whom he made the *ataliq-i kull* of Balkh before returning to Bukhara. The Ming had become identified with the western *iqta's* of Balkh under their leader Uraz Bi, who was one of the three most influential *amirs* of the Tuqai-Timurids during the 1630s. Centered in Maimana, Shibarghan, Andkhui, and Chichaktu, the Ming became the counterpart of Qataghan power and rivalled Mahmud Bi's attempts to establish control over the city of Balkh during the last decade of the seventeenth century. After 'Ubaidullah's conquest of Balkh in 1707, they became the most influential group in Balkh proper. 'Ubaidullah's assertion of Tuqai-Timurid authority at Balkh and Andkhui was of a fleeting nature and could not obscure the increased power of the amirid groups. Mahmud Bi's stronghold in Qataghan, the Ming territory, and Kahmard under the Alchin *amirs* were beyond his administrative grip. While the Chingizid dispensation continued to carry some weight, Balkh proper also became virtually autonomous after 'Ubaidullah Khan's death in 1711.[51]

The occupation of Lesser Turkistan by Nadir Shah not only 'tolled the death knell for the Chingizids at Balkh,'[52] but also marked the decline of the city of Balkh as a center of commerce and politics. With the discovery of the sea route to India and the opening of a trade route across Siberia, it had already lost its focal role as a trading city in the early eighteenth century.[53] During the Nadirid occupation from 1737 to 1747 Balkh was finally reduced to a minor provincial town furnishing supplies for Nadir Shah's army. Meanwhile, the former Uzbek *iqta's* continued to prosper, and Andkhui, Maimana, Khulm, and Qunduz emerged as regional urban centers. The Uzbeks furnished a major section of Nadir Shah's army and thus continued to play a prominent role in the politics of Lesser Turkistan.

The Qataghan *amir* Hazara Khan, for example, was in charge of executing Nadirid economic policies in eastern Balkh. With the decline of Iranian power in the region, he became increasingly independent.[54] Among the Ming, Haji Bi moved to the forefront. Having served with the future Durrani king Ahmad Shah in the army of Nadir Shah, he was able to gain the appointment as governor (*wali*) and chief tax collector (*sahib-i ikhtiyar*) of Maimana and Balkh from the Durrani ruler in 1750. Furthermore, Ahmad Shah awarded him the title 'khan'. The assumption of this title by the Qataghan and Ming leaders signalled a final departure from the Chingizid dispensation.[55]

Afghan Turkistan under the Sadozais

With the conquest of Maimana, Andkhui, Shibarghan, Balkh, and Badakhshan by Ahmad Shah's *wazir* Shah Wali Khan in 1751, the cis-Oxus regions formally became part of the Durrani empire.[56] At the same time, the rulers of Bukhara were unwilling to give up their claims to Lesser Turkistan and were to make intermittent attempts to enforce their authority there until they lost their independence to the Russians in 1868. Similar to Afghanistan, Bukhara witnessed the rise of a new dynasty in the wake of Nadir Shah's meteoric descent on India and Central Asia. While members of the Tuqai-Timurid dynasty continued to rule Bukhara nominally until 1785, the effective power in the khanate shifted to the chiefs of the Uzbek tribe Manghit, who had held the position of *ataliq* at the Bukharan court from the early eighteenth century on. Enjoying Nadirid patronage, Muhammad Hakim Bi Manghit (d. 1743) and his son Muhammad Rahim Bi (d. 1758) were able to assert their authority over Bukhara in the 1740s. During the reign of Muhammad Hakim Bi's brother, Daniyal Bi (r. 1758–1785), the Manghit administration became firmly established. Rather than styling themselves *khan*, Daniyal's descendants Shah Murad (nicknamed Amir-i Ma'sum, r. 1785–1800), Haidar (r. 1800–1826), Nasrullah (r. 1827–1860) and Muzaffar (r. 1860–1885) assumed the title *amir al-mu'minin*.[57]

In 1768 Bukharan interference with the politics of Balkh and Badakhshan caused Ahmad Shah to engage in a second campaign to Turkistan. While Shah Wali Khan was entrusted with the establishment of order in Qunduz and Badakhshan, Ahmad Shah asserted his authority in Maimana, Andkhui, Shibarghan, and Balkh and subsequently moved against Bukhara. At Qarshi, he reached an agreement with Daniyal Bi's son Shah Murad, which formally established the Oxus as border line between Bukhara and Afghanistan. As a symbol of his victory, the Durrani ruler received the *khirqa-yi mubaraka*, a piece of the Prophet Muhammad's cloak, from the Bukharan ruler.[58]

The agreement between Ahmad Shah and Shah Murad formally designated the areas south of the Oxus as part of the Durrani empire. Nevertheless, Bukhara continued to make its presence felt in this region. During his reign at Bukhara, Shah Murad engaged in two confrontations with Ahmad Shah's successors Timur Shah and Shah Zaman, each of which finally resulted in the confirmation of the contract of 1768. In 1789 Timur Shah addressed a letter to Shah Murad in which he complained of intrusions in his dominions by the Bukharan ruler. Apart from reprisals against the Ersari Turkmens dwelling on the left bank of the Oxus, Shah Murad's recent attack on Merv and his deportation of 30,000 inhabitants were quoted as main offenses. Finding his warnings ignored, Timur Shah set out for Turkistan with 100,000 troops and defeated Shah Murad's brother 'Umar Qush Begi near Aqcha in the fall of 1790.[59] Immediately after Timur Shah's death in 1793 Shah Murad was tempted by the power struggles which beset Shah Zaman's early reign and invaded Balkh. Unable to displace the Afghan garrison there, he gave up further designs on the areas south of the Oxus for the time being.[60] At the turn of the nineteenth century, he was able to occupy Balkh a final time.[61]

Subsequent to the conquest of Afghan Turkistan, Shah Wali Khan is reported to have appointed Afghan and Uzbek governors in the other newly conquered regions.[62] In addition, a garrison of Afghan soldiers (known as *kuhna naukar*)[63] was stationed at Balkh and Aqcha 'to keep the inhabitants in awe'.[64] But, rather than imposing a new order, the Afghan ruler more likely found himself drawn into the ongoing power struggles among the local elite. In appointing Haji Khan Ming as governor of Maimana and Balkh, Ahmad Shah probably merely acknowledged the fact that the Ming leader had already assumed control of the region in question immediately after Nadir Shah's death. Ahmad Shah's support of Haji Khan placed the Ming in a favorable position in their rivalry with the Qataghan Uzbeks, who suffered a decisive defeat at the hands of the Afghan army in July 1753.[65]

This defeat notwithstanding the Qataghan were not removed from the political map of Afghan Turkistan. The 1760s and 1770s were characterized by the rivalry between the Mirs of Badakhshan and the controversial governor of Qunduz, Qubad Khan.[66] While Qubad Khan's exact tribal affiliation is not clear, the available evidence indicates that he belonged to a Qataghan lineage competing for influence with the family of Mahmud Bi.[67] Other Qataghan leaders of the region continued to play an important role by assisting Qubad Khan's rival, Mir Sultan Shah of Badakhshan, in his conquests of Taliqan and Ishkamish. Shah Wali Khan's campaign to Qunduz and Badakhshan in 1768 turned the tide in favor of Qubad Khan. One of Qubad Khan's most powerful local supporters was a Qataghan military leader, his namesake Qubad Chechka. During the 1760s Qubad Chechka played an important role in Qubad Khan's repeated expeditions against Badakhshan. But a few years later, in the face of an Afghan military campaign to the region, he was instrumental in turning away public support from Qubad Khan in favor of Khuda Nazar Beg, a relative of Mahmud Bi. Khuda Nazar Beg assumed control of Qunduz with the backing of the Afghans, thus reestablishing the predominant position of his family until 1800.[68]

Enforced by garrisons of Afghan soldiers, the Sadozai presence in Lesser Turkistan was most pronounced in Balkh and Aqcha. On the whole, the Sadozai rulers seem to have exerted little immediate control over their new possessions in the north. This is reflected by the fact that little, if any, revenues flowed from this region to the Sadozai capital. The only condition placed on Haji Khan Ming's appointment as governor of Maimana and Balkh was that he furnish troops in times of need.[69] Badakhshan undertook to submit the income derived from the lapis lazuli, jasper, and ruby mines of Badakhshan to the Durrani kings in lieu of taxes.[70] The revenues collected by Ahmad Shah's successor Timur took the form of a nominal tribute, consisting of horses and sheep submitted by Maimana and fifty horses and a certain sum of money sent in by Balkh.[71] Andkhui furnished military support to Timur Shah during his confronation with Bukhara.[72] Beyond this, Ferrier describes Timur Shah's grip over Balkh and Aqcha as 'feeble'. The governor appointed there by the Durrani ruler only enjoyed nominal powers and was not in a position to collect taxes. The annoyances connected with the governorship of Balkh and Aqcha allegedly were so great that it was difficult for Timur Shah to fill this post. According to Ferrier, the king's weak position in this region became a subject of public ridicule: 'The Loutis, who wandered from town to town with monkeys and other animals, taught them to cast earth on their heads (a sign of deepest grief among the Asiatics) when they were asked whether they would be governors of Balkh or Aqcheh.'[73]

The most detailed data concerning the fiscal relationship between Afghan Turkistan and Kabul stem from Shah Zaman's reign. During this period, Balkh and its dependencies did not even yield a 'copper' to the state coffers because all the revenues were used up by the local Mirs. Moreover, the administrative costs of this region had to be covered by subsidies from Kabul.[74] Ghulam Sarwar, who visited Shah Zaman's court in 1793–95, reported that Balkh and Aqcha required an annual subsidy of 115,000 and 70,000 rupees respectively. During the same period, a yearly tribute in kind was due from Maimana (200 horses and 11,000 sheep), Andkhui and Khulm (1,000 horses and 15,000 sheep) and Qunduz (1,000 horses and 10,000 sheep).[75] During Shah Shuja''s reign from 1803 to 1809 the revenues of Balkh were entirely consumed for local expenses, such as religious grants, pensions, the expenses of the governor and the pay of the *kuhna naukar*.[76] With the decline of the Sadozai empire in the early nineteenth century the political linkage between Lesser Turkistan and Kabul became even weaker. While the rulers of Bukhara were to use the political turmoil engulfing Afghanistan to reassert their authority in Balkh, their presence in the region was neither continuous nor overly imposing. In the following section I will investigate how the Uzbek leadership fared during this period of shifting political configurations.

THE UZBEK PRINCIPALITIES OF THE EARLY NINETEENTH CENTURY

The end of Shah Zaman's reign in 1800 and the subsequent power struggle between the Sadozais and Muhammadzais signalled the end of the empire established by Ahmad Shah and eventually resulted in the creation of three independent centers of Durrani power in Kabul, Qandahar, and Herat. Only in the late 1830s Kabul under Dost Muhammad Khan and Herat under the leadership of Yar Muhammad Khan were able to enter the political scene and to exert mounting pressure on Afghan Turkistan. In the north, the Bukharan Amirs Haidar and Nasrullah maintained Bukhara's historical claims to the cis-Oxus region and took possession of Balkh twice, in the years 1817 and 1837/38, also bringing the Chahar Wilayat into their fold.[77] Most of Bukhara's energies, however, were devoted to the prolonged endeavor to subjugate the Transoxanian principality of Shahr-i Sabz, which was able to maintain its independence until 1856.[78] Accordingly, a new sort of equilibrium evolved in Lesser Turkistan during the first third of the nineteenth century. Assuming an increasingly independent position, the Uzbek leaders primarily sought out the support of Bukhara or other neighboring powers in order to gain an edge over their local rivals. By the middle of the nineteenth century, the political landscape of Lesser Turkistan was characterized by ten or twelve Uzbek khanates locked into permanent competition.[79] In 1845, Ferrier depicted the region as a land in upheaval:

> The amount of rivalry and intrigue that exist amongst the petty khans of Turkistan is perfectly incredible to any one who has not been in the country; and, instead of trying to decrease or modify either, they exert their intelligence to the utmost to complicate and carry out their paltry schemes. The certain consequence is a permanent state of warfare... They recognise the suzerainty of the princes of Herat, Bokhara, or Khulm [at the time of Mir Wali], only because they have not sufficient power to throw it off; or, that occasionally it happens to be to their interest to acknowledge it. They will change their protectors as often as it suits them... but they rarely pay their tribute to whichever suzerain they attach themselves for the time, and he is generally obliged to present them with khalats, or in other ways propitiate their transient good-will. If they furnish him a contingent for a war they receive an indemnity from him, and are otherwise repaid bay a portion of the plunder.[80]

In this section, I will discuss the position of the most important of these Uzbek rulers, their relationship with the other principalities in the region, and the strategies they employed in their interaction with the surrounding greater powers. At first sight, the constantly shifting alliances and the accompanying warfare seem to be the most distinguishing features in the interaction of the Uzbek principalities. But beyond this apparent turmoil a peculiar sort of stability may be discerned. While forming a constant threat, the interference by Herat, Bukhara and Persia during this period was mostly too short-lived to upset the existing balance in favor of one prinicipality or the other. Although the relative economic and military strength of the individual Uzbek rulers varied, the distribution of power remained essentially decentralized. Even the most powerful among them were unable to unseat their rivals on a permanent basis but had to base their claims to authority on a loose system of allegiances.

Maimana

Ruled by the descendants of Haji Khan Ming, Maimana continued to be the most influential principality among the Chahar Wilayat, though on a reduced scale compared to the eighteenth century. By 1775 Haji Khan's son Jan Khan (r. 1772–1795) had lost the right to farm the revenues of Balkh.[81] The principality of Maimana itself still was of significant proportions during Timur Shah's reign, extending to the upper reaches of the Murghab in the southwest and including Sar-i Pul in the east. Sometime after 1814, however, Sar-i Pul was able to assert its independence from Maimana, possibly because of the relative weakness of Maimana's newly installed ruler ʻAli Yar Khan (r. 1814–1829), a ten-year-old grandson of Jan Khan. During Mizrab Khan's reign from 1831 to 1845, Maimana lost the upper reaches of the Shirin Tagau and relinquished control of the areas between Qalʻa-yi Wali and the Murghab.[82] By 1863 Chichaktu formed the western border of the khanate, which consisted of ten villages at that point.[83] Located at the intersection of the trade routes from Herat and Iran on one side, Kabul and Balkh on the other, and Andkhui and Bukhara on the third, Maimana city was a commercial center of some importance, deriving a substantial income from custom duties and slave trade.[84] During the reign of Mizrab Khan, the four districts of the khanate were subject to regular revenue collection and taxation and yielded more than one hundred and fifty thousand (Kabuli?) rupees.[85] The available data concerning Mizrab Khan's military strength as compared to the other principalities of the Chahar Wilayat vary widely.[86] In the 1840s Ferrier estimated that Mizrab Khan had a household guard of 2,500 men and was able to call out 8,000 to 10,000 men if necessary. Mahmud Khan of Sar-i Pul entertained a standing force of 2,000 horsemen and 2,000 foot. The permanent forces of the rulers of Andkhui and Shibarghan hovered around the mark of 2,500 men.[87]

After their assertion of independence, the rulers of Sar-i Pul maintained friendly relations with Maimana until 1830. A sister and a daughter of Zulfaqar Sher Khan, who ruled Sar-i Pul until 1840, were given in marriage to 'Ali Yar Khan's branch of the family. This amicable relationship came to an end, however, when Mizrab Khan, who belonged to a rival branch of Haji Khan's descendants, came to power in Maimana. In the attempt to eliminate all rival contenders for the throne, he had (among others) Zulfaqar Sher's sister killed and thus provoked a war with Sar-i Pul. In his ongoing contention with Sar-i Pul, Mizrab Khan was aided by Shibarghan's ruler Rustam Khan (d. 1851), who was a steadfast enemy of Zulfaqar Sher and his son Mahmud. After Mizrab Khan's death in 1845 a realignment of coalitions within the Chahar Wilayat took place. His sons Hukumat Khan and Sher Khan formed an alliance with Sar-i Pul and took Shibarghan from Rustam Khan, who had in turn interfered with the affairs of Andkhui.[88]

Mizrab Khan's reign was not only characterized by his rivalry with Sar-i Pul. The growing interference by his more powerful neighbors in Kabul, Herat, Iran, and Bukhara, as well as greater Russian and British activities in the region forced the rulers of the Chahar Wilayat to cooperate at times and to play off one power against the other in order to maintain their independence. In November 1840, Mizrab Khan gave the following description of his situation to the British traveller Conolly: 'No doubt you know the saying that it is difficult for a man to sail with his legs in two boats, but how can a man escape drowning who is obliged to shift them among five, according as the wind changes?'[89] The winds that Mizrab Khan felt blowing came from the Persian siege of Herat of 1837–1838, Bukhara's occupation of Balkh during the same period, and the beginning of the First Anglo-Afghan War. With the onset of the Persian siege of Herat, Mizrab Khan responded to the request for help addressed to him by Nadir Mirza, the son of Kamran, ruler of Herat. As part of the Iranian army approached under its general Allahyar Khan Asaf al-Daula, Mizrab Khan was able to overcome his differences with Sar-i Pul and organized a numerous army by forming a coalition with the other Uzbeks of the Chahar Wilayat, as well as Turkmen, Hazara, Jamshedi, and Ferozkohi leaders. After their defeat near Bala Murghab, Mizrab Khan and the other chiefs of his confederacy submitted to Asaf al-Daula and sent their sons as hostages to the Qajar king.[90]

When the Persian siege had ended, the government of Herat followed in Iran's footsteps and, supported by British political officers, began to lay claim to the Chahar Wilayat in the 1840s.[91] At the time of Mizrab Khan's death in 1845 Maimana was nominally under the authority of the Herati ruler Yar Muhammad (r. 1842–1851), who promptly interfered in the struggle of succession between Mizrab Khan's sons, Hukumat Khan and Sher Khan. Yar Muhammad Khan's representative intervened on behalf of

Sher Khan by placing him in control of the army and citadel of Maimana, whereas Hukumat Khan had to content himself with the authority over the mercantile and agricultural population of the khanate. Subsequently Yar Muhammad's *ishik aqasi* apparently attempted to strengthen Herat's position in Maimana by establishing a Tajik military contingent.[92] Two years later Yar Muhammad used Hukumat Khan's plea for assistance as a pretext to start a military campaign to the region. He plundered Chichaktu, forced Sher Khan out of Maimana and installed Hukumat Khan (r. 1847–1862) as ruler there.[93] Nonetheless, Yar Muhammad Khan's plan to establish a more permanent military presence in the Chahar Wilayat came to naught. His attacks on Andkhui and Aqcha devastated the region to such an extent that he was unable to procure supplies for his army of nearly ten thousand soldiers. As Shibarghan and Maimana closed their gates on his army, he was forced to retreat to the Murghab, losing thousands of his soldiers to exposure and starvation.[94] Again two years later, in 1849, Yar Muhammad had gathered sufficient forces to besiege Hukumat Khan in Maimana because of the latter's failure to submit revenues. But the city successfully resisted all attacks of the Herati army. In September 1850 Yar Muhammad had to give up his siege of eleven months without having attained his goal. Despite repeated military campaigns to Maimana, he had been unable to translate his claims to authority into actual control of the Chahar Wilayat. While Maimana, Andkhui, and Shibarghan continued to formally accept Yar Muhammad's sovereignty until his death in 1851, they were actually able to maintain a precarious independence. How precarious this independence was became clear with the advent of Dost Muhammad Khan's troops in Afghan Turkistan in the year of Yar Muhammad's last retreat from Maimana. Devastated by Yar Muhammad Khan's repeated invasions, the Chahar Wilayat had few resources at their disposal to ward off the growing Muhammadzai presence.[95] In a field of shrinking political options, the Uzbek *khans* were to adhere to their time-honored strategy of containment, alternating nominal pledges of allegiance with spurts of spirited military resistance.

Qilich 'Ali of Tashqurghan (Khulm)

In the eastern part of Turkistan, Tashqurghan and Qunduz were the two major centers of power in the first half of the nineteenth century. Qilich 'Ali, a Uzbek chief of the Muitan tribe,[96] apparently rose to prominence in Tashqurghan in the late 18th century, most likely during Shah Zaman's reign. Qilich 'Ali's career seems to have been fostered in great part by his friendly relationship with the Sadozai court. Elphinstone describes him as a 'zealous and useful servant of the crown of Caubul.'[97] Other sources, however, view his loyalty to Shah Shuja' rather as 'ostentatious.'[98] While he had the *khutba* read in the name of the Sadozai king, he submitted no revenues whatsoever.[99] Qilich 'Ali also maintained some connection with the court of Bukhara, as his officials accompanied a delegation from Amir Haidar to Kabul in 1805.[100] Furthermore, he bolstered his position by entering marriage alliances with the chiefs of Qunduz and Maimana.[101] While interfering with the politics at Balkh, he retained his hometown as his seat of power. The choice of Tashqurghan as capital can be seen as an indicator of Balkh's declining status as economic and political center.[102] Tashqurghan, on the other hand, had become the most important mart in Lesser Turkistan, being conveniently located at the crossroads of the caravan routes from India, China, Bukhara, and Khurasan.[103] During Qilich 'Ali's reign, this rich agricultural oasis yielded a revenue of 150,000 rupees after deducting the expenses for his standing army of 2,000 men. Together with the troops maintained by local chiefs as part of service grants and the soldiers furnished by Qunduz, the ruler of Tashqurghan controlled a total army of 17,000 men.[104]

From his base in Tashqurghan, Qilich 'Ali was able to subject the neighboring petty states of Aibak, Ghori, Saighan, Kahmard, and Darra-yi Juz.[105] In the east, he gained ascendancy over Hazrat Imam and Qunduz.[106] In Balkh, Qilich 'Ali successfully challenged the authority of the governor appointed by Shah Shuja'. His takeover of the government of Balkh became more or less complete in 1809 when the support the abovesaid governor gave to Shah Shuja''s half brother and rival Shahzada 'Abbas furnished the Uzbek chief with a pretext to expel him from the city of Balkh. Subsequently Qilich 'Ali's eldest son, Mir Baba Beg, was appointed governor of Balkh by Shah Shuja'.[107] Balkh seems to have formed the westernmost point of Qilich 'Ali's sphere of influence. Burnes reports that his seven-year-long attempt to conquer Shibarghan met with no success.[108] Qilich 'Ali's small empire fell apart with his death in 1817, when his sons, Mir Baba and Mir Wali, began to fight each other for the possession of Tashqurghan.[109]

Mazar-i Sharif and Balkh

One of the petty states annexed by Qilich 'Ali was the city of Mazar-i Sharif located twelve miles east of Balkh. In 1481 the purported rediscovery of the grave of Muhammad's son-in-law 'Ali b. Talib at this site had led to the erection of a shrine and a religious endowment on the part of the Timurid administration.[110] Having formed part of the appanage of Balkh during Shaibanid and Tuqai-Timurid times, the shrine began to assume an increasingly independent political function with the end of the Nadirid occupation. While the shrine itself continued to attract a wide spiritual following at the beginning of the nineteenth century, the role of its chief administrator (*mutawalli*) was comparable to that of other small rulers in the region. Similar to Tashqurghan, Mazar's political and economic importance seems to have risen with the decline of Balkh. At the turn of the nineteenth century, the *mutawalli* of the shrine, Mirza 'Aziz, was reported to entertain his own troops.[111] Shuja' al-Din (d. 1849),[112] who was in charge of the shrine from the 1820s on, was described by Harlan in 1839 as the 'wealthiest chief in the province', second in importance only to the ruler of Qunduz, Mir Murad Beg. While the Mutawalli had lost much of his spiritual role compared with earlier shrine administrators, Harlan attributed his political success in part to his 'sacred character' which enabled him 'to concentrate at all times a military force by combination amongst his disciples sufficiently potent for the maintenance of a firm opposition.'[113] Controlling between 900 and 1,250 cavalry[114], Shuja' al-Din played an active role in the changing politics of the region. According to Harlan, his policy was 'to temporize with any power superior to and likely to conflict with this interest, but no political attachments are sufficiently strong to bias his judgement in the crafty pursuit of individual advantage.' After Qilich 'Ali's death Shuja' al-Din became independent and cooperated with Mir Murad Beg in negotiating a settlement between the sons of the Uzbek ruler in the 1820s, giving Tashqurghan to Mir Wali and Aibak and Darra-yi Suf to his half brothers Mir Baba Beg and Mir Sufi Beg.[115]

Shuja' al-Din was related by marriage to the governor of Balkh, Ishan Sayyid Parsa Khwaja Naqib (generally known as Ishan Naqib, d. 1838). A dignitary of the Naqshbandi order, Ishan Naqib belonged to the line of Gauhari shaikhs based in Qasan near Qarshi on Bukharan territory.[116] Subsequent to Qilich 'Ali's death in 1817, Ishan Naqib gained the governorship of Balkh with Bukharan support. His eldest son, Sayyid Muhammad Oraq (d. c. 1889), was appointed governor of Aqcha at this time. Nominally tributary to Bukhara, Ishan Naqib ruled Balkh more or less independently until 1837, when the pressure exerted on the eastern part of the Hijdah Nahr system by the ruler of Qunduz, Mir Murad Beg, triggered direct Bukharan interference. In November 1837 Amir Nasrullah conquered and destroyed the city and deported Ishan Naqib along with numerous citizens to Bukhara. Ishan Oraq fled to Tashqurghan and was able to retake Balkh with the assistance of Mir Wali and Shuja' al-Din in 1840. His younger brother, Ishan Sudur (d. 1868) became governor of Aqcha.[117] Apart from a short-lived attempt at annexation by Mir Wali in 1841, Ishan Oraq governed Balkh in the name of Bukhara until the advent of the Afghan troops in 1849.[118] Under the Muhammadzais, Ishans Oraq and Sudur were deprived of their governorships and spent extended periods of time in exile. Nonetheless, they continued to play a prominent role in the politics of Afghan Turkistan, eventually meeting violent deaths at the hands of Muhammadzai administrators.[119]

Mir Murad Beg of Qunduz

Subsequent to Qilich 'Ali's death one of his former lieutenants, Mir Murad Beg of Qunduz (r. 1817–1840?),[120] a Kessemir Qataghan, became the dominant figure of eastern Turkistan. A descendant of Mahmud Bi, Mir Murad advanced from his basis in Rustaq, where his father had been a tributary of the Mir of Badakhshan. He conquered Taliqan, Khanabad and Qunduz and was recognized as leader of the Qataghan tribe by the ageing Qilich 'Ali.[121] During the height of his power in the 1820s and 1830s, his realm comprised all the areas north of the Hindu Kush and the mountains north of Bamiyan. North of the Oxus, Kulab, Qurghan Tepe, and Qubadian were part of his sphere of influence. While nominally under the authority of Bukhara, Balkh and Mazar were subject to frequent plundering expeditions by Mir Murad Beg's army, which caused a great part of the population to flee to Maimana.[122] Qilich 'Ali's sons continued to hold Tashqurghan, Aibak, and Darra-yi Suf as governors under the authority of Qunduz, while the remainder of Qilich 'Ali's former possessions was given to Murad Beg's 'confidential followers' in *jagir*.[123] The Tajik chiefs Muhammad 'Ali Beg of Saighan and Rahmatullah Beg of Kahmard acknowledged Mir Murad Beg's claims to authority but apparently also submitted a nominal tribute to Kabul.[124] The focus of Murad Beg's military efforts seems to have been Badakhshan, which had been able to retain its independence apart from the fleeting military presence of Ahmad Shah's troops in 1751 and 1768 and the subsequent intrusion by Qubad Khan. Similar to his ancestor Mahmud Bi, Murad Beg mounted repeated military expeditions to this region from 1821 on, only to find his authority called into question by several rebellions. In 1829, the Qunduz ruler was finally able to subjugate Badakhshan and to extend his authority to the remote areas of Roshan, Shighnan, and Wakhan. Because of its prolonged resistance, Badakhshan was the region hardest hit by Mir Murad's policies. Its ruler was taken prisoner, the capital of Faizabad was totally destroyed, and about 20,000 families were deported in a vain attempt to people the swamps of Qunduz and Hazrat Imam.[125]

Firmly entrenched in Qunduz and Badakhshan and controlling a military force twice as strong as that of Maimana, Mir Murad Beg was by far the most powerful local ruler of Turkistan in his day. His possession of the important trade routes linking Turkistan with India added to his standing. The strategic importance of his position is reflected in part by the relative frequency of British visitors to his court. The reports left by these travellers furnish us with a greater amount of information on his style of government in comparison with the circumstances in the Chahar Wilayat during the same period. The following description of his character, his relationship with other tribal leaders, and the organization of his government bears greater detail than the above discussion of the Chahar Wilayat not only because his relative strength made his person intrinisically more important to the political structure of Turkistan but simply because more information is available on his reign.

The descriptions given of the ruler of Qunduz vary considerably according to the perspective of the beholder. Moorcroft, who faced detainment in Qunduz in 1824, noted Murad Beg's 'forbidding countenance' and the respectful bearing his courtiers assumed in his presence.[126] Lal, who never met Mir Murad Beg, claimed that his indulgences of various kind had left the Kessemir leader a mere wreck: 'Debauchery, which he had carried to an extreme point, has now produced fits, which succeed each other at frequent intervals, and have rendered him unable to transact business.'[127] In 1839 Dr. Lord painted a more favorable picture of his host:

> Murad Beg though in his 59th year, is to all appearance perfectly unbroken. He has never injured his constitution by excesses of any kind, unless we apply that name to the fatigues he has undergone, nor except habitual haemorrhoids and an occasional attack of cholic probably induced by repletion, can I learn that he has ever suffered from any illness. To the climate of Kundooz he seems perfectly inured, and merely takes the precaution of removing from it to Khana-abad during the intense heats of summer and autumn.[128]

While Tashqurghan formed the most important city of his realm,[129] Mir Murad Beg retained his capital at Qunduz. In 1837, Wood described Qunduz as 'one of the most wretched of his dominions. Five or six hundred mud hovels contain its fixed population, while dotted amongst these, and scattered at random over the suburbs, are straw-built sheds intermixed with the Uzbek tent or kirgah.'[130] Moorcroft gives the following description of Murad Beg's court:

> On the right was an area, of which three sides were flanked by a broad veranda with a flat roof, supported by wooden pillars; the floor was raised above the level of the court about three feet. In this, on our left, was seated Mir Mohammed Murad Beg, in the centre of a line of some thirty or forty courtiers, who were seated on their knees, with their feet to the wall, their bodies inclined forwards, and their looks directed to the ground. On the floor of the area stood a long line of attendants in front of the chief, some with white wands, and all bending their bodies slightly forward, and declining their heads. Between them and the veranda, immediately opposite the chief, sat the Arz begi, or presenter of petitions. The whole was orderly and respectful... The Mir sat upon a cushion of China damask, which raised him above his courtiers.[131]

In contrast with the deferential position his courtiers assumed, Mir Murad Beg was reclining on his silken pillow and 'stretched out his legs covered with huge boots, in contempt of all eastern rules of decorum.'[132]

The British Indian visitors had little favorable to say about Murad Beg's style of government. In 1832, Lal characterized him as 'unacquainted with justice and mercy.'[133] Five years later, Wood gave a more detailed description of the ruler of Qunduz and his policies. In particular, he noted the apparent contradiction between Mir Murad Beg's absolute authority over his subjects and the fact that he merely seemed to function as the 'head of an organized banditti,' a coalition with the other tribal leaders of the Qunduz region.[134] While abhorring Mir Murad Beg's 'predatory warfare,' Wood was not entirely unaware of the fact that the plunder procured by attacks on areas on the fringes of his dominions gave the Uzbek ruler the necessary means to maintain his authority within the Qataghan tribe:

> Not the least remarkable trait in the character of this man is the contrast afforded by his well ordered domestic government, and the uninterrupted course of rapine which forms the occupation of himself and his subjects, whose 'chuppaws', or plundering expeditions embrace the whole of the upper waters of the Oxus, from the frontier of China on the east, to the river that runs through Balk [sic]... on the west. His government is rigidly despotic, but seldom is absolute power less misused. The rights and property of his subjects are respected, merchants are safe, and trade is encouraged. Punishment for crime, whether against individuals or the state, is most summary; for theft and highway robbery, if the highway be *in their own country*, for that makes a wonderful difference, the only award is death... Countries in former times closed to the traveller, may now, with Murad Beg's protection, be as safely traversed as British India.[135]

Mir Murad Beg's conquests of the neighboring regions thus aimed first of all at securing a following among his immediate relatives and the other tribal leaders of the Qataghan Uzbeks:

> Murad Beg, aware that his description of force was ill-calculated to retain conquests when made, razed every hill fort as they fell into his hands, but reserved the Uzbek strongholds in the plain. These, Tash Kurghan excepted, are held by members of his family, or by men whose interest is identified with his own.[136]

The tribal leaders participating in Murad Beg's plundering expeditions received not only part of the booty but also grants of land for a nominal tribute. The only condition tied to these privileges was that the tribal leaders had to furnish troops and, according to Burnes, to maintain a part of Murad Beg's own army.[137] When called out, the entire army at his disposal amounted to 15,000 to 20,000 cavalry.[138] Harlan even claims that up to 100,000 cavalry were available in times of emergency. By contrast, Murad Beg's guard of 500 cavalry formed the only standing army. During military campaigns, the assembled troops carried their own subsistence, thus looking more like 'a karrovan prepared for passing a desert than a body of light cavalry for active service.' The decentralized organization of the army also meant that the troops usually could not be kept together for more than fifteen days:

> The people are punctual in meeting at the appointed time; they proceed upon the expedition martialled under their respective village leaders, and on the day their time of service expires everyone scampers off and returns to his native village without the ceremony of leave-taking or dismissal. It sometimes happens, when unlooked-for obstacles retard their operations, that the chief is obliged to leave unfinished an important enterprise, and hurry away with his dispersing force to the shelter of his stronghold.[139]

The ruler of Qunduz only had direct access to the revenues of the regions controlled by his immediate family, for the other areas of his dominion were distributed as *jagir* to regional leaders as part of his system of military tenure. His main sources of income were grain received as tax or quitrent from his own lands and the house tax levied in the districts of Qunduz, Taliqan and Hazrat Imam, as well the customs and transit duties collected in Tashqurghan. Wood's travelling companion Lord concluded that his total income of 396,000 rupees a year was negligible in comparison with his military weight.[140] Apart from generating a political following and the concomitant military support, booty most likely also formed a major part of Murad Beg's revenues. Slave raids furnished another important source of income. Mir Murad Beg not only carried on slave trade with Hazarajat, Chitral, and Kafiristan but also required part of his revenues to be paid in slaves. The revenue assessment for Saighan and Kahmard was one slave for every third family, thus encouraging the local governors Muhammad 'Ali Beg and Rahmatullah Khan to engage in slave raids on the adjacent Hazara regions in the south and to advance as far as Dai Zangi.[141]

Mir Murad Beg also attempted to enhance the trade in other items between Kabul and Bukhara via Tashqurghan. The transit duty levied at Tashqurghan at the rate of two and a half percent (*chihil yak*) for Muslims and five percent for non-Muslims conformed with Islamic precepts and was, according to Lal, 'not extortionate' in comparison with the rates levied in the wider region. The trade passing through Tashqurghan in the 1830s was considerable. Harlan estimated that Tashqurghan yielded 100,000 rupees per year in excise duties.[142] But there is evidence that the ruler of Qunduz did not have direct access to this sum. Lord reports that the right to collect customs and transit duties along the caravan road from Bukhara to Kabul rested with Mir Murad Beg's Hindu *diwanbegi* Atma Ram, who initially obtained this privilege in exchange for 25,000 rupees yearly. In the late 1830s the farm for the transit duties had risen to 40,000 rupees.[143]

Because of the low density of population in the Qataghan region, the ruler of Qunduz attempted to invite voluntary settlers in addition to the people brought there by force. In order to make agricultural pursuits attractive, he assessed only one tenth to one eighth on the production of the soil instead of the customary third.[144] The sheep of the Uzbek nomads were only assessed at one percent to two percent.[145] Due to its depopulation, Badakhshan furnished only little revenue. According to Wood, Mir Murad Beg also gave up working the ruby and lapis lazuli mines of that region for lack of profit.[146]

Confronted with Mir Murad Beg's powerful position, the other Uzbek rulers of Turkistan sought to curb his westward aggression. In the fall of 1824 Mir Baba Beg b. Qilich 'Ali, Zulfaqar Sher of Sar-i Pul, Ishan Naqib of Balkh, and Shuja' al-Din, the *mutawalli* of Mazar, formed a short-lived military coalition against the ruler of Qunduz.[147] While Baba Beg had to accept Murad Beg's supremacy, the other petty Uzbek rulers were eager to invoke Bukharan assistance in order to maintain a balance of power in the region. At the same time, however, they were not interested in Murad Beg's total destruction, recognizing his value as a counterweight to Bukharan interference in the region which would insure their own independence.[148] Until the late 1830s Mir Murad Beg had little contact with the rulers of Kabul. In the winter of 1832/33 Haji Khan Kakar spent several months at the court of Qunduz, negotiating a treaty by which Kahmard, Saighan, and Ajar were incorporated into his government at Bamiyan. As Haji Khan Kakar had acted without Dost Muhammad Khan's instructions and possibly only aimed at enhancing his own position in the Hazarajat, Amir Dost Muhammad Khan ignored the treaty concluded with Mir Murad Beg and relieved Haji Khan Kakar of his government of Bamiyan.[149] In 1837 there were reports that Dost Muhammad Khan and Mir Murad Beg had entered a double marriage alliance. Moreover, the ruler of Qunduz was said to have pledged his financial and military support in case of a war against the Sikhs.[150] According to Wood, the presents brought to Kabul by an emissary of Mir Murad Beg in October of the same year 'enlisted the warmest sympathy of Dost Mohamed Khan.'[151] Lord, on the other hand, noted that the relationship between the two rulers, while 'pacific,' was devoid of all 'cordiality'.[152] In 1838 Dost Muhammad Khan apparently became increasingly concerned with the powerful position of the Mir of Qunduz. Fearing a possible southward push by Mir Murad Beg towards Bamiyan, the Amir ordered a military campaign against the Qataghan ruler. As a result of this expedition, Mir Murad Beg had to give up control over Kahmard and Saighan and relinquish his claim on the transit duties collected in Tashqurghan. In the treaty concluded Mir Murad Beg described himself as 'the younger brother of the Ameer', thus acknowledging Dost

Muhammad Khan's claims to control over the Balkh region. Apart from his reduced income this loss of prestige diminished his power among the Qataghan Uzbeks. Many of his former allies threw off their allegiance and a struggle for succession sprang up between his son and his nephew.[153]

Mir Wali of Tashqurghan

The main beneficiary of Dost Muhammad Khan's intervention was Qilich 'Ali's son Muhammad Amin, known as Mir Wali (r. 1838–1850), who had supported Dost Muhammad Khan's military campaign. He was placed in possession of the regions given up by the ruler of Qunduz and was to share the transit duties of Tashqurghan with Dost Muhammad Khan. As a token of his rising power he was appointed by the Amir of Bukhara to settle the ongoing war of succession among Mir Murad Beg's relatives, just as Murad Beg had assumed the role of arbitrator among Qilich 'Ali's sons some twenty years earlier.[154]

During the First Anglo-Afghan War, Mir Wali was able to widen his sphere of influence north of the Hindu Kush considerably by alternately defying the British invaders and cooperating with them. Apart from giving shelter to Dost Muhammad Khan and his family on their flight from Kabul, he allowed the deposed Amir and his relatives to collect the caravan duties of Tashqurghan until Dost Muhammad's surrender to the British in November 1840. But his military support of the Muhammadzai ruler mainly seems to have been a facade for his plan to deprive his half brothers Mir Baba Beg and Mir Sufi Beg of their possessions of Aibak and Darra-yi Suf. Shortly after his reluctant participation in the battle of Bamiyan he succeeded in this venture by concluding a treaty with the British on September 28, 1840. The British dropped their support of Baba Beg and Sufi Beg and gave Mir Wali control over Aibak and Darra-yi Suf, as well as Kahmard. Claiming to act in the name of the British, the Mir of Tashqurghan conquered Balkh during the following year. Owing to British pressure, he gave up the direct occupation of Balkh shortly afterwards but his suzerainty was acknowledged by the Ishan of Balkh.[155] In the years following the departure of the British, Mir Wali was able to incorporate the former dominions of Mir Murad Beg into his realm. One of Mir Murad Beg's sons continued to function as his governor in Qunduz. Badakhshan was held by Mir Wali's son Ganj 'Ali Beg (d. 1868). Linked by marriage alliance to the ruler of Sar-i Pul, Mir Wali was also able to interfere with the politics of Andkhui and Shibarghan. In 1845 Ferrier described Tashqurghan as the major force in Afghan Turkistan, its power being comparable to that of Kabul, Herat, or Bukhara. Although this statement appears somewhat exaggerated, it points to Mir Wali's relative strength in the region. While his military force had consisted of 4,000 horse in the late 1830s, he was able to call out 8,000 cavalry and 3,000 infantry in 1845. Ferrier estimated his total revenues at approximately 750,000 rupees.[156] The comparative wealth of Tashqurghan during this period is reflected by the fact that its present-day bazaar, the Tim, and its major buildings, for example, the Madrasa-yi khishti were constructed during this period.[157]

Apart from his military campaign against Mir Murad Beg in 1838, Dost Muhammad Khan was not able to interfere much in Afghan Turkistan prior to the First Anglo-Afghan War. Until his renewal of interest in the region in 1845 the Aqrubat and Ghandak passes north of Bamiyan formed the northern boundary of his dominions.[158] While far from isolated, Tashqurghan and Qunduz were sufficiently distant from the greater centers of power at Kabul and Bukhara to pursue independent policies. The relative length of the reigns of Qilich 'Ali, Mir Murad Beg, and Mir Wali indicates that they were not exposed to major challenges by outsiders. Badakhshan excluded, all three rulers laid claim to roughly the same territories. The fact, however, that neither Qilich 'Ali nor Mir Murad Beg were able to establish an uninterrupted dynasty by handing over their dominions to members of their families indicates that their power was far from absolute. The above discussion has shown that Mir Murad Beg did not attempt to unseat the local rulers but tied them into a system of allegiance to the court of Qunduz. His system of military tenure in exchange for rent-free grants of lands gave a great degree of autonomy to his military leaders and administrators, who continued to play a great political role as allies and potential rivals. In 1839 Lord predicted that the leadership of northeastern Turkistan would pass to Mir Wali with the death of Mir Murad Beg. In his opinion, the ruler of Qunduz was 'the sole link that holds together the discordant elements of which his government is composed, and their dissolution will be a necessary consequence of his.'[159] The politics of eastern Turkistan during the first half of the nineteenth century were thus characterized by the continuously changing balance of power between the Muitan and Kessemir leaders. No matter whether Tashqurghan or Qunduz formed the seat of power, the dominant rulers were unable to displace the other Uzbek leaders, as is shown by Mir Murad Beg's acceptance of Mir Wali as governor of Tashqurghan and Mir Wali's acceptance of Mir Murad Beg's son as governor of Qunduz. What held true for the centers of power could be applied to the fringes of the Uzbek dominions as well: While Saighan and Kahmard were formally incorporated into the dominions of Qilich 'Ali, Mir Murad Beg, and Mir Wali, their local rulers stayed in power. An exception has to be made for Badakhshan, which, bearing the brunt of Mir Murad Beg's plundering expeditions, was deprived of its ruler and his sons. Nevertheless there is evidence that Mir Murad Beg employed another member of the ruling family as local governor, who held Jurm on a military tenure on terms similar to those held by the remainder of Mir Murad Beg's followership.[160]

DOST MUHAMMAD KHAN'S INTERVENTION IN TURKISTAN

The progress and effects of Amir Dost Muhammad Khan's occupation of Afghan Turkistan have received varying interpretations. The Afghan historian Reshtia views the transition of power to the Afghans as comparatively smooth. In McChesney's analysis, on the other hand, the political interests of the Afghan state and those of the petty Uzbek principalities were diametrically opposed to each other. Rather than being incorporated into the Afghan state, these petty rulers resisted the extension of Muhammadzai authority. Ultimately 'redundant' in the Afghan conception of government, they eventually lost their dominions.[161] In this section, I will attempt to trace the expansion of Muhammadzai authority until 1863 and the reactions it elicited.

The Beginnings of Afghan Administration

Dost Muhammad Khan's northward thrust initially concentrated on the regions along the route to Balkh. In 1843 he was able to reestablish control in Bihsud and Bamiyan. Shortly afterwards he began to exert pressure on his former ally, Mir Wali of Tashqurgan.[162] In 1848 Amir temporarily gave up his designs on Turkistan, as his attention was riveted on the crumbling of Sikh power in Punjab.[163] With the incorporation of Punjab into British India in 1849, the ruler of Kabul relinquished his hope of regaining Peshawar and returned to his ventures in Turkistan with renewed energy. In the same year his son Muhammad Akram Khan was able to defeat a coaliton of Uzbek Mirs near Saighan and to establish himself at Balkh. In 1850 Muhammad Akram Khan's half brother Ghulam Haidar occupied Tashqurghan and forced Mir Wali to flee across the Oxus.[164]

Following Muhammad Akram Khan's conquest of Balkh many local leaders, such as Ishan Oraq of Balkh and Nimlik, Ishan Sudur of Aqcha, Mir Baba Beg of Aibak, Ghazanfar Khan of Andkhui, Hakim Khan of Shibarghan, Mahmud Khan of Sar-i Pul, Mir Wali's son Ganj 'Ali Beg, and and Mir Murad Beg' son Shah Murad Beg (also known as Mir Ataliq, d. 1865) of Qataghan formally declared their submission to Afghan authority by offering presents and receiving robes of honor.[165] This show of obedience was repeated in 1851 when 'the Meers of Toorkistan from Akhchah to Budakshan, and Kashkar and the son of Meer Morad Beg [probably Mir Ataliq] came and made their salam to Dost Mahomed Khan bringing valuable presents.'[166] In August 1851 Ghulam Haidar reported that 'all was favourable in Turkistan.'[167] Three years later his cousin 'Abd al-Ghiyas Khan (b. Nawwab 'Abd al-Jabbar Khan) observed that the people of Turkistan 'had all become good subjects and were content.'[168] While noting that the imposition of Afghan authority sparked some rebellions, Reshtia reflects the view given in the above sources. In his opinion, all of Turkistan, with the exception of Maimana and Badakhshan, had submitted to Kabul at the time of Muhammad Akram Khan's death in March 1852. Reshtia also characterizes the situation in Turkistan under Muhammad Akram's successor Muhammad Afzal Khan as 'relatively peaceful'.[169] An overview of Dost Muhammad Khan's conquests in the region suggests that Afghan authority proceeded in a linear manner, albeit more gradually than the above accounts would indicate. In 1851, Aqcha and Sar-i Pul were taken. In 1854 and 1856, Shibarghan and Andkhui respectively tendered submission to Afghan authority. In 1859 Qunduz was annexed and Badakhshan was forced to recognize Afghan suzerainty. At the time of Dost Muhammad Khan's death in 1863, only Maimana had been able to maintain its independence.[170]

But a closer look at the administrative measures taken by the Afghans reveals that the intrusion of Afghan authority into Turkistan did not proceed unchallenged and raises questions about the exact nature of the submission of the Uzbek Mirs. According to Reshtia, Muhammad Akram Khan's military campaign in 1849 was caused by the refusal of the petty Uzbek principalities to adhere to a previously existing arrangement for the submission of revenue to Kabul.[171] *Siraj al-tawarikh*, on the other hand, states that the administrative measures taken by the Sardar in 1849 were rather cautious and merely served as a prelude to the intended subjugation of Turkistan, thus suggesting that the idea of revenue payments was being newly introduced to the region. Muhammad Akram Khan contented himself with assessing taxes 'little by little' (*andak andak*) on the lands of the Mirs and awarded a portion of these taxes to them as a service grant (*jagir*).[172] The somewhat fragmentary information furnished by *Siraj al-tawarikh* on the Sardar's policies does not allow any firm conclusions on the actual scope of his intervention in the Uzbek principalities. The caution which characterized his measures may be taken as an indication that his authority was more or less restricted to Balkh and Mazar and that he was in no position to unseat local rulers or to meddle with their prerogative of revenue collection in 1849. At the same time, his formal claims to the revenue of the entire region intimated to the Mirs that he was not going to be satisfied with mere tokens of submission in the long run. On their part, the Uzbek rulers were unwilling to follow their ready pledges of allegiance with revenue payments and responded to the Sardar's actual or threatened intervention with intermittent rebellions. *Siraj al-tawarikh* only mentions one concrete example of the policies imposed by Muhammad Akram Khan. The author links the *amirs*' rebellion at Aqcha in 1849/50 directly to the 'just government' (*husn-i hukumat*) imposed by the Sardar. Interfering with their methods of revenue collection, he had allegedly prevented them from oppressing their subjects.[173] Possibly reflecting the wishful thinking of the Kabul government, the author may have overstated the extent of

Muhammad Akram Khan's intervention and its effects. The question of the efficaciousness of the Sardar's policies apart, the rebellion at Aqcha indicates that his intentions triggered deep resentment among the local rulers of Turkistan.

McChesney views the clash between the expectations of the Afghan government and the attitudes of the local rulers of Turkistan as the result of an 'unbridgeable gulf' between the structure of the Afghan state and the political organization developed in the regions north of the Hindu Kush during the Chingizid era. While allowing for the 'importance of tribal identification' in the Afghan system of government, he points out that its institutions were modelled after those of Iran and Mughal India and thus were essentially hierarchically and centrally organized, as opposed to the egalitarian principles underpinning the Chingizid system. Given their roots in the Chingizid appanage system, the local Uzbek *amirs* 'probably expected that they would recognize Afghan sovereignty, present the usual tokens of fealty, and in turn be confirmed in their local prerogatives.' But with the increasing interference of the Afghans from the 1850s on the inherent tension between the Chingizid dispensation and the administration imposed by the Sardars led to the ultimate demise of the Uzbek khanates. The decentralization typical of the Chingizid system did not allow the Uzbek Mirs to form lasting coalitions. Thus they were easily manipulated by Afghan interests and could be easily eliminated once the Sardars became strong enough to impose direct control.[174]

McChesney's analysis aptly describes the mechanism underlying the imposition of Afghan control in Turkistan. The organization of the Durrani state indeed differed from the Chingizid system. Being newcomers to the region, the Muhammadzais were not interested in forming loose alliances but wanted to gain new sources of revenue. But despite these conceptual differences the question remains whether the *structure* of Dost Muhammad Khan's government was so radically different from the Uzbek states as McChesney would have it. At least for Dost Muhammad Khan's early reign the argument may be made that, on a somewhat grander scale, the organization of his state and his methods of gaining followers closely resembled those of his Uzbek contemporary Mir Murad Beg. Dost Muhammad Khan's weakness in relation to the Pashtun leadership forced him to portray himself rather as a tribal leader than an autocratic ruler and to organize his court–externally at least–on egalitarian principles. In the early years, the system of government of the Amir of Kabul had little in common with that of his more powerful Sadozai forebears. The institutions of the Sadozai state had crumbled during the prolonged power struggle which eventually brought Dost Muhammad Khan to power. In his attempt to obliterate all traces of the Sadozai past, Dost Muhammad Khan destroyed the last vestiges of their administration. During his early reign powerful government institutions were practically nonexistent. Still the fact remains that the Amir's insistence on his role as *primus inter pares* during the 1830s stemmed less from deeply held convictions than political exigencies. While he would have liked to impose a more centralized rule, his lack of power forced him to grant a great degree of independence to his provincial governors and to content himself with formal statements of allegiance from those groups entirely beyond his grip. But this decentralization was involuntary and was based on different conceptions than the appanage system of the Chingizids. With the conclusion of the First Anglo-Afghan War and the removal of traditional rivals for power, Dost Muhammad Khan was in a better position to live up to his aspirations and his state began to show more resemblance with the formula suggested by McChesney. The Afghan presence in Turkistan soon became stronger and more intrusive than during the Sadozai era. Even so it would be wrong to adhere to a rigid juxtaposition between a hierarchically organized Afghan state and essentially decentralized Uzbek principalities. As will be seen below, Dost Muhammad Khan's administration of Turkistan was fraught with power struggles among his sons.

As for the political circumstances prevailing in Lesser Turkistan in the middle of the nineteenth century, the trauma caused by the Muhammadzai invasion is best understood from the point of view of legitimacy. There is little evidence that the Uzbek Mirs continued to adhere to Chingizid ideals per se in the changing political landscape of the nineteenth century. At the time of Dost Muhammad Khan's aggression about one and a half centuries had elapsed since Maimana and Qunduz had become factually independent from the Tuqai-Timurids. It may therefore be argued that the decentralization of power among the Chahar Wilayat and the principalities of eastern Turkistan was no longer a product of Chingizid policies but was brought about by the absence of sustained interference by any superior power whatsoever. The political relationship between the cis-Oxus Uzbeks and the rulers of Bukhara was further affected by the collapse of the Chingizid system of government during the Nadirid period. With the accession of the Manghits, a lineage of Uzbek chiefs came to power who no longer could base their claims to authority on Chingizid prerogatives.[175] Despite these changing constellations of power the political outlook of the Uzbek leadership of Lesser Turkistan continued to be informed by the historically grown relationship between Bukhara and the former appanage of Balkh. In the nineteenth century, Bukhara not only represented a center of political gravity but also enjoyed far-reaching fame for its religious institutions. The linkage between the elite of both sides of the Oxus was reflected by the conclusion of marriage alliances and the flow of scholars to and from Bukhara. Given their recent appearance in the political arena of Afghanistan, the Muhammadzais, by contrast, could only have seemed as intruders. The clash brought about by the advent of the Afghan troops thus had less to do with contradictory philosophies of government than the trauma caused to the Uzbek leadership by the severance of their traditional ties with Bukhara and Samarqand and their forceful incorporation into a statehood considered alien.

The Extension of Afghan Authority in Western Turkistan

The events which unfolded in Lesser Turkistan subsequent to the arrival of the Muhammadzai army in 1849 indicate that the strategy of the rulers of the Chahar Wilayat was motivated not so much by their adherence to Chingizid ideals than the all too familiar necessity of changing boats at the right time. Given the Bukharan pressure on Balkh and Herat's designs on the western parts of Lesser Turkistan, the ambition of the Afghan king to extend his territory northward may have seemed, initially at least, more like an opportunity than a threat. Muhammad Akram Khan appeared to be only one of many players in the arena north of the Hindu Kush. Because of the ongoing rivalry between Kabul, Qandahar, and Herat, his position was far from powerful after the conquest of Balkh in 1849.[176] His army was also weakened by deaths and desertions and he often found his authority restricted to the vicinity of Balkh.[177] The poor condition of the Afghan forces did not seem to call for the formation of lasting coalitions against them among the petty rulers of Turkistan. Rather than facing the task of overcoming long-standing rivalries with their immediate neighbors, the individual *amirs* considered it more expedient to pledge formal and temporary allegiance to the new rulers of Balkh, whose presence, after all, might not be permanent. As reinforcements continued to arrive from Kabul and Afghan authority continued to extend into Turkistan, this strategy backfired. The advantages of the cooperation with the Afghans turned out to be short-lived, as the rulers of Aqcha, Sar-i Pul, Shibarghan, and Andkhui one by one lost their independence.

On their part, the Sardars perceived the lack of cohesion among the Uzbek *amirs* as an opportunity to further their administration by indirect means. The first 'beneficiary' of the Afghan presence was Mahmud Khan of Sar-i Pul. Along with Ishan Sudur of Aqcha and Ishan Oraq of Balkh and Nimlik, he was considered the main instigator of the rebellion at Aqcha in 1849/50. After the conquest of Aqcha in early 1851, these three leaders were taken prisoner. While Ishan Sudur and Ishan Oraq were transported to Kabul by Sardar Ghulam Haidar Khan, Muhammad Akram Khan refused to give up Mahmud Khan. Citing his great experience, he made him governor of Aqcha, apparently because he hoped to utilize his services in the administration of the wider area.[178] In 1852, shortly after Sardar Muhammad Afzal had become governor of Turkistan, Mahmud Khan again rose in rebellion. Earlier the same year, the Sardar had assumed direct control of Mazar-i Sharif, apparently unseating the Mutawalli. While the

Afghan occupation of the shrine caused great resentment among the Uzbeks in general, Mahmud Khan's rebellion may have been encouraged by the fear that his days as petty ruler were numbered. Indeed, Muhammad Afzal Khan turned all his attention to the reconquest of Aqcha. Shortly afterwards, he was able to capture Mahmud Khan and put him to death. Aqcha and Sar-i Pul were placed under direct Afghan administration.[179] In his military campaign against Mahmud Khan, the Sardar was aided by Mir Hakim Khan and Ghazanfar Khan, the rulers of Shibarghan and Andkhui. In return for their assistance, they received robes of honor and were confirmed as rulers of their hereditary dominions.[180]

After the conquest of Aqcha and Sar-i Pul, Sardar Muhammad Afzal Khan's claims to authority over Lesser Turkistan were put to a test by a rebellion centered in Shibarghan. In September 1854, Mir Hakim Khan of Shibarghan, whose attitude to Sardar Muhammad Akram Khan had been less than reverential,[181] admitted Mir Wali of Tashqurghan along with more than 1,000 Bukharan troops into his citadel.[182] Since his defeat by Sardar Ghulam Haidar Khan in 1850, Mir Wali had been a fugitive but had retained a measure of influence in the regions of Tashqurghan, Qataghan, Badakhshan, and Kulab.[183] According to Lee, his activities at Shibarghan were supported by Sher Muhammad Khan of Maimana and Ghazanfar Khan of Andkhui.[184] Faced with such a strong coalition, Sardar Muhammad Afzal began to lose confidence and ground. The troops commanded by his half brother Muhammad Zaman Khan had to abandon Nimlik and fell back on Balkh. Sardar Wali Muhammad Khan and his troops found themselves besieged at Aqcha. The presence of the Bukharan troops at Shibarghan disrupted the supplies required for the Afghan troops. Although the Mir of Qunduz did not participate in the uprising, Muhammad Afzal Khan saw his influence in the wider area at risk. In a letter to Dost Muhammad Khan he attempted to add urgency to his request for reinforcements by observing that the 'whole tribes around have got such wind in their heads that they will obey no orders.'[185]

The crisis brought about by the Bukharan interference was defused when a dispute arose between Mir Wali and the envoy of the Amir of Bukhara present at Shibarghan. With the departure of the Bukharan envoy, the position of the rebels at Shibarghan was so much weakened that they readily gave in to Muhammad Afzal's army which arrived outside the gates of the city during the final days of November 1854.[186] Mir Wali submitted a letter of apology to Dost Muhammad Khan, was pardoned, and received a *jagir* near Balkh. In spite this apparent conciliation with Afghan sovereignty Mir Wali probably was still considered a threat by Sardar Muhammad Afzal Khan. When the ex-Mir of Tashqurghan died of dysentery on May 9, 1855 there were widespread rumors that he had been poisoned by the Sardar.[187]

Mir Hakim Khan of Shibarghan seemed, initially at least, to be more fortunate. He readily submitted to Muhammad Afzal Khan and agreed to give up his arms and all the deserters of the Afghan army who had joined him in Shibarghan. Moreover, he undertook to submit a tribute of 5,000 tilas or 30,000 rupees and to have the *khutba* read in Amir Dost Muhammad Khan's name instead of the Bukharan Amir. In exchange, Sardar Muhammad Afzal Khan invested him with a dress of honor and restored the government of Shibarghan to him.[188] Yet, by April 1856 Mir Hakim Khan was reported to have fled to Maimana.[189] The sequence of the intervening events is not quite clear. In early December 1855 Sardar Muhammad Afzal Khan ordered Sardar Wali Muhammad Khan to take over the fort of Shibarghan. Muhammad Afzal Khan gave contradictory reasons for this move. To Kabul, he reported that the military occupation of Shibarghan had been necessitated by the fact that Mir Hakim Khan had 'repaired' to Maimana.[190] But shortly afterwards Mir Hakim Khan paid a visit to Muhammad Afzal Khan and complained that he had been deprived forcefully of his government despite his loyalty to Amir Dost Muhammad Khan. This seems to suggest that he had been present in Shibarghan until the advent of the Afghan troops. In his response, Muhammad Afzal Khan denied that he had any intentions of taking over the civilian government of Shibarghan. Sardar Wali Muhammad's military presence was merely intended to discourage threatened Bukharan activities in the region south of the Oxus. Mir Hakim Khan obviously did not trust these assurances. Shortly afterwards he sought Persian assistance with the help of the Mir of Maimana.[191] In January 1856 Mir Hakim Khan was reported to have assembled a force of 4,000–5,000 horsemen at Maimana with which he was plundering villages in the vicinity of Shibarghan and seizing Sardar Wali Muhammad's revenue collectors in the region.[192] Subsequently the ex-ruler of Shibarghan raised additional troops among the Uzbeks and Turkmens of Maimana so that he controlled a total force of 8,000 men. On February 2, 1856 a battle took place between Mir Hakim Khan's supporters and the Afghan troops garrisoned at Shibarghan, which ended with a narrow victory for Sardar Wali Muhammad Khan.[193] Mir Hakim Khan's troops were disbanded. A month later 'the people' of Andkhui – probably the local leadership – signalled to Muhammad Afzal Khan their willingness to deliver the person of Mir Hakim Khan to the Afghans. Moreover, they tendered their submission to Afghan authority and offered to pay revenues.[194]

With the conquest of Shibarghan and the submission of Andkhui, Maimana became the last bastion of Uzbek resistance in the Chahar Wilyat. After Mir Hakim Khan's defeat Ishan Oraq, the former governor of Balkh and Nimlik, became the focus of activities against the Afghans. Having spent four years in Kabul, Ghazni and Qandahar as a prisoner of Amir Dost Muhammad Khan, Ishan Oraq was able to escape to Maimana in March 1856. His presence there had an 'extraordinary effect' on the local population, probably in great part because of his reputation as a

Naqshbandi dignitary.[195] In April 1856 he set out for Andkhui and Shibarghan at the head of 6,000 soldiers. After an initial defeat at the hands of the Afghans, Ishan Oraq was able to rout Sardar Wali Muhammad Khan and to besiege him at the fort of Shibarghan. Another Uzbek force advanced towards Aqcha. Sardar Muhammad Afzal, worried by the fact that Ishan Oraq's total troops exceeded 12,000 men, resorted to intrigue. He released the son or nephew of the former Mutawalli of Mazar, restored him to his erstwhile possessions, and successfully bribed him to sow dissension among the ranks of the Uzbeks while Afghan reinforcements were approaching Shibarghan. Sardar Muhammad Afzal remains silent on the strategies employed by his stooge and the reward he received. He only goes on to say that the conspiracy worked and that the majority of the Uzbek soldiers were either killed or taken prisoner.[196]

The Mir of Maimana, Hukumat Khan, was able to maintain his independence despite Ishan Oraq's defeat. This was in part due to the relative remoteness of Maimana from Afghan strongholds and its relative proximity to the alternative centers of gravity at Herat and Bukhara. Bukharan activities in Afghan Turkistan peaked again with the conquest of Shahr-i Sabz in 1856. Numerous Turkmens and Uzbeks from the Maimana region joined the Bukharan army during the final siege on Shahr-i Sabz and Amir Nasrullah's son Muzaffar al-Din demanded a tribute of 12,000 Tangas (Bukharan currency) from Sardar Muhammad Afzal Khan. In July 1856 the people of Maimana and Andkhui renewed their attack on Shibarghan, this time with the support of 5,000–according to some sources, 10,000–Bukharan troops. The people of Shibarghan opened the gates to the intruders, and the Afghan general and his garrison had to flee to Balkh. Shortly afterwards Sardar Muhammad Afzal Khan reported to Kabul that the Bukharan troops controlled Maimana, Andkhui, and the Turkmen areas in between and were levying contributions there. All roads in Turkistan were unsafe, as the Uzbeks were in a general state of 'excitement'. But the Bukharan intervention in Afghanistan was not to last. In August 1856 Amir Nasrullah informed Dost Muhammad Khan that he did not intend to proceed further south and invited him to form an alliance against the Persians and the 'Christians,' that is, the British, with whom Dost Muhammad Khan had concluded a treaty during the previous year, and the Russians, whose hegemony Amir Nasrullah had come to fear.[197] As this proposal did not come to fruition, Bukhara returned to its policy of intermittent interference with the Chahar Wilayat. In early 1860 Hukumat Khan of Maimana took the leadership of a rebellion in the Chahar Wilayat with Bukharan encouragement.[198] Subsequent to Amir Dost Muhammad Khan's death in June 1863, Hukumat Khan's son Husain (r. 1862–1876) accepted a subsidy of 10,000 tilas or 60,000 rupees from the Amir of Bukhara and began to challenge Afghan possessions in the Chahar Wilayat.[199]

Persian interests made themselves felt in Maimana during the events leading up to the occupation of Herat of 1856–57 and Persia's subsequent efforts to suppress the Tekke Turkmens. The immediate effect of the failed Persian campaigns against Merv in March 1858 and October 1860 on Maimana is not clear. While Lee dismisses all reports that Persia exerted direct military pressure on Maimana in 1855 and 1858–60 as fictions created by Dost Muhammad Khan's officials, the available information points to the fact that Persia continued to be considered an important factor in the politics of Maimana and Herat.[200] Despite his narrowing options Mir Hukumat Khan was able to play off Persian/Herati interests against those of the Muhammadzai rulers until his death in 1862.[201]

Another group to be mentioned within the sphere of Afghan, Persian, Bukharan, Khivan and, eventually, Russian interests are the Turkmens, many of whom migrated to northern Afghan Turkistan simultaneously with the Afghan expansion in the Chahar Wilayat.[202] Until the 1880s the term 'Turkmen' carried the universal connotation of relentless plunderer and slave dealer in Khorasan and Central Asia. The Sariq and Ersari were mostly held responsible for depopulating the northern frontier of Afghan Turkistan from 1845 on well into the 1880s.[203] Based in Merv and Akkal, the Tekke, on the other hand, were infamous for their devastating raids on the Persian and Herat frontiers until the 1870s, which caused the local people to reckon history in terms of Tekke forays. The Russian campaign against Khiva in 1873 led to the suppression of slave trade in Khiva and Bukhara and caused the Tekke raids to subside in frequency and scope. Even so, Turkmen forays continued to block the trade route between Khiva and Krasnovodsk until the Tekke were defeated at Gök Tepe in January 1881 and Merv and Sarakhs submitted to Russian supremacy in 1884. The expansion of Russian authority in Turkmenia, in turn, led to the exodus of a large number of Turkmen refugees to Afghanistan, mainly to the region of Herat.[204]

During the events of 1855/56 the Turkmens of Afghan Turkistan seem to have shifted allegiances frequently in order to evade the tightening grip of the surrounding greater powers. In February 1855 Sardar Muhammad Afzal Khan reported to Amir Dost Muhammad Khan that the Turkmens from Andkhui and Shibarghan had joined the Turkmens on the other side of the Oxus as mercenaries in the army of Bukhara.[205] In the winter of 1855/56 the trans-Oxine Turkmens were rumored to have transferred their submission to the Shah of Persia and Shahzada Muhammad Yusuf, the ruler of Herat, arguing that Bukhara could no longer offer them sufficient protection in the face of growing Persian and Afghan pressure. This move allegedly provoked Bukhara to prove its military might in the region and to force these Turkmen groups to take refuge in Maimana and Andkhui in early 1856.[206] It was possibly from among these groups that Mir Hakim Khan raised his army in his last attempt to gain control of Shibarghan.[207]

The Turkmens who joined the Bukharan campaign against Shahr-i Sabz and Shibarghan later during the same year may very well have been identical with those driven across the Oxus by the Bukharan army a few months earlier.

The role of Persia and Bukhara in the power politics of Afghan Turkistan as described in the above paragraphs has mostly been gleaned from reports submitted from Turkistan to Kabul by Sardar Muhammad Afzal and his brothers. This raises the question how to assess the real extent of Persian and Bukharan interference in Afghan Turkistan at any given point in time. Possibly Muhammad Afzal Khan exaggerated some of the information on the threat posed by these powers in order to justify his policies and to give greater urgency to his requests for military reinforcements. As a rule, his hostile moves against an individual Uzbek leader were prefaced with the accusation that this man was secretly conspiring against Afghan rule with Bukhara and/or Persia. On the other hand, given the narrowing options of the Uzbek rulers in the face of expanding Afghan influence, they may indeed have cast about for outside support. While Muhammad Afzal Khan's reports may have distorted the actual dimensions of Persian and Bukharan involvement (importance of correspondence conducted, number of soldiers sent, etc.), they do reflect accurately the insecurity that characterized Afghan rule in the Chahar Wilayat in the 1850s. Contrary to the common assumption in Afghan historiography,[208] Bukhara and Persia had not relinquished their claims to Lesser Turkistan with the advent of the Muhammadzais north of the Hindu Kush: Sardar Muhammad Afzal was but one of many players in the region–and not a very strong one at that. Out of a total army of 9,000 in Afghan pay in Turkistan only 500 were present in the garrison of Shibarghan at the time of the Bukharan attack of 1856.[209] Morale was low in the army in general, as most of the troops had been in continuous service in Turkistan since 1850.[210] In the years between in 1854 and 1856 Amir Dost Muhammad Khan was unable to supply Muhammad Afzal with reinforcements because all his energies–and available troops–were directed to his effort to establish supremacy in Qandahar. Accordingly, all outside interference in Turkistan was noted with misgivings by the Sardar and his brothers. In 1855, at the time of the Persian activities in Maimana, Sardar Wali Muhammad Khan observed that a general rebellion against Afghan rule in Turkistan had only been prevented because most of the major Uzbek leaders had accompanied Muhammad Afzal on a visit to Kabul.[211] A month later Sardar Muhammad Amin at Tashqurghan reported to Amir Dost Muhammad Khan that the people of Turkistan had 'taken great airs' due to the Persian presence at Maimana. In order to prevent unrest Muhammad Amin Khan felt obliged 'to use every effort to attach them by presents.'[212]

The Conquest of Qunduz

Maimana owed its continuing independence not only to Hukumat Khan's successful balancing act between Bukharan and Persian interests but also to the fact that the Afghan governor was also kept busy in the eastern territories of Lesser Turkistan. From 1858 on, Sardar Muhammad Afzal Khan devoted a great part of his resources to the conquest of Qunduz and Badakhshan. Both principalities had formally submitted to Afghan rule in 1849 and 1851. What did their relationship with the Afghan governor of Turkistan look like during the remainder of the 1850s? The evidence on the role of Qunduz within the Afghan state prior to its conquest 1859 is somewhat contradictory. On the one hand, it seems as though the submission of its ruler, Mir Ataliq, was not purely nominal and entailed some form of revenue payment. But we only learn about these revenue payments from the fact that Mir Ataliq decided to withhold them in 1851 in order to protest the rough treatment Ishan Oraq and Ishan Sudur, the former chiefs of Balkh and Aqcha, had received from Sardar Ghulam Haidar.[213] The exact nature and amount of these revenue payments are not clear. *Siraj al-tawarikh*, again probably reflecting the viewpoint of the Afghan government, claims that the Qataghan Uzbeks refused to submit 'royal taxes' (*mal-i diwani wa kharaj-i sultani*) during that year.[214] Other sources suggest that the goods submitted by the ruler of Qunduz amounted to a nominal tribute rather than regular revenue payments. In winter 1855, for example, Mir Ataliq paid a visit to Sardar Muhammad Afzal at Tashqurghan. As on earlier occasions, he brought along presents for the Sardar–this time 14 horses and 21 camels–and received a robe of honor from him. This exchange reflects that Mir Ataliq formally accepted Afghan superiority without giving up the authority over his own domain. Sardar Muhammad Afzal also reported to Kabul that he concluded an 'advantageous' treaty with the ruler of Qunduz on this occasion.[215] While we are kept in the dark about the exact nature of the treaty, its conclusion is a further indication that Qunduz was treated as a separate entity, a vassalage, by the Afghan governor. Another hint of the nature of the relationship between Mir Ataliq and Sardar Muhammad Afzal in the early 1850s is provided by the claims the Sardar began to press against Qunduz at some point in 1858. According to *Siraj al-tawarikh*, he 'invited' Mir Ataliq to become 'obedient': he should have the *khutba* read in Amir Dost Muhammad Khan's name and allow royal officials to collect the taxes of the province directly from the peasants (*ra'iyat*). In a last attempt to defend his independence, Mir Ataliq sent his younger brother to Sardar Muhammad Afzal Khan. Apart from the customary presents due to the Sardar, Mir Ataliq's brother submitted a message to the extent that the Afghan governor should 'content himself with these presents and forgo the intentions and passions he was harboring [against Mir Ataliq], otherwise he would be afflicted with dangers hundredfold.'[216] While Mir Ataliq's poorly veiled threats did not deter Sardar Muhammad Afzal from pursuing his ambitions, this verbal confrontation indicates that Qunduz had been free from major intervention by the Afghan state up to that point.

Another argument adduced by Sardar Muhammad Afzal Khan for the final subjection of Qunduz was that Mir Ataliq was interfering with the principality of Ghori, which properly belonged to Afghanistan.[217] Moreover, the Sardar resorted to the customary accusation levelled against the local leaders of Turkistan, namely, that Mir Ataliq was intriguing against Afghan rule with Bukhara and the other Uzbek principalities of Afghan Turkistan.[218] On his part, Mir Ataliq had cautiously maintained at least an outside show of allegiance to the Kabul government. Apart from his protests against Sardar Ghulam Haidar's policies towards the local leaders of Balkh and Aqcha, he ventured to defy Afghan rule openly only once. In 1852 the ruler of Qunduz temporarily joined a popular movement against the Afghans which had emerged around the person of a local religious leader generally known as the 'Khalifa' in response to the Muhammadzai occupation of Mazar-i Sharif and the execution of Mahmud Khan. But he was only too willing to give in to Sardar Muhammad Afzal's attempts at conciliation, thus robbing this opposition movement of its impetus.[219] Like the rulers of the Chahar Wilayat, Mir Ataliq was looking to Persia and Bukhara as allies against the Afghans, but his contacts with these powers were weak in comparison. In August 1855 the ruler of Qunduz and his southern neighbor, Shah Pasand Khan Doabi, allegedly dispatched letters to Persia pledging their allegiance and active assistance in case of a Persian advance.[220] His contacts with the Persians notwithstanding, Mir Ataliq did not dare to challenge Afghan sovereignty openly. When Sardar Wali Muhammad accused his younger brother of having joined a Persian force at Maimana, Mir Ataliq insisted that he still was a 'servant of the Ameer' and that he should not be held responsible for the acts of his disobedient brother.[221] The British documents reveal no evidence that Mir Ataliq received any direct assistance from Bukhara. Shortly before the Afghan conquest of Qunduz, Muhammad Afzal Khan reported gleefully to Kabul that Mir Ataliq had been turned away from the court of Amir Nasrullah after a final desperate attempt to gain Bukharan support against the Afghans.[222] According to Muhammad Afzal Khan's son 'Abd al-Rahman Khan, the Bukharan Amir merely furnished Mir Ataliq with a flag and a tent, and the promise that these emblems of Bukharan power would be sufficient to frighten away the Afghans.[223] Bukhara only seems to have evinced interest in the fate of Qunduz when its conquest by the Afghans was already a fait accompli. Amir Muzaffar al-Din (r. 1860–1885) encamped with his army at Charjui in order to ascertain the extent of the military activities of the Sardars in Afghan Turkistan. But after minor clashes between the

Bukharan and Afghan border patrols Amir Muzaffar al-Din returned to Bukhara and abandoned Qunduz to its fate.[224]

As Sardar Muhammad Afzal Khan's complaints against Mir Ataliq kept mounting, the ruler of Qunduz attempted to ward off the impending Afghan invasion by sending his brother as an emissary to the court of Kabul in August 1858.[225] The emissary from Qunduz took great pains to discredit Muhammad Afzal Khan's reports about Mir Ataliq's hostilities and begged Dost Muhammad Khan to continue to respect the treaty concluded in 1855. Mir Ataliq's strategy of bypassing Muhammad Afzal Khan initially seemed to pay off. Dost Muhammad Khan advised the governor of Turkistan to abstain from further interference with Qunduz. But this move was probably prompted less by regard for the fate of Mir Ataliq than the Amir's reluctance to commit more troops to military ventures in Turkistan while affairs on the Indian border remained unsettled in the aftermath of the Mutiny of 1857.[226] In the meantime, hostile reports from Sardar Muhammad Afzal kept arriving. In early September the 'hawks' in Dost Muhammad Khan's council, foremost among them Sardar Sher 'Ali Khan, were able to convince the Amir that Qunduz was a 'thorn in the side of Toorkistan' which had to be removed.[227] Shortly afterwards Dost Muhammad Khan sent Sardar Muhammad A'zam, Muhammad Afzal Khan's full brother, the acting governor of Kurram, Khost and Zurmat, with his troops to Turkistan. In the spring of 1859 reinforcements under the Amir's other sons, Sardars Muhammad Aslam Khan and Muhammad Sharif Khan, as well as his nephew Shams al-Din Khan (b. Amir Muhammad Khan) followed.

The main source on the Afghan conquest of Qunduz are the memoirs of Sardar, later Amir, 'Abd al-Rahman Khan,[228] who acted as commander in chief (*sipahsalar*) under his paternal uncle Muhammad A'zam Khan. According to 'Abd al-Rahman, the forces under his command amounted to 20,000 men.[229] In their first stage, the military operations focussed on the disputed territory of Ghori. Mir Ataliq, allegedly accompanied by 40,000 horsemen, was beaten twice and was forced to retreat to Qunduz. Shortly afterwards the fort of Ghori surrendered to the Afghan besiegers. Mir Ataliq sought shelter with his eastern neighbor, Mir Yusuf 'Ali of Rustaq, leaving Baghlan and Qunduz to be occupied by the Afghan invaders.[230] With the help of the reinforcements under Sardars Muhammad Aslam Khan and Shams al-Din Khan, the Afghan forces advanced to the eastern border of the khanate of Qunduz in the summer of 1859.

The occupation of Khanabad and Taliqan established the Afghan forces in close proximity of Badakhshan. Both Faizabad and Rustaq had become factually independent with the deposal of Mir Wali in 1850 and had remained untouched by the struggles between the Afghans and the Uzbek principalities so far. Confronted with the possibility of an Afghan invasion, Mir Shah of Faizabad (r. 1844–1864) and his brother Mir Yusuf 'Ali of

Rustaq resorted to a dual strategy. On the one hand, they attempted to ward off Afghan ambitions in their direction by sending protestations of friendship to Sardar Muhammad Afzal Khan and offering to furnish troops to the Afghan government in exchange for nonintervention in their territories.[231] On the other hand, they actively assisted Mir Ataliq's efforts to expel the Afghans from Qunduz. Accordingly, the Afghan position in Qunduz and surroundings was far from secure in the beginning. Shortly after the conquest of Taliqan a rebellion broke out in the Baghlani towns of Khost and Andarab, which could only be quelled with the help of the recently arrived reinforcements under Sardar Muhammad Sharif, that is, a combined force of about 8,000 men. Sardar 'Abd al-Rahman Khan attributed this rebellion to the combined activities of Mir Ataliq and the Mirs of Badakhshan.[232] Mir Ataliq was not only supported by the Mirs of Badakhshan but also by his relative Mir Suhrab Beg, the ruler of the Transoxanian principality of Kulab. According to 'Abd al-Rahman Khan, the combined assistance of Kulab and Badakhshan enabled Mir Ataliq to raise a total force of 20,000 cavalry in addition to his own 2,000 followers. These troops were to challenge Afghan authority in Hazrat Imam and Taliqan constantly during the following two years.[233] In 1860, the continued harrassment by the Uzbek and Badakhshani troops caused the Afghan governor of Taliqan, Sardar Muhammad Amin Khan, to abandon the Afghan outpost.[234] 'Abd al-Rahman Khan, not stingy with praise of his own valor, describes how his subsequent arrival in Taliqan finally tipped the scales in favor of the Afghans. In the first instance, he was able to outwit the 'Ishan', a spiritual leader from the vicinity of Taliqan, who invited the Sardar to his home hoping to separate him from the remainder of his troops. 'Abd al-Rahman Khan became aware of this plot and was able to thwart the intended ambush. The Ishan and a number of local leaders from Rustaq and Qataghan, who were present at the Ishan's house, were taken prisoner. The leaders of Rustaq were quickly released with a message to Mir Yusuf 'Ali that further resistance to the powerful Afghan army was useless. The Ishan was sent to Sardar Muhammad A'zam Khan at Khanabad as a prisoner. 'Abd al-Rahman Khan also continued to hold the leaders of Qataghan in order to induce 2,000 families which had fled to Bukhara to resettle in Taliqan.[235] Mir Ataliq and his allies made a final stand against the Afghans by resorting to a two-pronged attack on Chal and Taliqan, but were beaten in both locations.[236]

This signal defeat convinced the Badakhshani Mirs of their inability to beat the Afghans on the battlefield and they renewed their negotiations with the Afghans, offering Mir Shah's cousin (*dukhtar-i 'amu*) to Sardar Muhammad A'zam Khan in marriage.[237] Muhammad A'zam Khan accepted this arrangement despite protests by 'Abd al-Rahman Khan, who insisted that the Badakhshanis were untrustworthy allies and that it was necessary to take that region by force. As part of the formal submission of Badakhshan, Mir Yusuf 'Ali arrived in Khanabad with, in 'Abd al-Rahman Khan's words, 'many promises and a few presents.'[238] One of his promises was to hand over the control of the ruby and lapis lazuli mines to Afghan officers.[239] Approximately a year later (in 1861/62) the Mirs of Badakhshan renewed their pledge of allegiance by sending a present (*peshkash*) of six slaves, nine horses with saddles and silver fittings, nine skins of honey, five hawks, and two hounds to 'Abd al-Rahman Khan at Taliqan. The Sardar accepted these presents and sent robes of honor to the Mirs. But he also reminded them of their promise to submit the Badakhshani mines to his control, thus renewing the historical treaty Shah Wali Khan had concluded with Badakhshan in 1768.[240] Furthermore, the rulers of Badakhshan were to desist from corresponding with other states, to furnish soldiers in times of need, and to submit a nominal tribute (*nazrana*). By means of this formal submission, Badakhshan was able to evade further encroachment by the Afghans for the time being. During the political confusion which followed Dost Muhammad Khan's death in 1863, Badakhshan became fully independent again. Mir Shah's successor Mir Jahandar Shah, being closely allied with the faction of Sardars Muhammad Afzal Khan and Muhammad A'zam Khan, was even able to gain possession of Qunduz in 1866/67. Shortly afterwards he was temporarily evicted from Badakhshan by Sher 'Ali's ally Sardar Faiz Muhammad Khan, who raised a *nazrana* of 40,000 rupees from his new Badakhshani appointees (Jahandar Shah's nephew Mizrab Shah and the sons of Yusuf 'Ali of Rustaq) on the occasion. From 1869 to 1872 Mir Mahmud Shah (a paternal cousin of Mizrab Shah) asserted his authority in Badakhshan with the help of the newly established Afghan ruler Amir Sher 'Ali Khan. In exchange, he sent 80,000 rupees and 500 horses to Kabul during the first year of his reign. In 1870 he undertook to pay an annual *nazrana* of 50,000 rupees. In the following years another 15,000 to 16,000 rupees were submitted as 'present' to the governor of Turkistan. In 1872 Mir Mahmud Shah sent 90,000 rupees to Kabul.[241] From 1873 on Badakhshan was directly administrated by the governor of Turkistan, Na'ib Muhammad 'Alam Khan, and the local cultivators experienced an almost twofold increase in revenue demands.[242] In 1877–78 the combined revenues of Badakhshan and Rustaq were assessed at 300,000 Kabuli rupees.[243]

THE EFFECTS OF THE AFGHAN ADMINISTRATION

By 1863, only Badakhshan and Maimana had been able to withstand the Afghan invasion. This section will focus on the question how the Afghan presence affected the political and social landscape in those principalities which had passed into Afghan possession at that point. What were the administrative measures implemented by the Afghans, and how did they affect the local power structure? What did the relationship between Kabul and its new province look like? What did Dost Muhammad Khan gain from his new possessions? Did Afghan administrative measures have a visible economic impact in Turkistan? Unfortunately, many of these questions can only be answered imperfectly, as most of the sources consulted focus mainly on the military progress of the Afghan army in Turkistan and offer few details on the policies adopted by the Afghan officials after their successful conquests. In great part, this can be attributed to the nature of the sources. Both the Persian sources and the British documents reflect the perspective of the Afghan court, which was mostly preoccupied with the need to expand its authority. The main goal was to secure the new conquests militarily, and little attention seems to have been paid to the exact nature of the administrative arrangements in the new possessions. Two main factors can be adduced as explanations for this attitude. First, the daily procedures required for the administration of the new province were considered routine and were thus simply less interesting from the imperial point of view than the special effort required for military conquests. This makes sense in light of the fact that most of Dost Muhammad Khan's reign was devoted to gathering sufficient military strength for the expansion of his territory. Little opportunity was left for attention to administrative procedures or the development of new ones. The conquest of Qunduz, for example, only preceded the Amir's death by four years. Linked to the first, the second factor stems from the structure of Dost Muhammad Khan's government. Formally treated as service grants (*jagirs*), the individual provinces were leased to the Amir's sons for a fixed sum of money. Apart from checking the accounts of the governors and listening to complaints by locals, the Amir had little impact on the activities of his governors. As the governors obtained possession of a region in exchange for a fixed sum, they had little interest in communicating their procedures in a detailed manner to the Amir. Sardar Muhammad Afzal Khan's independent position in Turkistan, for example, enabled him to carve out a stronghold for himself in this region, which was to play a crucial role for his success in the power struggle subsequent to Dost Muhammad Khan's death.

Administrative Measures Taken by the Afghan Government

With the conquest of Qunduz, the Muhammadzai expansion in Lesser Turkistan had reached its height for the time being. In this process many of the former Uzbek chiefs had been removed from power. Yet this displacement was by no means complete, as the events subsequent to Amir Dost Muhammad Khan's death were to show. In the ensuing struggle for the control of Kabul, which pitted the heir apparent Sher 'Ali Khan against his half brothers Muhammad Afzal Khan (d. October 1867) and Muhammad A'zam Khan (d. October 1869), both parties to the conflict entered alliances with the Uzbek elite. This is reflected by two series of gubernatorial appointments which reinforced the historical distribution of power in Lesser Turkistan. In 1864 Sardar Muhammad Afzal attempted to strengthen his position vis-à-vis Sher 'Ali Khan (then in control of Kabul) by reinstating the hereditary leadership of the Chahar Wilayat and Qunduz. From May 1866 to August 1868 Kabul passed to the possession of Sardars Muhammad Afzal Khan and Muhammad A'zam Khan, forcing Sher 'Ali Khan to make his headquarters in Lesser Turkistan and to grant substantial concessions to the local leadership in exchange for financial support.[244]

By and large the Uzbek leadership was able to maintain its position until the final 'Afghanization' of the Chahar Wilayat in 1875/76. In the following, I will attempt to give a brief sketch of the political developments in the individual Uzbek principalities up to that point. Until 1855 Tashqurghan and Balkh formed the bases of Dost Muhammad Khan's generals and their troops. After his appointment in 1852 Sardar Muhammad Afzal sought to concentrate the administration of Turkistan in his hands and constructed his new capital of Takhta Pul in the vicinity of Mazar-i Sharif.[245] Not surprisingly, the local leadership was most strongly affected in this core area of Afghan control. Mazar-i Sharif was apparently absorbed in the administration of Balkh. Nonetheless, the sons of the former Mutawalli, Shuja' al-Din, seem to have maintained a prominent position in the administration of the shrine.[246] When Ishans Oraq and Sudur, the former governors of Balkh and Aqcha, were removed to Kabul in 1851, Sardar Wali Muhammad Khan was placed in control of Aqcha.[247] In 1864 Ishan Oraq was released by Sher 'Ali Khan and began to play an active role in the politics of Afghan Turkistan and Bukhara again. Yet Sher 'Ali Khan's promise to return the governorship of Aqcha to him did not materialize. Tashqurghan and Aibak seem to have passed only briefly to the control of Mir Wali's sons Ganj 'Ali and Ghulam Beg in 1867.[248] In 1876 Tashqurghan was governed by the Qizilbash official Mirakhor Ghulam Muhammad Riza Khan Muradkhani.[249]

The rulers of the Chahar Wilayat continued to sail with the changing winds emanating from Kabul. During Dost Muhammad Khan's reign Sar-i Pul and Shibarghan became the *jagirs* of the Muhammadzai Sardars Muhammad Zaman Khan and Wali Muhammad Khan in 1852 and 1856 respectively.[250] In 1863 Mir Muhammad Khan Beglarbegi (d. 1886), the brother of the former ruler Mahmud Khan, gained possession of Sar-i Pul after Sardar Muhammad Zaman Khan had given up his governorship there and joined Sher 'Ali Khan's faction. Apart from an exile in Bukhara in 1864/65, Mir Muhammad Khan was able to maintain his authority at Sar-i Pul until 1875.[251] Mir Hakim Khan (d. 1876), who had lost Shibarghan to the Muhammadzais in 1856, apparently returned to his principality as early as 1859.[252] The hereditary ruler of Andkhui, Ghazanfar Khan,[253] and his son Daulat Beg remained independent in the internal administration of their principality in exchange for yearly 'offerings' to the governor of

Turkistan.[254] Husain Khan Ming, the ruler of Maimana (r. 1862–1876, 1884–1889) sided consistently with Amir Sher ʻAli Khan during the 1860s. As a result, the city of Maimana found itself besieged by Sardar ʻAbd al-Rahman Khan in April-May 1868.[255] In the long run, Husain Khan's faithful stance towards Sher ʻAli Khan could not protect him against the ambitious policies of the Amir's governor of Turkistan, Naʾib Muhammad ʻAlam Khan (d. July 1876). In late October 1875 Naʾib Muhammad ʻAlam Khan laid siege to Maimana. In December he accused the Mirs of Sar-i Pul, Shibarghan and Andkhui of colluding with Husain Khan and exiled them to Kabul. Husain Khan followed them when his citadel fell to the Afghan troops on 14 March 1876.[256] With the onset of the Second Anglo-Afghan War two years later, Sher ʻAli Khan was again forced to seek out the support of the traditional Uzbek leaders and to promise them independence in the internal affairs of their prinicpalities in exchange for military support, this time against the British. Husain Khan Ming of Maimana, Muhammad Khan Beglarbegi of Sar-i Pul, Hakim Khan of Shibarghan, and Rustam Khan of Mazar-i Sharif accepted the Amir's terms and once more took the front stage in the political affairs of Afghan Turkistan.[257]

In the eastern part of Lesser Turkistan, the removal of Mir Ataliq from Qunduz proved to be only of a temporary nature. Until the death of Amir Dost Muhammad Khan, Qataghan was administered by members of the royal family, viz. Sardar ʻAbd al-Ghiyas Khan (d. 1861/62) and Sardar ʻAbd al-Rahman Khan.[258] In 1864 Mir Ataliq was able to regain control of Qunduz. At the time of his death in June 1865 the government of Qataghan passed on to his sons Sultan Murad (in charge of Qunduz), ʻAbd al-Rahim Khan (in charge of Taliqan or Nahrin), and ʻAbd al-Karim Khan (in charge of Ghori). Sultan Murad continued to hold the Qataghan region as 'fief' from the Afghan Amir until he sided with Ishaq Khan's rebellion in 1888.[259] The neighboring region of Badakhshan was more strongly affected by the changing politics in Kabul and Lesser Turkistan, as the two rivals contending for power there – Mir Jahandar Shah and Mir Mahmud – were linked to the different factions of the Muhammadzai family. Mir Jahandar Shah, who was closely connected with the interests of Sardar Muhammad Afzal Khan, came to power in Badakhshan in the early 1860s. In 1869 he was deprived of his intermittent government of Badakhshan by his relative Mahmud Shah, who enjoyed the support of Amir Sher ʻAli Khan.[260]

The Nature of the Muhammadzai Administration

While they are mostly silent on the circumstances in the Chahar Wilayat, *Taj al-tawarikh*, *Siraj al-tawarikh*, and the British documents offer a few insights into the nature to the Afghan administration of Qunduz and its dependencies between 1859 and 1863. We are told that Sardar Muhammad

A'zam Khan appointed governors, *qazis* and muftis to the districts (*mahall*) of Qataghan in 1859.[261] During the same year efforts were made to assess the revenue of Qunduz and to reestablish a military tenure there.[262] The continuation of service grants indicates that – apart from the removal of Mir Ataliq – the Muhammadzai presence did not challenge the next level of leadership among the Qataghan Uzbeks. Likewise, the appointment of *qazis* most probably had little impact. While the *qazis* needed government backing to enforce their judgements, they were generally chosen from among the local population. The fact that Sardar 'Abd al-Rahman employed the Qazi of Qunduz in negotiations with the local people in 1863 indicates that this was a respected religious leader who enjoyed a long-standing relation with the local population, and not a newcomer to the region.[263]

As for the local governors (*hukkam*) set up by the Afghans, it is not apparent whether they were local leaders already in place or whether the new rulers appointed them in addition to the local leaders, thus establishing a dual power structure. On the one hand, there are some indications that the local leadership was confirmed by the Afghan government. Both *Taj al-tawarikh* and *Siraj al-tawarikh* state that all the local leaders were assured of 'Abd al-Rahman's support, received robes of honor and were dismissed to their villages. In the administration of Qunduz the Afghan administrators continued the system of military tenure and the rates of revenue that had been instituted by Mir Murad Beg in the 1820s.[264] On the other hand, it is likely that the *function* of the local leadership changed. There are indications that the revenue collection in Qataghan moved from local middlemen to Afghan officials and officers in the Afghan army, as had been one of the motives for Sardar Muhammad Afzal's aggression against Qunduz. This is shown by 'Abd al-Rahman's complaint that the local governors had embezzled part of the local revenues during Sardar 'Abd al-Ghiyas Khan's administration. The revenue collectors named were officers of the Afghan army stationed at Taliqan.[265] While it is hard to establish the exact scope of Afghan intervention on the local level, the rebellion of the Mir of Andarab in 1859 points to the possibility that the policies of the new governors were not only resisted out of solidarity with Mir Ataliq but because they were considered intrusive.

'Abd al-Rahman stresses the fact that he was able to subjugate eastern Turkistan entirely during his governorship in the 1860s. But while the position of the local leadership certainly changed, this group was not displaced entirely. A look at later developments in the region points to the fact that the Afghan administrators continued to rely on the cooperation of local middlemen in administrative and military matters. The relative weakness of the Afghan officials was in great part a result of the poorly developed communications across the mountain ranges which separated Turkistan from Kabul. This, in conjunction with Amir Dost Muhammad

Khan's military efforts elsewhere, had the effect that the Afghan presence north of the Hindu Kush remained thin. Prior to Amir 'Abd al-Rahman's large-scale resettlement schemes in the late 1880s, estimates of the Afghan population in Lesser Turkistan varied between two and four percent.[266] Kushkaki's description of Qataghan and Badakhshan indicates that practically all important administrational positions on the provincial and district level had passed to Pashtun or Qizilbash administrators during the era of Amir 'Abd al-Rahman Khan.[267] These changes affected the political role of the autochthonous elite but did not diminish the prestige of its members on the village level. The outsiders who were appointed to positions in the upper echelons of government often only stayed in the region for short periods of time and were dependent on local middlemen for the completion of even the most rudimentary administrational tasks, such as collecting taxes and recruiting soldiers.[268] Kushkaki's lists of influential men in Qataghan reveal that, in addition to mostly Pashtun and Qizilbash newcomers to the region, the former elite was still in place in the 1920s. It included worldly leaders, among them relatives of Sultan Murad, as well as men of religious standing.[269] The same can be said about Badakhshan.[270]

The importance of the local elite is reflected by the policies of the Muhammadzai governor of Turkistan, Sardar Muhammad Ishaq Khan b. Muhammad A'zam Khan (1880–1888), who continued to rely on auxiliary military contingents organized by traditional Uzbek, Hazara and Turkmen leaders. Having been influenced by the Naqshbandi order, Ishaq Khan was also partial to other members of the traditional elite, the ulama. The continuing influence of the traditional elite is reflected by Ishaq Khan's reaction to Amir 'Abd al-Rahman Khan's policy of imposing greater taxes and confiscating religious endowments. He refused to interfere with the possessions of the spiritual elite and rebelled against the Amir with the support of administrators, army officers, and the local leadership. The defeat of Ishaq Khan's troops at Ghaznigak in 1888 put an end to the rebellion and Ishaq Khan's successor imposed Amir 'Abd al-Rahman's reforms successfully. Even so he could not dispense with the cooperation of local middlemen entirely. The traditional elite continued to function as middlemen but its role was reduced to the village level.[271]

The Socio-Political Setting in Qataghan and Badakhshan

Siraj al-tawarikh and *Taj al-tawarikh* mostly refer to the leadership of Qataghan generically as 'heads of the province' (*ruasa-yi wilayat*,), 'nobles of the land' (*a'yan-i mulk*), and the 'dignitaries of each group' (*ashraf-i har qaum*).[272] Another term used for the local leadership of Qataghan is 'whitebeard' (*aqsaqal*).[273] Kushkaki also lists the titles of *mir*, *khan*, *beg* (*bai*), and *ming bashi*. Who were these local leaders and what groups did they represent? In the following section I will attempt to shed some light on the organization of the Qataghan Uzbeks on the basis of observations made by European visitors in the nineteenth and twentieth centuries. Among the modern-day anthropologists, the works of Centlivres, Centlivres-Demont, and Rasuly-Paleczek are particularly noteworthy. Although their studies furnish us with some valuable data on the origin of the Qataghan Uzbeks and their way of life in the nineteenth century, the total available picture of Qataghan organization continues to lack depth. In order to place our existing knowledge of the Qataghan Uzbeks into context, I will also take a look at the nature of leadership among the Tajiks in Badakhshan. Forming the designated border between British and Russian interests, Badakhshan has been studied in considerably greater detail than its geographically marginal position would suggest. Comparing the results of the studies on Badakhshan with the material available on Qataghan, I will argue that the broad outlines of organization were similar in both regions.

Uzbek Organization

Literally translated as 'people', 'nation', 'tribe', 'sect', 'group of followers',[274] the term *qaum* is common among various ethnic groups in Afghanistan. Orywal defines it, along with the term *ta^ʾifa*, as the 'basal unit of identification' of Afghan society.[275] Overwhelmingly used as a mark of distinction vis-à-vis outsiders, it designates solidarity groups of varying sizes. According to context, that is, according to the social/spatial distance between the informant and the questioner, it may be employed to describe multiple levels of local organization.[276] Thus the term *qaum* can emphasize the mutual support afforded by kinship units of different sizes, referring 'to the whole hierarchy of segmentary descent groups extending upwards from the nuclear family to the ethnic totality.'[277] Among the Chechka Qataghan resident west of the confluence of the Kokcha river and the Oxus, for example, this designation is variously used for the wider family (*khesh-i qaum*), the subdivisions (*urugh*) of the Chechka, as well as the entire group of Chechkas vis-à-vis other Uzbeks.[278] Among groups with little emphasis on agnatic or genealogical relationships, *qaum* may assume a wider sociological meaning, signifying any solidarity group or 'aggregation of dependents.'[279] Thus it may also stand for the cohesion among the residents of a quarter (*qaum-i guzar*) or a village (*qaum-i qishlaq*), or delimit the followership of a village chief (*qaum-i arbab*).[280] While allowing for kinship as the original organizing principle, Kussmaul has defined the term *qaum* as representing a community of villages linked by tradition among the Tajiks of Badakhshan.[281]

Because of their elasticity, the designations *qaum*, *taʾifa*, and *urugh* per se offer little information on the organization of the Qataghan Uzbeks. For the Uzbeks of the sixteenth and seventeenth centuries, McChesney has noted that the term *qaum*, along with the words *taʾifa*, *oimaq*, *qabila*, *batn*, *buluk*, *il*, *ulus*, and *ahl* was devoid of any distinct or technical meaning. It only served to designate 'the non-Chingizid groupings or factions identified by a specific name.' While these Uzbek groupings may have been organized along tribal lines, they displayed little solidarity vis-à-vis other groupings.[282] Historical studies concerning other tribal groups of Inner Asia likewise point to the fact that genealogy is but one of many factors determining their organization. Barfield views tribal organization as the result of an interplay between kinship structure, ecological conditions, and the power of the adjoining sedentary states. Accordingly, the Turco-Mongolian tribal confederations interacting with the Chinese empire were more complex and more hierarchically organized than the Arabian tribes of North Africa, which confronted comparatively small regional states. In the Turco-Mongol setting, relationships at the higher echelons of tribal organization tend to be shaped strongly by political exigencies.[283] In a similar vein, Lapidus points out that while the Turkic speaking societies of Inner Asia were conceived in terms of kinship and genealogy, 'the actual units of social organization were based on loyalty to successful warrior chieftains'.[284]

This concept seems to be confirmed by the observations Wood made among the Qataghan Uzbeks in 1837. He concluded that they seemed to attach less importance to genealogical descent than their political role as adherents of Mir Murad Beg:

> among the Uzbeks though the tribes are numerous and distinct, we do not detect that attachment between individuals of the same clan, or that devotion to its common head which has ever been the bond of union in all countries where this primitive arrangement prevails. When the Kattaghan indeed, mentions his tribe, it is with a conscious felling [sic] of superiority, but Murad Beg the ruler of Kunduz is a Kattaghan, and the pride of the Kattaghan is founded on their belonging to the tribe of their Chieftain, and not on their own ancestral lineage.[285]

Moreover Wood's companion Lord noticed that tribal leaders among the Qataghan derived their standing from their appointment by Mir Murad Beg rather than their descent.[286] But more recent anthropological studies concerning the Uzbeks of Lesser Turkistan show that no blanket statement can be made concerning their organization. Centlivres shows that the sedentary Uzbek population of Tashqurghan had lost its genealogical structure by the nineteenth century. The Qataghan Uzbeks, by contrast, continued to adhere genealogical principles.[287] The Gazetteer of 1882 attributes the origin of this group to their eponymous ancestor Qata. The subdivisions (*urugh*) of the Qataghan tribe sprang from his sixteen sons.[288] Centlivres identifies the Qataghan subdivisions of the Burka and the Temuz (in the region of Nahrin-Ishkamish), the Semiz and the Kessemir (of Bangi and Chal), the Jangataghan (of Rustaq), as well as the Chechka, as tribes 'possessing a genealogical tribal structure with complex ramifications and segmentations.' The Burka section resident at Nahrin, for example, continue to view the tribal structure of the Qataghan Uzbeks as a genealogical tree, the sons of the eponymous ancestor forming the major branches, and the sons of these sons bringing forth the sections, etc. The individual subdivisions were ranked hierarchically according to the seniority of the founding ancestor among his brothers. The segments formed by this genealogical tree coincided with the territorial distribution of the subdivisions and their sections. According to Centlivres, the subdivision which had its origin with the eldest brother in the genealogical tree was expected to furnish the chiefs of the tribe or clan, called *begs*. The assumed lack of 'tribal' organization among the Qataghan Uzbeks may possibly attributed to the fact that these structures were not always readily perceived by visitors to the region.[289] Rasuly-Paleczek, on the other hand, points out that descent may not be the only factor determining Qataghan organization. Like its Tajik neighbors in Badakhshan, the present-day *qaum* of the Chechka attaches little importance to genealogical configurations. Rasuly-Paleczek concludes that, nowadays at least, such knowledge has little bearing on the ability to compete for local resources.[290] Prior to the Afghan invasion the Chechka were nominally dependent on the Mir of Qunduz and submitted tribute to him. The whole group was organized under a *beg*, while the needs of the lower levels of organization, that is, the individual kinship units (sub-*urughs*) were looked after by *aqsaqals* (also known as *musafed*).[291]

Good 'birth' seems to be the most important factor distinguishing the Uzbek leadership. According to Centlivres and Centlivres-Demont, the *begs* (sometimes also called *khan*) derive their standing in great part from their genealogical background, the numerical strength of their family, and their ability to secure powerful positions for their relatives. Wealth is an important element in the quest for power but material possessions alone do not qualify an individual for the assumption of this role.[292] Azoy emphasizes that the *beg*'s office is not fixed and requires two basic qualities, *haisiyat* ('character') and *i'tibar* ('credit'). The first of these is established by 'the behavioral display of piety, generosity, and wisdom.' The second one denotes the ability of the *khan* to get things done for the community and to create a followership for himself.[293] Influential men attempt to bolster their position further by the arrangement of strategic marriage alliances with other leading families. Among the Burka, for example, marriages are mostly concluded within the section with a preference for cousin marriage. The *begs* of the same group, by contrast, often marry daughters and sisters of other *begs* from different sections.[294] Such strategies are also documented for the Chechka Qataghan. The *beg* of the Chechka, Sahib Nazar Ishikaqasi, sought to regain his influence in Qataghan after returning from Bukhara in the 1920s by entering marriage alliances with the family of

Sultan Murad Beg, the *beg* of the Qarluq, as well as *musafeds*, *begs* and religious dignitaries among the Chechka.[295]

There is little information on the role of the Qataghan *begs* prior to the Afghan invasion. On the village level, the *aqsaqals* or *musafeds* seem to have functioned as mediators in local conflicts and organizers of socio-economic tasks, such as the maintenance of irrigation channels and arrangement of festivities and weddings. It is not clear how they were appointed and what their linkage with the *beg* families was. After the Afghan conquest, in particular during the period of Amir Amanullah Khan (r. 1919–1929), so-called *arbabs* became the officially recognized local representatives on the village level. The *aqsaqals* or *musafed-i qishlaq* retained an informal position as village spokesmen. The former *begs* generally came to be known as *musafed-i qaum* and continued to play an important, albeit unofficial, role as mediators between the government and the local setting.[296]

The Socio-Political Circumstances in Badakhshan

In contrast to the Qataghan Uzbeks, the Tajiks of the adjacent region of Badakhshan have been dealt with in a thorough manner by Kussmaul (1965), Holzwarth (1980) and Grevemeyer (1982), whose studies draw on fieldwork, Persian sources, and materials compiled by Russian scholars. According to these authors, three levels of political leadership may be perceived in Badakhshan. From 1657 until the 1880s Faizabad was ruled by members of the Yarid dynasty. The central ruler usually carried the title 'Shah', 'Mir', or 'Amir.' Also known as 'Mir-i Shah,' he was recognized as ruler of all of Badakhshan, but his actual authority was limited to central Badakhshan.[297] The next level of leadership rested with two groups of regional leaders. The fertile regions of Badakhshan (Kishim, Rustaq, Ragh, Jurm) were controlled by other members of the Yarid dynasty. The mountainous areas (Ishkashim, Zebak, Wakhan, Shighnan) were mostly ruled by native rulers with the consent of the Mir of Faizabad. Both groups carried the title 'Mir' or 'Shah'.[298] The third level was furnished by the local leadership which acted as an intermediary between local and regional interests. Most sources offer contradictory information on the process which led to the appointment of these local leaders, known as *aqsaqals*. While it is said about Wakhan that local officials, such as *aqsaqals*, *qazis* and *diwanbegis* were elected by the population and then confirmed by the Mir, it is in most cases not clear whether these leaders obtained their positions primarily by virtue of their local standing or by appointment from the local ruler. The former *aqsaqal* of the central Badakhshani districts of Zardiu and Baharak, for example, informed Kussmaul that his family had been traditionally appointed to this post by the Mirs of Faizabad. Nevertheless, Kussmaul allows for the possibility that this leader was elected for life by the local population.[299] This ambiguity points to the dual function of the *aqsaqals*. More powerful than the Uzbek *aqsaqal*, the Badakhshani leader could be at the top of the local hierarchy not only of a village but possibly of a whole valley. On the one hand, he was in charge of intra-community affairs, presiding over villages councils, settling conflicts over land and water rights, leading the community in local military disputes, administrating the village guest house etc.[300] On the other hand, he was closely linked to the regional elite by marriage alliances and was a member of the council of the regional ruler.[301] Furthermore, the *aqsaqal*'s connection with the elite is documented by the fact that his title stood for the command of a military division. Being equated with the term *mir-i hazar*, it denoted the leadership of 1,000 soldiers. Apparently this title was also awarded for special military exertions. The ruler of Faizabad, for example, appointed successful warriors among his troops as *aqsaqals* to their home regions. Another vital element in the connection between the elite and the *aqsaqals* was the fact that the latter were in charge of collecting the revenues in the areas under their jurisdiction and submitting them to the regional ruler. They also organized the forced labor needed for the exploitation of some of the local mines, the proceeds of which also went to the local rulers.[302]

Given the close linkage between the *aqsaqals* and the regional rulers, Kussmaul characterizes the next lower level of local organization as the truly indigenous institution. The *musafed-i qaumi* were older members of local influential families. They obtained their leadership position neither by decree from above nor by local election but solely on the basis of their prestige. In Baharak and Zardiu there were four such *musafeds,* who functioned as intermediaries between their regions and the higher levels of government. They assumed a rather independent position vis-à-vis the *aqsaqal* and were likely to bypass him in favor of higher authorities in critical matters. Their political success in turn tended to enhance their standing among their followers. On the village level, the *musafed-i qaumi* were in charge of recommending individuals for the positions of village head (*arbab*), overseers of irrigation, and shepherds. The *arbabs* were elected for life by the village community. Their position was clearly subordinate to that of the *aqsaqal*.[303]

Holzwarth and Grevemeyer agree with earlier studies that Badakhshani society was characterized by a rigid distinction between the aristocracy (*khawass*) and the common people (*'awamm*). Apart from submitting agricultural products, the common people, known as 'peasants' (*ra'iyat*) and 'poor people' (*fuqara*), had to provide forced labor. In Shighnan, slavery was also common.[304] The aristocracy, on the other hand, was not only exempted from the payment of tribute but had the right to collect revenues. In exchange for military and administrative services its members received titles, as well as gifts in money and lands. As members of the military and service class (*naukaria*), the *arbabs* and *aqsaqals* formed one of the lower echelons of this aristocacy. As both military and administrative functions tended to be hereditary offices, outsiders had few avenues for social mobility, and the aristocracy tended to be 'shut off genealogically' from the remainder of the population.[305]

The relationship between the Mir of Badakhshan and the regional rulers was that of a *primus inter pares*. Pandit Manphul, who visited Badakhshan in the late 1860s, listed the political divisions of Badakhshan and added,

> All [these are] dependencies of Badakhshan, held by the relations of the Mir, or by hereditary rulers, on a feudal tenure, conditional on fidelity and military service in time of need; the holders possessing supreme authority in their respective territories, and paying little or no tribute to the paramount power.[306]

The relative autonomy of the regional rulers was reflected by the fact that their courts mirrored the administrative institutions of the court in Faizabad.[307] Another symptom of the lack of centralized power was that the whole army was only assembled in times of war. The scarcity of available troops at Faizabad caused in 1870 the Greek visitor Potagos to reach the conclusion that any rebel who could muster 15 followers was theoretically able to deprive the Mir of Badakhshan of his power.[308] The Mir's authority being based on the somewhat tenuous allegiance of the regional rulers, he was in no position to institute an uninterrupted administrative chain of command for the collection of revenue reaching from the central court all the way to the village level. Rather, the relation between Faizabad and the regional courts was formulated on the basis of friendship expressed by a reciprocal, and often symbolical, exchange of goods. Holzwarth characterizes the posture the Mir of Badakhshan assumed in the interaction with the regional and local elite as fluctuating between 'the ostentatious magnanimity of the gift giver and imperious demands for tribute.' Once a year the ruler of Faizabad distributed robes of honor (*khil'at*) to the *aqsaqals* and other influential men. The acceptance of such a garment implied a pledge of allegiance on the part of the recipient. In exchange, the members of the aristocracy submitted a formal tribute to the central ruler. Among the regional rulers this present to the Mir of Faizabad was known as *tartuq*, an 'inbetween between a gift and tribute.' The formal alliance existing between the Mir and the regional rulers tended to be further emphasized by the conclusion of marriages. The exchange of robes of honor for services and (nominal) tribute is not only documented for Badakhshan but also for Qunduz, Bukhara, and Kabul.[309] It is also in this light that the 'submission' of the Mirs of Badakhshan to the Afghan generals in 1860/61 is to be understood. By accepting 'offerings' and a proposed marriage alliance, Sardar Muhammmad A'zam Khan assumed the role of a friendly, though superior ally. By receiving robes of honor and undertaking to furnish a tribute and soldiers in times of need, the Mirs of

Badakhshan entered a relation with Kabul which formed an extension of the power constellations existing in their own territory.

Badakhshan and Qataghan Compared

Holzwarth attributes the political decentralization of Badakhshan in great measure to ecological factors. In the mountainous areas the available arable land was extremely scarce. The lack of natural resources combined with continuous internal warfare resulted in an economic system, for which, according to Holzwarth, even the term 'subsistence' would be a euphemism. The absence of any substantial agricultural surplus precluded the development of centralized governing institutions. Furthermore, the abundance of water meant that no complex irrigation systems were necessary, which would have required a more extensive system of administration, as was the case in Bukhara. The mountainous territory also formed an effective barrier for invading armies, rendering military operations extremely difficult for the central ruler. Qunduz, on the other hand, was characterized by level country, a theoretically unlimited amount of arable land, and an extensive irrigation system, which facilitated both the development of a more complex bureaucracy and military movements.[310] The northeastern regions of Qataghan indeed offered favorable conditions for extensive agricultural production. While the town of Qunduz was depicted as a peninsula jutting out into a 'sea of swamps' at the beginning of the twentieth century,[311] the surrounding country allowed intensive agriculture with the help of irrigation channels from the Qunduz and Khanabad rivers.[312] In the 1830s Harlan described the land in the vicinity of Qunduz as 'fertile, well cultivated and full of flourishing gardens.'[313] Hazrat Imam in the north was located in a productive plain irrigated by canals from the Oxus. In the east, the region around Taliqan was known for its fertility.[314] Therefore, the nature of the ecological/economical setting in this region may rightly be adduced to explain Mir Murad Beg's 'overpowering influence' over his subjects[315] and the 'well ordered domestic government' of these areas, which either formed his immediate possession or were controlled by his son, Mir Ataliq, and his brother, Muhammad Beg.[316] But not all of Qataghan lent itself as easily to centralizing forces. The region south of Hazrat Imam was taken up by a waterless wilderness (*chul*) which could only be used for grazing in spring. The areas adjoining Qunduz in the southeast extended to the lower reaches of the Hindu Kush and are depicted as 'hilly' and 'mountainous.'[317] These areas were partly cultivated for dry farming, but the Uzbek population mostly made its living raising sheep, horses and camels, engaging in seasonal movements in search of pasture. Wood noted that the Shorab valley southeast of Qunduz was dotted with Uzbek encampments.[318] Harlan reported that the 'nomadic classes' of the Qataghan Uzbeks spent their winters in Ghori and their summers on the slopes of the Hindu Kush.[319] The Burka section of the Qataghan moved back and forth between the lower regions of Baghlan and the mountains between Nahrin and Khost and even ascended to the upper reaches of the Hindu Kush around the Pass of Khawak in the nineteenth century.[320] The city of Taliqan likewise served merely as a winter quarter for the Uzbeks of the region who migrated with their flocks to the neighboring highlands in summer.[321] In the region of Khanabad, 1,000 sedentary and 4,000 nomad families were listed in the 1870s. Among the Chechka of Khwaja Ghar 300 families were sedentary, while 400 followed a nomadic lifestyle at that time.[322] While the ecological/economic conditions prevailing in these areas did not provide as impressive a barrier to the advancement of centralizing tendencies as the mountain regions of Badakhshan, they must have encouraged the local Uzbek and Tajik chiefs to assume a relatively independent position in relation to the paramount ruler of the region, as, for example, Mir Murad Beg.

At any rate, certain parallels between the socio-political organization of nineteenth-century Badakhshan and Qataghan under Mir Murad Beg may be discerned. Mir Murad Beg's military power was equal or slightly superior to that of Badakhshan;[323] the organization of his army was based on a system of military tenure comparable to that of Badakhshan.[324] In Qunduz, as in Badakhshan, the relationship between the supreme ruler and the regional leadership was less that of an absolute ruler demanding taxes from his subjects than that of the leader of a confederation, a phenomenon which caused Wood to speak of Mir Murad Beg as 'the head of an organized banditti.'[325] The Qunduz ruler was able to gain the allegiance of other tribal sections of the Qataghan by offering them part of the booty and rent-free grants of land. Like the Badakhshani rulers, Mir Murad Beg and his successors fostered the allegiance of local leaders by accepting presents and awarding *khil'ats*. In this manner the relationship between the Qunduz rulers and their followers was conceptualized not as a hierarchy engendering a clear chain of command but as a friendship requiring constant renewal by the exchange of gifts.[326] The paucity of available data does not allow any firm conclusions on the situation of the lower echelons of the society of Qataghan. Comparing the social situation of the Uzbeks of Lesser Turkistan with that of the Bukharan Uzbeks, Elphinstone reaches the conclusion that the former 'are as subservient as elsewhere.'[327] Wood contrasts the Qataghan Uzbeks with the Afghans and points to the relatively strong position of the Uzbek chiefs: 'Of the freedom enjoyed by the Afghans, the Uzbeks know nothing. The liberty of the slave they capture is not more at their disposal than their own life is in the hands of their chief or Beg.'[328] Harlan also notes that the leaders generally enjoy great respect. But, with the exception of Mir Murad Beg, they never resort to violent measures to enforce their authority: 'The people are submissive, respectful to their superiors, alert and crafty from the necessity of guarding agains the caprice of their rulers. Their chiefs seldom abuse their power, being patriarchs in fact as they are in theory.' Thus it is unlikely that Qataghan society displayed a marked split as that between the *'awamm* and *khawass* observed in Badakhshan. The only instance where a clear social and genealogical distance between the common people and the rulers is documented is the district of Qunduz, the situation of which most probably formed an exception to the rule: 'The population consists chiefly of slaves, who have been removed in large bodies from distant and refractory districts.'[329]

The Organization of the Afghan Administration

I will now turn from the socio-political setting in Afghan Turkistan to the circumstances under which the Muhammadzai invaders operated. The northward extension of Afghan authority certainly implied increased power for the Muhammadzais. But while the acquisition of this new province meant a net profit for Amir Dost Muhammad Khan, the task of administrating it had the effect of exacerbating the power struggle among his sons. Another topic to be discussed is the situation of the Afghan army in Turkistan as a reflection of the state of administrative affairs. Finally, I will briefly address the question of the economic effects of the Muhammadzai presence north of the Hindu Kush.

The history of the Afghan government of Turkistan from 1849 on was for the most part characterized by the rivalry between the two most powerful sons of Dost Muhammad Khan and their full brothers. Ghulam Haidar Khan, the heir apparent, played a great role in the acquisition of Tashqurghan in 1850. After his return to Kabul in spring 1851 and after the death of his half brother Muhammad Akram Khan in March 1852, Ghulam Haidar retained his influence in Tashqurghan by appointing his full brothers Muhammad Sharif and Muhammad Amin on successive governorships there.[330] Ghulam Haidar's eldest half brother and greatest rival, Muhammad Afzal Khan, on the other hand, was placed in control of Balkh. Soon after his appointment in 1852 Muhammad Afzal began his efforts to oust Ghulam Haidar's brothers from Tashqurghan. Despite Muhammad Sharif's cooperation with Muhammad Afzal in the conquest of Aqcha in 1852 Muhammad Afzal frequently complained to Kabul of his hostile attitude. In 1854 and 1855 Muhammad Afzal accused Muhammad Sharif of having consistently undermined his government at Balkh since 1852. In 1854 an agent of Ghulam Haidar reported that Muhammad Afzal was planning to remove Muhammad Sharif from Tashqurghan by force.[331] Muhammad Afzal apparently did not feel threatened by the presence of his other half brothers, Wali Muhammad and Muhammad Zaman, at Aqcha and Nimlik respectively.[332] Both men acted as local governors for Muhammad Afzal Khan until the death of Amir Dost Muhammad Khan and profited from the expansion of Afghan influence in the Chahar Wilayat. In 1854 it was even rumored that Muhammad Afzal Khan was planning to rebel against Dost Muhammad Khan in collaboration with Wali Muhammad and Muhammad Zaman.[333]

The conflict between Ghulam Haidar Khan and Muhammad Afzal Khan came to a head in June 1855 when Muhammad Afzal went to Kabul to renegotiate the terms of his governorship of Turkistan. Interestingly, little attention was paid to the Uzbek leaders who had accompanied Muhammad Afzal to Kabul. Rather, most of Dost Muhammad Khan's energies were taken up by the effort to balance the conflicting claims of his most powerful sons. The bidding for the 'farm' of Turkistan which ensued during the next two months not only reveals the rivalry between Ghulam Haidar and Muhammad Afzal but is also instructive on the way business was conducted at the court of Kabul. On June 28, shortly after his arrival in Kabul, Muhammad Afzal submitted 'rarities' from Turkistan worth 60,000 rupees to the Amir. We are not told whether any regular revenue was submitted at this time, but the subsequent negotiations indicate that Muhammad Afzal had farmed the province of Turkistan for 2.5 million rupees (25 *laks*) per year, from which administrative and military expenses were subtracted. In addition to the remainder of the revenues of Turkistan, Muhammad Afzal possibly also retained a measure of control in his former *jagir* of Zurmat, the governorship of which had passed to his full brother Muhammad A'zam.[334] On July 10 Dost Muhammad Khan began the bidding process by asking Muhammad Afzal to define his sphere of influence in Turkistan and to 'fix its revenue.' Muhammad Afzal proposed to maintain the current revenue but to deduct one *lak* of rupees in order to finance the planned military expedition against Qunduz. As for his sphere of influence, he repeated his previous request that Turkistan should be placed under his sole control and that 'no colleagues should be associated with him in the Government.' To this end, he and his full brother Muhammad A'zam should be allowed to exchange their *jagirs* in Zurmat, Kurram, Khost, and Logar for equivalent possessions in Turkistan. He also asked for an additional contingent of 6,000 Kabuli troops to be permanently stationed in his province. Ghulam Haidar responded to Muhammad Afzal's obvious attempt to carve out an independent base of power north of the Hindu Kush by offering an 'amendment': One of his own brothers should always be present in Turkistan, and Muhammad Afzal should pay the same amount of revenue exclusive of the income derived from Tashqurghan. But Muhammad Afzal refused to give up his ambitious stance and insisted on a complete separation of jurisdictions: 'If you think the farm of Toorkistan is too profitable suppose you and your brothers take it and give up Cabul to me and my brothers, in which case I will pay 2 lakhs a year more than you now pay for it.' Four days later, Dost Muhammad Khan accepted Muhammad Afzal's requests in toto under the condition that the total revenue of Turkistan should be raised to 27 *laks*.[335] But this did not put an end to the maneuvering on all three sides. Ghulam Haidar protested indignantly that he, as heir apparent, should be given a greater role in the affairs of Turkistan. Dost Muhammad Khan justified his decision by quoting Muhammad Afzal's 'eminent services' in conquering Turkistan and submitting valuable presents to the court of Kabul. Furthermore, Muhammad Afzal, being the older brother, would never listen to Ghulam Haidar's commands. Still, if Ghulam Haidar insisted, he could obtain the government of Turkistan for an additional two *laks* of rupees. On July 23 Dost Muhammad Khan informed Muhammad Afzal that Ghulam Haidar had bidden 1.5 million rupees more for the farm of Turkistan. If Muhammad Afzal wanted to continue with his governorship he should engage to submit an equal amount of money, or else he would have to recognize Ghulam Haidar's supremacy over Turkistan. On Muhammad Afzal's refusal to engage in further bidding, Ghulam Haidar was formally invested with the combined governments of Kabul and Turkistan and confirmed as heir apparent on August 3.[336] But two weeks later, reacting to the news of the Persian siege on Maimana, the Amir in effect removed this agreement by convincing Ghulam Haidar that he was not in the position to control two provinces simultaneously. Muhammad Afzal, who was the only one 'competent' to govern Turkistan, should be given his old provinces at the increased rate of revenue. Furthermore, it was agreed that Muhammad Afzal Khan and Muhammad A'zam Khan were to give up the *jagirs* they held in the vicinity of Kabul. On August 17, Dost Muhammad Khan ordered Ghulam Haidar to select a *khil'at* for Muhammad Afzal's investment with the government of Turkistan.[337]

In bestowing the government of Turkistan on Muhammad Afzal, Ghulam Haidar formally assumed a superior position to his eldest brother. Muhammad Afzal, on the other hand, got what he wanted. While the *jagirs* in question were apparently never transferred,[338] his other requests were granted. In the winter of 1855 Dost Muhammad Khan appointed Muhammad Afzal's son 'Abd al-Rahman governor of Tashqurghan in the place of Ghulam Haidar's full brother Muhammad Amin, who returned to Kabul.[339] Thus the spheres of influence of Dost Muhammad Khan's most powerful sons were separated entirely. The strong position of Muhammad Afzal and Muhammad A'zam in Turkistan was to bar the emergence of central authority under Ghulam Haidar's younger brother Sher 'Ali effectively for a prolonged period after the Amir's death. The bidding game which unfolded between Dost Muhammad Khan, Muhammad Afzal, and Ghulam Haidar during the summer of 1855 is indicative of the Amir's relationship with his sons. While Dost Muhammad Khan assumed the position of a neutral referee, he actually encouraged the rivalry between his two sons by raising the price of the governorship of Turkistan with each new bid. It is not clear whether the increases in revenue gained in this process were ever submitted by Muhammad Afzal Khan and furnished the Amir with a net increase in his income.[340] But Dost Muhammad Khan's interaction with his sons shows that he considered them strong rivals. The bidding process, which formed the central issue at the court during the two months in question, gave the Amir the opportunity to conciliate each of his sons and to keep them at bay simultaneously. By confirming Ghulam Haidar as heir apparent, he garnered his support in the administration of Kabul and the pending invasion of Qandahar. Muhammad Afzal's criticism of Ghulam Haidar's privileged position, on the other hand, was silenced by giving him virtually free hand in the regions north of the Hindu Kush.

While Turkistan had formally become part of Dost Muhammad Khan's possessions, it really formed the domain of Muhammad Afzal Khan and his immediate relatives. In the course of his governorship Muhammad Afzal gained direct access to the revenues of Balkh, Mazar-i Sharif, Tashqurghan and Qunduz. Unfortunately, there are few details available on the amount of revenue obtained and the manner in which it was collected.[341] 'Abd al-Rahman merely informs us that he allowed certain reductions in tax (*takhfif-i maliyati*) after bad harvests for locals connected with his government in Tashqurghan. But these favors were at least partially reversed when Sardar Muhammad Afzal arrived in Tashqurghan about two years after his return from Kabul to check his son's accounts. Arguing that the expenses of the army outweighed the receipts of revenue in the province,[342] Sardar Muhammad Afzal recovered 100,000 rupees from the local 'peasants' (*ra'aya*).[343] Sardar 'Abd al-Rahman Khan, who resisted his father's measures at the time, later became as astute as Sardar Muhammad Afzal in collecting revenues. He claims that the leaders of Qataghan thanked him for imposing a fine of only 1.2 million rupees after a rebellion in 1863. Furthermore, he collected an ernomous sum in arrears at that time.[344]

According to Sardar 'Abd al-Rahman Khan, he used the arrears collected to pay the army under his command. The reports on the number of troops stationed in Afghan Turkistan vary. In 1856 the British official Ghulam Ahmad stated that a total of 9,000 regular troops were stationed in Turkistan under the command of Sardar Muhammad Afzal Khan and Sardar Wali Muhammad Khan, consisting of 6,300 cavalry and 2,700 infantry.[345] Sardar 'Abd al-Rahman, who must have had intimate knowledge of the affairs in Turkistan but possibly also an interest in exaggerating his military might, claims that the army of Turkistan consisted of 15,000 regulars (cavalry, infantry, artillery) and 15,500 militia ('Uzbek, Durrani, Kabuli') in 1857.[346] 'Abd al-Rahman describes the relationship between the Muhammadzai rulers of Turkistan and their troops in romantic terms. Upon his return to Qataghan in 1861/62 he inspected the troops and conveyed the following message from Sardar Muhammad Afzal to them: 'My father considers all of you his sons and feels the same affection for you as he does for me.' The soldiers allegedly responded with equal warmth, shouting that each of them was ready to sacrifice his life for his father, Sardar Muhammad Afzal Khan.[347] Despite this protestation of loyalty not all was well in the army of Turkistan. In particular, those contingents left behind by Ghulam Haidar in 1850 found themselves in friction with Sardar Muhammad Afzal and left for Kabul without his permission in 1854.[348] In August 1858 officers of Sardar Muhammad Afzal's army complained to Dost Muhammad Khan that they had been kept without pay for one and a half years. Another grievance was that local Uzbek leaders were being given a role in the army.[349] During the governorship of 'Abd al-Ghiyas Khan in Qataghan the revenues intended for the pay of the troops were embezzled by a number of army officers. The warm welcome the troops gave Sardar 'Abd al-Rahman may be attributed to the fact that they hoped to finally receive the pay due to them for the past twelve months. The responsible officers at Khanabad resented the loss of independence occasioned by the return of Sardar 'Abd al-Rahman and rebelled shortly after the death of Amir Dost Muhammad Khan.[350]

The Economic Impact of the Muhammadzai Presence

Only fourteen years elapsed between Sardar Muhammad Akram Khan's invasion of Turkistan and the death of Amir Dost Muhammad Khan. For this early period of Muhammadzai domination, it is difficult to pinpoint the economic effects of the fiscal measures taken by the Afghans. The traces left by the frequent military campaigns needed for the subjugation of Turkistan are more readily apparent. But even before the advent of the Afghans Ferrier noted that the 'permanent warfare' among the 'petty khans' had 'precluded the development of the resources of the country.'[351] In the northeast, only the era of Qilich 'Ali Beg was known for its comparative tranquility.[352] Subsequently, the constant plundering expeditions by Mir Murad Beg had done lasting damage. In 1832 Mohan Lal observed that the country around Mazar-i Sharif was largely uncultivated. He attributed this state of affairs to the fact that most of the population had been carried into slavery by Mir Murad Beg. Possibly the depressed state of agriculture had in turn caused the local economy to mirror that of Qunduz: 'Second, the villagers, being addicted to plunder, are very careless of agriculture, every man of the village has a few horses to ride on for the purpose of making these chapaws [plundering expeditions].'[353] In western Turkistan the military campaigns of Yar Muhammad Khan in the 1840s and the subsequent Turkmen raids apparently had a similar impact. According to Centlivres, the plundering expeditions of the Turkmens in particular may have hurt the economic position of the towns in this region and have encouraged a resurgence of semi-nomadism.[354]

The question whether the events of the nineteenth century had a clear impact on the lifestyle of the population of Lesser Turkistan cannot be answered in a satisfactory manner. For the Hijdah Nahr region, McChesney points out that a general shift from agriculture to animal husbandry may have taken place much earlier, more than a century before Mir Murad Beg's time. The exact reasons for this development are not clear. McChesney raises the possibility that economic developments in the wider region may have been a factor. The increasing demand for horses in the trade with China and India possibly encouraged stockbreeding at the expense of agricultural pursuits. On the other hand, the constant struggles for the control of Balkh and the concomitant weakening of the local political structure may have allowed more and more pastoralists to enter the region.[355]

But even if the Afghans did not initiate the current economic trend in the region their presence did little to undo the havoc wreaked by their predecessors. In the 1880s Yate observed that the only thing the Balkh region lacked was cultivators:

> the more one sees of this Turkistan plain the more fertile does the land seem to be. The Balkh river... which emerges out on the plains through the gorge in the Alburz range, some 15 miles south of Balkh, flows northwest to Akchah, and there expends immense volumes of spill-water in the desert beyond, all of which might be utilised were there only people to utilise it. But the people have all apparently been killed off.

To show a case in point, Yate recounts the fate of Nimlik near Balkh, which not only suffered two military attacks by the Afghans but literally lost its foundations when Sardar Muhammad Afzal Khan used its woodwork and other building materials for the construction of his capital at Takhta Pul.[356] Centlivres points out that the towns of Turkistan suffered stagnation and regression during the time of the military campaigns directed at Lesser Turkistan during the reigns of Dost Muhammad Khan and Sher 'Ali Khan. Because of the low level of population, both urban and rural, as well as the insecurity of communications, trade in grain practically came to a standstill during this period.[357] But in the long run, the Afghan presence seems to have had a stimulating impact on the development of commerce in Turkistan. Until the period of Amir 'Abd al-Rahman Khan the caravan trade passing through along the grand overland routes had scarcely affected the local economic development in Badakhshan, Qataghan and Hazarajat. Accordingly, local trade was poorly developed and mostly based on barter. Cash currency was hardly known; tribute and luxury items were often reckoned in terms of slaves, horses and sheep.[358] A positive side effect of the Afghan military campaigns in the region was a greater demand for wheat, meat and fodder and the creation of a market for local products. Furthermore, the establishment of Afghan garrisons in Balkh, Takhta Pul, Tashqurghan, Nahrin, Dihdadi, Rustaq, and Yangi Qal'a attracted numerous merchants from Kohistan, the region of Jalalabad, and the greater towns of Turkistan. This process encouraged the commercial penetration of areas which had previously been marginal to the market economy.[359]

SUMMARY

In this chapter I have analyzed the socio-political circumstances in the region known as 'Lesser' or 'Afghan' Turkistan in the nineteenth century. When Dost Muhammad Khan began to extend his influence beyond the Hindu Kush from the late 1840s on, this area consisted of almost a dozen of petty principalities, the most powerful among which were Maimana under the leadership of the Ming Uzbeks, Tashqurghan under the Muitan Uzbeks and Qunduz under the Kessemir Uzbeks. These khanates primarily owed their existence to land grants made by members of the Tuqai-Timurid dynasty (1598–1740/1785) to their Uzbek military leaders known as *amirs*. With the decline of the Tuqai-Timurid dynasty from the late seventeenth century on, these *amirs* were able to assume an independent political role. Their separation from their Chingizid overlords seemed to have become complete when Lesser Turkistan was conquered by Ahmad Shah Sadozai in 1751. Nonetheless the formal incorporation of this region into the Sadozai empire did not affect the local configurations of power in a significant manner. While submitting a nominal tribute to the Sadozai capital, the Uzbek leadership remained more or less independent and continued to maintain its cultural ties with Bukhara and Samarqand. On their part, the Uzbek rulers of Bukhara were not ready to relinquish their claims to their former appanage of Balkh and intermittently made their military presence felt until the middle of the nineteenth century. With the decline of the Sadozai empire the Uzbeks were able to maintain a precarious independence between the competing interests of Kabul, Bukhara and Herat.

The setting in early nineteenth-century Turkistan may be characterized as one of 'political segmentation'. Although the relative economic and military strength of the individual Uzbek rulers varied, even the most powerful among them were unable to unseat their rivals on a permanent basis and had to base their claims to authority on a loose system of allegiances. The relationship between the powerful Uzbek leaders and their vassals was conceptualized not as a hierarchy engendering a clear chain of command but as a friendship requiring constant renewal by the exchange of gifts. In practical terms, the lesser chiefs had to by remunerated for their loyalty with rent-free grants of land and a share of the booty captured in the course of military campaigns. This system of service grants and loose alliances had the effect that relatively few troops were permanently present at the court of the ruler. His claims to supremacy rested with his ability to raise an army sufficiently large to impress his followers and neighboring principals. As soon as doubts concerning his political clout or even physical health arose allegiances tended to shift in favor of another contender for power who showed greater promise of securing adequate advantages for his followers.

During Dost Muhammad Khan's invasion of Lesser Turkistan the Amir's representatives were able to use the rivalries prevailing among the various Uzbek khanates to conquer them one by one. By 1863 only Maimana in the far west and Badakhshan in the east remained independent. The imposition of the Muhammadzai administration was accompanied by an unprecedented degree of Afghan interference in local affairs. Sardar Muhammad Afzal Khan, the governor of Turkistan, was first based at Balkh and later constructed a new capital for himself at Takhta Pul. Furthermore, he created regional governorships in the major towns of Afghan Turkistan. With the exception of Andkhui, these governorships were held by members of the royal family. The Muhammadzai intrusion into the local affairs of the region was partly reversed during the power struggle which erupted among Dost Muhammad Khan's sons after his death in 1863. Yet the political developments of the 1850s essentially prefigured the 'Afghanization' which continued to proceed during the reign of Amir Sher 'Ali Khan and culminated in the removal of amirid rule in the Chahar Wilayat of Sar-i Pul, Shibarghan, Andkhui and Maimana in 1875/76. But even in the regions where the former Uzbek elite was deprived of its power the Afghan officials continued to rely on the cooperation of the next lower echelon of the local leadership in the collection of revenues and the raising of troops.

Chapter 3

THE POSITION OF THE PASHTUN TRIBES IN THE MUHAMMADZAI STATE

From Turkistan, I will now retrace my steps across the Hindu Kush. This chapter will deal with groups that were much closer to the lords of Kabul than the Uzbeks, both in terms of kinship and geography. While the Ghilzais and the so-called eastern or border tribes are linked to the common apical ancestor Qais 'Abd al-Rashid by a less distinct lineage than the Sadozai and Muhammadzai rulers, these groups are generally recognized as belonging to the greater group of Pashtuns, or Afghans, as they were generally referred to until the nineteenth century.[1] From the late sixteenth century on the Pashtun tribes enjoyed a good degree of interaction with the rulers of Qandahar and Kabul. Unlike the Uzbek khanates of Lesser Turkistan, which owed their existence to the power vacuum brought about by the decline of Tuqai-Timurid dynasty, the Pashtuns were able to maintain their position within, and as formal partners of, the Durrani empire founded by Ahmad Shah Sadozai. As they controlled the trade routes linking Kabul with Qandahar and Peshawar, their goodwill was an essential ingredient for the ability of the Durrani kings to assert their claims to authority in Kashmir, Punjab, Sind, and Baluchistan, and to win the necessary resources for the maintenance of their empire. Going a step further, Ahmad Shah even claimed that the strong position of these Pashtun leaders lay at the root of his expansionist policies. According to Elphinstone, he 'had the penetration to discover that it would require a less exertion to conquer all the neighbouring kingdoms, than to subdue his own countrymen.'[2]

The Pashtuns are generally described as fiercely independent individualists who are as 'rugged' as the mountains they inhabit.[3] Both ethnographic and historical accounts tend to give the impression that there is little in Pashtun tribal organization that would lend itself to penetration by outsiders. Yet, the identity and political strategies of the Pashtuns have been shaped in great part by their interaction with greater powers. Even the most unruly groups profited less from a situation of 'splendid isolation' than their strategic position on the fringes of greater powers, for example, the Mughal and Safawid empires. In the eighteenth century the Sadozai rulers of

Qandahar and Kabul formally acted as heads of a Pashtun tribal confederacy. The dependencies of Kashmir and Punjab, as well as regular campaigns to India not only served to maintain the fiscal needs of the empire but also secured the allegiance of the Pashtuns by offering the prospect of plunder.[4] Apart from a light or symbolic revenue payment, the allegiance of these groups to the Sadozai kings was expressed by the duty to furnish a fixed number of soldiers in times of need. By comparison, the service grants and subsidies they enjoyed were much greater. When Dost Muhammad Khan gained possession of Kabul in 1826, he was in no position to emulate the policies of his Sadozai predecessors. His lack of resources, combined with the rise of the Sikh empire on the eastern border, precluded the possibility of profitable military campaigns into India while at the same time the sources of revenue in those regions had dried up. Kabul had become a small regional state, confronting independent principalities of equal size in Qandahar and Herat. The Ghilzais and the 'border' tribes had profited from the crumbling of Sadozai power and established a firm grip over the trade routes in the region. The effort to regain control of these routes formed an important aspect of Dost Muhammad Khan's attempt to expand the borders of his kingdom. Furthermore, the Ghilzais and border tribes lost part of their traditional subsidies. But contrary to the Durranis of Qandahar, previously the closest allies of the Sadozais, who were firmly incorporated into the revenue apparatus of Qandahar prior to the first Anglo-Afghan War, these groups suffered relatively few inroads into their tribal domains. In particular the Ghilzai rebellions were formulated less as an attempt to avoid contact with the royal court than as a challenge of the legitimacy of the Muhammadzai rulers. In many cases the leading groups among the Ghilzais did not wish to evade government control but rather wanted to receive a greater share in it.

Viewed as 'tribe' par excellence, the Pashtuns have been studied in greater detail by British colonialists and travellers than any other group in the region known as Afghanistan today. Even so, there is little reliable material on the social and economic organization of the Pashtuns in the nineteenth century. The sources tend to emphasize the 'turbulent' aspects of tribal behavior (feuds, rebellions, and military strength). Little is said about the underlying structures which allow the tribes to behave the way they do. Accordingly, Tapper has pointed out the need of cautious 'extrapolations' from more recent ethnographic studies.[5] There is general agreement among historians and anthropologists that the interplay of local tribal structures and the larger political setting produce a specific sort of 'tribal' behavior, though there is considerable controversy how much weight should be ascribed to either ingredient. Moving from the general to the specific, and from the 'ethnographic present' to the historical past, this chapter presents an attempt at approximation. I will start out with the question what constitutes a 'tribe'. On the basis of modern ethnographic studies I will then attempt to point out some of the formative factors of Pashtun tribal organization. By exploring the role of kinship structure, styles of leadership and mediation as well as the economic/ecological factors shaping Pashtun political behavior, I hope to set the stage for the historical section to follow. As will be seen below, the available anthropological studies pay special attention to those elements in Pashtun organization which foster egalitarian tendencies and render state interference difficult. In the historical section I will add a range of examples concerning the political behavior of the Pashtun tribes in the nineteenth century. Taking the 'bird's-eye view', I will single out individual influential leaders and discuss the origins of their power and their position within the Muhammadzai kingdom. The argument will be that court patronage can bring about a marked stratification in the tribal setting. Dost Muhammad Khan's endeavor to establish royal authority brought about a direct confrontaion with the well entrenched leading lineages controlling the approaches to Kabul. The 'wild' tribes located beyond the commercial arteries, by contrast, played an insignificant role in the politics of the nascent Muhammadzai kingdom.

PASHTUN ORGANIZATION IN THE LIGHT OF MODERN ANTHROPOLOGY

The Concept of 'Tribe'

The nature of tribally organized societies has formed a lasting topic of debate among historians and anthropologists alike. While there is general agreement that there is such a thing a tribe, it is difficult to provide a clear-cut definition for this phenomenon. For one thing, the word 'tribe' is generally used as a translation for a variety of Middle Eastern terms (*il*, *ta^cifa*, *qabila*, *qaum* etc.) which are often used interchangeably in the local literature and may denote various levels of organization.[6] Tribal societies display a broad spectrum of divergent modes of socio-economic, political, and cultural organization ranging from 'totally acephalous societies to kingdoms.'[7] Furthermore, tribal boundaries may be vague and may expand and shrink according to the fortunes of a particular group and its leadership.[8] The endeavor of colonial administrators and anthropologists to classify and label tribal groups as distinct demographic or geographic units has therefore justly invited the criticism of 'ethnographic fiction.'[9]

The discussion concerning the nature of tribal societies revolves around several issues. For one thing, the formulation of what constitutes a tribe is affected by the perspective of the speaker. Eickelman points out that the concept of tribe receives varying interpretations from government officials, anthropologists and the tribal people themselves. Moreover, there may be a tension between formal tribal ideologies elaborated by the socially and politically dominant sections of a tribe and the role of unspoken, practical notions guiding the everyday conduct of tribesmen.[10]

Tribal identities are overwhelmingly formulated in relation, often opposition, to neighboring groups and the state. A great part of the debate concerning the nature of tribes in the Middle East revolves around the question to what extent they are organized around genealogical principles and what role external political stimuli play in their formation. Is the tribe to be perceived as a social and political formation preceding the state, or is it created by the state?[11] In the Iranian context, Beck situates tribal formation at 'the intersection of dependence on resources (land for pastoralism and agriculture, water, migratory routes, trade routes, markets), external powers and pressures, and mediating agents (tribal leaders, government officials, regional elites, foreign agents...).'[12] Therefore, questions concerning the the 'internal' profile of a tribe (its economic/ecological basis, size, definition of membership, operative units, distribution of power, the role and status of leaders and religious figures) also need to be related to the larger framework of tribe-state relations. Special interest surrounds the role of the local leaders who act as middlemen between these two entities. What are the origins of their power and how do they position themselves in relation to their fellow tribesmen and the state? Another point of discussion is in which ways the internal organization of a tribe is affected by the nature of the state it interacts with. Factors of space and time form related issues. The geographic location of a tribe (the terrain, distance from, or proximity to, lines of communication and centers of power) may have a fundamental impact on its relationship with the state. We also have to ask how such a relationship evolves over time and to what extent the historical 'memory' of a group affects its actions in the presence.

Before I proceed to summarize some of the voices in the debate it will be useful to set down some working definitions concerning 'tribe', its constituent elements, and 'state'. I will start out with the concept of 'lineage' and move on to increasingly higher levels of inclusion. Unless noted otherwise, these definitions are based on Tapper (1983: 9–11).

A *lineage* is a localized and unified group of people who can trace their common ancestor.

A *clan* comprises several lineages. The claims of its members to common ancestry may be more weakly developed and may only be putative.[13]

A *tribe* is 'the largest unit of incorporation on a genealogical model'.[14] Its members consider themselves culturally distinct in terms of customs, dialect or language, and origins. Leadership is not necessarily centralized.

A *confederacy* is composed of a number of tribal groups which may be of heterogeneous origin. It comprises up to hundreds of thousands of people and is politically unified, usually under a central authority.

A *state* is defined by territorial frontiers (however vaguely defined), a central government (however weak and limited in its aims) and a heterogeneous population.

In the discussion of tribalism the theory of segmentary lineage organization as elaborated in the African context by Evans-Pritchard, Sahlins and Gellner has been of great impact, so much so that it has been identified as a 'gatekeeping concept' for Middle Eastern anthropology.[15] This theory casts the tribe as an essentially egalitarian formation. As relationships within a tribe are determined by notions of lineal descent from a common ancestor, each tribesman is entitled to the same political prerogatives as his fellows and will seek coalitions with them at different levels of common descent according to circumstances. This brings about, as Evans-Pritchard has called it, a system of 'balanced opposition', in which groups at each level of tribal organization are balanced by others of equal strength. Such a setting precludes any lasting centralization and thus provides no 'handle' for a sustained interference by the state. The tribe forms, in Gellner's words, 'an alternative to the state'. As will be seen below, the theory of segmentary lineage organization is not without its critics. The voices in the debate, in as far as they are relevant to the question of the relationship between state and tribe, fall into three major categories. Firstly, there are those who feel that this theory has been applied too uncritically to a wide variety of tribal settings. A second major issue is the question whether this theory reflects circumstances as they exist 'on the ground' or whether it merely adopts a tribal ideology of how things 'should be'. Finally a number of studies demonstrate that tribes described as 'segmentary' may display a certain degree of inherent stratification and/or may experience lasting changes because of state interference. The arguments outlined above make it clear that the theory of segmentary organization is not suitable as the single explanatory model for all aspects of tribalism. Nonetheless it provides a useful concept for understanding some of the mechanisms at work, in particular at the lower echelons of tribal society. In the following, I will begin with a summary of this theory and then will echo some of the criticisms it has elicited.

In his study of the Moroccan Berbers of the Central High Atlas, Gellner lists three elements as the decisive determinants of tribal organization:

> If (a) only one sex is allowed to be significant in ancestry, and (b) only shared ancestry is allowed to define groups, and (c) the whole group ('tribe') shares one ultimate ancestor, it follows that the individual is a member only of a series of 'nested' groups, the largest defined by the most distant ancestor (and so on downwards), with no groups of which he is member cutting across each other. From the viewpoint of the total group, what follows is that, at each level of size, there are groups opposing, 'balancing' each other.[16]

Gellner adds that, with the exception of the Tuareg, patrilineal descent is the main organizing principle among the tribes of 'arid-zone Islam'.[17] A tribe is thus characterized by a tree-like structure. Originating from a founding father, lines of male descendants ramify like the branches of a tree, forming successively smaller units. From the viewpoint of the individual, each ancestor defines a segment of this tree. Collective action is justified by common ancestry: 'an individual determines his relationship with another individual and that of his group with other groups by tracing back, as best he can, to the common ancestor and then back down again to the second individual or group.'[18] Linking himself to increasingly remote ancestors, a tribesman may thus identify himself in an ascending order as the member of a certain family, a lineage, a clan, or a tribe. This genealogical knowledge may be Occamist: 'the individual knows the name of his father and of his grandfather: after that, he will name or know of only those ancestors who perform the useful task of defining an effective social group.'[19] It is this 'telescoping' to a remote common ancestor along with the readily presentable knowledge of the crucial links within the genealogy which distinguish tribal groups from non-tribal peasant societies.[20] The segmentary lineage organization not only provides the basis for collective action but also determines access to tribal resources in land or pasture.[21]

Segmentary organization entails an ongoing process of opposition and balancing between structurally similar components. This mechanism precludes the emergence of lasting political specialization within the tribe. Rather, the tribe forms a self-contained 'mutual aid association whose members jointly help maintain order internally and defend the unit externally', thus performing tasks which would lie with specialized state agencies in other social contexts. Providing 'stability without government,' the tribe thus functions as a political alternative to the state.[22] Lineages, clans, and tribes only take profile as groups when threatened from outside. In his work on the Nuer, Evans-Pritchard points out that political allegiances tend to shift as different levels of interaction provoke the formulation of different sets of loyalties:

> Any segment sees itself as an independent unit in relation to another segment of the same section, but sees both segments as a unity in relation to another section; and a section which from the point of view of its members comprises opposed segments is seen by members of other sections as an unsegmented unit. Thus there is... always contraditction in the definition of a political group, for it is a group only in relation to other groups. A tribal segment is a political group in relation to other segments of the same kind and they jointly form a tribe only in relation to other Nuer tribes and adjacent foreign tribes which form part of the same political system, and without these relations very little meaning can be attached to the concepts of tribal segment and tribe.[23]

In the absence of external stimulation, the tribe will automatically return to a state of disunity. In such a setting, '[l]eadership beyond the small –

normally, the primary – segment can only be ephemeral because organized action above this level is ephemeral.'[24] Tribal leaders act as representatives of their own people to the outside world but command little authority within their own group.[25] In order to win the allegiance of their tribesmen, they have to rule them 'kindly and to avoid antagonizing them,' as the fourteenth-century Maghribi philosopher Ibn Khaldun (1332–1406) put it.[26]

While there may be some economic differences within the segmentary tribe, it does not lend itself to permanent stratification. All tribesmen are formally equal and are entitled and obliged to participate in all affairs concerning the tribe. Consisting of a very broad, relatively undifferentiated stratum, tribal organization is thus set apart from feudalism, in which politics and violence are the prerogative of a small group of warriors. Even so, the tribal setting is not devoid of hierarchies. In Gellner's opinion, a pure segmentary system with its egalitarianism and internal rivalries can only be maintained with the help of a superimposed layer of outsiders. Among the Moroccan Berbers, 'saints', religious specialists belonging to the Ahansala marabout family, provide the tribes with political continuity, supervise elections and mediate between groups in conflict. On the other end of the scale, 'subject minorities of slaves, oasis cultivators and petty artisans are to be found, with whom tribesmen ideally do not intermarry... '[27]

According to Gellner, segmentary structures are most likely to develop among pastoralists, whose mobile property allows them to evade political domination effectively. But this form of organization may be successfully 'emulated' by sedentary groups physically shielded from government interference, for example, by mountains. Yet segmentary organization does not emerge in a total vacuum. Only where there is a certain amount of existing tension, as generated by the competition for resources, do genealogical principles assume a formative role.[28] In a similar vein, Sahlins views segmentary lineage organization as a 'social means of intrusion and competition in an already occupied ecological niche.' For Sahlins, this competition takes place between tribal societies.[29] Gellner, on the other hand, views the state as one of the possible contestants. In his opinion, segmentary lineage organization is most clearly articulated in regions with intermittent state interference. The state has to keep up with a proliferation of tribal *khans* who are much harder to eliminate than an entrenched feudal aristocracy. By contrast, segmentary structures disappear in spheres where state influence is either very weak or very strong. In the first case, there is no need for clearly defined groups; in the second case, they are destroyed by the state.[30]

Segmentary lineage theory has shaped much of the anthropological debate on tribalism in the Middle East. Yet for some its implications and applications have been stretched too far. While acknowledging 'the existence of segmentary concerns in Middle Eastern societies', Abu-Lughod feels that this school of thought has taken up 'an inordinate amount of anthropological space.' To her, the discussion around this topic is a self-limiting enterprise which draws its justification in great part from a long line of male anthropologists. In her opinion, the pervasive influence of this theory has to be attributed to 'a felicitous correspondence between the views of Arab tribesmen and those of European men [which] has led each to reinforce particular interests of the other and to slight other aspects of experience and concern.'[31] Appadurai points to the possibility that the 'appeal of the small, the simple, the elementary, the face-to face' has made segmentation a 'prestige zone of anthropological theory.' He also raises the question whether this model may have been applied uncritically to settings outside the Maghrib: 'Did the African model of segmentation excessively dominate accounts of social structure in the Middle East, the New Guinea highlands and elsewhere?'[32]

Within the North African/Arabian setting the model of segmentary lineage organization has received a number of revisions. One group of authors emphasizes the notion of honor as operative principle of tribal social action.[33] Another group of critics views the ideal of patrilineal kinship as idiom of organization as a tribal ideology rather than a political reality.[34] In his study of the Bedouins of Cyrenaica, Peters, for example, raises several objections to the 'folk model' of segmentary lineage organization. While the Bedouin explain their world in genealogical terms, their reasoning allows for a wide spectrum of strategies which do not necessarily follow the simplistic pattern of fission and fusion the segmentary model would suggest. Economic and ecological factors have a decisive impact on the shape the interaction of tribal segments takes at different levels of organization. Moreover, genealogical reasoning primarily serves as a posterior justification of existing relationships rather than as a determinant of future political action. Peters also notes that the notion of 'balanced opposition' should not be understood as a balance of power. Although two segments may be formally equal in genealogical terms they may display gross inequalities in terms of numbers and economic prowess. The model of segmentary lineage organization fails to account for the presence of powerful leaders among the Bedouin of Cyrenaica. Another important point Peters makes is that this theory attaches little importance to kinship ties created through women.[35]

Marxist criticism also takes its departure from the question whether tribal societies really are as egalitarian and as impervious to state interference as the segmentary lineage model suggests. Rather than being enhanced, egalitarian structures tend to give way to stratification even in places where state control is weakly developed. Talal Asad points to the example of the Kababish Arabs of Sudan. Located in a relatively remote frontier region, this group witnessed the emergence of a dominant lineage in 19th century. Acting as middlemen for the colonial administrators, the

Awlad Fadlullah were able to assume a powerful position as rulers over their fellow tribesmen.[36] Hammoudi, who has studied the same groups as Gellner, grants that genealogical principles profoundly influence tribal action on an ideological level. But while the Ait-Atta claim that all members of their tribe are 'absolutely equal', their genealogy carries in itself the seeds of social stratification. Contrary to Gellner, Hammoudi is of the opinion that the tribes of High Atlas have integrated a high number of immigrants and conquered people who occupy a subordinate position in tribal society. This is expressed by a differential access to leadership on the basis of 'good birth'. Although in theory every tribesman displaying the requisite qualities of generosity and bravery may become a supreme leader, this office usually falls to a member of one of three or four powerful families in the tribe and is thus a stable, inheritable position. Hammoudi also takes issue with Gellner's artificial model of an egalitarian tribal society and a superimposed 'hagiarchy'. Rather, the members of holy lineages are part of the stratification already present in the tribe itself: 'Far from being a necessary excrescence of the social structure, the saints are in fact well and truly part, in an unambiguous way, of a recognised stratifcation and hierarchy.' On the basis of historical material from the seventeenth and eighteenth centuries, Hammoudi demonstrates that the role of the saints was not limited to mediation on the tribal level. Rather than assuming the role of pacifistic outsiders, they engaged in forthright political action which allowed them to act as middlemen between the central power and the tribe. Given this linkage with the state, the tribe should not be viewed as a 'simple segmentary anarchy' but as a 'reservoir of political renewal and challenge to the established powers.'[37]

The above criticism amply demonstrates the shortcomings of Gellner's model for understanding the origins of tribal leadership and its interaction with the state. The question under what conditions and by what mechanisms egalitarian tribal structures give way to stratification remains largely unanswered. Nonetheless the theory of segmentary lineage organization is a useful means for understanding other aspects of tribal organization. Bruinessen primarily detects segmentary patterns at the lower levels of tribal organization: 'If one looks from the bottom up instead of from the top down, the role of kinship is more obvious.' The higher echelons of Kurdish organization, on the other hand, provide the linkage with central powers.[38] Barfield is likewise of the opinion that genealogical principles function most vigorously at the lower levels of tribal organization. On the higher levels of the same structure relationships tend to be of a political origin and include 'client or slave descent groups that have no proper genealogical connections but are nevertheless an accepted part of the tribe; alliances or rivalries between descent groups that appear to violate genealogical charters; cooperation among networks of people that crosscut kinship relations; or the blatant rewriting ... of genealogies.' For

Barfield, the organization of a tribe is greatly influenced by the power and organization of the state it opposes. Accordingly he distinguishes between the ideal types of 'Arabian' and 'Turco-Mongol' tribal organization, which display different levels of complexity. The 'Arabian' type, which is characterized by the segmentary lineage organization as outlined above is mostly to be found in contact with the small regional states typical of the arid/mountainous setting of North Africa and Arabia. Although the combined population of such a tribe may reach tens of thousands, it rarely acts collectively at this level. Political cooperation commonly takes place at a lower level, the lineage functioning as the operative unit. The Turco-Mongol type, on the other hand, developed in the course of the interaction between the nomadic tribes of Inner Asia and the Chinese empire from the third century BC on and was introduced to the Iranian/Anatolian plateaus subsequent to the thirteenth century. It was characterized by a more hierarchical mode of genealogical organization (the 'conical clan') and a complex confederate character. By means of a substantial income siphoned off from its Chinese neighbors it was able to incorporate hundreds of thousands of tribesmen under powerful leaders. The high degree of centralization required for the confrontation with the Chinese empire also affected tribal organization. While the local leaders furnished their own tribal contingents, the higher levels of military administration cut across genealogical lines. Thus greater political units were formed 'by division from the top rather than alliance from the bottom'.[39]

Segmentary structures may thus be more pronounced in certain tribal settings and at certain levels of tribal organization. In addition, Salzman draws attention to the possibility that lineage solidarity and balanced opposition are not so much characteristics of pure segmentary systems than what he calls 'lineage-plus' models. As cases in point he names two tribally organized societies which rely on mechanisms other than segmentary fusion and fission to maintain their internal equilibrium. The Somali of the Horn of Africa, for example, are able to counter demographic imbalances by relying both on notions of patrilineal and matrilineal descent in their alliances. The Yomut Turkmen of northeastern Iran are distributed in a checkerboard pattern. This resolves the dilemma that in a typical segmentary setting competition for resources would automatically involve close relatives: 'by alternating close kin groups with distant ones ... genealogical solidarity can be maintained in spite of conflict between neighboring groups.'[40] Another mechanism to be observed in a number of tribal settings is a clear dichotomy cutting across segmentary patterns of opposition and alliance. In the Kurdish emirate of Hakkari, for example, such a dichotomy caused all tribes of the region to be grouped 'as those of the left and those of the right' and also extended into the towns of the emirate. Bruinessen describes this phenomenon in the following manner:

> Even at the level of the tribe, unity against outsiders may remain restricted to the domain of ideology... In cases of conflict between two tribes it may happen that a section of one makes common cause with the other. This may be either because of an internal blood feud that is taken very seriously, or (more frequently) because the section's headman has an axe to grind with the paramount chieftain. Especially before central governments severely curtailed the chieftains' powers in this century, there were perpetual struggles for leadership of the tribe. Each of the rivals tried to manipulate the socio-political environment in order to get the better of the others. For such ambitious chieftains the important dichotomy was not between 'the rival tribe' and 'my own tribe' but 'the power sources my rivals are tapping' vs 'the power sources I might tap'. From a very early date this environment included not only other tribes and powerful chieftains but also powerful states.

While the rivalries among chieftains make it easy for other governments to find access to tribal areas and to assume nominal control there, this form of polarization simultaneously limits the scope of government interference: 'Full control ... appeared extremely difficult to achieve, since every chieftain who became "loyal" had his rivals, who were thus forced into "rebellion".'[41]

As will be seen below, such dichotomies are also to be found among the Pashtun tribes. Segmentation thus only forms one, albeit important, avenue to an understanding of tribal organization and strategy. Moreover, tribes should not be seen in isolation, or fixed in space or time. I concur with Beck that tribes are 'historically and situationally dynamic' and therefore should not be identified as either socially egalitarian or complex: 'The task of the analyst is ... not to define tribes rigidly but to discover the conditions under which a decentralizing or centralizing tendency was dominant within a society at any given time and then trace the transformations through time and in response to particular circumstances.' [42] Before I move on to give the historical profiles of a number of Pashtun tribes, I will attempt to highlight some aspects of Pashtun tribal organization from the perspective of modern anthropology.

The Pashtuns

The available historical literature only makes very general references to the economic, political and social structure of the Pashtuns in the nineteenth century. Most information stems from British accounts, the viewpoints of which tended to shift along with changes of imperial strategy. From this perspective, the Pashtuns emerge alternatively as 'noble savages' or as bloodthirsty, treacherous and greedy bandits.[43] These accounts only give a partial description of Pashtun attitudes and political behavior and have contributed to the creation of the most enduring clichés concerning this group. Yet, however biased and incomplete, they point to certain elements of Pashtun organization also detected by present-day anthropologists.[44] Elphinstone's characterization of the Ghilzais and the border tribes as 'republican' and fragmented into 'little societies',[45] as well as the attributes of 'democracy' and 'disunity' applied by later authors,[46] prefigure the functionalist concept of segmentary lineage organization. Although the nineteenth-century authors tend to place too much emphasis on the effectiveness of the chain of command extending from the king downwards, their description of the tribal leadership as comparatively weak and exchangeable coincides fairly closely with modern anthropologist views. The characterization given by Harlan in the 1830s is representative of similar statements to be found in other works from the nineteenth century:

> The chief is to be viewed as an executive officer, and administers the laws of the tribe, which are the result of usage arising from expediency strictly in consonance with the customs of the people. He can levy no revenue; there are in fact no expenses of government... The attachment of the people is to the community, and not to the chief, who is liable to be removed by a council of the tribe for any flagrant misconduct. The chief represents the tribe in their foreign relations, calls out and commands the militia, who maintain themselves, and administers the judicial system of his tribe.[47]

The Pashtun ethos of independence and equality forms a theme both among nineteenth-century authors and modern anthropologists. The following characterization of a typical 'uncivilized' Pashtun given by Oliver displays a mixture of admiration and disdain which has colored European descriptions of the North-Western Frontier up to the present day.

> The style of the Tribesman is a little after the manner of Rob Roy – 'my foot is on my native heath,' and 'am I not a Pathan'? Even when he leaves his native heath behind, he takes his manners with him. He will come down, a stalwart, manly-looking ruffian, with frank and open manners, rather Jewish features, long hair plentifully oiled under a high turban, with a loose tunic, blue for choice – the better to hide the dirt – worn very long, baggy drawers, a *lungi* or sash across his shoulders, grass sandals, a sheep-skin coat with the hair inside, thickly populated, a long heavy knife, and a rifle... He is certain to be filthy and may be ragged, but he will saunter into a Viceregal durbar as proud as Lucifer, and with an air of unconcern a diplomatist might envy.[48]

While the British sources dedicate a lot of space to the enumeration of Pashtun subdivisions, their fighting strength, and the most promising strategies to cope with them, they offer little information on internal mechanisms that may affect the political behavior of a tribe, such as the nature of leadership and the local distribution of power. These aspects are addressed in a much more detailed fashion by twentieth-century anthropological studies. By discussing the most important ethnographic accounts concerning various Pashtun groups, such as the Yusufzais, the Mohmands, the tribes of Khost, and the Ghilzais, I hope to arrive at a clearer understanding of the pertinent elements of Pashtun organization.

Before moving on to specific case studies, I will use the next few paragraphs to cover a few broader aspects of Pashtun tribalism. There is general agreement that common descent, along with the *pashtunwali* (the Pashtun code of ethics), is the formative element of Pashtun identity. The Pashtuns have been described as 'the largest tribal society on earth'.[49] All thirteen million Pashtuns living in present-day Afghanistan and Pakistan[50] trace their origin to one putative ancestor, Qais 'Abd al-Rashid, who converted to Islam in the seventh century and married the daughter of Khalid bin Walid, one of the most famous generals of early Islamic history.[51] Despite these common roots the Pashtuns have never acted collectively at such a high level of organization.[52] That is why Tapper is of the opinion that the entire group of Pashtuns should be referred to as a *nation* or *ethnic group*. At the next lower level of organization the major subdivisions of the Pashtuns, such as the Mohmands, Ghilzais, Durranis, etc., are to be found. Although they are culturally relatively homogeneous, they should be called *confederacies* because of the large numbers of people they combine. The use of the term *tribe* should be reserved for the subdivisions of these confederacies.[53] Among the Ghilzais, there are seven such major tribes: Hotak, Tokhi, Nasir, Taraki, Kharoti, Andar, and Sulaiman Khel. Each of these tribes is divided into a number of patrilineages variously called *khel* or *-zai*.[54]

According to Tapper, the Pashtun have 'perhaps the most pervasive and explicit segmentary lineage ideology on the classic patterns, perpetuated not only in written genealogies but also in the territorial framework of tribal distribution.' Even so, the distribution of power within a group may vary considerably. Tapper contrasts the 'republican' organization of the border tribes with that of the sedentary Abdalis/Durranis whose well established tribal aristocracy had more in common with the leadership of the Kurds rather than that of the other Pashtun groups.[55] What kinds of factors can be held responsible for his degree of variation? The following two studies by Ahmed and Glatzer point to an interplay of ecological and historical variables which can produce widely variant political settings.

On the basis of his work among the eastern Pashtuns (the Yusufzais and the Mohmands) Ahmed emphasizes the formative impact of ecological factors on tribal organization. He distinguishes between two types of societies, those characterized by the principle of *nang* ('honor') and those organized on the basis of *qalang* ('rent', 'tax'). The tribal groups which inhabit the barren and unirrigated lands in the mountainous areas and support themselves by primitive modes of production fall into the *nang* category. Because of their restricted economic base wealth is fairly evenly distributed within these groups and they tend to be egalitarian in nature. In this setting, territorial boundaries coincide with segmentary lineages. In the absence of economic channels of power and mobility, tribal life revolves around the notion of honor as it is embodied in the *pashtunwali*. The egalitarian structure of these groups gives little authority to their leaders. Most commonly they are referred to as *maliks*, 'headmen', 'petty chiefs', or *mashars*, 'elders' rather than *khans*.[56] The *maliks* mostly represent the tribe in the interaction with outsiders but cannot interfere in internal matters, most of which are settled in *jirgas*, assemblies attended by all members of the tribe. On the other hand, *qalang* groups like the Swati Yusufzais and the sedentary Barakzai and Popalzai Durranis inhabit the fertile plains. Here irrigation produces a sufficient surplus to allow a hierarchical society to develop in which social status is linked to the economic base of the individual. This setting gives rise to powerful *khans*. Ahmed concedes that the emergence of a more stratified organization in a tribe cannot be explained by economic factors alone. Nevertheless he maintains that societies of the *qalang* type are more open to hierarchization in the interaction with outsiders. *Nang* groups, on the other hand, consistently defy all attempts at penetration.[57]

Pashtun tribalism has often been equated with nomadism. Indeed the Pashtuns are more strongly nomadic than the other ethnic groups of the region, furnishing eighty to ninety per cent of the total nomadic population of present-day Afghanistan. The most important nomadic groups are to be found among the Ghilzais and the Durranis. Among the Ghilzais, members of the Sulaiman Khel, Taraki, Nasir, and Kharoti carried on trade with the Indus basin and were economically more closely linked with northern India than the remainder of Afghanistan in the nineteenth century.[58] The Nurzai, Ishaqzai and Achakzai subdivisions of the Durranis are also known for their nomadic lifestyle. In his study of the Durrani nomads, Glatzer raises three important points which make it clear that Pashtun tribalism cannot be pressed into simplistic formulas.

Firstly, Glatzer points out that nomadism is not an essential aspect of Pashtun tribalism. Even among Pashtun groups with sizeable nomadic components, the majority of the population continued to rely on farming for their livelihood.[59] Secondly, the organization of the Durrani nomads fails to conform with the ideals of segmentary lineage organization despite the fact that they operate in a setting characterized by intertribal competition as described by Sahlins. While the patrilineal descent system may be used to explain relations with the settled population and to stress membership in the Pashtun nation, it is of little use for the definition of territorial divisions. Segmentary lineages play a negligible role in the formation of raiding parties and herding groups which tend to be extremely flexible in composition and to be based on common economic interest and close family relations rather than the fixed precepts of a ramifying genealogy.[60]

Leadership among the Pashtun nomads is an ephemeral office. The Nasir and Sulaiman Khel Ghilzais elected magistrates endowed with great authority, the so-called *tsalweshtis*, only in times of war or during their migrations which took them through the country of the hostile Wazir tribe.[61] Among the Durrani nomads, whose herding units tend to regroup frequently, those individuals who can secure access to summer pastures become 'seasonal' *khans*. In Glatzer's opinion, the extreme decentralization among the Durrani nomads is not only the result of economic and ecological factors but is occasioned by their relative distance from the state. Forming minorities within their respective tribes, the nomads were peripheral not only on the tribal level but also on the state level. Neither the Ghilzais who seized the Safawid throne in the eighteenth century nor the Durrani rulers of Qandahar and Kabul were of nomadic origin. While the Durrani nomads enjoyed some royal protection from the 1880s on, their pastures between the upper courses of the Murghab and Hari Rud rivers were located in remote regions which were of no strategical interest to the rulers of Kabul other than as a possible boundary cordon against the Russians. Accordingly, government presence remained minimal until the 1970s, allowing the nomads to remain 'a quasi-foreign matter in the administrative body of the state.' This leads to Glatzer's third thesis: the degree of hierarchization present within a tribe is directly linked to the intensity of its interaction with the state.[62]

Before moving on to specific case studies of sedentary Pashtun groups, one more general phenomenon of Pashtun organization needs to be mentioned, that of dichotomy. Like the Kurds many Pashtun groups align themselves with either of two larger blocs in their region. The Ghilzai tribes, for example, tend to polarize around two major *khans*.[63] In the nineteenth century Broadfoot observed that the Sulaiman Khel Ghilzais were split into two great blocs called *shammal* and *kaiser*.[64] According to Robinson, the Kharoti Ghilzais identified themselves as *tor gund* ('black faction'), as opposed to the Sulaiman Khel, who were *spin gund* ('white faction').[65] The Pashtun tribes of Khost and the Turis of Kurram are likewise divided into *spin* ('white') and *tor* ('black') alignments.[66] The eastern Pashtuns, particularly the Afridis, Orakzais, Bangash, Zaimukht, and Wazir are split into the *gar* and *samil* alliances.[67] In his analysis of the Yusufzais of Swat, Barth focussed on the formation of two great political blocs cutting across all tribal segments. It is his work which will form the point of departure for the following case study.

The Yusufzais of Swat

The Yusufzai case is somewhat peripheral to the Afghan setting both in terms of organization and history. Nonetheless this group has formed a lasting subject in the anthropological debate on tribes in the region. Barth's landmark study of 1959 and the criticisms (Asad 1972, Ahmed1976) and further anthropological research (Lindholm) which followed it have had the, certainly unintended, side effect of casting the Swat example as the paradigm of Pashtun organization. As the themes recurring in the discussion of Yusufzai organization mirror many of the topics already encountered in the above general introduction to the question of tribalism, a short summary of the different voices in the debate will be useful for the purposes of this chapter. The anthropogical studies concerning Swat fall, roughly speaking, into two camps. Barth and Lindholm emphasize the levelling mechanisms at work in Swati society and view it as acephalous and segmentary. Asad and Ahmed, on the other hand, stress the factors which set the landowning Yusufzai elite apart from the lower echelons of society. Another point of discussion concerns the authortiy exercised by the religious leaders and their relationship with the tribal elite. In the case of Swat, the threat of colonial intervention in the nineteenth and early twentieth centuries allowed Sufi dignitaries and their descendants to gain a broad followership and to set up centralized political institutions.

Characterized as 'the most numerous and powerful of the eastern Afghans,'[68] the Yusufzai Pashtuns of the Swat valley present an extreme version of Ahmed's *qalang* type. They entered the Swat valley as conquerors in the 1520s and formed a thin tribal aristocracy. While they only furnished one fifth of the total population, they controlled virtually all land, having forced the local population to become their clients or to take flight. The lush Swat valley with its intensive grain cultivation allowed the development of quasi-feudal conditions under which the Pashtun landowners collected as much as three fourths or four fifths of the gross grain crop from their tenants and were able to amass a big surplus.[69] Thus the Yusufzai of Swat are set apart from the other Pashtun groups in the region, which do not display such a strong social stratification. The Swati case also is peripheral to the history of Afghanistan. Relatively distant from the Sadozai centers of power, the Yusufzais of Swat did not even give nominal allegiance to the Durrani rulers.[70] From the middle of the nineteenth century on the British were the greatest political power in the region. But until the turn of this century, the administrators of Peshawar refrained from direct interference in Swat and simultaneously sheltered the leadership there from the interests of the Muhammadzai rulers of Kabul.[71]

Taking the social stratification of the Yusufzai setting into account, Barth characterizes the Pashtun overlords as a sharply delineated social group, an 'ethnic caste' in a hierarchical framework determined by parentage.

Internally, the Yusufzai Pashtuns are organized along segmentary lines. While landownership per se is the prerogative of the individual Pashtun household, access to land is defined on the basis of membership in a particular patrilineal descent group, a *khel*.[72] According to Yusufzai tradition, the original allotment of land took place immediately after the conquest of Swat in the sixteenth century. Shaikh Malli, a prominent religious dignitary, assigned different parts of the Swat valley to the major Yusufzai patrilineages, thus replicating their segmentary structure on the ground. In order to avoid inequalities, Shaikh Malli ordered that the lands should not become the permanent property of the lineages in question but should be re-allotted periodically within the *khels*. In this system of *wesh* each landowner was not entitled to certain fields but rather owned shares (*brakha*) representing a certain proportion of the total area redistributed. Barth claims that, until the 1920s at least, this system had actually operated among the eleven major Yusufzai lineages he studied.[73]

Thus the Yusufzai landowners were forced to migrate distances of up to thirty miles every ten years or so, whereas the tenants cultivating the ground stayed on. This confronted the landowners with the constantly arising need to create a new following for themselves. Barth characterizes this endeavor on the part of the individual Yusufzai landowners as the attempt to 'organize a central island of authority' in a 'politically amorphous sea of villagers'. On the basis of his claim of ownership to all land, the Pashtun *khan* attempts to bind as many followers as possible to himself on the basis of economic and house tenancy contracts. Another important institution is the men's house (*hujra*) presided over – and in great part financed – by the chief. By partaking of the *khan's* hospitality, the villagers formally acknowledge his political authority. Barth emphasizes the voluntary nature of these contracts between tenants and landlords: 'there is nowhere any *a priori* reason why a man should attach himself to any particular leader.' The landlord thus finds himself constantly competing for leadership with other Pashtuns residing on similar 'islands of authority'. One of the major factors for success in this rivalry is ownership in land, which not only secures a certain number of tenants but also generates sufficient wealth for prestige enhancing acts of hospitality. In addition, a Pashtun leader derives authority from his good reputation based on the notions of honor (*'izzat*) and shame (*sharm*): 'The ideal personality of a leader is virile and impetuous, given to extremes rather than compromise, sometimes unwise, but always brave.'[74]

Besides the leadership of the *khan,* Barth detects a 'saintly' style of leadership exercised by all men of religious standing, be they Sufi *pirs*, *sayyids*, *miyans* or mullahs.[75] The saints are outsiders to Pashtun organization and have no access to Yusufzai assemblies (*jirgas*). In return for their services as mediators in conflicts between individuals or bigger groups they receive non-circulating lands called *siri*. Unlike the lands allotted to the Sanusi mediators in Cyrenaica, the saints' property is not to be found in regions separating two hostile groups from one another. Rather, they receive land of inferior strategic and agricultural quality. Furthermore, the system of *wesh* requires that land alienated to a saint in a particular unit be equalized among the members of the segment. Thus the saints' holdings tend to be 'dispersed without particular reference to the borders between units in the land re-allotment system.'[76] While chiefs gain their standing on the basis of their reputation for honor, the saints make a name for themselves on the basis of their piety:

> Pride, rivalry and virility is expected of chiefs: such behaviour the Pathan villagers remember, encourage and admire. But these characteristics are relative, and are most clearly conceptualized in terms of their opposites: moderation, reasonableness and meekness. This complementary type of behaviour is expected of Saints, and the opposition is carried through to a remarkable extent – for example in the spectacular hospitality of chiefs as opposed to moderation bordering on miserliness among Saints, or in the immaculate white clothes of Saints in contrast to the showy brightness of the garments of many chiefs.[77]

Yet Barth also stresses the political nature of saintly leadership. As landowners they have a similar relationship with their tenants as their Pashtun counterparts. Apart from mediatory skills, a saint may rely on the numbers of followers he can bring to the field of contest. Furthermore, he may be linked to the prominent Pashtuns of his area by marriage alliances. But the dispersal of his property allows the saint to develop an alternative form of authority:

> [W]hile the dependants of a chief tend to be concentrated in his own ward and those immediately adjoining it, so that his political influence is contained within the segmentary hierarchy of re-allotment-units, the dependants of Saints are dispersed. Saints own much less land than chiefs and thus control far fewer dependants; but their channels of communication and influence extend much further. They spread their web of direct political influence over a much wider area. While the lands of chiefs help them to build a solid nucleus of control for purposes of adminstration and military dominance, the lands of Saints enable them to extend their influence over many communities, for purposes of arbitration, mediation, the collection of information, and political intrigue.[78]

In Barth's opinion, Yusufzai organization is segmentary and acephalous. But unlike the North African model, the Swat system does not maintain its balance by processes of fusion and fission fitting the theory of lineage organization. Rather, both chiefs and saints position themselves within a larger system of dichotomy. Thus the whole Yusufzai region is organized in a two-party system of blocs (*dala*) cutting across all segments of society. While their membership may vary, these blocs are permanent features which may be mobilized at times of conflict. Barth attributes the growth of this phenomenon to the allotment of land on the basis of segmentary principles which is bound to lead to tensions among agnatic collaterals. Paternal cousins find themselves working adjacent pieces of land and contending over unresolved issues of division. This underlying conflict is reflected in Pashtun kinship terminology, the word *tarbur*, 'father's brother's son' denoting rivalry and enmity. As coalitions between cousins are difficult or impossible, their families will seek alliances with outsiders.[79]

Yusufuzai organization automatically puts a ceiling on the amount of land, and, hence, power a Pashtun leader can accumulate: 'In the segmentary organization, a leader trying to expand the group of persons directly under his control creates opponents more rapidly than he creates supporters.' According to Barth, the constant balancing of power among the Pashtun leaders has precluded the emergence of any lasting stratification, such as the development of a centralized Khanate, among the Yusufzais. Yet he is aware that his model does not account sufficiently for the development of a Swati state with centralized government institutions in the 1920s. Barth attempts to solve this dilemma by claiming that the administrative machinery introduced by the newly established ruler with its centralized army, tax collection and modern communication had no significant bearing on the organization of the Yusufzai leadership. The ruler, Miangul 'Abd al-Wadud, a grandson of the famous Akhund of Swat (1794–1878), still was only able to maintain his power by continuously balancing bloc interests against each other. For Barth, Swat continued to be a land of 'freedom and rebellion' (*yaghistan*) even at the time of his fieldwork in 1954. In his view, the tribal system of opposed blocs still functioned vigorously on all levels below the superimposed administrative system.[80]

Talal Asad disputes Barth's notion that the ongoing balancing between two opposing blocs should be seen as the formative component of the political system of Swat. In his opinion, the Pashtun chiefs should not be conceptualized as individual 'islands of authority' but as members of a dominant class of landowners exploiting the landless. He also questions Barth's thesis that the political system rests on a web of dyadic contractual relationships of a voluntary nature. The fact that most land had become concentrated in the hands of a few Yusufzai landlords by the 1950s gave potential tenants little freedom of choice which leader to interact with. Thus Asad sees little reason for insecurity in the position of the dominant landlords of the region and, hence, the need of maximizing policies on their part. The only ones experiencing insecurity are small landholders and tenants:

> [I]n a society where a small group of landowners owns most of the land, where all subsistence is ultimately based on agriculture, where

> there is high population density, under-employment and land scarcity, where most non-landowners live barely above subsistence level, the landlord's dominant position is not problematic. The Pakhtun maintains his position by virtue of his control of land, not by cajoling the landless into accepting his authority.

Asad also misses the historical perspective in Barth's analysis of Swat society. While he agrees that there may have been a close coincidence between genealogical structure and landownership at the inception of Yusufzai rule in Swat, he points to the possibility that class differences became more pronounced with the arrival of the British in the nineteenth century, as the advent of cheap medicines and expensive modern firearms created a greater gap in wealth and political power.[81]

Like Asad, Ahmed doubts that Yusufzai society offers a great scope of maximizing strategies to those composing its lower strata, i. e. the tenants and peasants: 'A client, in theory, may have choices and strategies open to him but in practice, depending as he does for his land tenancy, "hujra" membership and a measure of protection on the Khan, would find it difficult to break the contract unilaterally.' In Ahmed's opinion, the vision of Swati society as based on 'social contracts' reveals not only Barth's own ethnocentrism but also the fact that he only had contact with the khanly minority of the Swat valley. Yusufzai organization lacks important criteria that would render it an acephalous, segmentary society. For one thing, the notion of unilineal descent is limited to a feudal military aristocracy which is set apart from the remainder of Swati society by ethnic and functional criteria. This stratification is reflected by the economic system which gives a pivotal position to the *khans* and is based on 'redistributional' rather than 'reciprocal' mechanisms. Furthermore, there are significant differences of status even among those claiming common descent. While accepting that the system of periodic re-allotment of lands may have had an equalizing effect in the past, Ahmed casts doubt on Barth's assumption that *wesh* formed a fundamental aspect of Pashtun organization well into the twentieth century. Rather, he points to evidence that – with the possible exception of a few 'pockets' in the Swat valley – this system gave way to a feudal, hierarchical stratification early in the nineteenth century. The official freezing of *wesh* by 'Abd al-Wadud in the 1920s finally made land alienable and thus eroded the role of the segmentary descent group as organizational principle once and for all.[82] Ahmed also disagrees with Barth's conclusion that the central state instituted by 'Abd al-Wadud from 1917 on remained exterior to Pashtun tribal organization. The establishment of a powerful centralized army combined with the disarmament of all potential rivals to power meant a significant blow to the Pashtun leadership. By taking over the collection of a fixed proportion of the taxes traditionally paid to the landlords the government assumed their redistributional powers to a great extent. For the remainder of 'Abd al-Wadud's reign (he abdicated in favor of his son in 1949) the Yusufzai *khans* saw their political choices dwindle: '"Maximizing" man was up against the strait-jacket structural framework of a highly centralized state.'[83]

Ahmed attributes Barth's failure to account for the emergence of the State of Swat and its pervasive impact on Yusufzai social structure to his limited view of the role of charismatic religious leadership. In particular, he takes issue with Barth's application of the same frame of reference for the political roles of 'Khans' and 'Saints'. The 'saintly' category as created by Barth does not distinguish between the various men of religious standing active on the village level, that is, the mullahs running the village mosques and the *miyans* or *sayyids*, and the ideal of true saintly leadership exercised by Sufis who place themselves outside the material world of the village. For Ahmed neither the village 'mullah' nor the Sufi saint enjoy the political prerogatives typical of the Yusufzai leadership. Yet they may emerge as influential leaders in times of great religious crisis brought about by the confrontation with British colonialism. The Akhund of Swat, Mastan Mulla and Miangul 'Abd al-Wadud spearheaded movements against British intervention and were able to create a broad followership for themselves at different times in Swat history, thus overriding the customary leadership of the Yusufzai *khans*. Ahmed points to the political systems instituted by the Akhund of Swat and his grandson as proof that Yusufzai society in the nineteenth and twentieth centuries was not as acephalous as Barth would have it.[84]

Contrary to Ahmed, Lindholm feels that religious leadership does not contradict segmentary structures. Rather, this system of 'ordered anarchy' with numerous and ephemeral small-scale leaders in every village presupposes the emergence of saintly mediators at certain conjunctions.[85] For Lindholm, the Yusufzai society of Swat valley represents 'a typical, and perhaps prototypical' acephalous segmentary system.[86] By comparison, the dichotomous bloc formation as described by Barth plays only a secondary role in determining political action. The egalitarian principles of segmentary organization allow for two possible forms of leadership, both of which are generated by the confrontation with outsiders on the regional level.

1) Secular leadership. This form of leadership emerges at times of aggression against outsiders in a setting reminiscent of that of 'predatory expansion' described by Sahlins. The war against weaker neighbors, so for instance, against the Kohistanis north of Swat, gives prominent men the opportunity to enhance their standing by proving their fighting abilities and securing spoils which in turn guarantee a larger following.[87] This form of authority only lasts as long if offers benefits to the followers:

> Because domination is thought to be simply the temporary rule of a co-equal, Pukhtun are willing to accept secular rulers with a minimum of moral outrage. Yet, simultaneously, they do not give them any

loyalty; ties to the leader are purely pragmatic and are justified solely in terms of the advantages gained by submission.[88]

2) Charismatic religious leadership. While hostilities within the village fall into the jurisdiction of the *jirga* or are allowed to run their course, confrontations between villages call for the mediation by a saint. Saints will also take a leading role in times of aggression by powerful outsiders. During the three recorded wars with the kingdom of Dir saintly leadership provided the Yusufzais of Swat with the necessary unity to beat back the invaders.[89] While his political role will recede with the passing of the crisis, the saint will maintain his reputation of authority transcending segmentary differences: 'Religious leadership never disappears; it is merely subordinated.'[90]

Lindholm's comparison of the political systems of Swat and Dir is of particular interest for the purposes of this chapter. Both valleys are sheltered from the main routes of invasion in the region by rugged mountain ranges. The Yusufzai Pashtuns are dominant in both regions and display a parallel social organization. Yet, their political structures display profound differences. Interestingly, Lindholm's analysis turns Ahmed's concept of *nang* and *qalang* on its head. In his opinion, the lush Swat valley is characterized by an almost prototypical segmentary organization. The ecological setting in Dir, on the other hand, is 'dry and harsh', allowing only for a low density of population. But contrary to Swat, the leadership in Dir was well entrenched, forming a petty princedom. Lindholm attributes this high degree of variation to differences in the larger political setting. The ongoing confrontation with the neighboring kingdom of Chitral forced the Painda Khel Yusufzais of Dir to develop a more complex political organization, a so-called secondary state:

> Instead of the rough and impoverished Kohistani... the primary enemy of the Painda khel was the Kingdom of Chitral. This ancient Kingdom of uncertain origins had developed as a center of the slave trade and as a parasite on caravans to China. While the Swati Yusufzai were struggling to defeat a society which was, organizationally, even more fragmented than their own..., the warriors of Dir were attempting to conquer a relatively complex and stratified society with a hereditary King. In emulation of their more centrally organized and hierarchical opponents, the leaders of the Painda khel were also granted extraordinary powers by their followers.[91]

Likewise the concentration of power Swat witnessed with the rise of Miangul 'Abd al-Wadud was the product of external pressure. The British alliance with Dir in the early twentieth century caused the Yusufzai *khans* to lend their support to the grandson of the Akhund of Swat, allowing him to gain a lasting ascendancy.

The case of Swat amply demonstrates how much the opinions differ on the applicability of the model of segmentary lineage organization to the Yusufzai example. Likewise the question of tribal resilience vis-à-vis the state receives varying interpretations. On the one hand, Barth views the tribe as impervious to centralizing tendencies. While disagreeing on the degree of stratification already present in Swat in the nineteenth and twentieth century, Asad, Ahmed and Lindholm, on the other hand, point to a clear linkage between internal stratification and the external pressure generated by the British colonialists and other powerful neighbors. In the next case study, I will discuss Ahmed's work on the Mohmands, a tribe which has been able to limit penetration by larger imperial systems and successfully adhered to the typical characteristics of *nang* organization until the 1970s, the time of Ahmed's fieldwork.

The Mohmand Agency

The Mohmands exemplify a typical 'border' tribe because they are to be found in equal numbers on both sides of the Durand line established in 1893. In the 1960s their total number was estimated at 400,000.[92] Ahmed's study focusses on the groups residing on, or contiguous to, Pakistani territory. Accordingly, he distinguishes between the encapsulated 'Settled Area Mohmands' (SAM) who were incorporated by the Pakistani government in 1951 and the 'Tribal Area Mohmands' (TAM) who were placed beyond direct government control from this date on. The comparison of SAM and TAM on the basis of their adherence to *pashtunwali*, the formative element of *nang* society, forms the core of Ahmed's study. His main thesis is that tribal ideal and empiric reality coincide closely in the TAM setting, where the tribesmen have only accepted partial economic penetration by the government while 'jealously guarding social and political autonomy' as well as tribal values.[93] Although the elements considered typical of Pashtun organization tend to undergo some change among the Settled Area Mohmands, they remain basic aspects of Pashtun identity and tend to be observed particularly by the dominant lineages. Like Barth, Ahmed assigns a formative impact to cousin rivalry (*tarburwali*) but locates the resulting dichotomy at a lower level of tribal organization.

Both TAM and SAM represent *nang* societies. The Mohmands arrived in the Peshawar valley in the early part of the sixteenth century, subsequent to the Yusufzais. In 1550 they lost the fertile regions of Hashtnagar and Mardan to the latter and were pushed to the barren, inaccessible mountains which form their present location. Thus Mohmand identity was formulated not only in the confrontation with the surrounding greater empires, such as the Mughals, Durranis, Sikhs and British, but also in antagonism to their wealthy Yusufzai cousins controlling all the rich agricultural land of the region. As their lands only yielded a limited subsistence, the Mohmands took to raiding the flatlands and taxing passing caravans as an additional source of income. Until the decline of the Mughal empire in the middle of the eighteenth century a great number of Mohmands found employment as soldiers of fortune in India. With the establishment of the British in Peshawar in 1849, Mohmand economic strategies became more limited, and many tribesmen were forced to become tenants of their Yusufzai neighbors.[94]

Unlike the Yusufzais of Swat, the Mohmands did not conquer their lands from a sizeable autochthonous population. Furnishing between 92 and 96 percent of the population, they form a broad stratum of gun-carrying tribesmen. Ahmed views the Mohmands as 'an acephalous, segmentary, egalitarian tribal society... in the classic mould of British social anthropology.' He distinguishes various levels of tribal organization, extending from the tribe (*star qam*), i.e. the Mohmands, over the clan (*qam*) to the household (*kor*), which forms the basic unit of production. In his analysis of Mohmand organization, Ahmed does not limit himself to the local terminology because of its lack of specificity. Below the level of the clan, he lists the sub-clan, the section, and the sub-section, all of which are referred to as *khel* by the Mohmands. Despite its segmentary organization Mohmand political behavior does not fit neatly either into the North African pattern or Barth's model of a pervasive bloc formation. The strong impact of cousin rivalry (*tarburwali*) makes a relatively low level of Mohmand organization, the sub-section defined by three or four ascendants held in common, the primary arena of conflict. Groups involved in a confrontation will rather seek outside alliances than conform with the ideal of fission and fusion suggested by the segmentary model. This bloc formation, again, is limited to the level of the sub-section and never includes the tribe as a whole: 'the killing is restricted to and done by members sharing close unilineal descent'. The intensity of *tarburwali* limits the amount of wealth and power a tribesman may acquire. Yet this practice is less motivated by material gain rather than concepts linked to honor: shame (*ghairat*), prestige (*'izzat*) and Pashtun identity (*pashtu*). While creating conditions seeming anarchic to the outsider, the enactment of *tarburwali* essentially serves to reconfirm the key principles of *nang* society and thus reproduces an internal sense of order.[95]

For Ahmed, the position of Mohmand leadership fits neatly into his concept of *nang* society. Technically, every male member of the tribe may aspire to leadership. This office is not inherited: 'The good and great qualities of a leader are buried with him in his grave.'[96] Generally recognized leadership qualities are bravery, generosity, concern for the lineage and wisdom in council. Ahmed distinguishes four kinds of tribal leaders:

1) *malik* – 'petty chief', 'headman',[97]
2) *mashar* – 'elder' (a more informal position than *malik*),[98]
3) government appointed *malik* (usually recruited from either of the first two categories),
4) *kashar* – 'young man' (a less influential leader who challenges, but simultaneously aspires to, the authority of the *malik* and the *mashar*).

A fifth style of leadership listed by Ahmed only comes to the fore at times of great emergency. Religious leaders only assume a leading role in times of supratribal crisis. But on the tribal level religious men ordinarily play a subordinate part. Islam is seen as an integral part of Mohmand identity, having been 'inherited' from the apical ancestor of the Pashtuns, the Muslim Qais 'Abd al-Rashid. Yet, given the formative role of *pashtunwali* for tribal behavior, little importance is attached to questions of doctrine or religious status. Unlike Yusufzai society, there is no 'saintly' class to be found among the Mohmands. Ahmed differentiates two groups of religious men, that of the *sayyids* or *miyans* and that of the mullahs. Forming a quasi endogamous group, the *miyans* assume a neutral role in the tribal setting. Their lands are located at the interstices of Mohmand sections or subsections. While their outward characteristics resemble those of the Barthian saint, the position of the *miyans* in the Mohmand region is basically insecure. Contrary to Gellner's *igurramen*, they have no part in the political processes in the village, such as the election of chiefs. During times of intratribal conflict they lack the coercive force to effect a settlement between the warring sections. Their religious status only allows them to keep the lines of communication open and to evacuate the wounded and sick as well as women and children. While the *miyans* claim social equality with the Mohmands, the mullahs are complete outsiders to, and entirely dependent on, tribal society. Unlike the *miyans*, who have a steady residence in the region and alternative sources of income, the mullahs are brought to the village for a fixed period of time on a contractual basis. Their duty is to look after the village mosque and to perform routine functions during rites of passage.[99]

In their relationship with the outside powers, the Mohmands are protected by the inaccessibility of their terrain and its uninviting economic prospects. An invasion of their country would require great efforts while yielding little booty in return. But this does not entail that the Mohmands should be seen as a small-scale isolated primitive community: 'Astraddle across the Agency-District border and the international border, the Mohmands interact with the state to their own advantage and when and how it suits them.' Mohmand tribal identity was not formulated in a setting of splendid isolation but in the process of 'battle sequences' with larger systems. For this reason, Ahmed is of the opinion that Mohmand tribal life is better described as 'institutionalized dissidence' than as a state of 'ordered anarchy'.[100] In the sixteenth and seventeenth centuries the Mohmands were able to hold their position by alternately supporting and defying Mughal interests. Although they were not able to pose a lasting challenge to Mughal rule by themselves, they were just one of many tribes in the region following a similar strategy. Ahmed holds the cumulative effect of the continuous rebellions by all the border tribes responsible for the ultimate decline of the Mughal empire.

Rather than attempting to establish direct authority in the region, the Mughals and their successors contented themselves with a system of indirect control on the basis of large allowances. After the advent of the British, the border tribes were able maintain their independence by formally accepting British sovereignty in exchange for non-interference. The treaties concluded with the British in the nineteenth century continue to be honored by the Pakistani government to the present day. From the beginning of the twentieth century on, the British government began to interfere in the tribal setting by appointing local leaders as *maliks* and tying them into a system of allowances and political favors. The authority of these government-created *maliks* was never quite accepted by the other tribesmen, and they remained little more than 'glorified tourist chiefs.' Their authority was also limited by their general profusion. In the 1970s every appointed Mohmand *malik* represented an average of 43 tribesmen. While the appointment of leaders opened a 'window' to tribal society for the British, it was not an effective means of controlling its political behavior: 'Mohmand raids and imperial reprisals form the ebb and flow of Mohmand history until the departure of the British in 1947.'[101]

For Ahmed, the high degree of continuity in Mohmand tribal life is the direct outcome of their segmentary, acephalous organization. Whereas he accepts the validity of a Marxist approach for stratified settings such as that of Swat, he is of the opinion that conflict in Mohmand society cannot be analyzed appropriately on the basis of class divisions. Ahmed is strongly aware of the impact of administrators on present-day local politics. Yet he feels that their role should not be overstated. While a Political Agent may influence the course of politics in tribal areas, he is not in the position to change the inherent social structures that gave rise to a particular conflict in the first place. Nonetheless Ahmed's comparison of the divergent developments in TAM and SAM after 1951 point to a pervasive impact of the progressive encapsulation of Mohmand society by the Pakistani government. First of all, the incorporation of SAM into the Pakistani administration affected the economic life in the region:

> Over the last 400 years TAM and SAM functioned within a similar geo-political situation. Their sources of income were in the main similar: 1 primitive agriculture; 2 raids into the richer Settled Areas and robbing caravans; 3 allowances (from Kabul and/or the British); 4

> taxes which they claimed either on caravan routes through the Gandab... or... on goods brought down the Kabul river; and 5 migration and money remitted home. Today divergences between TAM and SAM sources of income have emerged largely as a consequence of the political division in 1951. In TAM the sources of income are: 1 primitive agriculture; 2 political allowances, which are small, and hardly matched by increasing prices and increasing demands; 3 trade, national and international, legal and illegal; and finally 4 government employment. SAM sources of income, on the other hand, are largely based on agriculture and their fields. They have neither allowances nor trade to fall back on although many Belawals have successfully found government employment.[102]

Consisting overwhelmingly of small landholders, SAM society as yet lacks the exploitative relations typical of peasant societies. Still, the SAM tribesmen are clearly disadvantaged in comparison with their relatives in the tribal areas. Located in the regions immediately beyond the Pakistani administration, the TAM have been showered with a disproportionate amount of government favors in the form of electricity, schools and dispensaries. The introduction of development schemes in the 1970s did not coincide with the influx of outsiders to the region but rather benefitted junior lineages at the cost of the established *maliks*. The SAM regions were mostly bypassed by these developments. The relatively disadvantaged position of SAM is also reflected in their internal organization. The SAM leaders are not as powerful as those of the TAM. Their functions have been taken over to a great extent by government agencies such as the police. SAM relations with the government are characterized by dependence and are usually limited to the lower echelons of the administrative hierarchy. The TAM leadership, on the other hand, interacts with the head of the local administration frequently and on a footing of equality and friendship.[103]

Ahmed predicts that the sudden availability of large sums of money and new sources of employment in the TAM setting are bound to affect traditional Pashtun values. He maintains, however, that TAM life still coincided closely with the norms of *pashtunwali* at the time of his fieldwork. Despite their encapsulated state SAM also continued to adhere to key concepts of *pashtunwali*, such as *tor* (the protection of female modesty) and *tarburwali*. But other aspects of tribal organization had become weakened in the SAM setting. Despite the fact that SAM still derived their identity from the principles of their tribal code Ahmed observed that their behavior displayed an increasing split between 'speaking' and 'doing' *pashtu*.[104] While SAM still attempted to live up to the ideals of *pashtunwali*, their TAM counterparts dismissed these efforts as futile. Ahmed's list of TAM and SAM perceptions of themselves and each other makes clear that TAM formulated their ideal of tribal behavior as antithesis of SAM whom they categorized as 'soft'. SAM, while admitting that they had lost their former freedom, emphasized that they were more 'civilized' in comparison to the 'rough' and 'uncultured' TAM. According to Ahmed the dependent status and comparative poverty of SAM is also reflected in physical features, such as body size and weight. He even detects differences in general bearing which would seem to confirm TAM prejudices towards their settled relatives. SAM are 'stooped in posture' and 'reflect a state of anorexia towards life'. The 'untrammelled and unbound'[105] TAM man gets a much better rating. Walking 'straight with head erect' and displaying a 'continuing zest and appetite for life,' he emerges as a closer match to Ahmed's ideal of tribal man. The following characterization of the Tribal Area Mohmand is oddly reminiscent of the romantic description given by Ahmed's colonial forebear Oliver, which I have quoted in the introduction to this section.

> In the most profound sense he is an intellectual and cultural nomad. He travels light and carries his social intheritance in his genealogical charter and his political inheritance in his Code and the two, so closely interlinked and interrelated, are always at hand at all times for reference. He is free and being free as no peasant can be he is imprisoned in his Code; he is defined only within its boundaries – outside them he looks the world in the eye and owns no masters or position superior to his.[106]

TAM man is not bound to accept hierarchies imposed by outsiders. The egalitarian structure of his tribe, along with the low productivity and inaccessibility of his land do not lend themselves to any lasting stratification. Although the British managed to bring forth a class of privileged leaders, they were unable to give these leaders legitimacy in the eyes of their fellow tribesmen or to affect the general distribution of power on a permanent basis.

The Pashtun Tribes of Khost

The following two case studies concern groups located in regions belonging to present-day Afghanistan. The Khost basin in Paktia province lies immediately west of the border between Afghanistan and Pakistan. Surrounded by mountains 7,500–10,500 feet high, the basin itself has an altitude of approximately 3,000–4,000 feet and is traversed by the river Samul from west to east. A caravan route frequented by Ghilzai nomads partly follows the course of the river and partly crosses the uncultivated plain on the outskirts of the basin.[107] While Khost is not completely isolated it is located sufficiently far from all regional centers of power to allow the development of a social structure similar to that of the Mohmands. The works of Janata, Hassas and Steul portray the organization of the heterogeneous Pashtun tribes of Khost in terms very close to Ahmed's characteristic *nang* society. Again we are presented with a close match with the ideal of segmentary lineage organization. The patterns of leadership observed among the Khost tribes approximate those of Mohmands closely. As in the Mohmand setting, the Pashtun code of honor plays a decisive role in shaping the tribesmen's attitudes towards their fellows and the outside world.

The trade passing through the basin of Khost has had a minimal impact on the local economy. The life of the overwhelming majority of the population of approximately 100,000 souls revolves around agriculture. In particular, the irrigated lands along the river Samul are considered prime agricultural land and allow the production of a small surplus.[108] While the society of Khost thus lacks the 'severe economic poverty' Ahmed lists as a characteristic of the *nang* setting,[109] it is in many ways comparable to that of the Mohmand groups. Steul describes the Pashtuns of Khost as an 'acephalous society of the segmentary type'. Like the Mohmand groups described by Ahmed they form a broad tribal stratum, furnishing 96 percent of the population. The distribution of land is similar to that of the Mohmands, consisting of small average holdings.[110]

The titles and functions of the leadership among the Pashtuns of Khost coincide with the examples given by Ahmed for the Mohmands. The head of the fraternal joint family is the *mashar.* Steul distinguishes between two kinds of leaders with the title *malik*. On the lower level men with the title *malik* represent the village in the interaction with outsiders. With greater government interference in the twentieth century, the *malik* came to function as synapsis between village and government interests. His position increasingly resembled that of an elected mayor, with the exception that his authority within the village was limited. The *jirga* attended by all tribesmen continued to be in charge of all village matters and the *malik* was solely entrusted with the execution of its decisions concerning communal projects. The decisions taken in these assemblies are greatly influenced by a higher level of leadership categorized by Steul as *khans/Maliks*.[111] The *khans* are set apart from the *Maliks* by their comparative wealth in landed property. Situated in the rich irrigated regions of Khost, they are able to create a followership for themselves from among their clients, a situation reminiscent of Swat. But the majority of the leaders in the region are *Maliks* who derive their influence less from their wealth than from their reputation as *ghairatman*, men who live up to the ideals of *pashtunwali.* While landownership is an important aspect of Pashtun identity, the *amount* of land controlled has no bearing on a man's influence. The position of the *khans/Maliks* strongly resembles that of their Mohmand counterparts. They have to prove their leadership qualities continuously by offering protection to their followers in times of conflict or material need. On the basis of their reputation as powerful men and exemplary Pashtuns they are able to act as 'opinion leaders' on the village level and thus shape the process of decision making. But given the egalitarian structure of Khost society it would be unthinkable for a *khan/Malik* to act against the will of his tribesmen. Functioning as the spokesman of his group, he represents its collective authority but is not set apart from his fellow tribesmen otherwise. The Pashtun concept that each man is sovereign precludes concentration of power. Tribal councils are attended by all men of the community and decisions are made strictly on the basis of consensus. The relationships between the next higher levels of organization, family, lineage, clan, etc. are characterized by a similar notion of self-determination and equality. Pashtun genealogy thus primarily forms the basis for the development of solidarity groups on the basis of common descent but does not allow for any kind of institutionalized hierarchization.[112] Yet Janata points out that the acephalous organization of Pashtun society should not be understood to imply 'anarchy' or 'democracy'. While a Pashtun leader may only act as a *primus inter pares,* his voice will gain added weight with increasing age. Noting the respect accorded to the opinions of elder men, Janata therefore prefers to describe the Pashtun political system as a 'gerontocracy of whitebeards'. Moreover, he points to the existence of dominant lineages with hereditary leadership (*khan khel*) in other regions of the province of Paktia.[113]

The strong role of *pashtunwali* limits the authority of the religious leadership in a similar manner as in the Mohmand setting. Thus the role of the mullahs of the Khost basin can be compared to that of their counterparts in the Mohmand region in all respects. The *sayyids* of Khost, by contrast, appear to enjoy a position somewhat more powerful than the *sayyids/miyans* among the Mohmands. Most of them are prosperous landowners and enjoy a high reputation for their generosity as expressed by their hospitality and almsgiving. Unlike the possessions of the Barthian saints their lands tend to be concentrated around their residence. The broad followership of the *sayyids* thus cannot be explained by their economic position as powerful landowners. Rather, it is their reputation for piety reaching in some cases beyond the province of Paktia which generates their following. While outsiders to Pashtun society, they play an important role in the politics of Khost basin and, unlike their Mohmand counterparts, they have a voice in the *jirga*.[114]

According to Steul, the *pashtunwali* is not a fixed legal code but may vary according to socio-economic factors, such as nomadism or intermixture with non-Pashtuns. He agrees with Ahmed and Janata & Hassas that the *pashtunwali* consists of more than judicial sanctions. Governing all aspects of Pashtun behavior, it serves as a marker of Pashtun identity.[115] For the Pashtuns of Khost, the notions of *nang* and *tura* can be identified as the key concepts by which the standing of a Pashtun man is measured. *Nang* implies the altruistic aspect of ideal Pashtun behavior. A *nangialai* will protect the honor (*namus*) of his family, lineage, clan, and even the entire Pashtun nation as well as the integrity of its land, thus ensuring the continued existence of his group in a hostile world. *Tura* ('sword') on the other hand, involves the protection of individual interests. It is an aggressive principle by which a Pashtun prevents all attacks on his honor and his property by fellow tribesmen. The fact that the majority of conflicts among the Khosti tribes revolve around real or supposed attacks on land at first sight seems to confirm the often quoted proverb that *zan* ('woman'), *zar* ('gold), and *zamin* ('land') form the basis of all altercations in Pashtun society. Yet Steul and Janata & Hassas second Ahmed's view that conflict is not necessarily motivated by material gain. Ownership in land forming the basis of Pashtun identity, every invasion of it, whether real or perceived, implies an attack on a man's prestige and is bound to elicit an aggressive response.[116]

The Ghilzais

Anderson's fieldwork concentrated on the regions of Ghazni and Logar. Nonetheless his articles concern general issues of Pashtun organization and his observations seem to concern the entire Ghilzai confederacy. He portrays Ghilzai society as acephalous and segmentary. While contact with other tribes or larger polities may bring about a certain amount of internal centralization, this is not a permanent feature and does not necessarily entail greater authority. Moreover, Anderson points to an interesting tension in the way leadership is conceived of at the various levels of tribal organization.

The Ghilzais are an overwhelmingly sedentary group and occupy the regions traditionally known as the core of 'Afghanistan', in addition to the adjacent areas acquired in the course of their history:

> Ghilzai are a group of patrilineally related, territorially contiguous, named tribes whose homeland (*wtan*) is that portion of the total Pakhtun country lying south of the Kabul River, between the Spin Ghar [Safed Koh] and Takht-i Suleyman ranges on the east and the Hazarajat on the west down to the vicinity of Kandahar.[117]

Whereas there have been increases in population density, the basic distribution of the Ghilzai tribes has remained the same since the early nineteenth century. Ranging in altitude from 4,500 to 6,000 feet, their country lends itself to wheat and hay farming on the basis of rainfall and irrigation. The specialized nature of their production has the effect that the Ghilzais depend on trade with the surrounding bazaar towns for their daily neccessities.[118]

The identity of the Ghilzais was mainly formed in their competition with the Abdalis/Durranis which is documented from the early Safawid period.

In 1722 they were able to take the center stage by conquering Isfahan under the leadership of the Hotak tribe and bringing Safawid rule to an end. Yet subsequent to their seven-year hegemony at the former Safawid capital the Ghilzais found their political fortunes increasingly eclipsed in favor of their Abdali/Durrani rivals. Anderson points to some variation in leadership styles among the Ghilzais. In his opinion, the hereditary khanship found among certain groups can be explained by the nature of their interaction with surrounding polities. The *khan khel* ('lord lineage') of the Hotak, for example, was formed by the family which played a leading role in the interaction both with the Safawid and Durrani rulers. The case of the alleged *khan khel* among the Jabbar Khel of Hisarak is less clear. While pointing to the possibility that such a dominant group evolved during Jabbar Khel resistance to the British presence during the First Anglo-Afghan War, Anderson suggests that the notion of this group as the 'rulers' of the Ghilzais may have been the product of the British preoccupation with the need to keep the approaches to Kabul open.[119] For Anderson, these and other examples of centralized leadership among the Ghilzais form an exception rather than the rule. Contrary to the Durranis with their entrenched stratification between landlord and peasant, the Ghilzais form a broad tribal stratum which fulfills all of Gellner's requirements for a segmentary society.[120]

Like Ahmed and Steul, Anderson lists three categories of leadership: *mashar*, *malik*, and *khan*. The Ghilzai *maliks* may be compared to their counterparts in the Khost setting. They simply function as 'the government's termini of official communication'. True leadership rests with the *mashar*, the head of the household (*kor*), and the *khan*. Although the Ghilzais conceptualize the higher levels of tribal organization as extended versions of the household, Anderson points out an inherent tension between the styles of leadership associated with the persons of the *mashar* and the *khan*. On the household level, the *mashar* exercises a nearly absolute authority:

> The mashar owns the land, commands those who work on and subsist from it, represents them to others as an integral unit that is an extension of his person, and generally derives their identities from his own in a metaphor of 'fatherhood'. Sons, for example, have no independent economic or political identities apart from their father during his lifetime... [121]

The *khan*, by contrast, is in no position to command his fellow tribesmen or demand taxes from them. His position reflects 'influence rather than power',[122] and is primarily based on achievement. As a 'self-financed public servant' he creates a following for himself by 'feeding people', that is, providing hospitality and patronage for his fellows. His second attribute, the ability 'to tie the knot' refers to his ability to mediate among his followers and to represent the group in its interaction with outsiders. At the time of Anderson's fieldwork in the 1970s this ideal of khanly leadership was becoming further and further removed from reality, as influential men increasingly used modern agricultural machinery for the purpose of maximizing their own profit instead of employing it for the good of their community. This raises the question whether such khanly qualities are more closely identified with a 'golden past' rather than the political realities in the tribal setting. Nevertheless, Anderson's discussion reflects that the *conceptualization* of leadership among the Ghilzai closely coincides with the ideal of segmentary organization. But the Ghilzais do not mirror Gellner's theory that an egalitarian tribal setting requires a superimposed layer of religious specialists. Similar to that of the Mohmands, Ghilzai organization leaves little room for the development of a pronounced religious leadership. Mullahs are outsiders to tribal society, holding a rank similar to that of the village barbers. Mullahs, *sayyids* and Sufi pirs alike are 'assiduously' kept out of tribal affairs. Anderson makes no mention of any form of mediation on their part. Yet he allows for a greater scope of activities for religious dignitaries on the fringes of Ghilzai territory where tribal allegiances have become diluted because of intermixture with other groups.[123]

This brings my review of ethnographic studies on the Pashtuns to an end. The material presented helps to understand the relationship between the Pashtun leaders and their fellow tribesmen, as well as certain aspects of Pashtun political behavior. One important feature is the lack of centralization. While the Pashtuns are aware of belonging to a larger nation (*ulus*), political unions above the level of the tribe tend to be short-lived. The egalitarian structure of an ideal *nang* type society does not allow sustained military efforts or permanent conquests. Among the Afridis, for example, internal dissensions were only put aside during times of external aggression. But even at times of war there was no centralized military command, as

> each party is headed by its own Malik. On taking to the field, each man brings with him a sheepskin full of flour, and the amount of ammunition that he can manage to collect; but, should hostilities be protracted beyond the time that the supply of provisions will last, the tribes are either kept together and fed by contributions from villages in the neighbourhood, or disperse for a few days to make ammunition and to replenish their commissariat; but, should the latter course be adopted, it frequently happens that mistrust in each other and the fear of treachery in their neighbours prevent their again uniting.[124]

Ahmed likewise notes the 'blitzkrieg' aspects of Pashtun warfare, as well as its 'seasonal' nature:

A typical clash ... is a short raid, usually at sunrise or sunset, culminating in the capture of the village or booty like cattle. The glory of participation in an encounter, not the setting up of a dynasty or the lengthy involvement with administration that it implies, is the motivating factor.

[Tribal warfare] is invariably linked with the pattern of crops and cultivation. Engagements tend to be fought before or after the harvest and many a leader has discovered to his dismay that his followers have melted away at the climax of a battle if the current crop has to be harvested.[125]

Wars taking place at a higher level of organization unfolded according to similar dynamics. For the events surrounding the power struggles between various Sadozai princes in the early nineteenth century Elphinstone observed that the armies involved were comparatively small, never exceeding 10,000 men on either side. Moreover, battles were often decided by shifting allegiances rather than bloodshed: 'The victory is decided by some chief's going over to the enemy; on which the greater part of the army either follows his example or takes to flight.'[126]

As Barth has convincingly argued, segmentary organization automatically puts a ceiling on the amount of power a Pashtun leader may accumulate. His position rests with his ability to maintain followers rather than personal wealth. This also applies to the theoretical head of all Pashtuns, who had to portray himself as a *primus inter pares* in order to gain the allegiance of his fellow tribesmen. In this sense, the role of the Muhammadzai kings may be compared to that of the Mongol *khans* of the twelfth to fourteenth centuries, who gained their followership less by means of a coercive administrative machinery but on the basis of personal followership:

The steppe khan was surrounded by no pomp, ceremony, or mystery to clothe his kingship in a nimbus of the divine in the way that Iranian, Roman, or Chinese emperors were revealed. His purpose was down-to-earth: to obtain and distribute wealth. Great emphasis was placed on the quality of generosity... Even more basic was the quality of warrior and leader of men... [new paragraph] In a steppe empire... the bond between the khan and the tribal chief was the bond between leader and follower... but between the two men as persons not as offices. So personal was this bond... that at the khan's death, unless his successor recreated the empire on a similar personal basis, the empire soon dissolved.[127]

But can all tribal behavior be predicted on the basis of a particular social structure? Is there anything specifically 'Pashtun' in the identity and political stance of the groups under review? Gellner's dictum of the 'dragon-teeth quality' of the leadership in a segmentary society certainly suggests that such a setting is able to withstand centralizing policies more easily than societies which display a greater degree of inherent stratification. Therefore it might be argued that the strategies of tribes organized on the basis of segmentary lineage organization take a specific shape which sets them apart from other groups. The previous chapter has shown that the society of Lesser Turkistan and Badakhshan was characterized by a greater degree of hierarchization on the basis of genealogy and/or wealth than that of the Pashtuns. The selection of the Uzbek leadership was based in great part on notions of genealogical seniority. The Uzbek *begs* or *khans* were said to possess more authority than their Pashtun counterparts. Forming part of Mir Murad Beg's chiefdom, they enjoyed military grants and collected revenues. Studies on Badakhshan document a great social distance between the ruling elite and the subjects. Yet on a different level certain parallels between the relations of power among the Uzbeks or Tajiks on the one hand and the Pashtuns on the other may be discerned. Both in Lesser Turkistan and Badakhshan the relationships between the leading families display a great degree of dispersion of power which might be appropriately termed as 'political segmentation'. For the Uzbek leaders at least, there is little evidence that their political roles fundamentally differed from those of the Pashtuns. Nor do we know whether their positions were effectively more stable. Because of its brokerage position between local interests and external political forces, the contours of tribal leadership – whether Pashtun or Uzbek – are in great part shaped by the larger political setting, possibly more so than by 'grown' genealogical relationships. Another important aspect of Pashtun identity is the struggle against hierarchy, oppression and state. Indeed the rejection of all external authority can be linked to Pashtun notions of equality and honor.[128] Yet this phenomenon is by no means specific to societies characterized by a segmentary lineage organization but has also been documented for groups with a less pronounced tribal structure, such as the Chechka Uzbeks of Takhar and Qunduz.[129]

Despite the reciprocal mechanisms commonly at work all Pashtun behavior cannot be explained solely as the outcome of a fiercely egalitarian 'groundswell'. The cases described in this section make it clear that tribal life is impinged on by a number of variables which should not be viewed in isolation from each other. It is evident that the conjunction of a particular set of ecological and historical factors brought about the political structure unique to Swat. The formation of tribal structures is not only influenced by local ecological/economic variables but also by the historical developments within a particular tribe, such as its previous migrations and its intermixture with other groups in the course of its settlement.[130] Most importantly, the forces encountered in the wider political setting play a crucial role in the creation of relationships of power and the articulation of tribal identity. While there is some difference of opinion concerning the resilience of individual tribes to centralizing tendencies, there is nowadays general agreement that tribal positions are overwhelmingly formulated in relation to the next larger political entity no matter how close or distant, or how powerful it may be. 'Tribe and state,' says Tapper, 'are best thought of as two opposed modes of thought or models of organization that form a single system.'[131]

THE PASHTUNS IN HISTORY

So far I have looked at the Pashtuns through the lens of twentieth-century anthropology, attempting to arrive at an understanding of the pertinent aspects of their organization and gaining a few historical insights on the way. In the case of Afghanistan, modern ethnographies form a valuable resource for exploring the socioeconomic factors shaping tribal life, an aspect that is hardly touched upon by historical sources. Moreover, they shed light on the distribution of power at the lower echelons of tribal organization and the way relationships between leaders and followers are conceived from an inner-tribal perspective. Now the focus of my discussion will shift to the tribes as political entities within the Muhammadzai state. The following historical narrative draws on colonial records and travelogues and, to a lesser degree, on Afghan chronicles. Contrary to the modern anthropological studies summed up above, the works produced in the nineteenth and early twentieth centuries primarily view the Pashtuns in the light of government interests and concentrate on the highest level of Pashtun organization, that is, prominent leaders conspicuous for their cooperation with, or opposition to, the rulers of Kabul. While the theory of segmentary lineage organization emphasizes the levelling mechanisms at work in tribal society, the historical sources take the opposite approach and seek to indentify local hierarchies which would seem to fit best into a chain of command emanating from the center. My combined approach on the basis of anthropological and historical sources thus illuminates different aspects of Pashtun tribalism.

Given the mediatory role of the local leadership between tribe and state, any endeavor to understand the political landscape in nineteenth-century Afghanistan requires an analysis of the position of the prominent tribal chiefs and the origins of their power. In order to convey a sense of the variability of local organization and the cumulative processes at work in Dost Muhammad Khan's realm, I will present historical data concerning a range of Pashtun settings among the so-called border tribes and the Ghilzais. The main question to be investigated is whether tribe-state relations evolve according to a distinctive pattern. In this context Glatzer's proposition that the degree of hierarchization within a tribe is directly linked to the intensity of its contact with the state offers itself as a promising hypothesis. Applied to the Pashtuns, it would suggest that the leadership of the groups to be dealt with would become more powerful with increasing proximity to the government but would also be more vulnerable to state interference. Of course, it would be a mistake to expect a linear progression of hierarchization. For good reason Glatzer calls the suggested pattern 'seemingly simple'.[132]

What follows, then, is a detailed look at the mechanisms involved in state-tribe relations. Going back to Mughal times, I will investigate in which ways the state made its presence felt locally. I will attempt to find out how 'allegiance' to the central rulers was formulated and what the practical implications of this relationship were for the 'ruled'. Which regions were subject to demands for revenues and soldiers? How were these demands enforced? Which strategies did the local leaders employ and what were the rewards for their cooperation with the central power? How did the recipients of government largesse position themselves within their tribes and how lasting was their leadership? A closer investigation of the history of the so-called border tribes reveals a fascinating variety in terms of political outlook and internal organization within a relatively small geographical area. The following profiles of some of the leading families also demonstrate that the political processes within a tribe are affected by numerous elements. Apart from segmentary mechanisms, one pattern frequently to be observed is that of dichotomy, often encouraged by cousin rivalry (*tarburwali*). Moreover, horizontal cleavages may occur because of the generational conflict between father and son. Another factor not to be discounted is the powerful influence maternal relatives, particularly the maternal uncle (*mama*), may exert on behalf of a contender for power.

Before moving on to a more detailed discussion of the political fortunes of individual groups, I will begin with a few general observations regarding the origin of the greater group of Pashtuns and their attitude towards the states they had to arrange themselves with. Tracing their descent to the Prophet's contemporary Qais, the overwhelming majority of Pashtuns are Sunni Muslims. Only some of the border tribes, such as the Turis of Kurram, some Orakzais of Tira, and certain Bangash clans are of Shi'i persuasion. Popular legend has it that the Pashtuns are of Semitic origin, as Qais was the 37th in descent from Saul, King of Israel.[133] More generally, however, the Pashtuns are identified as Indo-European. There is evidence that the present-day Pashtuns have assimilated various outside groups in the course of their history.[134] Yet all of them are linked by a common genealogy, in which the border tribes are allotted a somewhat peripheral position, their ancestor having allegedly been only adopted three generations after Qais. The Abdalis/Durranis, along with the eastern Afghan tribes of the Peshawar valley and the Yusufzais, consider Qais's eldest son Sarbanr their forefather. Qais's second son gave rise to the Ghilzais, as well as dynasties of the Lodi (1451–1526) and Sur (1539–1555) at Delhi, by marrying his daughter Bibi Mato to a non-Pashtun (Shah Husain of Ghor). Qais's third son

Ghurghusht is reckoned to be the ancestor of diverse Pashtun groups, such as the Kakars dwelling in the area east of Qandahar and in Baluchistan, and the Safis of Peshawar, Bajaur and Kunar. Karlanri, who was adopted by a grandson of Sarbanr, brought forth the border tribes, that is, the Utman Khel, Orakzais, Afridis, Mangals, Khugianis, Turis, Jajis, and Wazirs.[135]

The relatively wide dispersion of groups closely related by genealogy can be attributed in great part to their migrations which started sometime around the fourteenth century. In the sixth and seventh centuries the Afghans/Pashtuns are mentioned by Indian and Chinese sources as inhabitants of the Sulaiman mountains east of Ghazni.[136] These mountains form an 'irregular parallelogram', extending from the Khyber in the north to Sibi in the south and separating Qandahar and Ghazni from the Derajat. Raverty is of the opinion that this region, generally known as 'Ghar' or mountainous country, more likely formed the original homeland of the Pashtuns than the often quoted region of Ghor located in central Afghanistan.[137] This notion is confirmed by Ghaznawid sources. The famous medieval scholar Al-Biruni (d. 1050) describes the Pashtuns as the inhabitants of the same mountain range.[138] His contemporary Al-'Utbi (d. 1040) informs us that they interacted closely with the Ghaznawid rulers, alternately defying their authority and furnishing troops to them.[139] According to the Mughal historian Ni'matullah, the eastward migration of the Pashtuns was initiated by the Ghorid ruler Mu'izz al-Din (also called Shihab al-Din, r. 1173–1206) in the course of his military campaigns to India.[140] Raverty, on the other hand, is of the opinion that there were no Pashtun settlements in the Peshawar valley and the regions adjoining north of it prior to the reign of Timur Gurkan (r. 1369–1404).[141] Information concerning the sequence of the Pashtuns eastward migration is sketchy. Certain of the border tribes, such as the Wazirs, are thought to have arrived in their present locations at the close of the fourteenth century.[142] According to their local traditions, the Mohmands, Tarklanris and Yusufzais migrated from the region around Qandahar to Kabul, and then onwards to the Jalalabad valley and the northern slopes of the Safed Koh at the end of the fifteenth century.[143] In 1504 the Mughal emperor Babur noted that Pashtun settlers were well established in the regions of Laghman, Peshawar, Hashtnagar, Swat, and Bajaur.[144] Many of these Pashtuns were fleeing the confrontation with Babur's troops. The migration of the Yusufzais to Swat via Peshawar and Bajaur, for example, was occasioned by an attack on them by Babur's uncle Mirza Ulugh Beg, the governor of Kabul.[145] The Mohmands, who were to move to the Peshawar region subsequent to the Yusufzais, resisted Mughal troops in Muqur (south of Ghazni) at that time. The eastward movement of the Pashtuns seems to have continued throughout Babur's era and beyond. In 1519 the Afridis were reported as having recently settled on the Bara river in the Khyber region. At that date, the Tarklanris, the future inhabitants of Bajaur, and the Utman Khel, the future inhabitants of the Peshawar border, were still dwelling further west in the region of Nangarhar.[146]

The westward movement of the Pashtuns towards the region of Qandahar and Herat apparently started in the fifteenth century. According to Raverty, the Abdalis/Durranis moved to the Qandahar region during the reign of the Timurid ruler Shah Rukh (r. 1404–1447), precisely in the year 1418.[147] In the sixteenth century the area around Qandahar formed a bone of contention between the Ghilzais and Abdalis. During the reign of Shah 'Abbas I, the Abdalis gave in to Ghilzai pressure and moved toward Herat. This relocation further west was not only brought about by the rivalries among the Ghilzais and Abdalis but was assisted and possibly initiated by the Safawid administration.[148]

The Pashtun expansion led to the displacement or subjugation of the local autochthonous populations. One of the groups strongly affected were the Tajiks, the ancient sedentary, non-tribal population of the region.[149] Prior to the Pashtun migration to the Kabul River valley, they had formed the dominant population of Kabul, Nangarhar and Laghman. Before the advent of Ghilzai nomads of the Ahmadzai division sometime in the late sixteenth century, the Logar valley located south of Kabul had also been a Tajik stronghold.[150] In the Kunar and Laghman valleys near Jalalabad the original Pashai and Kafir populations were pushed to the less fertile mountain regions by successive waves of Pashtun immigrants.[151] Prior to the sixteenth century the regions east and south of Ghazni were domains of the Hazara, groups of Central Asian origin who had entered Afghanistan during the Mongolian conquests in the thirteenth and fourteenth centuries.[152] The Ghilzai stronghold Qalat-i Ghilzai, for example, was populated by Hazaras at the time of Babur and was known as Qalat-i Barluk. The Hazaras also lost their foothold in the present-day province of Wardak when it was invaded by a Pashtun tribe with that name sometime in the course of the seventeenth century.[153] Because of the predominant position of the Ghilzais and Abdalis in the Qandahar region the local population of Farsiwans, Hazaras, Kakars and Baluch lost part of their previous possessions and were forced to pay revenues to their Pashtun overlords.[154] In those areas where the Pashtuns did not displace the local populations entirely the latter were likely to be reduced to the status of 'peasants' (*ra'iyat*) or 'tenants' (*hamsaya*).[155]

With the rise of the Mughal dynasty in India (1526–1707) and the Safawid dynasty in Iran (1502–1732), Afghanistan became the site of imperial rivalry. Kabul had been a Mughal possession since Babur's arrival from Ferghana in 1504. Many of the border tribes, such as the Afridi, Orakzais, the Wazirs, and the Daurs were also incorporated into the Mughal administration at least formally.[156] Mughal and Safawid interests overlapped in the region of Qandahar and Qalat-i Ghilzai. Having been conquered by Babur in the early sixteenth century, Qandahar changed hands several times after 1558, finally falling to the Safawids in 1649.[157] In the course of these events the Abdalis were able to enhance their position by taking over administrative tasks for the Safawids. The Abdalis were eventually able to translate their privileged position into supremacy over Afghanistan. Accordingly, this group came to derive its world view from its linkage to the ruling house. The other groups, by contrast, took a more independent stance and formulated their identity in opposition to the surrounding governments. Therefore the 'rebelliousness' of the Ghilzais and the border tribes was not only a label applied to them by imperial outsiders but an essential ingredient of their own identity. Both groups continued to describe themselves as *yaghi*, 'rebellious', well into the nineteenth century. This identity was formulated in a dialectical confrontation with the state and thus required its presence in a continuous process of self definition. This tension is expressed by juxtaposition in word pairs like *yaghistan* ('land of insolence') and *hukumat* ('government'), as well as *ghair 'ilaqa* ('alien territory') and *sarkar 'ilaqa* ('government area').[158] In this relationship of opposition tribal life was conceptualized as all that government is not, and vice versa: 'Yaghistan is where no man is above another, in contrast to hukumat where there are governors and governed.'[159] The usage of this term also entered the language of all governments in the region, be they Mughal, Durrani or British.[160] In his description of the North West Frontier the nineteenth century author MacGregor employed it as a formal term for all the Pashtun groups lying beyond the reach of British administration.[161] Others were less happy with such a generic application. Raverty, for example, made the critical remark that the extensive use of the term *yaghistan* tended to obscure the actual relationship between the tribes in question and the British government:

> 'Yaghistan' appears to be a very extensive tract, according to Colonel C.M. MacGregor. It seems that any tract of county [sic.] independent of the British Government is 'Yaghistan'... [This] is scarcely a happy term, to say the least of it, to apply to all parts not subject to British rule, and whose people, never having been British subjects, have never been in the position to rebel. If all independent people, and such as love their independence quite as dearly as Englishmen love theirs, are 'yaghi', there are a vast number of insubordinate rebels in Asia and other parts of the world. The mere fact of people 'never having obeyed any one' does not constitute them as rebels.'[162]

While Raverty's criticism exposes the extended imperial claims of the colonial administration, it obscures the fact that many of the groups mentioned by MacGregor had indeed defined themselves as *yaghi* prior to the advent of the British. In the following section I will take a look at the relationship of the so-called border tribes with their imperial neighbors, the Mughals, Sikhs and British on the one hand and the Durrani rulers on the other.

The Border Tribes

The term 'border tribes' has commonly been employed for the Pashtuns inhabiting the region extending along the Durand line from Bajaur to Waziristan. Running practically the whole length of eastern Afghanistan, this mountain country has been characterized as 'unutterably rugged and unattractive'.[163] Accordingly, Ahmed categorizes its inhabitants as 'almost entirely' *nang*.[164]

In the 1870s C. J. East discerned the following geographical entities from north to south:

> The small range of Khyber may be said to separate the plain of Peshawar from the valley of the Kabul river; its highest peak is 3,500 feet above the plain. It is pierced through at two places, on the south by the valley of the Khyber, and further north by the Kabul river.
>
> The Safed Koh or Spin Ghur range commences at Peshawar, and runs in a westerly direction to within thirty miles of Kabul. It throws out two large spurs to the north, one the Khyber... and the other the Kurkutcha. Its general aspect is one of greatest sterility, but it encloses numerous well-watered and fertile valleys.
>
> The Solimani mountains have a general direction parallel to the Indus; their southern limits may be taken at the Bolan Pass [in Baluchistan], whilst on the north they extend near Bunoo. The highest point of this range, that of Tukht-i Suliman, is 11,000 feet above sea level.[165]

While presenting a formidable barrier, this mountain country is far from impenetrable. 'It forms no great water-divide, for all the big rivers which pass through its limestone gates, cutting across the main strike of its hills, come from the highlands of Afghanistan.'[166] The northernmost region of Bajaur is located north of the Kabul river and adjoins the Kunar range in the east. Enclosed on every side by 'lofty and difficult mountain ranges',[167] its Tarklanri population relied mostly on agriculture and cattle breeding for its livelihood.[168] Further south and east the Mohmands occupied the banks of the Kabul river 'for about fifty miles of its course above its exit into the Peshawar valley at Fort Michni'.[169] This group mainly derived its income from the trade passing along and on the Kabul river. The Kohat Pass and the eastern portion of the Khyber Pass were controlled by the Afridis, who also profited greatly from tolls levied on the transit trade.[170] Inhabiting the western portion of the Khyber Pass, the Shinwaris were 'the most industrious carriers of goods between Peshawar and the other marts on the way to Kabal [Kabul]'.[171] Further south, the Orakzais and Bangash occupied the country lying north of the Kurram valley and west of Kohat.[172] The population of the Kurram valley was predominantly Turi. The region around the crest of the Paiwar Pass was inhabited by Jajis and Mangals.

The Kurram valley formed part of a trade route leading to Logar and Kabul but was mostly used for local traffic only.[173] Even further south, the Gomal river passing through the country of the Wazirs was considered the most isolated of the routes across the border land. Yet, connecting Ghazni with Sind and lower Punjab, it was passed every year by thousands of nomad traders (*powindas*). The Wazirs, whose subsistence was based partly on cattle breeding and partly on rain-fed agriculture, were greatly dreaded by the passing nomads for their attacks on their caravans.[174] Although proponents of the Forward Policy greatly stressed the commercial and strategic importance of the Gomal Pass, the Khyber pass, the roads through the Mohmand hills and the Kabul river itself formed the most vital connection between Kabul and Peshawar.[175] The groups inhabiting these parts were of primary concern for the powers seeking to maintain their supremacy in the region. They derived their income not only on the basis of transportation, transit and escort dues (*badraga*), or plundering raids on caravans, but also received allowances in exchange for not obstructing the important lines of communication passing through their country.

During the Mughal period, the Wazirs and their Daur neighbors formed districts of the province of Kabul but remained factually independent. During Akbar's reign (1556–1605), the tribes of the Khyber (the Afridis and Orakzais) and their Khatak neighbors, on the other hand, formed the administrative unit (*toman*) of Bangash and were supposed to furnish altogether 20,000 footmen and 1,200 horsemen for militia purposes.[176] But even in this region Mughal control was intermittent at best and was punctuated by severe military defeats. In the late sixteenth and early seventeenth centuries the Mughals faced a sustained challenge at the hands of the Raushaniyya sect.[177] With the rapid population growth of the border tribes in the seventeenth century, the Mughals faced almost yearly insurrections. In the years between 1672 and 1675, they suffered four decisive defeats at the hands of the Afridis, Khataks, and Bajauris. In their attempt to keep their line of communication to Kabul open, the Mughals resorted to all the strategies which the British were to use 250 years later: the erection of large fortified garrisons, the deployment of mobile columns, and the imposition of blockades. Most importantly, the cooperation of the tribes was ensured by the payment of large allowances. It is estimated that these groups received a total of 600,000 rupees annually during Aurangzeb's reign (r. 1658–1707). In the sixteenth century, the Afridis alone collected 125,000 rupees per year from the Mughal rulers.[178] The Khatak leadership received land grants and gained control of the ferry tolls levied at Attock in exchange for keeping the road to Kabul open. The 'Ali Khel *khans* of the Muhammadzais (not to be confused with the nineteenth-century rulers of Kabul) held the district of Hashtnagar in military *jagir*.[179]

With the decline of the Mughal empire, Nadir Shah sought to establish control over the border tribes. In 1739 he forced the Mughal emperor,

Muhammad Shah (r. 1719–1748), to give up the regions west of the Indus to him.[180] Nonetheless he had to pay the border chiefs for his passage through the Khyber region both when going to and returning from Delhi.[181] A few years later Ahmad Shah Durrani was able to use the political vacuum caused by Nadir Shah's death in 1747 to extend his dominions as far east as Sirhind. With the exception of the Wazirs and the majority of Yusufzais, all border tribes recognized his sovereignty. While the Wazirs refused to pay any allegiance whatsoever, the Yusufzais accompanied Ahmad Shah and his successors on their military campaigns to India.[182] The authority of the Sadozai king among the remaining border tribes was also limited. Rather than acting as an absolute ruler, he cast himself as a tribal leader, assuming the highest military command at times of war. The allegiance of the border tribes was mostly a formal one and found its expression in the willingness to furnish a fixed number of soldiers when such a necessity arose.

The tribes of the Khyber region, that is, the Afridis, Shinwaris and Orakzais, described themselves as *naukaran* ('servants') of the Sadozai kings. Their 'service', however, pales in comparison with the privileges they enjoyed. In Ahmad Shah's military register the Afridis are mentioned with 19,000 fighting men. But it is not clear whether they ever furnished such a great number of soldiers.[183] During the reign of Timur Shah they held a *jagir* in return for guarding a portion of the Khyber Pass and were exempt from tax or tribute. The Orakzais obtained *jagirs* in the Peshawar region for similar services.[184] At the time of Shah Zaman, the combined *jagirs* of the Afridis, Shinwaris and Orakzais were worth 12,000 rupees annually. In return they furnished a total of ten thousand men, two thousand of whom were Afridi infantry, during Shah Zaman's final military campaign to Punjab in 1798.[185] A few years later they were reported to be 'zealously attached' to the reigning Sadozai king Shah Shuja' (r. 1803–1809), but they were no longer furnishing troops to the royal leader at that time.[186] The privileges of the Bajauris are comparable to those of the Khyber tribes. During the Sadozai era their *khan* received 12,000 rupees of the revenue of Peshawar as well as an assignment of 500 *kharwars* of grain from Jalalabad in exchange for furnishing 500 footmen accompanied by some cavalry. Yet Strachey notes that the *khan* never quite fulfilled his part of the agreement.[187]

Other groups enjoyed an even closer linkage with the Sadozai court. During Ahmad Shah's reign Zain Khan, a Tarakzai Mohmand of La'lpura, played a prominent role, acting as military commander and governor of Sirhind. His grandson Arsalan Khan, by contrast, is mainly known for his prolonged rebellion during Timur Shah's reign. With the assistance the Afridis, he was able to take total control of the Khyber region and to close it to the Sadozai military, exacting transit duties from passing merchants on his own behalf. Among the Mohmands, both the Tarakzai division and the Baezai division under Dindar Khan of Goshta were supposed to furnish troops to Timur Shah.[188] The Muhammadzais of Hashtnagar, the Khataks, and the Babar Pashtuns were similarly privileged. The Muhammadzai leaders were important nobles at the court of Ahmad Shah Durrani and his successors. In addition to their *jagirs*, they received large salaries from the Sadozai kings.[189] Several of the Khatak chiefs paid no taxes at all but furnished troops to Timur Shah and his successors.[190] During the reign of Shah Zaman, Nurullah Khan Khatak was an influential military commander.[191] The Babar Pashtuns dwelling east of Takht-i Sulaiman were exempted both from paying taxes and furnishing troops because their famous fellow tribesman, Nur Muhammad Khan Babar Amin al-Mulk, played an important role as finance minister during the reigns of Timur Shah and Shah Zaman.[192]

Nonetheless revenue collection was not totally unknown in the region. During the Sadozai era Kurram was administered as 'Upper' Bangash, as opposed to 'Lower' Bangash located in Kohat.[193] Apart from soldiers furnished by all tribal segments, Kurram yielded a revenue of 100,000 rupees per year to Timur Shah's treasury. The neighboring tribes of Khost submitted 14,000 rupees annually during the same period.[194] During Shah Zaman's reign the tribes of Bangash and Daman were described as 'very obedient' in the payment of revenues.[195] This is not to say that revenue was given willingly in the entire region. A historical account of the eighteenth century describes the Bannuchi neighbors of the Wazirs and Khataks as 'great blockheads' in government affairs, who would not allow their chief, Sharafat Khan, to gather the yearly revenue of 25,000 rupees due to Timur Shah: 'The upshot is that a Thasil-dar [sic] or Collector from Kabul comes to aid him, and from each person much more is collected than his share would have been had he paid according to his assessment.'[196] With the decline of the Sadozai empire, or perhaps even earlier, the Afghan rulers gave up their claims to direct control over these regions. During Shah Shuja''s reign influential Durrani *sardars* collected the revenues of Upper and Lower Bangash, as well as those of Bannu and Daur, entirely on their own behalf.[197]

With the end of the Sadozai empire in 1818, the cities of Kabul, Jalalabad and Peshawar became the seats of competing sets of Muhammadzai Sardars. In the confusion accompanying the struggle for the control of Kabul, the border tribes lost their allowances. Meanwhile the Sikhs increasingly made their presence felt. From 1824 to 1834 Sardars Yar Muhammad Khan and Sultan Muhammad Khan were able to retain their hold over Peshawar by paying a yearly tribute of 110,000 rupees to Ranjit Singh.[198] From 1834 to 1837 the Sikh governor Hari Singh Nalwa assumed direct control of Peshawar and pursued a harsh policy against the border tribes, forcing even the Wazirs to pay revenue. In general, however, Sikh authority was limited to the valley of the Indus.[199] After Hari Singh's death in the battle of Jamrud the Peshawar Sardars resumed their role as local administrators, particularly in the region of Kohat. Apparently secure from Sikh inroads, the chiefs of Bajaur and Kunar maintained a friendly relationship with Ranjit Singh throughout the Sikh era.[200]

When the British took over the Sikh possessions in 1849 they maintained the same border line with the tribes of the region as their Sikh predecessors. The British strategy towards the border tribes up to the 1870s has been summed up as a 'system of non-intervention, varied by expeditions'. In accordance with the promulgated policy of 'forbearance', the British rulers abolished the Sikh poll tax and held forth boons like free medical treatment and employment in the police and army. These advantages notwithstanding the Pashtuns were not convinced of the beneficial nature of British rule.[201] Between 1847 and 1863 alone, no less than 22 major military expeditions had to be mounted against one or the other of the border tribes. By 1884 the frontier was dotted with a line of 54 fortified posts.[202] The military campaigns of the British tended to have only a temporary effect. The other measures they resorted to, such as fines, blockades and allowances, were not entirely successful either. This is shown, for example, by their frustrating efforts to keep open the Kohat Pass, which lay at the intersection of Afridi, Orakzai and Bangash interests. In 1849 an agreement was reached with the Adam Khel Afridis whereby they were to keep open their portion of the road between Peshawar and Kohat in exchange for an allowance of 5,700 rupees annually. During the next four years certain sections of the Adam Khel Afridis kept violating this agreement. British responses included a military campaign, a blockade against the misbehaving sections and an attempt at 'divide and rule'. In 1853 the neighboring Bangash, who claimed that they had been in charge of the pass in Mughal times, were asked to hold it against the other tribesmen of the region. After a strong Afridi attack had put an end to this experiment an agreement was worked out according to which sections of the Afridis, Orakzais and Bangash were to control the pass jointly in exchange for a total annual allowance of 14,600 rupees. Nonetheless the passage of this pass tended to be disturbed for decades to come.[203] In 1877 Lord Lytton, the viceroy of India, commented on the fitful nature of British control in the entire border region with the following dramatic words,

> I believe that our North-Western Frontier presents at this moment a spectacle unique in the world; at least I know of not other spot where, after twenty-five years of peaceful occupation, a great civilised power has obtained so little influence over its semi savage neighbours ... that the country within a day's ride of its most important garrison (Peshawar) is an absolute *terra incognita* and that there is absolutely no security for British life a mile or two beyond our border.[204]

What was happening 'a mile or two' beyond the British frontier? I will delineate the political fortunes of some of the border tribes during the time of Dost Muhammad Khan and his successor Sher 'Ali Khan. In this context I will attempt to identify the most prominent leaders and, to the extent possible, I will discuss the origins of their power and the nature of their relationship with the Kabul government.

The Tribes of the Khyber Region

Following the riverbeds of two small streams flowing towards Peshawar and Kabul respectively, the Khyber route consisted of a series of small passes. While it was fairly level and direct compared with the other routes of the region, its dramatic aspect as related by travellers lay rather in the fear of plundering raids by the locals hiding in the mountain spurs encroaching on the Pass. In his description of these mountain spurs Oliver used the image of two old combs placed with their teeth pointing inward, at times creating narrow passages.

> Thus at Kadam, the real gate [of the Khyber], some three miles from Jamrud – the hills begin to close in, and the Pass is only some 450 feet wide; a little further and it narrows to 250 feet. Then a few teeth [of the combs] have been knocked out; but approaching the spring and mosque of Ali ['Ali Masjid] ... it has diminished to forty feet, with slaty perpendicular cliffs 1,300 feet high on either side, and a fort, called after the mosque below, stands on an isolated hill commanding the road. Another six or seven miles and the Latabeg Valley [Gadhi La'l Beg] has opened to a mile and a half wide, only to close a little beyond, to less than ten feet between quite perpendicular walls of rock. Over the Landi Khana Pass ... probably the most difficult part of the road – it rises by a steep ascent between steep cliffs less than 150 feet apart, and down again till the valley of the Kabul river is reached at Dhaka.[205]

The two major strategic points in the Khyber Pass were Jamrud and 'Ali Masjid. Located at its eastern entrance, Jamrud had become a Sikh possession in the 1830s. After the Afghan-Sikh battle at Jamrud in 1837, Amir Dost Muhammad Khan asserted his claims to supremacy over the Khyber region by erecting the fort at 'Ali Masjid and placing a permanent garrison in it. Dakka, where the Khyber route joined with the other major trade routes of the region, was a Mohmand stronghold and did not form part of the Khyber Pass itself. Between Jamrud in the east and Landikhana in the west, the Khyber Pass proper extended through 25 miles of Afridi and Shinwari land.[206] The eastern parts of the pass were held by five of the eight major Afridi tribes, i.e. the Sipah, the Kuki Khel, the Malikdin Khel, the Kambar Khel, and the Zakha Khel. MacGregor estimated their total fighting strenth at 13,000.[207] The 'Ali Sher Khel Shinwaris occupying the western part of the pass were thought to consist of 3,000 fighting men.[208]

The Orakzais had no direct access to the Khyber Pass but shared the same upland valleys with the Afridis.[209] In the late nineteenth century estimates of their fighting strength ranged from 18,000 to 25,000.[210]

Travellers who passed through the Khyber Pass in the nineteenth century noted that it bore evidence of constant internal warfare. The land of the 'Ali Sher Shinwaris, for example, was studded with protective towers from which hostilities were carried on between individual families.[211] The dwellings of the Afridis also resembled little forts. The constant feuding among these 'highlanders' and the limited authority they accorded to their *maliks* form two major themes in all descriptions of the Khyber Pass.[212] The general diffusion of power among the Khyber tribes became apparent at the beginning of the First Anglo-Afghan War when Shah Shuja''s eldest son, Muhammad Timur, prepared to enter Afghanistan through the Khyber with British support. In April 1839 it turned out that the Khyber *maliks* who had received a total of 50,000 rupees in bribes in order to ease the British entrance into the region lacked the influence or the will necessary to fit tribal interests to the British agenda. Moreover, the leadership showed little inclination to share its newly acquired wealth with its fellow tribesmen.[213] Yet certain Khyber *maliks* stand out as leading figures in all accounts of the First Anglo-Afghan War. Among them are Khan Bahadur Khan Malikdin Khel, who had been ignored when the first round of British bribes was paid out, as well as 'Abd al-Rahman Kuki Khel and 'Alam Khan Orakzai.

While 'Alam Khan was a personal friend of Amir Dost Muhammad Khan, Khan Bahadur Khan was closely allied with Shah Shuja'.[214] According to Masson, Khan Bahadur Khan 'attained eminence amongst his tribe from the circumstance of his attendance at court during the sway of the Sadu Zais.' He had given one daughter in marriage to Shah Shuja' and had sheltered him when his political fortunes were on the decline.[215] During Shah Mahmud's first reign a group of Khyber leaders actively supported Shah Shuja''s claims to power.[216] On the eve of the First Anglo-Afghan War, or perhaps even prior to it, Khan Bahadur Khan's influence extended well beyond the Malikdin Khel tribe. In 1838 Shah Shuja' named Khan Bahadur Khan, Jum'a Khan Khalil and Sa'adat Khan Mohmand as the most powerful tribal leaders in the border region.[217] With the British presence in the Khyber from July 1839 on Bahadur Khan's position became even stronger. Immediately prior to his death in October 1841 he was able to bring about an Afridi-Orakzai alliance in the dealings with the British which turned out to be as short-lived as the British ascendancy itself.[218]

The attitudes and strategies of the Khyber leaders during the First Anglo-Afghan War were not solely based on personal loyalties felt either for Amir Dost Muhammad Khan or Shah Shuja'. Although many of them addressed encouraging letters to Shah Shuja' prior the onset of the war, they were slow to follow their professions of friendship with more tangible evidence of allegiance once the British troops arrived at Peshawar. One of the reasons given for their caution was that the Amir's son Muhammad Akbar Khan still held Afridi hostages. Furthermore, the Afridi chiefs quoted fears of a pending Sikh invasion of the Khyber Pass. Yet all of them, with the notable exception of Khan Bahadur Khan accepted the *khil'ats* the British sent to them in April 1839. The British Indian observer Shahamat Ali attributed the hesitant attitude of the Khyber chiefs to the fact that they were waiting for the result of the British advance on Qandahar before committing themselves to the cause of either the Muhammadzais or Sadozais.[219] But even after the fall of Qandahar the Khyber tribes did not welcome Shahzada Muhammad Timur to their land. When British and Sikh forces entered the Pass in July 1839 they met with a spirited resistance on the part of the Malikdin Khel and Kuki Khel Afridis. Afterwards continued attacks by the Malikdin Khel and other Afridi tribes rendered the British hold over the Khyber Pass precarious. This resistance may in part be attributed to the resentment triggered by the threatened dominion by unbelievers, be they Sikh or British. Yet the Afridis had not abhorred practical dealings with the Sikhs in the past. To the chagrin of Muhammad Akbar Khan they had been receiving payments from the Sikhs for allowing water to reach the fort at Jamrud up to 1838.[220] The prolonged Afridi resistance of 1839 rather had the pleasant effect that the British were willing to 'buy peace' by means of liberal allowances. Malleson is of the opinion that the Afridi attack on 'Ali Masjid of October 1839 can be attributed to the fact that the subsidy previously offered by Macnaghten fell much short of the sum of 80,000 rupees allegedly promised by Muhammad Timur.[221]

Thus the resistance to the entrance of the British in 1839 and the formation of the Afridi-Orakzai alliance in 1841 may primarily be seen as a method of 'bargaining' with the British for greater allowances. Whatever the personal attitudes of individual tribal leaders to Dost Muhammad Khan may have been, their actions prior to, and during, the First Anglo-Afghan war were motivated by a form of 'realpolitik'. Between 1839 and 1841 the British were simply more powerful and had more to offer than the Muhammadzai Amir. Dost Muhammad Khan had cut all Khyber allowances after coming to power in Kabul in 1826, most probably because of lacking funds. Accordingly, the Khyber Pass was closed to all trade and even to the Amir's half brothers, the Peshawar Sardars.[222] Dost Muhammad Khan began to pay greater attention to the Khyber tribes from the mid-1830s on because of his confrontations with the Sikhs. After the establishment of his garrison at 'Ali Masjid he paid 20,000 rupees a year to the Khyber tribes.[223] In 1838 Jum'a Khan Khalil and Bahadur Khan Malikdin Khel were reported to enjoy personal allowances of 4,000 rupees each.[224] These amounts pale in comparison with the allowances granted by the British during the First Anglo-Afghan War. After the Afridi attack on 'Ali Masjid in October 1839 Mackeson, the British officer in charge of the Khyber, agreed to pay a total of 80,000 rupees annually, the Malikdin Khel,

Kuki Khel, Zakha Khel, and 'Ali Sher Shinwari *maliks* receiving 16,000 rupees each. Another 16,000 rupees were allotted to the remaining Khyber tribes. By 1840 Khan Bahadur Khan Malikdin Khel enjoyed a personal allowance of 10,000 rupees and 'Abd al-Rahman Kuki Khel received at least 8,000 rupees annually. By the end of 1840 Mackeson was paying out more than 100,000 rupees a year in allowances.[225] In exchange, the transit duties of the region were to be controlled by the British puppet Shah Shuja'.[226]

Neither the generous sums of money doled out nor military action were able to secure a lasting peace for the British in the Khyber region. Immediately subsequent to the disastrous retreat of the Kabul garrison in January 1842 all the influence gained by arduous efforts in the course of the two past years evaporated. The Khyber tribes opened negotiations with Dost Muhammad Khan's son Muhammad Akbar.[227] After the Amir's return to Kabul the allowances to the Khyber tribes approximately returned to their pre-war level. The Afridi *maliks* received 18,000 rupees.[228] The 'Alisher and Sangu Khel Shinwaris enjoyed an allowance of 7,000 rupees.[229] In 1857 the British estimated that the total allowances of the Khyber tribes in cash and kind reached 40,000 rupees per year.[230]

Prior to the Second Afghan-Anglo War of 1878–1880 the Afridis described themselves as 'servants' of the Muhammadzai Amirs.[231] Yet this allegiance was more of a formal nature and their connection with the court of Kabul was limited to the collection of allowances. For the most part, the Khyber tribes continued to use the competition between British and Muhammadzai interests in their lands for their own benefit. In 1850, for example, the Afridis and other Khyber tribes reminded Dost Muhammad Khan that the allowances due to them had not yet been disbursed by the Governor of Jalalabad, Sardar Ghulam Haidar Khan. They ended their letter with the nonchalant offer to make arrangements with the British in case their services were no longer required by the Amir. Dost Muhammad Khan immediately sent orders to Ghulam Haidar Khan to pay the Khyber tribes in order 'to keep them in good humour.'[232] Two years later the Afridi and Shinwari chiefs were able to use the proposed British activities against the Michni Mohmands to extract a 'small increase' to their allowances from Ghulam Haidar Khan.[233]

Throughout Amir Dost Muhammad Khan's second reign both the Afghan and British governments disputed the other's ability to control the Khyber region. In the fall of 1853 the Amir noted gleefully that, in spite of their wealth and power, the British had been unable to subdue the border tribes sufficiently. Ironically, Dost Muhammad Khan was reminded of his own weakness in the same area shortly afterwards when he was informed that a caravan from Kabul had been plundered in the Khyber Pass. The only 'protection' the Amir could offer to merchants on their way across the Khyber Pass was to help recovering their possessions *after* they had been plundered.[234] In early 1857 the king himself faced resistance when he was on his way to Peshawar for negotiations with the British. Even so, he felt that the payment of allowances was the only way to keep the passage through the Khyber pass open.[235] During the last three years of his reign Dost Muhammad Khan finally suspended the allowances of the Khyber tribes because of their 'continued misconduct'.[236]

The Afghan government was only able to make its presence felt intermittently in the Khyber region. Moreover, its effectiveness diminished in proportion to the distance of the tribal groups from the provincial capital of Jalalabad. Thus, among the Afridis, the idea of revenue payments to the king was entirely unheard of. Being located more closely to the government seat of Jalalabad, the Shinwari tribes, on the other hand, were not able to restrict their relationship with the government to occasional polite visits to Jalalabad. The Manduzai, considered the weakest of the Shinwari tribes, had even paid revenues to the Amir prior to the First Anglo-Afghan War.[237] Other Shinwari tribes were also listed in the revenue register of the king. Yet a great part of the revenues formally due to the government was given up in the form of allowances. The Sangu Khel Shinwaris of Saroli and Naziyan, for example, owed a revenue of 8,000 rupees to the Amir. Half of this sum was retained by their chiefs as a personal allowance. Dost Muhammad Khan was only able to put greater pressure on the Khyber tribes during personal visits to the region, as the presence of a fairly large army accompanying him gave additional weight to his claims to supremacy. This was the case in February of 1859 when the Amir arrived at Jalalabad and summoned all Khyber chiefs to his residence. While the Afridi *maliks* got away with their customary assurances of allegiance, the promise not to accept subsidies from the British and to restore plundered goods to their rightful owners, the Sangu Khel Shinwaris soon found themselves pressured to allow their lands to be measured for a regular revenue assessment. Upon their resistance the Amir prepared a military expedition against them, ordering 4,000 troops as well as a militia of approximately 10,000 Mohmands, Khugianis and Jabbar Khel Ghilzais into the field. Threatened with the devastation of their lands, the elders of the Sangu Khel Shinwaris came in to the Amir 'carrying the Koran on their heads'. A staff of *munshis* entered the Sangu Khel possessions and worked out a revenue assessment of two rupees per *jarib* to be paid to the king.[238] We are not told whether the newly assessed revenue was ever paid to its full amount after Dost Muhammad Khan's departure for Kabul. Despite his claims to revenue, the governor of Jalalabad had little power to interfere with internal tribal matters. On several occasions the Afridis and Shinwaris made it perfectly clear to him that he had no business in attempting to settle intratribal affairs, let alone exact fines for local quarrels.[239]

In spite of his weakness in the Khyber region the Amir took exception to British endeavors to exact punishments for tribal misbehavior. This was the case when the British representative Khan Bahadur Fatih Khan Khatak was shot at by a Sangu Khel Shinwari in the summer of 1856. In order to demonstrate the efficiency of his government, Dost Muhammad Khan immediately reported to the British that he had mounted a successful military expedition against the fellow tribesmen of the offender. Yet the British only considered the matter settled after having obtained a fine of 1,000 rupees from the Sangu Khel Shinwaris.[240] In 1857, prior to the outbreak of the Mutiny, a British officer was killed by a group of Kuki Khel Afridis near the entrance of the Khyber. After they had been blockaded for the remainder of the year the Kuki Khel finally settled the issue by paying 3,000 rupees to the British. Dost Muhammad Khan, who had resisted all pressure to use the Mutiny to reclaim former Afghan possessions from the British, reacted angrily. He pointed out that the border tribes were under his authority and that the British had no business conducting independent negotiations with any of them.[241]

During the unrest following Amir Dost Muhammad Khan's death in 1863 the Khyber tribes were able to retain their privileges. In 1865 the new Amir, Sher 'Ali Khan, paid an annual allowance of 22,900 rupees to the Afridis. Furthermore, they were allowed to levy transit duties on all caravans passing through the Khyber.[242] After the interregnum of his half brothers Sardars Muhammad Afzal and Muhammad A'zam from 1866 to 1868 Sher 'Ali Khan was able to strengthen his position in Kabul. His tribal policies became accordingly more intrusive. In 1869, during negotiations with the Khyber *maliks* in Kabul, he offered to raise their allowance to 40,000 rupees per year. In exchange, the collection of transit dues was to pass to the Afghan government. Furthermore, Sher 'Ali Khan planned to place altogether 600 militia in three posts between Landi Khana and 'Ali Masjid.[243] By October 1870, 21 Khyber *maliks* resided as hostages in Jalalabad.[244] These measures apparently met with some resistance on the part of the Khyber tribes. In the spring of 1871 Shinwaris, Ghilzais and other tribes from the vicinity of Jalalabad were employed by the government in a military operation against the Afridis.[245] In December of the same year, continued robberies in the Khyber pass caused the governor of Jalalabad, Shahmard Khan, to send a number of *maliks* as prisoners to Kabul. Here the Amir personally fastened irons to their legs and ordered them to perform hard labor until they were willing to give up the property they had plundered. These men were still reported to be in confinement in October 1873.[246] Despite these harsh measures plundering raids in the Khyber Pass continued.[247] The days of Aghan supremacy in the Khyber region came to an end during the Second Anglo-Afghan War. In May 1879 the treaty of Gandamak placed the Khyber region, Michni, and Kurram under British protection. Two years later the British signed an agreement with the Khyber tribes according to which the protection of the Pass was to be secured by a corps of local riflemen under the command of British officers. The control of the transit duties levied also passed to the new overlords. In exchange for maintaining peace, the Khyber tribes, on their part, retained their independence and received an annual allowance of 80,000 to 90,000 rupees.[248]

Kurram, Khost and Zurmat

Contrary to the Khyber tribes, the groups inhabiting Kurram and the adjacent regions of Khost and Zurmat had traditionally paid revenues to the Sadozai rulers. Already during his first reign, Dost Muhammad Khan began to raise demands for revenue in these regions. In 1850 they became the *jagir* of Dost Muhammad Khan's son Sardar Muhammad A'zam Khan and thus formed one administrative unit.[249] Kurram and Khost were known for their comparative fertility. Apart from wheat both valleys produced high-quality rice exported to Bannu and Kabul. The Turis formed the dominant group of the upper Kurram valley, having reduced the older Bangash population to *hamsayas* in the early eighteenth century.[250] The Turis, as well as the Bangash population of Kurram were overwhelmingly Shi'a. This led to the rise of four dominant families of *sayyids*, to one of which each Turi was linked as a disciple.[251] Otherwise there was no entrenched leadership. The typical Turi was described as 'an absolute democrat who thinks himself as good as his neighbour, and cannot bear to see anybody in authority over him'.[252] The historical sources mention a few prominent families without furnishing great detail on their political activities. In the 1850s Malik Zarif of Paiwar was an important ally of Sardar Muhammad A'zam Khan.[253] The *malik* of Shalozan was linked to the court by a marriage alliance with Amir Dost Muhammad Khan.[254]

While Muhammad A'zam attempted to strengthen his position in neighboring Khost by marrying the daughter of a local chief, Kurram formed the stronghold of his administration.[255] During his governorship Kurram was administered by his son (Sardar Muhammad Sarwar Khan?) and a deputy (*na'ib*).[256] The post of deputy was filled by outsiders to Kurram society, first by Azad Khan Ghilzai of Tizin and then by his son (?) Ghulam Muhammad Khan (or Ghulam Jan).[257] The government presence in Kurram was secured by the erection of a fort at Ahmadzai and the establishment of a strong garrison.[258] Manned by 150 matchlockmen and 50 cavalry, the Afghan garrison at Khost was considerably weaker.[259] By themselves, however, these outposts were not strong enough to guarantee the authority of the Afghan governors. Revenues could only be collected with the assistance of armies sent from Ghazni or Kabul which 'swept the whole country clean', 'eating up' everything in their reach. In the 1850s Lumsden estimated the revenue due from Kurram at 60,000 rupees annually, including 12,000 rupees collected as transit duties on caravans.[260] In Khost the revenue collection had been the prerogative of a local chief until the early nineteenth century.[261] Under Sardar Muhammad A'zam the region was supposed to pay an annual revenue of 12,000 rupees, which amounted to one rupee per inhabitant.[262] While Zurmat was officially assessed at 150,000 rupees a year during Dost Muhammad Khan's second reign, it is unlikely that the Sulaiman Khel and Mangal population of this region submitted regular revenue payments to the government.[263]

Throughout the reign of Dost Muhammad Khan, reports of rebellions in Kurram and Khost reached the capital of Kabul. In great part this resistance can be seen as a reaction to the revenue collecting 'raids' conducted by the Afghan governor at irregular intervals. In 1851, for example, the Turis took possession of the fort (*burj*) at the Paiwar Pass for three months. Their refusal to give in to the mediation by the deputy was mainly triggered by the fear that they would by held accountable for two years of revenue as well as the provisions plundered from the fort. Their rebellion only came to an end when Amir Dost Muhammad Khan despatched Sardar Muhammad A'zam Khan with a strong force to the region.[264] Three years later 8,000 Turis blockaded the same pass, quoting their fear of oppression at the hands of Muhammad A'zam Khan's approaching army. The Sardar, on the other hand, reasoned that he could obtain the revenue due to him only by force. During the ensuing military confrontation at the Paiwar Pass the Turis suffered a decisive defeat.[265] The revenue collection was far from regular in the years to come, and continued to be resisted whenever Sardar Muhammad A'zam or his representatives began to press their claims.[266] Another major confrontation took place in April 1858 when Chamkani on the upper Kurram was threatened by a revenue collecting raid for the first time in twenty years.[267] Nevertheless Sardar Muhammad A'zam's officials could count on the cooperation of certain Turi *maliks* when their attempts at imposing their overlordship were directed at outsiders. In April 1857 Ghulam Muhammad Khan reported that an insurrection of the nearby Jajis had been 'suppressed amicably' by the Turi *maliks*.[268] A year later Sardar Muhammad A'zam Khan was assisted by Malik Zarif of Paiwar against the rebellious population of Baliyamin in adjacent Miranzai.[269] Apart from revenue collection, another factor triggering local resistance was the resentment of the *na'ib's* interference with local affairs. The Turi 'mutiny' of May 1855, during which Na'ib Azad Khan Ghilzai found himself besieged in his fort at Ahmadzai, was caused by the latter's support of the Sunni minority living around the fort. Peace was restored by the mediation of the influential *sayyid* Mir Ziya al-Din Shah, who extracted the promise from Azad Khan not to meddle with internal Turi disputes in the future.[270]

The willingness of certain Turi *maliks* to cooperate with their Muhammadzai overlords may in part be attributed to the fact that they were set apart from the neighboring groups by their Shi'i faith. In March 1856 the Turis were assisted by the son of Sardar Muhammad A'zam Khan against incursions by the neighboring Khostwals and Darwesh Khel Wazirs.

The attackers justified their action with the Turi refusal to join their rebellion against the Muhammadzai administration.[271] While taking place unaided by the Turis, the Khost rebellion of 1856–57 was motivated by concerns similar to those felt by the population of Kurram. After some minor resistance in February, approximately 5,000 to 6,000 Khostwals and Wazirs besieged the fort of Khost in March 1856.[272] The first reports reaching Kabul indicated that this siege had the primary object of reducing the physical presence of the Muhammadzai administration. After mediation by Sahibzada Ziya al-Din, who was respected both in Khost and Waziristan, the tribes of Khost declared that they were willing to pay revenues under the following three conditions,

1) Na'ib Ghulam Muhammad Khan was not to govern their territory because he was a tyrant.
2) Lands which had been sequestered by the government after their original owners had fled (probably in the attempt to evade revenue payments) were to be returned.
3) The government forts erected in Khost should be abandoned and the garrison withdrawn.[273]

Although the son of Sardar Muhammad A'zam Khan accepted these conditions, the rebellion continued. In July the revenue officials were driven out of Khost 'naked and disarmed'. Sardar Muhammad A'zam's son received orders from Kabul to advance no further demands for revenue for the time being.[274] Despite these attempts to mute government activities resentment against Ghulam Muhammad Khan continued to run deep. In August he was driven out of Khost by approximately 1000 attackers. During the negotiations which followed it turned out that the resistance of the Khostwals had not only been triggered by the impostion of revenue payments but the fact that Ghulam Muhammad Khan had abducted three local women.[275] Thus the Khost rebellion which continued until early 1857 may be seen as a reaction to twofold attack by the government on the Pashtun notion of honor. The Muhammadzai government, in particular the activities of its representative Ghulam Muhammad Khan, had directly interfered with the *namus* of the Khostwals, as represented by their women and their land.

The reasons for the participation of the Darwesh Khel Wazirs (possibly the Kabil Khel Utmanzai section of neighboring Birmal) in this rebellion are less clear. While Birmal had suffered occasional plundering raids by Sardar Muhammad A'zam in the 1840s, the country of the Wazirs, consisting of Birmal in the west and Waziristan in the east, was more or less secure from inroads either by the Afghan or British governments.[276] Dwelling in 'an extensive tract of very mountainous country – about one hundred and twenty miles in length from north to south and about eighty in breadth in its widest part – some of the most strongest and most difficult in the

Afghanistan,' the Wazirs were able to evade all outside interference well into the twentieth century.[277] Little is known about Dost Muhammad Khan's attitude to the Wazirs of Birmal. In 1849 he ordered an army of 10,000 men to be sent to the assistance of Sardar Muhammad Afzal, who proposed to enter Birmal by force. At the same time, the wisdom of a military confrontation with the Wazirs was very much doubted by his advisor Sardar Sultan Muhammad Khan.[278] In 1855 part of the region on the Tochi river, inhabited by the Daur Pashtuns, was ceded to Afghanistan by the British. But even in this region the sovereign rights of Kabul remained largely 'imaginary'.[279] In 1875 Dost Muhammad Khan's successor Sher 'Ali Khan did not even dare to raise the issue of revenue payments with a delegation from Daur visiting his court.[280] Likewise, his relations with the Darwesh Khel Wazirs were more or less limited to the attempt to make them his 'well-wishers' by granting allowances to them.[281] The only commitment the Darwesh Khel entered was to submit a certain number of soldiers for Amir Sher 'Ali Khan's infantry regiments. During a visit to the court in the spring of 1873 they, along with the Khugiani leaders present, agreed to furnish a total of 630 recruits.[282]

By comparison, Kurram, Khost and Zurmat were more firmly, if uncomfortably, incorporated into Sher 'Ali Khan's administration. Kurram was governed by the Amir's half brother Wali Muhammad Khan, whose mother was a Turi, from 1869 on. Zurmat, Khost, and Katawaz were controlled by the Amir's trusted foreign minister Arsalan Khan Jabbar Khel Ghilzai and his son Ma'azullah Khan. With Sher 'Ali Khan's efforts at establishing a more centralized administration, local resistance to revenue collection considered excessive began to take the shape of direct complaints to the court of Kabul. In 1870 the *maliks* of Kurram complained to the king that Sardar Wali Khan's extortions were unendurable. In May 1876 a delegation from Kurram accused the Sardar of raising one extra rupee per one and a half acres on his own behalf on top of the regular land revenue, of paying nothing for the fodder requisitioned for his horses, and of levying disproportionate fines on light and trumped up offences. This complaint had the effect that Sardar Wali Muhammad Khan was dismissed from the governorship of Kurram.[283] Similar charges were brought against Ma'azullah Khan. He was accused of having appropriated 350 000 rupees in excess revenue in the region of Zurmat. But because of Arsalan Khan's powerful position at his court, Amir Sher 'Ali Khan did not dare to take any steps against Ma'azullah Khan. To solve the issue, the prime minister advised Arsalan Khan to present an offering (*nazrana*) to the Amir in order to keep the Amir from lending his ear to the elders of Zurmat. In any case, the governorship of Ma'azullah Khan was never seriously called into question.[284] In 1877 Sher 'Ali Khan sought to bring Kurram more firmly under control by establishing a regular postal service to that region.[285] But with the Second Anglo-Afghan War which started a year later, Kurram was to slip entirely from Muhammadzai control. With the treaty of Gandamak, Kurram became a British possession. After the conclusion of the war the British granted independence to the region but finally annexed it in 1893.[286]

Bajaur

Let us return to the Kabul river and the area north of it. The next two regions to be discussed, the Mohmand country adjoining the Kabul river and Bajaur, display certain parallels. Both settings are characterized by their relatively rich agricultural land and their trade relations with the Peshawar plain. True to Ahmed's *qalang* ideal, the leadership of both regions was firmly entrenched. Although both groups were linked to the Muhammadzai family by marriage alliances, their political strategies and fortunes differed fundamentally in the nineteenth century. The Mohmand chiefs of La'lpura, on the one hand, profited from their close interaction with Amir Dost Muhammad Khan and 'policed' the Khyber region in cooperation with the governor of Jalalabad. This linkage turned out to be disadvantageous during the reign of Dost Muhammad Khan's successor, as the *khan* of La'lpura increasingly found himself subject to efforts by Sher 'Ali Khan to curb his power. The khanly family of Bajaur, on the other hand, was able to stay aloof of Kabul politics and retained its independence even after the region was ceded to the British in 1893.

Located north of the Mohmand territory, Bajaur was somewhat removed from the strategically important Khyber region. Its independence and remoteness is reflected by the fact that, apart from the British Chitral Relief Expedition of 1895 and some troops passing through in 1897, no colonial officer visited this region in the nineteenth century.[287] Bajaur consists of a series of valleys, the most fertile of which is the Rud valley. Because of its comparative fertility, Bajaur produced a surplus in wheat, barley and pulses and was also able to export sheep and goats, as well as ghi, hides and wool. Another trade item was iron ore.[288] The Tarklanri Pashtuns, who had entered the region in the sixteenth century, formed the dominant element of the population. Yet in the early nineteenth century, Elphinstone also reported that there was a sizeable non-Tarklanri population in Bajaur:

> Bajour belongs to the Afghaun tribe of Turcolaunee... but it also contains other inhabitants; the upper hills being inhabited by converted Caufirs, the lower by Hindkees, and the plain by a mixture of all tribes and nations, counfounded under the common name of Roadbaurees. The number of the Turcolaunees amount to ten or twelve thousand families, and those of the other inhabitants may be guessed at thirty thousand souls.[289]

Oliver understood the Rudbaris to represent the former autochthonous population of Bajaur. But it also is possible that this term was used for the heterogeneous Pashtun groups, such as the Safis, Mohmands and Utman Khel, who inhabited the Rud valley alongside the Tarklanris.[290] The fact that the chief of Bajaur received tribute from the Kafirs, taxes from the Hindkis, and rent from the Rudbaris points to the possibility that the Tarklanris formed a tribal aristocracy comparable to that of the Yusufzais of Swat. Indeed, Bajaur resembled the Swat example in displaying a marked stratification between Pashtun landowners and landless groups. Furthermore, the *khans* enjoyed a powerful position and were set apart from their fellow tribesmen by considerable wealth and political eminence in both settings.[291] But contrary to Swat, where several sets of *khans* were competing for power, all claims to authority in Bajaur were concentrated in the hands of one leading lineage, the Ibrahim Khel. Elphinstone even credited the chief of Bajaur, who carried the title of *baz* ('falcon') or *badshah* ('king'), with 'absolute' authority over his people: 'He administers justice in his tribe, with power to banish, beat or bind.'[292] In 1901 McMahon and Ramsay described the power of the chief of Bajaur as 'autocratic'. At the same time, they noted that the amount of control he exercised throughout Bajaur varied according to his ability to make his military presence felt. Although the Mamund Tarklanris inhabiting the poorer and more inaccessible valleys of Chaharmung and Watalai paid nominal allegiance to the chief of Bajaur, they challenged his authority almost constantly. Nonetheless the relative strength of the leading lineage of Bajaur is reflected by the fact that its members were in the position to collect revenues. At McMahon's time, the region was divided into eight minor khanates held by the chief of Bajaur and his relatives. In each of these subdivsions the ruling family was entitled to collect an *'ushr* ('tithe') varying from one tenth to one fifth of the produce. Moreover, the local population owed military service to the *khans*.[293] Elphinstone estimated the revenues of the chief of Bajaur at 100,000 rupees. This enabled him to maintain a standing army of 'some hundred horse and a body of foot'.[294] In the 1870s MacGregor reported that the chief of Bajaur controlled 13 guns, 40 camel artillery (*shahins*), 700 rifles, 8,000 infantry and 2,000 cavalry.[295]

In 1859 Amir Dost Muhammad Khan explained to the British *wakil* that the ruling family of Bajaur enjoyed a particularly privileged position because it was linked to the Muhammadzai family by a threefold marriage alliance. During the reign of Shah Mahmud the Bajaur chief Mir 'Alam Khan had entrusted a young daughter of his to Dost Muhammad Khan's eldest brother Fatih Khan. In exchange, the *wazir* had convinced Shah Mahmud to exempt Bajaur from revenue payments. Two more daughters had been wed to the Peshawar Sardars Sultan Muhammad Khan and Pir Muhammad Khan. It was for this reason, the Amir continued, that he had refrained from any incursions into the territory of Bajaur. This romantic portrayal was not believed by the Commissioner of Peshawar, who drily noted that Bajaur's continued independence had to be attributed less to the

Amir's munificence than to his inability to penetrate its inherently strong position.[296] Indeed it was reported in the early 1830s that Dost Muhammad Khan much 'coveted' the possession of Bajaur. In 1831 Mir 'Alam Khan was able to avert a threatened invasion from the ruler of Kabul by submitting a sum of 10,000 or 12,000 rupees. A year later he expressed his submission to the Sardar by paying a reluctant visit to Kabul. Soon afterwards he 'joyfully took his departure, inwardly determined never again to trust himself to the power of Dost Mahomed Khan.' The latter was able to strengthen his position in the border region by seizing Jalalabad from his nephew Nawwab Muhammad Zaman Khan in 1834. Fearing renewed pressure by Dost Muhammad Khan, Mir 'Alam Khan increasingly relied on his alliance with the Peshawar Sardars and maintained contact with Ranjit Singh. On the eve of the First Afghan War he readily sided with Shah Shuja'.[297]

In the 1830s, the rivalry between Dost Muhammad Khan and his half brothers in Peshawar was mirrored on a local level in the power struggle between Mir 'Alam Khan and his cousin Amir Khan. While Bajaur had been under the control of a single ruler in the past, two separate centers of power had already crystallized at the time of Elphinstone's report.[298] Mir 'Alam Khan held the northern region and Amir Khan controlled Nawagai and the southern portion of Bajaur. Amir Khan apparently was the weaker of the two and was forced to seek the assistance of the *sayyids* of Kunar and of Dost Muhammad Khan himself in order to be able to withstand the pressure Mir 'Alam Khan began to exert in 1824. At the beginning of the First Anglo-Afghan War the ruler of Nawagai invited Muhammad Akbar's infantry into his fort. Yet the British advance on Kabul tilted the scales in favor of Mir 'Alam Khan and Amir Khan found himself temporarily displaced from Nawagai. In March 1841 he was able to regain his former possessions with British approval.[299] With the conclusion of the First Anglo-Afghan War, Bajaur was allowed to lapse into its former independence. In 1843 Sardars Muhammad Akbar Khan and Muhammad Afzal Khan had to give up their attempt to conquer the region. According to *Siraj al-tawarikh*, their Durrani, Ghilzai, Qizilbash and Kohistani troops were unable to cope with the difficult terrain and the 'heroic activity' of the Bajauris.[300] The distribution of power in Bajaur seems to have remained the same up to the Second Anglo-Afghan War. In 1877 Dilaram Khan of Bajaur and Habo Khan, the son of the chief of Nawagi (Haidar Khan ?)[301] presented a *nazrana* of 3,000 rupees to Amir Sher ʿAli Khan and were granted an allowance of 6,000 rupees each.[302]

The Mohmands of La'lpura

Occupying the land north and south of the Kabul river, the Mohmands were able to exert pressure on the plains of Nangarhar and Peshawar. In particular the groups among them which controlled several of the most important trade routes between Kabul and India were subject to continuous attention by the rulers of the region. Unlike the chiefs of Bajaur, these *khans* chose to cooperate closely with the rulers of Kabul. Their relationship with the British, by contrast, was one of unequalled contention. Possibly because of their 'troublesome' disposition they have been described in greater detail by British sources. In particular, the study compiled by Merk in 1898 gives a remarkable amount of information on the position of the La'lpura *khans* and their political fortunes. As these men and their followers played an important role during the reigns of Dost Muhammad Khan and his successor, some of the material furnished by Merk and others merits summing up here.

Merk observed that the Mohmand country consisted of two distinct geographical settings. The first was formed by

> the rich alluvial lands along the banks of the Kabul river from Jalalabad to Lalpura; the fringe of fertile soil commences at the pretty, but rather swampy, irrigated valley of Kama, and gradually dwindles in proportions down the river, till at Dakka the sterile hills close in upon it.
>
> The second, and by far the most extensive part of Mohmand territory, is comprised in the glens and valleys that radiate from the mountains of Tartara, south of the Kabul (6,400'), and Ilazai north of the river (9,000' high), and drain into the Kabul and Swat rivers.[303]

While the mountainous part of the Mohmand country had little to offer in terms of livelihood, the Kabul river and its environs, supplying water for irrigation and functioning as a conduit for the trade between Peshawar and Kabul, was the 'principal source of Mohmand wealth'.[304] Unlike the Mohmands studied by Ahmed, the tribal groups inhabiting these fertile regions fit into the *qalang* formula. The Tarakzais of La'lpura and the Baezais of Goshta who form the focus of Merk's study can justly be characterized as more 'aristocratic' in their organization than their fellow tribesmen living in the hills, or their Afridi and Shinwari neighbors in the Khyber region. One major factor contributing to the comparative power of the *khans* was their wealth generated by irrigated lands and transit duties, which even enabled the leaders of La'lpura to maintain mounted troops.[305] Another factor was their close linkage to the Afghan court. From Sadozai times on, the *khans* held their position with the confirmation of the rulers of Kabul and enjoyed considerable favors.[306] As a negative consequence of this intimate connection, royal interference with the appointment and dismissal of these chiefs became increasingly common in the latter part of the nineteenth century.[307]

With 10,000 to 12,000 fighting men the Baezais were the largest tribe in the Mohmand region. Their lands were also considered the most fertile.

During Amir Dost Muhammad Khan's first reign, their leader, Khalid Khan of Goshta, enjoyed a royal *jagir* worth 8,000 rupees annually.[308] In the late 1870s the total income of Khalid Khan's grandson, Mughal Khan (d. 1893), was estimated at 20,000 rupees.[309] Yet the influence of the *khans* of Goshta was eclipsed entirely by the numerically insignificant Tarakzai section which furnished the *khans* of La'lpura.[310] The Morcha Khel were considered the leading lineage not only by other Tarakzai sections but were also influential among the other Mohmand tribes living in the wider region, such as the Halimzais, Dawezais, Utmanzais, and eastern Baezais. According to local tradition, the Morcha Khel Tarakzais owed their predominant position to the fact that their founding ancestor Malik Morcha had obtained a saintly blessing for an act of chivalry.[311] Morcha's employment in the Mughal army may also have helped somewhat to enhance his position. After successful service with the emperor Akbar he was placed in charge of the Mughal fort at Dakka, the command of which seems to have become hereditary in his family. The Morcha Khel were further aided by the commercial position of Dakka, where the Khyber route met with the other major trade routes of the region (via Tartara, Karapa, and Abkhana). Like other Mohmand tribes, the leaders of La'lpura also acquired valuable *jagirs* in the Peshawar valley during Mughal times.[312]

The La'lpura *khans* were able to maintain their prominent position under the Sadozais. The importance of Malik Morcha's descendant Zain Khan during the era of Ahmad Shah has been mentioned above. Despite the rebellion of Zain Khan's grandson, Arsalan Khan, his family continued to hold a *jagir* in the time of Timur Shah.[313] The strength of the La'lpura *khans* also affected the neighboring regions. Apart from a military confrontation which culminated in the conquest of Nawagai by Zain Khan, the relationship between La'lpura and Bajaur seems to have been friendly. Nawagai was returned to Bajaur when Arsalan Khan entered a marriage alliance with the chiefly family of Bajaur. Sa'adat Khan, who was *khan* of La'lpura at the time of Dost Muhammad Khan, continued this friendly alliance by marrying a sister of the chief of Nawagai. Conversely, the relationship with most of the Shinwaris was overtly hostile.[314] From the Mughal period on, the Morcha Khel exerted pressure on the region between Landi Kotal and Pesh Bolak, gradually depriving the Shinwaris of their lands. During the reigns of Amirs Dost Muhammad Khan and Sher 'Ali Khan they cooperated with the government in all measures directed against the Shinwaris, as was the case in the above mentioned revenue assessment of the Sangu Khel in 1859. Clearly, the *khans* of La'lpura were considered formidable enemies by the Shinwaris:

> Summoned by the Hakim of Jalalabad to punish the savage robbers of the Sufed Koh or to collect revenue from outlying and recusant villages, the Mohmand horse and foot would come suddenly over the

> Kabul river in force, harry the country up to the foot of the hills, and then retire behind the protection of the deep stream, which their enemies knew not how to cross. These exploits, their intimate relations with the Kabul Government, the minitaure pomp and state of their Khans, and their power of united action have given them a martial reputation among the people out of all proportion with the facts.[315]

The income of the *khans* of La'lpura was formidable. During the reign of Dost Muhammad Khan, Sa'adat Khan derived an annual income of 60,000 rupees from nine villages in Tappa-yi Shahi of Nangarhar which he held in *jagir.* Furthermore, he received valuable presents from the Amir during his visits to Kabul. Sa'adat Khan collected another 10,000 rupees in transit dues and ferry fees levied at La'lpura.[316] In 1882 the total income of his grandson, Akbar Khan, was estimated at 100,000 to 120,000 rupees per year, approximately half of that amount being obtained from the trade passing through by the Mohmand and Khyber routes.[317] A list of the cash allowances given out by the Kabul government to the various Mohmand tribes in 1898 clearly demonstrates the privileged position of the *khans* of La'lpura: While the *khan* of La'lpura and his family received 40,000 rupees a year, the Khwaezais and Baezais had to content themselves with 2,400 and 3,200 rupees respectively.

Sa'adat Khan's receipts on trade consisted of transit dues levied at Dakka (4,000 rupees) and La'lpura (3,000 rupees) and ferry fees (3,000 rupees). However, these figures do not reflect the entire income generated by trade in his time. Firstly, Sa'adat Khan did not raise these dues himself but farmed the collection rights out to his agents at fixed rates. Secondly, a portion of the income generated in Mohmand country was reserved for his fellow tribesmen. According to Merk, the *khan* of La'lpura received one third of all transit dues levied on the roads. Another third went to his tribal section, the Dadu Khel Tarakzais, the privileged Morcha Khel receiving half of the resultant sum. The final third was reserved for the Halimzai Mohmands.[318] While the bulk of the trade between Peshawar and Kabul took place along the overland routes, the Kabul river was an important conduit for the local trade from Kunar, Bajaur, Kafiristan and Chitral. During the warm season traffic on the river was brisk. Bajaur and Kunar exported wax, hides, ghi, rice, walnuts and honey; Bajaur also sent large quantities of iron ore to Peshawar; finally, gold dust, hawks, falcons and slaves from Kafiristan and Chitral floated down the river. In order to pass through the entire length of Mohmand country, each wooden raft had to pay a total of 120 rupees.[319] The *khan* of La'lpura collected one third of this amount, out of which he gave two rupees to the Halimzais. On rafts made of inflated skins he levied a toll of four rupees. His total income from this source amounted to 7,000 rupees annually, for which amount he farmed out the right to collect the river dues.[320]

Just as they farmed out the collection of their trade revenues, the chiefs of La'lpura relied on a miniature administration for the management of their landed estates. The revenues from their *jagirs* were collected by so-called *faujdars* in kind. These agents not only controlled the storage and disbursement of these revenues but were also in charge of raising local fines and fees.

> [The *faujdars*] stored the grain in granaries on the spot. The Khan paid his retainers and expenses by cheques on the *faujdars*, who honoured them in cash or in kind as directed, and accounted for the balance annually to the head accountant at Lalpura. In addition the *faujdars* levied fines (which were credited to the Khan) in the jagir villages, for grave offences committed by any of the inhabitants, e.g., Rs. 400 for murder, Rs. 50 for a broken arm or foot, varying sums for theft, & c.; and collected the market dues *tarazudari*, and the marriage and burial fees from the Hindu residents. In large villages like Hisarshahi, Lalpura or Baru, the fines and fees amounted to considerable sums, and were farmed out to contractors.

The *khans* of La'lpura used their income to bolster their position among their fellow tribesmen. The Halimzais, for example, were paid an annual cash allowance of 9,000 rupees. Other Mohmand chiefs received varying sums of money as personal favors.[321] Another part of the surplus generated was used to maintain a body of mounted troops. In the 1890s the *khan* of La'lpura was said to employ 140 horsemen for escort duties in the Khyber region from Dakka to Landi Khana.[322] According to their pecuniary means and their reputation as leaders, the *khans* of La'lpura had varying degrees of influence among their fellow tribesmen. Theoretically they were in the position to settle the internal affairs of all the Tarakzai, Halimzai, Dawezai and Utmanzai Mohmands. But 'only a strong Khan would attempt to do so, and then not without the secret co-operation of the clan-elders, who would privately receive part of the fines imposed by the Khan.' Nonetheless, the role of the Morcha Khel as *khan khel* was never questioned by the surrounding Mohmand tribes. When Sher 'Ali Khan began to interfere with the appointment of the chiefs of La'lpura in the 1870s he was unable to displace the ruling family entirely and could only limit their power by reducing their allowances and cultivating the Baezai *khan* of Goshta as a counterpoise.[323]

The course of La'lpura politics in the nineteenth century is best viewed in the light of an internal split among the Morcha Khel which brought about the existence of two leading families vying for the control of La'lpura. The two main rivals during Amir Dost Muhammad Khan's reign were Sa'adat Khan and Tura Baz Khan, who, according to most accounts, were *tarburs*, patrilateral parallel cousins. Their enmity dated back to the Sadozai period, their fathers being brothers of the famous Arsalan Khan. The rift between the two cousins was generally attributed to the fact that Sa'adat Khan's father Sadullah had murdered Tura Baz Khan's father Ma'azullah.[324] Sa'adat Khan became chief of La'lpura shortly after the death of Fatih Khan Barakzai in 1818. As Sa'adat Khan pursued a close linkage with the Muhammadzai court, Tura Baz Khan was ready to side with Amir Dost Muhammad Khan's enemies. At the beginning of the First Anglo-Afghan War Tura Baz Khan joined Shahzada Timur, while Sa'adat Khan sought to obstruct the British advance at the Tartara and Abkhana passes. When the British forces took possession of Dakka and La'lpura in August 1839, Tura Baz Khan was installed in the government of the region. Subsequent to the war Sa'adat Khan was able to regain the chiefship, while Tura Baz Khan received a *jagir* at Kama after submitting to Amir Dost Muhammad Khan. Yet the enmity between the two branches of the family continued unabated. At the beginning of Amir Sher 'Ali Khan's reign, Tura Baz's son Riza Khan was able to gain the chiefship of La'lpura for one and a half years. Subsequently the power passed to Sa'adat Khan's son Sultan Muhammad Khan, who was killed by Riza Khan's son, Malang, in 1871.[325]

Sa'adat Khan retained the chiefship of La'lpura for the remainder of Dost Muhammad Khan's second reign. During this period he was said to be at the height of his prosperity. He enjoyed a close relationship with Sardar Muhammad Akbar Khan and gained considerable influence by entering a marriage alliance with Dost Muhammad Khan. His daughter Qamar Jan was married to the future Amir, Sher 'Ali Khan, and gave birth to two of his most influential sons, Sardars Muhammad Ya'qub and Ayub Khan. By this connection, Qamar Jan's full brothers Nauroz Khan and Sultan Muhammad Khan were maternal uncles of the two young Sardars, a linkage that was going to prove crucial during the reign of Amir Sher 'Ali Khan.[326]

Apart from the vertical split occasioned by the enmity between Sa'adat Khan and Tura Baz Khan, generational tension was another source of conflict in the chiefly family. While Sa'adat Khan cooperated closely with his son Nauroz Khan, his relationship with Sultan Muhammad Khan was extremely troubled. In 1855 he reported to Amir Dost Muhammad Khan that Sultan Muhammad Khan had killed his eldest son by the same wife, Fatih Muhammad. Furthermore, Sultaṇ Muhammad had sought British support for his plan to do away with his father. Fearing an attempt on his life, Sa'adat Khan requested that Sultan Muhammad be sent to Turkistan to serve with Sardar Muhammad Afzal Khan.[327] In December 1863 Sultan Muhammad Khan turned against the British and joined the Akhund of Swat in the Ambela campaign .[328]

In great part Sa'adat Khan owed his pivotal position in the border region to the fact that the trade routes leading through his land formed an important alternative to the often disrupted connection through the Khyber Pass. At times Dost Muhammad Khan even suspected Sa'adat Khan of fomenting unrest in the Khyber region in order to enhance his own standing. Be that as it may, the routes through the Mohmand region were considered much safer than the Khyber Pass during the time of Dost Muhammad Khan.[329] While Sa'adat Khan was not able to prevent robberies on caravans moving from Peshawar to Kabul, Bajaur and Kunar, he strongly cooperated with the governor of Jalalabad in the restoration of the plundered property.[330] The British subsidies of 100,000 rupees a month which were sent to Amir Dost Muhammad Khan in the course of 1857 as part of the Anglo-Afghan Treaty of Friendship, were transported through Mohmand rather than Khyber country.[331] As part of his cooperation with the governor of Jalalabad, Sa'adat Khan was given a virtually free hand in all dealings with the Shinwaris.[332]

Until the annexation of Punjab by the British the Halimzais and the Tarakzai chiefs of La'lpura, Michni and Pindiali held *jagirs* around the confluence of the Kabul and Swat rivers.[333] While these possessions had not been meddled with during Sikh times, most of them were confiscated by the British in 1851 and 1854. The reason given for this move was the hostile attitude of the Mohmands. Indeed, the relationship between the British and the Mohmands was one of continuous conflict in which Sa'adat Khan and his sons Fatih Khan and Nauroz Khan played an important role. They were aided by their relatives Nawwab Khan and Rahimdad Khan, the chiefs of Pindiali and Michni, who had lost their *jagirs* to the British in 1850 and 1854 respectively.[334] In the early 1850s Amir Dost Muhammad Khan openly encouraged the Mohmands in their activities against the British.[335] Yet his attitude shifted somewhat as his son Ghulam Haidar prepared to enter negotiations with the British in the spring of 1855. Aware of Sa'adat Khan's opposition to a government agreement with the British, Ghulam Haidar and Dost Muhammad Khan tried to show that their negotiations at Peshawar also served Mohmand interests. Both of them took the conclusion of the Anglo-Afghan treaties of 1855 and 1857 as an opportunity to plead the case of Rahimdad Khan.[336] When the British remained firm in their refusal to restore the *jagirs* in question, Dost Muhammad Khan advised the Mohmand tribes under his jurisdiction not to challenge his agreements with the British. He informed Sa'adat Khan that he would only retain his *jagir* in Nangarhar if he refrained from raiding the British frontier.[337] In 1857 when Sayyid Amir Badshah, a relative of the *sayyids* of Kunar, was inciting the Michni Mohmands to engage in jihad against the British, Dost Muhammad Khan had him removed from Mohmand territory. Otherwise, the Amir took few practical steps to stop the 85 raids committed by the Mohmands on British territory between January 1855 and March 1860.[338] His successor Sher 'Ali Khan, on the other hand, was more willing to listen to British remonstrances. After a major military confrontation between the Mohmands and the British at Shabkadar on 2 January 1864, Sher 'Ali Khan seized Sa'adat Khan and Nauroz Khan and took them to Kabul. A few months later, Sa'adat Khan died in captivity 'from the effects of the inclement climate of Kabul'.[339]

Sher 'Ali Khan's decisive action against his father-in-law was indicative of a general shift in the royal policies towards the Mohmands. The new Amir showed little interest in 'conciliating' the Mohmands as his father had been wont to do. On the contrary, Sher 'Ali Khan felt that the regular entertainment of Mohmand elders at the court was a waste of money and he generally was stingy with presents to them.[340] Moreover, he attempted to deemphasize the trade routes through the Mohmand region in favor of the Khyber Pass. Another, yet more unrealistic, project was to shift part of the trade with Peshawar to the Kurram valley.[341] Sher 'Ali Khan's cautious attitude towards the Mohmands in general may have been a reflection of his uneasy relationship with Nauroz Khan, the maternal uncle of his son, Sardar Muhammad Ya'qub Khan. Contrary to Dost Muhammad Khan, Sher 'Ali Khan viewed his Mohmand relatives with a good measure of distrust and jealousy and attempted to reduce their influence. With the imprisonment of Nauroz Khan in 1864 the Amir tried to strengthen the position of Tura Baz's branch of the family by appointing Tura Baz's son, Riza Khan, to the chiefship of La'lpura. Yet finding that Riza Khan was unable to command the followership of his fellow tribesmen, Sher 'Ali Khan gave this office to Nauroz's full brother, Sultan Muhammad Khan, who held it until his death in 1871. In the meantime, Nauroz Khan was released and joined Sardar Muhammad Ya'qub Khan, who was the governor of Herat at that time.[342] Henceforth his fortunes were to rise and fall with those of his nephew. When Muhammad Ya'qub Khan rebelled in 1870 because of the appointment of his younger half brother, 'Abdullah Jan, as heir apparent, Sher 'Ali Khan reacted with the temporary confiscation of Nauroz Khan's possessions.[343] Subsequent to Ya'qub Khan's reinstatement as governor of Herat in 1871, Nauroz Khan succeeded Sultan Muhammad Khan as chief of La'lpura. Yet he was only able to gain this office after the Amir had had to acknowledge that his appointee Muhammad Shah Khan (b. Sultan Muhammad Khan), whom he favored for his youth and weak position, was not accepted as a leader by the Mohmands. Even after awarding the chiefship of La'lpura to Nauroz Khan, Sher 'Ali Khan attempted to cultivate Sultan Muhammad Khan's family as a local counterpoise by stipulating that it was to receive a fixed share of his income.[344] Nonetheless Nauroz's khanship was characterized by 'vigour and energy'.[345] Emulating the policies of his father, he guaranteed the safety of the roads through his territories. His activities against the Shinwaris and Khugianis were coordinated at times with those of Amir Sher 'Ali Khan's foreign minister Arsalan Khan Ghilzai and the governor of Jalalabad.[346] The relationship between Nauroz Khan and Sher 'Ali Khan began to deteriorate again in the fall of 1873. The Amir dismissed Nauroz Khan from the chiefship of La'lpura and imposed a fine of five thousand rupees on him.[347] Nauroz Khan was able to regain his office shortly afterwards. Yet the imprisonment of Sardar Ya'qub Khan in 1874 caused him to throw off any show of allegiance to Sher 'Ali Khan and to flee from La'lpura. Until his death in 1877 he was reported to be moving around Gandau and Bajaur, disrupting the trade in the region.[348]

Nauroz Khan's rebellion provided Sher 'Ali Khan with a welcome opportunity to undermine the power of the leading family of La'lpura and to keep tribal affairs in an unsettled state. One step in this direction was the appointment of Zardad and Lal Khan, nephews of Sa'adat Khan, to the joint leadership of La'lpura. Having chosen weak leaders, the Amir soon began to reason that they deserved smaller allowances than their powerful predecessors. In 1876 his prime minister used the inability of the two brothers to provide for the safety of the trade routes as a pretext for withholding their allowances and thus undermined their position even further.[349] In 1877 Muhammad Shah Khan b. Sultan Muhammad Khan was able to gain the chiefship of La'lpura. In exchange for his appointment he had to accept a considerable reduction of the income linked to the chiefship. Apart from an allowance of 8,000 rupees he only retained half the revenues of one of the nine villages which had traditionally formed the *jagir* of the chiefs of La'lpura. When Nauroz Khan's elder sons, Muhammad Sadiq Khan and Muhammad Akbar Khan, forfeited their combined allowance by leaving for Peshawar Muhammad Shah Khan's total allowance was raised to 20,000 rupees.[350] Compared to his predecessors, Muhammad Shah Khan thus found his income much curtailed and was unable to garner support for his claims to leadership by handing out generous allowances to his fellow tribesmen.[351] Simultaneously, Amir Sher 'Ali sought to bolster the position of the Baezai Mohmands, whose allowance he raised to 12,000 rupees annually after Nauroz Khan's rebellion. In return Taj Muhammad Khan (d. 1877), the chief of Goshta, and his half brother, Sayyid Amir Khan of Chardeh, as well as the local Baezai *maliks* and some Halimzai leaders supported the Amir in his activities against Nauroz Khan.[352]

Sher 'Ali Khan also began to meddle with other prerogatives of the chiefs of La'lpura. As the appointment of a new *khan* was pending after Sultan Muhammad Khan's death in 1871 the Amir sent Shahmard Khan, the governor of Jalalabad, to La'lpura to safeguard the security of the trade routes.[353] Moreover, disputes between the chiefs of La'lpura and the Shinwaris were no longer seen as 'off limits' for the government. When unrest broke out concerning the possession of Qal'a Sahibzada on the Shinwari border, Shahmard Khan was simply ordered to annex the disputed territory.[354] Finally, Sher 'Ali Khan attempted to use Nauroz Khan's rebellion to take direct control of the collection of transit duties in the region. During the chiefship of Zardad Khan and Lal Khan these revenues were placed under the direct management of the governor of Jalalabad. However, it soon became clear that the government lacked the strength to back up this measure. While the leadership of La'lpura was weak, the greater group of Mohmands saw no reason to give up their hereditary rights. The net result was that the traders passing through the region had to pay transit dues in two locations, once to the government officials at Dakka, and a second time when encountering the Mohmands in the hills.[355] When Muhammad Shah Khan obtained the khanship in 1877 he also regained the right to levy the tolls on the river and road traffic.[356]

Altogether Sher 'Ali Khan's attempts to curb the power of the *khans* of La'lpura only met with limited success. While he played a considerable role in the choice of the leadership, he was in no position to deprive the descendants of Sa'adat Khan Mohmand of their claims to power. Subsequent to the Second Anglo-Afghan War the chiefship of La'lpura was in the hands of Nauroz Khan's son, Akbar Khan, who enjoyed all of the family's traditional sources of income. But Sher 'Ali Khan's attempt at interference may be seen as a prelude to similar policies to be pursued by Amir 'Abd al-Rahman Khan. From 1885 on the Amir began to establish direct contact with the Mohmand tribes, such as the Halimzais, who used to be under the management of the *khans* of La'lpura. Furthermore, Akbar Khan faced reductions of his *jagir* and lost control of the trade revenues. In part, the loss of power of the La'lpura family may also have been caused by the declining importance of the trade routes leading entirely through Mohmand country. With the establishment of the Durand Line, La'lpura remained part of the Afghan state but many of the tribal groups formerly under its sphere of influence, such as the other Tarakzai sections, as well as the Halimzais, Dawezais and Utmanzais, were placed under British authority and began to receive allowances from their new overlords.[357]

From the 'feudal' leadership of Bajaur and La'lpura to the 'democratic' tribes of the Kurram and Khyber region, the cases discussed in this section span a whole range of possibilities of tribal organization and political strategies which make it clear that Pashtun tribalism cannot be pressed into a neat formula. Perhaps the Afridis of the Khyber region and their not too distant neighbors, the Mohmands of La'lpura, form the most striking contrast. Although both groups occupied strategically important positions and received allowances from the rulers of Kabul, only the *khans* of La'lpura, in particular Sa'adat Khan, can truly be described as 'servants', albeit well paid ones, of the Muhammadzais. The British presence during the First Anglo-Afghan war did bring forth a greater coalition under the leadership of Khan Bahadur Khan Malikdin Khel among the Afridis, but this group lapsed back into a state of 'institutionalized dissidence' with the retreat of the British. While formally pledging allegiance to the Muhammadzai rulers, the Afridis essentially maintained a bargaining position between the competing interests of the Afghan kingdom and the colonial administration of Punjab. These two examples show that 'proximity' to the state, as well the hierarchization accompanying it, cannot solely be seen as a spatial phenomenon. Historically grown relationships with the local rulers, the formulation of identity in opposition to, or in consonance with, their policies are important diacritics in the evolution of tribal politics.

Among the border tribes discussed, only the Shinwaris of the Khyber region, the Turis of Kurram and the tribes of Khost were subjects to the Muhammadzai kings in the sense that they were placed under the authority of administrators sent from Kabul and had to pay revenues. Even so, government presence in these regions was usually limited to small garrisons barely able maintain themselves. Revenue collection required the presence of a larger military force sent from the next larger towns. Such military expeditions occurred at irregular intervals and took the form of military raids. Apart from enforcing the payment of revenues they also served to feed the soldiers who were scouring the land. While little is known about the tribal leadership in these regions, it is apparent that it did not cooperate with the state forces. Rather, any pending revenue collection was seen as an imposition by outsiders, to be evaded or fought off if possible. Faced with with an approaching revenue collecting army, the local population had three possible strategies to resort to. Firstly, to abandon the land and to disappear into the 'hills' with all movable property. Secondly, to fight the advancing troops and possibly attain a better bargaining position in the ensuing negotiations, or thirdly, to submit to the local crops being 'eaten up' by the invading army, which might, after all, soon go away. Once government troops or hostile tribal militias arrived the scales were tilted entirely in favor of the government. Yet the methods both sides resorted to basically took the form of tribal raid and counter raid. In particular during the lulls between major military campaigns the tribal forces could become formidable enemies for the local government representatives left behind.

The Western Reaches of the Kabul River

After mastering the Khyber pass, the caravans travelling to Kabul had a journey of a bit less than two weeks or 130 miles ahead of them.[358] Ever since the conclusion of the First Anglo-Afghan War the route leading to Kabul via Gandamak reminded British travellers of the terrors the Kabul garrison had experienced during its disastrous retreat in January 1842. Accordingly, their accounts of this region consciously or unconsciously reverberate with the horrible fate their forebears had met with in the deepest winter:

> At Jelalabad – ninety miles from Peshawur – the cross ranges of hills are, for a change, replaced by a well-watered fertile stretch of country, a score of miles long by a dozen wide, dotted with towers, villages and trees; and where the Kabul river – that has all along had to struggle

> through mere cracks – becomes a broad clear stream 100 yards wide. Thence the route lies through a thoroughly unattractive country again, over long stony ridges, across rocky river-beds, varied with an occasional fine valley like Fathabad, or an oasis like Nimlah, to Gandamak, which by way of comparison with what is beyond again, is a land flowing with milk and honey: for on by Jagdalak and the Lataband Pass or Tezin and the Khurd Kabul, is a wide waste of bare hills, surrounded by still more lofty and forbidding mountains: the teeth become more closely set together; the road narrower; the stony ridges change to bleak heights from 7,000 to 8,000 feet high, the river-beds, deep valleys, or narrow defiles, like the fatal Jagdalak, almost devoid of verdure, and in whose gloomy ravines the winter sun can hardly penetrate – these are the outworks that have to be negotiated before the gardens and orchards, the bazaars and forts of Kabul, can be approached.[359]

In this section I will focus on the political setting in two of the 'fertile stretches' along the Kabul river. The first of these, the Kunar valley, is located immediately east of Jalalabad. It provides a point of contrast with the cases covered so far in that its Pashtun population derived from various tribal origins and was not politically dominant. The rulers of the small khanates of Pashat and Asmar were not Pashtuns. The second area to be discussed is that of Laghman. Far more accessible than Kunar, this region had traditionally served as a *jagir* of the Sadozai kings, who in turn enhanced the political fortunes of the Ghilzai Pashtuns of the area at the expense of the local population. Therefore, the political developments in Laghman are best viewed in connection with the two dominant Ghilzai sections also at home in the adjacent regions along the Kabul river, the Jabbar Khel and the Babakr Khel.

Kunar

The Danish anthropologist Christensen, who has authored the most recent study on Kunar, gives the following description of the valley:

> The Kunar area is situated on the southern watershed of the Hindu Kush mountains, and contains the southern part of the Kunar river drainage area. Altitude varies from about 6,000 m. in the northern part of the area to about 600 m. in the lower Kunar valley. Because of the terrain climate is a function of altitude, and the areas below 1,000 m., which include the whole of the Kunar valley and the lower Pech valley, are within the subtropical region of eastern Afghanistan... The Kunar province contains the largest forest areas in Afghanistan outside Paktia. These forests are situated between 1,800 m. and 3,400 m. and contain cedar, pine and spruce. In the upper part of the forest

belt and above, there are mountian meadows that are utilized for grazing in a pattern of transhumance between these and lower areas. Below the coniferous forest at altitudes between 1,000 m. and 1,800 m., a vegetation comprising different species of evergreen oak are found and below this semi-steppe vegetation.

Two different socioeconomic settings may be distinguished in Kunar. The region known in the nineteenth century as the khanate of Pashat extended along the valley proper from Shewa near the confluence of the Kabul and Kunar rivers to Chigha Sarai (known as Asadabad today) in the north. Here the descendants of the original Dardic speaking population of the area, who were generally referred to as 'Tajik' or 'Dehgan', lived alongside Pashtuns.[360] The valley bottom was mainly irrigated and produced a sufficient surplus of rice to allow its export to the Mohmand region. Other products were wheat, barley, and corn.[361] In conformity with Ahmed's *nang-qalang* model, the core region of the khanate of Pashat displayed a great amount of centralization and stratification. By comparison, the tributary valleys of Kunar were characterized by a much more egalitarian organization.[362]

The Pashtuns dwelling in the hilly areas were of heterogeneous origin and had entered their lands in successive waves of immigration. The Safis living on the right bank of the Kunar river and in the Pech valley had conquered their lands from the local Kafir population some time after the sixteenth century and continued to spread westward. The Adram Khel and Shubul Khel Shinwaris displaced the Kafirs living along the western tributaries of Shin Koruk and Shigal after they had been forced out of their own lands by intertribal conflicts (possibly with the Mohmands?) in the late eighteenth century. The Shinwaris who settled above Shigal were in turn driven out by Mashwani Pashtuns. The Mamund Tarklanris began to settle on the eastern side of the Kunar river in the region between Sarkanai and Sangar (north of Asmar) in the beginning or middle of the seventeenth century. In the 1820s they began to push into Chigha Sarai and Shigal with the support of Mir ᶜAlam Khan Bajauri. The Kabul Tsappar mountains along the southern end of the Kunar river were inhabited by Baezai Mohmands of the Khuga Khel Usman Khel subdivision.[363]

The Tarklanris living in the region north of Chigha Sara fell under the authority of the khans of Asmar, who held sway in the Bashgul portion of the Kunar river and were said to control 2,000 fighting men.[364] The Mohmands, Shinwaris and Safis paid allegiance to the rulers of Pashat, who had authority over 8,500 fighting men.[365] The *padshahs* of Pashat belonged to a line of *sayyids* who came to power when the 'Arab' rulers of Bajaur and Kunar were displaced by the Tarklanris entering Bajaur in the middle of the 16th century. At that point Mir 'Abbas, a 'dervish' living in Kunar, 'came forth from his recluse's cell, and stretched forth his arm,' successfully using the existing power vacuum in his region to establish his own authority. During the Nadirid period, the sphere of influence of Mir 'Abbas's son Mir 'Ubaidullah seems to have extended into Nangarhar.[366] Initially the town of Kunar formed the seat of government of the Sayyids. At the time of Sayyid Nazif (b. Sayyid Latif b. Mir 'Ubaidullah b. Mir 'Abbas), who ruled the valley approximately from 1770 to 1825, Pashat had become the administrative center.[367] The rulers of Kunar mostly raised their revenues in the valley proper. According to most accounts their annual income fluctuated between 60,000 and 80,000 rupees in the late eighteenth and early nineteenth centuries.[368] Because of their holy descent the rulers of Pashat also commanded special respect among the Pashtuns in the surrounding areas, including the Ghilzai groups resident along the Kabul river.[369] But only the Shinwaris of the region of Shigal are documented as paying a regular revenue to them. The contributions submitted by the other Pashtun groups, such as the Safis, seem to have been of a nominal nature:

> No regular revenue is obtained from the mountains to the west of the valley. In many places each family contributes at every harvest a dish full of corn [grain] containing about five seers, this they consent to do on the score of charity adverting to the sanctity of their chief's character.[370]

The interaction between the Sayyids of Kunar and the Sadozai kings seems to have been limited to the submission of a small tribute and possibly the provision of a number of horsemen in times of war.[371] But with the decline of the Sadozais and the rise of the Muhammadzais at the beginning of the nineteenth century, Kunar began to face increasing pressure from the lords of Kabul. This was in part the result of Sayyid Nazif's active interference in the power struggle between Shah Zaman and his half brother Shah Mahmud. In 1800 he was instrumental in tilting the scales in Shah Mahmud's favor by opposing Shah Zaman militarily. For this reason, he faced a retaliatory invasion of his territory as soon as Shah Zaman's full brother Shah Shuja' came to power in 1803. Fortunately, his friendship with the commander of this military expedition, 'Arzbegi Akram Khan Popalzai, allowed him to hold on to his possessions unscathed after paying a bribe of 5,000 rupees. With the civil war following Shah Mahmud's deposal from power in 1818, a number of Dost Muhammad Khan's relatives and rivals began to depend in large part on the country around Jalalabad for their pecuniary resources. During the time of Sardar Muhammad 'Azim Khan's ascendany at Kabul, his nephew, Sardar Nawwab Muhammad Zaman Khan, used his base in Jalalabad to begin a military confrontation with Sayyid Nazif. In 1821 Muhammad 'Azim Khan himself entered Kunar, deprived Sayyid Nazif of possessions worth 85,000 rupees and forced him to cede the district of Shewa to the governor of Jalalabad.[372]

After the death of Sardar Muhammad 'Azim Khan in 1823, all attention of the Muhammadzai clan was riveted on the heated fight for the possession of Kabul. Meanwhile, Sayyid Nazif found himself caught up in a power struggle of an entirely regional nature, facing increasing pressure from the ruler of Bajaur, Mir 'Alam Khan. Sayyid Nazif's troubled relationship with Mir 'Alam Khan demonstrates that marriage ties may serve to foster existing alliances but also carry the seeds of conflict. Sayyid Nazif was married to Mir 'Alam Khan's sister, who had given birth to his sons Faqir, Amir, 'Abbas and Shahbaz. This formal alliance notwithstanding, Mir 'Alam Khan was inclined to push his influence into Kunar by more practical means. He was aided in his designs by the sons of his sister, particularly Sayyid Faqir. From 1824 on the politics of Kunar were characterized by Sayyid Faqir's rivalry with his half brothers Muhiy al-Din, Baha al-Din, Hashim, and Husain, and his attempts to seize power with the assistance of his maternal uncle and Amir Khan of Nawagai. This conflict entered a decisive phase when Sayyid Nazif proceeded to Nawagai with his sons in order to dissuade Mir 'Alam Khan from his hostilities against Amir Khan. While in Nawagai, Sayyid Faqir used the occasion of a tribal assembly to stab and kill his half brother Muhiy al-Din. While this move eliminated one of Sayyid Faqir's most powerful rivals, it initially weakened his position in Kunar. Sayyid Nazif removed him and his full brothers from their governorships in the south of Pashat and stationed them in the poorer northern regions of Chigha Sarai, Shigal, Sarkanai and Dunai.[373] Moreover, Sayyid Nazif began to rely more strongly on Baha al-Din, whom he placed in control of the town of Kunar. Shortly afterwards Sayyid Faqir rebelled openly. He offered Chigha Sarai and Shigal to Mir 'Alam Khan in exchange for his assistance in unseating Sayyid Nazif. Amir Khan of Nawagai was to obtain Sarkani and Dunai for similar services. Mir ᶜAlam Khan and Amir Khan readily availed themselves of the areas offered to them but failed to keep their part of the contract. Though left to his own resources, Sayyid Faqir was able to imprison and kill his father approximately in the year 1825. The town of Kunar passed into his possession, but the southern part of the valley remained under the authority of Sayyid Baha al-Din. This state of affairs continued until 1834 when Dost Muhammad Khan seized Jalalabad from his nephew Nawwab Muhammad Zaman Khan. As Sayyid Faqir had been an ally of Muhammad Zaman Khan, he was removed to Charbagh in Laghman. Sayyid Baha al-Din, who undertook to submit 19,000 rupees a year, became the sole ruler of Kunar.[374]

Yet a few years later, at the beginning of the First Anglo-Afghan War, the Amir suspected Sayyid Baha al-Din of harboring a British spy and corresponding with Shahzada Timur. He ordered Sardar Muhammad Akbar, at that time governor of Jalalabad, to seize the ruler of Kunar and to send him to Kabul. It is not clear whether these accusations were truly based on Dost Muhammad Khan's fear of the British or whether they merely served as a pretext for the expansion of his authority. At any rate, Sardar Muhammad Akbar took the following military expedition to Kunar as an opportunity to avail himself of 100,000 rupees-worth of Sayyid Baha al-Din's property, which must have formed a welcome addition to his war chest. The impression that the move against Sayyid Baha al-Din was strongly motivated by financial considerations is supported by the fact that the Sardar made the Sayyid's full brother Hashim governor of Kunar in exchange for 9,000 rupees more in revenue.

With the British invasion, the tables were turned in favor of Sayyid Baha al-Din again. Although Sayyid Hashim held on to Kunar tenaciously throughout the year of 1839, Baha al-Din was able to displace him with British help in January 1840. Sayyid Hashim subsequently accepted a pension from the British.[375] Sayyid Baha al-Din remained in power in Kunar throughout Dost Muhammad Khan's second reign.[376] In 1866 he was succeeded by his younger son Mahmud, who held Pashat as a government grant at least until 1883. At that time his possessions were assessed at 30,000 rupees in taxes, out of which 16,000 rupees were assigned to him as an allowance. Other portions of Kunar were farmed to members of the Muhammadzai family.[377] Sayyid Mahmud Khan had been a close ally of Sardar Muhammad Akbar Khan and was married to his daughter. During the power struggle of 1866–1868 he was a steadfast supporter of Sher 'Ali Khan[378]. In 1870 Sayyid Mahmud was named as one of the thirteen members making up the newly instituted advisory council at Sher 'Ali Khan's court. Acting as the Amir's middleman in his dealings with the *khans* of Bajaur and Dir, he also seems to have enjoyed a fairly strong position in the border region.[379] The only source of conflict between Sher 'Ali Khan and Sayyid Mahmud mentioned in the available sources was the latter's refusal to give up part of the revenues of Kunar in favor of his elder brother Hisam al-Din. Rather than forcing the issue, the Amir gave in and assigned a separate piece of government land west of Kunar to Hisam al-Din, in essence granting him an annual government allowance of 12,000 rupees.[380]

The Jabbar Khel Ghilzais

The region around Surkhrud, Gandamak, Jagdalak and Tizin was inhabited by two prominent sections of the Ahmadzai Ghilzais, the Jabbar Khel and the Babakr Khel.[381] Accounts from the nineteenth century describe the Jabbar Khel as the leading lineage of this region.[382] Anderson attributes this reputation to the prominent role the Jabbar Khel had played under 'Aziz Khan during the First Anglo-Afghan War.[383] Yet a look at the events of 1840–1842 shows that the participation of the Babakr Khel in the rebellion against the British was at least as crucial for the outcome of the war. Moreover, there are indications that the Jabbar Khel entered the political stage of the Kabul basin as early as the seventeenth century. At that time an Ahmadzai leader by the name of Jabbar, possibly the founder of the Jabbar Khel patrilineage, was appointed to the khanship over his tribe in exchange for the protection of the thoroughfare between Jalalabad and Kabul.[384] While known for their 'republican government', the whole group of Ahmadzais differed from the Khyber tribes in their 'perfect obedience' to the kings.[385] Throughout the Sadozai and Muhammadzai periods the Jabbar Khel in particular cooperated closely with the masters of Kabul, entered marriage alliances with them and accepted public offices.[386]

The Jabbar Khel were centered in the region of Qabr-i Jabbar (or Khak-i Jabbar) between Jagdalak and Khurd Kabul, and about Surkhpul and Hisarak.[387] The region of Hisarak was comparatively fertile, and its chief products of wheat and barley found a 'ready market' in the adjoining hills. This area had become *mu'afi*, that is,. exempt from revenue payments, at the time of Ahmad Shah in recognition for services rendered by the then Jabbar Khel leader, Langar Khan. While this privilege was lost during the reign of Amir Dost Muhammad Khan, it was regained at the time of his successor for reasons to be explained below.[388] During Dost Muhammad Khan's time 'Aziz Khan b. Ahmad Khan of the Mariyam Khel subdivision became the most prominent leader among the Jabbar Khel. Ahmad Khan (d. 1818) had been in the service of Dost Muhammad Khan's eldest brother, Fatih Khan, and had secured a sizeable *jagir* in the southernmost portion of Laghman. At the time of Ahmad Khan's death 'Aziz Khan inherited two thirds of his possessions and the *jagir* bestowed by Fatih Khan henceforth came to be known as Kats-i 'Aziz Khan.[389] 'Aziz Khan's standing among the Ahmadzais was further enhanced by the fact that his sister was married to Dost Muhammad Khan.[390] During the First Anglo-Afghan War 'Aziz Khan remained loyal to the Amir and rebelled during the early part of 1840. In September 1841 he precipitated the insurrection against the British by declaring jihad together with Muhammad Shah Khan Babakr Khel.

Little is known about 'Aziz Khan's fortunes during Dost Muhammad Khan's second reign. In spite of his short-lived involvement with the rebellion of Muhammad Shah Khan Babakr Khel he seems to have continued undisturbed in his possessions until his death during hajj sometime prior to 1855. In the summer of 1856 his somewhat less influential brother, Karim Khan, took offense after Dost Muhammad Khan had reduced his allowance by transferring some of his lands to another Jabbar Khel leader. He left Kabul and joined the cause of Muhammad Shah Khan Babakr Khel for some months, attacking Charbagh and the fort of 'Aziz Khan, and threatening to disrupt the traffic between Jalalabad and Kabul from a base in Usbin. Contrary to Muhammad Shah Khan, however, he soon gave in to attempts at reconciliation by the son of 'Aziz khan. In 1857 he was reported to be loyal to the government again.[391]

During Sher 'Ali Khan's reign 'Ismatullah Khan (b. 'Aziz Khan) became the acknowledged leader of the Jabbar Khel. Carrying the title Hashmat al-Mulk, he acted as a minister at the court of Kabul and was held responsible for the security of the portion of the Kabul road passing through Jabbar Khel territory. At the same time he was able to use his position at court to shield his fellow tribesmen from undue impositions of taxes and the threatening recruitment of soldiers.[392] But 'Ismatullah's influence in the capital was eclipsed by that of his relative and rival Arsalan Khan (b. Mahabbat Khan).[393] Arsalan Khan had been a steady ally of Sher 'Ali Khan during his power struggle with his half brothers Afzal Khan and A'zam Khan. The Amir appointed him *wazir-i kharija* and chose him as one of his close councillors. The governorship of Zurmat, Khost and Katawaz provided Arsalan Khan and his son Ma'azullah Khan with a substantial income and gave them a measure of influence among the Pashtun groups clashing in the overland trade to India, i. e. the Kharotis, Sulaiman Khel and Wazirs.[394] He was also in charge of a military campaign against the Hotak Ghilzais.[395] Like 'Ismatullah Khan, Arsalan Khan was able to use his high position at court to further his standing among the Jabbar Khel. It was during his tenure as *wazir* that his home region of Hisarak was restored to the revenue free status it had enjoyed prior to Dost Muhammad Khan's time.[396]

Throughout the reigns of Dost Muhammad Khan and his successor, a certain rivalry between the Jabbar Khel Ghilzais and the Mohmand *khans* of La'lpura may be observed. The period of Dost Muhammad Khan was characterized by a close linkage of the Morcha Khel Mohmands to the court. Accordingly, Sa'adat Khan was called in to assist the governor of Jalalabad whenever trouble was brewing in the Jabbar Khel region.[397] During the reign of Sher 'Ali Khan this relationship was reversed as Nauroz Khan's political fortunes began to decline along with those of his nephew, Sardar Muhammad Ya'qub Khan. In 1874 'Ismatullah Khan and Arsalan Khan played a crucial role in bringing about Ya'qub Khan's submission and imprisonment in Kabul. Arsalan profited greatly from Nauroz Khan's subsequent rebellion. He was ordered by Amir Sher 'Ali Khan to occupy La'lpura with government troops and to erect a fort at Dakka. The rift between Nauroz Khan and the Amir not only enhanced Arsalan Khan's political career but also provided him with an additional source of income. He is said to have made such a fortune by contracting the construction of the government fort at Dakka that he had enough money left over to build a new fort and pleasure garden for himself at Rozabad. Arsalan Khan's life and times more or less coincided with those of his benefactor. He died six months prior to the onset of the Second Anglo-Afghan War. The fort at Rozabad, which symbolized his close relationship with Sher 'Ali Khan, was torn down by Amir 'Abd al-Rahman Khan in 1885.[398]

The Babakr Khel Ghilzais

The prominent position of the Babakr Khel of Tizin can be traced back to the eighteenth century, when they ingratiated themselves with Nadir Shah by showing 'instances of personal and tribal devotion'. It is not clear, though, exactly what kind of privileges they received in return for their services. During the Sadozai period the Babakr Khel submitted a nominal revenue to the government and received allowances for protecting the roads leading to Kabul via Haft Kotal, Chinari and Lataband.[399] Both the Jabbar Khel and the Babakr Khel seem to have expanded into the region of Laghman in the course of the eighteenth century. In the nineteenth century the Jabbar Khel were concentrated in the region south of the Kabul river, whereas the Babakr Khel were the dominant Ghilzai group in the valley proper.[400] Although Laghman was generally referred to as 'Ghilzai' by the Durrani rulers, the original Tajik/Pashai population had not been displaced entirely by the advent of the Pashtuns. In the nineteenth century Laghman consisted of two subdivisions for revenue purposes, Laghman-i Afghania and Laghman-i Tajikia. In order to come to a closer understanding of the political circumstances in Laghman, let us take a look at the geographical setting:

> The district of Laghman is about 26 miles from east to west, and on an average 32 miles from north to south. It may be said to begin near Darunta and, skirting the northern base of the Siah Koh, extends in a westerly direction up to Badpakht. The valley takes a northern direction at Mandrawar, and proceeding straight up to Tirgarhi, bifurcates into two portions – one going up the Alingar, and the other up the Alishang valley. Its boundaries on the north are the Kafiristan mountains, on the east the hills of Kashmund, on the south the Siah Koh range, on the west the Usbin river... On the eastern side a chain of spurs runs down from the Kashmund range, terminating in the Ambir hills just above Charbagh. The aspect of the country in this direction is dreary to a degree, and consists of sandy hillocks without any cultivation or vegetation on them, till they are finally lost in the Gamberi desert. The southern end of the valley, though it has some cultivated lands and flourishing villages, has nothing to boast of in the way of beauty; and the same remarks may apply to the western portion, but nothing can equal or surpass the beauty and grandeur of its northern parts. Looking northwards from Tirgarhi, the eye rests on the beautiful Alishang valley, with its numerous villages, forts, and river... To the northeast extends the Alingar valley, with its villages and forts belonging to different Ghilzai chiefs, the whole bounded by a mass of snowy mountains... .[401]

While the Alingar valley up to Kulman, Chilas and Niyazi was dotted with Ghilzai forts and villages, the Alishang valley formed a stronghold of the

Tajiks. The southern portion of the Laghman valley was inhabited by Pashtuns and Tajiks, the Pashtuns holding villages on both sides of the Kabul river, whereas the Tajiks were concentrated in the villages of Charbagh, Haidar Khani, Mandrawar and Tirgarhi.[402]

At the beginning of the nineteenth century the Tajikia portion of Laghman was governed by Ibrahim Khan Bayat, a Qizilbash leader. Both the Tajik and Pashtun population were described as 'quite obedient' at the time of the Elphinstone mission.[403] This view was contradicted seventy years later by Warburton, who noted that the revenue collection by the government pitted Pashtun and Tajik leaders against each other:

> It has been always a difficult undertaking for the Governor of Lughman to realize not only his own jaghirs, but the different 'barats' [drafts] issued from Kabul on Lughman Afghania by the Amir of Kabul, from the troublesome Ghilzai chiefs, who swarm in that quarter of Afghanistan, and invariably set the Hakim's authority at defiance. The Governor has never had more than 200 khasadars [irregular foot soldiers] to maintain his rule, so in collecting the revenue he had to depend a great deal on the friendly assistance of the Tajik Chiefs: several times the late Amir Sher 'Ali had to send a strong force to Tigri [Tirgarhi], to enable his deputy to secure some quota of the revenue for the public chest.[404]

Why this difference of opinion between the informant of the Elphinstone mission and Warburton? Of course, certain room has to be allowed for the fact that the two speakers, the first a resident of Kabul, the second a colonial administrator, described the situation in Laghman from different perspectives.[405] But it also raises the possibility that the political circumstances in Laghman had indeed changed during the period which had elapsed between the two statements. Unfortunately, there is no information on the development of revenue demands in this region during the Muhammadzai era. Perhaps the imposition of new revenue demands lay at the root of Ghilzai recalcitrance. However, there is also the strong possibility that not the revenue payments per se formed a source of conflict but the Ghilzai assumption that Amir Dost Muhammad Khan lacked the legitimacy to raise such demands at all. This at least was the reasoning Muhammad Shah Khan Babakr Khel of Badi'abad, the most influential chief among the Ghilzais of Laghman, assumed at the onset of his twelve-year long conflict with Dost Muhammad Khan. Prior to the First Anglo-Afghan War Muhammad Shah Khan apparently had had no doubts concerning the righteousness of Dost Muhammad Khan's reign. He was a close ally of the Amir's eldest son, Muhammad Akbar Khan, to whom he gave his daughter in marriage and with whom he sided throughout the First Anglo-Afghan War. In the power struggle ensuing after the departure of the British garrison and the death of Shah Shuja', Muhammad Shah Khan was instrumental in tilting the scales in favor of his son-in-law, so much so that he was described as 'the right hand and head of Mohamed Akbar'.[406]

Muhammad Shah's influence with Sardar Muhammad Akbar and his strong position in Laghman caused him to be viewed with distrust by the Amir. Shortly after his return to Kabul in 1843 Dost Muhammad Khan began to take steps against the Babakr Khel leader. Warburton gives the following account of the first phase in the confrontation between the Amir and Muhammad Shah Khan:

> Muhammad Shah Khan, in the process of time [i.e., during the First Anglo-Afghan War], secured sway over nearly all of Lughman, until his castles in the air were knocked down by the Dost. He was seated one day at Shewakai, a fort and village near Kabul, with Gul Muhammad Khan, Khoda Baksh Khan, Malik Hamid Abdul, Katumzai, and Malik Shergal, when a horseman was seen urging his steed at full speed towards the fort from the direction of Kabul, who on near approach turned out to be Aziz Khan, Jabbarkhel. Dismounting quickly, he appeared, and, taking Muhammad Shah Khan aside, informed him that Amir Dost Muhammad Khan had arranged to make prisoners all the Ghilzai Chiefs then present in Kabul. The assembly broke up quickly, and all the Chiefs made off towards Lughman, where they all joined Muhammad Shah Khan.[407]

No matter what the Amir's actual designs may have been, Muhammad Shah Khan's sudden departure for Badi'abad indicated a rift between him and the king, as court etiquette required all nobles to remain in attendance at the capital until formally dismissed. Muhammad Shah Khan's rebellion entered a decisive stage with the death of Sardar Muhammad Akbar Khan in February 1847. As mentioned in Chapter One, Muhammad Shah Khan refused to give up the treasure his son-in-law had deposited with him. He is also said to have laid claim to Muhammad Akbar Khan's title of *wazir*, which the deceased had been awarded by Shahzada Fatih Jang during the final phase of the First Anglo-Afghan War, and to his wives, as he had been connected to the Sardar by an oath of brotherhood.[408] But the Amir blankly refused to consider Muhammad Shah Khan's ambition for an influential position at court. Muhammad Akbar Khan's possessions, his titles and troops were transferred to the new heir apparent, Ghulam Haidar Khan.

Muhammad Shah Khan's rebellion can thus undoubtedly be attributed to his frustrated efforts to bolster the privileged position he had gained during Dost Muhammad Khan's first reign and the Anglo-Afghan War. The government, on the other hand, insisted that all his claims were baseless. Interestingly, the court historian Faiz Muhammad attempts to portray the reasoning advanced by both parties of the conflict. According to the government perspective, Muhammad Shah Khan had shown several instances of treason which Dost Muhammad Khan had graciously overlooked out of regard for Muhammad Akbar Khan. Once the Sardar was dead, the Babakr Khel leader began to fear royal punishment, rebelled and barricaded himself at Badi'abad. Muhammad Shah Khan, on the other hand, justified his quest for power by pointing out that the Ghilzais had as much right to rule the country as the Muhammadzais:

> [Muhammad Shah Khan] gathered a group of Ghilzai brigands and told them, 'The Ghilzai people [*mardom-i Ghiljai*] cannot bear to live under the rule of the Muhammadzai tribe [*ta'ifa-yi Muhammadzai*]. That is why it behoves us to use some foresight concerning our own position, to deprive the Amir of his grip over the government, to topple the foundation of his kingdom by the strength of our tribal unity (*ittifaq-i qaumi*), and to occupy the king's throne.'[409]

It may be argued that these words were merely put into Muhammad Shah Khan's mouth by a biased court historian. Yet there is a letter by Muhammad Shah Khan himself to the Commissioner at Peshawar which also emphasizes the inherent weakness of Dost Muhammad Khan's claims to supremacy: 'the Ameer is a Sirdar and King so long only as the times are quiet... If trouble arise, he will do nothing, but, poor as we Ghilzyes seem, we can do much.'[410]

While court sources dismissed Muhammad Shah Khan's followership as a group of 'starving libertines and vagrants who served merely to get a piece of bread', Muhammad Shah claimed in his letter to Peshawar that he had one thousand steady followers.[411] Who were the allies and adherents of the Babakr Khel chief? Within Laghman, Muhammad Shah Khan was linked by marriage alliance to Ibrahim Khan, a Tajik *malik* of Alishang, who was reported to support his cause in the years of 1852 and 1856.[412] Among the neighboring Ghilzais the support for Muhammad Shah Khan soon crumbled. His most influential ally, 'Aziz Khan Jabbar Khel, returned to the government fold even prior to Dost Muhammad Khan's military expedition into Laghman in April 1849.[413] Karim Khan Jabbar Khel's short-lived union with Muhammad Shah Khan has been discussed above. Apart from Muhammad Shah Khan's immediate relatives, such as his sons, his brothers Khwaja Muhammad Khan and Dost Muhammad Khan, and their sons, no other Ghilzai leaders are mentioned as steady participants in the rebellion.[414] Muhammad Shah Khan's rebellion thus can certainly not be characterized as some sort of 'national' Ghilzai uprising against Muhammadzai hegemony. On the other hand, it was not confined to Laghman alone. In some cases it was actively carried into other regions by Muhammad Shah Khan and his relatives. In others, independent tribal unrest was encouraged indirectly by Muhammad Shah Khan's example.

According to *Siraj al-tawarikh*, Muhammad Shah Khan's rebellion was extinguished in April 1849 when Dost Muhammad Khan and Ghulam Haidar mounted a major military expedition to Laghman. Muhammad

Shah Khan was forced to hand over Badi'abad and to remove himself to the region of Farajghan in the upper Alishang valley.[415] The Babakr Khel chief is also said to have given up some of Muhammad Akbar Khan's treasures and to have submitted some sons as hostages to the king.[416] In his place, Ghulam Haidar Khan became governor of the Ghilzai portion of Laghman. Laghman-i Tajikia was assigned to Sardar Sultan Muhammad Khan, who had returned to Afghanistan because of the decline of the Sikh empire.[417] Sardar Muhammad Akbar's son, Jalal al-Din, was placed in control of the neighboring regions of Tagau and 'Safi'.[418]

Despite, or more probably, because of, this decisive blow to his status Muhammad Shah Khan continued to make his presence felt in Laghman. From the early 1850s on his actions clearly dominated the entries of the Jalalabad and Kabul newswriters. In 1853 it was reported that Muhammad Shah Khan was about to attempt to recover the lands lost to the Amir.[419] In September 1854 he was accused of having incited his brother and son present at Kabul to make an attempt on the king's life. The Amir reacted by dismissing the Babakr Khel hostages from court and formally confiscated Muhammad Shah Khan's remaining estates.[420] Since 1852 the governor of Jalalabad and the Amir had ordered several military raids on Laghman.[421] By far the largest campaign was the one conducted by Sardar Ghulam Haidar Khan in April 1855. The heir apparent defeated Muhammad Shah Khan in the Alingar valley, arrested two of his sons and occupied his remaining forts. But neither during this nor any other expedition to the region, the government troops were able to seize Muhammad Shah Khan, who had a way of vanishing into or across the mountain ranges enclosing the Laghman valley.[422]

At the beginning of his rebellion Muhammad Shah Khan seems to have enjoyed considerable sympathy among the population of the Alingar and Alishang valleys. Apart from Ibrahim Khan of Alishang, the Niyazis of the upper Alingar valley openly supported the Babakr Khel leader.[423] But as these regions became subject to nearly constant raids by the rebel and his followers, the general opinion soon turned against him and the inhabitants of these regions sought for government assistance.[424] After Ghulam Haidar's expedition to Laghman the Niyazis undertook to capture Muhammad Shah Khan for a reward of 10,000 rupees.[425] As he was losing local support, Muhammad Shah Khan attempted to portray his raids in Laghman not as a rebellion against the government but as a matter of personal enmity with the local groups in question. When threatened by yet another government expedition he justified his recent raids in the Alishang region as a necessary measure to punish the Niyazis and Aroki Babakr Khel.[426]

Muhammad Shah Khan's rebellion also spilled into the adjacent regions of Tagau, Nijrau and Usbin. Mazu Tagawi, the leading chief of Tagau had been forced to acknowledge Amir Dost Muhammad Khan's sovereignty and to pay him revenues in 1831 and 1846.[427] In 1854 Mazu's son (Malik Shahdad Khan?) apparently opposed being incorporated into the government of Sardar Jalal al-Din and entered an alliance with Muhammad Shah Khan.[428] The population of neighboring Nijrau sheltered the Babakr Khel leader against Dost Muhammad Khan's forces.[429] Closer to Laghman, Muhammad Shah Khan's alliance with the leaders of Usbin posed a more serious threat to Kabul interests. In 1855 the caravan traffic near Jagdalak was seriously disrupted by plundering raids Muhammad Shah Khan's nephew organized with the help of the population of Usbin.[430] The crisis reached a climax in November 1855 when Muhammad Shah Khan's nephew managed to capture the Amir's nephew, Shah Muhammad b. Sardar Pir Muhammad Khan, near Tizin. Sardar 'Usman Khan, the Amir's deputy at Kabul, reacted angrily, as he felt that the captivity of Sardar Shah Muhammad in Muhammad Shah Khan's hands was 'derogatory to the honor of the Barukzye family'. Yet he could not convince the *ishik aqasi* Khan Gul Khan to proceed to Laghman and to negotiate for Sardar Shah Muhammad's release. Khan Gul Khan reasoned that such an enterprise would be pointless: Muhammad Shah Khan would not give up his royal hostage as long his two sons and one nephew were held prisoners by Sardar Ghulam Haidar Khan. At best he would consent to an exchange of captives.[431] Muhammad Shah Khan had thus demonstrated again how tenuous the Barakzai claims to authority were. Rather than imposing their order on the Babakr Khel leader, the Amir and his family found themselves locked into a petty war of retaliation and mutual kidnappings with him.

The plundering raids on the Kabul-Jalalabad route continued. In the following year, Shahmard Khan, the governor of Jalalabad, was reported to be in 'constant alarm' of Muhammad Shah Khan. No caravan could pass the Jagdalak region without an armed escort.[432] Government measures against the Babakr Khel leader took the shape of scattered military reactions to his plundering raids rather than coordinated offensives. This can be attributed in part to the fact that most of the Amir's resources were devoted to his campaign to seize control of Qandahar from autumn 1855 on. During this period, Muhammad Shah Khan's rebellion gained added significance not only because the Amir's military strength had shifted to Qandahar but because he was seen as a useful ally by the Qandahar Sardars. In August/September 1855 it was reported that Muhammad Shah Khan was active on behalf of the Qandahar Sardars the region of Zurmat. He allegedly raised a body of 3,000 Jadrans by offering a salary of eight rupees per month and raided the town of Gardez with their assistance shortly afterwards.[433] It is not clear whether the Babakr Khel chief had actually been supplied with the sum necessary for collecting such a large group of followers by the Qandahar Sardars. When he returned to the Niyazi region two months later, he was still accompanied by 3,000–4,000 horsemen.[434] Subsequently there was no further news of a wide Jadran following. Nonetheless Muhammad Shah Khan's activities in the Zurmat region seem to have had some effect on the Ghilzai population there. In November 1855 a rebellion of the Sulaiman Khel and Sohak Ghilzais was thought to be linked to Muhammad Shah Khan's recent presence in the region.[435]

Meanwhile the government attempted to contain Muhammad Shah Khan's influence by threats and promises. In September 1855 it issued an order that any tribe not opposing Muhammad Shah Khan's passage would be fined 5,000 rupees.[436] In March 1856 Sardar Muhammad Amin Khan, the Amir's second deputy at Kabul, offered a liberal reward to the son of the Khanan of Ahmadzai if he or his fellow tribesmen apprehended the son of Muhammad Shah Khan; if not, they would be fined 1,000 rupees. Shortly afterwards the Ishik Aqasi and the son of the Khanan of Ahmadzai delivered the son of Khwaja Muhammad Khan to the government. Muhammad Shah Khan's son was able to flee and to join the fugitive Qandahar Sardar, Rahmdil Khan, at Nawa.[437]

The activities of Muhammad Shah Khan's family peaked for a last time in the late summer of 1856. In August the nephew of the Babakr Khel leader incited the residents of Gulbahar and Parwan to rebel against the revenue collectors dispatched by the government. Shortly afterwards Sardar Muhammad Amin's son and his military force of 200 cavalry, 100 infantry and one gun, faced night attacks by the rebellious Kohistanis who, together with the neighboring people of Salang and Panjsher and the following of Muhammad Shah Khan's nephew, numbered close to 5,000 men.[438] But with Dost Muhammad Khan's subsequent return to Kabul, the odds were turned against Muhammad Shah Khan again, and the Babakr Khel leader addressed the British for assistance in October 1856. While Muhammad Shah boasted of his successes, his letter also rang with despair and weariness. 'Show me some kindness here,' he wrote,

> or else invite me into your own territory and give me dry bread to eat. If both these requests be refused, at least give me leave to come into your territories and settle down in some quiet corner till it please God to turn my night into day. For 12 years now I have been driven about the hills from door to door... I have no apprehension of the Ameer, for he can do nothing against me if it goes on for 10 years more; but as your Government is mighty, I think it best to take hold of your skirt. Dost Mahomed gives many pledges and swears many oaths but I cannot trust him.

As Muhammad Shah Khan was turned away by the British, he prepared to seek reconciliation with the Amir.[439] In December the Amir forgave Muhammad Shah Khan's nephew and restored him to his *jagir*. At the same time he announced that Muhammad Shah Khan himself would not be spared royal punishment.[440] Yet after some correspondence between Muhammad Shah Khan and Sardar Ghulam Haidar – who had become his new son-in-law by marrying Muhammad Akbar Khan's widow – the Amir decided to pardon the Babakr Khel leader. As a pledge to Muhammad Shah's safety, Amir Dost Muhammad Khan sent two of his sons and the Ishik Aqasi Khan Gul Khan to Laghman, thus acknowledging the importance of Muhammad Shah Khan's quest for peace.[441] Muhammad Shah Khan seems to have died soon afterwards, but his conflict with the Amir continued to smolder and affected other members of his family.[442] In September 1861 Dost Muhammad Khan arrested Khwaja Muhammad Babakr Khel, 'claiming from him the property of the late Wuzeer Mahomed Akbar Khan.'[443] Shortly afterwards Sher Muhammad b. Muhammad Shah Khan was imprisoned by the governor of Laghman, while his other brothers fled to Bajaur. Muhammad Shah Khan's family returned to favor for a short period during the time of Amir Sher 'Ali Khan. In 1873, Haji Sahib of Bajaur, a *khalifa* of the Akhund of Swat, interceded with the Amir on behalf of Faiz Muhammad Khan b. Muhammad Shah, who was prisoner at Kabul, and his remaining brothers living in Bajaur. It is not clear whether the conflict between Sher 'Ali and Faiz Muhammad Khan dated back to the period of their fathers, or whether the Babakr Khel clan had given new reason for offence. According to Warburton, Faiz Muhammad Khan was locked into a family feud with 'Ismatullah Khan Jabbar Khel. On the eve of the Second Anglo-Afghan War Faiz Muhammad Khan was appointed civil governor of 'Ali Masjid, where he obstructed the progress of the British representative Cavagnari in September 1878.[444]

The cases discussed in this section – the Sayyids of Kunar, the Jabbar Khel, and the Babakr Khel – again make it clear that the relationship between the Muhammadzai rulers and the local leadership could take a variety of forms. Kunar was able to remain more or less independent until the early nineteenth century. Muhammadzai interference began in the 1820s, taking the form of annexation of regions close to Jalalabad (Shewa), occasional plundering raids against the Sayyids and interposition in rivalries among the members of the ruling family. Nevertheless, the Sayyids continued to control their core possessions until the 1880s. During Amir Sher 'Ali Khan's reign the ruling Sayyid enjoyed a certain allowance and acted as a middleman for the Amir in all dealings with the even remoter regions of Bajaur and Dir. The Jabbar Khel Ghilzais, on the other hand, had traditionally interacted closely with the Durrani rulers as guardians of the trade route between Jalalabad and Kabul. 'Aziz Khan Jabbar Khel owed a large part of his possessions and influence to his father's friendship with Dost Muhammad Khan's eldest brother, Fatih Khan, and seems to have retained his influential position during the Amir's second reign. In Sher 'Ali Khan's time 'Aziz Khan's son 'Ismatullah Khan and his relative Arsalan

Khan Jabbar Khel continued to profit from this policy of cooperation. Muhammad Shah Khan Babakr Khel of Badi'abad has to be characterized as the only truly 'troublesome' Ghilzai in the Kabul watershed. His case, comparable to that of Nauroz Khan Mohmand, makes it clear that a close linkage to the court did not present an unqualified voucher for success but also carried the potential for conflict.

Despite their divergent political fortunes the leaders in question have certain characteristics in common. They do not fit the often-quoted cliché of the 'hungry' tribesman perched in his barren hills, ready to raid the fertile plains below.[445] The rulers of Kunar and the influential Jabbar Khel and Babakr Khel leaders controlled rich agricultural lands. Their main motivation was not to avoid government contact but to use it to their advantage. In the cases of Sayyid Mahmud, 'Aziz Khan Jabbar Khel and Muhammad Shah Khan Babakr Khel the linkage to the court was bolstered by marriage alliances. Unfortunately the available sources yield few clues concerning the relationship between these leaders and their fellow tribesmen. Nor do they discuss the strategies employed by the less prominent local leaders. Nonetheless the above narrative concerning the tribal origins of the prominent leaders in the Kabul basin and their political fortunes under Amirs Dost Muhammad Khan and Sher 'Ali Khan allows the important conclusion that segmentary structures may give rise to a powerful tribal leadership. The crucial factor for such a development clearly is the linkage to the court. It is accompanied by royal favors which in turn enhance the leader's standing within his own group. At the same time, this relationship is characterized by an inherent tension, as a powerful tribal leader may use his influence to challenge the king's authority at any given moment. This phenomenon has been discussed by Bendix in his study on kingship in medieval history. On the one hand, the kings required the assistance of notables in governing their realm: 'Rulers were typically torn between the need to delegate authority and the desire not to lose it.' Servants of the crown were rewarded with grants of land and/or ranks and offices. The recipients of such favors, on the other hand, 'could use their status and their resources to develop their own power, sometimes to such an extent that kings and aristocrats became bitter enemies. . . .'[446] The cases of Muhammad Shah Khan Babakr Khel Ghilzai and Nauroz Khan Mohmand clearly fit into this scenario. Both men had gained important positions at the royal court. Their rebellions began when the Amir became fearful of their influence and sought to curtail their power. At this point they withdrew to the 'hills' and began to conform with the romantic image of the fierce tribesman. Muhammad Shah Khan and Nauroz Khan took to a policy of raiding, paralyzing the trade between Kabul and Peshawar. While they had lost their standing at the court, they were thus able to demonstrate that royal pretensions to authority in the tribal regions could only be lived up to with their cooperation.

The Hotak and Tokhi Ghilzais

So far I have been dealing with the groups located along the eastern approaches to Kabul. Now I will turn to the area south of the capital and take a look at two famous Ghilzai tribes located along the trade route to Qandahar. The caravans travelling southwards from Kabul had to pass through the territories of the Wardaks, the Ahmadzais, the Andars, Tarakis, Tokhis, and Hotaks. With the exception of the Wardaks, all these tribes belonged to the Ghilzai confederacy. In the early nineteenth century, only the northern groups found themselves within the sphere of influence of Kabul and Ghazni and paid revenues.[447] In the 1830s the region of the Hotaks and Tokhis was disputed between the Amir and his half brothers at Qandahar, and these two groups were entirely independent. The Hotaks and Tokhis had been the most important rivals of the Abdalis/Durranis ever since Safawid times. In this section, I will investigate the origins of their power and their attitudes towards the rulers of Kabul in the nineteenth century.

The country south of Ghazni is characterized by three streams flowing in southwesterly direction, the Arghandab, the Tarnak and the Arghastan-Lora. The major intervening mountain ranges are the Gul Koh in the west and the Rozanai Hills in the east. South of Muqur, the route to Qandahar followed the valley of the Tarnak river, a plain roughly sixty miles long and twenty miles wide. Between Ulan Rubat and Pul-i Sangi, this plain was inhabited by the Tokhis, their chief settlement being Qalat-i Ghilzai, also known as Qalat-i Tokhi. The adjoining Gul Koh range and the valleys of Nawa, Margha, and Arghastan were also Tokhi territory. The Tokhis living in the central Tarnak valley were mostly agriculturists and made their living by cultivating grain and alfalfa. The hilly Tokhi lands were used for pasture. Diwalak, located 14 miles east of Qalat-i Ghilzai on the highroad to Kabul, was considered the boundary between the Tokhis and the Hotak Ghilzais.[448] The Hotaks inhabited the southeastern portion of Ghilzai country bordering on the Durranis and Kakars. Their income mostly derived from almond groves, agriculture, commerce and sheep breeding.[449]

Elphinstone estimated that the Tarakis, Andars and Tokhis were equal in strength, each tribe numbering 12,000 families. On the other hand, he and other authors considered the Hotak tribe to be much smaller and to comprise only 5,000 to 7,000 families. At the same time, Elphinstone noted that this relative weakness was a recent phenomenon, pointing out that the Hotaks had formerly been a 'numerous clan'.[450] Prior to the eighteenth century, the Hotaks had been equal in number with the Tokhis. The history of these two tribes needs to be viewed in conjunction, as they were linked both in their competition for royal favors and their cooperation with each other in times of rebellion. The leading families of both groups were also connected with each other by marriage alliances.[451] Another dimension of the political outlook of the Tokhis and Hotaks was their rivalry with the Abdalis, particularly the leading Sadozai clan, from the early Safawid period on.

The Historical Origins of the Leading Families

During the sixteenth and early seventeenth centuries, the Hotaks and Tokhis profited from the shifting influence of the Safawids and Mughals in the region. At the time of Shah 'Abbas I (r. 1587–1629) the Ghilzais – we are not told which groups – entered center stage after a large section of the Abdalis had been transferred from Qandahar to Herat.[452] In the seventeenth century, roughly at the same time that Jabbar Khan gained influence among the Ahmadzais of the Kabul basin, the Tokhi leader Malakhi Khan Babakrzai cooperated with the Mughals in securing the lines of communication leading through his territory against Hazara robbers and was formally appointed to the leadership of the Ghilzais.[453] The Hotaks, on the other hand, began to interact with the Safawid administrators, thus gaining prominence among the Ghilzais and Afghans in general.[454] In 1702 the newly arrived Safawid governor of Qandahar, Gurgin Khan, succeeded in weakening the still influential Sadozais of his province by fostering the position of Amir Khan, an Ishaqzai Hotak, popularly known as Mir Wais. Yet subsequently the Safawid governor was unable to curb the power of the leader of his own making. In 1709 Mir Wais murdered Gurgin Khan and proclaimed the independence of Qandahar: 'Three powerful Persian armies, one after the other, were sent against him, but Wais inflicted crushing defeats on them and made his independence secure.'[455] After his death in 1715, Mir Wais was succeeded by his brother Mir 'Abd al-'Aziz. Two years later the power within the family passed to Mir Wais's sons Mir Mahmud and Mir Husain. Despite ongoing rivalries with the Abdalis of Herat, who had also rebelled against the Safawids in the meantime, Mahmud was able to maintain control of Qandahar. During the following years he began to strike out against the heart of the weakened Safawid empire. In October 1722 he deprived the Safawid ruler Husain Sultan Shah of his capital Isfahan and made his brother Mir Husain governor of Qandahar. Ghilzai rule in Persia was limited to the towns and communications in the southeastern part of the country and turned out to be short-lived. In April 1725 Mir Mahmud was killed and succeeded by his cousin Ashraf b. 'Abd al-'Aziz. Four years later Tahmasp Quli (to become known as Nadir Shah in 1737) reconquered Isfahan and placed the Safawid Tahmasp II on the throne. In 1732 he took full control of Herat, and in March 1738 Qandahar surrendered to him after a prolonged siege.[456]

After the conquest of Qandahar Husain Hotak and his fellow tribesmen were exiled to Iran at least temporarily.[457] Meanwhile Malakhi's relative Ashraf Khan Babakrzai Tokhi, who had joined Nadir Shah's army during the siege of Qandahar, moved to the forefront in the Ghilzai region, acting as the *beglarbegi* of Qalat-i Ghilzai and Ghazni.[458] In spite of the setback suffered during the Nadirid period the family of Mir Wais continued to be highly esteemed among the greater group of Ghilzais and had access to influential positions at the Sadozai court. Timur Shah made Nurullah Khan b. Haji Angu (or Angur), a nephew of Mir Wais, leader of the Hotaks and bestowed the title *ikhlas quli khan* on him.[459] Nurullah Khan was reckoned one of the most influential men at Timur Shah's court and enjoyed the enormous revenues of Dera Isma'il Khan, Bannu, Daman, Urgun as a service grant.[460] His son 'Abd al-Rahim farmed the revenue of the same districts (possibly with the exception of Urgun) and received an allowance of 150,000 rupees.[461] At the time of Shah Zaman, 'Abd al-Rahim Khan is reported to have paid 225,000 rupees annually for the right to collect the taxes of Dera Isma'il Khan.[462]

The Babakrzai Tokhis also maintained their influential position during the Sadozai period and received the right to collect taxes from all caravans passing between Kabul and Qandahar in exchange for protecting the highroad.[463] In return for their privileges, the Tokhis furnished 1,500 to 2,000 horsemen to the king, whereas the Hotaks were only required to provide 500 to 700.[464] Ashraf Khan Babakrzai Tokhi continued to control Qalat-i Ghilzai during the first part of Ahmad Shah's reign.[465] During the period of Timur Shah, Muhammad Amir Khan b. Ashraf Khan, also known as 'Amu' Khan, was recognized as paramount chief of the Tokhis and received an allowance of 160,000 rupees in addition to the revenues of some Durrani lands in the region of Jaldak.[466] At the time of Shah Zaman's reign Wali Ni'mat b. Amu Khan Babakrzai was appointed to the khanship of the Tokhis by the king. All three sons of Amu Khan, that is, Wali Ni'mat, Fatih and Mir 'Alam, continued to enjoy especial respect at Shah Zaman's court and were addressed as '*umdat al-khawanin al-kiram* ('the most excellent of the noble chiefs') in all royal edicts. Despite the royal backing Wali Ni'mat Khan enjoyed, his authority among the Tokhis was challenged by another member of his family. Shihab al-Din Tokhi was a grandson of Ashraf Khan's brother, Allahyar Khan, and thus a cousin of Wali Ni'mat. His claims to power were encouraged by the court faction around the finance minister, Nur Muhammad Khan Babar Amin al-Mulk, who harbored a personal enmity against Wali Ni'mat Khan. Apparently Shihab al-Din Khan did not derive his influence among the Tokhis solely on the basis of funds given to him by Amin al-Mulk, as he had already gained a certain reputation among the Tokhis and in Kabul prior to Wali Ni'mat's row with the finance minister. The ensuing fight between Shihab al-Din and the descendants of Amu Khan split the Tokhis into two factions and was to cost Wali Ni'mat his life. Nevertheless Shah Zaman continued to honor the historical claims to power advanced by the brothers of Wali Ni'mat and appointed Fatih Khan to the khanship of the Tokhis. Shah Zaman's support of Fatih Khan notwithstanding the tribal war between the two Tokhi factions continued to smolder and flared up whenever the king was away on military campaigns.[467] The balance of power between the descendants of Amu Khan and Shihab al-Din is reflected by the fact that the income from the trade between Kabul and Qandahar was split between them. Fatih Khan collected the transit dues from the caravans moving from Qandahar to Kabul and Shihab al-Din received the dues from the ones travelling in the opposite direction. With the confusion accompanying the decline of the Sadozai empire, both chiefs began to levy fees on *all* caravans travelling through their territories.[468]

Both the Tokhis and the Hotaks entered marriage alliances with the Sadozais. ʿAbd al-Rahim Hotak gave one of his daughters to Shah Zaman.[469] Shah Shujaʿ was married to a sister or daughter of Fatih Khan Babakrzai.[470] Although the Ghilzai leadership enjoyed considerable privileges, its support for the Sadozais was not unequivocal. Shah Mahmud's relationship with the Hotaks and Tokhis was particularly troubled. It is not clear whether the resistance Shah Mahmud encountered during his first reign was linked to any loss of allowances on the part of the Ghilzai elite. In part Shah Mahmud's lack of popularity can be attributed to the general confusion which prevailed in Afghanistan subsequent to his accession to the throne. Another major source of discontent was the enhanced role of Fatih Khan Muhammadzai and his brothers at the royal court.[471] ʿAbd al-Rahim Khan Hotak's rebellion began at a time when Fatih Khan Muhammadzai was absent from Kabul. In the autumn of 1801, as Fatih Khan was busy collecting the revenues of Peshawar, the Hotak leader rose together with the population of Logar and proclaimed himself king. Shihab al-Din Tokhi allegedly acted as his *wazir*.[472] By assuming a royal title ʿAbd al-Rahim clearly attempted to remind his fellow tribesmen of the historical claims of his family to leadership among all the Pashtuns in the Qandahar-Kabul region. But it is doubtful whether this move was designed to question the legitimacy of the Sadozai dynasty as such or aimed more specifically at challenging Shah Mahmud's claims to authority. Both ʿAbd al-Rahim Khan's rebellion and Shihab al-Din Tokhi's subsequent attack on Qandahar coincided with Shah Shujaʿ's ongoing efforts to topple his half brother Mahmud from power. The events which followed were only to heighten the favorable attitude of the Hotak and Tokhi leadership to Shah Shujaʿ. Fatih Khan Muhammadzai, on his part, relied on the assistance of the Durrani leadership to subdue the Hotak-Tokhi rebellion. A military force under the command of Sher Muhammad Khan Bamizai Mukhtar al-Daula fought several battles with the insurgents and defeated them decisively in November 1801. In early 1802 Fatih Khan Muhammadzai inflicted two crushing defeats on the combined Ghilzai forces. 3,000 (according to some accounts, 6,000) Ghilzais lost their lives during the most important battle at Qalʿa-yi Shahi near Kabul.[473] The Hotaks and Tokhis suffered most from the 'punishment' inflicted on the Ghilzais by the government troops. Shah Mahmud attempted to discourage further Ghilzai unrest by having 'Abd al-Rahim Khan Hotak and two of his sons blown away from a cannon. Moreover, he followed Nadir Shah's example in constructing a minaret of Ghilzai skulls. The effects of the great 'Ghilzai War' continued to be felt for years afterwards. In the course of the repeated military campaigns all major Ghilzai forts had been destroyed. In 1809 Elphinstone observed that formerly flourishing villages in the Tokhi region were still in a state of decay.[474] Needless to say that Shah Mahmud's demonstration of his military prowess lost him the last vestiges of Ghilzai support. In 1803, on the eve of the Sunni-Shi'i riot in Kabul, Shukrullah Khan (a grandson of Nurullah Hotak), Fatih Khan Tokhi, and Shihab al-Din Tokhi jointly entered an alliance with Shah Shuja', thus enabling him to remove Shah Mahmud from the throne.[475] While Shukrullah Khan Hotak and Fatih Khan Tokhi subsequently paid allegiance to Shah Shuja', Shihab al-Din Tokhi continued to assert his independence and refused to have any dealings with the court of Kabul.[476] Thus the rivalry between the Fatih Khan and his cousin remained the determining factor in the political outlook of the Tokhi leadership at the beginning of the nineteenth century.

With the end of the Sadozai empire the Hotaks and Tokhis witnessed the emergence of two independent principalities in Kabul and Qandahar, and thus found themselves on the fringes of two centers of gravity again. From the 1820s on Kabul and Ghazni were controlled by Dost Muhammad Khan and his full brother Amir Muhammad Khan. Qandahar, on the other hand, had passed to the 'Dil' brothers, Purdil, Sherdil, Kuhandil, Rahmdil, and Mihrdil Khan. While Dost Muhammad and Amir Khan were backed by the Qizilbash leadership of Kabul, the Qandahar Sardars could rely on the assistance of their maternal uncle Khuda Nazar Khan Ghilzai.[477] When Dost Muhammad Khan gained control of Kabul in 1826, he and the leaders of Qandahar agreed that Qalat-i Ghilzai was to form the border between the two principalities.[478] As both sets of Muhammadzai brothers continuously sought to widen their respective spheres of influence, their interests overlapped in the territory of the Hotaks and Tokhis. Although the Qandahar Sardars attempted to use the Ghilzais as a counterpoise to Dost Muhammad Khan and employed a number of them in their army, they were unable to exert any direct control over the Ghilzai groups in their region.[479] Prior to the First Anglo-Afghan War their troops were defeated by the then most influential Hotak leader Gul ('Guru') Muhammad Khan.[480]

The Position of the Leadership in the Early Nineteenth Century

As the most detailed descriptions of the political circumstances in the region between Ghazni and Qandahar stem from the First Anglo-Afghan War and the period immediately prior to it, I would like to take a short look at the leading personalities of that time and their scope of authority. At the onset of the First Anglo-Afghan War, Lynch reported that the members of the prominent Hotak and Tokhi families still enjoyed a special respect among their fellow tribesmen: 'In both the tribes of Hotak and Tokhy, there are aristocratic clans... out of which the chiefs of both the tribes are invariably chosen. They are supposed by their tribes to be incapable of doing wrong and blood shed by them is not considered revengeable.'[481] Roughly at the same time as Lynch, Broadfoot gave the following sketch of the political landscape in the region south of Ghazni:

> Shahabudin Khan of the Tokhis established twenty-five years ago a kind of rule from Kelat-i Ghilzi to Kattawaz; he levied taxes on travellers and merchants, and plundered the tribes who opposed him. He is represented as a tall, stout man, kind and hospitable at home, but harsh and oppressive abroad. After his death, his son Abdurrahman in connection with Gul Muhammad Khan of the Hotakis, and heir of the Ghilzi monarch, carried on the same system. The Mama of Wazikhwah timidly joined them; the Khan of the Tarakkis was the quietest and best of the Ghilzi chiefs. The Suliman Khel have no regular head, but Mehtar Musa Khan had influence enough to lead formidable parties to a foray. The Anders and Tarakkis generally submitted to Dost Muhammad and seldom plundered.[482]

Little is known about Gul Muhammad Khan Hotak's previous political career except that he was a descendant of Mir Wais. Masson, who passed through the Tokhi region in the late 1820s, offers some information on the position of the two most important Tokhi chiefs, Shihab al-Din and Fatih Khan Babakrzai, at that time. As mentioned above, both chiefs derived most of their income from the overland trade, using the weakness of the Sardars of Kabul and Qandahar to levy transit dues manifold higher than those they were allowed to raise in the Sadozai period.[483] On the basis of their income from the trade between Kabul and Qandahar and their historical link with the Safawid and Durrani empires the position of the two most prominent Tokhi leaders may be compared to that of the Morcha Khel Mohmands of La'lpura. Nonetheless certain distinctions need to be made. Contrary to the *khans* of La'lpura, the Ghilzai leadership had always maintained a critical distance to the Durranis. The historical Ghilzai claims to authority had relaxed somewhat for the most part of the Sadozai period, as both the Tokhi and Hotak elite received ample favors from the rulers. With the rebellion against Shah Mahmud, however, old Ghilzai grievances had gained a renewed stringency. Shihab al-Din Tokhi also assumed a historical reasoning when formulating his opposition to the Muhammadzai lords of Kabul and Qandahar:

> Shahabadin Khan, in common with all the Ghiljis, execrates the Duranis, whom he regards as usurpers, and pays no kind of obedience to the actual sirdars of Kandahar and Kabal, neither does he hold any direct or constant communication with them. They, on their part, do not require any mark of submission from him, it being their policy to allow an independent chief to be between their respective frontiers, or that they distrust their power of supporting such a demand. As it is, the Ghilji chief sets them at defiance; and, boasting that his ancestors never acknowledged the authority of Ahmed Shah, asks, why should he respect that of traitors and Ahmed Shah's slaves?[484]

Fatih Khan Tokhi, on the other hand, was not opposed to Durrani rule as such. His hostile attitude to the Muhammadzai Sardars was attributed to his marriage alliance to Shah Shuja', by virtue of which he was the maternal uncle of Shahzada Muhammad Timur. This shows that the historical Ghilzai claims to power per se did not bring forth a steadfast enmity towards the kings and lay dormant as long as the interests of the leading Hotak and Tokhi lineages were honored. Despite their traditional rivalry with the Durranis, the Hotak and Tokhi leaders had cooperated with the Sadozai rulers throughout the eighteenth century. At times of crisis, however, their historical grudges were easily evoked and provided convenient material for the formulation of opposition, in this manner determining the pattern of political action.

Unlike the *khan* of La'lpura, Shihab al-Din Tokhi received no favors from the rulers of Kabul in the early nineteenth century. Therefore, it is unlikely that he disposed of a 'miniature administration' comparable to that of Sa'adat Khan Mohmand. Masson described his residence at Khaka as a modest dwelling which could be easily rebuilt in case it was destroyed during times of conflict. Shihab al-Din maintained 200 to 300 horsemen in regular pay and was said to be able to assemble upwards of 40,000 tribesmen in times of crisis. But such large forces were bound to diperse fairly quickly, for he and the other Ghilzai chiefs lacked the means to maintain a numerous army over a prolonged period. At the time of Masson's visit, there were indications that Shihab al-Din's ability to impose his will on his fellow tribesmen was limited: '[T]here is much distrust of the severe Khan entertained by many of the tribe, of which his factious sons profit to create themselves parties. Such a state of things manifestly operates to diminish the power of all... '[485] This statement would seem to clash with Lynch's above quote concerning the scope of authority of the *khan khel* among the Tokhis and Hotaks. Yet already in 1809 Elphinstone had noted that the Hotak and Tokhi leadership seemed to be in a state of transition. At the same time, he raised the possibility that the prominent role of this elite in the dealings with external powers – whether Pashtun or Iranian – might never have translated into a corresponding amount of authority at home:

> [The Ghilzai chiefs] have now lost the authority which they possessed under their own royal government. There is great reason to doubt whether that authority ever was so extensive as that which has been introduced among the Duranis on the Persian model. It is more probable that the power even of the king of the Ghilzaes was small in his own country, and that the tumultuary consent of his people to support his measures abroad was dictated more by a sense of the interest and glory of the tribe than by any deference to the king's commands. Some appearances, however, warrant a supposition that his power was sufficient to check murders and other great disorders. Whatever the power of the king may have been formerly, it is now at an end, and that of the aristocracy has fallen with it; and though it has left sentiments of respect in the minds of the common people, yet that respect is so entirely unmixed with fear that it has no effect whatever in controlling their actions.

But Elphinstone was also aware that the Tokhi and Hotak chiefs still enjoyed a more powerful position than their counterparts among other Ghilzai tribes. He perceived a clear correlation between the intensity of a chief's interaction with the government and the amount of authority he enjoyed at home. Thus the style of leadership among the groups located in the vicinity of the trade route between Kabul and Qandahar essentially differed from the role of the chiefs among the tribes, such as the Sulaiman Khel, which were further removed from government interference.

> The degree in which this want of government is felt is not the same throughout the tribe. Among the people round Kabal and Ghazni, the power of the king's governor supplies the place of internal regulation. In many tribes more distant from cities than the neighbourhood, one of the king's kazis induces one party to have recourse to the... Mahommedan law... With the Ohtaks and Tokhis and generally with the Ghilzaes on the great roads, the authority which the chiefs derive from the Durani government, and perhaps the respect still paid to their former rank, enables them to prevent general commotions, though they cannot suppress quarrels between individuals... [new paragraph] Among the eastern Ghilzaes, and especially among the Solimaun Khails, the power of a chief is not considerable enough to form a tie to keep the clan together, and they are broken into little societies... which are quite independent in all internal transactions.[486]

This observation was confirmed thirty years laters by Broadfoot, who noted that the income and authority of a Ghilzai chief tended to vary with his proximity to the king:

> It is understood that the head of the senior 'Khel' is chief of the tribe, and the king often grants him the title of khan. He dares not collect any income from his tribe, but lives on the produce of his own lands; and by appropriating by fraud part of the duties on infidels and merchandise, and in the obedient tribes, part of the royal taxes. Among the eastern tribes (who are always in rebellion or rather in a state of independence) he uses his influence to head plundering expeditions and procure a good share of the spoil. His seniority in birth makes the Afghans pay him the respect of an elder brother, but nothing more.[487]

Dost Muhammad Khan's Policies towards the Hotaks and Tokhis

Let us return to the political developments in the middle of the nineteenth century. The First Anglo-Afghan War temporarily interrupted the power struggle between Dost Muhammad Khan and the Qandahar Sardars. On their part, some of the Hotak and Tokhi leaders used this opportunity to assert their independence of the Amir and to offer their support to Shah Shuja'.[488] Despite their protestations of friendship for the Sadozai king most of these leaders were reluctant to submit to him once he had entered the country with British support. Just as in the other cases discussed so far, the British upset the local balance of power by inserting themselves into existing power struggles. The newly appointed chiefs received their positions primarily because of their reputation of being 'trustworthy servants' of Shah Shuja'.[489] Mir 'Alam Khan b. 'Abd al-Rahim Hotak, who had already joined Shah Shuja' in Shikarpur, replaced Gul Muhammad Khan as chief of the Hotaks and was appointed governor of Qalat. Khalil Khan Babakrzai received the leadership of the Babakrzai Tokhis. Among Shihab al-Din's descendants, the chiefship shifted from 'Abd al-Rahman Khan first to Samand Khan Tokhi, and subsequently to 'Abd al-Rahman's younger brother Pakhar Khan.[490] Yet British support alone was not sufficient to create a new leadership. In different ways, both Gul Muhammad Khan Hotak and 'Abd al-Rahman Tokhi continued to play an important role in Ghilzai politics. After his initial flight to Kohat, Gul Muhammad Khan returned to his home region in March 1840 and began to coordinate his activities against the British with the brothers of 'Abd al-Rahman Khan Tokhi. While 'Abd al-Rahman Khan himself was handed over to the British authorities by the Sikhs in October 1840 and was unable to play an active political role inside Afghanistan, his example spread the fear among the remaining Ghilzai leaders that they also might be exiled to India. Apart from the British attempt to establish a fortified garrison at Qalat-i Ghilzai, it was this fear of deportation which triggered the Hotak/Tokhi rebellion of 1841.[491] During the final phase of the First Anglo-Afghan

War the focus of the anti-British activities shifted to other Ghilzai groups in the region. From October 1841 on, the Andar, Taraki, and Sulaiman Khel tribes laid siege to the British garrison of Ghazni. The Tokhis and Hotaks, on the other hand, remained relatively quiet, attacking Qalat-i Ghilzai only in May 1842.[492] Despite his obvious role as a British puppet, Mir 'Alam Khan Hotak was able to hold on to his influential position even after the end of the First Anglo-Afghan War. In 1843 he resided in Qandahar, where he sided with Kuhandil Khan against the Sadozai regent, Shahzada Safdar Jang. In return he gained a formal appointment to the leadership of the Hotaks from the Qandahar Sardars.[493] Among the Tokhis, the leadership seems to have reverted to 'Abd al-Rahman Khan.[494]

Following the return of the Qandahar Sardars and the reestablishment of Dost Muhammad Khan on the throne of Kabul, the rivalry between the principalities Qandahar and Kabul began to intensify again, with the scales gradually tilting in favor of the Amir. While the Amir attempted to make his presence felt at Qalat-i Ghilzai by sending his sons Ghulam Haidar and Sher 'Ali there, his half brothers at Qandahar continued to claim the whole Tokhi territory as their sphere of influence and to foment unrest in the region.[495] In 1852 Rahmdil Khan challenged Dost Muhammad Khan to come and fight for the possession of Qalat and Qandahar, reminding him that the region south of Muqur could not be as easily conquered as the regions north of the Hindu Kush.[496] This conflict subsided for a few months, as the Amir and the Qandahar Sardars reached a compromise whereby Qalat was to become neutral territory. But in the summer of 1853 the power struggle between the lords of Kabul and Qandahar flared up again when a major Tokhi rebellion which was supported by the 'Dil' brothers gave the Amir a welcome pretext to strengthen his hold on the trade route to Qandahar and to rebuild his fort at Qalat.[497]

While centered in Tokhi territory, this uprising was apparently not limited to Tokhi tribesmen. In June 1853 Sardar Sher 'Ali Khan reported that he was confronted by a force of 40,000 Tokhis and Hotaks.[498] At the same time, it is not clear whether Mir 'Alam Khan Hotak assumed an active role in the rebellion.[499] The Tokhis also attempted to gain the support of the neighboring Kakars, Andars, Tarakis and Sulaiman Khel. The reasoning adopted for the rebellion followed the pattern discussed above. The letters addressed to the neighboring tribes argued that the aim of the uprising was to restore the historical kingdom of the Ghilzais. For one thing, the letters pointed out, Dost Muhammad Khan's claims to kingship were not legitimate:

> during the reign of the Dooranees [i.e., the Sadozais] the Tokhees and Hotukkees were obliged to submit to the Government as they were then powerless, but now that there was no Dooranee on the throne, nor a single Dooranee of any consequence in the kingdom, they were quite able to cope with Dost Mohomud Khan.

The historical argument adopted also revealed the current grievances of the Tokhis. Whereas Nadir Shah had deprived the Ghilzais of their former power, the reasoning went, Ahmad Shah had treated them on equal terms with the Durranis. Dost Muhammad Khan, however, had 'not only dispensed with their services, but oppressed them very much and now wanted to impose on them the tax levied from Hindoos, and that death was preferable to such a life.'[500]

Although the Tokhis and Hotaks had profited from the competition between Kabul and Qandahar prior to the First Anglo-Afghan War, they had started to feel Dost Muhammad Khan's tightening grip from the early 1850s on. With his successful conquests in Afghan Turkistan, the Amir had become stronger than his adversaries in Qandahar and had begun to push his influence southward. The increased government presence heralded the enforcement of revenue demands among the Tokhis and Hotaks, who had traditionally expressed a 'great dread and dislike' to paying taxes to the Durranis. The leading subdivisions of the Hotaks and Tokhis had never submitted any revenues to the Durrani kings.[501] In the early 1850s the government of Kabul began to make its plans known to introduce a poll tax (*sar mardi*) similar to the one already being collected among the 'Ali Khel, Andar and Taraki Ghilzais. It is in this light that the Tokhi refusal to being treated like 'Hindus' needs to be understood.[502]

After six military engagements Sher 'Ali Khan was finally able to inflict a decisive defeat on the Ghilzais at Shamalzai, a village close to the border between the Ghilzai and Taraki lands. His first step was to weaken the Tokhi leadership by seizing 'Abd al-Rahman Khan and two of his sons and having them blown from a cannon.[503] 'Abd al-Rahman's brother Sultan Muhammad Khan, who succeeded to the chiefship, was subsequently accused of stirring up a renewed rebellion and was imprisoned in February 1856.[504] From the winter of 1853 on the Amir imposed a fairly regular tax collection among the Tokhis and Hotaks. Furthermore, he began to press revenue demands on the Sulaiman Khel of Katawaz, 'who had hitherto never paid revenue to any government.'[505]

The Amir's growing influence in the region south of Ghazni is reflected by his ability to ensure the safety of the caravans using the highroad. Already in 1852–53 Sardar Sher 'Ali Khan enforced a contract with the leaders of the Hotaks and Tokhis according to which they were held responsible for the restitution of all merchandise plundered by their fellow tribesmen.[506] With Dost Muhammad Khan's occupation of Qandahar in November 1855 the traffic between Kabul and Qandahar was even less likely to be disrupted. In 1857 Lumsden noted in the region of Ghazni that the local traders seemed to be 'driving their cattle totally unarmed and in apparent security'. The watchtowers on the Sherdahan Pass north of Ghazni were manned by Sulaiman Khel tribesmen, 'who were formerly famous for their depredations on the road, till Sirdar Sher Ali Khan [then governor of Ghazni] one day surrounded them and inflicting a severe chastisement obliged the clan to come to terms which have been religiously adhered to ever since.'[507] Even so, the Amir's authority was far from complete. While Lumsden claimed that the Hotak and Tokhi Ghilzais had become 'as quiet and well behaved a tribe as is to be found in the Ameer's dominions,'[508] Dost Muhammad Khan was unable to dictate the terms of the revenue settlement with these two groups in the winter of 1853/54. Whereas the Amir would have liked to raise a poll tax of four rupees per man, the Hotaks and Tokhis were only willing to pay half as much.[509] The Sulaiman Khel also resisted all attempts at a regular revenue assessment. This group responded to the Amir's demand of 100,000 rupees per year with the modest offer to submit 10,000 rupees in exchange for being 'left in undisturbed possession of their country'.[510]

Despite their repeated defeats the Hotaks and Tokhis remained a force to be reckoned with. During Amir Sher 'Ali Khan's reign Mir 'Alam Khan Hotak and Muhammad Aslam Khan (a grandson of Shihab al-Din Tokhi) were the most influential Ghilzai leaders. As mentioned above, Mir 'Alam Khan had retained his leadership of the Hotaks by siding with the Sardars of Qandahar in 1843. Although he had been able to retain his prominent position at court during the early part of Sher 'Ali Khan's reign, he sided with the rivals of the Amir during the final phase of the power struggle of 1866–68. Subsequent to Sher 'Ali Khan's assumption of power both Mir 'Alam Khan Hotak and Muhammad Aslam Khan Tokhi rebelled and began to collect the revenues of their regions on their own behalf. There are different viewpoints concerning the origins of this rebellion. Reflecting the court perspective, Sher 'Ali Khan's contemporary Nuri attributes Mir 'Alam Khan's uprising simply to his 'faithlessness' (*namak harami*) and dismisses his endeavor to reestablish a Ghilzai kingdom as a wild dream. The British newswriter at Kabul, on the other hand, quotes rumors according to which this rebellion was encouraged by the hostile attitude of the Qandahar ulama to Sher 'Ali Khan. Both sources agree that Mir 'Alam Khan Hotak and Muhammad Aslam Khan Tokhi failed to gain widespread support among their respective tribes.[511] Despite two successive defeats in early October 1869 both leaders kept up their resistance for several months. Mir 'Alam Khan Hotak and his two sons, 'Abdullah and Muhammad Afzal, submitted to the Amir in the course of the spring of 1870 and received their former privileges.[512] Muhammad Aslam Khan, by contrast, seems to have been unwilling to give up his rebellion at that time.[513] On the eve of the Second Anglo-Afghan War the Hotaks and Tokhis were part of a larger Ghilzai rebellion against Sher 'Ali Khan's unprecedented efforts to enlist soldiers and to bring in revenues.[514] In 1887 Mir 'Alam Khan Hotak's grandson Muhammad Shah Khan assumed a leading role in the Ghilzai rebellion against Amir 'Abd al-Rahman Khan.[515]

As with the other examples discussed so far, the case of the Hotak and Tokhi Ghilzais demonstrates that Amirs Dost Muhammad Khan and Sher

'Ali Khan had to cope with Pashtun tribal structures which had emerged in Mughal/Safawid times and had become entrenched during the Sadozai era. Unlike his Sadozai predecessors, Dost Muhammad Khan only controlled a 'miniature' kingdom and felt the pressing need to make his presence felt among those groups which had hitherto defined themselves as partners rather than as subjects of the lords of Kabul. The role and the attitudes of the tribal leadership changed accordingly. While the descendants of Mir Wais Hotak and Ashraf Khan and Allahyar Khan Babakrzai were able to defend their historical claims to leadership among their fellow tribesmen, these offices were no longer 'bestowed' on them by the king, nor did they necessarily translate into influential positions at court and the concomitant sources of income. The Amir, on the other hand, found himself unable to displace the leading lineages among the Hotaks and Tokhis and began to use his relative military strength to impose revenue payments on them. These measures, incomplete and detested as they were, represented an unprecedented degree of government interference in the regions south of Ghazni, causing the Hotaks and Tokhis to be placed on nearly the same footing as the 'obedient' Ghilzai tribes residing closer to Kabul.

Revenues Raised among the Ghilzais

While the poll tax exacted from them may have reminded the Hotaks and Tokhis of the *jizya* imposed on non-Muslims, they – along with the other Ghilzai tribes within the reach of the government – continued to enjoy a privileged position in comparison with the other revenue-paying groups in the wider region. In order to gain an understanding in which ways the Muhammadzai administration affected the position of the greater group of Ghilzais, I will attempt to give a short overview of the revenue policies instituted both east and south of Kabul. The only fairly detailed data available concern the revenues collected in Jalalabad, Laghman, Logar, and Ghazni and are based on materials gathered either during the Second Anglo-Afghan War or shortly afterwards. In general, it may be said that the dealings of the Muhammadzai rulers concentrated on the powerful tribal groups controlling the trade routes linking Kabul with Peshawar and Qandahar. Along these routes, government interference diminished with increasing distance from the administrative centers of Kabul, Jalalabad, Ghazni, and (after 1855) Qandahar. In the regions further removed from the major trade routes government presence tended to dwindle almost entirely. Even in the areas which were fairly firmly incorporated into the Muhammadzai administration government presence tended to be thin. The governor (*hakim*) of Jalalabad, for instance, employed three revenue accountants (*diwans* or *daftaris*).[516] In Laghman, the local governor (*hakim*) was assisted by two *diwans*. His military consisted of 200 *khassadars* (irregular foot soldiers).[517] The governor of Ghazni commanded one regiment of regular infantry and 300 militiamen (*jazailchis*).[518] The subdivisions (*tappa*) of Wardak, 'Ali Khel and Andar were administrated by subordinate *hakims* who handed over the revenues which were submitted to them (or possibly their agents) by the village headmen (*maliks*).[519]

According to the figures available, the gross revenues of the regions in question reached the following amounts:[520]

Jalalabad	697,638	Kabuli rupees[521]
Laghman	477,914	Kabuli rupees[522]
Logar	450,000	rupees
Wardak	100,000	rupees
Maidan	200,000	rupees
Ghazni	100,000	rupees
Shilgar	120,000	rupees
Muqur	40,000	rupees

The Tokhi Ghilzais were assessed at 150,000 Kabuli rupees, but it is not clear whether this amount was ever collected in full. Molloy informs us that the revenues due from the tribes of Zurmat (assessed at Rs. 150,000) and Katawaz (assessed at Rs. 30,000) were rarely realized.[523]

A substantial part of the gross revenues was redistributed to the local elite in the form of allowances. Apart from assignments of revenue in the form of *jagirs,* the Pashtun *khans* also enjoyed a special allowance called *tankhwah-i wilayati* ('provincial allowance'), which formed the biggest item on the list of fixed expenditures. In the Ghazni district Hasings noted that the leading chiefs collected an additional salary known as *tankhwah-i rikabi* ('stirrup allowance') which was intended as a remuneration for the provision of a certain number of horsemen in times of war. The village headmen received an allowance called *malikana.* Furthermore, an allotment of grain and cash known as *wazifa* was generally set aside for the support of the religious establishment. In the case of Jalalabad 37% of the gross revenues were given out in the form of such allowances, the *tankhwah-i wilayati* forming the largest item in the list of expenditures:

tankhwah-i wilayati	167,715	Kabuli rupees
jagir	15,858	Kabuli rupees
malikana	16,521	Kabuli rupees
wazifa	56,621	Kabuli rupees[524]

In Laghman, 16,512 rupees were deducted from the gross revenue to pay the salaries of the administrators and to cover the table allowance of the governor. The remaining expenditures comprised close to 90,000 rupees, the most important items being:

tankhwah-i wilayati (paid to the Ghilzai leadership)	63,685	Kabuli rupees
malikana (paid to the headmen in the Tajikia subdivision)	11,142	Kabuli rupees
wazifa	12,783	Kabuli rupees[525]

Amir Dost Muhammad Khan's efforts to gain additional sources of revenue were thus hampered by the need to adhere to the traditional system of allowances and exemptions which had been instituted by Ahmad Shah. Even in regions where government authority was established fairly firmly, the Ghilzais continued to hold on to their privileged position. Hasting's statement for the Ghazni district that the Ghilzais were treated 'with consideration' by the government and enjoyed a favorable revenue assessment also held true for other regions. In 1845 Ferrier noted that the Pashtuns generally considered military service their only debt to the government, whereas other ethnic groups were subject to high taxes.[526] As a rule, Dost Muhammad Khan and his successor adhered to the revenue system instituted by Ahmad Shah and Timur Shah. The *jam'bast* assessment, also called *jam'-i qalandar khan* (after a revenue administrator of Ahmad Shah), was for the most part reserved for the Pashtuns. Consisting of a fixed quota in cash and kind, it entailed little or no government interference on the village level. Furthermore it was extremely light in comparison with the rates collected from non-Pashtuns. The *kot* system, which was applied to the other ethnic groups, implied that a fixed share of the gross produce had to be handed over to the government. It fluctuated with the amount of crops harvested and its assessment gave a more direct role to government officials. Most commonly the revenues were submitted according to the settlements of *se kot* ('three shares') and *char kot* ('four shares'), on the basis of which one third or one fourth of the harvest was handed over to the government.[527] At the beginning of the nineteenth century Strachey noted that the Ghilzais residing in the province of Kabul generally paid a revenue of one tenth of the produce, whereas the Tajiks had to submit as much as one third (*se kot*) of their harvest.[528] The differential treatment of Pashtuns and non-Pashtuns seems to have been even more pronounced in Logar, where the Pashtun landholders paid less than one tenth of the revenues submitted by the Tajiks and Qizilbash.[529] In the Ghazni district, almost the entire *tappa* Tajik was assessed according to the *se kot* system. The districts inhabited by 'Ali Khel Ghilzais and Wardaks were overwhelmingly administered according to the principles of *jam'bast*, whereas the Tarakis and Andars mainly seem to have paid a poll tax.[530] In the region of Jalalabad, the Khugianis paid revenues on the basis of *jam'-i qalandar khan* and most Ghilzai villages submitted no revenues whatsoever.[531]

At the same time, Amir Dost Muhammad Khan's efforts to bring new Pashtun groups into the fold of government control only met with limited success. Although he was able to secure the trade route to Qandahar, he made little headway among the tribes located further east which had traditionally evaded government control. The Kharoti Ghilzais at home in the mountains north of Katawaz and Urgun, for example, had avoided revenue payments to Timur Shah with the argument that they could only offer him a handful of pine nuts as tribute, as this was the only product of their country.[532] This tribe also seems to have remained entirely independent during Dost Muhammad Khan's time. Wherever revenues were paid to the Amir, their collection was cumbersome. Lynch reported that certain Ghilzai tribes gave up a 'tithe' to their chief, 'who wanders about the country during harvest time more like an Irish friar than a chief and begs rather than demands what is frequently given with a very bad grace.'[533] During Dost Muhammad Khan's first reign, the Sulaiman Khel Ghilzais of Zurmat and Katawaz were supposed to submit one in forty camels to the Amir.[534] Yet the revenue agents had to fear for their lives if they actually ventured into Sulaiman Khel country to collect the government dues. In the 1830s Broadfoot reported that no taxes had been raised 'for a long time', possibly since the decline of the Sadozai dynasty. Even when revenues were submitted the contributions which eventually made their way into the government coffers were meagre. Broadfoot gives the following characterization of a typical revenue collection in Katawaz:

> The khan directed the Khels to bring their quota, and presently saw lots of rotten sheep and toothless camels arrive at his gate. These were bought on the king's account at high prices and sold for what they fetched. Blankets, grain, and a little money, made up the remainder. There was always a deficiency in the amount, and the khan usually took half of what he received, and gave the king the rest with an apology; sometimes the king allowed him to take a certain share.[535]

During his second reign, the Amir was able to collect some revenue among the Sulaiman Khel. This success notwithstanding his attitude to these tribes remained cautious and he did not dare to use coercive measures to induce the neighboring Ahmadzais and Sohaks to do the same.[536] In Amir Sher 'Ali Khan's time the Sulaiman Khel continued to remain largely beyond the reach of the government.[537]

SUMMARY

The historical materials I have presented in this chapter make it clear that Pashtun tribal structures cannot be pressed into neat patterns. If one were to make broad generalizations concerning the types of organization prevailing among the Pashtuns in the nineteenth century, three tribal 'belts' may be distinguished. Firstly, the so-called border tribes, as well as the Ghilzais located at a distance from the major trade routes, displayed the dispersion of power typical of segmentary lineage organization. Further north, the regions of Swat, Dir and Bajaur formed another setting, in which the Yusufzai and Tarklanri Pashtuns represented a thin tribal aristocracy superimposed on a local population of heterogeneous origin.[538] The neighboring valley of Kunar presented a related case, with the difference that the elite was furnished by a family of non-Pashtun *sayyids* who had seized power in the course of the sixteenth century. Finally, the Ghilzai and Mohmand groups controlling the southern and eastern approaches to Kabul were characterized by an entrenched leadership which had crystallized under Safawid/Mughal patronage.

While the Pashtuns engaged in migrations and conquest movements in earlier times, their tribal boundaries have not changed substantially since the nineteenth century. For this reason, modern anthropological works provide useful information concerning the ecological/economic determinants of tribal life. What cannot be projected into the past, however, is the political position of the tribal leadership. For the Ghilzais, Anderson has pointed out that their political identity underwent significant changes in the twentieth century, as the notion of a separate Ghilzai identity was subsumed by a larger 'Pashtun' one.[539] The attitudes of the Hotak and Tokhi Ghilzais described in this chapter thus were the product of political configurations unique to the eighteenth and nineteenth centuries. For this reason, present-day data can only shed a limited amount of light on the political setting in nineteenth-century Afghanistan. At the same time, modern anthropological studies have furnished us with a *concept* useful for the understanding of tribal society which may also be applied to the past. The theory of segmentary lineage organization gives us a sense of the political decentralization prevailing at Dost Muhammad Khan's time. The notion of segmentary fusion and fission helps to explain the aspects of the historical narrative often so bewildering to the Western reader, such as the multiplicity of political actors, the vast range of often short-lived coalitions and, to follow the prevailing stereotype, a Pashtun penchant for warfare. As my historical materials show, the groups located immediately beyond the reach of the government, such as the Khyber tribes, the Turis of Kurram and the Sulaiman Khel Ghilzais, approximated segmentary ideals most closely. Here the avenues to power were open to a large pool of contenders and no lasting stratification can be observed. Among the Ghilzai and Mohmand groups which displayed a greater degree of internal stratification, the competition for the paramount leadership also often unfolded according to segmentary principles, with the important distinction that the candidates for power exclusively belonged to the entrenched leading lineages. Similar rivalries were also at work within the various strands of the royal family. The political conflict unfolding in these settings often followed the pattern of cousin rivalry (*tarburwali*), or was influenced by jealousies among brothers and half brothers.

The distribution of power within Dost Muhammad Khan's realm may likewise be viewed in terms of segmentation. As will be seen in the following chapter, the Amir's autocratic control over Kabul and its surroundings was offset by his limited reach into the regions making up the provinces of his kingdom. Given the limitations this system of goverment placed on the resources available to the king, the need to raise revenues and soldiers constantly put his abilities as a ruler to a test. Outside Kabul, royal claims to authority could only be maintained by a network of personal loyalties, the strength of which was a function of the Amir's ability to remunerate the services rendered. Accordingly, Dost Muhammad Khan was confronted by the conflicting needs of gaining access to revenues while simultaneously conciliating his tribal allies. The relationship between the Amir and the Pashtun nobles was characterized by an inherent tension and was subject to constant reassessment. As the recipients of royal favors could use the resources placed in their hands to carve out separate bases of power, the king watched his strongest allies with misgivings, well aware that they might challenge his authority at any given moment. The relative weakness of the king is also reflected by the fact that the military confrontations with such powerful allies-turned-foe tended to drag on for extended periods of time, taking the form of tribal raid and counter raid.

The theory of segmentary lineage organization allows us to understand the equalizing mechanisms at work at various levels of Afghan society. At the same time, the view of tribal politics as the outcome of a balancing process between the various segments of a ramifying lineage system only gives a limited a role to the external factors shaping local configurations of power. My discussion of the Ghilzai and Mohmand groups located along the major trade routes in Dost Muhammad Khan's realm shows that segmentary structures had given way to an entrenched leadership by the nineteenth century. The crucial factor for this development was court patronage, which, giving individual families privileged access to economic resources, produced a lasting stratification within the tribes concerned. Having crystallized during the Mughal/Safawid period, the leading lineages of the Morcha Khel Mohmands and the Jabbar Khel, Babakr Khel, Tokhi and Hotak Ghilzais were tied to the Sadozai rulers by a system of service grants comparable to the medieval European institution of the *feudum*. The privileges individual chiefs obtained allowed them to enhance their position locally by extending generosity and protection to their fellow tribesmen. While the social differences between the Pashtun *khan* and his tribal followers never became as pronounced as in feudal Europe, the competition for leadership and its equalizing effects were no longer open to all members of the tribe but became confined to the aristocratic families. Although unable to impose tribal chiefs from above, the Sadozai government promoted individual contenders for power, mostly heeding hereditary claims to leadership. The rival branches of the leading families in turn sought to enhance their chances for success by cultivating different factions at the royal court.

The interaction with the state thus has a formative impact on the development of local relationships of power. As demonstrated by the emergence of entrenched leading lineages, the genealogical principles typical of the segmentary organization tend to give way to relationships of a more political nature at the higher levels of tribal organization. The local configurations of power in nineteenth-century Afghanistan are best understood in the light of Glatzer's proposition that the degree of hierarchization within a tribe is directly linked to the intensity of its interaction with the state. Yet this phenomenon is not to be understood in strictly linear terms, implying that the most formidable tribal leaders are to be found in the immediate vicinity of the centers of power. Given their long-standing incorporation into the Sadozai and Muhammadzai administrations, the leaders of the 'obedient' Pashtun tribes in the neighborhood of Kabul and Ghazni had little opportunity to maneuver vis-à-vis the state. The most powerful Ghilzai and Mohmand chiefs, on the other hand, rose at a certain *distance* from the royal and provincial capitals, particularly in strategically important regions where the rulers were unable to exert permanent control and required local assistance in advancing their claims to supremacy. Intermittent government presence thus had the effect of enhancing the position of the existing local leadership and encouraging the emergence of leading lineages. Furthermore, 'proximity' to the state should not be seen as a purely spatial phenomenon. As the contrasting modes of organization of the Khyber tribes and the Morcha Khel Mohmands show, historically grown relationships with local rulers, the formulation of identity in opposition to, or in agreement with, their policies are important diacritics for the political developments within a particular tribe.

The prerogatives the great Pashtun leaders enjoyed under the Sadozais invite the comparison with the position of the *ilkhanis* or paramount chiefs of the great tribal confederacies of Iran. The Qashqai confederacy, for example, grew during the Safawid period in a process of amalgamation, the local tribal leadership being able to create an increasingly large following for itself. While receiving government titles and privileges, the paramount Qashqai chiefs apparently derived their power in the first place from their tribal base and were recognized by the government primarily on the basis of their local influence.[540] This would suggest a development parallel to the one which took place among the great Pashtun groups in the eighteenth century. Yet two important differences in the organization of Pashtun tribes and the Iranian confederacies and their relationship with the rulers of their time stand out. Firstly, the role of the Iranian kings seems to have been stronger in the delineation of tribal confederacies and the shaping of their leadership. Garthwaite points out that the tribal policy of the Qajars also included the attempt to forge tribal groups into fairly centralized administrative units. This endeavor could also entail the appointment of outsiders to the paramount leadership. The Khamseh confederacy, for example, was formed by royal order and was controlled by a merchant family of Shiraz.[541] No such imposition of an external leadership from the top is documented for the powerful Pashtun groups which interacted with the Mughal/Safawid and Sadozai rulers.[542] In these regions the court or its representatives promoted the claims to leadership advanced by men of local standing and subsequently encouraged the formation of leading lineages by bestowing similar privileges on the descendants of the erstwhile leaders. The only active effort to delimit tribal boundaries is documented for the early Sadozai era, when Ahmad Shah attempted to weaken the Barakzai Durranis by separating the Achakzais from them. The second difference concerns the composition of the tribal groups in question, and their scope of organization. The Pashtun groups organized under a paramount leader tended to be much smaller in scale and more homogeneous in composition than the Iranian confederacies, which comprised hundreds of thousands of people of various ethnic backgrounds.[543] While Ahmad Shah was formally recognized as the leader of the Durrani and Ghilzai Pashtuns, effective leadership took place on the level of the tribe or its subdivision, involving groups whose populations generally amounted to no more than several thousand families.

Amir Dost Muhammad Khan's relations with the more distant tribes, such as the Turis of Kurram and the Sulaiman Khel and Mangals of Zurmat were limited to irregular revenue collection campaigns. His efforts to establish control over the major lines of communication in his realm, by contrast, brought him into fairly close contact with the entrenched lineages guarding the highroads. The task of finding a new sort of equilibrium with the powerful leadership he had inherited from the Sadozai era constituted a major challenge for the newly established Amir. Viewed by the greater part of the Pashtun elite as usurpers, the Muhammadzai family was more preoccupied with consolidating its bases of power than honoring the traditional prerogatives of the tribal aristocracy. The former Sadozai empire having shrunk to a small regional state, Dost Muhammad Khan was unable, and unwilling, to continue a full-fledged system of service grants. The loss of the revenue-rich Indian provinces also compelled him to seek new sources of revenue within the confines of his kingdom and to make his presence felt among those Pashtun *khans* who had hitherto defined themselves as partners or rivals, rather than as subjects, of the lords of Kabul. The Pashtun groups to feel Muhammadzai pressure for revenues most acutely were the Hotak and Tokhi Ghilzais and, as will be seen in the following chapter, the Durranis of Qandahar. On the whole, however, Dost Muhammad Khan and his successor Sher 'Ali Khan were unable to introduce significant changes to the lenient tax rates the greater group of Pashtuns had been accustomed to since the time of Ahmad Shah Sadozai. In his effort to consolidate his authority, the Amir was able to play on the existing rivalries between certain groups, such as the Jabbar Khel Ghilzais and the Morcha Khel Mohmands. If caught by the government, openly rebellious tribal leaders were likely to be imprisoned or executed. Even so, Dost Muhammad Khan was unable to affect the internal organization of the tribes he was interacting with. The Tokhi and Hotak Ghilzais are a case in point. Subsequent to the Tokhi uprising of 1853 the Amir eliminated the instigators of the rebellion and imposed unheard-of tax collections among these two groups. Even so, the remaining members of the leading lineages continued to command the respect of their fellow tribesmen and were to reemerge on the political arena and to vaunt their historical claims to power as soon as signs of weakness emanated from the center.

Chapter 4

DOST MUHAMMAD KHAN'S OCCUPATION OF QANDAHAR AND HIS ADMINISTRATION

During the Sadozai period the Durranis of Qandahar, in particular the Popalzai, Barakzai and Alikozai tribes interacted closely with the royal court. Assuming high positions in the administration and the military, their leaders enjoyed great influence both in the Sadozai capital and at home. Yet from the middle of the nineteenth century on British observers noted with surprise 'the paucity of influential chiefs' among these very groups.[1] In the first part of this chapter, I will investigate how the decline of the Durrani leadership was brought about during the reign of Dost Muhammad Khan's half brothers at Qandahar from 1818 until 1855. As will be seen below, the Muhammadzai rulers viewed the former state supporting elite as rivals and sought to undermine their hereditary privileges in every possible way. While proximity to the court had been advantageous for the Durrani leaders in the eighteenth century, they now found themselves more vulnerable to state interference than the other Pashtun groups interacting with the first generation of Muhammadzai rulers.

The second part of this chapter concerns the nature of Dost Muhammad Khan's administration. The Amir's difficult position in southern Afghanistan subsequent to his occupation of Qandahar in November 1855 is symptomatic of the problems besetting his reign in general. For this reason, I will proceed from a specific description of his situation in Qandahar to a more general analysis of his administration. Despite his impressive territorial gains Dost Muhammad Khan was unable to back up his military conquests with centralized government institutions which would have allowed him to tap local resources in an efficient manner. Only a fraction of the surplus produced locally reached the higher level of administration by way of revenue payments.[2] The difficulty of drawing together adequate supplies also affected the king's ability to provide for his army. As the example of Qandahar will show, Dost Muhammad Khan's resources there were insufficient for sustaining a powerful army over a prolonged period.

THE DURRANIS

Durrani History and Organization

In this section I will explore some of the milestones of Durrani history, paying particular attention to the 'imperial' factors shaping tribal organization. The fortunes of the Durranis were linked to their Safawid and Nadirid overlords even more closely than those of their Hotak rivals. The Durranis themselves viewed their origins in 'saintly' terms. Known as 'Abdali' until the Nadirid period, they were said to have adopted this name from Ahmad Shah's ancestor Shaikh 'Arif, who had received from a Chishti saint the title *abdal* denoting the fifth rank in the hierarchy of Sufi saints.[3] In the sixteenth century the Arghastan valley east of Qandahar seems to have formed the 'homeland' (*watan-i asli)* of the Abdalis.[4] During the same period parts of this confederacy followed a nomadic lifestyle, migrating between Qandahar and the valley of Toba and Zamindawar in the northwest and Qarabagh, Ghazni and Kabul in the northeast.[5] At the time of the Safawid ruler Shah 'Abbas I (r. 1587–1629), the most important Abdali leader was Sado (Asadullah, b. 1558), the progenitor of the Sadozai branch of the Popalzai tribe. In the course of the competition between the Safawids and the Mughals for the possession of Qandahar, Sado and his descendants mostly sided with the Safawids. The Popalzai leader is first mentioned in the year 1589 when Shah 'Abbas entrusted him with the protection of the highroad between Herat and Qandahar. At that time he also received the title of *mir-i afaghina* ('lord of the Afghans'). Sado seems to have maintained his leading position even after the possession of Qandahar passed to the Mughals in 1595. In 1622 he assisted Shah 'Abbas in his reconquest of Qandahar and was awarded the Safawid title *sultan.*[6] According to Leech, Shah 'Abbas declared the persons of Sado and his descendants to be 'sacred' and gave him so much authority that he had the 'power of life and death' not only over the Popalzais but the entire Abdali confederacy. His duties also seem to have included the collection of revenue on behalf of the Safawid governor. Despite the strong Safawid backing he enjoyed, Sado's attempts to raise revenues met with resistance among the Barakzai Abdalis who had traditionally challenged Popalzai claims to leadership among the Abdalis.[7] Throughout the sixteenth century, Sado's descendants were able to maintain a leading position in the region in exchange for assisting the *beglarbegi* of Qandahar in the revenue collection among the Abdalis and adjacent regions. Yet their influence withered when Gurgin Khan assumed the governorship of Qandahar in 1702 and began to encourage rival claims to regional leadership advanced by other members of the Sadozai division and the Hotaks under Mir Wais. Within a few years the Abdali leaders Daulat Khan and his son Rustam Khan, both direct descendants of Sado, were put to death. In 1707 the remaining Abdalis of the Qandahar region were either killed or driven away during a massacre organized by Gurgin Khan. Despite these decimations the Abdalis were said to consist of 60,000 families in the early eighteenth century and thus continued to outnumber the Ghilzais.[8]

For the next thirty years, Herat was to form the center of Abdali activities. In 1709 the Abdalis reacted to Mir Wais's rebellion by offering military assistance to the Safawids. In 1716/17 they asserted their independence at Herat. The following years were taken up by military confrontations with the Persian army and the Ghilzais. Another important political development among the Abdalis was the rivalry between two sets of Sadozai leaders. The grandsons of Daulat Khan Sadozai, Zu'l-Faqar Khan and Ahmad Khan, were based in Farah. They enjoyed the support of Zu'l-Faqar Khan's maternal uncle, 'Abd al-Ghani Alikozai. Zu'l-Faqar Khan's claims to leadership among the Abdalis were directed against another, closely related, Sadozai lineage controlling Herat.[9]

Nadir Shah's conquest of Herat on 16 February 1732 initially weakened the Abdalis. As a punishment for their unwillingness to submit to his rule, 6,000 of them were deported to Mashhad, Nishapur and Tus. In Iran a number of them entered Nadir Shah's army under the leadership of 'Abd al-Ghani Khan Alikozai, and their contingent rendered him valuable service during his military campaign to Daghistan in 1734–35. Following the conquest of Qandahar on March 12, 1738, Nadir Shah rewarded the Abdalis for their services by restoring them to their old possessions near Herat and allowed them to move to the region of Qandahar, Qal'a-yi Bist and Zamindawar, where he granted them the lands he had recently confiscated from the Hotak Ghilzais.[10] The Abdalis profited in several ways from their association with Nadir Shah. The lands given to them in the vicinity of Qandahar were *tiyul*, fiefs given in remission of crown revenues in exchange for the supply of 6,000 cavalry. In addition, they received lands known as *khushkaba* (dependent on an uncertain supply of irrigation) in the valleys of the Tarnak, Arghastan, Kadanai, and Dori rivers. These lands were assessed at one-tenth of their produce and independent of military service.

After Nadir Shah's death in June 1747 Ahmad Khan was able to gain the leadership of the Abdalis at a *jirga* held in the vicinity of Qandahar. The main reasons quoted for his election were his direct descent from Sado and the fact that his second next ancestor, Khwaja Khizr b. Sado, was generally venerated by the Abdalis as a saint. After his assumption of power Ahmad Shah sought to weaken his most powerful Abdali rivals, the Barakzais, by splitting off the Achakzai subdivision from them and turning it into a tribe of its own right within the Abdali confederacy. Otherwise, the composition of the tribes previously known as Abdali did not change significantly. According to most accounts, Ahmad Shah made his imperial claims known by renaming this confederacy 'Durrani' corresponding to the title of *durr-i dauran* ('pearl of the age') or *durr-i durran* ('pearl of pearls') which he assumed henceforth.[11] Yet there also are indications that the name 'Durrani' had been current among the Abdalis of Herat prior to the period of Ahmad Shah and that it became common among all Abdalis subsequent to his rise to power.[12] Another source traces the name 'Durrani' to the Abdalis' custom of wearing a small pearl studded ring in the right ear.[13] The renaming of the Abdalis did not reflect any internal reorganization but more probably signified a change in their political identity. The term *durr*, 'pearl', while not a common indicator of royal legitimacy, may have reflected Ahmad Shah's claims to worldy authority and foreshadowed his intended leap from tribal politics to imperial ones. Simultaneously, casting himself as 'pearl among pearls', he emphasized his close linkage to the former Abdali confederacy, portraying his relationship with his fellow tribesmen as one of equality and partnership. While he adopted the major outlines of the Safawid and Nadirid systems of administration, Ahmad Shah successfully incorporated the Abdali *khans* into the structure of his nascent state by bestowing all major offices on them.[14] Ahmad Shah's successors Timur Shah and Shah Zaman generally followed the policies instituted by the founder of the Durrani empire. At the same time, they were constantly aware of the drawbacks of being entirely dependent on the support of their fellow tribesmen for their exercise of power. Fearing that the Durrani chiefs might use their powerful position at court to advance separate claims to leadership, Timur Shah and Shah Zaman strove to check their influence by fostering less influential tribal outsiders who posed no threat to their authority. One of Timur Shah's most quoted policies is the removal of his capital from the Durrani heartland of Qandahar to Kabul. Furthermore, he sought to create a military counterpose to the Durranis by expanding his Qizilbash bodyguard to 12,000 men and choosing non-Durrani counsellors.[15] While Shah Zaman initially adhered to the precept of appointing Durrani nobles to leading positions, he attempted to weaken their grip on hereditary government posts and to centralize his administration during the final phase of his reign. The continued strength of the Durrani leadership is reflected by the fact that these measures led to Shah Zaman's downfall.

During Ahmad Shah's reign the Durranis became even more firmly entrenched in southern Afghanistan. They were allowed to continue in the possession of the *tiyuls* awarded by Nadir Shah. Moreover, Ahmad Shah relinquished formal government claims on their produce by allotting regular pay for military services rendered. The *khushkaba* lands became hereditary (*maurusi*) possessions and were eventually claimed by the Durranis as 'ancestral' lands. The assessment of one-tenth of the produce was substituted with the small amount of grain or chaff the Durrani occupants had to furnish the army with on occasion of its passage. Furthermore, many Durranis received *khalisa* (crown lands) in the immediate vicinity of Qandahar and the tax receipts of recently cultivated lands (*nauabad*) as military pay or gratuity for past services. Their share in the *khalisa* lands was half (*nisfakari*) or two-thirds (*sekot*); the *nauabad* territories were assessed at one-tenth. The policies of Nadir Shah and Ahmad Shah led to a considerable displacement of the native Farsiwan, Hazara, Kakar and Baluch cultivators by the Abdalis/Durranis, who also controlled the revenue collection in the region. Whereas the crown lands were almost exclusively cultivated by non-Durranis at the beginning of Ahmad Shah's reign, three-fourths of them had been transferred to Durranis at the time of his death. The Durranis were also able to extend their *khushkaba* possessions considerably, leaving only a small portion of these lands to the native peasantry.[16]

There is conflicting information on the size of the entire Durrani confederacy in the nineteenth century. In the 1830s Rawlinson estimated it at 235,000 families, as opposed to the 100,000 families mentioned for the period of Ahmad Shah. Twenty years prior to Rawlinson, Elphinstone was of the opinion that the Durranis still numbered 100,000 families and made up at least half of the entire population of 800,000 souls in their lands. At the end of the nineteenth century Raverty thought the Durrani confederacy to consist of 300,000 souls, including 60,000 men capable of bearing arms.[17] The region claimed by the various Durrani tribes covered an extensive tract of land bounded in the east by the Ghilzais, in the north by the Hazara highlands and in the west and south by the deserts adjoining Persia and Baluchistan. The eastern part of this area is divided into two distinct geographical sections by the Kadanai-Dori-Argandab river which flows in a westerly direction until it joins the Helmand at Qal'a-yi Bist (Bost). The hilly country north of this river is divided by a number of valleys which run southwest and are watered by the rivers Arghastan, Tarnak, Arghandab, Kushk-i Nakhud and Helmand. With the exception of the regions bordering the Helmand river, Khash Rud and Farah Rud, the southern parts of the Durrani dominions are overwhelmingly arid.

Located on a plain on the left bank of the Arghandab, the city of Qandahar belonged to the more fertile region of the province:

> The country round Candahar is level, naturally of tolerable fertility, irrigated both by water-courses from the rivers and by Caureezes, and the most industriously cultivated. It in consequence abounds with grain, and its gardens contain good vegetables and excellent fruit, besides melons, cucumbers, &c. which are cultivated in the fields... Madder, assafœtida, spusta (lucerne) and shuftul (a kind of clover) are also abundant. The tobacco of Candahar has a geat reputation. The country near the hills is probably the most fertile, and that round the town is best cultivated; the country to the west is sandy at no great distance from the city, and that to the south becomes dry and unproductive within a march of Candahar: that to the east is fertile

> and much better cultivated than the rest of the valley of the Turnuk...[18]

The lands around Qandahar were inhabited by all Durrani tribes in 'nearly equal proportions'.[19] While Nadir Shah's distribution of land had taken tribal affiliations into account it was nonetheless artificial in nature and had the effect of placing the various Pashtun tribes in the immediate vicinity of each other. The subsequent acquisition of *khushkaba*, *khalisa* and *nauabad* lands by the Durrani leadership further eroded the notion of clearly delineated tribal domains. Moreover, there was a sizeable component of *ra'iyats*, the original cultivators of the region, who either belonged to other ethnic groups like the Hazaras, Tajiks, and Baluches or less powerful Pashtun tribes like the Kakars. Needless to say that the population of Qandahar city was even more heterogeneous in composition, a great part of it being furnished by non-Pashtun Farsiwan and Hindus.[20]

In the regions located at a distance from Qandahar an equal amount of intermixture of the various Durrani tribes was to be observed. During Nadir Shah's time the 'Alizais under their leader Nur Muhammad Khan received Zamindawar northwest of Qandahar. In the nineteenth century this region was also inhabited by Barakzais. The neighboring regions of Deh Raud and Tirin Kot housed Alikozais, Popalzais and Nurzais. The Alikozais received lands on the Arghandab and Tarnak rivers northeast of Qandahar from Nadir Shah and Ahmad Shah. The Sadozais were likewise awarded *khushkaba* lands in the Tarnak valley. Other Popalzai groups and the Barakzais were able to take possession of the Arghastan valley further east. The Barakzais also held Maiwand and Girishk west of Qandahar. The Achakzais shared the land irrigated by the Kadanai and Dori streams south of Qandahar with the Nurzais. The Nurzais also inhabited Garmser, Khash Rud and Farah. Lash Juwain in the extreme southwest of the Durrani territory was home to a mixture of Ishaqzais, Achakzais and Popalzais.[21] The lifestyle of the individual Durrani groups depended on the fertility of their soil. Inhabiting the barren lands located in the southern and western tracts of the Durrani country, the Achakzai, Nurzai and Ishaqzai tribes were mainly known for their nomadism. In the nineteenth century the greater part of the Barakzais were also reported to lead a pastoral lifestyle. The Alikozais and Popalzais, along with the 'Alizais of Zamindawar, mostly were agriculturists.[22]

The geographical distribution of the Durrani tribes also affected their position within the Sadozai empire. In the early nineteenth century Elphinstone made the following observation:

> The clans near Candahar probably look up most to the King, while those who inhabit remote and unfrequented countries (as the Noorzyes and the Atchikzyes), are more attached to their Sirdars. Even in those tribes the Sirdar derives a great part of his power from

> the King, but he exercises it subject to less control than the chiefs of tribes near the royal residence, and he is less apt to be eclipsed, or set aside, by the immediate intervention of the sovereign.[23]

Beyond regional differences, the above passage reveals that the entire Durrani confederacy was incorporated into the Sadozai military and adminstrative apparatus more closely than any other Pashtun group. Holding almost all their lands as service grants, the Durranis had little opportunity to evade government control in the long term. Their close linkage to the court also engendered a greater amount of internal hierarchization. Subject to appointment by the king, the paramount Durrani leaders were recruited from among a limited number of prominent families. These *sardars* and the next echelon of leadership, the *khans*, enjoyed much more authority among their fellow tribesmen than their counterparts in other Pashtun groups. Among the Durranis, British observers detected little of the 'democratic spirit' they accorded so readily to other Pashtun tribes. In their opinion, the Durrani leadership was far removed socially and economically from the lower echelons of tribal society: 'At present the peasantry of the Dooranee tribes look up to the *mulliks* as their guardians and masters, and through the *mulliks* they are led to regard the person of the Khan with feelings both of fear and reverence.'[24]

Even so, it would be wrong to assume a clear chain of command reaching from the Sadozai kings to their Durrani troops. While the Sadozai rulers were theoretically able to affect the internal organization of the Durrani tribes by nominating outsiders as *sardars*, the next lower echelon of tribal organization usually resisted the imposition of chiefs from above. Moreover, the military contingents of the Durranis continued to be organized on the basis of tribal affiliation rather than being imposed from above. Finally, the Sadozai kings depended on the support of the Durrani nobility against rival claimants to the throne. The strength of the Sadozai kings thus rested in great part with their ability to reconcile this powerful aristocracy.

> [T]he dynasty of Suddozye is mainly upheld by the Dooraunees, and the crown would be transferred without a struggle from one member of it to another by a general combination of that tribe; consequently the King is in a great measure dependent on the good will of the Dooraunee chiefs, and is obliged to conciliate that order by bestowing on it a large portion of power and honour, though in reality he views it with jealousy, and is continually employed in indirect attempts to undermine it.[25]

With the ascendancy of the Muhammadzai Sardars in Kabul and Qandahar, however, the Durrani nobility was to face unprecedented attacks on its prestige and economic standing. In the following section, I will take a closer look at the policies of Dost Muhammad Khan's relatives in the principality of Qandahar during the first half of the nineteenth century.

The Policies of the Qandahar Sardars

Dost Muhammad Khan's half brothers Purdil, Sherdil and Kuhandil took control of Qandahar and its surroundings in 1818 immediately after Shah Mahmud had hastened his own downfall, and that of the Sadozai dynasty, by executing the eldest and most influential member of the Muhammadzai family, Wazir Fatih Muhammad Khan. Henceforth known as the 'Qandahar Sardars', this set of brothers was able to maintain its hold over the city and to claim authority over a great part of the Durrani lands for more than three decades to come, only interrupted by the British intervention of 1839–1842. While Purdil Khan was the eldest brother, Sherdil Khan, the second eldest of the Qandahar Sardars, seems to have played a leading role in the politics of Qandahar in the early Muhammadzai period. He acted as the commander in chief of the troops of this principality and managed to hold on to the erstwhile Sadozai possession of Sind. Moreover, he actively interfered in the struggle for the control of Kabul, and it was only after his death in July 1826 that Dost Muhammad Khan could make a more successful bid for power in the former Sadozai capital.[26]

Sherdil Khan was succeeded by Purdil Khan, whose government of Qandahar has been described in certain detail by the British traveller Masson. Unlike Sherdil Khan, Purdil Khan was unable to challenge Dost Muhammad Khan's position at Kabul. Nevertheless his possessions, combined with those of his younger brothers Kuhandil, Rahmdil and Mihrdil, were formidable enough to place him on an equal footing with the Amir in the late 1820s. Purdil Khan's claims to sovereignty are reflected by his assumption of the title of *padshah* in his communications with foreign states. Even so, his authority in Qandahar was far from absolute and was challenged at times by his younger brothers, who would give expression to their opposition by holding court independently of the head of the family.[27] Their independent bearing was further enhanced by the fact that they enjoyed their own sources of revenue which they administrated through their own agents. According to Masson, Kuhandil Khan was in charge of Qandahar's frontier with Herat and the territories to the north. He controlled Garmser, the 'Alizais of Zamindawar, the Nurzais of Deh Raud, and the Hazara territories north of Qandahar. Mihrdil Khan was entitled to the revenues of the regions bordering on the lands of the Tokhi and Hotak Ghilzais in the northeast. To the south of Qandahar, the authority of the Sardars extended as far as Sibi, as Sind and the Baluch/Brahui principality of Qalat had slipped from the control of the Qandahar Sardars with the death of Sherdil Khan.[28] The revenues of Sibi, along with those of Pishin and Shorabak, were alloted to Rahmdil Khan, who resumed all crown lands from the local *sayyids* for his personal use.[29] Despite the decentralized nature of the administration of their principality the younger Qandahar Sardars were not quite as self-sufficient as they would have liked. The problems of revenue collection in certain regions such as Shorabak and Sibi, as well as Deh Raud and Zamindawar, required the 'Dil' brothers to combine their forces for punitive expeditions. By comparison, Purdil Khan's revenues were much vaster and more accessible, being concentrated in and around Qandahar. Purdil Khan not only controlled the property he had seized after the death of Sherdil Khan but also received most of the income of Qandahar city and the fertile districts bordering immediately on it. Supported by a well-paid army of 3,000 horsemen, Purdil Khan thus faced few lasting challenges to his position as the leading Sardar of Qandahar.[30] After Purdil Khan's death in 1830 the remaining brothers were locked into a 'triumvirate' of jealousy in which the elder Kuhandil Khan took the leading position. Another important figure in the policies of Qandahar was Khuda Nazar Khan, the maternal uncle of the Sardars, who enjoyed particular influence with Rahmdil Khan and held the position of *mukhtar*, or chief manager, at the time of Masson's visit.[31]

Qandahar had risen to importance subsequent to the destruction of the old Ghaznawid winter capital of Bost by the Ghorids in 1150.[32] In the nineteenth century it constituted a vital link in the trade between India and Persia and was one of the most important trade centers in Afghanistan. Prior to the First Anglo-Afghan war estimates of the entire revenue, including the income from customs and taxes levied in the city, varied from Rs. 800,000[33] to 1,200,000.[34] Yet the Qandahar Sardars were reported to 'live from hand to mouth', levying not only all sorts of taxes imaginable, but also extorting additional funds from the Hindu merchants and other wealthy citizens on a daily basis.[35] While the city seems to have continued to prosper in the 1830s, its trade declined subsequent to the First Anglo-Afghan War. European observers attributed this development, as well as the emigration of a great number of Kuhandil's subjects, to the Sardars' harsh government.[36]

Besides the denizens of Qandahar, the Durranis inhabiting the countryside were another group to suffer from the policies of the 'Dil' brothers. In order to understand the position of the Durrani leadership during this period, I will briefly trace its political fortunes from the early nineteenth century on, when the power struggle of the last Sadozai rulers, Shah Mahmud and Shah Shuja' unfolded. Initially at least, the Durrani leadership seemed to suffer little from the political unrest taking hold of the Sadozai empire. During Shah Mahmud's first reign from 1800 to 1803 it was able to gain the renewal of many of the grants originally bestowed by Ahmad Shah. Moreover, certain groups, such as the 'Alizais of Zamindawar, managed to enlarge their landed holdings significantly at the cost of the last remaining *ra'iyats* in their region. The Nurzai and

Popalzai tribes were able to hold on to their lands in Deh Raud and Tirin which they had seized from the Hazaras during Timur Shah's time. Nevertheless the majority of the Durrani *sardars* continued to be partial to Shah Shuja', and they were instrumental in bringing him to power in 1803. During Shah Shuja''s reign from 1803–1809 the position of the Durrani leadership seemed to be stronger than ever before. Because of the ruler's dependence on their support, the most influential *sardars* prospered both financially and politically. During the final phase of Shah Shuja''s reign Elphinstone noted that the king had little control either over the appointment of his Durrani ministers or the way they exercised their powers.[37] In the long run, however, the general political instability was bound to affect the position of the Durrani leadership negatively. The frequent struggles between Shah Shuja' and his rivals for the possession of Qandahar caused altercations and many deaths among the Durrani elite. This situation was exacerbated during Shah Mahmud's second reign, which was characterized by the king's great partiality to Fatih Khan Muhammadzai and his brothers. Between 1809 and 1818 Shah Mahmud's son Kamran acted as the governor of Qandahar and, apparently encouraged by Fatih Khan, 'absolutely butchered' the Durrani leadership.[38] During the early phase of Shah Mahmud's second reign the Durranis also faced the first inroads into their tax exempt status. Quoting the lacking revenue receipts from the more distant Durrani province of Sind, the governor of Qandahar resorted to the unheard-of measure of forced revenue collections from certain Durrani chiefs.[39] But on the whole Shah Mahmud seems to have respected the financial privileges of the Durrani leadership, and the only taxes imposed on a regular basis were of a rather nominal nature.

It was only with the accession of the Muhammadzai Sardars in 1818 that the priviliged position of the Durrani leadership began to crumble seriously. According to information gathered by Rawlinson, the British political agent for Qandahar during the First Anglo-Afghan War, the 'Dil' brothers aimed consistently at weakening the non-Barakzai tribesmen and at undermining their financial and political privileges during the first twenty years of their reign. The great offices of state were taken away from the prominent noble families and were given to Durranis of more obscure backgrounds. As in earlier periods, the supervision of the revenue collection rested with an influential Farsiwan family which had first gained this position during the reign of Timur Shah. The Durrani cavalry, which had rarely been called out as a military force after the era of Ahmad Shah, was now formally divested of its function. Instead, the lords of Qandahar created an independent force of 3,000 mercenary horsemen who could be employed to harass the Durrani leadership.[40] By various measures of coercion they gradually forced the Durrani landowners to accept a tax assessment of their lands which was to increase Qandahar's net revenues by 300,000 rupees.[41]

In order to gain a better understanding of the measures taken by the Qandahar Sardars, let us take a closer look at the administrative structure of Qandahar. For tax purposes, the principality of Qandahar was divided into two entities, firstly, the *qariyajat*, or 'suburbs' dependent on the city of Qandahar, and secondly, nineteen *mahallat*, or 'districts'.[42] The 6,000 *qulbas* ('ploughs') of land distributed among the Durranis by Nadir Shah were to be found in both subdivisions. For example, the cultivable land of the Barakzai fief (*tiyul*) consisted of a total of 933 *qulbas*, 542 of which were located in the *qariyajat* and 391 in the *mahallat*. Up to Shah Mahmud's second reign, all Durrani *tiyuls* were exempt of revenue payments. The lands originally set aside for the *ra'iyats* made up roughly one third of the Durrani lands. They were mostly located in the vicinity of villages and were assessed at one tenth of the produce or five *kharwars* per *qulba*. The *khalisa*, or crown, lands were rented out to the *ra'iyats* at the rate of half the produce (*nisfakari*) and a third of the produce (*sekot*) in the *qariyajat* and *mahallat* respectively. Because of their privileged position the Durrani leaders were able to take over many of the *ra'iyat* and *khalisa* lands even before the end of Ahmad Shah's reign. While the *tiyuls* were exempt of revenue payments, the Durranis had to adhere to the existing assessments of the *ra'iyati* and *khalisa* lands they acquired. Moreover, there were certain taxes Pashtun and non-Pashtun landlords alike had to pay from Ahmad Shah's time on. These included taxes on the operation of mills, shops for cleaning rice, leases of orchards, melon grounds, etc. The taxes imposed on the Durranis during Shah Mahmud's second reign consisted of commutations for services previously rendered, such as the supply of chaff for the royal cavalry (*kahbaha*) and the provision of labor for the maintenance of an important irrigation channel (*ju-yi shah*).[43]

In their effort to widen their tax base the Qandahar *sardars* moved ahead gradually. While their first measures primarily targeted the non-Durrani population and only affected the Durrani landlords in an indirect manner, they prepared the ground for increasingly intrusive revenue policies. One such move was the imposition of a capitation tax called *khanawari*. Originally known as *khanadudi*, this tax had been levied by Ahmad Shah solely among ethnic outsiders, such as groups of Kakar, Ghilzai, Baluch origin, who entered the Qandahar region as shepherds or cultivators. The Qandahar Sardars raised this tax substantially by collecting 3 to 15 rupees per family instead of the 2 rupees required by Ahmad Shah. Furthermore they extended its imposition to the entire non-Durrani population including the *ra'iyats* who had become landless laborers during the Sadozai period. Likewise the tax assessment on flocks, known as *sargalla*, was increased substantially and applied to the previously exempt *ra'iyats*.[44] Another measure, the tripling of the *anguri*, or tax on *ra'iyat* gardens, affected the Durrani landowners more directly, as many of them had taken over *ra'iyat* lands.[45]

In the following years the Qandahar Sardars took further steps to force the Durrani landlords to accept a regular revenue assessment of their fiefs. They began by doubling and tripling the assessement on the former *ra'iyat*, *nauabad* and *khalisa* lands in Durrani possession. The imposition of revenue payments on the traditional Durrani fiefs was prepared by a policy of harassment. In the eyes of the Qandahar Sardars, these fiefs had ceased to fulfill their function as service grants because the Durrani cavalry had been supplanted by an independent mercenary force. The maintenance of these troops provided a convenient pretext for levying forced contributions from the Durrani landholders, thus eventually compelling them to request a regular revenue assessment of their fiefs in order to avoid the Sardars' frequent and unpredictable extortions. It was agreed that the Durrani landowners were to submit three *kharwars* of grain for every *tiyul qulba* loacted in the *qariyajat* and two *kharwars* for every *tiyul qulba* located in the *mahallat* to the government of Qandahar. This arrangement, again, was soon followed by an array of new or modified taxes and fees. For example, the revenue agents made demands under the heads of 'agency charge'[46], 'storage'[47] and 'difference in weight' on top of the regular assessment.[48] The imposition of the 'price of chaff' (*kahbaha*) instituted by Shah Mahmud was extended from the *qariyajat* to the *mahallat* and its rate was raised from eight to nine rupees per *tiyul qulba*. The lands in the vicinity of Qandahar were subject to further arbitrary fees.[49]

All the above quoted taxes and fees were introduced by the Muhammadzai Sardars prior to the First Anglo-Afghan War. Altogether they had the effect of placing nearly equal financial demands on the Durranis as the other tax-paying groups in the region. Only the Barakzais, being fellow tribesmen and allies of the rulers of Qandahar, were granted a total exemption from revenue payments and were thus better off than during any other period since the time of Nadir Shah. The remaining Durrani leadership, particularly the Popalzais, readily sided with Shah Shuja' when he conquered Qandahar with British support in April 1839. Initially Shah Shuja' gratified Durrani hopes of regaining their old privileges. They temporarily gained a reinstitution of their former service grants cum cash allowances of varying sizes.[50] In the long run, however, the British presence in Afghanistan ended up weakening the financial prerogatives of the Durranis and their claims to political influence. While there is little information on the tax policies of the Qandahar Sardars subsequent to the First Anglo-Afghan War, it is likely that they continued in much the same manner as prior to the interregnum by Shah Shuja' and the British.

It may thus be justly said that Durrani interests declined with those of their Sadozai overlords. From 1818 on the Durrani leadership was not only deprived of royal patronage and offices at court but also had to face the aggressive policies of the new proprietors of Qandahar. Certain groups, such as the 'Alizais of Zamindawar, the Nurzais and Popalzais of Kushk-i Nakhud, Nesh, Deh Raud and Tirin, as well as the Alikozais of Arghandab were able to resist government interference in their fertile lands located at a certain distance from Qandahar.[51] The groups living in the heart of this Muhammadzai principality, by contrast, were more firmly incorporated into its administrative structure. In this region, where the revenue was often assessed on the basis of consumption of water and its collection farmed out to contractors, the unprecedented financial pressures caused many Durranis to give up their lands to *ra'iyats* or even to the government.[52] The financial difficulties many of the Durrani landowners experienced were accompanied by the loss of political prerogatives. Like Dost Muhammad Khan at Kabul, the lords of Qandahar sought to concentrate all political clout in the hands of their immediate family. The next lower military and administrative positions were mostly filled by non-Durranis (Ghilzais, Farsiwan, Qizilbash), and a few Barakzais.[53] Thus the affairs of government, previously accessible to the greater part of the Durrani elite, became more specifically a domain of the Muhammadzais. This development is reflected by the fact that the title *sardar*, which the Sadozai rulers had awarded to the highest leaders of the Durrani tribes as a military rank, came to be reserved almost exclusively for the members of the royal family.[54] But while it is evident that the Durrani elite suffered political and financial reverses under the rule of the Qandahar Sardars, Rawlinson's emphasis on the 'poverty and depression' it experienced during the period immediately prior to the First Anglo-Afghan War should be treated with caution. Being the British political agent, this author had a vested interest in emphasizing the horrors of Muhammadzai rule and thus casting British policies vis-à-vis the Durranis in a comparatively favorable light. Despite the hostile attitude of the Qandahar Sardars towards them the Durranis continued to represent a 'strong economic segment' in southern Afghanistan well into the twentieth century.[55] Along with other Pashtun leaders, certain non-Muhammadzai Durranis had access to administrative posts not only in their home regions but also in Lesser Turkistan.[56] While they had lost certain traditional privileges, the Durranis had by no means ceased to be a political force, and none of the Muhammadzai rulers could afford to overlook their interests.

Dost Muhammad Khan's Occupation of Qandahar

During Purdil Khan's time the Durrani leadership attributed the extortionist policies of the Qandahar Sardars to the fact that these rulers felt that their political future was insecure and, fearing to lose their hold over Qandahar, were filling their coffers as fast as possible.[57] But even though they lacked the legitimacy attached to Sadozai rule, the 'Dil' brothers and their Muhammadzai Barakzai kinsmen continued to represent the strongest political group in southern Afghanistan. Therefore they were able to regain control of Qandahar subsequent to the First Anglo-Afghan War and remained the Amir's most powerful rivals. In the early 1850s, as Dost Muhammad Khan sought to establish control over the Tokhi and Hotak Ghilzais and began to toy with the idea of annexing Qandahar, Kuhandil Khan was busily extending his territory further westward at the cost of the weak ruler of Herat, Sa'id Muhammad Khan b. Yar Muhammad Khan (r. 1851–1855). In March 1852 he was in control of Lash Juwain, Farah and Sabzawar and pushed his influence to within sixty miles of Herat.[58] Kuhandil Khan's link to the government of Persia was another deterrent to Dost Muhammad Khan's designs to gain possession of Qandahar.[59] Apart from lacking funds the Amir was hampered by the unsettled position of his conquests north of the Hindu Kush and the consistent opposition some members of his court, notably his half brother Sultan Muhammad Khan and his son-in-law Hafiz Ji b. Mir Wa'iz, voiced to any open move against the rulers of Qandahar.[60]

Despite their continued strength the Qandahar Sardars did not present a united front and discontented members of the family were likely to seek the support of Dost Muhammad Khan. This was the case in 1851 when Rahmdil Khan left Qandahar for Kabul against Kuhandil Khan's wishes.[61] In the following years the rivalries existing within the Qandahar 'triumvirate' were exacerbated by the fact that the sons of the 'Dil' brothers began to advance their own claims to political power. Most prominent among the second generation of the Qandahar Sardars were Purdil Khan's son Mir Afzal, Kuhandil Khan's sons Muhammad Sadiq, Muhammad 'Umar and Sultan 'Ali, and Rahmdil Khan's son Ghulam Muhammad.[62] In 1855 several events allowed Dost Muhammad Khan to increase his pressure on Qandahar. On March 30 his son Ghulam Haidar concluded a treaty of friendship with the British at Peshawar, which encouraged the Amir in his efforts to extend his authority within the borders of Afghanistan.[63] In Qandahar, the deaths of Mihrdil Khan and Kuhandil Khan in March and August 1855 brought about a power struggle in which the last surviving member of the old generation, Rahmdil Khan, and the sons of Purdil Khan and Mihrdil Khan were pitted against Muhammad Sadiq Khan and his brothers.[64] Muhammad Sadiq Khan, who was characterized as a 'flighty, eccentric character' by a British newswriter in 1856, had become known for his restless political ambition even prior to his father's death and had joined the court of the Amir in early 1855. Yet when he found out that Dost Muhammad Khan merely intended to use his presence to exert pressure on Kuhandil Khan to relinquish his Persian connections, the young Sardar left Kabul again and returned to Qandahar, en route plundering the inhabitants along the road linking Kabul and Ghazni and visiting the Tokhi Ghilzais, with whom he had collaborated against the Amir three years earlier. Subsequently Muhammad Sadiq Khan regained his position in Qandahar and was deputed to the Persian court by the Qandahar Sardars.[65] The news of Kuhandil Khan's impending death reached him while he was at Mashhad. When Muhammad Sadiq Khan arrived in Qandahar a whole week had elapsed since his father's demise. Nonetheless he immediately advanced his claims to political leadership and took possession of Kuhandil Khan's wealth and the citadel of Qandahar. In the ensuing confrontations between the factions of Muhammad Sadiq Khan and his uncle Rahmdil about 200 men lost their lives.[66] In the early days of September the fighting subsided because of the intervention of the ulama and *sayyids* of the city, who argued that Rahmdil Khan, being the oldest member of the family, should take over the government of Qandahar. While Kuhandil Khan's sons initially refused to consent to such a settlement, Rahmdil Khan was able to silence their opposition at least temporarily by winning Ghulam Muhyi al-Din Khan, one of Muhammad Sadiq Khan's brothers, over to his side.[67]

On 8 September 1855 Rahmdil Khan confidently informed Amir Dost Muhammad Khan that Kuhandil Khan's sons had given up all claims to a share in the government of Qandahar and had contented themselves with the possession of the *jagirs* previously allotted to them. This letter was very different in tone from his earlier communications to Kabul, in which he had urgently requested the Amir's support against Muhammad Sadiq Khan. Perhaps Rahmdil had become aware that he himself might be deprived of all claims to power if he invited the Sardars' long-standing rival Dost Muhammad Khan to Qandahar. In any event, this letter did little to change the Amir's determination to take an active part in the political developments in Qandahar, as Rahmdil Khan's initial calls for help had provided him with an ideal pretext to set his army in motion. When Dost Muhammad Khan received Rahmdil Khan's letter announcing the end of the crisis at Qandahar he was not to be dissuaded from his chosen course of action and justified his continued approach on Qandahar with his distrust of Muhammad Sadiq Khan's ulterior political designs.[68] The Amir's position was confirmed by reports according to which turmoil was reigning supreme in Qandahar. Within the city Rahmdil Khan was said to be incapable of imposing order, while without its limits all economic life was paralyzed by the plundering raids of his rivals. Supported by 300 Barakzai soldiers who had deserted from the newly created 'Persian' regiments in Qandahar, Muhammad Sadiq Khan and his brother Sultan 'Ali had effectively cut off the trade routes to Herat and Seistan.[69] The political situation of Herat had changed in the meantime, as Shahzada Muhammad Yusuf, a grandson of Shahzada Haji Feroz al-Din Sadozai, had deposed the Alikozai ruler Sa'id Muhammad Khan during the second week of September. This interregnum, in combination with Dost Muhammad Khan's occupation of Qandahar, was to lead to the Persian siege of Herat in April 1856 and the conquest of the city on 26 October 1856.[70] In September 1855, however, the shift of power at Herat allowed Dost Muhammad Khan to move against Qandahar without having to fear the active interference of the Persian government on behalf of the Qandahar Sardars.

Thus the Amir marched towards Qandahar 'outwardly for the sake of [reaching a] compromise, inwardly with the determination to annex'.[71] According to the Commissioner of Peshawar, he would not be stopped either by critics at his own court or by any of the measures the Qandahar Sardars resorted to:

> [T]he chiefs of Khandahar patched up their own disputes, and tried to unite in opposing the Ameer... Every argument of dissuasion; cash compensation for the expenses of his march; flat prohibition to cross their border; and even firing upon the van of the Ameer's army; was tried in vain. With a mixture of firmness and fair words the Ameer held on his course.[72]

Upon his arrival in Qandahar on 14 November, the Amir took possession of the citadel and shortly afterwards announced his decision that none of the local contestants was to play a role in the future government of the city. Rather, they were to receive allowances on the basis of the net revenues of Qandahar after the necessary deductions for the administration and the upkeep of the military.[73] Ten months later, in September 1856, Dost Muhammad Khan handed over the control of the city to his son Ghulam Haidar and returned to Kabul. Despite the apparent facility of the Amir's occupation of Qandahar the length of his stay there indicates that the actual transfer of power to his hands was fraught with problems. For one thing, the old elite was not ready to accept the passive and, in their eyes, demeaning position as royal stipendiaries. Secondly, Dost Muhammad Khan's occupation of Qandahar was accompanied by severe economic problems.

By early January 1856 it was clear that the Amir faced a severe crisis, and the British newswriter summed up the prevailing mood with the following words, 'The chiefs and soldiers are displeased with the coming of the Ameer and the Ameer himself seems ashamed of it.' At that point in time only three members of the former ruling family remained in Qandahar. With the exception of Rahmdil Khan, Mir Afzal Khan and Ghulam Muhyi al-Din, all the Qandahar Sardars had shown their disaffection by quitting the city or the country altogether. Muhammad Sadiq Khan, whose fort of Mahmudabad near Kushk-i Nakhud had been destroyed by Dost Muhammad Khan, was rumored to have left for Turkey but later turned out to have withdrawn to Baluchistan. His brothers Sultan 'Ali and Muhammad 'Umar, along with Khushdil b. Mihrdil Khan were encamped at Mala Khan in the Garmser with 600 horsemen after a failed conspiracy against Dost Muhammad Khan. Shortly afterwards Rahmdil Khan himself left Qandahar in protest and raided a grain caravan intended for Qandahar. Dost Muhammad Khan's interference in the affairs of Qandahar was not only resisted by the Sardars but also members of the religious establishment. The Amir's attempt to silence his critics by imprisoning a number of religious dignitaries, such as Sahibzada Gudri, Qazi Ghulam and Akhundzada 'Azizullah, only worsened his situation, as the remaining ulama of Qandahar continued to voice their opposition, denouncing him as a servant of the British and proclaiming jihad against him.[74]

Dost Muhammad Khan's situation seemed to ease somewhat in early May when Hafiz Ji conducted successful negotiations with Rahmdil Khan and induced him and all of his sons, with the exception of Muhammad 'Alam Khan, to return to Qandahar. Roughly at the same time the Amir's son Muhammad Sharif Khan was able to beat Muhammad 'Umar Khan and his companions and to bring them back to Qandahar. Dost Muhammad Khan's victory seemed complete when Muhammad Sadiq Khan gave up his resistance in Baluchistan and made his entry into the city in early August. But while the Sardars' open rebellion seemed to have come to an end the Amir faced new problems, as he was unable and unwilling to fulfill their expectations concerning an adequate financial reward for their obedience. During his negotiations with Hafiz Ji, Rahmdil Khan had demanded a *jagir* worth 500,000 rupees in exchange for relinquishing his claims to the government of Qandahar in favor of Ghulam Haidar Khan. This amount possibly was merely intended as a bargaining tool in the impending settlement with the Amir. Yet the stipend Rahmdil Khan ended up collecting from the Amir in 1856 fell far short of all his expectations, amounting only to 1,000 Kabuli rupees per month for him and his son Ghulam Muhammad. In 1857 Rahmdil Khan's allowance was raised to 80,000 rupees per year.[75]

The resistance of the Qandahar Sardars flared up again immediately after Dost Muhammad Khan had left Qandahar in September 1856. In early October Ghulam Haidar Khan reported to Kabul that Muhammad Sadiq Khan had used the Persian siege of Herat to wrest the city of Farah from the Amir's governor, Khairullah Khan. In a letter to Mirakhor Ahmad Khan, Muhammad Sadiq Khan threatened to hand over Farah to the Persians unless Ghulam Haidar Khan granted him the possession of his old *jagir*, assisted him in rebuilding the fort of Mahmudabad along with 500 *ra'iyat* houses destroyed by the Amir and gave him an allowance of 8,000 rupees. Ghulam Haidar Khan responded by sending Jalal al-Din Khan b. Sardar Muhammad Akbar Khan with 2,000 cavalry, one infantry regiment and six guns to Farah. On his part, Muhammad Sadiq Khan had been able to collect a force almost equally strong. With the help of his brothers, Muhammad 'Umar and Sultan 'Ali, and his cousin, Muhammad 'Alam Khan b. Rahmdil, who had previously joined the Persian ranks, he was able to procure reinforcements from Herat. Another powerful ally of his was Sultan Ahmad Khan b. Sardar 'Azim Khan, a former member of Dost Muhammad Khan's court and future ruler of Herat. As Farah was located in a region of overlapping

Muhammadzai and Persian interests, Muhammad Sadiq Khan was able to rally the support of certain Barakzai, Achakzai, Ishaqzai and Nurzai chiefs. While none of the Achakzai leaders are mentioned by name, it is likely that Akram Khan b. 'Abdullah Khan Achakzai was among them, as he had been part of Sultan 'Ali Khan's and Khushdil Khan's failed plot against the Amir of January 1856. Another ally of Muhammad Sadiq Khan was Samand Khan, the brother of Ahmad Khan, the Ishaqzai chief of Lash Juwain. The allegiance of the local Nurzai chiefs was split. While three of them were reported to be active on behalf of Muhammad Sadiq Khan, the remainder of the tribe, along with most of the Ishaqzais and Alikozais did not 'stir' against Ghulam Haidar Khan. Despite the support he enjoyed Muhammad Sadiq Khan's effort to reestablish himself in the changing political arena of Afghanistan failed. On 30 October, four days after the fall of Herat to the Persians, Ghulam Haidar Khan reported to the British government that his nephew Jalal al-Din had been able to defeat Muhammad Sadiq Khan and his allies and had regained control of Farah.[76]

While this military success allowed Ghulam Haidar Khan to regain control of Farah, his position remained difficult. In 1856–57 most of the areas under his jurisdiction were experiencing a severe famine, which was most pronounced in the city of Qandahar, where roughly ten thousand soldiers needed to be fed subsequent to the arrival of Dost Muhammad Khan. Another major point of concern was the garrison of Farah, which housed 2,000 soldiers.[77] Immediately after Dost Muhammad Khan's occupation of Qandahar the problems of procuring supplies for the troops had seemed ordinary enough. This sort of shortage was a common occurrence even in the capital of Kabul, where the Amir avoided keeping the entire army in the vicinity of the city, particularly in winter when provisions tended to be scarce. At Qandahar, the problem of bringing in adequate resources for the upkeep of the troops became even more pronounced as Dost Muhammad Khan had already overextended his means during his long march from Kabul and was now preoccupied with establishing control over the administration of his new province. As his revenues in cash and kind were poor, he did little to discourage his soldiers from plundering the countryside to make up for their lack of income. Pillaging by soldiers was a regular occurrence, and the British representative Bahadur Khan Fatih Khan Khatak likened the behavior of the Amir's troops in the surroundings of Qandahar to a flock of birds denuding a field of millet.[78] In early 1856 the problem of collecting food supplies for the city of Qandahar could still be resolved by requisitioning from the surrounding countryside.[79] But during the following months the situation of the troops, city dwellers and farmers became increasingly serious. In May Ghulam Haidar reported a general scarcity of wheat, barley and hay, noting that the horses of Dost Muhammad Khan's cavalry were so malnourished that barely one fifth of them could be used for active duty. Moreover, it became increasingly clear that the unusually hot and dry weather for the season was about to destroy most of the spring harvest.[80] The situation in Qandahar worsened as the summer wore on. At the same time, no grain imports from less afflicted areas reached the city. Unable to alleviate the situation of his subjects, the Amir resorted to the greatest of his governing skills, a policy of 'soft words', to maintain order: 'In the midst of all this [misery] the Ameer is never abused. He conciliates all with soft words. 'My son' or 'my brother', or 'my child' goes further than a rupee.'[81]

The situation in Qandahar did not improve significantly after Dost Muhammad Khan had returned to Kabul with part of his troops. As Ghulam Haidar succeeded to the government of Qandahar, he took active steps to procure grain from places as far away as Ghazni, which was located 231 miles to the northeast and could be reached by a camel caravan in ten to twelve days, and Sabzawar, which was 300 miles distant to the northwest.[82] Between September 1856 and April 1857 he was said to have brought in as much as 50,000 loads of grain from the Ghazni region, thus draining the Amir's resources there.[83] These efforts notwithstanding grain prices in Qandahar continued to rise dramatically, increasing as much as tenfold.[84] The scarcity was not confined to the city of Qandahar alone. Ghulam Haidar Khan's letters to the Amir bear ample witness to the fact that more or less all districts of his province, 'from the confines of Kilat [Qalat-i Ghilzai] to Furrah,' were afflicted.[85] While Farah was better off than Qandahar, Ghulam Haidar Khan was unable to collect more than hundred *kharwars* of grain there in January 1857.[86] The countryside had been drained by a vicious circle in which plundering by the stationed troops caused shortfall in revenues, which in turn resulted in even more devastation at the hands of the soldiers:

> The allowance for the troops employed at Furrah has been fixed by Your Highness at 90,000 Rs. In consequence of the distress in which they are involved, owing to the scarcity of provisions, all pray for payment. The revenues of the country, on the other hand, cannot be estimated at more than ten or twelve thousand rupees. The country has been overrun by troops and desolated and the people ruined.
>
> Every month the sowars and footmen are paid respectively 10 and 5 rupees each, for their support, and the chiefs are also paid at different rates according to their position. Still in consequence of the dearth of provisions, the troops are miserable, and I am wondering how this state of things will end.[87]

Ghulam Haidar Khan's description of the situation in Qandahar was even more dramatic, as hoarding exacerbated the prevailing fear of famine.

> The scarcity of provisions at Candahar is inexpressable. If it were procurable at 2 Rs. a maund, the people would buy and sell among

themselves. The worst is that the people imagine that they have been visited with famine. Those that have grain in store, do not take it out, those that have not are in distress. People live now upon vegetables. Even carrots sell at four maunds per rupee. Beast and bird have become mad with hunger. It is difficult to dine at home in consequence of the efforts of the cat and the fowl to help themselves to a morsel. The eldest men cannot bring to recollection any time when such a scarcity prevailed... The troops are in distress, and the people in a yet greater misery. Both horse and man may be compared to those figures in the game of chess.[88]

Despite the concern Ghulam Haidar expressed for the well-being of the 'people' his efforts to procure grain mainly benefitted his soldiers, to whom he continued to supply grain at rates well below the prevailing market rates until the spring harvest of 1857 promised a better supply of provisions.[89] Accordingly, his popularity seems to have been limited more or less to his troops, whose assistance he required desperately to maintain control over the province of Qandahar. While a great part of Ghulam Haidar Khan's revenues were devoted to the upkeep of the army, the payment of the troops remained irregular. Thus the soldiers mostly used military expeditions to 'indemnify' themselves for their troubles by acquiring livestock and plunder of all descriptions.[90]

Little is known about the other aspects of Ghulam Haidar Khan's administration, except that he modeled his court in Qandahar after that of his father in Kabul.[91] But the few data available create the impression that little changed for the population of the former principality of Qandahar after the 'Dil' brothers had been deprived of their power. Rather, the government had simply passed to a new set of Sardars, as Ghulam Haidar administrated the newly acquired province with the assistance of his full brother Sher 'Ali Khan (the governor of Ghazni) and his nephew Jalal-Din Khan (in charge of Zamindawar and Girishk).[92] In his attempts to raise revenues, Ghulam Haidar Khan clearly emulated some of the policies of his uncles, and introduced a few novelties besides, such as the auctioning of irrigation water to the highest bidder at the height of summer.[93] The periodic issuing of new copper coins, which took place as often as five times a year, was already known to the citizens of Qandahar from the reign of the Qandahar Sardars.

Some of the Sirdar's financial strokes of policy are more effective than foresighted, but he is after all only following the footsteps of his predecessors, who, when in difficulties on account of the lowness of the exchequer, immediately ordered a new copper coinage depreciating that in circulation at the time to about one half its value by a simple order, and issuing new specie at the full rate; besides charging one anna per rupee for the trouble of the transaction. This is

> frequently done with the copper currency, although rupees also undergo an occasional revision. The mint is entirely in the Sirdar's hands.[94]

The members of the British Qandahar Mission of 1857–58 deplored Ghulam Haidar Khan's oppressive revenue-raising measures, including his reliance on high transit duties as source of income. At the same time, they grudgingly acknowledged his efforts to foster the trade with Herat and India by improving the safety of the local merchants.[95] The head of the mission, Major H. B. Lumsden, even reached the conclusion that the general difficulties which beset Ghulam Haidar Khan's administration severely curtailed the range of policies open to him:

> Went over to the Sirdar's house and found him, as usual, in the midst of a throng of chiefs, moonshies, and litigants; each striving by power of lungs to impress his own ideas on the mind of the Sirdar, who was evidently glad of the excuse of our arrival to get a little respite. A Governor of any district in Affghanistan has a most difficult game to play, and the wonder is how such machinery works at all. On the one hand he has the Ameer at Cabul calling on him for revenue accounts and a surplus. The army screaming for pay; chiefs pleading for maintenance for themselves and retainers, and the executives from different quarters clamorous for cash to repair and build forts, and other necessary public works, while on the other hand he has charge of a country yielding little revenue, and the treasurer consequently reports an empty exchequer, and the government dues already overdrawn; merchants threaten to leave the country owing to oppressive taxation; and crowds of people howl all day for protection from the exactions of needy and unscrupulous landed proprietors. In short, these rulers always appear to live in a crisis, and their only hope is to stave it off from day to day, until a revolution in some corner affords a plausible excuse to repudiating a considerable portion of the goverment liabilities; and thus enables them to commence a fresh account.[96]

DOST MUHAMMAD KHAN'S ADMINISTRATION

In 1857 Dost Muhammad Khan's political fortunes looked more promising than ever before. In the course of the last fifteen years he had been able to expand his realm considerably beyond his core possessions of Kabul, Bamiyan, Jalalabad and Ghazni. North of the Hindu Kush, Tashqurghan, Balkh, Shibarghan, and Sar-i Pul were fairly firmly incorporated into his administration. With the occupation of Qandahar the Amir had been able to bring the southern trade route entirely under his control and to extend his authority as far west as Sabzawar. This allowed him to exert increasing pressure on Herat, which eventually was to pass to his possession on 27 May 1863, barely two weeks prior to his death on 9 June.[97]

The Amir's increasing political power can be linked in great part to his improved relationship with the British. With the annexation of Punjab in 1849, the British had extended their territory as far west as Jamrud and had become immediate neighbors of Afghanistan. Until 1855 contacts between the two governments remained limited. While the caravan trade continued to flow the border remained closed to travel and diplomatic communication. This atmosphere, characterized by Governor General Dalhousie as one of 'sullen quiescence', improved on March 30, 1855 with the conclusion of the Anglo-Afghan Treaty between Ghulam Haidar Khan and the Chief Commissioner of Punjab, John Lawrence.[98] During the negotiations preceding the agreement the Afghan delegation failed to gain its foremost objectives, which were the inclusion of Herat into the treaty, an assurance of British assistance in troops and money in case of Russian or Persian aggression, and the restoration of Sultan Muhammad Khan's former fiefs. The resultant treaty offered few favors to the Afghan government, postulating peace and friendship between the two governments and binding Dost Muhammad Khan 'to be the friend of the friends and enemy of the enemies of the Honourable East India Company'. Nonetheless the British commitment to nonintervention proved beneficial for the Amir, as Dalhousie's implicit sanction enabled him to proceed with the occupation of Qandahar.[99]

With the Persian siege of Herat in the summer of 1856 British sentiments tilted more strongly in favor of the Afghan government. In August Governor General Canning supplied Dost Muhammad Khan with 4,000 muskets, bayonets and ammunition, and, in addition, a subsidy of 500,000 Company's rupees. This aid arrived too late to tempt the Amir to interfere with the Persian occupation of Herat. Nonetheless Dost Muhammad Khan readily took up the idea of providing troops for a military campaign against the Persians at Herat in exchange for British funds. During the negotiations which followed at Jamrud in early 1857, however, the British decided for a less costly option. Rather than attempting to remove the Persians from Herat, the Amir was to concentrate on securing his western frontier against possible Persian encroachments. On 26 January 1857 the Chief Commissioner of Punjab and the Amir signed the Anglo-Afghan Treaty of Friendship, which stipulated that the Afghan government was to receive an immediate subsidy of 100,000 Company's rupees per month and an additional gift of 4,000 muskets. A delegation of British officials (the Qandahar Mission of 1857–58) was to supervise the expenditure of the subsidy for military purposes. Finally, the treaty provided for the permanent exchange of (non-European) representatives (*wakils*) at Peshawar and Kabul. Although the subsidy to the Afghan ruler was solely intended for the duration of the Anglo-Persian War, it ended up being continued for one and a half years after the conclusion of the Anglo-Persian Peace Treaty on 4 March 1857. Between August 1856 and October 1858 the British government paid a total of 2.6 million Company's rupees to the Afghan government and supplied it with equipment and ammunition worth 164,115 rupees.[100] When Dost Muhammad Khan renewed his pressure on Herat in the summer of 1862, he received no active support from the governments of London and India. Nonetheless his conquest of Herat was facilitated by their tacit approval of his westward push, as it discouraged the Persian government from interfering on behalf of the Herati ruler, Sultan Ahmad Khan.[101]

No doubt British assistance facilitated Dost Muhammad Khan's consolidation of power. Yet while bolstering him financially, the British subsidies in particular made the Amir vulnerable to accusations by his countrymen that he had placed his 'tail' into British hands. On his part, Dost Muhammad Khan felt the constant need to downplay his relations with the British in order to appease public opinion.[102] Yet the criticism became even louder during the Indian Mutiny of 1857 when the Amir opted to continue to receive the British subsidy rather than giving in to the insistence of Sardar Sultan Muhammad Khan and certain followers of the recently deposed 'Dil' brothers that this was the opportunity to renew his claims to the possession of Peshawar. Other proponents of a jihad against the British were the ulama of Zurmat, Qandahar and Kabul, most prominent among them Hafiz Ji b. Mir Wa'iz.[103] Having weathered the Mutiny, the British cut off Dost Muhammad Khan's subsidy in October 1858, causing him to lose face among his courtiers and, moreover, forcing him to reduce his military expenditures.[104] Thus the British subsidies were by no means an unqualified boon for the Amir. The funds received from 1856 until 1858 indeed enabled him to enhance his coercive power within Afghanistan by creating new military contingents and/or paying existing ones. At the same time, however, the British aid primarily functioned as a stopgap and did not allow the Amir to bring about lasting changes in the organization of his government. The growth of his military was not accompanied by the development of a corresponding administrative machinery that could have secured a smooth flow of revenues. In the following section, I will take a look at various aspects of Dost Muhammad Khan's government, such as the distribution of power within his family, the organization of his army, and his revenues on the basis of taxes and customs.

The Structure of Dost Muhammad Khan's Government

There is general agreement that the administrative system of the Sadozai kings was closely modelled on that of the Safawid and Nadirid states.[105] At the same time, it was set apart from the Iranian example by the fact that it gave a strong role to the Durrani *khans*. While Ahmad Shah acted as the supreme commander of his army and controlled the revenues and redistribution of plunder, the paramount tribal commanders, called *sardar* or *amir-i lashkar*, had a voice in all major decisions. In particular, seven Durrani chiefs and two Ghilzai leaders formed a council (*majlis*) which advised Ahmad Shah on all major questions of policy. Although the Sadozai kings officially bestowed the court offices on tribal leaders, their freedom of choice was severely restricted by the fact that a number of government positions were considered the hereditary right of certain Durrani families.[106] During Shah Zaman's reign, for example, three of the four supreme ministerships were controlled by families belonging to the Bamizai and Sadozai subdivisions of the Popalzai Durranis.[107] Along with other Pashtun nobles, the Durrani *sardars* also played a pivotal role in the administration of the provinces. Acting as provincial governors and/or military commanders, they enjoyed a considerable amount of independence as long as they maintained order and regularly submitted the local revenues to the royal exchequer.[108] Given this high degree of decentralization, the Sadozai kingdom 'resembled much more a federative republic... than an absolute monarchy'.[109] Elphinstone noted that the king's authority was felt in different ways by the various segments making up the population of Afghanistan. Along with the Indian provinces, the urban areas forming the core of the empire yielded most of the royal revenues. The Pashtun tribes, on the other hand, considered themselves partners rather than subjects of the king. The viewpoints concerning the role and prerogatives of the king differed accordingly:

> [T]here is some distinction of interests between the King and the nation, and a still greater difference of opinion regarding his legal powers: The King, the Courtiers, and the Moollahs, maintaining that he has all the authority possessed by Asiatic despots; and the people in the tribes considering him a monarch with very limited prerogatives...
>
> The government of the tribe of Dooraunee centres in the King, though even there, he is generally obliged to attend to the wishes of the heads of the clans. He also interferes in the interior government of the tribes on the plains, and near the great towns; but he contents himself with levying his supplies of men and money from the rest, without any further interference in their affairs than is occasionally required to preserve the public tranquillity... With the exception of the republican government of the Ooloosses, the situation of the Afghaun country appears to me to bear a strong resemblance to that of Scotland in ancient times: the direct power of the King over the towns and the country immediately around, the precarious submission of the nearest clans, and the independence of the remote ones, the inordinate

> power and faction of the nobility most connected with the court, and the relations borne by all great lords to the crown, resemble each other so closely in the two states, that it will throw light on the character of the Dooraunee government to keep the parallel in view.[110]

The shift of power from the Sadozais to the Muhammadzais in the early nineteenth century and the accompanying political turmoil caused the former empire to break up into local principalities and cut off the former state-supporting elite from its traditional avenues to power. Apart from formalities like the striking of coins and the insertion of the Amir's name in the *khutba*, the administration of Dost Muhammad Khan's nascent state showed little resemblance with that of the bygone Sadozai empire and was extremely rudimentary in nature. As if to obliterate all traces of Sadozai supremacy, Dost Muhammad Khan even did away with the physical remnants of that era, such as the office of records. During his reign, as during that of his successor, there were no government offices, and the state officials worked in their homes, carrying scraps of paper around in their pockets when reporting to the king.[111] Moreover, only a few of the formerly prominent Durrani families continued to figure in the Amir's administration. For his first reign, merely two, non-Pashtun, officials are mentioned. While Dost Muhammad Khan never awarded the title of *wazir* to anyone, Mirza 'Abd al-Sami' Qizilbash, the most powerful official at the court, was generally recognized to be filling the equivalent of this position. His son, Mirza Muhammad Husain Khan, acted as *mustaufi* or finance officer. During Dost Muhammad Khan's second reign another official, Mirza 'Abd al-Razzaq was considered both *wazir* and highest revenue officer (*mustaufi al-mamalik*). During this period, Mirza Husain Khan was in charge of the internal administration of the revenue department.[112] The only ranking Durrani officials mentioned for the period subsequent to the First Anglo-Afghan War are Sherdil Khan Barakzai, Ghulam Muhammad Khan Bamizai, and Mirakhor Ahmad Khan Ishaqzai. Acting as court chamberlain (*ishik aqasi*), Sherdil Khan also had considerable influence in the internal administration of the country.[113] Ghulam Muhammad Khan was recognized as the Amir's chief adviser in military matters.[114] Mirakhor Ahmad Khan Ishaqzai (not to be confused with Ahmad Khan Ishaqzai of Lash Juwain) was closely associated with Ghulam Haidar Khan's administration of Jalalabad and Qandahar.[115]

Dost Muhammad Khan's efforts to concentrate all power in the hands of his immediate family is also reflected by the composition of his council, the only non-Muhammadzai members of which were Ghulam Muhammad Bamizai, Hafiz Ji b. Mir Wa'iz and Khan Shirin Khan Qizilbash (d. 1859). Yet by no means were all the Amir's numerous brothers, nephews and sons included in the deliberations at court. The council members most often admitted were the Peshawar Sardars (Sultan Muhammad Khan and Pir

Muhammad Khan), Nawwab Jabbar Khan (d. 1854) and the Amir's nephews Muhammad Zaman Khan and Muhammad 'Usman Khan. The attendance of Dost Muhammad Khan's sons was irregular, as many of them tended to be away on governing duties or military campaigns in the provinces. Among them, only Muhammad Afzal Khan, Muhammad A'zam Khan, Ghulam Haidar Khan, and Sher 'Ali Khan, being the eldest and most influential, seem to have voiced their opinions in council.[116] In many ways, the institution of this council reflected the conflicting pulls the Amir experienced in his administration. On the one hand, he needed to conciliate his brothers by showing deference to their greater age and formally involving them in all government decisions. Accordingly he gave his court the appearance of a tribal *jirga*, which had little in common with the ritualized court proceedings of the Sadozais.[117] Below this veneer of respect to his relatives and fellow tribesmen, on the other hand, lay Dost Muhammad Khan's stark determination to retain a firm grip on the reins of government. As a result, the Amir's council did not really work as a consultative body but was merely designed as a formality to gain additional sanction for policies *after* they had been formulated by the Amir. Thus, according to the British informant Sayyid Hisam al-Din of Kunar, the members of the council were 'all name and no body':

> Everything here is first settled between Ameer Dost Mahomed Khan and his son Gholam Hyder Khan, and when they have quite made up their minds, they go through the form of sending for the Peshawur Sirdars and Osman Khan, and Hafiz Ji, to give their advice. Be assured there is not among them the man who dares to say 'No' when the Amir says 'Yes'.[118]

Statements of this nature may be taken to support assessments of Dost Muhammad Khan as an 'absolute' ruler,[119] who 'could introduce changes in the administration as he saw necessary'.[120] In practice, however, the Amir displayed a curious mixture of autocracy and powerlessness in his administration. As mentioned above, the counsels of Sultan Muhammad Khan and Hafiz Ji did play a role in dissuading the Amir from attacking Qandahar in the early 1850s. Moreover, once a decision had been reached in the council it was by no means certain that the Amir would be able to implement it. Often the nobles flatly refused to follow the Amir's orders.[121] As depicted by the British documents, the court seems to have been the scene of constant haggling. Administrative procedures were often paralyzed for months at a time, as military leaders declined to call their armies to muster and the Amir's eldest sons jostled for the possession of the strategically important and revenue-rich provinces of Kabul, Ghazni and Qandahar.

Following the popular Afghan precept that 'a man is helpless in his tribe without the assistance of his *qaum*, in his *qaum* without the assistance of his brothers, and among his brothers without the assistance of his sons', the Amir relied almost exclusively on his sons in the administration of his realm.[122] With the exception of Shahmard Khan (d. 1878), the governor of Jalalabad, whose tribal background is not clear, all provincial governments were held by sons of Dost Muhammad Khan. There is contradictory information concerning the legal status of the provinces. According to *Siraj al-tawarikh*, their revenues were bestowed on the Amir's sons as service grants (*jagir*). The British sources, on the other hand, characterize them as 'leases' (*ijara*), which were farmed out to the Sardars in exchange for a fixed sum of money.[123] The following account depicting the conflict between the Amir and Ghulam Haidar Khan concerning the latter's obligations to the king points to the possibility that the exact status of the provinces was subject to differing interpretations from the points of view of the Amir and the provincial governors.

> 26 April 1858
> The Ameer ordered Gholam Hyder Khan to produce his account of receipts and disbursements of the Candahar revenue for the past year. Gholam Hyder Khan in reply said, that the disbursement was higher than the receipts, and that as he had understood the Province of Candahar was held by him as a grant [*jagir*] and not as a farm [*ijara*], he made no demand for the excess expenditure. But if he held it as a farm he wished to be paid his full demand; and for the next year he would not hold the Province, and the Ameer might appoint any one else he pleased. The Ameer got provoked and annoyed, and so was Sirdar Gholam Hyder Khan, who on leaving the court said to the Ameer, 'I know that you don't need me now; but I also don't care for you.'[124]

No doubt the provincial governors owed the king a certain amount of revenues after deductions for administrative expenditures and the upkeep of their own m ilitary contingents. The notion that the Sardars were bound to the king by some sort of contract is reinforced by the fact that the apportionment of provinces took place in a bidding process in which the contenders often accused the current officeholders of embezzlement and promised to submit a greater net revenue in case they gained the appointment. Even so, Reshtia's assessment that the Amir 'did not permit his sons to exercise any administrative power in the provinces'[125] is not supported by the available evidence. While Dost Muhammad Khan was in the position to shuffle and reshuffle the available governorships and to play on the existing rivalry among his sons, his ability to intervene in the internal policies of the provinces was limited to the exertion of pressure for the payment of revenue. Thus his position vis-à-vis his provincial governors was by no means stronger than that of his Sadozai forebears. In this light, Ghubar's characterization of the provincial governors as 'little kings' mirrors the distribution of power in Dost Muhammad Khan's kingdom more accurately.[126] Entertaining their own military contingents, the Sardars were more or less independent in their methods of revenue collection and the fixing of local allowances. All the Amir's efforts to gain information about the fiscal situation of his governors met with determined resistance. Aware that the Amir depended on their support as much as they did on his, the Sardars usually responded to any pressure by their father with the threat to resign their offices if not left alone in the administration of their provinces. The above quotation concerning the quarrel between Dost Muhammad Khan and Ghulam Haidar Khan represents a typical exchange between the Amir and any of his governors at revenue collecting time.

In the distribution of the available provinces Dost Muhammad Khan favored two sets of sons in particular. In 1857 the Amir's eldest son by a Bangash wife, Muhammad Afzal Khan, was in charge of Turkistan. His younger brother, Muhammad A'zam Khan, was governor of Khost, Zurmat and Kurram. Most of the remaining provinces were reserved for the sons of the Amir's favorite wife Khadija, who stemmed from an important Popalzai lineage. Ghulam Haidar Khan, previously in charge of Kabul, had become the governor of Qandahar in 1856. He was assisted by his nephew Jalal al-Din Khan b. Muhammad Akbar Khan, who was in charge of Zamindawar and Girishk. Sher 'Ali Khan held the province of Ghazni and had delegated the governorship of Qalat-i Ghilzai to Muhammad Akbar Khan's eldest son, Fatih Muhammad Khan. Muhammad Sharif held Muqur and 'Ali Khel. Sardar Muhammad Amin was in charge of Kohistan. Among the Amir's 26 remaining sons, many of whom were still too young to take on administrational tasks, only three held governorships. Muhammad Aslam Khan, whose mother was a Jawansher Qizilbash, was in charge of Bamiyan and 'Hazara'. Muhammad Zaman Khan, son of a Sadozai mother, held Nimlik and Sar-i Pul in Turkistan as a *jagir.* Wali Muhammad Khan, son of a Turi mother, governed Aqcha from 1851 until he received the government of Shibarghan in 1856. Wali Muhammad Khan's full brother Faiz Muhammad Khan acted as the commander of artillery in Kabul.[127]

As the eldest son of the Amir, Muhammad Afzal Khan enjoyed a highly influential position as the governor of Turkistan. Ghulam Haidar Khan and his full brothers, on the other hand, controlled almost the entire region south of the Hindu Kush. In 1857 Lumsden noted that Muhammad A'zam Khan's territories of Khost, Zurmat and Kurram yielded a negligible income in comparison with Sher 'Ali Khan's neighboring province of Ghazni:

> There is... a marked difference perceptible between the administration of the districts under Sirdar Mahomed Azim Khan in Koorum and those of Sirdar Sher Ali Khan in Ghuznee, in the former there is an evident scarcity of money; all government functionaries as well as

troops are in arrears, while in the latter everything required is easily procured and no grumbling or complaints are heard. Perhaps this is not so much attributable to the difference of character of the individuals carrying on the administration, as to a part of the policy of the Ameer who by placing the richer provinces in the hands of the family of the heir apparent is strengthening their hands for a day of trial. . . [128]

This differential treatment was also reflected by the distribution of troops among the Sardars. Shortly after the First Anglo-Afghan war Dost Muhammad Khan placed the newly created regiments of regular infantry exclusively under the command of Muhammad Akbar Khan and his full brothers.[129] British assistance in the form of weapons and subsidies also primarily benefitted the heir apparent, his full brothers, and nephews.[130] Three of the four military contingents created subsequent to the Anglo-Afghan Treaty of Friendship of 1857 were controlled by Sher 'Ali Khan, while the fourth was under the nominal command of the Amir himself.[131] Throughout his reign Dost Muhammad Khan stuck to his decision that one of Khadija's sons should be his successor. Immediately after the First Anglo-Afghan war he nominated Muhammad Akbar Khan heir apparent. Subsequent to Muhammad Akbar Khan's death in 1847, Ghulam Haidar Khan gained control of his position and possessions.[132] When Ghulam Haidar died on 2 July 1858, the Amir made it public that Sher 'Ali Khan would be his successor. Sher 'Ali Khan inherited his late brother's annual allowance of 20,000 rupees and gained command of his troops and territorial charges. Dost Muhammad Khan attempted to strengthen Sher 'Ali Khan's position further by decreeing that his former allowance of 12,000 rupees per year, along with the governorship of Ghazni should not pass to Muhammad Amin and Muhammad Sharif but to Sher 'Ali's son, Muhammad 'Ali Khan, who also received the command of Jalalabad and 'Ghilzai' (Laghman).[133]

By concentrating almost all power in the hands of his sons, Dost Muhammad Khan was able to establish his family as the new ruling dynasty of Afghanistan. Yet this policy also carried the seed of constant conflict among his closest relatives. Almost half a century later, the Amir's grandson, 'Abd al-Rahman Khan (r. 1880–1901), was to point out that while Dost Muhammad Khan had been able to consolidate his rule over all of present-day Aghanistan his exclusive reliance on his sons produced tensions among them which ultimately led to civil war after his death:

Dost Mohammad Khan made the same mistake [as Timur Shah] in dividing the kingdom of Afghanistan among his sons, giving to each one of them a separate army. In consequence of this policy the sons were placed by their own father in the position of being able to fight against each other.[134]

Indeed, Dost Muhammad Khan's administration was fraught with constant power struggles. As discussed in Chapter Two, the rivalry between Muhammad Afzal Khan and Ghulam Haidar Khan over the control of Turkistan and its 'settlement' by the Amir immediately preceded the occupation of Qandahar. Kabul formed another bone of contention, and the ongoing bidding for its control also strained the relationship between full brothers. From 1854 on Ghulam Haidar Khan and Sher 'Ali Khan were locked into a dispute about their respective governorships of Kabul and Ghazni, each of them resorting to the usual accusations of embezzlement and endeavoring to drive up the Amir's revenue demands on his opponent.[135] With the departure of Dost Muhammad Khan and Ghulam Haidar Khan for Qandahar in autumn 1855, Muhammad 'Usman Khan acted as the Amir's deputy in Kabul but faced several challenges to his authority by Muhammad Amin Khan, the governor of Kohistan.[136] As Ghulam Haidar Khan was appointed to the government of Qandahar in 1856, Sher 'Ali Khan gained the governorship of Kabul and the competition between the two brothers resumed, lasting until the death of Ghulam Haidar Khan in July 1858.[137] When Sher 'Ali Khan was nominated heir apparent by the Amir, he faced the rivalry of his younger full brothers Muhammad Amin and Muhammad Sharif. Both resisted Sher 'Ali Khan's plans to make them governors of Qandahar and Girishk respectively. While Muhammad Amin Khan preferred to hold on to the government of Kohistan in the vicinity of Kabul, Muhammad Sharif Khan began to bargain for the governorship of Ghazni.[138] Meanwhile in Qandahar, Sher 'Ali Khan's nephews Fatih Muhammad Khan and Jalal al-Din Khan also resented the fact that their uncle, combining his former governorships with those of Ghulam Haidar Khan, was about to become the most powerful man south of the Hindu Kush. Nonetheless Fatih Muhammad Khan, Sher 'Ali Khan's former governor of Qalat-i Ghilzai, opted to be loyal to the new heir apparent and agreed to act as his deputy at Qandahar. Jalal al-Din Khan, by contrast, embarked on a prolonged rebellion from his base of Girishk and finally left the country in the spring of 1859. As Fatih Muhammad Khan was unable to maintain control of Qandahar and its districts on his own, Sher 'Ali Khan was forced to take over the government of Qandahar in late 1858. In August 1859 Muhammad Amin Khan finally agreed to become the governor of Qandahar, thus allowing Sher 'Ali Khan to return to Kabul. Muhammad Sharif Khan accepted the governorship of Girishk, Zamindawar and Farah.[139]

Throughout these disputes Dost Muhammad Khan assumed the role of an arbitrator, constantly exhorting his younger sons to respect the existing distribution of power which was based, he argued, on seniority and ability. During his negotiations with the Chief Commissioner of Punjab in 1857 the Amir portrayed himself as a helpless victim of the continuous conflicts among his sons:

> 'See these coarse garments,' said Dost Muhammad, opening his vest, 'how old and patched they are. Are these the proper robes for a ruling prince? This shawl around my head is the sole piece of finery I possess. I have no money whatever. My sons and my chiefs take everything I have. They leave me nothing, and they tear me into pieces with their dissensions. I live from hand to mouth among them, a life of expedients. I wish to heaven I could turn Faquir and escape from this heavy lot.'[140]

While the Amir's exclamation was clearly intended to impress the need of pecuniary assistance on John Lawrence, it certainly contained a grain of truth. Operating from a limited base of power, Dost Muhammad Khan had no other option but to foster his sons as his closest allies. An obvious drawback of this policy was that these allies tended to become strong rivals. Just as the Durrani *sardars* during the Sadozai period, the sons of the Amir were 'at one and the same time the strength and the curse of the monarch'.[141] It was for good reason that Dost Muhammad Khan's successor, Sher 'Ali Khan, barred many of his relatives from his administration. In his time, contrary to that of his father, Muhammadzai claims to royal authority had become well consolidated, and he could afford to widen his base of support beyond his immediate family. In his administration he secured his power by seeking out the support of the Qizilbash, Jabbar Khel and Wardak leadership.[142] Nonetheless the question remains whether Dost Muhammad Khan really was as helpless in the face of the smoldering conflicts among his sons as he claimed. Given the decentralized nature of his administration, the Amir may have used the ongoing competition among his sons as a mechanism to prevent the most powerful contenders for power from challenging his own position. While fostering the political careers of his eldest sons by making them military commanders and/or governors, he also saw to it that they were kept at a distance from his capital and had little opportunity to interfere with the proceedings of his non-Muhammadzai court officials. Dost Muhammad Khan's attitude towards his sons thus mirrored his relationship with other tribal leaders: While he required their support in maintaining his claims to authority he had to find means to keep them at bay. Although it was to create instability in the long run, this policy served the Amir as an expedient in his effort to secure his reign over Afghanistan.

The Army

Dost Muhammad Khan is credited by Afghan historians in particular for having laid the foundation of a 'regular' Afghan army (*'asakir-i nizamiya*), as opposed to the military system of the Sadozais, which relied in great part on tribal cavalry (*sawara-yi gushada*) and local militias (*piyada-yi sakhlau*).[143] The Sadozai army was indeed highly decentralized in nature and gave a great role to the tribal levies under the command of local leaders, which were only called out at time of war. Singh is of the opinion that only one third of Ahmad Shah's army of up to 120,000 men consisted of regular contingents. Both the regular and the tribal units were mostly composed of cavalry, one fourth being furnished by foot soldiers.[144] According to Ghulam Sarwar, Timur Shah's standing army numbered close to sixty thousand men. The combined armies of Bahawalpur, Sind and the Baluch Khan of Qalat amounted to 80,000 men, 30,000 of which were foot soldiers.[145] During his military campaigns Shah Zaman could summon more than 100,000 cavalry, the infantry amounting to 30,900 men.[146] In the early nineteenth century, almost the whole of Shah Shuja''s regular troops were reported to be horsemen. The Durrani tribal levies also consisted solely of cavalry.[147] The Sadozais relied on two kinds of militia, *iljari* (mostly foot soldiers) and *qara naukar* (mostly cavalry), which were mostly raised in the vicinity of the great towns.[148]

In his effort to establish greater government control over his army, Dost Muhammad Khan employed three foreign advisers. In 1830 he appointed 'Abd al-Samad Tabrizi, a former Qajar officer.[149] Four years later, during Shah Shuja''s unsuccessful bid to regain to the throne, the Amir captured one of his rival's British officers, Campbell, who converted to Islam and became Muhammad Afzal Khan's commander in chief in Turkistan.[150] The American doctor Josiah Harlan apparently joined Dost Muhammad Khan's court in 1836 and received the command of the regular troops.[151] With the assistance of his advisers, Dost Muhammad Khan introduced British-type uniforms and a European-style drill in his army.[152] His most important reform was the establishment of regular infantry regiments, the total number of which was estimated between 1,000 and 1,500 men prior to the First Anglo-Afghan War.[153] At the beginning of his second reign the Amir raised five infantry divisions of 800 men, placing two of them under the command of Muhammad Akbar Khan and distributing the remaining three among Sher 'Ali Khan, Muhammad Amin Khan and Muhammad Sharif Khan.[154] In 1857 Lumsden recorded a total of 14 regular regiments of infantry but noted that they rarely reached their nominal strength of 800 but more likely consisted of 600 soldiers each.[155] Besides the regular infantry, Dost Muhammad Khan continued to rely on militiamen called *jazailchi* after the matchlock they carried. In the 1830s the Amir was thought to be able to raise 2,000–2,500 *jazailchis*.[156] Subsequent to the First Anglo-Afghan War their number rose to 3,500. 2,500 of them were attached to the Sardars, whereas the remaining 1,000 were commanded by local chiefs.[157]

Despite these innovations, the major part of the Amir's army continued to consist of cavalry. While the Qizilbash *ghulam khana* had ceased to exist as a separate body, Dost Muhammad Khan sought to create another division of cavalry under direct government supervision, the *'amala-yi sarkari*. Contrary to the tribal cavalry (the so-called *khud aspa*), the soldiers in this group received their entire pay and their horses from the government. The supply of horses by the government had been unheard of prior to Dost Muhammad Khan's time.[158] In the 1830s the *'amala-yi sarkari* furnished 3,000 out of the Amir's total cavalry of 12,000.[159] During the Amir's second reign, the cavalry at his disposal officially consisted of 15,300 men and his entire infantry, including *jazailchis*, amointed to 9,250 men. The following list, prepared by the British official Ghulam Ahmad in August 1856, gives an overview of the strength of Dost Muhammad Khan's army and its distribution at the time of his occupation of Qandahar:

1) *Troops of the Amir*

200 cavalry (Amir's own)
700 cavalry (nominal contingent of Sardar Sultan Muhammad Khan and paid out of his allowance; only 300 really kept up)
500 cavalry (nominal contingent of Sardar Pir Muhammad Khan; only 200 really kept up)
200 cavalry (nominal contingent of Sardar Sa'id Muhammad Khan; only 80 really kept up)
120 cavalry (nominal contingent of Shams al-Din b. Amir Muhammad Khan and his brother, Nazar Muhammad; only 80 really kept up)
400 cavalry (nominal contingent of 'Abd al-Ghani Khan b. Nawwab 'Abd al-Jabbar Khan and his five brothers; nearly all kept up)
300 cavalry (nominal contingent of Shah Daula Khan and Nizam al-Daula Khan, sons of Nawwab Muhammad Zaman Khan)
40 cavalry (nominal contingent of Nur Muhammad b. Muhammad Quli Khan b. Fatih Khan)
540 cavalry (nominal contingent of miscellaneous chiefs, such as Ghulam Muhammad Khan Bamizai and his son Taj Muhammad Khan; 'Abd al-Salam Khan Popalzai; 'Abd al-Wahhab Khan Barakzai; Sherdil Khan Ishik Aqasi and his brother 'Ataullah Khan, etc.; all kept up)
200 *khassadars* (*jazailchis* attached to the Amir's person).

2) *Troops of Sardar Ghulam Haidar Khan*

500 cavalry (contingent of Jalal al-Din Khan b. Muhammad Akbar Khan)
200 cavalry (contingent of Shah Sawar Khan b. Muhammad Akram Khan)
130 cavalry (contingent of 'Abd al-Ghias Khan b. Nawwab 'Abd al-Jabbar Khan)
? cavalry (contingent of Sultan Ahmad, Muhammad 'Umar, Muhammad Sadiq, sons of Sardar Muhamamd 'Azim Khan, Sardar-i Kalan)
1,870 cavalry (contingent of miscellaneous chiefs)

200 cavalry (*'amala-yi sarkari*)
500 bodyguard *jazailchis*
1,600 regular infantry.

3) *Troops of Sardar Sher 'Ali Khan*
400 cavalry (furnished by the Tajiks and Andar Ghilzais near Ghazni)
900 cavalry (Durranis)
800 regular infantry
100 infantry (carabineers?)
50 *jazailchis*.

4) *Troops of Sardar Muhammad Sharif Khan*
800 cavalry (of different tribes)
800 regular infantry.

5) *Troops of Sardar Muhammad Amin Khan*
600 cavalry
800 regular infantry
250 *jazailchis*.

6) *Troops of Sardar Muhammad A'zam's troops*
500 regular infantry
100 *jazailchis*.

7) *Troops of Sardar Muhammad Hasan Khan*
400 regular infantry.

8) *Troops of the sons of Sardar Nawwab 'Abd al-Samad*
400 cavalry
150 *jazailchis*.

9) *Troops of Sardar Fatih Muhammad Khan b. Muhammad Akbar Khan*
300 *jazailchis*.

10) *Troops of Sardar Muhammad Afzal Khan*
1,500 cavalry from Kabul
4,000 cavalry from Balkh
800 regular infantry from Kabul
800 regular infantry from Balkh
300 *jazailchis*.

11) *Troops of Sardar Wali Muhammad Khan*
800 cavalry
800 regular infantry.[160]

All foreign observers detected a gap between the nominal cavalry figures given in the muster rolls and the actual amount of troops kept up. In his discussion of Dost Muhammad Khan's tribal cavalry, Lumsden noted that

> they are not so easily computed, as it is notorious that they are never kept up to the full complement required from each chief... Were this not the case, Kandahar and its dependencies should furnish eight thousand Jagirdari Horse; Ghazni 5000; Cabul, including Jellalabad, Logar and the Koh-i daman, 15,000; while Balkh with its Uzbegs could give 10,000 more, making a total of 38,000. But if we consider the actual state of affairs I think that 20,000 may be calculated as an extreme estimate of this description of force in the country.[161]

This problem had its roots in the system of allowances and land grants given to the tribal leadership in exchange for the maintenance of a specific number of troops, which was an incentive for the military leaders to inflate the numbers of soldiers kept on their rolls. Already during Shah Shuja''s first reign it had become a common practice among the *khans* to borrow men from each other's contingents, to mount their servants, and to hire common people when their troops were mustered by the king. At that time the number of soldiers maintained by the government was thought to be nearly double of that which really served.[162] Lumsden's quote shows that this problem still persisted in the 1850s. In his efforts to modernize the army, Dost Muhammad Khan placed certain divisions under the direct supervision of his immediate family. But on the whole the economic basis of the majority of the military forces remained unaltered well into Sher 'Ali Khan's reign.[163]

In order to place Dost Muhammad Khan's policies in perspective, let us take a short look at mode of payment in the Sadozai army. The army officers, mostly being furnished by Durranis, enjoyed land grants called *jagir*, *tiyul* or *suyurghal* which could include cash allowances.[164] On the next lower level, the pay of the Durrani horsemen was also covered partly by *tiyul* and partly by a cash allowance.[165] The pay of the *ghulams* originally seems to have been as high as that of the Durrani cavalry, but it was apparently less often backed up by grants of land and had suffered some reductions by the time of Shah Shuja''s first reign.[166] The *qara naukars* were furnished by the landownders at a fixed rate in exchange for the remission of their land revenues. While the cash components of the military salaries could theoretically be drawn from the royal treasury, they most commonly took the form of written assignments (*barat*) on certain amounts of grain to be issued by the local tax collectors in the countryside. Rather than collecting these items, the recipients of such *barats* were often more willing to sell them to the government agents in question at a 'prodigious discount', thus essentially suffering great reductions of their income. For this reason, the most favored option among the horsemen was to receive as much pay as possible in commutation for revenue.[167]

In the course of military campaigns the provisions of the army were in theory looked after by the officers in charge, who received cash or assignments on the revenues of the provinces along the way.[168] Yet in 1809 Elphinstone noted that the army officers rarely took the trouble of providing grain for their soldiers, and that plunder was the order of the day whenever the army was on its march. At the same time, there seems to have been an unwritten rule that whereas provisions could be simply seized in the Indian provinces, they thad to paid for scrupulously in the region west of the Khyber pass.[169] When Dost Muhammad Khan gained control of Kabul in 1826, the eastern provinces of the former Sadozai empire had fallen away from Afghan control and no longer formed a field of activity and a potential basis of income for the Afghan army: 'During the [Sadozai] monarchy,' Burnes observed, 'the Affghans went, in the course of their service, to Peshawer, Sindh, Cashmeer, and to the other provinces and brought back with them their savings. No such opportunities now present themselves: the Koh-Damaun, Jellalabad and Lughman are their Sindh and Cashmeer.'[170] Prior to the First Anglo-Afghan War Dost Muhammad Khan was preoccupied with his effort to consolidate his hold over Jalalabad and Ghazni, as well as mounting a military campaign against Shah Shuja' in 1834, and engaging the Sikhs at Peshawar in 1835 and 1837. Accordingly, all of his resources were concentrated on the upkeep of his army. Dost Muhammad Khan cut the expenses of his court to the 'economical scale' of 5,000 rupees a month and endeavored to raise further income by reducing allowances, increasing duties and taxes, resuming *waqf* lands which had no heirs, arbitrarily taking loans and fines, and letting Haji Khan Kakar's sizeable *jagirs* lapse.[171]

The following rates of pay are recorded for Dost Muhammad Khan's first and second reign: the regular infantry, the *jazailchis* and the horsemen carrying loads earned five rupees a month. Among the regular infantry as much as two months' pay was deducted for clothing and equipment. The pay of the cavalry amounted to 10 rupees per month.[172] Just as in the Sadozai army, only a small part of the pay of Dost Muhammad Khan's soldiers consisted of cash. The Sardars and the local chiefs were entitled to land assignments and remissions of revenue for maintaining their quotas of horsemen and militia. The regular regiments received a mixture of cash and assignments of grain, grass, sheep, blankets and butter for their services. As a rule, the pay was irregular and assignments were issued by the government in anticipation of future income to be generated by the upcoming harvest or an impending revenue collection campaign.[173] The general profusion of such *barats* during Dost Muhammad Khan's first reign earned them the epithet of 'stag's antlers', meaning that payment was about as likely as catching a stag by its antlers.[174]

Dost Muhammad Khan's efforts to create an efficient standing army were further hampered by the lack of an infrastructure which would have allowed him to draw together sufficient supplies for his soldiers. Lumsden noted that there was no such thing as a commissariat in the Afghan army:

> [I]n districts where the revenue is paid in grain a certain proportion is allotted to each fort, and parties receive orders... on the headmen of villages when marching. In this way all troops on the line of march must be fed by the nearest villages, the latter getting credit for the amount of grain, &c. supplied, when the revenue comes to be collected. In disturbed districts, or foreign countries, Affghan troops always live on their enemies and pay for nothing. On any great occasion of public danger, when the whole available force may be collected en masse, each district has to furnish a certain amount of grain, as well as its contingent of militia, each soldier receiving a seer of flour daily from the common store; so long as this lasts, the militia consider themselves bound to remain with their standards, but the day that this allowance ceases, the whole retire to their respective homes.[175]

The prevailing methods of acquiring supplies had the effect that the villages located along the highroads had to bear the brunt of the military requisitioning and often found their resources totally exhausted. Subsequent to military campaigns it was a common occurrence that armies which retraced their steps to Kabul along the same route they had already passed through when going out to action found it next to impossible to collect provisions. The general dearth of provisions also had the effect that a large number of the troops were constantly preoccupied with gathering supplies rather than fighting.[176] While it was most difficult to provide sufficient forage and food for the army when it was engaged in military campaigns, its presence in the main garrisons also meant a constant challenge for the local governors. Kabul for example was afflicted by famines from time to time, in particular during the winter when the lines of supply were closed by snow. In early 1856, as the impending famine was making itself felt in the Qandahar region, the capital was also experiencing a scarcity of grain.[177] Aware of the pressure the presence of a large army placed on the resources available at Kabul, Dost Muhammad Khan generally saw to it that a great part of his troops were sent away from the city in winter. While some contingents retired to the warmer region of Jalalabad, others were sent to Tagau and Bangash for the purpose of revenue collection.

Revenue collection thus also served as a mechanism for feeding the royal troops.[178] More often than not, however, the soldiers had to take the initiative for their maintenance. Plunder was considered an ordinary occurrence wherever large garrisons of troops were maintained and was often even encouraged by the military leaders. On the occasion of the conquest of Herat in May 1863, Dost Muhammad Khan rewarded his army by allowing 4,000 soldiers 'chosen expressly for the purpose from different tribes and regiments' to plunder the city of Herat.[179] The news of an approaching army, whether friend or foe, usually caused the villagers to abandon their houses and to take their livestock with them:

> As the troops have no regular pay and during their period of service generally speaking live on plunder, it is difficult to say which is the most disastrous to the people, its own army or that of a foreign invader, for both one and the other abandon themselves to all kinds of excesses, devastate the country, and leave behind the most fearful traces of their passage.[180]

Dost Muhammad Khan's sons were well aware of the problems besetting the organization of their army and the need for regular payments. This necessity they also sought to impress on British observers whenever possible in order to encourage offers of financial aid. In June 1856 Muhammad Sharif Khan played on British concerns over the Persian siege of Herat by pointing out to the British envoy Bahadur Khan Fatih Khan Khatak that the Afghan army would only be able to interfere with the affairs of Herat if assisted by the British:

> Just see what soldiers we have! The finest anywhere. But then we have no money. If we had but money, we should have no difficulty in thrashing the Persians... But if by tomorrow's dawn we reached Heerat [sic], we could not give breakfast to the troops; by dinner time the army would be starved, and next day broken up. Thus we should lose even the country in our rear. Otherwise we are at the service of the British.[181]

In the same vein, Ghulam Haidar Khan observed to Lumsden that only well-fed troops could be expected to form an efficient army, as it was 'useless to offer any amount of grain to a starved horse at the foot of a steep ascent'.[182] Ghulam Haidar Khan seems to have followed this realization at least in part with practical deeds. Among all the troops in Dost Muhammad Khan's kingdom, the regiments under his command were said to be the best paid. Even so, the payment of his soldiers fluctuated with the state of his exchequer and was doled out in petty installments, often only immediately prior to military campaigns.[183]

The components making up Dost Muhammad Khan's army received varying judgments concerning their efficiency. Temple, the Secretary to the Chief Commissioner of Punjab, praised the Amir's infantry as the 'flower of the force'.[184] While acknowledging that the regular soldiers were drilled to a certain extent, Lumsden considered the irregular cavalry the strongest component of the Amir's army. By contrast, he estimated the regular cavalry to be an 'almost useless body'.[185] Despite his critical view of the Afghan troops Lumsden was ready to concede that Dost Muhammad Khan's restricted resources did not allow him to do a better job:

> The plain fact is that the Ameer's postion is a most difficult one, for the country of Affghanistan does not yield revenue sufficient to support its innumerable chiefs and their families and at the same time to keep the army requisite to keep such a turbulent population in order and these chiefs are far too powerful to be restricted in their allowances beyond a very wide margin, so that the whole system of government finance is a succession of expedients and shifts and at the end of every two or three years the accounts of the country come to a dead lock and the rulers are obliged to repudiate a certain proportion of the public debt and commence a fresh set of accounts.[186]

In his effort to create a stronger army the Amir was not only hampered by the financial demands placed on him by the Sardars and their families. The conflicting needs of simultaneously raising additional taxes and soldiers also met with local resistance. At times when Dost Muhammad Khan attempted to collect additional militiamen for the purpose of revenue collection or military campaigns, the population of the areas called upon most often on such occasions (Kohistan and Logar), offered him the choice between soldiers and revenue payments, making it perfectly clear that the Amir could not have both.[187]

Thus Dost Muhammad Khan's attempt at modernizing his army only met with limited success. Certainly the concentration of military power in the hands of the Amir is undeniable. Throughout his reign, he acted at least in theory as the supreme military commander, rendering obsolete the position of *sipahsalar* (commander in chief), as it was known in the periods of Ahmad Shah and Timur Shah. During Dost Muhammad Khan's period, this title was only bestowed on the provincial army generals subservient to the Sardars, such as Campbell in Turkistan and Faramarz Khan in Qandahar.[188] But the above discussion has shown that Dost Muhammad Khan only assumed the active high command of his army during major military campaigns. Under usual circumstances his sons were in direct command of the troops scattered in various provinces. The ongoing rivalries among the Muhammadzai Sardars continued to bear ample centrifugal potential, which also affected the attitudes of their subordinates:

> From their system as well as the nature of Affghans generally, great jealousies exist between the contingents of different Sirdars, which frequently break out into serious conflicts when these troops are by any accident brought together. The subdued feelings of the chiefs towards each other will invariably be found to pervade their followers down to the smallest drummer-boy in a regiment, who, though he does not hesitate to abuse his master soundly among his companions, would consider it a personal insult for the follower of a rival chief to do so.[189]

In the long run, the main element of Dost Muhammad Khan's modernization, the creation of regular infantry regiments permanently maintained in garrisons, was bound to loosen tribal ties and to weaken the traditional military leadership. Amir Sher 'Ali Khan continued his father's centralizing policies. During his administration the regular infantry regiments were expanded at the cost of the tribal cavalry and were arranged according to body height or age rather than tribal allegiance. Moreover, he sought to establish greater control over the payment of his troops by abolishing the *barat* system.[190]

In the 1850s Dost Muhammad Khan's efforts at modernization had as yet borne little fruit. If Lumsden is to be believed, the irregular cavalry under tribal leaders, rather than the regular infantry regiments, continued to be the most effective component of the Amir's army. Therefore the tribal leaders, while having little access to the higher echelons of military administration, continued to play a vital role in all major military campaigns. The same can be said for the Qizilbash. Although the overall participation of the Qizilbash in the royal army declined with the disbandment of the *ghulam khana*, Dost Muhammad Khan continued to rely on their services in the form of 'tribal' contingents, which is reflected by the fact that their most prominent leader, Khan Shirin Khan Jawansher, continued to enjoy great influence at court as military leader and council member. Thus, far from enjoying, 'absolute' power, the Amir found his ability to maneuver highly restricted. Consisting of a 'succession of expedients', his policies were aimed at political survival and did little to affect the underlying socioeconomic structures inherited from the Sadozai period.

The Amir's Revenues

The available data on Dost Muhammad Khan's income are too scanty to allow a detailed analysis of the mechanisms of revenue collection and redistribution. For this reason I will restrict myself to a few general observations. As already seen in the case of the Ghilzais, the Amir only managed to introduce insignificant changes to the revenue system instituted by Ahmad Shah. I will start with a discussion of the revenue system of the Sadozais, the kinds of lands involved, and the taxes raised both by them and their Muhammadzai successors. The second part of this section will be devoted to a summary of the policies pursued by Dost Muhammad Khan.

The most detailed information concerning the nature of Shah Zaman's revenues is available from the accounts of the British agent Ghulam Sarwar and the Herati historian Imam al-Din Husaini. Strachey, a member of the Elphinstone mission, compiled an overview of the fiscal situation of the Afghan empire during Shah Shuja''s first reign and compared it with the earlier, more glorious periods of Sadozai history. Though fragmentary and in parts contradictory, the available data allow certain conclusions concerning the relationship between the Sadozai court and its provinces. In his analysis of the information furnished by Ghulam Sarwar, Gankovsky backs Elphinstone's observation that the Sadozai kings mostly relied on their possessions east of the Khyber for their income.[191] According to Gankovsky, the revenue-rich provinces of Kashmir, Peshawar, Dera Ghazi Khan, Dera Isma'il Khan and Multan submitted not only a much greater total amount of revenues but also a greater percentage of the taxes collected locally than the western provinces of the Sadozai empire. But even the Indian provinces sent in no more than 50 percent of the revenues raised locally. While Bahawalpur and Sind remained in the hands of local chiefs, the above mentioned provinces were farmed out to Durrani and Hotak nobles, who were entitled to make deductions for the payment of troops, expenses incurred on behalf of the king, e.g. during military campaigns, and for religious endowments. The revenues potentially due to the crown were further diminished by the fact that a large proportion of the available lands was turned into service grants. In the late eighteenth century Husaini observed that Multan furnished little revenue to Shah Zaman because part of its territores had fallen to the Sikhs and Bahawal Khan II of Bahawalpur (r. 1771–1811), while the remainder formed Sadozai *jagirs*.[192] On the basis of Ghulam Sarwar's data Gankovsky reaches the conclusion that 48 percent of the revenues of Multan were taken up by *jagirs*. In Dera Isma'il Khan 55 percent of the revenues were apportioned to service grants. These figures are comparable with those available for the Durrani stronghold of Qandahar, where 43 percent of the total income were devoted to *jagirs*. In effect, however, the Sadozai treasury received less than a quarter of the revenues collected in the province of Qandahar, as another 300,000 rupees were consumed for administrative expenses and religious endowments. In Herat close to 40 percent of the available revenues were taken up by service grants. According to Ghulam Sarwar, roughly a third of the local revenue, or 400,000 rupees, was intended for the royal treasury.[193] Strachey points out that this amount was assigned as an allowance to the governor of Herat, Shahzada Qaisar b. Shah Zaman, and thus was not available at the capital.[194] Given the decentralized nature of the Sadozai administration, the net revenues of Timur Shah and Shah Zaman were relatively low in relation to the vastness of their possessions, amounting to approximately ten million rupees a year.[195]

The following sets of figures given by Husaini and Strachey allow us to form an impression of the gap between the local revenues and those directly available to the crown as well as the relative amounts of money involved. According to Husaini, Shah Zaman farmed out Kashmir for 2.4 million rupees before deductions for administrative costs and *jagirs*. The receipts of the governor, Mukhlis al-Daula 'Abdullah Khan Alikozai, were estimated at four million rupees. Dera Ghazi Khan was farmed for 700,000 rupees. Dera

Isma'il Khan, the revenues of which were estimated at 400,000 rupees, was assigned to 'Abd al-Rahim Hotak in exchange for 225,000 rupees. Shah Zaman's net revenue from Multan under Muzaffar Khan Sadozai amounted to two or three hundred thousand rupees. The region of Peshawar was governed by Zardad Khan Popalzai and was assessed at 700,000 rupees a year.[196] Strachey estimated that the entire revenue of Kashmir amounted to 4.5 million rupees until Shah Zaman's reign. After deductions for *tiyuls* and *jagirs* it was farmed for 2.1 million rupees, out of which 700,000 rupees were deducted for local expenses, leaving a balance of 1.4 million rupees to be paid to the king. The revenues of Sind reached five million rupees, out of which 1.5 million were submitted to Ahmad Shah. During Timur Shah's reign this amount dropped to 1.2 million. Shah Zaman, by contrast, had little control over the revenues of Sind, as they were almost entirely at the disposal of his minister Rahmatullah Khan Sadozai Mut'amid al-Daula.[197] Multan, assessed at 350,000 rupees, submitted 200,000 rupees to Timur Shah; during Shah Zaman's reign the revenue paid directly to the king decreased to 100,000 rupees. From Dera Ghazi Khan 600,000 out of 750,000 rupees were due to the royal treasury. Dera Isma'il Khan was expected to pay 250,000 out of its assessment of 600,000 rupees. Out of Peshawar's assessment of 700,000 rupees 180,000 reached Timur Shah's exchequer and 100,000 were paid to Shah Zaman. During Shah Shuja''s first reign the lands of Peshawar were almost entirely given out in *tiyul*. After Shah Zaman's removal from power in 1800 the decline of the Sadozai empire was heralded by the increasing unwillingness of local governors to furnish troops to the king and to pay revenues. During his first reign Shah Shuja' received practically no regular income from Kashmir, the Derajat, Multan, Shikarpur and Sind.[198]

The principal sources of Sadozai and Muhammadzai income were land revenue, the produce of crown lands, and the duties and customs levied in the towns. Generally speaking, three kinds of land were distinguished, crown lands (*khalisa*), private property (*mulk*), and religious endowments (*waqf*). Ghani points out that it is difficult to determine the exact proportion between these three forms of landownership in the course of time but reaches the conclusion that most of the lands of Afghanistan were in the possession of private landowners during the eighteenth and nineteenth centuries.[199] This opinion is supported by evidence from materials collected by the Elphinstone mission, according to which the greater part of the crown lands was concentrated in the immediate environs of Herat, Qandahar, Kabul and Peshawar. Moreover, a lot of these lands had been alienated to private individuals by the time of Shah Shuja''s first reign.[200]

The basic unit of land used for the tax assessment was a measurement called *qulba*, 'plough', indicating the amount of land a team of oxen could plough. The decisive factor influencing the amount of tax paid was the ethnic origin of the landholder. As mentioned in Chapter Three, the revenue system of Ghazni and Jalalabad mostly relied on two kinds of assessments. The *jam'bast*, a fixed quota in cash and kind, was for the most part reserved for the Pashtun landholders. The *kot* system, according to which a fixed share of the yearly produce was levied by the government, applied to the remaining population. The *kot* system varied according to the amount of water available for irrigation. The agricultural lands were categorized as *abi* or *rudi*, 'irrigated' and *lalmi*, 'rain fed'. In the 1880s Raverty observed that the Tajik population of the province of Nangarhar paid one third (*se kot*) of the harvest in kind or one quarter (*char kot*) in cash for irrigated lands, whereas lands dependent on rain were assessed at one tenth in kind.[201] On *khalisa* lands the government levied half of the harvest (*nim kot*) but assessments reaching two thirds or five sixths of the gross produce also were common.[202] Two further agricultural taxes raised both by the Sadozai and Muhammadzai rulers were the *jaribi*, a horticultural tax which was paid by the *jarib*, and a tax on livestock, variously called *sargalla* and *shakh shumari*.[203] While the *jaribi* seems to have been levied on Pashtuns and Persian speakers alike, the *sargalla* was exclusively imposed on ethnic outsiders. In Qandahar, for example, it was reserved for 'stranger colonists' during Ahmad Shah's time, whereas the local Durranis and Farsiwan were exempt. During the reign of the Qandahar Sardars it was extended to include all non-Durranis.

The tax terminology discussed so far is devoid of Islamic elements. Kakar's observation that the *jam'bast* is better understood as the product of conditions peculiar to Afghanistan rather than Muslim influence points to the fact that certain elements of the fiscal system instituted by the Sadozai rulers departed from the provisions of the *shari'at* and possibly reflected existing local customs more strongly.[204] While the available sources on the administrative systems of the Sadozai and Muhammadzai periods do mention some properly Islamic tax categories such as *kharaj*, *zakat*, *'ushr*, *khums* and *jizya*, there is evidence that their actual application differed somewhat from the original Islamic precepts. A case in point is *kharaj*, a land tax which was levied on conquered territories during the early Islamic period and was higher than the canonic alms tax (*zakat*) raised in territories 'inherited' by Muslims since pre-Islamic times. According to Fragner, the *zakat* on cultivated lands was fixed at ten percent (*'ushr*, 'tithe') of the harvest .[205] In medieval Persia *kharaj* became the basic term for land tax.[206] The use of *kharaj* in Afghanistan is less clear. In *Siraj al-Tawarikh* this term is merely used formulaically, denoting 'royal taxes' (*mal-i diwani wa kharaj-i sultani*) in general.[207] Gankovsky is of the opinion that *kharaj* was a land tax levied at the rate of one tenth on the crops of unirrigated fields as opposed to a tax of one third (*salisat*, apparently the equivalent of *se kot*) on irrigated lands.[208] Ferrier, on the other hand, identifies *kharaj* as a form of poll tax (*sarkhana*) among some of the non-Pashtun rural population of southern Afghanistan, such as the Farsiwan, during the era of Dost Muhammad Khan. The Farsiwan and Hindus living in the town were exempt from this imposition but had to pay a special tax on their shops.[209]

In nineteenth-century Afghanistan, *zakat* was levied according to Islamic precepts on the livestock of the nomadic and sedentary population at the rate of 2½ percent. Called *chihilyak*, the same rate was collected from Muslim traders as transit duty. Non-Muslims usually had to submit twice as much.[210] The *jizya*, a poll tax paid by non-Muslims, formed a source of revenue even in the smaller towns of Afghanistan, as Hindus played a preponderant role in the local and long-distance trade throughout the country.[211] The traditional Islamic tax of *'ushr* is recorded for the Sadozai period but there is no clear evidence concerning its application.[212] The case of *khums* ('one fifth') is similarly problematic. According to Gankovsky, the Sadozai kings levied this tax on the profits of mining.[213] During Amir 'Abd al-Rahman Khan's reign the taxes on lands, mills, vineyards and estates yielding interest were collected under the headings of *'ushr*, *khums* and *zakat*.[214] Neither precedent for the collection of *khums* conforms with Sunni jurisprudence, which stipulates that this tax should be levied on the spoils of wars against non-believers.[215]

Apart from custom duties (*chabutara*, *sayir*) and *jizya*, the urban regions were subject to a multitude of other impositions, the most important ones of which were taxes on shops, trades (*asnaf*), auction dues (*dallali*), and cattle sold in the market. Finally there was the mint tax, known as *zarbkhana*, which was raised by the periodic calling in of copper coins. The right to collect these taxes, as well as public offices such as that of the *kotwal*, or chief of police, were farmed out by the government for a fixed sum of money.[216] Only one of the following accounts stems from the period of Dost Muhammad Khan. Although they concern various locations and are reckoned in different currencies, I list them here in full because in combination they give some idea of the relative proportions of the various taxes collected. In 1857 Lumsden recorded the following tax items in the city of Qandahar:[217]

custom duties collected at city gates	60,000 Qandahari rupees per year (1 Qandahar rupee ≈ ½ Kabul rupee)
907 tax-paying shops at 1.25 rupees per month	13, 605 rupees per year
silk weavers	7,000 rupees per year
grain dealers	2,500 rupees per year
dyers	3,000 rupees per year
tanners	8,000 rupees per year
butchers	1, 400 rupees per year
cap and *pustin* makers, saddlers	1,200 rupees per year

poll taxon non-Pashtuns at 5 rupees per year	total amount not listed
jizya	6,000 rupees per year
cattle sold in the market	5,000 rupees per year
kidney fat (of all goats and sheep slaughtered in the city; used for soap manufacture)	amount not known
gambling houses	5,000 rupees per year

During the Second Anglo-Afghan War, O. St. John estimated the revenues of Qandahar city as follows:[218]

custom duties	800,000 Qandahari *kham* rupees per year (1 Qandahar *kham* rupee ≈ 5/6 Qandahari *pukhta* rupee)
custom duties in Pishin	72,000 rupees per year
tax on provisions sold in city	115,000 rupees per year
sargalla on flocks of nomad tribes	205,000 rupees per year
soap manufacture	90,000 rupees per year
tax on shops	42,000 rupees per year
tax on sale of horses, cattle and sheep	37,000 rupees per year
manufacture of leather	25,000 rupees per year
tax on shops and industries in environs	21,200 rupees per year
export of asafoetida	20,000 rupees per year
duty on sale of caps and shoes	16,000 rupees per year
zarbkhana	15,000 rupees per year
tax on cultivated lands near city	14,000 rupees per year
manufacture of sesamum oil	12,000 rupees per year
manufacture of snuff	9,000 rupees
sale of silkworm's eggs	8,000 rupees per year
gambling houses	5,000 rupees per year
dyers in city	4,000 rupees per year
dyers outside city	2,300 rupees per year
cultivation of hemp	3,000 rupees per year
khanawari (tax on non-Durrani males)	72,000 rupees per year
jizya	4,600 rupees per year

During the same period, Hastings gave the following account of the taxes levied in the city of Ghazni:[219]

custom duties	46,333 (Kabuli?) rupees per year
kalladagh (tax on meat killed and brought into the city)	1,166 rupees per year

zarbkhana	1,100 rupees per year
kotwali	500 rupees per year
asnaf	484 rupees per year
tarazudari (license to weigh grain during revenue collection)	410 rupees per year
dallali	400 rupees per year
reshm furushi (license for the right to sell silk)	216 rupees per year
tobacco license tax	200 rupees per year

The following figures for the revenues of Kabul city stem from Amir 'Abd al-Rahman Khan's reign:[220]

custom duties	950,000 rupees per year
grain duties	80,000 rupees per year
soap manufacture	50,000 rupees per year
zarbkhana	40,000 rupees per year
dallali	30,000 rupees per year
taxes on leather work	12,000 rupees per year
dagh-i postin (stamping of government mark)	12,000 rupees per year
kotwali	8,000 rupees per year
woven manufactures	8,000 rupees per year
jizya	6,000 rupees per year
market fees	4,000 rupees per year
goldwashing	1,000 rupees per year

Dost Muhammad Khan's consolidation of power was reflected by increasing revenues. Immediately prior to the First Anglo-Afghan War, following the incorporation of Jalalabad and Ghazni into his kingdom, the Amir's receipts amounted to 2.5 million rupees. In 1857, after the conquest of Qandahar and parts of Afghan Turkistan, Dost Muhammad Khan estimated his net revenue at 3,008,800 rupees, claiming that he derived 2,222,000 rupees from Kabul, 444,000 rupees from Qandahar, and 342,800 rupees from Turkistan.[221] Generally speaking, the amounts reaching the royal exchequer were negligible in comparison with the taxes collected locally by the provincial governors. As seen in Chapter Two, the province of Turkistan was farmed by Muhammad Afzal nominally for 2.5 million rupees, an amount seven times higher than the net revenue submitted to the Amir. Ghazni, the entire revenue of which was estimated at 750,000 to 800,000 rupees, submitted only a fraction of this amount to Kabul.[222] While Dost Muhammad Khan gradually succeeded in widening his sphere of influence in the region known as Afghanistan today, he was unable to introduce fundamental changes to the administrative system known from Sadozai times. Like his Sadozai predecessors, the Amir could only exert direct pressure on the regions forming the core of his realm. Apart from bringing new groups, such as the Tokhis into the fold of government control, he derived the bulk of his revenues from the regions located in the immediate vicinity of Kabul and along the major trade routes radiating out from his capital. From Dost Muhammad Khan's first reign on, these regions in particular were increasingly burdened with royal requests for revenues and soldiers.[223] This is reflected by Lal's estimate of the revenues during the Amir's first reign, which distinguishes between the 'just' amount of revenue (*'asl*) and extra demands raised by the king's officials (*bid'at*).[224] According to Lal, the revenues realized by Dost Muhammad Khan were as follows:

custom duties	299,920 rupees
khalisa	159,179 rupees
Kohistan and Logar[225]	606,826 rupees
Hazarajat and Bamiyan[226]	102,775 rupees
Jalalabad and Laghman	695,754 rupees
Ghazni and Maidan	458,169 rupees
Zurmat and Kurram[227]	179,251 rupees
Total	2,501,874 rupees

It is not clear which proportion of these revenues was deducted by the local governors for their own expenses. Moreover, not all the regions listed submitted their revenue on a regular basis. The areas located on the fringes of Dost Muhammad Khan's empire were most likely to resist government interference. This was the case in Zurmat and Katawaz, where the Amir only realized nominal taxes. After the conquest of Qandahar the revenue collection remained notoriously difficult in the region northwest of Qandahar, particularly in the districts of Nauzad, Zamindawar and Dehraud.[228] The Hazarajat, over most of which the Sadozai kings had only exerted nominal control,[229] also continued to remain largely beyond Dost Muhammad Khan's grip. In the Kabul region only the areas bordering on Kohistan and the trade route to Bamiyan, such as Turkoman, Parsa and Bihsud, paid any revenue to the Amir. In the region of Ghazni, the Jaghatu, Jaghori, Muhammad Khwaja and Chahardasta Hazaras are mentioned as paying tribute.[230] A great part of the revenues accruing from these areas were farmed out to the Qizilbash leadership in lieu of allowances.[231] During his second reign, the Amir also laid claim to the more remote Hazara regions of Dai Kundi and Dai Zangi but his control over this region seems to have been intermittent at best.[232] Even the Hazara regions subject to fairly regular revenue collections commonly resisted the impositions made by the government. In the Bihsud region, for example, it was a time-honored custom to offer the revenue agents *sang ya buz*, that is, the choice between being pelted with stones and accepting goats instead of the sheep required by the government.[233] Yet, if the government had sufficient troops at its disposal it tended to enforce its demands by feeding the soldiers on the land until its requests for revenue were fulfilled. In the 1830s, Harlan described the revenue collection in Bihsud as follows:

> The revenue of Beysoot under the [Sadozai] kings of Cabul was seventeen thousand rupees; Dost Mahomed increased it to the enormous sum, comparatively, of eighty thousand rupees, which was an assessment of two rupees for each family![234] This tax is levied upon the villagers by their own chiefs. A body of one thousand cavalry is annually sent to collect the revenue. This corps is dispersed over the district in small divisions, each one with orders to collect, and is quartered upon the husbandman, who is obliged to subsist the soldiers so long as the revenue remains unpaid! ... The revenue is collected in kind, the amount being paid in sheep, horned cattle, goats, horses, slaves, grain and berriks [*barak*] etc. The accumulated mass is dispatched to Cabul, which is the nearest mart of general commerce; a portion is sold for necessary cash expenses, another portion is traded off by means of reciprocal necessities and much of the grain is retained for family use. The slaves are sold by private contract, but the government levies... a percentage upon the amount of sale![235]

This process of revenue collection usually took four to six months.[236] Not all the revenues levied in the countryside reached the government coffers. The agents in charge usually received extra offerings in the form of horses, carpets and fabric which became their private property. Moreover, part of the collected livestock tended to get lost to plundering raids by the Hazaras during the return to Kabul.[237]

The main characteristics of the revenue collection in Bihsud as described above also applied to the other regions within the reach of the government. As a rule, the government agents spent several months in the region to which they were deputed, settling the revenue demands in lengthy negotiations punctuated by military confrontations as each side attempted to demonstrate its military strength. For this reason, revenue collection without the presence of sufficient troops to back up the government demands was unthinkable, and it stopped entirely whenever the Amir had to leave Kabul during major military campaigns.[238] In 1855–56, as Dost Muhammad Khan was preoccupied with the annexation of Qandahar, his deputies at Kabul had to cope with three major rebellions. The uprisings of Muhammad Shah Khan Babakr Khel and the leadership of Khost were followed by a rebellion in Bihsud and Dai Zangi.[239] Even in the regions considered 'obedient' to the Amir, revenue payments were essentially used as a means to reduce government interference to a minimum. Although the revenue year formally started on *nauroz* (21 March), the raising of taxes was an ongoing process, continuing as long as the weather allowed access to the regions in question. Winter, however, always was a critical period for the Amir, as the flow of his revenues on the basis of land taxes and custom receipts more or less dried up. During such periods of scarcity Dost Muhammad Khan resorted to exacting money from members of his court and local merchants.[240] Another source of income was the confiscation of the property of deceased persons.[241]

The greater part of the Amir's revenue was devoted to the upkeep of his army. Immediately prior to the First Anglo-Afghan War it was estimated that he used up 2.1 million out of his entire income of 2.5 million rupees for the pay of his soldiers.[242] After the conquest of Herat, as the revenue of the king rose to 7 million rupees, at least 4.3 million rupees were consumed for the maintenance of the army.[243] The remainder of the Amir's revenue was expended on his court and allowances for his numerous relatives to the extent that they were not covered by *jagirs*.[244] Once these immediate exigencies had been taken care of to the extent possible no funds were left over. Public works in the city of Kabul, while organized by the Amir, had to be paid by the local citizens.[245] Chronically short of money, the Amir likened his position to that of a hungry fox waiting in vain for a sheep's tail to fall off.[246] Although Dost Muhammad Khan's ascendancy over Afghanistan had become an undisputed fact by the 1850s, his supremacy found its expression only partially in the control of local resources. The need to maintain the loyalty of his family and friendly tribal leaders, such as Sa'adat Khan Mohmand, had the effect that large parts of the country continued to be tied up in the form of *jagirs*. Thus Dost Muhammad Khan's efforts to generate revenue and men concentrated on the towns of Kabul, Ghazni, Jalalabad and Qandahar and their surroundings. At the same time, his arbitrary control over the urban areas was offset by his inability to generate a regular flow of revenue payments from the regions beyond the highroads. The constant pressure exerted on the urban areas and the regions bordering on them, in turn, proved counterproductive in the long run, as the tax burden placed on merchants and non-Pashtun farmers alike discouraged the development of greater economic activities.

The Role of the Ulama

The British sources consulted alternately describe the Pashtuns dwelling on their borders as 'fanatical' and irreligious.[247] At the same time, they offer next to no information on the role of the ulama in Afghan society. Rarely, if ever, are religious dignitaries mentioned by name and even less is known about the education and family background of these men. For this reason, I will restrict myself to a few general remarks concerning the centers of religious learning, the role of the ulama in the judicial apparatus, and their relationship with the Muhammadzai rulers.

In the late eighteenth century Kabul was the seat of at least one significant *madrasa*. The Madrasa of Faiz Khan, also known as Madrasa-yi Uzbakan, drew students from as far afield as Tatarstan.[248] While there were three *madrasas* in Kabul at the beginning of the nineteenth century, no influential college of religious learning is recorded for this city during Dost Muhammad Khan's period.[249] In the wider region, Bukhara and Peshawar along with the neighboring town of Hashtnagar were the major centers of religious instruction. Clerical offices in Badakhshan and adjacent areas seem to have been filled by graduates of the *madrasa* in Faizabad.[250] In the 1830s Burnes reported that the three former colleges of Balkh were no longer active.[251]

Despite this decline of religious institutions, the position of the ulama still tended to be stronger in the parts of the country 'completely under royal authority'.[252] In the tribal areas their role was limited to the activities taking place in the village mosque, such as the daily prayers and the informal religious instruction of the youth. Given the strong role of *pashtunwali*, the administration of justice tended to rest with the village *jirga* rather than the mullah.[253] In the urban areas, by contrast, members of the religious establishment not only enforced public morality but also had part in the administration of justice. Both the Sadozai and Muhammadzai kings appointed *qazis* assisted by a number of muftis in all major towns of their realm.[254] Theoretically the *qazis* were in the position to decide both civil and penal cases. In practice, however, their control of penal matters was restricted to civil and minor criminal cases, and they mainly acted as assistants to the king or local governor in settling the cases brought to court.[255] Moreover, the enforcement of the *qazis'* judgments rested entirely with the government. Certain observers were of the opinion that the Muhammadzai king and his governors were particularly keen on handling cases which were likely to result in the payment of a fine to the government. At the same time the delineation of the respective juridical spheres of influence between Dost Muhammad Khan and his *qazi* seems to have been guided by the notion that the judgment of matters falling into the domain of *'urf*, or customary law, formed the prerogative of the king or his representative.[256] The precepts of *pashtunwali* nonetheless tended to affect the rulings reserved for the *qazis*. In the region of Qandahar, for example, the ultimate settlement of murder cases was routinely left to the family of the victim so that it could live up to the rules of *pashtunwali* by taking revenge on the family of the murderer.[257]

The government usually awarded the office of *qazi* to local dignitaries. In Kabul this post was held by members of the Barakzai tribe.[258] After the annexation of Qandahar, Dost Muhammad Khan removed Ghulam Khan, the *qazi* of the 'Dil' brothers, from office and imprisoned him for voicing criticism of the Amir's policies. The remaining ulama, who had previously opposed Kuhandil Khan's links with Persia, now assumed an equally critical attitude towards Dost Muhammad Khan's and Ghulam Haidar Khan's pro-

British policies.[259] Part of their discontent was also directed against the new *qazi* appointed by the Amir. Ghulam Haidar Khan responded by threatening to remove all ulama from office unless they were ready to prove their learning on the basis of *Durr al-mukhtar,* a well-known handbook of Hanafi *fiqh*. The conflict between the governor of Qandahar and the ulama came to a head in February 1858 over the issue of the forcible conversion of a Hindu boy to Islam. When it became known that Ghulam Haidar Khan had allowed the boy in question to escape from the city of Qandahar together with his family the ulama began to vent their discontent against the Lumsden Mission. Ghulam Haidar Khan reacted with a show of force, ordering the ulama in question to be expelled from Qandahar city. These, however, skillfully used to the governor's heavy-handedness to gain the support of the population of Qandahar. Having assembled with 500 to 600 of their religious students (*talib*) at the shrine of Hazrat Ji located near the Kabul gate,[260] they forced their reentry into the city, attacked the house of the newly appointed *qazi* and laid siege to the citadel. The situation was defused when the governor rescinded the order for the ulama's expulsion from the city. While the ulama had carried the day, Ghulam Haidar retaliated by forcing a number of them to accompany him to Kabul in March 1858.[261]

Despite these tensions neither Ghulam Haidar Khan nor any of his governor-colleagues took any active steps to curb the power of the religious establishment in general, as was to be the case during the reign of 'Abd al-Rahman Khan later in the nineteenth century.[262] While certain members of the religious establishment suffered reductions in income during Dost Muhammad Khan's first reign, the greater group of ulama continued to enjoy a privileged position.[263] Until the Second Anglo-Afghan War a considerable portion of the income of each region was set aside for allowances fixed for the religious establishment. In Qandahar the *wazifa* paid to this group amounted to 126,000 rupees in 1877/78.[264] During Dost Muhammad Khan's time by far the most influential religious leader in the Qandahar region was a Ghilzai *pir* known as Akhund Mulla Sahib al-Din. Residing at Mazra' five miles northeast of Qandahar in the Arghandab valley, Mulla Sahib al-Din had one thousand disciples and his followership in the wider region was estimated at 30,000 souls. He was also highly respected by the Qandahar Sardars Kuhandil and Rahmdil Khan but it is not clear whether he actively interfered with their policies.[265]

In the Kabul region, the most influential family was that of Sayyid Ahmad Mir Aqa. As mentioned in Chapter One, Sayyid Ahmad was the imam of the Jami' Masjid of Pul-i Khishti in Kabul until his death in 1807–8. During Shah Shuja''s first reign Sayyid Ahmad held the title of *mir wa'iz*, or head preacher, of Kabul.[266] According to Fofalzai, the Sadozai kings awarded this title to the most respected ulama of their time. The *mir wa'iz* was entitled to lead the congregational prayer and to pronounce the sermon on Fridays and on the occasion of *'id* and thus fulfilled a function comparable to that of the *imam jum'a* in the Iranian context. For the city of Kabul two men of this rank are mentioned for the period of Shah Zaman's reign, Mulla Ahmad Khan Durrani[267] and Sayyid Ahmad. Sayyid Ahmad, who held this title uninterruptedly until Shah Shuja''s first reign, was a Sufi who enjoyed a wide following among the Sunnis of Kabul and Kohistan.[268] Linked to Sher Muhammad Khan Mukhtar al-Daula, Sayyid Ahmad used his popularity among the Sunni population of Kabul and Kohistan to interfere with the power struggle between Shah Mahmud and Shah Shuja' in 1803. According to Elphinstone the title of *mir wa'iz* ceased to exist after Sayyid Ahmad's rebellion against Shah Shuja' and his subsequent execution.[269] Nonetheless his sons Mir Haji (Mir Ma'sum) and Hafiz Ji (Mir Darwesh) continued to play an important role in the political life of Kabul.[270] During the First Anglo-Afghan War Mir Haji assumed a prominent position in the uprising agains the British and the events subsequent to their withdrawal. Like his father, Mir Haji enjoyed a great amount of esteem among the Sunni population of Kabul and Kohistan during Dost Muhammad Khan's second reign. Until 1871 members of his family were in charge of the Friday and *'id* prayers but it is not clear whether they carried the title of *mir wa'iz*.[271] While Mir Haji's brother Hafiz Ji also seems to have profited from the religious reputation of his family, his activities mostly seem to have been of a political kind. Despite his marriage alliance with Dost Muhammad Khan, his allegiance to the Amir seems to have been far from unequivocal, as is shown by his revolt in favor of Shah Shuja' at the beginning of the First Anglo-Afghan War. During Dost Muhammad Khan's second reign he enjoyed an influential position at court as member of the Amir's council.

Little is known about the role of the Mujaddidi family at the time of Dost Muhammad Khan. This highly respected family traced its origins in Afghanistan to the reign of Sultan Mas'ud Ghaznawi (r. 1030–1040), who entrusted its ancestor Shaikh Shihab al-Din Farrukhshah with the task of spreading Islam in the region of Nijrau. In the middle of the fourteenth century members of this family became established in Sirhind under the leadership of Imam Rafi' al-Din. It was here that the name-giver of the family, Shaikh Ahmad Sirhindi (d. 1624), also known as 'Renewer of the Second Millenium' (*mujaddid alf-i sani*), attained fame as a teacher of Naqshbandi doctrines. Subsequent to his conquest of Sirhind in 1748 Ahmad Shah induced three descendants of Shaikh Ahmad named Shah Ghulam Muhammad, Shah 'Izzatullah and Shah Safiyullah to join him in Qandahar.[272] When Ahmad Shah's successor Timur Shah shifted his capital to Kabul he took along certain members of the Mujaddidi family and awarded lands in Kabul, Kohistan, Jalalabad, Qandahar and Herat to them.[273] As representatives of the Naqshbandi order, the Mujaddidi family enjoyed a widespread following in Afghanistan, including the nomadic

Sulaiman Khel Ghilzais.[274] Known as the 'Hazrats of Shor Bazar', they were also influential at the courts of Timur Shah and Shah Zaman. Their preponderant role as proponents of a jihad against the British during the Third Anglo-Afghan War of 1919 and as opponents to Amir Amanullah Khan's subsequent program of reform are well known. Yet the only member of the family mentioned for the nineteenth century is Hazrat Shah Miyan 'Abd al-Baqi (b. Hazrat Qayyum, d. 1870), who was a contemporary of Shah Zaman, Shah Mahmud, Shah Shuja', and Dost Muhammad Khan. Fofalzai describes him as a poet, *mujahid* and 'nationalist' (*milliyat khwah*) but furnishes no further details concerning his activities.[275]

Another important Naqshbandi *pir* was 'Abd al-Ghafur, the Akhund of neighboring Swat (1794–1878). In 1835 he supported Amir Dost Muhammad Khan in one of his campaigns against the Sikhs. Almost thirty years later he led the Yusufzais in a successful attempt to repulse the British during the Ambela campaign. Despite his popularity all over north-eastern Afghanistan the Akhund desisted from seeking direct access to secular power and formally remained an outsider to Pashtun tribal affairs. He initiated a number of Afghan disciples not only to the Naqshbandi order but also to the teachings of the Qadiri, Chishti and Suhrawardi orders. One of his *khalifas* was Hadda Sahib of Nangarhar who spearheaded an uprising against Amir 'Abd al-Rahman Khan in 1897.[276] Beyond this, I have been unable to locate detailed information concerning the activities of Sufi orders during Dost Muhammad Khan's period. A closer study of the organization and followership of these orders as well as their relationship with the temporal rulers clearly forms one of the desiderata for the understanding of the socio-political setting in nineteenth-century Afghanistan.

Trade

In the light of the downfall of the Sadozai dynasty, the concomitant territorial loss, and the breaking up of the core regions of the country into small principalities, both European and Afghan historians view the nineteenth century as a 'dark' period of political and economic disintegration. Gregorian, for example, sums up the situation of the country in the following manner,

> From the late eighteenth century on, the development of urban Afghanistan was impeded by the decline of overland trade, the growing economic isolation of the region, the political ascendancy of the Afghan tribes, and the growth of semifeudal, semipastoral tribal communities, with parochial notions of economic self-sufficiency and a tendency to lapse into a natural economy. The disintegration of central power, protracted civil wars, and hazards of travel in

Afghanistan contributed to the political fragmentation of the region and the decline of urban population and economy.[277]

Prior to the nineteenth century, by contrast, the cities of Afghanistan had been participants of a flourishing trade. Located at the crossroads of the trade routes linking Persia, Central Asia and India, Kabul, Qandahar and Herat had prospered during Mughal/Safawid times. Qandahar was located at the intersection of the trade routes leading south across the Bolan Pass to Sind and the coast of the Arabian sea, and west towards Seistan, Herat and Iran. Kabul, on the other hand, was connected with India by the commercial routes passing through Jalalabad and Ghazni, in the latter case via Kurram, Khost, or the Gomal Pass. To the north, Kabul was linked with Balkh, Qarshi and Bukhara by the Bamiyan route. In Afghan Turkistan the silk road leading from Yarkand across the Pamir to Faizabad, Qunduz, Tashqurghan, Mazar-i Sharif, Maimana and Herat needs to be mentioned.[278] While the overland trade was negatively affected by the increasing importance of the sea route from the early seventeenth century on, it did not grind to a halt entirely. Although the trade may have decreased in volume, Afghanistan continued to function as a thoroughfare for goods from Turkistan and Persia intended for India, and vice versa. The regions north of the Oxus primarily exported raw silk and silk fabrics, bullion, dried fruit, horses and Bactrian camels, as well as madder and spices to India, mostly via Kabul and in a lesser proportion by way of Qandahar. The caravans returning from India carried a merchandise of cotton piece goods, sugar, tea, indigo, shoes, metal, drugs and spices, a large part of which made its way to Bukhara. The Persian trade items sent to India by way of Herat and Qandahar consisted of silk, carpets, horses, saffron and copper utensils. Afghanistan mainly exported horses, wool and woollen manufactures, skins, furs, and agricultural products such as dried and fresh fruits, tobacco, hashish opium and madder to India. Another important trade item was asafoetida collected by Kakars in the vicinity of Farah and Herat.[279]

The trade passing through Afghanistan was distributed among various ethnic groups on the basis of trade route worked and the items held for sale. Most of the commerce between Qandahar, Herat and Mashhad, for example, was carried on by Persians. The trade in 2,000 to 3,000 horses yearly by way of Qandahar largely formed the domain of Baluch tribesmen and the Sayyids of Pishin, who imported English goods when returning to Afghanistan.[280] A great part of the trade conducted with India via the Bolan Pass and Jalalabad was controlled by Hindu merchants and bankers with mercantile connections reaching as far as Astrakhan, Yarkand, Calcutta and Hyderabad. The center of their financial web was Shikarpur on the Indus, which had thrived particularly under the patronage of the Sadozais during the eighteenth century and remained one of the most important trading towns in the Indus region during the nineteenth century.[281]

Another important group participating in the trade between India and Bukhara were the so-called *powindas*,[282] Pashtun nomads who mostly made use of the Gomal Pass and passed through the district of Dera Isma'il Khan on their way to India.[283] The most famous group participating in the nomad trade were the Lohanis who were based in Daraban near Dera Isma'il Khan. The other groups migrating in significant numbers mostly belonged to the eastern Ghilzai tribes, such as the Nasirs, Kharotis, Sulaiman Khel and Tarakis. All these tribes followed a fairly firm pattern of migration, moving in a fixed order to India in fall and returning to Afghanistan in the same sequence in spring. In autumn, when snow began to appear on the summits of the Sulaiman mountains east of Ghazni, they began to assemble on the upper course of the Gomal river, forming groups of up to 15,000 fighting men for the purpose of mutual protection during the migration through the hostile Wazir country. Having arrived in the district of Dera Isma'il Khan, the nomads dispersed into smaller groups. After settling their families in winter camps some of the nomads stayed in the region, hiring out their pack animals as local carriers of salt, earth, bricks, firewood etc.. A great part of the men, however, continued on their way to India and proceeded southward to Sind, Karachi, Bombay, Deccan and Mysore or took the eastern route to Lahore, Amritsar, Delhi, Agra, Benares and Calcutta. Another group of nomad traders went to Multan, Bahawalpur and Rajputana. In the April or May the *powindas* gathered again and returned to their grazing grounds in Zurmat and the region between Ghazni and Qalat-i Ghilzai, many of them engaging in trade with Kabul, Bukhara and Samarqand.[284]

During Dost Muhammad Khan's reign about 9,400 *powinda* men accompanied by 35,000 camels entered India each year.[285] Controlling much of the trade with Bukhara in sheep-skin coats and drugs, the Lohanis were considered the richest group among the nomad traders. They also had the longest history of participation in the long-distance trade, claiming that it dated back to Ghaznawid times. Their role as merchants is clearly documented from the early Mughal period on. Next in line, the Daftanis were reputed to be the 'most enterprising' merchants, specializing on the trade in expensive Indian fabrics and indigo. The Sulaiman Khel were known as brokers and wholesale merchants who went as far as Calcutta to conduct their business. Their deadly enemies, the Kharotis, sent about half of their men to India as merchants. The Nasirs, forming the most numerous group among the *powindas*, were also the poorest and mostly made their living as local carriers.[286]

While it is evident that the nomad traders played a considerable role both in the local and overland trade, it is difficult to fix the exact proportion of trade controlled by them. In the winter of 1838/39, at a time when the traffic in the region was disrupted by Britain's military preparations for the First Anglo-Afghan War, 4,000 camel loads of fruit arrived in India.[287] In the early 1830s Lal observed that the yearly Lohani caravan providing Kabul and Bukhara with English and Indian goods consisted of 600–700 camels.[288] Vigne, who travelled across the Gomal Pass during the same period, was of the opinion that besides the Lohanis five or six caravans crossed the Hindu Kush for Bukhara each year.[289] Dost Muhammad Khan's military forces proceeding to Turkistan in 1838–39 were accompanied by a caravan of 1,600 camels and 600 pack horses, which carried merchandise worth two million rupees, yielding a transit duty of 50,000 rupees to the Amir.[290] The English and Russian goods disposed of in Kabul fetched a total of 300,000 and 200,000 rupees respectively.[291] In 1840 the entry of Afghan goods worth 157,137 Indian rupees was recorded in the custom houses of the North Western Province. During the same period Indian goods worth 308,985 Indian rupees were sent off to Kabul. Furthermore, a survey of the trading activities of Kabuli merchants in Delhi concluded that British manufactures and imported spices worth 886,000 rupees made their way to Afghanistan.[292] In 1862 Davies estimated the Bukharan trade items reaching Amritsar to be worth a total of 275,000 Indian rupees. The Indian goods sent to Bukhara via Kabul had a value of 750,000 Indian rupees. In Davies's opinion the total volume of trade between British India and Afghanistan hovered around the mark of three million rupees for both countries.[293]

En route between India and Turkistan the *powindas* traded part of their merchandise to the local population and thus also fulfilled, as Ghani puts it, 'the functions of a regular seasonal market'.[294] On the whole, however, the long-distance trade was focused on the urban centers and mainly consisted of luxury items. The difficult communications, the reliance on pack animals, as well as the duties and other fees exacted at numerous customs stations made trade in bulkgoods unprofitable. The trade passing through Afghanistan was impeded by formidable physical barriers, such as the Hindu Kush and the highlands of Hazarajat. The travellers using the ancient Bamiyan road to Balkh had to follow a circuitous route traversing four major passes ranging in altitude from 9,000 to 12,000 feet.[295] While these passes were subject to snowfall during winter, they were still more easily accessible than the more direct routes leading across the eastern part of the Hindu Kush.[296] The Khawak Pass linking Panjsher and Andarab, for example, was closed entirely by snow from December to June and was only frequented by local traders.[297] Hazarajat lying beyond the control of the Muhammadzai rulers of Kabul, the closest trade route to Herat led through Qandahar. Although the highroad linking Kabul and Qandahar bore no particular difficulties it was closed to traffic for two to four months during the year because of snow.[298] The road from Kabul to Jalalabad via Khurd Kabul, Haft Kotal, Jagdalak and Gandamak was practicable throughout the year but caravans rarely traveled it in January and February.[299] Wheeled transportation being virtually unknown in Afghanistan, all goods were transported by camels, horses, ponies and donkeys. A good camel could go three miles per hour, and an average horse covered four miles per hour.[300] The pace of the caravans generally varied between 8 and 25 miles per day.[301] Thus the distance of 191 miles between Kabul and Peshawar was covered in two weeks.[302] Bukhara, 829 miles distant from Peshawar, could be reached in thirty to forty days by the Bamiyan road.[303] The route between Bukhara and Herat via Maimana took 25 days.[304] The distance of 308 miles between Kabul and Qandahar was considered a journey of 15 days. Caravans travelling from Qandahar to Herat via Girishk, Farah and Sabzawar took 16–20 days to cover a distance of 400 miles.[305]

The limited scope of economic integration in Afghanistan was reflected by the diversity of the currencies and weights used in the various commercial centers. Yet an even greater impediment to a free flow of trade were the numerous customs stations which usually did not content themselves with levying the Islamic rate of 2½ per cent for the sake of *zakat* but harassed the merchants with further exactions. A common measure resorted to by the Amir's officials was to overestimate the value of the merchandise, thereby raising the custom dues considerably.[306] Such extortions were most pronounced in Qandahar during the reign of the 'Dil' brothers, entailing a total duty of ten per cent. In Herat the merchants had to pay duty at a rate of nine per cent during the 1840s. During the same period, the duty imposed in Kabul was comparatively lenient, only amounting to a total of four per cent.[307] At the time of Dost Muhammad Khan's first reign Lal counted no less than 14 customs stations within the confines of the Amir's small realm.[308] The independent chiefs located along the trade routes levied additional customs and fees for safe conduct. In the Khyber Pass, which was generally avoided by merchants in Dost Muhammad Khan's time, travellers had to pay dues in seven locations.[309] Caravans bound for Turkistan encountered 17 customs stations between Kabul and Tashqurghan.[310] Until their defeat in 1853 by Dost Muhammad Khan's forces, the Tokhis freely collected custom duties on the highroad between Muqur and Qandahar, thus ridiculing all claims to control advanced by the Qandahar Sardars.[311] On the trade route between Qandahar and Herat duties were levied 'every three or four stages'.[312] The trade route between Maimana and Herat was also known for the heavy duties levied there not only by the ruler of Herat but also independent Jamshedi chiefs. The extortionate policies of the Qandahar Sardars and the rulers of Herat led to a general decline of trade in southern Afghanistan. Many Hindu merchants left Qandahar, and the trade across the Bolan Pass almost came to a standstill. While the Lohani trade across the Gomal Pass continued to flourish it was directed towards Kabul rather than southern Afghanistan.[313] The few merchants passing through the principality of

Qandahar generally avoided entering the city for fear of exactions by the Sardars.[314] Burnes even reported that the traders carrying Kashmir shawls preferred to send their merchandise to Mashhad via Bukhara rather than face the vicissitudes of the trade route between Qandahar and Herat.[315] The difficulties besetting the trade in Afghanistan are also reflected by the fluctuation of prices from region to region. Whereas grain tended to be scarce in Kabul, it was 40 per cent cheaper in the markets of Afghan Turkistan, where demand was extremely low.[316] English fabrics from Bombay were disposed of at a profit of 100 per cent and more upon prime cost at Kabul and Qandahar. Once they made their way to Bukhara they fetched a profit as high as 150 per cent to 200 per cent upon prime cost. At Herat British articles sold at four times their original price.[317]

The caravan trade had little impact on the economic development of the rural areas along its routes. This is shown by the fact that barter was the main medium of exchange outside the urban trade centers. In Hazarajat, for example, only the regions in the vicinity of the town of Qandahar, Ghazni and Kabul were involved in trade. Yet even here the demand for foreign goods was extremely low, as only members of the local elite were able to acquire luxury items. Imports to Hazarajat, such as salt, sugar, gauze, chintz of Kabul, European fine calicoes, white piece goods, indigo and cochineal, only reached a volume of 10,000 rupees annually. All trade was conducted by barter, the basic unit of reckoning being sheep.[318] In Badakhshan, Qataghan and on the northern slopes of the Hazarajat cash currency also was hardly known, and the trade likewise catered to the needs of a small local elite.[319] Caravans travelling along any of the great trade routes of Afghanistan had to procure their provisions by barter because the silver and copper coins current in the towns were not accepted in the countryside. On the Bamiyan road the merchants even had to carry their own provisions.[320]

The turmoil accompanying the rise of the Muhammadzais in the 1820s disrupted the flow of trade. Caravans could be detained in one location for months at a time either because of political disturbances or the whims of the local rulers.[321] East of the Khyber, the high duties demanded by Ranjit Singh along the trade route from Lahore to Peshawar likewise had the effect of driving commerce 'into circuitous channels.'[322] As a new balance of power evolved among the principalities of Kabul, Qandahar and Herat in the course of the 1830s, commercial enterprise in Afghanistan also began to recover. Even so, the trade volume did not reach the level of Sadozai times. In the early nineteenth century the customs receipts of Kabul had decreased 25-fold as compared to the late eighteenth century, dropping from 600,000 to 700,000 rupees annually to 25,000 rupees.[323] In the 1830s Burnes credited Dost Muhammad Khan with giving the 'greatest encouragement' to trade. During his first reign the Amir was able to raise his custom receipts of Kabul city from 82,000 to 222,000 rupees per year.[324] The custom receipts from his entire realm amounted to 415,500 rupees.[325] Dost Muhammad Khan's trade policy mainly consisted of his efforts to render the traffic along the major trade routes safer. While he was unable to bring the Khyber Pass under his control even during his second reign, he successfully secured the region between Kabul and Jalalabad by suppressing plundering raids in Jagdalak. On the trade route to Turkistan the Amir put an end to raids by the Shaikh 'Ali Hazaras in the area between Saighan and Kahmard.[326] After the incorporation of Qandahar into the Amir's realm the highroad leading to Kabul was considered generally safe, allowing caravans to travel unarmed day and night. The only exception was Haidar Khel north of Ghazni, were occasional plundering raids continued to occur. All highwaymen apprehended in the district of Ghazni were sent to Kabul and summarily executed in order to discourage disturbances.[327] Between Ghazni and Qalat-i Ghilzai small posts were established which served to protect travellers and to shelter twelve sets of postal runners who were said to be able to convey messages between Kabul and Qandahar within four days.[328]

The relative profitability of the trade in Dost Muhammad Khan's time is reflected by the fact a number of his relatives entered commercial enterprises through agents. Besides his function as the governor of Afghan Turkistan, Sardar Muhammad Afzal was also active as the largest trader in the region north of the Hindu Kush. He made a considerable profit by buying up all the cotton and silk produced in his province and selling it to the merchants of Afghanistan and Turkistan. In Kabul, his wife was known to engage in commercial speculations. The Amir's wife, Bibi Khadija (the mother of Sardar Muhammad Akbar Khan) likewise entered trade ventures. Other members of the Amir's family who were active in this manner were his half brother Sardar Pir Muḥammad Khan, his nephews Muhammad 'Usman Khan b. Nawwab Samad Khan and 'Abd al-Ghani Khan b. Nawwab Jabbar Khan, as well as his grandnephew Shahdaula Khan b. Nawwab Muhammad Zaman Khan.[329] The Amir thus had a vested interest in encouraging the trade in his realm. But while his efforts to prevent disturbances along the trade routes were fairly successful, he was unable to eliminate robberies altogether and even his own caravans were sometimes subject to depredations. In early 1859, for example, one of Muhammad Afzal Khan's caravans carrying merchandise as well as dried fruits and presents intended for the king lost all its goods and eight men to robbers from Ghorband.[330]

The consolidation of Dost Muhammad Khan's authority restored a certain measure of confidence among the merchants. Yet, beyond establishing a fair degree of security, the Amir pursued no particular economic policy to speak of. Moreover, the merchants engaging in long-distance trade found themselves subject to the whims of the Amir, his sons and officials once they had reached Kabul or one of the provinical capitals. In the 1830s Lal observed that extortions were the order of the day:

> The Amir has encouraged commerce indeed, but yet he has often forcibly extorted large sums of money from the merchants, wherewith to maintain his troops for sake of the extension and stability of his government. Whenever traders with shawls from Kashmir, or horses from Bokhara, pass on their way through Kabul, the Amir avails himself of the first description of the articles, and of the animals, and giving no value to all the cries of the owner, he pays any sum he likes; which, of course, is much less than the original price. The merchants bring a great quantity of gold in Russian ducats, and the Bokhara tilas for Amrat Sar and India... They bring these openly in the smallest quantity only, for fear of being seized by the Amir; and being thus forced they practise smuggling.[331]

The few recorded active efforts of the government to influence prices in the urban bazaars were directed at the local suppliers and took the crudest form possible. In the 1830s Dost Muhammad Khan threatened to 'grill some bakers in their own ovens' for short-weighing their Kabuli customers.[332] At times of scarcity prices were fixed in an arbitrary manner in order to prevent hoarding of grain, meat and fodder. If the traders resisted this policy they ran the risk of harsh physical punishment. During the final phase of the First Anglo-Afghan War, for example, Nawwab Jabbar Khan resorted to the following measure:

> The Navab sent for one man belonging to each of the different trades, as one butcher, one grass and grain seller, &c., and persuaded them to sell cheap, so as not to produce famine. They made an excuse, that their supply or store of grain is not in the vicinity, and that to bring it into the market requires a longer notice. The Navab gave no heed to such excuses, but ordered his men to pierce an iron nail through the corner of the trader's ear; and then in the case of the butcher, to fasten the point of it in the block of wood over which he used to hang the killed sheep in his shop. Thus he was forced to stand there for a whole day, passing a stream of blood from his ear; and the meat was next morning so cheap as to be within the reach of all classes. Such was the example put upon all traders, and the effect was satisfactory.[333]

Despite all the problems besetting commercial enterprises in Afghanistan the profits to be made once a caravan had reached its destination apparently were incentive enough for a fair flow of trade. According to Rathjens, the trade in Afghanistan flowered for a final time in the first half of the nineteenth century, as the modus vivendi which had developed between the interests of the government, the local chiefs and the caravans allowed all concerned to enjoy a measure of profit. Commercial activities only began to decline seriously in the second half of the nineteenth century when the trade between Turkistan and India ceased and the construction of a railway through Baluchistan made the transit trade through Afghanistan unattractive.[334]

SUMMARY

In this chapter I have argued that the 'consolidation' of Dost Muhammad Khan's power was not accompanied by a corresponding process of political and economic centralization. Instead, the organization of the Amir's government mirrored, and formed and extension of, the existing relationships of power which had become entrenched during the Sadozai period. Given the relative strength and status of the local leadership, the circumstances of Dost Muhammad Khan's reign are better viewed in the light of political segmentation and a concomitant economic fragmentation than by notions of linear growth or decline.

Dost Muhammad Khan departed from the example of his Sadozai predecessors by curtailing the role of the Pashtun elite in the organization of his government. Nevertheless the concentration of nearly all administrative and military power in the hands of his immediate family did not improve his ability to tap local resources of revenue and manpower. The distribution of provincial governorships and army divisions among the sons of the Amir engendered an equal, if not greater, amount of decentralization as compared to the Sadozai period. Apart from imposing previously unheard-of tax assessments on the Durranis and the Hotak and Tokhi Ghilzais, Dost Muhammad Khan found himself unable to change the system of service grants and tax exemptions inherited from the Sadozai era. The Amir's efforts to raise men and revenues concentrated on the regions most easily accessible from his base in Kabul. Beyond the highroads, however, his claims to control became more tenuous. His frustrations in attempting to open up sources of revenue are reflected by his often quoted description of Afghanistan as a country that produced little but men and stones.[335] The surplus generated at the village level was mostly redistributed locally and remained beyond the reach of the government. While there were plenty of men, they would not be harnessed to the vehicle of government but rather obstructed its progress by evading revenue payments, insisting on traditional privileges, or even clamoring for royal subsidies.

The overall decentralization of the Amir's government and the restricted nature of his cash funds is also documented by another element taken over from Sadozai times, the remuneration of soldiers on the basis of written assignments entitling them to collect a certain amount of local produce in the countryside. Of the revenue which did reach the royal treasury, a great part was expended on allowances for the numerous members of the royal family who had no immediate access to profitable government offices. Because of the chronic lack of funds the Amir's administration resembled a series of makeshift arrangements, constantly putting his negotiating skills and claims to leadership to test. His difficulties in drawing together adequate resources also affected the organization of his army. Aware that the idea of Muhammadzai sovereignty could only be impressed by the threatened or ongoing presence of troops, Dost Muhammad Khan concentrated most of the available funds on the upkeep and reorganization of his military forces. Even so, the efforts required for the maintenance of large numbers of soldiers during major military campaigns usually exceeded his resources. As a rule, the soldiers had to do without regular salaries and resorted to plunder for their upkeep.

Chapter 5
CONCLUSION

In the preceding pages I have attempted to reconstruct the political landscape of Afghanistan during the reign of the first Muhammadzai king, Amir Dost Muhammad Khan. Dost Muhammad Khan's rise to power was occasioned by the shift of authority from one powerful Durrani subdivision to another which began during the early years of the nineteenth century. While the Sadozai dynasty, which had furnished the kings of Afghanistan since 1747, remained in power until 1818, Dost Muhammad Khan's family under the leadership of Fatih Khan Muhammadzai was able to increase its hold over government affairs gradually from the turn of the century on. Characterized by a great amount of administrative and political decentralization, the disintegration of the Sadozai empire was hastened by rivalries between two sets of royal brothers, Shah Zaman and Shah Shuja' on the one hand and Shah Mahmud on the other. This process intensified following Fatih Khan's death and the deposal of Shah Mahmud in 1818 as similar power struggles erupted among Fatih Khan's remaining brothers. With Dost Muhammad Khan's seizure of Kabul in 1826 a sort of equilibrium was reestablished between the contending parties. In the course of these events the Sadozai empire, which had included Nishapur in the west and Kashmir, Punjab and Sind in the east during the period of its greatest extension, broke up into a number of principalities. The regions east of the Khyber Pass fell to the Sikh empire. In the 1830s Dost Muhammad Khan's sphere of influence was limited to Kabul, Kohistan, Jalalabad and Ghazni. His half brothers, the Sardars of Qandahar, controlled a principality of equal size in southern Afghanistan, while Herat became the dominion of Shah Mahmud and his son Kamran. During the same period the Uzbek khanates of Lesser Turkistan reasserted their independence. Eastern Turkistan, including Badakhshan, was the scene of a continuously changing balance of power between the Muitan and Qataghan Uzbek chiefs. Further west, in the so-called Chahar Wilayat, Maimana held a leading position.

After the First Anglo-Afghan War of 1839–1842 Dost Muhammad Khan concentrated his efforts on extending his sphere of authority. In this endeavor he received British backing, in particular subsequent to the conclusion of the Anglo-Afghan Treaty of 1855, although the Amir's military activities had begun as early as 1849 with the conquest of Balkh. By the time of his death, all of Lesser Turkistan, with the exception of Maimana and Badakhshan had been incorporated into his realm. In the region south of Kabul the Amir began to encroach on the sphere of interest of the Sardars of Qandahar by extending his authority over the Hotak and Tokhi Ghilzais in 1853. In November 1855 a dispute over the right to leadership broke out between the last remaining Qandahar Sardar Rahmdil Khan and his nephew Muhammad Sadiq Khan, thus providing Dost Muhammad Khan with an opportunity to annex the principality of Qandahar to his dominion. Finally on 27 May 1863, barely two weeks prior to his death, the Amir was able to gain control of Herat.

Dost Muhammad Khan's successful consolidation of power allowed him, roughly speaking, to lay claim to the regions forming present-day Afghanistan. The loss of the eastern provinces of Sind, Punjab and Kashmir, which used to furnish the bulk of the income of the Sadozai kings, forced him to exert greater pressure on the groups living in Afghanistan proper. Even so, his authority was far from absolute. The Hazaras, who had remained largely untouched by efforts to raise revenues and soldiers during the Sadozai period, successfully continued to ward off any sustained Muhammadzai interference in their central regions. Dost Muhammad Khan was only able to raise revenues in the Hazara regions bordering immediately on the provinces of Kabul, Ghazni and Qandahar. Further north, the prominent leadership of Lesser Turkistan, such as the Ming Uzbeks of Maimana and the Qataghan Uzbeks of Qunduz had also retained their influential position during the Sadozai period. The revenue payments submitted by them were of a purely nominal nature and did not even suffice to cover the expenses of the local administration. With Dost Muhammad Khan's invasion of this region the Afghan presence in Lesser Turkistan became stronger and more intrusive than during the Sadozai era. In the regions forming the core of Afghan control, that is Tashqurghan, Mazar-i Sharif, Balkh, Aqcha, Sar-i Pul and Shibarghan, the traditional leadership was superseded by Muhammadzai governors. Qunduz was also forced to pay revenues directly to Afghan officials. Even so, the local elite was not displaced entirely and reemerged during the power struggle which broke out among Dost Muhammad Khan's sons in 1863. In the regions which did remain under direct Muhammadzai control the local elite also continued to play a preponderant role in administrative and military matters.

Unlike the Hazaras and Uzbeks, the Pashtuns, foremost among them the Durranis, had cooperated closely with the Sadozai kings in the administration of the Durrani empire. Acting as military commanders, court officials and provincial governors, the prominent Pashtun leaders received sizeable service grants variously called *jagir*, *suyurghal* and *tiyul*, which in turn enhanced the respect they enjoyed among their fellow tribesmen. The latter partook to a certain degree in the privileges accorded to their chiefs, enjoying lenient revenue assessments, if they were subject to any form of revenue payment at all. The Durranis owed their special position among the Pashtuns largely to the policies of Nadir Shah Afshar and Ahmad Shah Sadozai. Holding a great part of their lands as service grants, they interacted closely with the Sadozai rulers and were entitled to the most influential government positions. While Ahmad Shah's successors Timur Shah and Shah Zaman made some efforts to curb their power, the Durrani leaders retained a great measure of influence in the political affairs of Kabul and Qandahar until the time of Dost Muhammad Khan. The emergence of the prominent Durrani families and the leading lineages of other Pashtun tribes can be traced to the late sixteenth and early seventeenth centuries. Located on the periphery of the Safawid and Mughal empires, the Pashtun tribes controlling the highroads linking Herat, Qandahar, Kabul and Peshawar enjoyed the lasting attention of the imperial powers vying for control in the region. In exchange for their cooperation in keeping the lines of communication open, local chiefs were officially awarded the leadership over their tribes, received service grants and were allowed to maintain their own troops. Functioning as a sort of subsidiary government in regions where state control was weak, they often were also entitled to levy transit dues and to collect revenues from the surrounding tribes. While the material benefits accompanying their appointment helped individual chiefs to further their claims to authority among their fellow tribesmen, the royal recognition of their leadership position as hereditary encouraged the emergence of entrenched leading lineages with a strong sense of the privileges historically 'due' to them by all those advancing claims to royal supremacy. The privileged status of these leading lineages was enhanced during the Sadozai period, as their role in the acquisition and administration of the Indian provinces further fostered their view of themselves as partners or rivals, rather than subjects, of the Sadozai rulers.

There is little information regarding the exact position of these leading lineages within their respective tribal groups. The available data strongly suggest that the claims to hereditary leadership advanced by these *khan khels* were generally accepted by their fellow tribesmen. The leadership of the Morcha Khel Mohmands, and the Hotak and Tokhi Ghilzais, for example, continued to rest within one family throughout the eighteenth and nineteenth centuries. Challenges to the power of an appointed chief only had a chance of receiving wide tribal backing if the contender was a member of the leading lineage, possibly belonging to a branch split off on the basis of rivalry between paternal cousins or half brothers. The leading lineages also tended to be set apart from their tribal fellows by considerable wealth derived from tolls and/or landed estates. The leadership of the

Morcha Khel Mohmands furnishes an excellent example of the fact that powerful tribal leaders used their income to act like miniature kings, doling out generous allowances in order to secure the allegiance of the surrounding tribes and developing small-scale administrations involving the employment of revenue collectors and mounted troops. The internal hierarchization fostered by a close connection with the court was most pronounced among the Durranis, where the tribal leadership was far removed socially and economically from the lower echelons of tribal organization. But even in such a stratified setting the ideal of tribal equality was not abandoned entirely, as all men were at least theoretically entitled to participate in the political affairs of their tribe. While Pashtun tribal structures allowed for the emergence of a powerful leadership, the resulting socioeconomic structure nowhere approximated to a feudal setting as known from Europe, in which politics and violence were the exclusive prerogative of a small warrior stratum.[1] Serfdom, another typical aspect of European feudalism, was practically unknown in Afghanistan.[2]

In the nineteenth century British observers and Afghan monarchs alike cast the Pashtun tribesmen as ignorant and unruly 'hillmen' who resisted all civilizing efforts exerted by government. While arguing from the tribal perspective, more recent anthropological studies tend to reinforce this notion of the 'untrammelled' Pashtun. In the light of the theory of segmentary lineage organization as elaborated by Evans-Pritchard, Sahlins and Gellner, the Pashtun tribes are viewed as highly egalitarian societies resilient to a lasting stratification. My analysis shows that the Pashtun tribes located in the regions beyond the immediate influence of the king, such as the so-called border tribes and the Kharoti and Sulaiman Khel Ghilzais indeed fit this image closely in the nineteenth century. Yet the groups feared most by Amir Dost Muhammad Khan as potentially 'troublesome' were the powerful, entrenched lineages controlling the trade routes east and south of Kabul. Given their long history of interaction with ruling dynasties, these influential chiefs were less interested in avoiding government contact than using it to their advantage in order to maximize their influence locally and at court. One major problem Dost Muhammad Khan faced in his effort to establish authority over these groups was the question of legitimacy. While his family had played a prominent role under the Sadozais, other tribal groups, among them the Hotak Ghilzais, could point to a similarly illustrious past. In their rebellions during the 1850s, the Tokhis and Hotaks, as well as Muhammad Shah Khan Babakr Khel, advanced separate claims to royal authority, arguing that the Amir's power was ill-gotten. But beyond easily evoked historical grudges the main motivation behind these uprisings seems to have been the fear of losing existing privileges, as the Amir found himself unable, and unwilling, to continue the policies of his Sadozai predecessors unaltered. The loss of the income derived from the former eastern provinces, combined with Dost Muhammad Khan's efforts to concentrate all power in the hands of his immediate family, left little room for extra favors to be handed out to the tribal elite. On the other hand, the prevailing distribution of power provided few opportunities for the Amir to open up new sources of revenue or to change the existing tax assessments in a significant manner. The need to strike a balance between control and conciliation thus became a more precarious undertaking than at any time during the Sadozai era.

In the Amir's policies several regional patterns may be observed. The regions bordering on Kabul, Jalalabad and Ghazni bore the greatest amount of pressure for revenues and soldiers. While the non-Pashtun groups were subject to the highest revenue rates in the country, the Pashtun groups inhabiting the region south of Kabul, such as the Wardaks and the Ahmadzai, Andar and Taraki Ghilzais were also generally characterized as 'obedient' to the government. At times these groups raised objections to tax impositions considered oppressive. In general, however, the tribal leadership found that it had little opportunity to maneuver vis-à-vis the government, and the revenue collection as such did not pose any serious problems in this region. The prominent Pashtun groups located along the trade route to Peshawar, by contrast, continued to enjoy certain privileges, if on a somewhat reduced scale compared to the Sadozai period. The Khyber tribes collected royal allowances in exchange for their avowed allegiance to the Amir. In reality, however, they assumed a more or less independent position, riding the tide between competing Muhammadzai and British interests. Closer to Kabul, the leaders of the Baezai and Morcha Khel Mohmands and the Jabbar Khel and Babakr Khel Ghilzais were more reliable allies of the Amir. At Dost Muhammad Khan's time Sa'adat Khan Morcha Khel and 'Aziz Khan Jabbar Khel maintained a close relationship with the court which was cemented by marriage alliances. While the Amir depended on the assistance of powerful tribal leaders to give substance to his claims of authority along the trade route between Kabul and Dakka, he also was vigilant in keeping them in check lest they use their power contrary to the interests of the government. This was the case with Muhammad Shah Khan Babakr Khel of Laghman, who, for Dost Muhammad Khan's taste, had concentrated too much power in his hands during the First Anglo-Afghan War, in great part due to his close connection with the Amir's son, Muhammad Akbar Khan. Subsequent to his return to power, Dost Muhammad Khan sought to remove Muhammad Shah Khan from the political arena, thus provoking him to engage in a lengthy rebellion. During the reign of Dost Muhammad Khan's successor Sher 'Ali Khan, the uprising of Nauroz Khan b. Sa'adat Khan Morcha Khel followed a similar pattern. Although both leaders in question largely owed their powerful position to court patronage, they turned into dangerous enemies once the Amir took active steps to curtail their power. Using their local influence to paralyze the trade passing through their regions, they proved to the king how fragile his claims to authority were outside the gates of Kabul. On a practical level, these rebellions impeded the flow of traffic and revenues. But beyond this they served as a constant reminder to the king that he was only one of many players in a game that constantly put his claims to leadership to a test.

Unlike the Jabbar Khel and Babakr Khel of the Kabul watershed, the Hotak and Tokhi Ghilzais inhabiting the region south of Muqur were famous for the critical distance they assumed in relation to the Sadozai and Muhammadzai rulers alike. Pointing to their role as conquerors of Isfahan, the Hotaks in particular advanced separate claims to kingship whenever they felt bypassed in the political process. Throughout the eighteenth century, the insistence of the Hotaks and Tokhis on a privileged position had been heeded by the Sadozai rulers. With the decline of the Sadozai empire in the early nineteenth century, however, these two groups were quick to rebel. It is not clear whether the Tokhi/Hotak uprising of 1801–2 was linked to any concrete loss of privileges but it seems to have been directed at least partially against the growing role of the Muhammadzais in government affairs. With the emergence of the competing Muhammadzai principalities of Kabul and Qandahar in the 1820s, the Hotaks and Tokhis asserted their independence. They were only incorporated into Dost Muhammad Khan's kingdom in 1853 when the governor of Ghazni successfully subjected them to the first regular tax assessment in their historical memory. Although considered oppressive by the groups concerned, the Amir's policies were limited to the imposition of new taxes and did not succeed in undermining the standing of the existing leadership.

Having traditionally identified most closely with the Sadozais, the Durrani groups resident in the vicinity of Qandahar were the ones most negatively affected by the rise of the Muhammadzais. The Muhammadzai Barakzai rulers of Qandahar, who held sway in southern Afghanistan between 1818 and 1855, formed a subdivision of the Durranis. Nonetheless they had little interest in sustaining the former state-supporting elite, which, if powerful enough, would have been able to challenge their right to rule. During the period prior to the First Anglo-Afghan War they disbanded the Durrani cavalry, divested the prominent noble families of their offices in the administration of Qandahar, and deprived the landholders within their immediate reach of their former tax-exempt status, thus placing them on the same footing as the non-Durrani tax-paying groups in the region. Only the tribes located at a certain distance from Qandahar, such as the 'Alizais of Zamindawar, the Nurzais and Popalzais of Nish, Tirin and Deh Raud, were able to retain a powerful position vis-à-vis the government and to resist tax collections successfully. Enjoying close genealogical links with the Sardars of Qandahar, the Barakzai tribe suffered no losses in income or political status and prospered instead. Subsequent to the annexation of Qandahar in 1855 Dost Muhammad Khan continued the policies of his half brothers. The transferral of power from the greater group of Durranis to the

Muhammadzai subdivision is reflected by the fact that the title *sardar*, previously a military rank awarded to the most prominent Durrani leaders of all tribal affiliations, now came to be reserved almost exclusively for the members of Dost Muhammad Khan's family. In spite of these reverses the Durrani elite was by no means eliminated as a political force and its members continued to exert influence on the political life of the country well into the twentieth century.

The circumstances accompanying Dost Muhammad Khan's rise to power forced him to 'meddle' with the Pashtun tribes of his domain to an unprecedented degree. With the shrinking of funds available as compensation for tribal loyalty and the concentration of the highest military and administrational offices in the hands of the Amir's immediate family, a great part of the tribal elite was deprived of its former avenues to wealth and power. At the same time, the Amir was unable to change the distribution of power between center and periphery in a significant manner. Just as in Sadozai times, the administration was characterized by a high degree of decentralization. While feared for his autrocatic power in Kabul and vicinity, the Amir had little control over the internal administration of his provinces, receiving only a fraction of the surplus produced locally. Dost Muhammad Khan's efforts to open up new sources of revenue only met with limited success. Apart from tax increases imposed on the Hazara regions close to Kabul, the only groups subject to new tax assessments on a significant scale were the Durranis and the Hotak and Tokhi Ghilzais. The other Pashtun tribes were mostly able to safeguard the lenient rates of revenue they had been accustomed to since the time of Ahmad Shah Sadozai. Another problem the Amir encountered in his administration was the lack of manpower. A great part of the royal army was distributed in the provinces. But even in the regions forming the core of his realm a steady presence of the king or his officials and their troops was required to create the semblance of order. More often than not, revenue collections took the form of military campaigns, and, once the troops withdrew with the supplies collected, the local communities were suffered to relapse into their 'natural' order. At times when large forces had to be assembled for the Amir's major military campaigns to Turkistan, Qandahar and Herat, the troops available for the routine procedures of administration shrank significantly, inviting local resistance to revenue collection and allowing ongoing uprisings to gain in scope.

Given the limited scope of his administrative control, the Amir sought to extend his reach into the tribal areas by a web of personal alliances reinforced by marriage ties. Favoring for the most part prominent Pashtun, Kohistani and Qizilbash families, this policy had the effect of strengthening, rather than weakening, certain segments of the local leadership. But even in those cases where Dost Muhammad Khan assumed a hostile attitude towards tribal groups he was unable to change their internal organization in a significant manner. Certainly the role of the influential Pashtun chiefs changed in the early Muhammadzai era. During the Sadozai period they had enjoyed an intimate connection with the ruling family, using court patronage as a stepping-stone for entering the highest echelons of the administration and the military apparatus, thus furthering their influence among their fellow tribesmen. With the general restriction of avenues to power during the period of Dost Muhammad Khan, the political role of the Pashtun chiefs devolved to a lower level of administration. While no longer acting as supreme commanders, the *khans* continued to play a fairly influential role as military leaders of their respective tribal contingents in the Amir's cavalry. The participation of non-Muhammadzai Pashtun officials in the administration of Lesser Turkistan is documented in Kushkaki's gazetteer of Qataghan and Badakhshan. In their capacity as local middlemen, the Pashtun leaders continued to negotiate the terms of contact between the government and their fellow tribesmen.

Despite these relative shifts in power the members of the entrenched leading lineages were able to defend their historical claims to leadership both in relationship to the king and within their tribe. Their role was not only defined by their present ability to fulfill the criteria considered necessary for effective leadership but also by a sense of hereditary legitimacy. The historical past of a tribe thus continued to inform its organization in the present. On one level, the historical role of the tribal leadership continued to be reflected by its comparative wealth and status. On another, the political behavior expected of this leadership was guided by the ongoing interpretation of past events. The formation and formulation of tribal identity reached back into the past, fixing instances of opposition to, or agreement with, government to generally known historical junctures. The strategies adopted by a tribe thus were not only influenced by the political exigencies of a given moment but also by a strong sense of the 'proper' mode of dealing with the government. Acting as miniature kings, the *khans* controlling the major trade routes used their local standing and their hereditary status as bargaining positions with the Amir. My research shows that the interaction between these tribes and the state is better understood as the product of historical relationships of power rather than an inherent state of 'dissidence'. For the greater group of the Pashtuns, I have demonstrated in a number of case studies that the interplay of historical, ecological and socioeconomic factors created a variety of tribal settings, allowing each group in question to develop a specific political profile in its relationship with the government. 'Tribalism' thus remains a complex phenomenon, and any attempt to capture it carries the risk of confusing a part for the whole or of freezing the organization of a tribe in space and time.

NOTES

INTRODUCTION

1 Canfield 1986: 80.
2 Waller 1990: 24.
3 Singer 1984: 99.
4 Poullada 1973: 28–29.
5 Janata 1975: 17.
6 cf. Grevemeyer 1990: 34.
7 *Waqi'at-i Shah Shuja'*; for a German translation see Zimmermann 1842: 181–201.
8 Lord 1839a: 104.
9 Minute by Governor General Dalhousie, 26 June 1855 (For. Sec. 31 August 1855 No. 53)
10 Edwardes to Temple 5 March 1856 (L/P&S/5/227 No. 16 of 22 April 1856 p. 358); Edwardes to Temple 17 May 1856 (L/P&S/5/227 No. 23 of 3 June 1856 pp. 679–684); Edwardes to Temple 9 June 1856 (L/P&S/5/228 No. 28 of 17 July 1858 pp. 30–43); Edwardes to Temple 26 August 1856 (L/P&S/5/228 No. 43 pp. 721–732)
11 Hall 1981: Appendix III; KN 11 April 1857 (L/P&S/5/232 No. 44 of 29 July 1857 p. 632); KD 13–21 October 1860 (For. Pol. B. December 1860 No. 531)
12 Bellew 1862: 221, 241.
13 QM 1 May 1857 (For. Sec. 30 April 1858 No. 31)
14 Richard Pollock quoted in Northbrook to Salisbury 7 June 1875 (L/P&S/7/4 Part I No. 19 of 7 June 1875 p. 3)
15 Lindholm 1980: 360.

1 AMIR DOST MUHAMMAD KHAN'S FIRST REIGN

1 At the beginning of the nineteenth century, the Qajars only controlled Mashhad (conquered in 1802), but by 1816, Fath 'Ali Shah (r. 1797–1834) was able to extend his control over Nishapur, Kuchan, Bujnerd, Tabas, Turbat i Haidaria, and Qa'in. (Ferrier 1858: 151–152)
2 Ranjit Singh's conquests proceeded in the following manner: Attock (1813), Multan (1818), Kashmir (1819), Dera Ghazi Khan (1819), Dera Isma'il Khan (1821), and Peshawar (1823).
3 Singh 1981: 318. Lahore was temporarily regained in 1797 and 1798.
4 The outcome of this battle, which took place in May 1818, was inconclusive. Iranian authors and Harawi, who resided at Mashhad, claim that the Qajar

army was victorious. (Champagne 1981: 84–85; Harawi 1990: 17–18) According to other accounts, the Afghan troops only gave up the pursuit of the fleeing Iranians after Fatih Khan Muhammadzai had been hit by a spent bullet. (Ferrier 1858: 147–157; Reshtia 1957: 28; Reshtia 1990: 53–54; ST 92–96)

5 Lockhart 1958: 87–97; Tate 1973: 41–43.

6 Elphinstone 1972 II: 99.

7 Singh 1981: 9–11, 270–271; ST 25.

8 The two Alikozais in question were Hukumat Khan and Muhammad 'Azim Khan, son of Mir Hazar Khan (one of Ahmad Shah's officers). (Reshtia 1957: 7) ST lists only Muhammad 'Azim Khan. (ST: 59–60)

9 Bellew 1973: 163; Masson 1974 III: 41.

10 According to Harawi and Faiz Muhammad, both Shah Mahmud and 'Ata Muhammad died in 1244/1828–9. (Harawi 1990: 23; ST 113) Ferrier places 'Ata Muhammad's death in 1830. (Ferrier 1858: 173)

11 Ferrier 1857: 145–146; Fofalzai 1958: 333–334, 351; Lal 1977: 107, 163 164; Reshtia 1957: 50–51; ST 190; TSu 284–288.

12 Elphinstone 1972 II: 97; Ferrier 1858: 67, 94; Singh 1981: 347–438.

13 Fofalzai 1958: 234–240, 243; Gankovsky 1985: 121; Husaini 1967: 26–27; Singh 1981: 29; ST: 10, 46, 61–62; TSu 172–173.

14 Fofalzai 1958: 221–225.

15 Ferrier 1858: 81–97; Ghani 1982: 365–366; Rashad 1967: 35–44; Singh 1981: 29, 99; ST 10, 16, 55.

16 According to Husaini, Sher Muhammad Khan was appointed to the leadership of the entire Durrani confederacy. (Husaini 1967: 27–28) Fofalzai, by contrast is of the opinion that the Durrani kings were unable to appoint outsiders to the leadership of tribal groups. Sher Muhammad Khan being a Bamizai, he was able to become chief of the Bamizais but not of the whole Durrani tribe. (Fofalzai 1958: 231, 238)

17 Fofalzai 1958: 229–233; Fofalzai 1967: 174–176; Ghubar 1981: 392–393; Raverty 1888: 57; Reshtia 1957: 13; Shah Shuja''s autobiography in Zimmermann 1842: 187–188; ST 46, 52–53, 62.

18 Muhammad 'Ali Khan Ayub (?) Bashi in Elphinstone Collection F 88 13 Kt, p. 191; Strachey, 'Revenue and Trade', f. 9.

19 Ghubar 1981: 395; Masson 1974 III: 43; ST 73–74; Na'imi, Appendix. In Kashmiri 1951: 243; Shah Shuja''s autobiography in Zimmermann 1842: 192 193, 195. Fofalzai attributes this rebellion to the fact that Sher Muhammad Khan felt that he was about to lose his influential position at Shah Shuja''s court to Muhammad Akram Khan Bamizai (Amin al-Mulk). After his death Akram Khan took over the administration of Sind. (Fofalzai 1958: 233–234; Strachey, 'Revenue and Trade', f. 9.)

20 The dates given for Fatih Khan's conquest of Kashmir are variously given as 1811 (Ferrier 1858: 148; Sykes 1981 I: 389–390), 1813 (Dupree 1980: 351; Ghubar 1981: 401; Reshtia 1957: 23) and 1815/16 (TSu 193–197).

21 Lal 1978 I: 106–107; 110–113; Masson 1974 III: 43–46; ST 100.

22 Reshtia 1957:1. Burnes' estimate of 60,000 Muhammadzai families in the 1830s is doubted by other authors. (Burnes 1834 II: 342; Hough 1841: 402)

23 Ferrier 1858: 120; Fofalzai 1967: 645; Gankovsky 1985: 121.

24 According to Lal, Reshtia and Sultan Muhammad Barakzai, Rahimdad Khan was relieved of his position due to complaints of fellow Barakzais (such as Mihrab Khan and Kado Khan) that he did not live up to the qualities of hospitality and mediation traditionally required of a Pashtun chief. (Lal 1978

I:11–12; Reshtia 1957: 3; Reshtia 1990: 12–13; TSu 151–52). Fofalzai, on the other hand, attributes Timur Shah's choice of Payinda Khan to his personal rivalry with Rahimdad Khan and the fact that he was married to one of Payinda Khan's sisters. (Fofalzai 1958: 240; Fofalzai 1967: 174n, 646–647)

25 Reshtia 1957:3–4. Certain tribal groups, such as the Ghilzais, Safis, Turis, etc., which were not administered as part of the 18 provinces of the Sadozai empire, were placed under the control of Durrani *sardars*, who did not reside in the areas apportioned to them but collected revenue. The *sardars* also assumed the military command over these tribal units at times of war. (Elphinstone 1972 II: 256, 269) Fofalzai quotes a *farman* of 1787 which entitles Payinda Khan to farm the revenues of the Ghilzais (*mustaʾjiri-yi maliyat-i taʾifa-yi Ghilzai*). (Fofalzai 1967: 647) In the nineteenth century, the term 'Ghilzai' referred not to the entire Ghilzai confederation but was used as an administrational term for the Pashtun portion of of Laghman, which was partly inhabited by Babakr Khel and Jabbar Khel Ghilzais and partly by Tajiks. (Ghubar 1981: 516; Masson 1974 III: 52; Reshtia 1957: 45, 52; Reshtia 1990: 78, 89; ST 108; Warburton 1880: 4–5) At the beginning of the nineteenth century the Ghilzais of Laghman had to furnish two thousand soldiers to the royal army. (Information by Muhammad 'Azim Baraki, Elphinstone Collection, F88 13Kt) Lal also mentions a Ghilzai contingent in the army. During his first reign Shah Shuja' attempted to win over Payinda Khan's son Fatih Khan by offering him the military command over this division. (Lal 1978 I: 39)

26 Fofalzai 1958: 305; Reshtia 1957: 4–5; Reshtia 1990: 15. The exact nature of this leadership is not clear. Was Payinda Khan in control of the revenue collection among all these groups? The figure of 80,000 rupees given by Reshtia for Payinda Khan's salary seems improbable when compared to Fofalzai's claim that the highest military commanders at the rank of *sardar* and *nawwab* received yearly 500,000 rupees under Shah Zaman. Ghulam Sarwar, who visited Shah Zaman's court in 1793–95 reported that Payinda Khan and his relatives governed Dera Ghazi Khan, Ghazni and Ghorband. (Gupta 1944: 273, 276)

27 According to Reshtia, kingship was to become an elective office. (1957: 7; 1990: 18). As the plot was hatched at the residence of Miyan Ghulam Muhammad, an *'alim* from Lahore resident at Qandahar, Ghubar concludes that it was encouraged by the British government. In his opinion, the plan was to place Shahzada Mahmud on the throne (Ghubar 1981: 386) Based on documents available at the court of Bahawalpur, Ali's account of this plot assigns a central role to Fatih Khan b. Payinda Khan, who had become a disciple of Miyan Ghulam Muhammad. According to this narrative, the conflict between Fatih Khan and Wafadar Khan was sparked by the hostile attitude of the Qandahari ulama to Miyan Ghulam Muhammad. (Ali 1848: 98 100) While the list of the participants varies with each author, *Siraj al tawarikh*, *Tarikh-i Sultani*, Ghubar and Reshtia agree on the following actors: Payinda Khan, Muhammad 'Azim Khan Alikozai, Nur Muhammad Khan Babar Amin al-Mulk, Islam Khan Popalzai, Hikmat Khan Sarkani, and Arsalan (or Aslan) Khan Jawansher. Others mentioned are Muhammad Rahim Khan 'Alizai, Sultan Khan Nurzai, Khizr Khan 'Alizai, Zaman Khan Popalzai, Ja'far 'Ali Khan Jawansher, and Yusuf 'Ali Khan (chief of eunuchs). (Ferrier 1858:122; Fofalzai 1967: 367; Ghubar 1981: 386; Reshtia 1957: 5–7; Reshtia 1990: 18; ST 59–60; TSu 168–169)

28 This chart is based on Ferrier 1858: 160, 192; Fofalzai 1958: 241–242; Lal 1978 I: 22–24, Masson 1974 III: 36, Reshtia 1957: 9–10n; ST 106, 108, 111,

113, 197, 216, 218; KN 5 June 1854 (For. Sec. 28 July 1854 No. 10); KD 20 October 1861 (For. Pol. A. November 1861 No. 130). Payinda Khan had four daughters, one of whom was a full sister of Dost Muhammad Khan. The most famous among them was the 'mother of Madad Khan,' who was active on behalf of Dost Muhammad Khan during the First Anglo-Afghan War. (Lal 1978 I 188–191; Reshtia 1957: 10n)

29 Fofalzai 1958: 174; Lal 1978 I: 23–25.

30 Gankovsky 1985: 131.

31 'Abd al-Jabbar Khan is mentioned in connection with the administration of the Derajat and Kabul. Sultan Muhammad Khan was possibly associated with the government of Peshawar even before Fatih Khan's military campaign against Kashmir. (Ali 1848: 167; Ferrier 1858: 148; Ghubar 1981: 401; Reshtia 1957: 21–23; ST 81, 85; TSu 193–197)

32 Lal 1978 I: 70, 76, 95.

33 Masson 1974 III: 27.

34 The accounts of Dost Muhammad Khan's transgression vary. According to Faiz Muhammad, Dost Muhammad Khan confiscated the jewelry of Haji Feroz al-Din's and Malik Qasim's wives, implying that the act of entering the harem itself represented a violation of the honor (*hatk-i hurmat*) of the women involved. (ST 93) Reshtia glosses over Dost Muhammad Khan's behavior by merely speaking of a 'rumor' (*afwah*) concerning the Sardar's disrespectful behavior in the royal harem. (Reshtia 1957: 28) Foreign observers are more graphic in their description. According to Lal, Dost Muhammad Khan did not content himself with despoiling the members of the household but 'committed an unparalleled deed by taking off the jewelled band which fastened the trousers of Prince Malik Qasim's wife... and treated her rudely in other ways.' (Lal 1978 I: 104; see Ferrier 1858: 153 for a similar account)

35 Fatih Khan was blinded at Herat and killed by gradual dismemberment at Sayyidabad located between Ghazni and Kabul later in the same year. (Ferrier 1858: 147–157; Harawi 1990: 15, 18–19; Lal 1978 I: 103–106; Reshtia 1957: 28, 32–33; Reshtia 1990: 53–54, 60; ST 93, 97)

36 Harawi 1990: 17, 19–20; ST 97.

37 Faiz Muhammad places these events in the year 1238–39/1823. (ST 106 108) According to the accounts of Moorcroft and Reshtia, however, Habibullah Khan's deposal must have taken place during the first six months of 1824. (Alder 1985: 320–321; Moorcroft & Trebeck 1841 II: 345–346; Reshtia 1990: 70–78)

38 Ferrier 1858: 192–193; Masson 1974 I: 288–289; Reshtia 1957: 42–45; Reshtia 1990: 74–78.

39 Burnes 1834 I: 99, II: 302–304; Dupree 1980: 351; Gankovsky 1985: 131 133; Reshtia 1957: 35, 39, 41–42; Reshtia 1990: 64, 69–71, 73–74; Singh 1990: 69–73, 80, 85, 90–92.

40 Ali 1848: 176; Ghubar 1981: 510; Reshtia 1957: 36n; Vigne 1982: 147.

41 Reshtia 1957: 31–32, 36; Reshtia 1990: 59, 65–66.

42 Ghubar 1981: 511–512; Lal 1978 I: 123–129; Reshtia 1957: 37–41; Reshtia 1990: 66–72. ST does not mention the clashes between Dost Muhammad Khan and Muhammad 'Azim Khan.

43 Reshtia 1957: 43–45; Reshtia 1990: 74–78; Lal 1978 I: 136–143; ST 106 108.

44 Balland *EIr*: 549; Ferrier 1858: 187–189; Ghubar 1981: 512–514; Lal 1978 I: 130–145; Reshtia 1957: 42–46; Reshtia 1990: 74–80; ST 106–109.

45 ST 111, 113.

46 Masson 1974 III: 257.

47 Ali 1970: 483; Burnes 1839a: 13.
48 Reshtia 1957: 30–31; Reshtia 1990: 57–58; Sykes 1981 I: 392.
49 Masson 1974 I: 284, II: 256–258.
50 Lal 1978 I: 169–172; Masson III: 307–309; Reshtia 1957: 59–60; ST 127.
51 Ferrier 1858: 68–69; Singh 1981: 25–27; According to *Siraj al-tawarikh*, Sabir Shah gave Ahmad Khan the title *padshah-i dauran*. (ST 10)
52 Masson 1974 III: 307; Reshtia 1957: 61; Reshtia 1990: 102.
53 Masson 1974 III: 309–310.
54 Masson 1974 III: 6–7, 310–314, 348–351; Lal 1978 I: 171–172.
55 Harlan 1842: 137.
56 Ghubar 1981: 531; Lal 1978 II: 233. In the 1830s Masson observed, 'I have heard that he [Dost Muhammad Khan] is not inimical to the restoration of the King Sujah al Mulkh, and it is a common saying with Afghans, 'How happy we should be if Shah Sujah were Padshah, and Dost Mahomed Vazir.' (Masson 1974 I: 253)
57 Masson 1974 I: 70–95.
58 Lal 1977: 42.
59 Burnes 1834 II: 332.
60 Harlan 1842: 126–129.
61 Wood 1841: 171.
62 Harlan 1842: 127; Gerard 1832: 4.
63 Masson 1974 I: 243–244, III: 86–87; Lal 1977: 26; Pearse 1898: 59.
64 Lal 1978 I: 206, 238; Harlan 1842: 146. Dost Muhammad Khan knew Turkish because of his Qizilbash background. (ST 153) Although many of the Qizilbash gradually adopted Persian as their primary language, many of them continued to speak Turkish. According to Ravan A. G. Farhadi, the Afshars located at Nanakchi north of the Kabul Silo still spoke Turkish up to the 1960s. (Personal communication)
65 Burnes 1839a: 8; Harlan 1842: 125–126. Dost Muhammad Khan's literacy is disputed by Bahadur Fatih Khan Khatak, who visited Qandahar in 1856 in order to ratify the Anglo-Afghan treaty concluded in March 1855. He claims that the Amir simply signed the treaty with an *alif* because of his inability to write. (L/P&S/5/228 No. 33 of 21 August 1856, pp. 223–224)
66 Masson 1974 III: 308–309.
67 Masson to Wilson 4 January 1835 (Elphinstone Collection F 88 15 B 12)
68 Harlan 1842: 129, 145.
69 ST 250.
70 Masson 1974 I: 252.
71 Lal 1978 I: 237. See also Burnes 1939: 18–19 for a similar statement.
72 Harlan 1842: 147.
73 Masson 1974 III: 308.
74 Ali 1970: 479–480.
75 Lal 1978 I: 236–237.
76 Masson 1974 I: 252; see also Harlan 1842: 129, Lal 1977: 42–43 for similar statements.
77 Masson 1974 III: 14–15, 87; Lal 1977: 42–43; Vigne 1982: 160.
78 Harlan 1842: 134, 144–145; Masson 1974 III: 15, 83–85, 212–216.
79 Burnes 1834 II: 330; Burnes 1839b: 15; Masson 1974 I: 252.
80 Pearse 1898: 58–73, 88.
81 Burnes 1834 II: 329; Lal 1977: 209–210; Lal 1978 I: 225; Masson 1974 I: 250–255.
82 Burnes 1839b: 14; Ghubar 1981: 517.

83 Ali 1970: 476–477; Hahn 1964: 16–17, 29–30; Masson 1974 I: 238 II: 288; Raverty 1888: 485.
84 Fofalzai 1967: 569; Habib 1987: 77–78; Hough 1841 284–285; Masson 1974 II: 251–257; Raverty 1888: 61, 65.
85 Burnes 1834 II: 335; Masson 1974 II: 259.
86 Masson 1974 II: 259, 261.
87 Lal 1977: 42.
88 Bechhoefer 1975.
89 Gaube & Wirth 1984: 60–69.
90 Hough 1841: 286; Malleson 1879: 6–7; Masson 1974 II: 259.
91 Masson 1974 II: 262. In present day Kabuli Persian the term *kucha bandi* has lost the connotation mentioned by Masson and only refers to narrow winding lanes in general.
92 Burnes 1834 II: 335; Burnes 1839a: 7; Masson 1974 II: 260; Vigne 1982: 165. Elphinstone estimated the Qizilbash population of Kabul at ten to twelve thousand souls. (Elphinstone 1972 I: 417)
93 Burnes 1839a: 7; Fofalzai 1967: 366–367, 656–658; Habib 1987: 84; Masson 1974 II: 260, III: 306.
94 Dupree 1984: 638; Ferrier 1858: 70; Kakar 1979: 158; Savory 1979: 245; Savory 1980: 19–20; Yazdani 1989: 90.
95 Dupree 1984: 639-Ferrier 1858: 70; Lal 1977: 43–44.
96 Masson 1974 II: 297; Singh 1981: 30.
97 The term *chindawul* (rearguard) was apparently used both for the army contingent in question and its commander. According to a *farman* issued in 1751, Wali Muhammad Khan Jawansher was addressed as *chindawul-i sarkar i khassa-yi sharifa*, 'the rearguard of the royal army.' The Rikas, who had been settled in the vicinity of Mashhad during Safawid times, were brought to Qandahar by Ahmad Shah in 1755. Later on they accompanied Timur Shah to Kabul and received lands close to the Bala Hisar at Rikakhana and Bibi Mahru. (Fofalzai 1967: 366–368, 726)
98 Husaini 1967: 38.
99 Elphinstone 1972 II: 267; Fofalzai 1958: 299–300; ST 56.
100 Singh 1981: 359.
101 Dupree 1984: 640.
102 Burnes 1839a: 8; Ferrier 1858: 99; Husaini 1967: 27–28; Raverty 1888: 329. Husaini lists the following *ghulam khana* divisions:
4,000 under Nur Muhammad Khan Babar; this contingent includes some Durranis;
3,000 under Hasan Khan Qizilbash Peshkhidmat;
3,000 under Sadiq Khan Peshkhidmat;
2,700 under Amir Khan of Chindawul and in other elite contingents, such as the *nasaqchis* (security forces);
500 under Iltifat Khan Khwaja Sara;
500 under Maqsud Khan Khwaja Sara;
300 Habashis;
1,000 under Mishkin Khan Khwaja Sara at the service of Shahzada Qaisar at Herat, mostly Qalmaqs and Hazaras.
103 Fofalzai 1958: 74, 188, 299, 306, 309–310; ST 56.
104 Fofalzai 1958: 175, 177; Reshtia 1957: 9; Reshtia 1990: 21; ST 61–62; TSu 172.
105 Burnes 1839a: 8; Burnes 1839b: 15; Elphinstone 1972 II: 267.
106 Masson 1974 II: 297.

107 Burnes 1839a: 8.
108 Ghubar 1981: 393.
109 Ferrier 1858: 132; Malleson 1879: 320; Masson 1974 III: 42; Lal 1978 I: 37.
110 Elphinstone 1972 II: 336.
111 According to *Siraj al-tawarikh*, Mir Wa'iz did not issue a *fatwa* but gave a binding order (*hukm*) for the destruction of the Qizilbash.
112 Ferrier 1858: 132–134; S. T. 66. Ferrier obtained his information from the writings of 'Abdullah Khan Harati, *peshkhidmat* to Shah Kamran, and from oral accounts gathered during his visit to Afghanistan in 1845.
113 Elphinstone 1972 II: 337; Fofalzai 1958: 216–217.
114 Little is known about the persons of Sayyid Ashraf and Sayyid 'Ata. Lal merely characterizes them as 'the great fanatics.' Sayyid Ashraf does not seem to be identical with the Sayyid of Opian (Ashrat), who was executed during Dost Muhammad Khan's governorship of Kohistan. (Lal 1978 I: 79–81, 99) Masson attributes the attempt to place Shahzada 'Abbas on the throne to Muhammad Shah Khan, a 'simple weaver' from Istalif, who entered Kabul at the head of 4,000 or 5,000 men. As neither Lal nor Massong give dates, it is not clear whether Masson's account refers to a separate event. (Masson 1974 III: 123)
115 Lal 1978 I: 130–131; Masson 1974 III: 73.
116 Burnes 1839a: 9, 12; Harlan 1842: 44.
117 Masson 1974 II: 229–230, 315.
118 Ali 1970: 483; Dupree 1984: 641; ST 151.
119 KI, n. d., received on 8 April 1852 (For. Sec. 30 April 1852 No. 97)
120 KN, n. d. , received on 18 February 1854 (For. Sec. 28 April 1854 No. 19)
121 ST 295–301, 317–318: Memorandum on Sardar Muhammad Isma'il Khan (For. S. I. 1869 No. 85)
122 Fofalzai 1967: 205; Masson 1974 II: 315.
123 Adamec 1985: 451; Dupree 1980: 12; Masson 1974 III: 153; Wood 1841: 173–174; Yapp 1962: 515.
124 Burnes 1839b: 19; Raverty 1888: 66.
125 Lal 1978 I: 94.
126 Masson 1974 III: 128
127 Ibid. III: 23–26, 126–128; Adamec 1975: 228; Burnes 1839b: 19; Lal 1978 I: 96–97, 223. According to Lal, Dost Muhammad Khan had entered marriage alliances with Baqa Khan and Khwaja Khwanji before murdering them. The upper Panjsher valley remained practically independent of the Amir's administration until the late 1830s. (Wood 1841: 413, 419–420)
128 Lal 1978 I: 147–152; Masson 1974 III: 81–85; Reshtia 1957: 50,52; Reshtia 1990: 86,88. According to Masson, the sum of 40,000 rupees collected by Dost Muhammad Khan was classified as a fee for the maintenance of the Amir's troops (*mihmani*).
129 ST 151, 158; Yapp 1962: 515. Lal lists the following participants in the rebellion: Mir Masjidi of Julgah, Mir Darwesh Khan, Mir Khwaja, Khaliq Ibrahim, Mir Sikandar Shah, Sail al-Din, Malik 'Isa Khan. (Lal 1978 II: 276–277)
130 Lal 1978 II: 274–277; Ali 1970: 314–315. Ghulam Khan Popalzai was the son of A'zam Khan Popalzai, the *nasaqchi bashi* (chief of security forces) of Shah Shuja'. (Fofalzai 1958: 308)
131 ST 151.
132 Lal 1978 II: 276–277; Habibi 1959: 803–810; Yapp 1962: 516, 520.
133 Masson 1974 II: 298–299.

134 Lal 1978 I: 192–197; Masson 1974 II: 301–304. According to Lal, Mir Yazdanbakhsh offered 100,000 rupees.
135 Harlan 1939: 127; Masson 1974 II: 304, 372.
136 Lal 1978 I: 133, 140; Masson 1974 III: 30; Reshtia 1957: 43.
137 Hough 1841: 87; Masson 1974 II: 305, 316.
138 Masson 1974 II: 307–312.
139 Haji Khan Kakar's troops consisted of 400 Kakar cavalry and 220 *ghulam khana*. (Ibid. II: 346)
140 Ibid. II: 346–347, 354, 368. The districts of Jirgai and Burjehgai, for instance, yielded 10,000 rupees.
141 Ibid. II: 371–373, 391, 409, 429–430.
142 Ibid. II: 319, 322, 360–361, 414–424, 430. Wakil Saifullah had killed Mir Yazdanbakhsh's father Mir Wali Beg in the early nineteenth century. At the time of his rise to power Mir Yazdanbakhsh had revenged the death of his father by slaying Wakil Saifullah. (Ibid. II: 295)
143 Ibid. III: 94–107; Lal 1978 I: 206, 212.
144 Masson 1974 III: 210–212; Reshtia 1957: 53–54; Reshtia 1990: 91.
145 MacGregor 1844: 877.
146 Lal 1977: 209–210; Lal 1978: 233; Masson 1974 I: 176. According to Lal 1977, the total annual income of Jalalabad was 900,000 rupees, of which 500,000 were collected by different chiefs for their own subsistence and 400,000 came into the Nawwab's treasury.
147 Jones 1976: 56–57; Masson 1974 I: 254–255, II: 222.
148 Masson 1974 III: 400–401.
149 Ibid. III: 402.
150 Harlan 1939: 127.
151 Burnes 1839b: 14–15; Hough 1841: 288; Lal 1978 I: 232–233.
152 Romodin 1985: 140, 144.
153 Dupree 1980: 376; Ghubar 1982: 521–522; Raymond 1848: 74–76. See Kaye 1857 I: 369–374 and Norris 1967: 451–452 for the full text of the manifesto.
154 Dupree 1980: 377–378; Durand 1879: 83–84, 92–93; Norris 1967: 295; Reshtia 1958: 78; Reshtia 1990: 126; Ali 1970: 387ff; Sykes 1981 II: 4–5, 14. Ghubar arrives at a total of 22,350 soldiers under British command in the army of the Indus. (Ghubar 1982: 523, 530) Faiz Muhamamd only lists 9,350 soldiers in the same unit. (ST 142) The Army of the Indus was accompanied by 38,000 camp followers. (Dupree 1976: 510; Romodin 1985: 138–139) In Romodin's opinion, the total strength of the Khyber army was 11,000 men. (Romodin 1985: 138–139)
155 Eyre 1879: 256; Singer 1984: 71–72; Sykes 1981 II: 33. Durand gives a total figure of 20,000 persons killed during the British retreat. (Durand 1879: 377). By contrast, Dupree is of the opinion that there were a number of survivors: 'Incidentally, contrary to popular belief and perpetuated in British writings on the period, Dr Brydon was not the only survivor of the retreat. In fact, about 20 members of Shah Shuja''s Force reached Jalalabad shortly after Brydon. In fact, the Afghans held the following prisoners: 35 British officers, 51 enlisted men and two civilians; 12 wives and 22 children... Ultimately, and over a period of several years, about 2000 sepoys and camp followers, generally slaves of Afghan tribesmen, made their way back to India.' (Dupree 1976: 507)
156 Reshtia 1957: 68; Reshtia 1990: 111; ST 129–130, 136.
157 Yapp 1980: 15–16.
158 Ghubar 1981: 444–446; 521.
159 Yapp 1980: 224.

160 Ibid. 228, 251; Durand 1879: 14–16, 67–68.

161 Yapp 1980: 201–217.

162 Durand 1879: 14–16, 24, 39–40, 44; Norris 1967: 154; Yapp 1980: 225 230, 245, 253.

163 Durand 1879: 40–41; Masson 1974 III: 456.

164 Burnes 1973: xiii; Yapp 1980: 89, 236–240.

165 Norris 1967: 167.

166 Yapp 1980: 240–253, 272, 286–287, 302–303.

167 Ibid. 212–215; Durand 1879: 18; Sykes 1981 I: 394–396; Bentinck to Secret Committee 5 March 1835 (L/P&S/5/8a No. 2)

168 Ferrier 1858: 263–4; Fraser-Tytler 1953: 95; Ghubar 1981: 521; Reshtia 1957: 76: Reshtia 1990: 122–123; Sykes 1981 I: 398; Wood 1841: 422; Yapp 1980: 224, 237–238.

169 Ali 1970: 305; Ghubar 1981: 529–530; Kaye 1857 I: 456, 472; Lal 1978 II: 247, 259–260, 268; ST 151.

170 Ghubar 1981: 532–533; Kaye 1857 II: 73, 77; ST 151–153, 157; Yapp 1962: 508.

171 The identity of Sultan Muhammad is not quite clear. Lal, ST and Yapp mention the person of Sultan Muhammad Angizai Barakzai, Dost Muhammad Khan's former governor of Kohistan, who was active on behalf of the ex-Amir in Kohistan. Ghubar, on the other hand, speaks of 'Sultan Muhammad Khan Nijrawi', which raises the possibility that there was a local chief by that name. (Ghubar 1981: 541; Lal 1978 II: 347, 358; ST 158; Yapp 1962: 518)

172 Possibly the son of Khwaja Khanji of Karzai, who was murdered by Dost Muhammad Khan during his governorship in Kohistan under Shah Mahmud. (Lal 1978 I: 97–98) Malik Saif al-Din and Mir Darwesh Khan had joined the rebellion thanks to the encouragement of one of Dost Muhammad Khan' sisters. (Reshtia 1957: 90)

173 An important exception was Khalifa Ibrahim of Istalif, who consistently sided with the British (Yapp 1962: 518)

174 According to Ghubar the Kohistani forces defeated three British cavalry squadrons (*kandak*) (Ghubar 1981: 542) Reshtia states that the British cavalry contingent (*qit'a-yi sawar*) was routed. (Reshtia 1957: 90) Faiz Muhammad reports that all 800 British cavalry were defeated and pursued by the troops under the leadership of Dost Muhammad Khan and his sons. (ST 158) The British sources, on the other hand, belittle the ex-Amir's military success. Yapp's analysis of the battle does not even raise the possibility of British defeat. (Yapp 1980: 517) According to Durand, the ex-Amir and his Kohistani forces only defeated two squadrons of the 2nd Bengal Cavalry before they were dispersed by the remainder of Sale's army: 'But Dost Mahomed...escaped from the field without pursuit or difficulty.' (Durand 1879: 293) Norris dismisses the notion of Dost Muhammad Khan's victoriousness as false romance: 'Let us say rather that he [Dost Muhammad Khan] left the field with his honour intact after a brief skirmish with part of Sale's brigade.' (Norris 1967: 335) Also see Stocqueler 1983: 132–137.

175 Faiz Muhammad puts the following words into Dost Muhammad Khan's mouth: 'Even if the tribes (*qabaʾil*) of the Waziris, Tarakis, Andaris, and the other Ghilzai tribes (*tawaʾif*) assemble and raise the banner of jihad they will not be able to resist and will disperse, as they are a tribal people (*ulusi*). (ST 158–159)

176 Ferrier (1858: 338–339) likewise points out that a mutiny generated by British intrigues forced Dost Muhammad Khan to abandon his troops.

177 Reshtia 1957: 91.
178 Ghubar 1981: 542–543.
179 The decision of the Qandahar Sardars to abandon the control of Qandahar to Shah Shujaʻ had been prompted not only by lack of Persian/Russian support but also by the desertion of men like Haji Khan Kakar, Ghulam Akhundzada (an influential ʻalim of Qandahar), ʻAbd al-Majid Khan (son of Shah Pasand Khan, governor of Lash), Habibullah Khan Sirkani, Faiztalab Khan Nurzai, Akhtar Khan ʻAlizai of Zamindawar, and Ramazan Khan Ghilzai to the cause of Shah Shujaʻ. After his coronation, Shah Shujaʻ also attempted to win the allegiance of Dost Muhammad Khan Ishaqzai of Garmser. (Fane 1842: 115, 123–126; Ghubar 1981: 529, Kaye 1857 I: 435–438; Lal 1978 II: 207–214; Norris 1967: 266–267; Peers 1954: 171–172; ST 142–143)
180 Kaye 1857 I: 373–374; Reshtia 1957: 70–71; Reshtia 1990: 115–116; ST 143; Yapp 1980: 268–270, 307, 309.
181 Kaye 1857 I: 440; Macnaghten claimed that 'all classes of his people' gave Shah Shujaʻ a 'reception the most cordial and loyal.' (Auckland to Secret Committee 23 May 1839, L/P&S/5/8b No 17) Likewise, Fane described the atmosphere in Qandahar as 'enthusiastic.' (Fane 1842: 126) Durand and Havelock, on the other hand, view the public attitude to Shah Shujaʻ as less flattering. Havelock raises the possibility that 'all the national enthusiasm of the scene was entirely confined to his Majesty's immediate retainers.' (Durand 1879: 156; Havelock 1840 II: 22–23).
182 With the exception of Macnaghten, all authors agree that the population of Kabul displayed no particular affection for Shah Shujaʻ on his entrance to the city. (Durand 1879: 187; Fane 1842 II: 185–186; Kaye 1857 I: 478–9; Kennedy II: 83; Peers 1954: 173–174)
183 Peers 1954: 175–176; Ali 1970: 479–480.
184 The verse originally read,
sikka zad bar sim o zar raushantar az khurshed o mah
nur-i chashm-i durr-i durran (or durr-i dauran) Shah Shujaʻ al-Mulk Shah.
and was changed to
sikka zad bar sim o tila Shah Shujaʻ-i armani,
nur-i chashm-i lat (or lard) (o) Burnes o khak-i pa-yi Company. (Ghubar 1981: 539; Reshtia 1957: 83; Reshtia 1990: 133; TSu 273) The British were generally known as *lard*, 'Lord', which quickly became *lat* in common usage. *Lat* also being the name of a deity of pre-Islamic times, the British, along with their servant Shah Shujaʻ, were identified as idolators.
185 ST 156. Lal offers a different interpretation of Mulla Shakur's behaviour. In his opinion, the minister intentionally emphasized Shah Shujaʻ's dependence on the British in order to create a separate base of support among the Durrani nobles for the king. (Lal 1978 II: 315–324)
186 According to Ghubar, Nizam al-Daula was appointed in March 1840. (Ghubar 1981: 539)
187 ST 155–156.
188 Durand 1879: 156, 306–307.
189 Lal 1978 II: 380; Yapp 1964: 339–340; Yapp 1980: 311, 314, 346–347.
190 Ghubar 1981: 540; Lal 1978 II: 343–344.
191 Reshtia 1957: 93; Reshtia 1990: 146; Sale 1985: 9; Yapp 1964: 339; Yapp 1980: 346–348. According to *Siraj al-tawarikh*, Nizam al-Daula sometimes simply withheld the allowances of individual chiefs, so, for instance that of Samad Khan Popalzai. In the author's opinion, Nizam al-Daula's actions were only partly guided by personal ambition. Colluding with Dost Muhammad

Khan's former official Mirza Imam Wirdi Khan Qizilbash, the hidden intent of his measures was to further opposition to Shah Shuja' and thus to abet the cause of the Barakzais. (ST 156, 161–162)

192 ST 162. For a description of the shrine see Einzmann 1977: 167–170.

193 Yapp 1980: 314. For a detailed account of the local uprisings of 1839–1841 see Yapp 1962 and 1963.

194 Lal 1978 II: 343; Yapp 1962: 519.

195 Kaye 1857 II: 144–161; Lal 1978 II: 380; Norris 1967: 362–364; ST 161.

196 The 17th being the date of the battle of Badr, this date is one of special significance during the month of Ramazan.

197 For the best account of the final months of the British at Kabul and their disastrous retreat, see Eyre 1879: 221–290.

198 Kaye 1857 II: 145, 152–154; Lal 1978 II: 385–386; Reshtia 1957: 93; Reshtia 1990: 147; ST 162–163; Yapp 1964; 334–335.

199 Kaye 1857 II: 153, 406–407.

200 Eyre 1879: 133–150.

201 Ibid. 82.

202 Habibi 1959: 868–870; Lal 1978 II: 380–381, 390–391; Reshtia 1957: 99; Reshtia 1990: 154; ST 163; Yapp 1964: 343.

203 Habibi 1959: 869; Lal 1978 II: 389–390; ST 156, 161; Yapp 1964: 337. Ghubar identifies Imamwerdi as Uzbek. (Ghubar 1981: 548)

204 Ghubar 1981: 548, 550; Reshtia 1957: 96; ST 163; Yapp 1964: 346 Ghubar even claims that Mir Haji and other ulama of Kabul helped to incite the attack of November 2 by declaring jihad at the time of the morning prayer.

205 Yapp 1964: 346–347. Ghubar and Reshtia are of the opinion that Nawwab Zaman Khan was established as leader of the rebellion *before* the attack of November 2. (Ghubar 1981: 549; Reshtia 1957: 99; Reshtia 1990: 155)

206 Kaye 1857 II: 289–290; Kohzad 1955a: 3; Yapp 1964: 347–348, 362.

207 Lal 1978 II: 439–442; ST 179–182; TSu 272–273; Yapp 1964: 350–353.

208 Ghubar 1981: 569; Kohzad 1955a: 3–8; Lal 1978 II: 443–444; ST 182–184; Yapp 1964: 353–356.

209 Lal 1978 II: 444–448; ST 183–185; Yapp 1964: 358–362.

210 Ghubar 1981: 570–571; Norris 1967: 414–415; Peers 1954: 184–185; Reshtia 1990: 184–185; Reshtia 1957: 120–121; ST 185–189; Yapp 1964: 364; Yapp 1980: 432–435.

211 Ferrier 1858: 384–385; Peers 1954: 185–186; Reshtia 1957: 122–123; Reshtia 1990: 186–189; Yapp 1980 430, 441.

212 Ghubar 1981: 539–540; 548–550; Reshtia 1957: 95–99.

213 Yapp 1964: 337, 365, 371–372, 379–381.

214 Ibid. 381.

215 Lumsden and Elsmie 1899: 174; EKN 19 May 1856 (L/P&S/5/228 No 28 of 17 July 1856 p. 65)

216 Ferrier 1858: 385–386; Reshtia 1957: 123–124; Reshtia 1990: 189; ST 187 188, 198, 200; Yapp 1964: 367–371.

217 'Abdullah Khan Achakzai still figures prominently in the popular memory of the First Anglo-Afghan War. His shrine at Rish Khor near Kabul is still visited for prayer and commemoration. (Einzmann 1977: 255)

218 Ghubar 1981: 554; ST 198.

219 Subsequently Sultan Ahmad Khan left for Iran and only returned to Kabul for a short period in 1847. In 1857 he was installed on the throne of Herat by the Persians. (Champagne 1981: 390–391, 432, 436, 473; Nuri 1956: 18–19; Reshtia 1957: 127 128, 136, 140–141; Reshtia 1990: 196, 208, 216–217; ST

192, 199–200; QM 7–13 August 1857, For. Sec. 30 April 1858 No. 66B; KD 11–17 June 1860, For. Pol. A. July 1860 No. 162; Diary of Nawwab Faujdar Khan 19 January 1858, For. Sec. 28 May 1858 No. 46)

220 Laurence to Curvie 29 February 1847 (L/P&S/5/190 No. 20 of 3 March 1847)

221 Ferrier 1858: 389–398; Reshtia 1957: 126–129; Reshtia 1990: 194–198; ST 198–201.

222 Harlan 1842: 135–136; Lumsden 1860: 6–10; Reshtia 1958: 127; Reshtia 1990: 195; ST 200, 209–210; KN 23 July 1855 (For. Sec. 30 November 1855 No. 44)

2 AMIR DOST MUHAMMAD KHAN'S POLICIES IN TURKISTAN

1 *Gaz.* IV: 5–6.

2 Wood 1841: 407.

3 In the seventeenth century the Hijdah Nahr system provided water for as many as 271 villages in its vicinity. During the first decade of the nineteenth century Elphinstone reported on the basis of secondhand information that the country around Balkh contained 360 villages watered by the Hijdah Nahr system. In the 1880s the Hijdah Nahr system only fed 185 villages. (Elphinstone 1972 II: 183; McChesney 1991: 21–26)

4 *Gaz.* I: 1–2.

5 Grevemeyer 1982: 22–24.

6 Ibid. 94–95; Holzwarth 1980: 181.

7 Hambly 1966: 14–16.

8 Holzwarth 1980: 181–183; Olufson 1904: 146.

9 Grevemeyer 1982: 249.

10 Ibid. 10–11, 249; Holzwarth 1980: 179; Pearse 1898: 107–108.

11 McChesney 1991: 257.

12 Centlivres 1972: 155–156.

13 *Gaz.* IV: 476.

14 Ibid. I: 20; Harlan 1939: 41; Merk 1886b; Wheeler 1979: 19; Wood 1841 206–207, 410–411. According to Harlan, however, Saighan and Kahmard were inhabited by Uzbeks. (Harlan 1939: 44) Lal also designates the population of Saighan as 'Turks'. (Lal 1977: 54)

15 Qarluqs, 'Turks', Chinaki, Chung, Moghol, Toghul.

16 Centlivres 1975: 29–32; Centlivres 1976a: 257, 266. Also see Lord 1839a: 109.

17 Grevemeyer 1982: 12.

18 Centlivres, however, holds that Uzbek populations did not extend further east than Rustaq. Apart from a few exceptions, the Turkophones resident in Badakshshan proper were 'Turks' or 'Moghols.' (Centlivres 1975: 28)

19 Pandit Manphul in Yule 1872: 448; Gordon 1876: 134; Shahrani 1984b: 145–147; Wood 1841: 369.

20 Kussmaul 1965b: 491.

21 The 'Kabulis' or 'Shamalis' were Persian speakers from Kabul and Kohistan who moved to Turkistan in the 1820s because of the turmoil brought about by the ongoing power struggle among the Muhammadzai Sardars. (Centlivres 1976b: 130; Moorcroft & Trebeck 1841 II; 451) During the same period the number of Kabuli emigrants to Bukhara increased significantly, their total number reaching 2,000. (Gregorian 1969: 52) In the 1830s Harlan estimated that there were 10,000 Kohistanis in the Balkh region, who had fled from 'exorbitant territorial taxes' levied by Amir Dost Muhammad Khan. (Harlan 1939: 65)

22 Centlivres 1976b: 130; Moorcroft & Trebeck 1841 II: 450–451, 481. According to Kushkaki, part of the trade in Badakhshan was carried out by pre-Uzbek Utranji Turks and Bajauris. (Kushkaki 1989: 105)
23 Harlan 1939: 65.
24 Centlivres 1976b: 130.
25 McChesney 1991: 257–260.
26 Barthold 1956: 1; Brentjes 1983: 54, 167–168; Ghubar 1981: 57; Gregorian 1969: 33; Schurmann 1962: 75.
27 Vambéry 1872 I: 177; Vambéry 1885: 346–350.
28 Grevemeyer 1982: 43–45; Hajianpur 1991: 170; McChesney, *EIr*: 178; Shalinsky 1986: 292.
29 Barthold 1935: 177; Shalinsky 1986: 293; Vambéry 1885: 347–348.
30 Barthold 1934: 294–295; Barthold 1935: 164–165; DeWeese 1994: 67–68; Erskine 1974: 24–25; Halperin 1985: 25–31; Sarkisyanz 1961: 182–183; Skrine & Ross 1899: 182–183; Weiers 1986: 345–351.
31 Akiner 1983: 267; Barthold 1934: 295; Barthold 1935: 176–177; Barthold 1956 I: 51; DeWeese 1994: 90–91, 101–103, 144–158; Erskine 1974: 26; Shalinsky 1986: 293; Spuler 1943: 87, 213–220; Weiers 1986: 361.
32 DeWeese 1994: 101–103, 144–158.
33 Vambéry 1885: 347.
34 DeWeese 1994: 105–121.
35 Barthold 1934: 294–295; Dickson 1960: 209; Lemercier Quelquejay 1991: 152; Sarkisyanz 1961: 182; Subtelny 1983: 121–122n. Tracing its descent from Shiban, this ruling clan should properly be called 'Shibanid'. Similarly, Muhammad Shaibani's should be Shibani. The usage of 'Shaibanid' became common in Muslim sources in analogy with the Arabic name.
36 Hambly 1991: 184; Vambéry 1885: 349, 353, 356–357. It is not certain whether all the Uzbeks present in the Oxus region today were followers of Muhammad Shibani. The Manghits, for example, were apparently brought to Khwarazm during the time of Chingiz Khan. During the Shaibanid era they settled in the region of Qarshi in the khanate of Bukhara. (Vambéry 1872 II: 146)
37 McChesney 1991: 50; McChesney, *EIr*: 177; Vambéry 1885: 349, 353–354
38 Barfield 1992: 206–209, 214; Barthold 1935: 183; Fletcher 1986: 26; McChesney, *EIr*: 176.
39 Barfield 1992: 212; Hambly 1991: 114–115.
40 Barfield 1992: 207; Barthold 1956: 44; McChesney, *EIr*: 176–177.
41 Anderson 1978: 168 –170; McChesney 1991: 54, 322.
42 Dickson 1960: 211
43 Ibid.; McChesney 1991: 55–56, *EIr*: 176–178.
44 McChesney *EIr*: 177.
45 Dickson 1960: 210–211.
46 McChesney 1983: 33–70; McChesney 1991: 57–58; Vambéry 1872 II: 127n.
47 McChesney 1991: 97–98.
48 Ibid. 114.
49 Ibid. 107–109, 114–116.
50 Ibid. 102–103, 114, 116–117, 162–168; TB: 1–2, 4, 6 7; Grevemeyer 1982: 49–54; Teufel 1884: 277, 284–304, 350.
51 McChesney 1991: 117, 160, 164–165; Teufel 1884: 294, 303–304.
52 McChesney 1991: 215.
53 Barthold 1935: 238–239.
54 McChesney 1991: 201, 214.

55 Ibid. 214n, 221; Adamec 1975: 162; Lee 1987: 124–125.
56 Singh 1981: 99; ST 16; Sykes 1981 I: 357.
57 Bregel, 'Bukhara III' in *EIr*; Bregel, 'Central Asia VII' in *EIr*; Bregel, 'Mangit' in *EI2*. Also see Boukhary 1876: 110–116; Faiz Buksh 1871: 66–67; Hambly 1991: 190 192; Khanikoff 1845: 295–302; Nazarov 1963: 14–18; Vambéry 1872 II: 139–147.
58 ST 27. According to Badakhshi, the *khirqa* was captured in Faizabad by Shah Wali Khan. (TB 5–6, 46–47) See McChesney 1991: 222–227 for a detailed discussion of the various traditions concerning this relic.
59 Boukhary 1876: 22–23, 139, 142; Fofalzai 1967: 271–277, 569; ST 41; TSu 156; Vambéry 1872 II: 157–158. According to Elphinstone, the encounter at Aqcha took place in 1789 and its result was inconclusive. (Elphinstone 1972 II: 305–306) Boulger views Timur Shah's campaign against Bukhara primarily as an attempt to intimidate the Qataghan Uzbeks of Qunduz. (Boulger 1879 I: 299)
60 Elphinstone 1972 II: 309–310; Fofalzai 1959: 47–50.
61 Wheeler 1979: 19.
62 Singh 1981: 99; ST 16.
63 Ahmad Shah is reported to have settled 5,000 *kuhna naukar* in Afghan Turkistan. In the 1790s Ghulam Sarwar noted that the Balkh garrison consisted of 2,900 Afghan cavalry and 11 guns while Aqcha was held by 1,000 cavalry and 4 guns. In the early nineteenth century Elphinstone claimed that the number of the *kuhna naukar* present in the city of Balkh had dwindled to 1,000. (Elphinstone 1972 II: 197–198; Gupta 1944: 278–279; Harlan 1939: 31; Lee 1996: 96n)
64 Ferrier 1858: 81.
65 Grevemeyer 1982: 65; Lee 1996: 81–84, 414; McChesney 1991: 220–221.
66 The various accounts of Qubad Khan's political career are widely divergent. For the versions given in Husain b. 'Ali's *Zeb-i tarikhha* and Gulistana's *Mujmal al-tawarikh*, see McChesney 1991: 227–230. My interpretation of the events of this period is based on Badakhshi, Fofalzai (1967), and Lord, all of whom focus on the rivalry between Qubad Khan and the Badakhshani Mirs and the role local Qataghan leaders assumed in the politics of the day.
67 Fofalzai describes him as a 'the khans of the northern region of Afghanistan' (*az khanan-i safahat-i shamal-i Afghanistan*), a contemporary of Ahmad Shah, and governor (*hakim*) of Qataghan. (Fofalzai 1967 I: 164) According to Lord, Qubad Khan's father had been *parwanachi* at the court of Qunduz under Mahmud Bi's relative Suhrab Beg. Assuming a different time frame than Badakhshi and Fofalzai, Lord reports that Qubad Khan distinguished himself in Timur Shah's Indian campaign of 1781. In return, he was rewarded with the district of Nahrin south of Qunduz. From there, he was able to expand his authority to Qunduz, the regions north of the Oxus, as well as Balkh and Shibarghan. (Lord 1839a; 98–100)
68 TB: 46–55; Fofalzai 1967: 164–165; Lord 1839a: 98–99. The dates given for these events vary. Badakhshi places the advent of the Afghan army in the year 1184/1770–1. Fofalzai emphasizes that it took place after Timur Shah had shifted his capital to Kabul in 1186/1772–3. Lord claims that Qubad Khan conquered Badakhshan in 1785 and that he was deposed in favor of Khuda Nazar Beg in 1792.
69 Adamec 1975: 162.
70 Grevemeyer 1982: 66–67.
71 Fofalzai 1967: 173–174; Lee 1987: 128; Strachey, 'Revenue and Trade', f. 136.

72 Boukhary 1876: 249.
73 Ferrier 1858: 101. Also see TSu 157.
74 ST 57. Also see Husaini 1967: 32. According to Strachey, Shah Zaman received 'some horses and no cash' from Balkh. (Strachey, 'Revenue and Trade', f. 136)
75 Gupta 1944: 268, 278–279.
76 Elphinstone 1972 II: 197. According to Schefer, however, one third of the 30,000 rupees raised in Balkh were submitted to Kabul. The other two thirds were split equally for the maintenance of the *kuhna naukar* and the payment of Uzbek troops engaged for military expeditions to areas outside of Balkh. (Schefer's appendix in Boukhary 1876: 260–261)
77 Howorth 1973 II: 868; Lee 1996: 122, 125, 163–164, 210–211; Stirling 1991: 231, 286.
78 Bregel, 'Central Asia VII' in *EIr*; Bregel, 'Mangit' in *EI2*.; Wheeler 1979: 22; KN 11–13 July 1855 (For. Sec. 28 September 1855 No. 40); EKN 4 July 1856 (L/P&S/5/228 No. 43 of 22 September 1856, pp. 684–685)
79 Centlivres 1976b: 122–123.
80 Ferrier 1971: 204.
81 Lee 1996: 92–93, 113.
82 Gupta 1944: 278; Lee 1987: 127–128; Lee 1996: 125 141; Schefer's appendix in Boukhary 1876: 261; Stirling 1991: 284–285.
83 Vambéry lists Alvar (Almar?), Kafir Qal'a, Qaisar, and Khwaja Kinti as the most important villages of the khanate. (Vambéry 1983: 304, 308)
84 Burnes 1839d: 42–43; *Gaz*. IV: 398; Lee 1987: 124, 129; Stirling 1991: 285. Vambéry also lists escort money (*qamchin pulu*) as source of income. (Vambéry 1983: 308)
85 Ferrier 1971: 198; Lee 1987: 130–131.
86 For a detailed discussion see Lee 1996: 136–140.
87 Ferrier 1971: 198–204, 225–226.
88 Burnes 1973: 226–227; Ferrier 1971: 202–204; 225–226; Lee 1987: 128–129; Matin-i Andkhui 1993a: 3; Matin-i Andkhui 1993b: 3rd installment.
89 Yapp 1980: 368.
90 ST 132–134. The Turkmen contingent in Mizrab Khan's confederacy consisted of 500 horsemen from Khiva under the leadership of Khalifa 'Abd al-Rahman Khan Turkmen. ST also mentions a group of Salor and Sariq Turkmens as participants in the battle. Maimana, Sar-i Pul, Andkhui and Shibarghan furnished 6,000 cavalry. Sher Muhammad Khan Hazara, Zaman Khan Jamshedi, and Shah Pasand Khan Ferozkohi brought about 4,000 foot soldiers and numerous horsemen into the field. During the final encounter with the Qajar army the combined Uzbek, Turkmen, Hazara, Jamshedi and Ferozkohi troops amounted to 20,000 men. For a detailed account see Lee 1996: 149–160.
91 Lee 1996: 190–205; ST 190; Yapp 1980: 367–368.
92 Ferrier 1971: 197–198.
93 Lee 1987: 131–132.
94 Ibid. 132; Vambéry 1864: 240–241; Yate 1888b: 346 347. Reshtia attributes Yar Muhammad Khan's hasty withdrawal from Turkistan to the fact that the eastern dominions of Herat (Ghor, Farah, and Bakwa) were threatened by the Qandahar Sardars. (Reshtia 1957: 132; Reshtia 1990: 202)
95 Lee 1996: 216–218; Wheeler 1979: 20–21.
96 Centlivres 1972: 19; Elphinstone 1972 II: 196; Harlan 1939: 36. According to Faiz Buksh, Qilich 'Ali belonged to the Som section of the 'Mu-i Tanikarama' or 'Karama' Uzbeks. (Faiz Buksh 1871: 11, 52) But Centlivres only lists the following subdivisions of the Muitan Uzbeks at Tashqurghan: Chushman,

Aghshiq, Chaghir, Teli, Garimseli, Kalcha, Qazioghli, Qaochin, Qipchak, Aimaq, and Qerghez.

97 Elphinstone 1972 II: 196–197, 199. Also see Gupta 1944: 279

98 *Gaz.* IV: 572.

99 Elphinstone Collection F 88 Kt, p. 79.

100 ST 69.

101 Centlivres 1972: 19–20, Elphinstone 1972 II: 196.

102 McChesney 1991: 232.

103 Centlivres 1976b: 125.

104 Elphinstone 1972 II: 199.

105 Ibid. II: 196; Harlan 1939: 43–44; Moorcroft & Trebeck 1841 II: 395.

106 Faiz Buksh 1871: 51; Lord 1839a: 100.

107 *Gaz.* IV: 572; Elphinstone 1972 II: 197.

108 Burnes 1973: 227.

109 Boukhary 1876: 73n; Centlivres 1972: 19; *Gaz.* IV: 572; Lord 1839a: 102; Moorcroft & Trebeck 1841 II: 399–400. Faiz Buksh places Qilich 'Ali's death in the year 1234/1818–19. (Faiz Buksh 1871: 52)

110 Boukhary 1876: 73–74; Frye, 'Balkh' in *EI2*; McChesney 1991: 30–35.

111 Husaini 1967: 32.

112 Lee 1996: 222.

113 Harlan 1939: 30, 33; McChesney 1991: 241, 244–245, 251.

114 Ferrier 1971: 208; Burnes 1834 I: 232; Harlan 1939: 33.

115 Harlan 1939: 32, 34–35.

116 Lee 1996: 119; Lord 1839a: 103; McChesney 1991: 233, 262. The Gauhari family owned considerable lands in the region of Qarqi. (Lee 1996: 302n)

117 Harlan 1939: 29–30; *Gaz.* IV: 586–587; Lee 1996: 119 122, 163–172; Lord 1839a: 105–106; Peacocke in *Gaz.* IV: 109.

118 Harlan 1939: 127; ST 206, 209; Yapp 1962: 513; letter by the *wakil* of Mir Wali, Lahore, n.d. (L/P&S/5/190 No. 20 of 3 March 1847, p. 686). Ferrier and Wheeler name Ishan Sudur as the governor of Balkh in the 1840s. (Ferrier 1971: 204, 207; Wheeler 1979: 21)

119 Lee 1996: 320, 552.

120 According to Lord, Mir Murad Beg was born in 1780. (Lord 1839a: 100, 123) The available information on the length of Murad Beg's reign is contradictory. The dates given for his death range from 1838 to 1846. (Boulger 1879 I: 304; *Gaz.* IV: 572; Grevemeyer 1982: 124; Grötzbach 1972: 54) Faiz Buksh reports that Mir Murad Beg was 'afflicted with insanity' from 1839 on and was put to death by his son Mir Ataliq in 1851. (Faiz Buksh 1871: 55, 57–58)

121 Burnes 1834 II: 346; Harlan 1939: 38–39. According to Faiz Buksh, Mir Murad Beg and his four brothers established themselves in Qunduz in 1810. Qilich 'Ali expelled them once in 1812 but subsequently 'relinquished' his claims on Qunduz in favor of the young, energetic general Murad Beg. (Faiz Buksh 1871: 51–52) Lord dates Mir Murad Beg's rise from 1815. (Lord 1839a: 100)

122 Harlan 1939: 28; Lord 1839a: 104–106, 110–111, 119 121. The Bukharan occupations of Balkh in 1817 and 1837–8 were triggered in large part by Mir Murad Beg's activities in the area. Subsequent to Qilich 'Ali's death, Mir Murad Beg entered Balkh and made his brother Ahmad governor there. Shortly afterwards Ahmad gave up the possession of Balkh in the face of approaching Bukharan troops. In 1837 Mir Murad Beg concentrated his troops on the western border of his amirate and seized on the the eastern canals feeding Balkh. (Lee 1996: 163–164; Lord 1839a: 103, 119; Wood 1841: 235–236)

123 Harlan 1939: 35.
124 Burnes 1834 I: 189–190; 193–194; Masson 1974 II: 306–307, 397–399.
125 Burnes 1834 II: 202–206; Grevemeyer 1982: 24, 54, 68, 124; Harlan 1939: 42–43; Lal 1977: 54–60; Pearse 1898: 103–104, 123–124; Lord 1839a: 111; Wood 1841: 247, 250–252; 392. The dates given for the final subjugation of Badakhshan are contradictory. Burnes places the conquest in the early 1820s. (Burnes 1834 II: 302) Grevemeyer (1982: 54) gives the date as 1829. Masson's account of Haji Khan Kakar's activities in Turkistan suggest that Mir Murad Beg finally subjugated Badakhshan in the winter of 1832/1833. (Masson 1974 III: 100) Harlan attributes Murad Beg's ire against the Badakhshis to haughty treatment he suffered while serving in the military of the Mir of Badakhshan. (Harlan 1939: 37) The tribute paid by Shighnan and Roshan was nomimal. According to Wood, the northern territory of Darwaz remained entirely independent. (Wood 1841: 378–379). In 1838 Murad Beg had the chief of Wakhan, Muhammad Rahim Beg, killed allegedly because he failed to render an adequate tribute. (Wood 1841: 329–330; 390–391)
126 Moorcroft & Trebeck 1841: 486.
127 Lal 1977: 59.
128 Lord 1839a: 123.
129 Dubeux 1848: 92. Whereas Elphinstone stated that Qunduz 'is a good town, and exceeds Taush Koorghaun in extent,' the figures given by Burnes in 1832 clearly show that Tashqurghan was economically far superior to Qunduz. Burnes gives a figure of 10,000 inhabitants for Tashqurghan, while he only estimates a population of 1,500 for Qunduz. (Burnes 1834 I: 205; II: 202; Centlivres 1976b: 125; Elphinstone 1972 II: 184) Likewise, Lord contrasts Tashqurghan favorably with Qunduz, describing the former 'a considerable commercial entrepot'. (Lord 1839a: 106)
130 Wood 1841: 214. The Gazetteer, on the other hand, stated in 1914 that Qunduz had been a large fortified town in the past, and 'must have been a remarkable place in its day.' (*Gaz.* I: 116)
131 Moorcroft & Trebeck 1841: 421–422.
132 Burnes 1834 I: 224. Also see Wood 1841: 214.
133 Lal 1977: 59.
134 Wood 1841: 216.
135 Ibid. 217–218.
136 Ibid. 217. Qunduz, Hazrat Imam, Khanabad, and Taliqan formed the core area of Mir Murad Beg's possessions. Hazrat Imam and Taliqan were governed by his brother, Muhammad Beg, and his son, Mir Ataliq, respectively. The Tajik Musa Yasawal, 'a household slave' of the Uzbek ruler, was entrusted with the government of Khanabad. Ghori and Ishkamish were in the hands of Qataghan leaders of the *urugh* of Munas. Chal was held by a leader of the Temuz (a subdivision of the Munas Qataghan). The governors named for Andarab, Khost, and Firing were Tajiks. (Lord 1839a: 105–107, 123; Wood 1841: 235, 240)
137 Burnes 1834 II: 348; Grevemeyer 1982: 55; Harlan 1939: 60–61; Lord 1839a: 113; Moorcroft & Trebeck 1841: 444.
138 Burnes 1834 II: 348; Harlan 1939: 39; Lal 1977: 59; Lord 1839a: 114–115; Wood 1841: 216. Lal, who gives the figure of 20,000 was of the opinion that Murad Beg's troops also included foot soldiers.
139 Harlan 1939: 60.
140 Lord 1839a: 106, 111–113.
141 Harlan 1939: 44–45, 82–83; Lal 1977: 54; Lord 1839a: 112, 115; Masson1974 II: 307. During Burnes's visit to the region in 1832 Rahmatullah

Khan was said to avoid slave raids into Hazarajat and rather sell his own subjects as revenue. (Burnes 1834 I: 193–194)

142 Tashqurghan exported up to 200,000 animal hides annually to Bukhara. The caravans to Kabul carried gold, silk, sheep, cotton and horses. (Harlan 1939: 39; Lal 1977: 59, 63–64; Lord 1839b: 128; Wood 1841, 404)

143 Lord 1839a: 112.

144 Burnes 1834 II: 350; Grötzbach 1972: 54; Lord 1839a: 111.

145 Lord 1839a: 111; Moorcroft & Trebeck 1841: 483.

146 Burnes 1834 II: 350; Moorcroft 1841 II: 482; Wood 1841: 250–252, 259, 266, 314–316.

147 McChesney 1991: 237–238; Moorcroft & Trebeck 1841: 444.

148 Harlan 1939: 30.

149 Lal 1978 I: 212; Masson 1974 III: 100–101.

150 Mir Murad Beg gave a daughter to be married to a son of Dost Muhammad Khan, who in turn affianced one of his daughters to the son of the Mir of Qunduz. (For. P.C. 11 September 1837 No. 34)

151 Wood 1872: 117.

152 Lord 1839a: 106.

153 Harlan 1939: 16, 36–41.

154 Ibid. 41.

155 Ferrier 1971: 207; *Gaz.* IV: 572; Yapp 1962: 509–513.

156 Ferrier 1971: 202–204; 211; Harlan 1939: 37. Ferrier gives the revenues of Tashqurghan as £24,000 in silver and £ 50,000 in grain.

157 Centlivres 1972: 20.

158 Masson 1974 II: 306.

159 Lord 1839a: 122.

160 Holzwarth 1980: 193; Lord 1839a: 107; Wood 1841: 241, 248.

161 McChesney 1991: 260.

162 ST 198, 201; Laurence to Curvie 19 February 1847 (L/P&S/5/190 No. 20 of 3 March 1847, pp. 685–688).

163 Alder 1974: 105; Reshtia 1957: 130–131; Reshtia 1990: 199–201.

164 *Gaz* IV: 572–573; Wheeler 1979: 20.

165 ST 206.

166 KN 9 August 1851 (For. Sec. 29 August 1851 No. 47); Wheeler 1979: 21.

167 Wheeler 1979: 21.

168 KN 5 June 1854 (For. Sec. 28 July 1854 No. 10.)

169 Reshtia 1957: 133.

170 Lee 1987: 133; ST 208–210, 227–239.

171 Reshtia 1957: 131–132; Reshtia 1990: 201. It is not clear whether this obligation to submit revenues stemmed from the formal commitments entered by the Mirs during the Sadozai era or had been imposed by Dost Muhammad Khan at a more recent date.

172 ST 206

173 Ibid. 208.

174 McChesney 1991: 257–260.

175 According to Vambéry, Daniyal Bi was related to the Tuqai-Timurids on the maternal side. (Vambéry 1872 II: 147)

176 Reshtia 1957: 132; Reshtia 1990: 202.

177 KN 18 April 1850 (For. Sec. 31 May 1850 No. 76); KI 11 November 1850 (For Sec 27 Dec 1850 Nos. 28–29); KN 30 March–15 April 1851 (For. Sec. 30 May 1851 No. 54)

178 Wheeler 1979: 21; ST 209.

179 Faiz Buksh 1871: 57; Lee 1996: 231–232; MacGregor 1871: 149; Wheeler 1979: 21. Wheeler is of the opinion that Muhammad Afzal Khan also executed the Mutawalli of Mazar-i Sharif at this time. According to Lee, however, Shuja' al-Din had already died in the autumn of 1849, prior to Sardar Muhammad Akram's conquest of Balkh. (Lee 1996: 222) Thus it is not clear whether Wheeler confounds two separate events, or whether a person other than Shuja' al-Din was put to death at this time.

180 Dost Muhammad Khan awarded the title of Nizam al Mulk to Mir Hakim Khan and bestowed a seal with the title of Amin al-Daula on Ghazanfar Khan. (ST 210) According to Reshtia, these two Uzbek rulers also assisted Muhammad Afzal's half brothers Muhammad Sharif and Muhammad Aslam in putting down a revolt instigated by Mahmud Khan in the Hazarajat. (Reshtia 1957: 133; Reshtia 1990: 203–204)

181 In April 1850 he had Muhammad Akram Khan's messengers 'Abd al-Sami' Khan and Na'ib Zulfaqar Khan put in irons. (KN 18 April 1850, For. Sec. 31 May 1850 No. 76)

182 KN 24 October 1854 (For. Sec. 26 January 1855 No. 100) According to another entry, the troops accompanying Mir Wali (including his own) to Shibarghan amounted to 8,000 men. (KN 6 September 1854, For. Sec. A 24 November 1854 No. 14)

183 KI 19 November 1850 (For. Sec. 27 December 1850 No. 29); KN 3 February 1851 (For. Sec. 28 March 1851 No. 42); KI 30 June 1851 (For. Sec. 25 July 1851 No. 54).

184 Lee 1996: 238.

185 KN 6 September 1854 (For. Sec. A 24 November 1854 No. 14); MacGregor 1871: 150; Wheeler 1979: 22.

186 KN 8 November–11 December 1854; Edwardes to Temple 19 December 1854 (For. Sec. 16 January 1855 Nos. 59, 111); Wheeler 1979: 22.

187 KN 21 January 1855 (For. Sec. 27 April 1855 No. 16); KN 21 May 1855 (For Sec. 31 August 1855 No. 58)

188 Lee 1996: 236–238; Edwardes to Temple 19 December 1854 (For. Sec. 26 January 1855 No. 59) According to another source, Mir Hakim Khan agreed to pay the expenses of the march of the Afghan army to Shibarghan. (Munshi of Sardar A'zam Khan to Major Coke November/December 1854, For Sec. 26 January 1855 No. 109)

189 KN 10 April 1856 (L/P&S/5/227 No. 25 of 17 June 1856, p. 810)

190 EKN 6 December 1855 (L/P&S/5/226 No. 9 of 22 February 1856, p. 833)

191 EKN 31 December 1855–8 January 1856 (L/P&S/5/226 No. 12 of 22 March 1856, pp. 926–927)

192 EKN 5 February 1856 (L/P&S/5/227 No. 16 of 22 April 1856, pp. 304–305)

193 EKN 29 February 1856 (L/P&S/5/ 227 No. 21 of 17 May 1856, pp. 603–604)

194 EKN 17 March 1856 (L/P&S/5/227 No. 21 of 17 May 1856, pp. 608–609); MacGregor 1871: 154–155.

195 MacGregor 1871: 155.

196 Lee 1987: 133; Lee 1996: 248–249; KN 10 April–1 May 1856 (L/P&S/5/227 No. 25 of 17 June 1856, pp. 810–820); EKN 25 May 1856 (L/P&S/5/228 No. 28 of 17 July 1856, p. 67). Ishan Oraq was taken prisoner again. (Wheeler 1979: 25–28)

197 MacGregor 1871: 158–160; EKN 4–16 July 1856 (L/P&S/5/228 No. 43 of 22 September 1856, pp. 684–690); EKN 3–14 August 1856 (L/P&S/5/229 No. 54 of 22 October 1856, pp. 247, 251)

198 Lee 1996: 272–275; KD 23–29 April 1860 (For. Pol. A. May 1860)

199 Vambéry 1864: 246–249; Vambéry 1983: 300–306.

200 Lee 1996: 244, 254, 263. In August 1855 Sardar Wali Muhammad Khan reported that a Persian army of 7,000 men had occupied Maimana after a short siege and temporarily relieved Hukumat Khan of his authority. (KN 16 August–6 September 1855, For. Sec. 28 December 1855 No. 72); EKN 21 October 1855, L/P&S/5/226 No. 3 of 22 January 1856, p. 526) In December 1856 Sardar Muhammad Afzal accused the leader of Maimana and Mir Ataliq of Qunduz of negotiating with Persia to 'concert measures about the capture of Oozbekia.' (EKN 16 December 1856 (L/P&S/5/ 230 No. 14 of 21 March 1857) Two years later Sardar Muhammad Afzal Khan reported that Mir Hukumat Khan had submitted to the government of Persia and undertook to pay revenues and to assist the Qajar government militarily during its planned military campaigns in Turkistan. (KN 15 August 1858, For. S. C. 26 November 1858 No. 21; KN 13 February 1859, For. S. C. 27 May 1859 No. 3; KD 20–26 August 1860 (For. Pol. A. October 1860 No. 5)

201 At the time of Hakim Khan's defeat by the Muhammadzais in February 1856, the 'Turkmens' of Maimana and Andkhui sought the support of the Muhammad Yusuf Khan Sadozai, who ruled Herat from fall 1855 until April 1856. (EKN 29 February 1856, L/P&S/5/227 No. 21 of 17 May 1856, pp. 603–604) In February 1858 the Mir of Maimana asked Sardar Muhammad Afzal Khan for assistance against the Persians. (KN 16 February 1858, For. Sec. 28 May 1858 No. 17) According to Faiz Buksh, Hukumat Khan submitted to Amir Dost Muhammad Khan in 1859 (?), receiving the title 'Shuja' al-Daula' from the Afghan king. (Faiz Buksh 1871: 58–59) In 1860 the Mir of Maimana attempted to ward off pressure by Sardar Muhammad Afzal Khan by submitting to the new ruler of Herat, Sultan Ahmad Khan Barakzai (r. 1857–1863). When the relationship with Herat soured, the Mir of Maimana again pledged allegiance to Sardar Muhammad Afzal Khan. (Lee 1996: 276–280) He is also reported to have formally accepted the sovereignty of Kabul in 1861 and 1862. (MacGregor 1871: 157–158)

202 These movements were not only the result of pressure exerted by the surrounding greater powers but were also brought about by rivalries among the various Turkmen tribes and their subdivisions. In the mid–1850s the Tekke assumed control of Merv. This forced the Sariq to migrate southwards to Yulatan and Panjdih. In the 1880s they were reported to have settled in the region of the confluence of the Kushk and Murghab rivers. The Salor were almost entirely scattered by the events at Merv and the southward push of the Sariq. In the 1880s the majority of them had been incorporated into the Tekke confederation. On Afghan territory, members of this tribe were to be found near Maruchaq on the upper course of the Murghab, south of the region inhabited by the Sariq. Small groups were also present in the vicinity of Maimana and Herat. The majority of the Ersari lived in Bukharan territory on the left hand of the Oxus. In the 1870s and 1880s groups of Ersari were reported to inhabit the region around Andkhui and the northwestern portion of Aqcha and Shibarghan. Andkhui was also the home of the Alieli. (Akiner 1983: 316; Barthold 1962: 35; Boulger 1879 I: 221–224; *Gaz.* IV: 47; De Blocqueville 1980: 55–57, 68, 83; Holdich 1885: 282; Jarring 1939b: 36–50; Lumsden 1885: 565–567; Marvin 1880: 127–130; Roskoschny 1982: 17; Skrine & Ross 1899: 267–270; Stewart 1881: 531, 534; Vambéry 1885: 396–401; Yate 1888b: 101, 117, 157–158, 184–189; Mashhad Agent to Thomsen 23 May 1876, For. Pol. A. July 1876 No. 208)

203 Planhol 1976: 282–284; Yate 1888b: 135–142, 342; KD 21–23 September 1869 (For. Pol. A Oct. 1869 No. 283); KD 10–13 March 1871 (For. Pol. A May 1871 No. 56).
204 Harawi 1990: 22; Lee 1996: 416–418; Marvin 1880: 128–130, 139; Skrine & Ross 1899: 284–286; Yate 1888b: 342.
205 KN 19 February 1855 (For. Sec. 25 May 1855 No. 37)
206 EKN 31 December 1855 (L/P&S/5/226 No. 12 of 22 March 1856, pp. 925–926); EKN 21 January 1856 (L/P&S/5/227 No. 16 of 22 April 1856, p. 299)
207 EKN 29 February 1856 (L/P&S/5/227 No. 21 of 17 May 1856 pp. 603–604)
208 Dupree 1980: 356; Reshtia 1957: 132.
209 Ghulam Ahmad 1856: 690, 732. Sardar Muhammad Afzal Khan's son 'Abd al-Rahman Khan claims that the regular army of Balkh consisted of 15,000 regulars in addition to 15,500 Uzbek, Durrani and Kabuli militia. (SM I: 5; TT 10) But the figure of 9,000 appears more realistic in the light of Sardar Muhammad Afzal Khan's constant requests for reinforcements from Kabul.
210 KN (Lahore, 30 November 1853) (For. Sec. 30 December 1853 No. 53); KN 5 June 1854 (For. Sec. 28 July 1854 No. 10); Wheeler 1979: 22.
211 KN 6 September 1855 (For. Sec. 28 December 1855 No. 72)
212 EKN 7 October 1855 (L/P&S/5/226 No. 11 of 8 March 1856, pp. 862–863)
213 KI 1–15 May 1851 (For. Sec. 25 July 1851 No. 54)
214 ST 209.
215 AKN 6 December 1855 (L/P&S/5/226 No. 9, p. 833); MacGregor 1871: 153.
216 ST 227. For a slightly different account, see SM I: 8–9.
217 Diary of Nawwab Faujdar Khan at Jalalabad 17–23 March 1859 (For. S. C. 27 May 1859 No. 7) Nawwab Faujdar Khan designates the disputed area as 'Ghorian' (located in western Turkistan). But it is more likely that the principality of Ghori, located south of Qunduz, formed the bone of contention between Sardar Muhammad Afzal Khan and Mir Ataliq.
218 KN 3 September 1858 (For. S. C. 26 November 1858 No. 21).
219 KN 27 March–9 April 1853 (For. Sec. 27 May 1853 No. 157); Wheeler 1979: 21.
220 KN 9 August 1855 (For. Sec. 30 November 1855 No. 44)
221 KN 16 August 1855 (For. Sec. 28 December 1855 No. 72)
222 MacGregor 1871: 161; Muhammad Afzal Khan to Dost Muhammad Khan, 10 February 1859 (For. S. C. 29 April 1859 No. 19); Nawwab Faujdar Khan at Jalalabad, 19–23 March 1853 (For. S. C. 27 May 1859 No. 7)
223 SM I: 9, 13; TT 14, 17. According to 'Abd al Rahman Khan, these items were given to Mir Ataliq by Amir Muzaffar al-Din. However, Muzaffar al-Din's father Nasrullah was still in power in Bukhara when the Afghan war against Qunduz began. Perhaps the primary intent of this anecdote is to point out the remoteness of Bukhara and Mir Ataliq's poor faculties as a ruler as reflected by his acceptance of this odd offer.
224 ST 235–236; SM I: 21–24.
225 Mir Ataliq's envoys to Sardar Muhammad Afzal Khan and Amir Dost Muhammad Khan are both described as 'a brother' of Mir Ataliq without the addition of any names. Therefore, it is not clear whether one or several of Mir Ataliq's relatives acted as his emissaries. The brother sent by Mir Ataliq to the governor of Turkistan was killed shortly afterwards by Mir Ataliq for having been coopted by Muhammad Afzal Khan. (ST 227) If the emissaries mentioned are identical the Qunduz mission to Kabul must have taken place prior to the one to Muhammad Afzal Khan. Faiz Buksh, on the other hand, claims that Mir

Ataliq killed his brother 'Ismatullah as early as 1853 for having cooperated with Sardar Muhammad Afzal. (Faiz Buksh 1871: 58; for a list of Mir Ataliq's brothers, see ibid. p. 70)

226 The plan to conquer Qunduz had formed a subject of discussion at the court of Kabul since summer 1855. (KN 14 July 1855, For. Sec. 28 September 1855 No. 40; KN 23 July 1855, For. Sec. 30 November 1855 No. 44)

227 MacGregor 1871: 161; KN 11 August–4 September 1858 (For. S. C. 26 November 1858 No. 21)

228 SM I: 10–27; TT 14–29. The account in ST 229–237, 239 closely approximates the narrative given in TT There are, however, variations in some details and the spelling of names. Therefore, it cannot be safely assumed that the author of ST based his account directly on TT

229 SM I: 10; ST 229; TT 15.

230 KD 2–8 July 1859 (For. S. C. 26 August 1859 No. 9); SM I: 11–14; ST 229–230; TT 15–17.

231 SM I: 18; TT 21; KD 29 August–5 September 1859 (For. S. C. 28 October 1859 No. 8)

232 SM I: 14; ST 231; TT 18; KD 29 August–5 September 1859 (For. S. C. 28 October 1859 No. 8)

233 SM I: 15; ST 232; TT 18–19. ST gives the name of the Kolabi ruler as Mir Sara Beg.

234 SM I: 15–16; ST 232; TT 19. According to ST, Sardar Muhammad Zaman Khan was governor of Taliqan at that point in time.

235 SM I: 17–19; TT 20–22. At this point, the account in ST diverges from that of TT According to ST, 'Abd al Rahman Khan continued to hold the prisoners both of Taliqan and Badakhshan because these areas 'were not properly controlled yet.' (ST 233–234)

236 SM I: 19–21; ST 234–235; TT 22–24.

237 SM I: 25; TT 27. According to ST, the daughter of Mir Shah was offered to Muhammad A'zam in marriage. (ST 236–237)

238 TT 27.

239 KD 23–29 April 1860 (For. Pol. A. May 1860)

240 According to TT and ST, the following mines were handed over to Afghan control: five gold, one lapis lazuli (located in the upper Kokcha valley), one agate or jasper (*sang-i sulaimani*, *yashb*), and one ruby (in Gharan). (TT 29; ST 239) It is not clear how productive these mines were. In 1837 Wood reported that Mir Murad Beg had given up working the ruby and lapis lazuli mines for lack of profit. (Wood 1841: 266; 315–316) In 1867 Pandit Manphul noted that the ruby mines had not been worked for twenty years. (Yule 1872: 443). In 1923, Kushkaki stated that neither the ruby mine of Gharan nor the one close to the Russian border were exploited. (Kushkaki 1989: 174) In 1873 the lapis lazuli mine was worked by fifty men and its yearly profit was estimated at 50,000 to 60,000 'Muhammadshahi' rupees. (KD 24–27 October 1873, For. Sec. March 1874 No. 8).

241 Faiz Buksh 1871: 59–63; Grevemeyer 1982: 69–70; Hensman 1978: 345–346; Holzwarth 1990: 41; Lee 1996: 309–310; Montgomerie 1872: 197; ST 281, 293; TB 80 83; Wheeler 1979: 30–34; KD 4 January 1869 (For. Pol. A. February 1869 No. 176); KD 30 September 1869 (For. Pol. A. October 1869 No. 285); KD 1–4 October 1869 (For. Pol. A. November 1869 No. 149); KD 20–22 January 1871 (For. Pol. A. February 1871 No. 489); KD 29 April–5 May 1870 (For. Pol. A. August 1870 Nos. 28–29); KD 2–4 July 1872 (For. Sec. August 1872 No. 23).

242 Naib Muhammad ᶜAlam Khan appointed General Hafizullah Khan governor of Badakhshan; Mir Mahmud became a state pensioner. (Gordon 1875: 339; Principal Events of 1875, For Pol. A March 1877 No. 608; KD 17–19 June 1873, For. Sec. July 1873 No. 66; KD 22–24 July 1873, For. Sec. October 1873 No. 97; KD 22 25 August 1873, For. Sec. November 1873 No. 21). The revenue assessment rose from four Badakhshani *sers* of grain per plough to seven Badakhshani *sers*. In addition Naᵓib Muhammad 'Alam Khan levied a poll tax of six rupees per marriage and attempted to exploit the lapis lazuli mine more extensively. (KD 24–27 October 1873, For. Sec. March 1874 No. 8)

243 Lambert 1886.

244 Khafi 1957 II: 4–5; Lee 1996: 310–313; McChesney 1991: 269; ST 296–297; Wheeler 1979: 31; KD 29 November–23 December 1867 (For. Pol. A January 1868 No. 49)

245 The exact date of the foundation of Takhta Pul is not clear. According to ST, the capital was built in 1269/1852–3. Sardar Muhammad Afzal Khan also established a school there for the instruction of the young 'Abd al-Rahman Khan. The construction of the entire capital took three years. (ST 214) 'Abd al-Rahman Khan states in his memoirs that one of the first buildings erected at Takhta Pul was a school. The construction began subsequent to the conquest of Shibarghan, probably in early 1855. (SM I: 1–2; TT 7–8) Faiz Buksh is of the opinion that the construction of the fortress of Takhta Pul began in 1858. (Faiz Buksh 1871: 12).

246 Lee mentions two of Shuja' al-Din' sons, Sufi Khan (executed in 1868) and Rustam Khan (d. 1878), describing Rustam Khan as the Mutawalli of the shrine from 1867 to 1875. (Lee 1996: 313, 331, 337, 352–353, 370). In his narrative of the events of 1867, Khafi names Mir Aslam Khan as the governor of Mazar-i Sharif and Hijdah Nahr. (Khafi 1957 II: 5) In 1871 Faiz Bakhsh describes Sayyid Sulaiman b. Shuja' al-Din as the head attendant. (Faiz Buksh 1871: 10–11)

247 Faiz Buksh 1871: 57; ST 210.

248 Lee 1996: 294, 308, 312–313, 338–339; Wheeler 1979: 25–26, 31. According to Khafi, however, Sher 'Ali Khan appointed Ishan Sudur as governor of Tashqurghan and Aibak and awarded the governorship of Aqcha to his son in fall 1867. (Khafi 1957 II: 5) Ganj 'Ali and Ghulam Beg were rumored to have been executed by Sardar 'Abd al Rahman Khan in fall 1868. (Lee 1996: 331; KD 24 September 1868, For. Pol. A October 1868 No. 121)

249 KD 17–30 October 1876 (For. Sec. December 1876 Nos. 65, 71) In 1876–77 Ghulam Muhammad Riza Khan served as the first Afghan governor of Maimana. (Lee 1996: 358 373; ST 335)

250 ST 210, 232.

251 Faiz Buksh 1871: 63; Hensman 1978: 179; Khafi 1957 II: 5; Lee 1996: 290, 294, 301–302, 307, 313, 459; ST. 261, 272–273, 298, 335; Wheeler 1979: 30–33; KD 11–14 March 1870 (For. Pol. A April 1870 No. 45); KD 17–20 June 1870 (For. Pol. A August 1870 No. 54).

252 Faiz Buksh 1871: 63; Lee 1996: 268–269, 274, 296, 307, 311; ST 298, 335; Wheeler 1979: 30–32.

253 The exact date of Ghazanfar Khan's death is not clear. According to British documents, Ghazanfar Khan died a natural death in late 1868 or early 1869 (KD 7 January 1869, For. Pol. A February 1869 No. 177; KD 2 June 1870, For. Pol. A August 1870 No. 44). Yet Faiz Muhammad lists Ghazanfar Khan among the Uzbek leaders who were forced to live in Kabul in autumn 1875. (ST 335)

254 Marvin 1880: 38–39; Wheeler 1979: 31–33; KD 17–19 June 1873 (For. Sec. July 1873 No. 66).

255 Khafi 1957 II: 41–43; Lee 1996: 306, 313, 325–330; Merk 1886a: 12; Nuri 1956: 75, 147; SM I: 95–96; ST 297–300; Wheeler 1979: 29–33;

256 Merk 1886a: 12–13; KD 21 March–3 April 1876 (For. Sec. May 1876 Nos. 41, 108–111); for a graphic account of the siege and its effect on Maimana see Lee 1996: 344 359. Ghubar and ST place these events in 1873–74. (Ghubar 1981: 596; ST 335)

257 Lee 1996: 362–363.

258 SM I: 28–30; TT 30–31.

259 Faiz Buksh 1871: 70; *Gaz.* I: 94–95; Kushkaki 1989: 14–16, 256; MacGregor 1871: 163–164; Rasuly-Paleczek, 'Kinship and Politics': 11; SM: 174; TT 158; Wheeler 1979: 28; Yate 1888b: 319.

260 The dates given for the beginning of Jahandar Shah's reign vary between 1860 and 1864 (Faiz Buksh 1871: 60; TB 80). Jahandar Shah concluded marriage alliances with Sardars Muhammad Afzal Khan and 'Abd al-Rahman Khan. He lost control of Badakhshan for the first time after his defeat at the hands of Sher 'Ali Khan's ally and half brother Sardar Faiz Muhammad Khan in 1867. Mir Jahandar Shah fled to Chitral and subsequently joined the court of Sardar Muhammad A'zam at Kabul in 1868. In October of the same year he was restored to the government of Badakhshan, only to lose it to his rival Mahmud Shah in September 1869. The following years he spent as an exile moving back and forth between Kulab, Bukhara, Samarqand, Tashkent, Khoqand, Wakhan and Chitral. In 1878 he was assassinated by his son Sherdil in Farghana. (Faiz Buksh 1871: 60–65; ST 293, 303; Hensman 1978: 345–346; TB 80–83; Wheeler 1979: 31; KD 4 January 1869, For. Pol. A February 1869 No. 176; KD 14–17 May 1869, For. Pol. A August 1869 No. 15; KD 30 September 1869, For. Pol. A October 1869 No. 285; KD 20–23 January 1871, For. Pol. A February 1871 No. 489; KD 10–13 March 1873, For Sec. April 1873 No. 16; KD 15–18 August 1873, For. Sec. October 1873 No. 117)

261 ST 231; TT 18; SM I: 14.

262 KD 1–7 August 1859 (For. S. C. 30 September 1859 No. 2)

263 SM I: 32; TT 34.

264 Lord 1839a: 111; MacGregor 1871: 162; Moorcroft & Trebeck 1841: 483; KD 1–7 August 1859 (For. S. C. 30 September 1859 No. 2) In 1871 the land revenue was still one tenth of the produce. The assessment on flocks had doubled. Instead of one sheep per hundred, one sheep in forty was collected. (Faiz Buksh 1871: 17) According to other sources, the assessment of 2.5% on sheep had already been current during Mir Murad Beg's time. (Grevemeyer 1990: 46–47)

265 SM I: 28–30; TT 30–32.

266 According to Khalfin, the Afghan population of Lesser Turkistan amounted to 11,750 souls while the Uzbeks, Tajiks, Turkmens and Hazaras of the region numbered 640,000. In 1885 the Gazetteer of Afghan Turkistan stated that Afghans in the province numbered less than 3,500 households out of a total population of 87,000 families. (Khalfin 1958: 254; Lee 1996: 480–484)

267 Kushkaki 1989: 16–19, 44, 60, 87, 98, 139, 170, 259.

268 Rasuly-Paleczek 1993a: 92–94.

269 Kushkaki 1989: 27, 36, 60, 69, 77, 83, 89, 97. The ulama not only derived their standing from their public role as learned men and mediators but were often important landowners and merchants. In 1824 Moorcroft described Qasim Khan, the Khwaja of Taliqan, as one of the most influential spiritual

leaders in the Qunduz region. He also had a measure of influence at the court of Qunduz, as Mir Murad Beg was both his *murid* and son-in-law. Moorcroft not only noted the steady stream of visitors to the residence of the Khwaja but also his mercantile activities: 'Notwithstanding his saintly character, he was a dealer in merchandise, and especially in slaves, of whom a portion taken in his forays were usually presented to his Pirzada by Murad Beg.... Besides the profits of trade, the Pirzada derives some advantage from his cattle, as he has one hundred brood mares, and several very large flocks of sheep.' (Moorcroft & Trebeck 1841 II: 476, 479–480) In 1839, Lord stated that the *pirs* among the Qataghan functioned like other local leaders, enjoying 'comfortable villages and jagheers' and furnishing altogether 1,000 soldiers to Mir Murad Beg's army. (Lord 1839a: 115, 118)

270 Holzwarth 1980: 223; Kushkaki 1989: 117, 122, 139, 141, 148, 152, 168, 170, 186, 199, 200, 210, 226.

271 Grevemeyer 1990: 45–51. For accounts of Ishaq Khan's rebellion, please see Kakar 1971: 142–153; Khafi 1957 II: 160–186; Lee 1996: 496–513.

272 ST 231; TT 18; SM I: 14.

273 ST 290.

274 Haim 1983.

275 Orywal 1986: 85. In his general discussion of ethnic identity in Afghanistan, Orywal considers the terms *qaum* and *ta'ifa* analogous. (Ibid. 84) In the case of the Daikundi Hazara, Schurmann observed that the term *ta'ifa* seemed to span the same range of meaning as *qaum* but also described relationships not determined by consanguinity. (Schurmann 1962: 142 n) But in northeastern Afghanistan *ta'ifa* appears to signify a subdivision of the *qaum*. (Centlivres & Centlivres-Demont 1988b: 239)

276 Bacon 1958: 129; Centlivres 1972: 158–159; Centlivres 1979: 35; Holzwarth 1980: 229; Roy 1988: 201–202; Schurmann 1962: 142n.

277 Azoy 1982: 31–32

278 Rasuly-Paleczek 1993b: 79–81.

279 Azoy 1982: 31.

280 Centlivres 1979: 35; Centlivres & Centlivres-Demont 1988b: 239. Also see Balland 1988: 139n, Canfield 1973: 34–35, and Roy 1988: 201–202 for further examples.

281 Kussmaul 1965a: 79–80; Kussmaul 1965b: 516, 518.

282 McChesney 1991: 57. Also see McChesney 1983: 34n; McChesney *EIr* 177.

283 Barfield 1990: 155–170.

284 Lapidus 1990: 33.

285 Wood 1841: 210–211.

286 'In affairs of internal policy Murad Beg seems particularly to attend to two objects – first, that as many of the sirdars as possible should be relatives or creatures of his own, and in this he is not a little assisted by the singular fact that the Ooroogbs or clans of the Uzbeks though so carefully distinguished have nothing like hereditary chiefs. "Who is the head of your clan?" said I to Mingh kul, the present governor of Ghoree, and a man of much influence int he great Ooroogh of Munas: "I am now," replied he, "but you may be tomorrow if the Meer wishes."' (Lord 1839a: 12) While this statement may have been intended to flatter Dr. Lord, it *does* emphasize Mir Murad Beg's relatively powerful position.

287 Centlivres 1976b: 130. This is not to say that all Muitan Uzbeks had settled down in the nineteenth century. Harlan reports that their 'pastoral classes' continued to engage in seasonal migrations in the regions south of Tashqurghan in the 1830s. (Harlan 1939: 59)

288 *Gaz.* I: 95; Lord 1839a: 108. Centlivres speaks of twelve subdivisions (Centlivres 1975: 35)
289 Centlivres 1975: 28–35.
290 Kussmaul 1965a: 75; Rasuly-Paleczek 1993b: 81.
291 Rasuly-Paleczek 1993a: 93–94.
292 Centlivres & Centlivres-Demont 1988a: 239, 242.
293 Azoy 1982: 35–36. Azoy's characterization of Uzbek organization has been criticized as more fitting for the Pashtuns than the Uzbeks of Afghan Turkistan. (See Canfield 1986: 101 fn 12)
294 Centlivres 1975: 35.
295 Rasuly-Paleczek, 'Verwandtschaft und Heirat': 12–13, 16.
296 The position of *arbab* seems to have existed among the Qataghan Uzbeks prior to the Afghan conquest. But its differentiation from that of the *musafid* is not clear. (Rasuly-Paleczek 1993a: 93–95) Among the Ersari Turkmens of Andkhui, Aqcha and Shibarghan the *aqsaqals* apparently continued to be formally recognized as local leaders. In the 1880s they were responsible for assessing revenuies and submitting them to the Afghan government. (Merk 1886b)
297 Grevemeyer 1982: 127; Holzwarth 1980: 188–189.
298 Grevemeyer 1982: 128; Holzwarth 1980: 191–192; Kussmaul 1965a: 81; Montgomerie 1872: 196; Yule 1872: 441.
299 Kussmaul 1965a: 81; Kussmaul 1965b: 517.
300 The nineteenth-century traveller Olufson characterized the *aqsaqa1* as the 'chief magistrate of the village.' (Olufson 1904: 144)
301 Kussmaul 1965a: 81; Kussmaul 1965b: 517.
302 Grevemeyer 1982: 128–130, 146–147; Holzwarth 1980: 211–214; Yule 1872: 443.
303 Holzwarth 1980 214–215; Kussmaul 1965a: 81–85; Kussmaul 1965b: 517
304 Grevemeyer 1982: 154–155; Olufson 1904: 131.
305 Holzwarth 1980: 197, 211, 214; also see Grevemeyer 1982: 134, 140, 158. Olufson considered the division of society so rigid that he spoke of 'castes'. (Olufson 1904: 145) Kussmaul, on the other hand, stresses the 'homogeneous' character of Badakhshani society. (Kussmaul 1965b: 517)
306 Yule 1872: 441.
307 Grevemeyer 1982: 130.
308 Holzwarth 1980: 197.
309 Ibid. 194–195, 200; Ferrier 1971: 204; Holdsworth 1959: 9.
310 Holzwarth 1980: 187.
311 *Gaz.* I: 116
312 Kushkaki 1989: 66.
313 Harlan 1939: 44.
314 *Gaz.* I: 4; Kushkaki 1989: 71.
315 Lord 1839a: 122–123.
316 Wood 1841: 216–217, 240.
317 Elphinstone 1972 II: 182; *Gaz.* I: 3–4; Harlan 1939: 41.
318 Wood 1872: 272.
319 Harlan 1939: 59.
320 Centlivres 1975: 35.
321 Moorcroft & Trebeck 1841 II: 482–483.
322 Grötzbach 1972: 126; Rasuly-Paleczek 1993b: 79.
323 Lord 1839a: 101; Wood 1841: 247.
324 Faiz Buksh 1871: 27; Harlan 1939: 60–61.

325 Wood 1841: 216.
326 Holzwarth 1980: 194, 200.
327 Elphinstone 1972 II: 190.
328 Wood 1841: 210; Wood 1872: 134.
329 Harlan 1939: 44, 58.
330 Muhammad Sharif was in charge of Tashqurghan from 1852 until 1854. Muhammad Amin was recalled from Tashqurghan in winter 1855. (ST 210; Wheeler 1979: 22)
331 KN 5 June 1854 (For. Sec. 28 July 1854 No. 10).
332 ST 210.
333 Sayyid Husain Khan to Ghulam Haidar Khan (For. Sec. 28 July 1854 No. 10)
334 ST 209–210.
335 KN 5 June 1854 (For. Sec. 28 July 1854 No. 10); KN 27 June–14 July 1855 (For. Sec. 28 September 1855 No. 40). MacGregor gives the figure of 37 laks. (MacGregor 1871: 152)
336 KN 22 July–14 August 1855 (For. Sec. 30 November 1855 No. 44)
337 KN 16–17 August 1855 (For. Sec. 28 December 1855 No. 72); MacGregor 1871: 153.
338 In 1857 Muhammad A'zam Khan was still reported to be in charge of Khost, Kurram and Zurmat. (Lumsden 1860: 8–9, 60–64; QM 11 April 1857, L/P&S/5/232 No. 44 of 29 July 1857, pp. 614–615)
339 ST 217; SM I: 2; TT 8.
340 British estimates of Amir Dost Muhammad Khan's net income from Lesser Turkistan vary between 300,000 rupees (in 1856, according to Ghulam Ahmad), 342,000 rupees (in 1857, according to MacGregor 1871 II: 65) and 350,000 rupees per year (according to Merewither, 'Note').
341 In 1877–78 Amir Sher 'Ali Khan collected the following gross revenues in Lesser Turkistan:

Tashqurghan, Aibak, Mazar-i Sharif, Hijdah Nahr, Darra-yi Suf, Sangcharak, Balkhab	Kabuli rupees	2,197,629
Shibarghan	Kabuli rupees	180,845
Maimana	Kabuli rupees	300,000
Sar-i Pul, Darzab, Sarchakan, Gurziwan	Kabuli rupees	251,111
Qunduz and Qataghan	Kabuli rupees	515,000
Badakhshan and Rustaq	Kabuli rupees	300,000
Total	Kabuli rupees	3,744,585

After deductions for administrative costs, religious endowments and the military establishment a net revenue of 900,000 Kabuli rupees remained. (Lambert 1886)
342 It is not quite clear whether the term *wilayat* used here refers to the entire province of Turkistan of just the district of Tashqurghan.
343 SM I: 3; TT 9.
344 Amir 'Abd al-Rahman claims that he collected 50 laks in arrears. (TT 35) According to Sultan Muhammad, 'Abdal-Rahman 'only' collected 15 laks of rupees at that time. (SM I: 33)
345 Ghulam Ahmad 1856: 731–732. This report was compiled on the basis of information gathered in Qandahar. In 1877–78 the troops stationed in Lesser Turkistan (Maimana excluded) numbered approximately 3,000 cavalry and 8,800 infantry. (Lambert 1886)
346 SM I: 5; TT 10.
347 SM I: 27; TT 29.
348 KN 5 June 1854 (For. Sec. 28 July 1854 No. 10)

349 KN 24 August 1854 (For. Sec. 26 November 1858 No. 21)
350 SM I: 29–30; TT 30–32.
351 Ferrier 1971: 204.
352 Elphinstone 1972 II: 198; Yavorski 1885 I: 98.
353 Lal 1977: 67.
354 Centlivres 1976b: 123.
355 McChesney 1991: 234.
356 Yate 1888b: 254–255, 318.
357 Centlivres 1976b: 127.
358 Ibid. 126; Gordon 1876: 133–134, 136–137, 147–148; Harlan 1939: 131–133; Holzwarth 1980: 181; Pearse 1898: 103–104; Wood 1841: 210. In a great part of Badakhshan, revenues were mostly collected in kind until the 1920s. (Holzwarth 1980: 223)
359 Centlivres 1976b: 120–121, 127.

3 THE POSITION OF THE PASHTUN TRIBES IN THE MUHAMMADZAI STATE

1 Caroe 1985: 8–24
2 Elphinstone 1972 I: 233.
3 Barfield 1990: 179; Tapper 1983: 6; Wylly 1912: 8, 51.
4 Gani, *EIr*, 558–559.
5 Tapper 1983: 7.
6 Bacon 1958: 128; Beck 1990: 187; Bruinessen 1992: 64; Evans-Pritchard 1949: 57; Tapper 1983: 6; Tapper 1990: 55–56.
7 Beck 1986: 16 fn. 7.
8 Bacon 1958: 127; Bruinessen 1992: 57, 116–118.
9 Tapper 1990: 51.
10 Eickelman 1981: 88–92.
11 Bruinessen 1992: 134.
12 Beck 1990: 189.
13 According to Bruinessen, the anthropological distinction between lineages and clans on the basis of real or invented claims of descent is largely artificial. Political allegiance may already start playing a role on the lineage level. (Bruinessen 1992: 51)
14 Barfield 1990: 156.
15 Appadurai 1986: 357–359.
16 Gellner 1969: 41.
17 Gellner 1983: 439.
18 Bacon 1958: 42.
19 Gellner 1969: 38.
20 Ahmed 1980: 128, 132–133.
21 Bacon 1958: 128; Bonte 1991: 656; Evans-Pritchard 1949: 55; Peters 1967: 262; Sahlins 1961: 327–328.
22 Gellner 1969: 41–42, 51; Gellner 1983: 438–440; also see Evans-Pritchard 1949: 59.
23 Evans-Pritchard 1956: 147.
24 Sahlins 1961: 326–327.
25 Evans-Pritchard 1949: 59–60.
26 Gellner 1981: 19.
27 Gellner 1983: 440. Also see Gellner 1969: 64, 74, 78.
28 Gellner 1983: 441–442.
29 Sahlins 1961: 323, 342.

30 Gellner 1983: 442–443.
31 Abu Lughod 1989: 280, 285.
32 Appadurai 1986: 357–359. For a similar criticism see Dresch 1988: 57.
33 Caton 1990: 91–92; Dresch 1986: 315–316; Meeker 1976: 254–255.
34 Bonte 1991: 657.
35 Peters 1967: 263–272.
36 Asad 1970: 161–171.
37 Hammoudi 1980: 283–298.
38 Bruinessen 1992: 51, 62.
39 Barfield 1990: 157–172.
40 Salzman 1978: 59–61.
41 Bruinessen 1992: 75–77.
42 Beck 1990: 190–191.
43 Ahmed 1978; Oliver 1890: 108, 183; Wylly 1912: 5–12.
44 Lindholm 1980.
45 Elphinstone 1972 I: 228, 230, 232, 235, II: 18, 69, 152.
46 Davies 1932: 47; Oliver 1890: 185.
47 Harlan 1842: 9–10. Also see Elphinstone 1972 I: 211–215.
48 Wylly 1912: 11–12.
49 Anderson 1978: 168.
50 Estimates of the Pashtun population on both sides of the Durand line vary widely. The above figure is based on estimates from the 1960s. (Dupree 1980: 59) Spain, who conducted his research in the 1950s gives the total Pashtun population as eleven million. In the 1970s, Ahmed arrived at a figure of fifteen million Pashtuns on Pakistani territory alone. (Ahmed 1976: 6) Harrison estimates the entire Pashtun population at 20 million, 10.99 million of which are native to Pakistan and 9 million native to Afghanistan. (Harrison 1986: 286)
51 Ahmed 1976: 7; Ahmed 1980: 128–129; Anderson 1983: 129; Barth 1959: 27; Caroe 1985: 7–24; Elphinstone 1972 I: 210; Glatzer 1977: 107–118; Glatzer 1983: 219–220; Janata 1975: 15; Neamet Ullah 1976 I: 37–38; Raverty 1888: Appendix p. 58–59; Spain 1985: 40–42; Steul 1980: 251; Steul 1981: 28.
52 Glatzer 1983: 226.
53 Tapper 1983: 9–10.
54 The suffix *zai*-'born of' is derived from Pashtu *ziy* ('sons). The term *khel*, from Arabic *khail* ('troop of cavalry') denotes among the Pashtuns lineages of various levels of inclusion. (Anderson 1983: 125, 129; Barth 1959: 13)
55 Tapper 1983: 43, 59–60.
56 Although there often are overlappings in terminology, it may be said that the word *khan* generally denotes a politically more influential position than the terms *malik* and *mashar*. The use of the term *malik* as a leadership position may either point to a relatively unstratified tribal setting or to the lower echelons of more complex societies, such as that of the sedentary Durranis. (Ahmed 1980: 120; Barth 1959: 72; Glatzer 1983: 223–224; Elphinstone 1972 I: 213–217; 234, II: 102–104; Steul 1981: 70; Yapp 1983: 160, 165)
57 Ahmed 1976: 73–82; Ahmed 1980: 116–125.
58 Kakar 1979: 124; Reisner 1981: 54–55; Robinson 1978; Hastings 1880.
59 Kakar characterizes Pashtun nomadism as a 'postagricultural phenomenon'. (Kakar 1979: 124). Glatzer is of the opinion that certain Pashtun groups adopted a nomadic lifestyle or possibly incorporated non-Pashtun nomads after migrating from their original homeland, the Sulaiman mountains. (Glatzer 1977: 127n) In the nineteenth century only a fraction of the Kharoti,

Sulaiman Khel and Taraki Ghilzais followed a nomadic lifestyle. (Raverty 1888: 493, 499–500, 503; Robinson 1978: 30) Nomadism expanded significantly between the 1890s and 1940s owing to 'a unique merging of interests of the nomads and the Afghan state'. (Pedersen 1994: 79) Nonetheless Balland and Janata have drawn attention to the fact that the figures given for the nomads tend to be exaggerated. Janata's research in Paktia showed that 170,000 nomads annually crossed the border with Pakistan in 1972. He reached the conclusion that the total number of nomads in Afghanistan did not exceed 1 million. (Balland 1988b: 266; Janata 1975: 12–14, 25; Janata quoted in Jawad 1992: 13)

60 Glatzer 1983: 219–222.

61 Broadfoot 1886: 359; Elphinstone 1972 II: 154, 174–176; Ferdinand 1962: 125; Kakar 1979: 125; Raverty 1888: 496; Steul 1981: 150. *Tsalwesht* means 'forty' in Pashtu. The *tsalweshtis* were groups of forty which formed a sort of militia led by an authoritarian *mir.* The sedentary Tani Pashtuns of Khost basin also form a militia called *tsalweshti*, ten men being furnished by each of its four subdivisions. At times of confrontation with the Wazirs, this militia may consist of more than forty men. The other Pashtuns of Khost maintain a similar militia called *arbaki.* (Steul 1981: 150)

62 Glatzer 1983: 212–213, 226–227.

63 Anderson 1983: 140.

64 Broadfoot 1886: 388.

65 Robinson 1978: 141.

66 Elphinstone 1972 I: 218, II: 54; Spain 1985: 50; Steul 1981: 54–55.

67 Davies 1932: 50–51; Elphinstone 1972 I: 218; Lumsden 1860: 59; MacGregor 1873 I, 1: 28; Oliver 1890: 143–144, 161–162; Spain 1985: 42, 47, 49; Wylly 1912: 15, 268–280, 349, 395–397; Yapp 1983: 151, 168, 172. The Orakzais and the Bangash furthermore display a split into Sunni and Shia. (Davies 1932: 51; Oliver 1890: 143–144; Wylly 1912: 352–362, 395)

68 Raverty 1888: 193. This author estimated the total group of Yusufzais at 200,000 families. In the 1950s Barth arrived at a figure of 400,000 Yusufzai inhabitants for the Swat valley alone. (Barth 1959: 5) According to Lindholm, the total population of Swat (apparently including non-Yusufzais) was 1 million in the 1970s and 1980s. (Lindholm 1982b: 23)

69 Ahmed 1976: 32–34; Barth 1959: 6–7,11, 30.

70 Raverty 1888: 193

71 Barth 1959: 8.

72 Ibid. 16, 23–25.

73 Barth 1959: 9–13, 65–68, 108; Elphinstone 1972 II: 15–17. The system of a periodic redistribution of land seems to have been limited to certain border tribes, such as the Tarklanris of Bajaur, the Yusufzais of the Swat valley, the Utman Khel, and the Afridis. (Davies 1932: 55; Kakar 1979: 116; McMahon & Ramsay 1981: 41–47, introduction by Christensen, pp. 11–12; Scott 1879: 601) *Wesh* was not as common among the Pashtuns living in the regions forming part of present-day Afghanistan. (Anderson 1975: 586; Hastings 1880; Janata 1975: 18; Merk 1984: 21; Reisner 1981: 47) In Kunar the term refers to the distribution of land which took place only once upon the immigration of the various Pashtun groups which make up the population of this valley today. (Christensen 1980: 80 fn. 4) Among the Khwaezai Mohmands a form of *wesh* seems to have survived until the 1880s. (Kakar 1979: 293n) During the same period, *wesh* was also still practiced in the villages of Hazarnao, Basawal and Girdi Kats in the Jalalabad region. (*Gaz.* VI: 289)

74 Barth 1959: 43–56, 69–73, 81–82, 90–91.
75 Ibid. 57.
76 Ibid. 99.
77 Ibid. 133–134.
78 Ibid. 99–103, 121.
79 Ibid. 104–110; also see Elphinstone 1972 I: 328.
80 Ibid. 126–132, 134.
81 Asad 1972: 85–90.
82 Ahmed 1976: 9–12, 37–48.
83 Ibid. 123–126.
84 Ibid. 14, 53–61, 87–109, 115–119.
85 Lindholm 1981: 148.
86 Lindholm 1982b: 21.
87 Lindholm 1981: 151–154; Lindholm 1982a: 78–82; Lindholm 1986: 347.
88 Lindholm 1990: 34–35.
89 Lindholm 1981: 153–154.
90 Lindholm 1982b: 27–30
91 Ibid. 22–23, 26.
92 Spain 1985: 44.
93 Ahmed 1980: 3, 11, 47–54, 307.
94 Ibid. 60–65.
95 Ibid. 6, 23, 47, 127–131, 160, 182–183, 201–210, 359.
96 Ibid. 146, 158.
97 This title was allegedly conferred by the Prophet on the family of the forefather of all Pashtuns, Qais 'Abd al-Rashid. (Ibid. 128)
98 While he stresses the ephemeral nature of Mohmand leadership, Ahmed also points out that '[t]he leader of the section or sub-section is almost invariably the living senior agnate.' (Ibid. 141–142)
99 Ibid. 120–129, 141–147, 161–167, 359.
100 Ibid. 11, 16.
101 Ibid. 60–70, 142–146, 308.
102 Ibid. 23, 302, 314.
103 Ibid. 147–150, 308–309, 326–345.
104 Ibid. 327. The genealogical memory was less pronounced and the institution of *melmastia*, hospitality, was dying. While continuing to play an important role in the social life, the *jirgas* had lost their judicial functions. (Ibid. 141, 150, 181, 335–336)
105 Ahmed 1975: xviii; quoted in Steul 1981: 153.
106 Ahmed 1980: 330–332.
107 Janata 1975: 13, 27; Steul 1981: 6.
108 Steul 1981: 3, 10, 15, 181.
109 Ahmed 1976: 75
110 Steul 1981: 12, 14, 55–56, 111.
111 Ibid. 17, 84–87. Steul uses the variant spelling of *malik/Malik* to distinguish between two levels of leadership denoted by the same term.
112 Ibid. 41, 70–71, 77–81, 97–98, 117–124, 178–181.
113 Janata 1975: 17; Janata & Hassas 1975: 87, 90.
114 Janata & Hassas 1975: 97; Steul 1981: 102–107.
115 Steul 1981: xiv, 131–135.
116 Janata & Hassas 1975: 85–89; Steul 1981: 139–143, 152–153, 182, 241 243.
117 Anderson 1983: 124.
118 Anderson 1975: 575–584.

119 Ibid. 577, 589; Anderson 1983: 139. There are more examples of dominant lineages among the Pashtuns, suggesting that this phenomenon was not purely the result of a skewed colonialist perception. Robinson lists the Ashraf Khel section of the Shai Khan Khel Nasirs as the khan *khel*. (Robinson 1978: 127) A dominant lineage is also documented for one of the subdivisions of the Ghulab Khan Khel of the Malikdin Khel Afridis. (MacGregor 1873 I,2: 345) Wylly mentions the Malikdin Khel istelf as the *khan khel* of the Afridis and also notes a hereditary khanship for the 'Alisherzai division of the Lashkarzai Orakzais (Wylly 1912: 269, 353) The Morcha Khel among the Tarakzai Mohmands of Lalpura are particularly famous as a leading lineage with a close connection to the Sadozai and Muhammadzai courts. (Merk 1984: 48) For the Pashtuns of Paktia, Janata & Hassas describe two coexistent styles of leadership, based on achievement and/or membership in a dominant lineage (*khan khel*). In their opinion, leadership based on achievement coincides with ancient Indo-European institutions whereas the notion of a leading lineage was possibly introduced by the Central Asian Turco-Mongol nomads in the course of their conquests. (Janata & Hassas 1975: 87, 90)

120 Anderson 1975: 588, 596; Anderson 1982: 7–8; Anderson 1983: 128–131, 143.

121 Anderson 1983: 133.

122 Wylly 1912: 13.

123 Anderson 1975: 599; Anderson 1978: 169–170; Anderson 1983: 132–138, 143–144.

124 MacGregor 1873 I, 1: 28. Also see Lumsden 1850.

125 Ahmed 1983: 197–198. Also See Dupree 1976: 511.

126 Elphinstone 1972 II: 276.

127 Fletcher 1986: 23.

128 Christensen 1980: 80; Steul 1981: 178–179.

129 Rasuly-Paleczek 1993b: 81.

130 Janata 1975: 16.

131 Tapper 1990: 68.

132 Glatzer 1983: 212.

133 Tate 1973: 10.

134 Janata 1987: 212; Spain 1985: 39.

135 Caroe 1985: 11–24; TSu 52.

136 Brentjes 1983: 24, 49. In 982 the earliest Persian geography, the *Hudud al 'alam*, also located the Afghans in this region. (Minorksy 1937: 19–20, 91 92)

137 Raverty 1888: 465–466. An alternative school of thought holds that the Pashtuns were the aboriginal inhabitants of the Peshawar valley, migrated from there to Qandahar in the fifth century A. D. and returned to their original homeland in the fifteenth century because of the pressure exerted by the Central Asian tribes. (See Ahmed 1980: 368–369)

138 Bosworth 1963: 113; Sachau 1888 I: 208.

139 Nazim 1971: 30, 76 Also see Brentjes 1983: 171, Neamet Ullah 1976: 39.

140 Neamet Ullah 1976: 40. Also see Caroe 1985: 125.

141 Raverty 1888: 388n.

142 Baden-Powell 1972 II: 647; Wylly 1912: 419.

143 Davies 1932: 60; McMahon & Ramsay 1981: 58, Plowden 1875: 177–182.

144 Raverty 1888: 127; Wylly 1912: 155–156.

145 Raverty 1888: 54, 100, 122–127. According to Farhang, Babur engaged in six military campaigns against the eastern Pashtuns between 1505 and 1521. (Farhang 1991 I: 42–43)

146 Raverty 1888: 53, 125n, 223.
147 Ibid. 604.
148 Fraser-Tytler 1953: 54; Lockhart 1958: 95.
149 Beattie 1982: 48; Dupree 1980: 183; Gregorian 1969: 33n; Janata 1975: 19 20.
150 Raverty 1888: 100, 682; Warburton 1880: 2–4.
151 Christensen 1980: 79; Ghani 1982: 310.
152 Janata 1975: 20–21; Raverty 1888: 66.
153 Leyden 1812: 397; Raverty 1888: 485n, 694; Röhrborn 1966: 14.
154 Rawlinson 1841: 823; QM 31 July 1857 (For. Sec. 30 April 1858 No. 63)
155 Raverty 1888: 693.
156 Raverty 1888: 54, 390.
157 Until the early sixteenth century Qandahar was held by the Arghun rulers in vassalage with the Timurids of Herat. In 1507 the first Mughal ruler Babur (d. 1530) occupied the city but it subsequently passed back to the possession of the Arghun princes, who ruled it in the name of Muhammad Shibani from that point on. In 1522 Babur was able to regain possession of Qandahar and made his second son, Mirza Kamran, governor there. In 1537 Qandahar passed to Safawid control but Kamran won it back shortly afterwards. In 1545 the Mughal ruler Humayun turned the city over to Persia as part of his effort to regain his throne in India. After the death of the commander of the Safawid army Humayun was able to retake Qandahar. In 1558 the Safawids under Tahmasp I (r. 1524–76) established control there. In 1595 the Mughal emperor Akbar (r. 1556–1605) conquered Qandahar. Having defeated the Uzbeks at Herat, the Safawid ruler Shah 'Abbas I (r. 1588–1629) captured the city in 1622. Sixteen years later the Safawid governor of Qandahar, 'Ali Mardan Khan, voluntarily gave up the city to Mughal control. In 1649 it finally fell to the Persians under Shah 'Abbas II (1642–1666). A third force in the region were the Uzbeks, who were able to take possession of Qandahar for a short period after the death of Shah 'Abbas I. (Riazul Islam 1970: 2–3, 15–18, 23 26, 41–48, 60, 82, 104, 111–112, Szuppe 1992: 113)
158 Ahmed 1980: 11, 60; Barry 1984: 115–116; Barth 1959: 133.
159 Anderson 1983: 125.
160 Kaye 1857: 154; Merk 1984: 33, 43; Wood 1841: 167; M. 'Azim Baraki in Elphinstone Collection F 88 13 Kt, p. 128; Qandahar News 30 November 1877 (For. Pol. A March 1878 No. 128)
161 MacGregor 1873 I, 2: 126, 145, 279.
162 Raverty 1888: 215.
163 Holdich 1909: 53–54.
164 Ahmed 1983: 200.
165 Ghani 1982: 164. The paragraphs are quoted in the reverse order.
166 Holdich 1909: 53–54.
167 Raverty 1888: 116.
168 MacGregor 1873 I,1: 145–146.
169 Scott 1879: 596.
170 Fofalzai 1967: 357; Gordon-Polonskaya 1960: 213; Scott 1879: 601.
171 MacGregor 1873 I, 3: 99.
172 Oliver 1890: 143–144; Scott 1879: 596.
173 *Gaz.* VI: 750. Lumsden 1860: 61–63; MacGregor 1871 II: 576–577; Oliver 1890: 160; Spain 1985: 26; Wylly 1912: 393; KD 11–14 August 1876 (For. Sec. September 1876 No. 60)

174 Ahmed 1983: 202; Broadfoot 1986: 392–394; Elphinstone 1972 I: 380–381; Ghani 1982: 313; Hamilton 1910: 284–286; Holdich 1909: 72; MacGregor 1873 I, 2: 307, 310; MacGregor 1873 I, 3: 9–14, 269–270; Rathjens 1962: 215; Raverty 1895: 157–158; Spain 1985: 26–27, 106; Vigne 1982: 78–79, 82–85; Wylly 1912: 78–83; 91–92; Strachey, 'Revenue and Trade', f. 54.

175 Ahmed 1983: 203; Oliver 1890: 206.

176 Oliver 1890: 123; Raverty 1888: 390.

177 Initiated in Hashtnagar by Bayazid Ansari (d. in the 1580s), a Baraki from Kaniguram, this movement enjoyed the support of the Khalils and was soon joined by the Afridis and Orakzais. It reached its height under the leadership of Bayazid's sons, Shaikh 'Umar (d. 1591) and Jalal al-Din (d. 1599–1600). In 1583 the Mughal forces suffered a major military defeat at the hands of the Yusufzais. In 1586–87 the Mohmands under the leadership of Jalal al-Din attacked the Peshawar district. Two years later a rebellion in Tira had to be subdued. In 1593–94 the Raushanis killed the governor of Kabul province. In 1599 or 1600 Jalal al-Din raided Ghazni. In 1611 Bayazid's grandson Ahdad b. Shaikh 'Umar even attempted to take over the city of Kabul. Fourteen years later he died while battling the Mughals in Tira. Between 1626 and 1628 Ahdad's son 'Abd al-Qadir (d. 1633) confronted the Mughals in the Khyber region and at Peshawar with the support of the Khalils, Mohmands, Yusufzais and Khataks. (Aslanov 1981: 29–31; Davies, 'Afridi', *EI* 2; Leyden 1812: 386–418; Raverty 1888: 45–46; Smith 1946: 34–37; Tate 1973: 23–24)

178 Singer 1984: 28–29; Spain 1985: 32–34, 46n.

179 Ahmed 1984: 8; Farhadi, 'Khatak', *EI* 2; Plowden 1875: 198.

180 Spain 1985: 228.

181 Malleson 1879: 270–272; Oliver 1890; 196.

182 Raverty 1888: 193, 534; Raverty 1894: 317–318; ST 39–40; Strachey, 'Revenue and Trade' f. 54; Elphinstone Collection F 88 13 Kt, pp. 80, 84. According to Caroe, the combined military strength of the Wazirs, Bhitannis and Daurs was estimated at 102,000 in Ahmad Shah's time. But it is not clear whether all of these ever served in the Durrani army. (Caroe 1985: 258)

183 Davies, 'Afridi', *EI* 2.

184 Fofalzai 1967: 357; Raverty 1888: 94–95.

185 Husaini 1967: 30; Masson 1974 I: 163–164; Raverty 1888: 44; Strachey, 'Revenue and Trade', f. 52. According to other sources, the receipts of the Khyber tribes were up to ten times higher during the Sadozai era, adding up to a total of 120,000 or 130,000 rupees for the Afridis and Shinwaris. (MacGregor 1873 I, 2: 130; Lord to Wade 24 October 1838, For. Sec. C. 16 October 1839 No. 70, p. 21.) Other figures quoted are 80,000 rupees per year during the period of Ahmad Shah (Malleson 1879: 390) and 60,000 rupees collected by the Khyber chiefs during Shah Shuja''s reign. (Lal 1977: 46) Could it be that the tribes themselves upgraded the amounts received during bygone eras in order to enhance their bargaining position vis-à-vis the British and Amir Dost Muhammad Khan? Dost Muhammad Khan – generally accused of being much more stingy towards the border tribes than his Sadozai predecessors – paid the Khyber tribes an annual allowance of 25,000 rupees during his second reign. (MacGregor 1873 I, 2: 131) In 1865 the Afridis received 22,900 rupees from Dost Muhammad Khan's successor Amir Sher 'Ali Khan. (Spain 1985: 46 fn 9)

186 Elphinstone Collection F 88 13 Kt.

187 Elphinstone 1972 II: 37; Strachey, 'Revenue and Trade', f. 65; Elphinstone Collection F 88 13 Kt, p. 83; Letter by Lumsden on 27 November 1838 (For. Sec. C. 16 October 1839 No. 78, p. 7)

188 Merk 1984: 48, 92; Raverty 1888: 121–122. According to Faiz Muhammad and Fofalzai, Arsalan Khan himself was the governor of Sirhind at Ahmad Shah's time. (ST 43; Fofalzai 1967: 280) But Husaini, Merk and Singh only mention Zain Khan as governor of Sirhind. (Husaini 1974: fs. 521b, 533b, 571a; Merk 1984: 48; Singh 1981: 281) There are several versions of Arsalan Khan's rebellion. According to the most detailed one by Fofalzai, Arsalan Khan was part of a plot on Timur Shah's life in 1776. After the failure of this plot he withdrew to Dakka where he withstood Timur Shah's attempts to subdue him for the next 16 years. In 1792 he submitted voluntarily after the *qazi al-quzat*, Faizullah Daulatshahi (d. 1793), had guaranteed his security. Having delivered Arsalan Khan to the Durrani court in Peshawar, Faizullah Daulatshahi broke his promise to ensure his safety. Timur Shah, listening to the complaints of the merchants who had suffered at the hands of Arsalan Khan, ordered the execution of the Mohmand leader. (Fofalzai 1958: 30–31; Fofalzai 1967: 280–281; see Raverty 1888: 122, TSu 159–160 for a similar account of Arsalan Khan's submission and death) Ferrier and Singh place Arsalan Khan's plot against Timur Shah in the year 1791. (Ferrier 1858: 102 103; Singh 1981: 388) On the basis of oral information collected among the Mohmands in the late nineteenth century, Merk came to the conclusion that Arsalan Khan rebelled at some point after assuming the leadership in the Dakka region in 1782. His greatest feat was said to be the successful robbery of Timur Shah's revenue collectors who were returning to Kabul from Kashmir and Punjab with a treasure of 700,000 rupees. (Merk 1984: 49)

189 Husaini 1967: 29; Raverty 1888: 217.

190 Raverty 1888: 427; Strachey, 'Revenue and Trade', fs. 68–69.

191 Fofalzai 1958: 87; Husaini 1967: 29.

192 Elphinstone 1972 II: 69; Fofalzai 1958: 188; Husaini 1967: 27; Raverty 1888: 328–329.

193 Elphinstone 1972 II: 257; Lumsden 1860: 62–63; MacGregor 1873 I, 1: 164–165.

194 Raverty 1888: 75–80.

195 Elphinstone Collection F 88 13 Kt.

196 Raverty 1888: 426.

197 Madad Khan Ishaqzai raised annually 40,000 rupees in Kurram and 30,000 rupees in Bannu and Daur. Amounting to 30,000 rupees per year, the revenues of Kohat were collected by a Nurzai *sardar.* (Strachey, 'Revenue and Trade', fs. 95, 98)

198 Burnes 1834 I: 99, II: 302–304; Dupree 1980: 351; Gankovsky 1985: 131 133; Reshtia 1957: 35, 39, 41–42; Reshtia 1990: 64, 69–71, 73–74; Singh 1990: 69–73, 80, 85, 90–92.

199 Broadfoot 1886: 399.

200 MacGregor 1873 I, 1: 18; Pearse 1898: 179, 184; Yapp 1983: 157–158.

201 Davies 1932: 22–28.

202 Wylly 1912: 17, 485–486.

203 MacGregor 1873 I, 1: 4–7, 72, 165–166; I, 2: 200–204, 213–218; Oliver 1890: 189–190; Wylly 1912: 278–285, 396.

204 Miller 1977: 97.

205 Oliver 1890: 197–198

206 Yapp 1983: 157, 188.

207 The estimates of the Afridi population vary. During the Sadozai era their number was given as 40,000 families. (Raverty 1888: 94) This figure was dismissed by Masson in the 1830s, who pointed out that the Afridis turned out 5000 fighting men at the most. (Masson 1974 I: 164) At the beginning of the

nineteenth century Elphinstone estimated the Orakzais, Afridis and Shinwaris at a total of 120,000 souls. (Elphinstone 1972 II: 43). According to Oliver, the Afridis had 26,000 fighting men. (Oliver 1890: 183) In the early twentieth century Wylly gave the fighting strength of the Afridis as close to 30,000. (Wylly 1912: 268–272) In the 1950s Spain estimated that the Afridis numbered 250,000 souls. (Spain 1985: 46)

208 MacGregor gives the following tribal distribution from east to west. 'The portions of the Khaibar held by different clans are said to be as follows: From Syad Mir's Choki, south-east of Jamrud, to Shahi Bagadi road, by Sipahs (1,000 strong). From Shahi Bagadi road to Sultan Tarah, by Kuki Khels (3,000 strong). From Sultan Tarah to Ali Masjid, Malikdin Khel and Kambar Khel (6,000 strong), From Ali Masjid to Garhi Lala Beg [Gadhi La'l Beg], Zakha Khel (3,000 strong). From Lala Beg to Haft Chah, Shinwaris (3,000 strong).' (MacGregor 1873 I, 2: 129) Consisting of four major subdivisions, the total number of Shinwari fighting men was estimated at 13,000 in the nineteenth century. (*Gaz*. VI: 736) In the 1950s Spain gave the Shinwari population as 50,000. (Spain 1985: 48).

209 Ali 1970: 287; Yapp 1983: 168.

210 Malleson 1879: 50; Oliver 1890: 163.

211 Masson 1974 I: 153.

212 MacGregor 1873 I, 1: 26–29; Masson 1974 I: 163; Oliver 1890: 185–186; 191–194.

213 Ali 1970: 215–216; 289–292; Yapp 1983: 160, 171.

214 Ali 1970: 285–287.

215 Masson 1974 I: 163.

216 ST 64; Shah Shuja''s autobiography in Zimmermann 1842: 184–185.

217 Lord to Wade 24 October 1838 (For. Sec. C. 16 October 1839 No. 70, p. 16)

218 Yapp 1983: 168–173.

219 Ali 1970: 211–213, 241–242, 288, 356, 383.

220 Letter by Lumsden of 27 November 1838 (For. Sec. C. 16 October 1839 No. 78, p. 5); KD 30 September–3 October 1870 (For. Pol. A Dec 1870 No. 349)

221 Malleson 1879: 391–392.

222 Masson 1974 I; 147; Raverty 1888: 44, 50.

223 Yapp 1983: 157.

224 Letters by Jum'a Khan and Khan Bahadur Khan to Lord in Lord to Wade 24 October 1838 (For. Sec. C. 16 October 1839 No. 70, pp. 16–21)

225 Havelock 1840 II: 203; Yapp 1983: 162, 174–175. MacGregor estimates the annual expenses of the British government in the Khyber at 125,000 rupees. (MacGregor 1873 I, 2: 131)

226 Ali 1970: 428; MacGregor 1873 I, 2: 131.

227 Yapp 1983: 180–181.

228 With an allowance of 7,000 rupees, the Malikdin Khel were the main beneficiaries. The Kuki Khel and Kambar Khel tribes shared 5,000 rupees a year. The allowance of the Sipahs amounted to 4,000 rupees. The Zaka Khel received 2,000 rupees. (MacGregor 1873 I, 2: 131)

229 MacGregor 1873 I, 2: 131.

230 Edwardes to Brandreth 17 October 1857 (For. Sec. 30 April 1858 No. 89)

231 JI 24 June–8 July 1853 (For. Sec. 30 September 1853 No. 53)

232 KI 16 March 1850 (For. Sec. 31 May 1850 No. 27)

233 The chiefs named are Khwaja Nur Khan, Misri Khan, and Shero Khan. An Afridi chief by the name of Allahdad Khan (possibly the eldest son of Khan Bahadur Khan Malikdin Khel), directly offered his services to the British.

Mackeson to Melvill 30 January 1852 (For. Sec. 27 February 1852 No. 54); KI received in Peshawar on 8 April 1852 (For. Sec. 30 April 1852 No. 97)

234 KN, received in Lahore on 27 December 1853 (For. Sec. 27 January 1854 No. 79); Nawwab Faujdar Khan at Jalalabad, 10–23 February 1859 (For. S. C. 29 April 1859 Nos. 5, 10); KD 2–8 July 1859 (For. S. C. 26 August 1859 No. 9)

235 KD 2 August 1857 (For. Sec. 30 April 1858 No. 89)

236 MacGregor 1873 I, 2: 131; KD 2–8 July 1859 (For. S. C. 26 August 1859 No. 9); KD 8–14 August 1859 (For. S. C. 30 September 1859 No. 5)

237 Yapp 1983: 173.

238 Nawwab Faujdar Khan at Jalalabad, 10 February–9 March 1859 (For. S. C. 29 April 1859 Nos. 5, 10, 14, 19)

239 JI 24 June–8 July 1853 (For. Sec. 30 September 1853); JN 12 October 1855 (L/P&S/5/226 of Jan-March 1856, p. 511)

240 Dost Muhammad Khan to Canning 11 June 1856 (L/P&S/ 5/228 No. 53 of 21 August 1856); Edwardes to James 25 October 1856 (L/P&S/5/229 No. 65)

241 JN 29 January 1857 (L/P&S/5 230 No. 14 of 21 March 1857); Paske to Edmonstone 27 October 1857 (For. Sec. 30 April 1858 No. 87); Edwardes to Brandreth 16 October 1857 (For. Sec. 30 April 1858 No. 88); Dost Muhammad Khan to his *wakil* at Peshawar 27 September 1857, Sardar Muhammad A'zam Khan to Nawwab Faujdar Khan, n. d.; Nawwab Faujdar Khan to Edwardes 29 September 1857; Edwardes to Nawwab Faujdar Khan 10 October 1857 (For. Sec. 30 April 1858 No. 89)

242 The levy consisted of 5 rupees per laden camel (3 rupees if the load was food), 3 rupees per horseman, and 1 1/2 rupees per unladen camel or pedestrian. (Spain 1985: 46n)

243 The transit dues were fixed in cooperation with the merchants of Kabul in the following manner: 4 rupees per loaded camel or pony, all kinds of goods, 2 rupees per load of dried fruits, 2 rupees per horse to be sold, 2 rupees per mounted traveller. KD 26 October–1 November 1869 (For. Pol. A. November 1869 No. 152); KD 26–28 July 1870 (For. Pol. A September 1870 No. 62)

244 KD 30 September–3 October 1870 (For. Pol. A. Dec. 1870 No. 349)

245 KD 31 March–10 April 1871 (For. Pol. A. May 1871 Nos. 462, 466)

246 KD 8–11 December 1871 (For. Sec. January 1872 No. 37); KD 28–30 October 1873 (For. Sec. March 1874 No. 9)

247 KD 14–17 April 1876 (For. Sec. May 1876 No. 115)

248 Oliver 1890: 203–204; Warburton 1900: 216.

249 Masson 1974 I: 250, II: 212; Wylly 1912: 411; Lumsden 1860: 60, 62, 64. According to Masson, the Sulaiman Khel of Zurmat had already been forced to pay a certain tribute during Dost Muhammad Khan's first reign. (Masson 1974 II: 212)

250 Bellew 1862: 116–120; *Gaz.* VI: 426–427; Lumsden 1860: 62; MacGregor 1873 I, 3: 217; Oliver 1890: 143–144, 159–160; Wylly 1912: 391–393, 411. In Timur Shah's time the Turis were thought to count 6000–7000 families. (Raverty 1888: 81) In the nineteenth century estimates of their fighting strength ranged from 3000 footmen and 500 horse (Lumsden 1860: 63) to 5000–6000 men (Oliver 1890: 145; Wylly 1912: 414), or even 8,000 men (Malleson 1879: 50). In the 1950s Spain gave their number as 20,000 souls. (Spain 1985: 49–50). The Bangash of the Kurram valley were estimated to comprise 5,620 (men?). (MacGregor 1873 I, 1: 167)

251 Spain 1985: 49–50; Wylly 1912: 414. Little is known about the leading *sayyids* during Amir Dost Muhammad Khan's era. The only names mentioned are those of Mir Ziya al-Din (?) Shah and Sayyid Madad Shah. (KN 29 May 1855,

For. Sec. 31 August 1855; KN 7 August 1858, For. F.C. 29 October 1858 No. 503)

252 Wylly 1912: 414.

253 KN 7 August 1858 (For. F.C. 29 October 1858 No. 503)

254 Wylly 1912: 393.

255 KN 27 July 1858 (For. F.C. 29 October 1858 No. 503)

256 EKN 6 January 1856 (L/P&S/5/226 No. 12 of 22 March 1856, pp. 926 927); EKN 19 February 1856 (L/P&S/5/227 No. 21 of 17 May 1856, p. 601); EKN 9 July 1856 (L/P&S/5/228 No. 43 of 22 September 1856, p. 688); EKN 5 August 1856 (L/P&S/5/229 No. 54 of 22 October 1856, pp. 248–249); EKN 7, 30 September 1856 (L/P&S/5/229 No. 64 of 22 December 1856, pp. 687, 693)

257 Bellew 1862: 129; KN 18 May 1855 (For. Sec. 31 August 1855 No. 58); Dost Muhammad Khan to Edwardes, n. d. (L/P&S/229 No. 59 of 22 November 1856, p. 473). Other sources give his name as Ghulam Jan. EKN 7 April 1857 (L/P&S/5/232 No. 44 of 29 July 1857, p. 631); KN 16 May 1857 (For. Sec. 30 April 1858 No. 36)

258 Wylly 1912: 411.

259 KN 26 March 1856 (L/P&S/5/227 No. 25 of 17 June 1856, p. 805)

260 Lumsden 1860: 60–62; Wylly 1912: 411.

261 Elphinstone 1972 II: 54.

262 Lumsden 1860: 60. During Dost Muhammad Khan's first reign, Lal estimated that the combined revenues of Kurram and Khost amounted to 95,000 rupees. (Lal 1978 I: 233) In 1856 the British official Ghulam Ahmad quoted the revenues derived from Kurram (possibly including Khost?) as 100,000 rupees. (MacGregor 1871) In the 1880s the tribes of Khost paid an annual revenue of 60,000 rupees. (Molloy 1883d: 6)

263 During Dost Muhammad Khan's first reign Muhammad Afzal Khan had to give up his efforts to enter Zurmat after having been defeated by the Sulaiman Khel. (Broadfoot 1886: 364) Dost Muhammad Khan's position in Zurmat does not seem to have improved much during his second reign. In the fall of 1858 the son of the government agent informed the Amir that only the Sulaiman Khel Ghilzais had submitted the revenue due to the royal family. The neighboring Ahmadzais and Sohaks, however, refused to do so. While Dost Muhammad Khan took steps to remove the traditional Ahmadzai leader, Daulat Khan, he advised the government agent at Zurmat 'not to coerce any tribe to pay revenue, and only to receive it from those who would willingly pay it, in order that disturbances might not arise.' (Elphinstone 1972 II: 149; *Gaz.* VI: 550, 823; Vigne 1982: 106; KN 25 August 1858, For. S. C. 26 November 1858 No. 21) In the 1830s Lal was of the opinion that the combined revenues of Zurmat, Gardez and Kharwar (a district in the region of Ghazni) amounted to 65,190 rupees. (Lal 1978 I: 233) In 1856 Ghulam Sarwar estimated the revenues of Zurmat at 150,000 rupees. (quoted in MacGregor 1871 II: 65) In the 1880s Molloy gave the same figure for the revenues of Zurmat. (Molloy 1883d: 6–7)

264 KI 18 January 1851 (For. Sec. 28 February 1851 No. 50); KN 30 March–15 April 1851 (For. Sec. 30 May 1851 No. 54)

265 KN 1–8 March 1854 (For. Sec. 26 May 1854 No. 30)

266 EKN 19 February 1856 (L/P&S/5/227 No. 21 of 17 May 1856, p. 601); EKN 14 January 1857 (L/P&S/5/230 No. 14 of 21 March 1857)

267 Lumsden 1860: 64.

268 EKN 7 April 1857 (L/P&S/5/232 No. 44 of 29 July 1857, p. 631)

269 KN 27 July, 7 August 1858 (For. F. C. 29 October 1858 No. 503)

270 KN 18–29 May 1855 (For. Sec. 31 August 1855 No. 58)
271 EKN 11 March 1856 (L/P&S/5/227 No. 21 of 17 March 1856, pp. 606–607)
272 KN 26 March 1856 (L/P&S/5/227 No. 25 of 17 June 1856, pp. 805–806)
273 KN 6 April 1856 (L/P&S/5/227 No. 25 of 17 June 1856, p. 808)
274 EKN 9 July 1856 (L/P&S/5/228 No. 43 of 22 September 1856, p. 688)
275 EKN 5 August 1856 (L/P&S/5/229 No. 54 of 22 October 1856, pp. 248 249); EKN 7–15 September 1856 (L/P&S/5/229 No. 64 of 22 December 1856, pp. 686–689)
276 Letter from Kabul 13–27 November 1849 (For. Sec. 25 January 1850 No. 35)
277 Raverty 1895: 157–158. Also see Ahmed 1983: 203; MacGregor 1873 I, 2: 310, 326–328; I, 3: 269.
278 Letter from Kabul 13–27 November 1849 (For. Sec. 25 January 1850 No. 35)
279 Wylly 1912: 429–431; Temple to Readen 23 July 1855, Nicholson to Temple 5 July 1855 (L/P&S/5/226 No. 3 of 22 January 1856, pp. 575B–579.
280 KD 3–6 December 1875 (For. Sec. January 1876 No. 30)
281 KD 5–7 December 1871 (For. Sec. January 1872 No. 33); KD 26–29 November 1875 (For. Sec. Jan 1876 No. 28)
282 KD 10–13 March 1873 (For. Sec. April 1873 No. 16)
283 Wali Muhammad Khan was replaced by Sardar Shahbaz Khan b. Muhammad Akram Khan as governor of Kurram. From 1876 until 1878 Wali Muhammad Khan played a role in the administration of Kabul. (Ramsay 1880 No. 319; KD 5–15 May 1876, For. Sec. June 1876 No. 34, 36; KD 20–22 June 1876, For. Sec. July 1876 No. 57; KD 27–29 June 1876, For. Sec. August 1876 No 60); KD 8–10 August 1876, For. Sec. September 1876 No. 59; KD 5–18 December 1876, For. Sec. January 1877 Nos. 57, 60)
284 KD 21–24 April 1876 (For. Sec. June 1876 No. 30); KD 4–7 August 1876 (For. Sec. September 1876 No. 58); KD 12–14 September 1876 (For. Sec. November 1876 No. 9); KD 2–4 January 1877 (For. Sec. February 1877 No. 27)
285 KD 26–28 January 1877 (For. Sec. March 1877 No. 36)
286 Caroe 1985: 380; Oliver 1890: 141–142; Wylly 1912: 415.
287 Caroe 1985: 381, 386; Christensen, Introduction to McMahon & Ramsay 1981: 18.
288 MacGregor 1873 I, 1: 147; McMahon & Ramsay 1981: 8–9, 48–49; Oliver 1890: 271.
289 Elphinstone 1972 II: 37.
290 Oliver 1890: 272; McMahon & Ramsay 1981: 9–10. In 1901 McMahon and Ramsay estimated the entire population of Bajaur at 100,000 souls.
291 Christensen, Introduction to McMahon & Ramsay 1981: 15; McMahon & Ramsay 1981: 33.
292 Elphinstone 1972 II: 37.
293 McMahon & Ramsay 1981: 9–10, 32, 35–36, 47.
294 Elphinstone 1972 II: 37.
295 MacGregor 1873 I, 1: 146.
296 Edwardes to Davies 24 February 1859 (For. S. C. 29 April 1859 No. 10); Diary of Nawwab Faujdar Khan, Jalalabad 10–16 March 1859 (For. S. C. 27 May 1859 No. 5)
297 Masson 1974 III: 89–91; Masson 30 June 1837 (For. P. C. 11 September 1837 No. 28); Lumsden 27 November 1838 (For. S. C. 16 October 1839 No. 78)
298 Elphinstone 1972 II: 38.
299 MacGregor 1871 II: 561; Yapp 1962: 500–504; Lumsden 27 November 1838 (For. S. C. 16 October 1839 No. 78)
300 ST 198. Also see Reshtia 1957: 127; Reshtia 1990: 195–196.

301 Jalalabad Newsletter 23 August–6 September 1857 (For. Sec. 30 April 1858 No. 89); Report by the Deputy Police Inspector at Tangi 15 Februar 1877 (For. Sec. March 1877 No. 41)
302 KD 23 February–15 March 1877 (For. Sec. May 1877 Nos. 14, 17, 18)
303 Merk 1984: 1–2.
304 Oliver 1890: 246.
305 Ahmed 1980: 122–123; Merk 1984: iii, 17.
306 Ali 1970: 420; Raverty 1888: 122.
307 Oliver 1890: 248.
308 MacGregor 1873 I, 2: 469, 474.
309 Merk 1984: 66.
310 According to MacGregor, the Tarakzai Mohmands were able to turn out 2,500 fighting men. (MacGregor 1873 I, 2: 468)
311 Merk 1984: 46–47.
312 Ali 1970: 417; Lal 1977: 35; MacGregor 1873 I, 2: 135, 475, 480, 488; Masson 1906: 160; Masson 1974 I: 147; Merk 1984: 26; Oliver 1890: 202, 210.
313 Raverty 1888: 122.
314 Merk 1984: 48–53; Oliver 1890: 248.
315 Merk 1984: 17–19.
316 This figure apparently did not include the receipts from the Khyber trade. Traditionally the Mohmands were entitled to one fourth of the transit dues collected in the Khyber Pass. (MacGregor 1873 I, 2: 473–474; Merk 1984: 4 5; KN received at Peshawar on 7 October 1853, For. Sec. 25 November 1853 No. 56; Diary of Khan Bahadur Khan Fatih Khan Khatak 6 May 1856, L/P&S/5/228 No. 28 of 17 July 1856, p. 34)
317 Merk 1984: 63–64.
318 Ibid. 5. Also see Masson 1974 III: 220–221. According to MacGregor, the proceeds from the transit duties were distributed somewhat differently, half being apportioned to the Morcha Khel, and half to the Dadu Khel and Kasim Khel Tarakzais. (MacGregor 1873 I, 2: 475) In Dost Muhammad Khan's time the rates for the transit dues (apparently identical with *badraga*, or 'safe conduct') were as follows:

Muslim foot passenger	1 rupee
Hindu foot passenger	2 rupees
horseman	2—4 rupees
laden horse	2–3 rupees
laden camel	3 rupees
package of goods	4 rupees

(Lal 1977: 215; MacGregor 1873 I, 2: 135, 475)
319 MacGregor 1873 I, 2: 474–475; Merk 1984: 3.
320 Merk 1984: 8, 22.
321 Ibid. 34–35, 63–64. Rs. 6,000 were paid to the Halimzais of Gandau, while the Halimzais of Kamali received 3,000 rupees. (Merk 1984: 23) MacGregor only mentions an annual gift of 3,000 rupees to the Halimzais. (MacGregor 1873 I, 2: 474)
322 Merk 1984: 64. In 1898 the *khan* of La'lpura received a cash allowance of Rs. 13,440 for the maintenance of his retainers, 200 foot and 20 horse. (Ibid. 24)
323 Ibid. 64–65; KD 28–30 March 1876 (For. Sec. May 1876 No. 110); KD 12 15 May 1876 (For. Sec. June 1876 No. 36); KD 30 June–3 July 1876 (For. Sec. August 1876 No. 65)
324 Merk 1984: 49–50. Shahamat Ali gives two contradictory versions of the conflict. According to one, Tura Baz Khan was the son of Ma'azullah Khan,

who was killed by Sa'adat Khan. According to the other, Tura Baz Khan was the grandson of Ma'azullah Khan, and his father, Nur Muhammad Khan was murdered by Sa'adat Khan. (Ali 1970: 303, 420)

325 Ali 1970: 220, 254, 303, 320, 326–328, 417–420, 522; Ghubar 1981: 530; Lal 1978 II: 270–271; Merk 1984: 25, 50–51; Wylly 1912: 227; KD 29 December 1871–1 January 1872 (For Sec. January 1872 No. 215)

326 Merk 1984: 55, 93. According to Adamec, the name of Sa'adat Khan's daughter was Mariyam. (Adamec 1975: Table 70)

327 Edwardes to Temple 7 September 1855, Minute by Dalhousie 1 November 1855, JN 28 July–23 August 1855 (For. Sec. 30 November 1855 Nos. 40, 41, 46)

328 MacGregor 1873 I, 2: 490 Sultan Muhammad Khan's incursions on British territory caused Sher 'Ali Khan to mount a military expedition against him. Faiz Muhammad Khan's description of the military confrontation at La'lpura in 1863–64 creates the impression that Sultan Muhammad Khan was the *khan* of the Mohmands at this time. (ST 262–263)

329 Davies 1862: 1, 46–47; Lal 1977: 35; KN 9 August 1851 (For. Sec. 26 September 1851 No. 24)

330 JI 24 June–8 July 1853 (For. Sec. 30 September 1853 No. 53)

331 Edwardes to Khan Bahadur Khan Fatih Khan Khatak 10 October 1857 (For. Sec. 30 April 1858 No. 89); Edwardes to James 16 May 1858 (For. Sec. 30 April 1858)

332 EJN 7–15 August 1856 (L/P&S/5/229 No. 54 of 22 October 1856, p. 258–259); JN 2 October 1858 (For. S. C. 26 November 1858 No. 23)

333 Ali 1970: 323; Merk 1984: 26.

334 MacGregor 1873 I, 2: 475–488; Edwardes to Temple 18 September 1855 (For. Sec. 28 December 1855 No. 24)

335 KN 20 March–4 April 1852 (For. Sec. 28 May 1852 No. 80); KN 6 June 1853 (For. Sec. 29 July 1853 No. 90)

336 Dost Muhammad Khan to Edwardes 28 August 1855; Edwardes to Temple 7 September 1855; Minute by Dalhousie (For. Sec. 30 November 1855 Nos. 40 41); Ghulam Haidar Khan to Edwardes 28 March 1856 (For. Sec. 27 June 1856 No. 6, L/P&S/5/227 No. 25 of 19 June 1856, pp. 779–781); James to Edmonstone 21 March 1857 (L/P&S/5/230 No. 14 of 21 March 1857)

337 MacGregor 1873 I, 2: 486–490; Diary of Khan Bahadur Fatih Khan Katak 6–7 May 1856 (L/P&S/5/228 No. 28 of 17 July 1856, pp. 34, 39–40); Edwardes to Faujdar Khan 10 October 1857 (For. Sec. 30 April 1858 No. 89)

338 MacGregor 1876 I, 2: 484–486; Edwardes to Brandreth 17 August 1857, Nawwab Faujdar Khan to Edwardes 29 September 1857 (For. Sec. 30 April 1858 Nos. 88–89)

339 Merk 1984: 27, 51. See ST 262–263 for Sher 'Ali Khan's campaign against Sultan Muhammad Khan during roughly the same period.

340 KN September 1877 (For. Sec. July 1878 Nos. 122–123)

341 KD 26–28 July 1870 (For. Pol. A. September 1870 No. 62); KD 25–28 March 1872 (For. Sec. April 1872 No. 128)

342 MacGregor 1873 I, 2: 491–492; Merk 1984: 51.

343 KD 9–10 October 1870 (For. Pol. A. December 1870 No. 351)

344 KD 29 December 1871–1 January 1872 (For. Sec. January 1872 No. 215); KD 19–21 March 1872 (For. Sec. April 1872 No. 126); KD 5–7 October 1872 (For. Sec. December 1872 No. 103)

345 Merk 1984: 52.

346 Ibid. 18; KD 13–16 December 1872 (For. Sec. January 1873 No. 10); KD 21–24 February 1873 (For. Sec. April 1873 No. 6); KD 22–24 July 1873 (For. Sec. October 1873 No. 97)
347 KD 12 September–2 October 1873 (For. Sec. February 1874 Nos. 71, 83)
348 KD 24–27 December 1875 (For. Sec. February 1876 No. 49); KD 30 December 1875 (For. Sec. January 1876 No. 29); KD 7–10 April 1876 (For. Sec. May 1876 No. 113); KD 28–30 November 1876 (For. Sec. January 1877 No. 55); KD 19–21 January 1877 (For. Sec. February 1877 No. 32)
349 KD 21–24 July 1876 No. 54 (For. Sec. September 1876 No. 54); KD 28–30 November 1876 (For. Sec. January 1877 No. 55)
350 KN September 1877 (For. Sec. July 1878 Nos. 122–123); Confidential Newsletter fom Attock 25 July 1878 (For. Sec. August 1878 No. 68) The village under Muhammad Shah's control was Girdi, located five miles west of Dakka. Among the villages lost to the government Baru, Hisarshahi, Hisarak, and Khan are named. Muhammad Shah even seems to have lost control of Dakka.
351 Political report of events in Afghanistan by Cavagnari, 23 December 1878 (For. S. S. January 1879 No. 500)
352 Merk 1984: 22, 67; KD 28–30 March 1876 (For. Sec. May 1876 No. 110); KD 12–15 May 1876 (For. Sec. June 1876 No. 36); KD 30 June–10 July 1876 (For. Sec. August 1876 Nos. 61, 63, 65)
353 KD 29 December 1871–1 January 1872 (For. Sec. January 1872 No. 215)
354 KD 16–18 September 1873 (For. Sec. February 1874 No. 72)
355 KD 7–10 July 1876 (For. Sec. August 1876 No. 63); KD 21–24 July 1876 (For. Sec. September 1876 No. 54)
356 KN September 1877 (For. Sec. July 1878 No. 122–123)
357 Merk 1984: 33–34, 40, 57–63.
358 Hensman 1978: 565; Warburton 1900: 261.
359 Oliver 1890: 198–199.
360 Christensen 1980: 79. Also see *Gaz.* VI: 157; Elphinstone 1972 I: 415–416; Lorimer quoted in Grierson 1919: 89; Ovesen 1983: 325–327; Wutt 1978: 43.
361 MacGregor 1871 II: 558–559.
362 Christensen 1980: 82.
363 Ibid.80–81; *Gaz.* VI: 43; MacGregor 1871: 559; Raverty 1888: 95, 105; Wutt 1978: 45.
364 Little is known about the organization of this khanate. It was ruled by a certain Hazrat 'Ali from ca. 1830 to 1886. He was succeeded by his son Tahmasp. (*Gaz.* VI: 43, 467–468)
365 This figure does not include the Shinwaris. MacGregor lists 2,800 Safis, 3,000 Mohmands and 2,700 Tajiks. (MacGregor 1871 II: 559)
366 MacGregor 1844: 875.
367 Raverty 1888: 106–107.
368 MacGregor 1871 II: 559; Raverty 1888: 107. Strachey's figure of 150,000 rupees is not confirmed by any other source. (Strachey, 'Revenue and Trade' f. 48) The main source of income was agricultural produce. But the exact nature of the assessment is not clear. According to an eighteenth-century source quoted by Raverty, the assessment was 50% in money on irrigated lands and 10% in kind on rainfed lands. (Raverty 1888: 107). The assessment quoted by Strachey is the most extreme: He is of the opinion that the ruler of Pashat collected two thirds of the grain harvested and received 5 rupees for the straw of each lot of grain trodden out by two bullocks. (fs. 48–49) In 1838 Sayyid Nazif's son, Sayyid Baha al-Din, received one third of the cultivation.

MacGregor mentions further sources of income:
'A poll tax on every Hindu, permanent resident Rs. 5
temporary resident Rs. 3
Tax upon tradesmen and manufacturers, each Rs. 3
The country furnishes the chief with 100 servants, or in lieu of each servant Rs. 50
The gold washing of the Kunar river farms at Rs. 50
Revenue is derived from emigrating Ghilzaies, who bring their flocks and herds to Kunar for winter pasturage, a flock of 300 gives the ruler of Kunar Seven sheep, one seer of butter and milk and one blanket.
Each camel furnishes a load of firewood.' (MacGregor 1871 II: 558)

369 Robinson 1978: 9.

370 Strachey, 'Revenue and Trade' fs. 49, 51. Also see Raverty 1888: 105.

371 According to Elphinstone, the rulers of Kunar were supposed to furnish 150 horsemen, as well as 'some revenue' to Shah Shuja'. (Elphinstone 1972 I: 415–416) Strachey is of the opinion that Sayyid Nazif submitted a sum of money instead of furnishing the 300 horsemen required by Shah Shuja'. (Strachey, 'Revenue and Trade', f. 48)

372 MacGregor 1871 II: 560–561.

373 It is not clear whether Sayyid Faqir had played a role in the government of Pashat up to that point. His brothers had held the regions of Kalmanai, Nurgul, and Kashkot.

374 MacGregor 1871 II: 561–563.

375 Ali 1970: 192–193, 442, 469, 512, 516; MacGregor 1871 II: 563–564; Yapp 1962: 505–506.

376 JN 24–30 May, 21 June 1855 (For. Sec. 28 September 1855 No. 38)

377 KD 14 October 1872 (For. Sec. December 1872 No. 108) The entire Kunar valley was assessed at 200,000 rupees. (Molloy 1883d)

378 ST 287, 290.

379 KD 19 October 1868 (For. Pol. A. December 1868 No. 37); KD 22–24 March 1870 (For. Pol. A. May 1870 No. 132); KD 6–9 November 1876 (For. Sec. Nov. 1876 No. 16); Report by Deputy Inspector of Police at Tangi, 15 February 1877 (For. Sec. March 1877 No. 41)

380 The land in question was assessed at 24,000 rupees, out of which Hisam al-Din was allowed to retain 12,000 rupees as his personal allowance. (KD 7–9 March 1871, For. Pol. A. May 1871 No. 56; KD 25–28 August 1871, For. Sec. September 1871 No. 19)

381 Anderson 1973: 576–577; Elphinstone 1972 I: 212; II: 148, 157; Oliver 1890: 199; Robinson 1978: 57–58, 196.

382 Warburton 1880 Appendix II: vi.

383 Anderson 1983: 139.

384 Ghani 1982: 321; Leech 1845a: 310.

385 Elphinstone 1972 II: 157.

386 Robinson 1978: 61–62.

387 In the 1930s they were thought to number 1,600 families. (Robinson 1978: 61)

388 Burton 1880.

389 This region is located south of the Kabul river, opposite of Qarghaie and Charbagh, and comprises the villages of Waliabad, Tiragar-Kanderzai, Rawat, and Aminabad. (*Gaz.* VI: 405)

390 Hensman 1978: 351–352; ST 202; Warburton 1880 Appendix II: iv; QM 19 October 1857 (For. Sec. 30 April 1858 No. 96)

391 Edwardes to Temple 21 August 1856 (L/P&S/5/228 No. 33 of 21 August 1856, pp. 278–279); EKN 7–31 July 1856 (L/P&S/5/228 No. 43 of 22 September 1856, pp. 687–693); EJN 3–16 September 1856 (L/P&S/5/229 No. 54 of 22 October 1856, p. 265); Muhammad Shah Khan to Edwardes, n. d. (L/P&S/5/229 No. 65 of 22 December 1856); JN 22 February 1857 (L/P&S/5/230 No. 18 of 22 April 1857)

392 Ghubar 1981: 594–595; Hensman 1978: 353; Warburton 1880, Appendix II: iv; KD 21–24 November 1873 (For. Sec. March 1874 No. 18); KD 30 June–3 July 1876 (For. Sec. August 1876 No. 61); KD 17–20 November 1876 (For. Sec. January 1877 No. 52); KD 26–28 January 1877 (For. Sec. March 1877 No. 36) 'Ismatullah Khan was executed by Amir 'Abd al-Rahman Khan in October 1882. (Kakar 1971: 117)

393 Faiz Muhammad describes both 'Ismatullah Khan and Arsalan Khan as maternal relatives of Sardar Muhammad Yusuf Khan, whose mother was a sister of 'Abd al 'Aziz Khan Jabbar Khel (ST 275, 284)

394 Ghubar 1981: 594–595; Warburton 1880, Appendix II: v; KD 20–23 September 1872 (For. Sec. October 1872 No. 67); KD 10–19 June 1873 (For. Sec. July 1873 Nos. 64, 66); KD 11–14 August 1876 (For. Sec. September 1876 No. 60); KD 12–15 February 1877 (For. Sec. March 1877 No. 41)

395 Nuri 1956: 181.

396 Burton 1880.

397 This was the case during the rebellion of Karim Khan Jabbar Khel. EKN 13 July 1856 (L/P&S/5/228 No. 43 of 22 September 1856, p. 688–689)

398 *Gaz.* VI: 218, 675; ST 339; Warburton 1880 Appendix II: iv-v.

399 Burton 1880.

400 Ali 1970: 459; Raverty 1888 Appendix: 72–73.

401 *Gaz. VI*: 477.

402 *Gaz. VI*: 485; Warburton 1880: 4.

403 Information by Muhammad 'Azim Baraki, Elphinstone Collection F 88 13 Kt, p. 127.

404 Warburton 1880: 9.

405 Yet Muhammad 'Azim Baraki does not hesitate to characterize other groups, such as the Kohistanis, as defiant of Shah Shuja''s claims to authority. (Information by Muhammad 'Azim Baraki, Elphinstone Collection F 88 13 Kt, p. 126)

406 Pottinger quoted in Yapp 1964: 362.

407 Warburton 1880, Appendix II: vi.

408 Ferrier 1858: 395; Gaz. VI: 218; Peshawar Political Diary 2 March 1847 (L/P&S/5/190 No. 21 p. 794)

409 ST 201.

410 Muhammad Shah Khan, Karim Khan (Jabbar Khel) to Edwardes, n.d. (L/P&S/5/229 No. 65 of 22 December 1856, pp. 761–762)

411 KN 1–8 March 1854 (For. Sec. 26 May 1854 No. 30)

412 JI 26 July–9 August 1852 (For. Sec. 24 September 1852 No. 117); AJN 24 January–5 February, 10 March 1856 (L/P&S/5/227 No. 21 of 17 May 1856, pp. 531–533, 554–555)

413 ST 201–202.

414 KN 6 September 1854 (For. Sec. A. 24 November 1854 No. 14); EKN 7 November 1855 (L/P&S/5/226 No. 3 of 22 January 1856, p. 532); EKN 21 November 1855 (L/P&S/5/226 No. 9 of 22 February 1856, pp. 827–828); EKN 27 December 1855 (L/P&S/5/ 226 No. 12 of 22 March 1856, p. 925); EKN 16 March 1856 (L/P&S/5/ 227 No. 21 of 17 May 1856 p. 608); EJN 24

March 1856 (L/P&S/5/227 No. 21 of 17 May 1856 p. 556); EKN 6–25 August 1856 (L/P&S/5/229 No. 54 of 22 October 1856 pp. 249–253); EKN 21 December 1856 (L/P&S/5/230 No. 14 of 21 March 1857). The following of Muhammad Shah Khan's sons are recorded by name: Sher Muhammad, Amir Muhammad, Faiz Muhammad, Samandar, Muhammad Akram, Pir Muhammad. (Warburton 1880, Appendix II: vi; KD 29 September 1861, For. Pol. A. November 1861 No. 69; KD 2–4 September 1873, For. Sec. November 1873 No. 24)

415 ST 202. For a similar account see Ghubar 1981: 576–577. Faiz Muhammad is of the opinion that Muhammad Shah Khan only handed over the fort of Badi'abad after being assured that it would not be destroyed. According to Warburton the Amir had the fort demolished as soon as it fell to his control. (Warburton 1880, Appendix II: vi)

416 Ferrier 1858: 396.

417 *Gaz.* VI: 218; Warburton 1880: 8–9.

418 KN, n. d., received on 18 February 1854 (For. Sec. 28 April 1854 No. 19) The population of the lower end of Tagau was Ghilzai; the upper portion of the valley was inhabited by 8,000 to 9,000 Safi families. (*Gaz.* VI: 773–774)

419 KN 27 March–9 April 1853 (For. Sec. 27 May 1853 No. 157)

420 KN 6 September 1854 (For. Sec. (A) 24 November 1854 No. 14)

421 JI 26 July–9 August 1852 (For. Sec. 24 September 1852 No. 117); JN 21 February–12 March 1854 (For. Sec. 28 April 1854 No. 28); KN 15 August–30 October 1855 (For. Sec. 28 December 1855 No. 72); EKN 27 December, 5 January (L/P&S/5/226 No. 12 of 22 March 1856, pp. 925–926); EKN 22 January 1856 (L/P&S/5/227 No. 16 of 22 April 1856, pp. 299–300); EKN 20 February 1856 (L/P&S/5/227 No. 21 of 17 May 1856, pp. 601–602); KN 29 March–9 April 1856 (L/P&S/5/227 No. 25 of 17 June 1856, pp. 806–811)

422 JN 18 April–20 May 1855 (For. Sec. 31 August 1855 No. 58); KN 19 September–3 October 1855 (For. Sec. 28 December 1855 No. 72)

423 KI 28 July–13 August 1852 (For. Sec. 24 September 1854 No. 119)

424 Warburton 1880, Appendix II: vii; KN 10 January 1855 (For. Sec. 27 April 1855 No. 8); EKN 3 November 1855 (L/P&S/5/226 No. 3 of 22 January 1856, pp. 530–531); AJN 18–30 November 1855 (L/P&S/5/226 No. 9 of 22 February 1856, pp. 820–821)

425 KN 7 May 1855 (For. Sec. 31 August 1855 No. 58)

426 KN 29 March–9 April (L/P&S/5/227 No. 25 of 17 June 1856, pp. 806–810)

427 ST 200.

428 KN n. d., received on 18 February 1854 (For. Sec. 28 April 1854 No. 19)

429 QM 26 February–4 March 1858 (For. S. C. 28 May 1858 No. 10)

430 EKN 7 November 1855 (L/P&S/5/226 No. 3 of 22 January 1856, p. 532)

431 EKN 21 November 1855 (L/P&S/5/226 No. 9 of 22 February 1856, pp. 827 828); EKN 27 December 1855 (L/P&S/5/226 No. 12 of 27 March 1856, p. 925)

432 EJN 2 September 1857 (L/P&S/5/229 No. 54, p. 265) Also see KN 20–26 September 1856 (L/P&S/5/229 No. 64, pp. 690–692)

433 KN 20 August–7 September 1855 (For. Sec. 28 December 1855 No. 72)

434 EKN 3 November 1855 (L/P&S/5/226 No. 3 of 22 January 1856, pp. 530–531)

435 EKN 11 November 1855 (L/P&S/5/226 No. 3 of 22 January 1856, p. 533); EKN 1 March 1856 (L/P&S/5/227 No. 21 of 17 May 1856, pp. 604–605)

436 KN 19 September–3 October 1855 (For. Sec. 28 December 1855 No. 72)

437 EKN 6–16 March 1856 (L/P&S/5/227 No. 21 of 17 May 1856, pp. 605–608); KN 23 April–2 May 1856 (L/P&S/5/227 Nol. 25 of 17 June 1856, pp. 816–820)

438 KN 6 August–1 September 1856 (L/P&S/5/ 227 No. 25 of 17 June 1856, pp. 249–255)
439 Muhammad Shah Khan, Karim Khan (Jabbar Khel) to Edwardes, n.d.; Edwardes to Muhammad Shah Khan 17 October 1856 (L/P&S/5/229 No. 65 of 22 December 1856, pp. 761–762)
440 EKN 21 December 1856 (L/P&S/5/230 No. 14 of 2 March 1857)
441 KN 28 April–14 May, 21 September–18 October 1857 (For. Sec. 30 April 1858 Nos. 36, 94)
442 Muhammad Shah Khan was buried at the shrine of Mihtar Lam in Laghman. (Warburton 1900: 95–96)
443 KD 22 September 1861 (For. Pol. A. October 1861 No. 222)
444 Warburton 1880, Appendix II: vii; Warburton 1900: 68; KD 28 May–7 June 1869 (For. Pol. A July 1869 No. 149).
445 See Caroe 1985: 321.
446 Bendix 1978: 7, 226.
447 Elphinstone 1972 II: 161; Broadfoot 1886: 355, 363–364; *Gaz.* VI: 730; Ghani 1982: 358–359; MacGregor 1871 II: 278; Masson 1974 II: 204–205; Strachey, 'Revenue and Trade' fs. 10–21, 134; Information from Muhammad Hasan Nur, Elphinstone Collection F 88 13 Kt, p. 85; Information from Muhammad 'Azim Baraki, Elphinstone Collection F 88 13 Kt, p. 130.
448 Anderson 1975: 580; Elphinstone 1972 II: 138–139; *Gaz.* V: 137, 312, 390 391, 485; *Gaz.* VI: 237, 554, 675, 704; Lal 1977: 198; Leech 1845c: 458; Lumsden 1860: 69; MacGregor 1871 II: 274, 276; Masson 1974 II: 204–205; Molloy 1883c; Raverty 1888, Appendix: 75; .
449 Elphinstone 1972 II: 139, 148; *Gaz.* VI: 204; Lynch 1841; Molloy 1883c.
450 Elphinstone 1972 II: 148; Gaz. VI: 204; Lal 1977: 198; Information from Muhammad Hasan Nur, Elphinstone Collection F 88 13 Kt, p. 85. In 1841 Lynch estimated the Hotaks at 14,850 souls and the Tokhis at 26,700 souls. Sixteen years later Lumsden was of the opinion that the combined Hotak and Tokhi population numbered 60,000 souls. (Lumsden 1860: 69; QM 19 October 1857, For. Sec. 30 April 1858 No. 96) In 1880 the Hotaks were reckoned to be about 12,000 families and the Tokhis 20,000. (Kakar 1971: 119)
451 Leech 1845a: 311, 316.
452 Fraser-Tytler 1967: 54; Lockhart 1938: 2.
453 Ghani 1982: 320–321; Leech 1845a: 310; Sultan Muhammad gives contradictory information on the date of Malakhi Khan's rise to leadership among the Tokhis. He describes Malakhi Khan as a contemporary of the Mughal ruler Aurangzeb (r. 1659–1707) but places his appointment as *khan* in the year 1034/1624. (TSu 60, 70)
454 Raverty 1888, Appendix: 74–75.
455 Singh 1981: 4–7; also see TSu 71–72.
456 Lockhart 1938: 3–4, 8–14, 31–54, 117–120; TSu 73–97.
457 Astarabadi 1962: 303; Lockhart 1938: 120; Singh 1981: 17; Perry 1975: 209.
458 Raverty 1888, Appendix: 52; TSu 91, 95. Ashraf Khan's success under Nadir Shah can in great part be attributed to Hotak-Tokhi rivalry for the possession of Qalat. (Leech 1845a: 315–317)
459 Fofalzai 1958: 187. Nuri gives Nurullah's title as *khawass quli khan*, 'slave of the elite'. (Nuri 1956: 179)
460 Fofalzai 1958: 187; Leech 1845a: 319–320; Raverty 1888: 85.
461 Lynch 1841.
462 Husaini 1967: 31. According to Faiz Muhammad, this region was farmed for 200,000 rupees. (ST 57)

463 Fofalzai 1958: 190–191; Ghani 1982: 358.

464 *Gaz.* VI: 204; Yapp 1963: 298. The figure of 1,500 cavalry provided by the Tokhis and 700 furnished by the Hotaks stems from Lynch. (Lynch 1841) Leech arrives at a total contingent of 1010 horsemen for the Tokhis, and 397 horsemen for the Hotaks. (MacGregor 1871 II: 275–276) Rawlinson reports that the Tokhis were supposed to provide 1061 cavalry, whereas the Hotaks furnished 507. (Rawlinson 1841: 826) According to an informant of the Elphinstone mission, the Tokhis supplied 3,000 horsemen to Shah Zaman. (Information from Muhammad Hasan Nur, Elphinstone Collection F 88 13 Kt, p. 95)

465 Leech 1845a: 317; Singh 1981: 356.

466 Fofalzai 1958: 188; Ghani 1982: 358; Leech 1845a: 319; Lynch 1841.

467 Fofalzai 1958: 188–189; Leech 1845a: 320.

468 Masson 1974 II: 199.

469 ST 57.

470 Shah Shuja' claimed that the Hotak and Tokhi leadership suggested a marriage alliance between the daughter of Fatih Khan and Shah Shuja' when they sided with him in his power struggle with Shah Mahmud in 1803. (Fofalzai 1958: 207–208; Shah Shuja''s autobiography in Zimmermann 1842: 186) According to Masson, the mother of Shah Shuja''s eldest son Timur was a sister of Fatih Khan. (Masson 1974 II: 198–199)

471 Fofalzai 1958: 212; Information from 'Umar 'Alikhel Ghilzai, Elphinstone Collection F 88 13 Kt, p. 229.

472 Lal 1978 I: 32; Leech 1845a: 321; Raverty 1888: 57. According to another account, 'Abd al-Rahim Hotak's son (Mir 'Alam Khan?) was proclaimed king. (Information from 'Umar 'Alikhel Ghilzai, Elphinstone Collection F 88 13 Kt, p. 229) The role of Fatih Khan Babakrzai is not quite clear. According to Lal, he was instrumental in winning Jabbar Khel support fro the rebellion. (Lal 1978 I: 34) Leech, on the other hand, is of the opinion that Fatih Khan Babakrzai went over to Shah Mahmud after the first Ghilzai defeat. (Leech 1845a: 321)

473 The Durrani leaders involved in the battles with the Ghilzais were, apart from Mukhtar al-Daula Bamizai, Ahmad Khan Nurzai, 'Abd al-Majid Khan Barakzai, Saidal Khan Alikozai, A'zam Khan Popalzai, Shadi Khan Achakzai, and Samandar Khan Bamizai. (Fofalzai 1958: 212; Leech 1845a: 321)

474 Elphinstone 1972 II: 138; Fofalzai 1958: 212; Lal 1978 I: 32–34; ST 65–66; Information from Muhammad Hasan Nur, Elphinstone Collection F 88 13 Kt, pp. 74–75; QM 14 April 1857 (L/P&S/5/232 No. 44 of 29 July 1857, pp. 617 618); QM, 16–22 October 1857 (For. S. C. 30 April 1858 No. 96)

475 Fofalzai 1958: 207–208; Shah Shuja''s autobiography in Zimmermann 1842: 186

476 Leech 1845a: 322.

477 The exact tribal affiliation of Khuda Nazar Khan is not clear. He is mostly simply referred to as 'Ghilzai'. (Leech 1839a: 59; Reshtia 1957: 10n) According to Masson, he was an Andar Ghilzai (Masson 1974 I: 286).

478 ST 110.

479 Leech 1839a: 63; Yapp 1963: 288.

480 Ghani 1982: 372; Lynch 1841.

481 Lynch 1841.

482 Broadfoot 1886: 355.

483 In the 1830s Fatih Khan Babakrzai's stronghold was in the area between Qalat-i Ghilzai and Katawaz. (Broadfoot 1886: 355) He levied 3 rupees per camel, 2

rupees per horse, 1 rupee per donkey, and a 20 rupee fee for the supplies used by the caravan (*mihmani*). Shihab al-Din resided near the village of Khaka, located 20 miles northeast of Qalat. He demanded 4 rupees per camel, 2 rupees per horse, and 1 rupee per donkey. (Masson 1974 II: 198 199, 202) At the time of Timur Shah, the Tokhis had been allowed to collect 1 Qandahar rupee per camel, 10 annas per horse, and 5 1/2 annas per donkey. (Lynch 1841)

484 Masson 1974 II: 209–210.

485 Ibid. II: 198–199, 210–212.

486 Elphinstone 1972 II: 150–152.

487 Broadfoot 1886: 359.

488 Among these, 'Abd al-Rahman b. Shihab al-Din Tokhi, Khalil Khan and Rahmat Khan Babakrzai, and Muhammad Akram Khan Hotak were the most prominent leaders. (Wade 25 December 1838, For. Sec. C. 16 October 1839 No. 70)

489 Yapp 1963: 289.

490 Ghubar 1981: 530; Nuri 1956: 179; Yapp 1963: 288–289; Lynch 1841.

491 Yapp 1963: 289–299.

492 Yapp 1964: 373.

493 Nuri 1956: 179–180.

494 QM 14 April 1857 (L/P&S/5/ 232 No. 44 of 29 July 1857, pp. 617–618)

495 KN 3 April 1850 (For. Sec. 31 May 1850 No. 75); KN 9 August 1851 (For. Sec. 29 August 1851 No. 47); KI 14–17 August 1852 (For. Sec. 29 October 1852 No. 84)

496 KN 6–13 July 1852 (For. Sec. 22 August 1852 No. 92)

497 Reshtia 1957: 133–134; Reshtia 1990: 204–205; ST 212–215; KN 27 March–9 April 1853 (For. Sec. 27 May 1853 No. 157); KN (Peshawar 7 October 1853, For. Sec. 25 November 1853 No. 56); KN 5 June 1854 (For. Sec. 28 July 1854 No. 10); Newsletter from Sayyid Hisam al-Din of Kunar (24 June 1854, For. Sec. 28 July 1854 No. 17; 5 July 1854, For. Sec. 25 August 1854 No. 31); JN 3 August 1854 (for. Sec. 25 August 1854 No. 45); Kabul Newsletter from the former Nizam al-Daula 5 August 1854 (For. Sec. 29 September 1854 No. 8)

498 KI 24 June–8 July 1853 (For. Sec. 30 September 1853 No. 55)

499 Mir 'Alam Khan had already turned away from the Qandahar *sardars* in 1267/1850 during an earlier Tokhi rebellion (*fisad-i taʾifa-yi Tokhi*). (Nuri 1956: 11–12, 180; ST 212)

500 KN 22 July–6 August 1853 (For. Sec. 30 September 1853 No. 57)

501 Lynch 1841.

502 In 1880 Hastings reported that the poll tax had been introduced a long time ago among the Ali Khel, Andar and Taraki Ghilzais in regions where it was difficult to institute a regular land assessment. In these regions, 'people were assessed, not the land.' The poll tax was levied on all grown males, allowing a lower rate for non-landowners. According to Hastings, only the following were exempted from the poll tax: 'mullahs, maliks, youths, the old, the blind and the cripple; all khans and women.' (Hastings 1880) Faiz Muhammad describes the revenue payments imposed on the Hotaks and Tokhis as 'land tax' (*maliyat-i arazi*). (ST 213)

503 QM 14 April 1857 (L/P&S/5/ 232 No. 44 of 29 July 1857, pp. 617–618)

504 KN 6 May 1854 (For. Sec 30 June 1954 No. 19); EQN 6 Februar 1856 (L/P&S/5. 227 No. 16 of 22 April 1856, p. 317.

505 KN (Lahore 27 December 1853, For. Sec. 27 January 1854 No. 79)

506 ST 212.

507 QM 7–8 April 1857 (L/P&S/5/232 No. 44 of 29 July 1857, pp. 601–602)

508 QM 14 April 1857 (L/P&S/5/232 No. 44 of 29 July 1857, pp. 617–618)

509 Even the settlement of four rupees per man would have been low in comparison with the rates paid by other Ghilzai groups along the route to Kabul. In 1880 Hastings reported that the 'Ali Khel settlers in the vicinity of Ghazni had to pay seven rupees, while nomads were assessed at three rupees annually. Andar landowners had to pay four to eight rupees, and men without land submitted three rupees per year. (Hastings 1880) It is not clear to what extent Dost Muhammad Khan interfered with the traditional Tokhi right to collect transit dues.

510 KN (Lahore 27 December 1853, For. Sec. 27 January 1854 No. 79)

511 Nuri 1956: 180; ST 288; KD 10–27 September 1869 (For. Pol. A. October 1869 Nos. 280–284)

512 Nuri 1956: 181–183; KD 8–11 October 1869 (For. Pol. A. November 1869 No. 149; KD 2–29 November 1869 (For. Pol. A. January 1870 Nos. 106, 110, 112, 113); KD 18–21 February 1870 (For. Pol. A. November 1869 No. 149); KD 22 April–2 May 1876 (For. Pol. A. August 1870 Nos. 26–28) Muhammad Afzal Khan's son Muhammad Shah was to play a leading role in the Ghilzai uprising against Amir 'Abd al-Rahman Khan in 1886–87. (Kakar 1971: 129 136)

513 KD 15–18 April 1870 (For. Pol. A.May 1870 No. 139)

514 Peshawar Confidential Diary 7 February 1878 (For. Sec. May 1878 No. 138); Memorandum by Sandeman 10 June 1878 (For. Pol. A. July 1878 No. 43)

515 Kakar 1971: 120–137.

516 *Gaz.* VI: 293; KD 1–3 August 1876 (For. Sec. September 1876 No. 57)

517 Warburton 1880: 8–9. The exact meaning of the administrative terminology is not clear. Jenkyn's opinion that the titles *diwan* and *daftari* referred to the same position, the first title being reserved for Hindu accountants, and the second being applied to Muslims holding the same office, is not borne out by other sources. (*Gaz.* VI: 293). Warburton informs us that there was a hierarchy between the offices of *diwan* and *daftari*. Moreover, the names of the two *diwans* listed by him, i.e., Mirza Dad Muhammad and Mirza Shirin b. Mirza Dad Muhammad, indicate no Hindu background.

518 Lumsden 1860: 11, 17.

519 Hastings 1880.

520 If not stated otherwise, the following figures stem from Molloy 1883c and 1883d.

521 *Gaz.* VI: 291–292; Ghani 1982: 386.

522 *Gaz.* VI: 495–496; Warburton 1880: 8.

523 Hastings 1880; Molloy, 1883c, 1883d.

524 *Gaz.* VI: 291–292; Ghani 1982: 386. In the early 1830s Lal estimated that the entire revenue of Jalalabad was 900,000 rupees, out of which 500,000 rupees were collected by the local chief as allowances and 400,000 reached the exchequer of the governor, Nawwab Muhammad Zaman Khan. (Lal 1977: 209–210)

525 *Gaz.* VI: 496–497; Warburton 1880: 8.

526 Ferrier 1858: 322–325.

527 Kakar 1979: 74–77.

528 Strachey, 'Revenue and Trade', fs. 21, 134.

529 On the basis of *jam'-i qalandar khan*, the Pashtun landholders paid approximately 1 1/4 Kabuli *ser* per *jarib*, whereas the Qizilbash and Tajiks submitted 12–22 *sers* per *jarib*. Only when Pashtuns acquired lands from these groups, had they to pay the same rate as the latter. (*Gaz.* VI: 516; Ghani 1982: 358–359)

530 Hastings 1880.
531 *Gaz.* VI: 290. As seen above, the Sangu Khel Shinwaris located in the vicinity of Jalalabad faced the first regular revenue assessment on their landed property in 1859.
532 Broadfoot 1886: 367, 399.
533 Lynch 1841.
534 Vigne 1982: 106–107.
535 Broadfoot: 363, 367.
536 KN (Lahore, 27 December 1853, For. Sec. 27 January 1854 No. 79); KN 25 August 1858 (For. S. C. 26 November 1858 No. 21)
537 KD 20–23 September 1872 (For. Sec. October 1872 No. 67)
538 Christensen, Introduction to McMahon & Ramsay 1981: 15.
539 Anderson 1983: 124–125.
540 Beck 1983: 288, 297; Garthwaite 1983: 320.
541 Garthwaite 1983: 319–320.
542 Fofalzai 1958: 231.
543 Beck 1983: 287–289, 308.

4 AMIR DOST MUHAMMAD KHAN'S ADMINISTRATION

1 O. St. John 1881.
2 Grevemeyer 1990: 35; Elphinstone 1972 I: 378–388; Ghani 1982: 184; Gani, *EIr*, 558.
3 Kieffer, 'Abdali' in *EIr;* Leech 1845c: 449; Nir Harawi 1964–65: 80–81; Romodin 1985: 121; Singh 1981: 1n.
4 TSu 59–60.
5 Ghani 1982: 336.
6 Caroe 1985: 223–225; Ghani 1982: 318; Raverty 1888: 603; TSu 56–57.
7 Leech 1845c: 445–456; TSu 58–59. Also see Elphinstone 1972 II: 96–97.
8 Lockhart 1958: 96; Tate 1973: 32–43; TSu 61–62.
9 Zu'l-Faqar Khan and Ahmad Khan were sons of Zaman b. Daulat b. Sarmast b. Sher b. Khwaja Khizr b. Sado. Allahyar Khan of Herat was son of 'Abdullah b. Hayat. Hayat Khan was the son of a brother of Sher Khan and thus the paternal cousin of Sarmast Khan. (Ghani 1982: 337; Leech 1845c: 463; Singh 1981: 7–13)
10 Astarabadi 1962: 303; Boukhary 1876: 14–15; Elphinstone 1972 I: 303, II: 100–101; Grevemeyer 1982: 58; Lockhart 1938: 120; Perry 1975: 209; Singh 1981: 15–18; TSu 95. According to Boukhary, the Hotak leader Shah Husain was taken to Mazandaran and executed there. The author of *Tarikh-i sultani* reports that Shah Husain was accompanied to Mazandaran by all his relatives and fellow tribesmen present with him in Qandahar. Perry and Singh concur with Lockhart's statement that the Hotak Ghilzais were exiled to Khurasan and 'settled on the lands vacated by the Abdalis.' Ravan A. G. Farhadi, by contrast, offers an alternative reading of Astarabadi's *Jahangusha-yi Nadiri* and concludes that the Hotaks were forced to settle in the vicinity of Muqur. In Anwar's edition the phrase in question is given the following way: *an jama'at [ta'ifa-yi Hotaki]-ra az Arghandab guzaranida, rawana-yi makan muqarrar sakhtand.* (Astarabadi 1962: 303) Farhadi holds that the word *muqarrar* should be read as *Muqur*: *an jama'at-ra ... rawana-yi makan-i Muqur sakhtand.* (Personal communication)
11 Nir Harawi 1964–64: 81; Singh 1981: 27.
12 Gregorian 1969: 30n.
13 *Gazetteer of Afghanistan* 1908: 73–74.

14 Ghani 1982: 338.
15 Elphinstone 1972 II: 300–301; Ferrier 1858: 98; Fofalzai 1958: 236; TSu 152.
16 Rawlinson 1871: 823–828.
17 Elphinstone 1972 II: 99–100; Rawlinson 1871: 829, 862; Raverty 1894: 326. In the 1950s and 1960s estimates of the Durrani population mostly hovered between 1 and 1.5 million souls. (Gregorian 1969: 416)
18 Elphinstone 1972 II: 88–93
19 Ibid. II: 99.
20 The available data on the size and composition of the population of Qandahar city in the nineteenth century are contradictory. The author of *Siraj al-tawarikh* quotes the figures of 60,000 and 80,000 souls mentioned in *Hayat i afghani* and *Jam-i jam* respectively. (ST 4) According to Strachey, the city of Qandahar consisted of 5,000 houses at the beginning of the nineteenth century, the Pashtuns only making up one fourth of the population and the majority consisting of Farsiwans. (Strachey, 'Revenue and Trade', f. 129) While Elphinstone felt 'utterly at a loss' how to fix the number of the inhabitants of Qandahar city, he was of the opinion that the greater part of them were Pashtuns. (Elphinstone 1972 II: 130, 133) According to Lal, the Persian population of 2,000 families was outnumbered by the Pashtuns. (Lal 1977: 184) During the 1830s and 1840s Masson, Kennedy and Ferrier estimated the entire population of Qandahar at 25,000 to 30,000 souls. (Hamilton 1906: 197; Kennedy 1840 I: 250)

In 1880 Protheroe gave the following account of the population of Qandahar:

Durrani	522 families
Ghilzai	611 families
Farsiwan	1,084 families
Kakar	275 families
Miscellaneous	828 families
Foreigners	566 families

without further clarifying the categories of 'miscellaneous' and 'foreigners'. (*Gaz.* V: 244–245)

In the early twentieth century Hamilton described the population of Qandahar as follows:

Durrani	4,390 families
Ghilzai	300 families
Kakar	550 families
Farsiwan	1,240 families
Hindu	300 families

His account also includes a description of the distribution of the Pashtuns in Qandahar: 'Kandahar is divided into districts which are in the occupation of the different tribes. The south western quarter of the city has four great divisions – the Barakzai Duranis, extending down the Shikarpur and Herat Bazaars, having south of them the Hindustani quarter and west that of the Halakozai [Alikozai] Duranis, while in the extreme south-west corner of the city, between the last two, there are the Nurzai Duranis. The south-eastern quarter appears to be occupied principally by Populzai Duranis. In the north-eastern quarter the portion stretching on the north of the Kabul Bazaar is occupied by the Ghilzais; north of them and to the north-east angle of the city is the Bar Durani quarter; while between them and the citadel is the Achakzai Durani quarter. In the south-western portion of the north-western quarter are the houses of the Alizais.' (Hamilton 1906: 194; also see Fofalzai1958: 234, 239; Reindke 1976: 71)

For a map of Ahmad Shah's citadel at Qandahar and the placement of his Pashtun troops around it see Fofalzai 1967: 199.

21 Astarabadi 1962: 303; Bellew 1973: 161–164; Elphinstone 1972 II: 97–99; Gregorian 1969: 47; Leech 1845c: 469; MacGregor 1871 II: 61; Orywal 1982: 38; Rawlinson 1871: 825; Reshtia 1957: 2–3; Singh 17–18; Tate 1973: 18 19n; Temple 1879:181.

22 Conolly 1834 II: 102; Elphinstone 1972 II: 97–99; *Gaz.* II: 5, 62, 85–86; 296; *Gaz.* III: 343; Yapp 1963: 301.

23 Elphinstone 1972 II: 103–104.

24 Rawlinson 1871: 866.

25 Elphinstone 1972 II: 101–104.

26 Reshtia 1957: 45; Reshtia 1990: 78–79; ST 108.

27 Masson 1974 I: 283–286.

28 Leech 1839a: 61–62; Masson 1974 I: 289.

29 Conolly 1834 II: 129; *Gaz.* V: 453; Masson 1974 I: 288.

30 Hough 1841: 140; Rawlinson 1871: 836, 838–839.

31 Leech 1839a: 51–59; Masson 1974 I: 286.

32 Caroe 1985: 123, 171.

33 Burnes 1834 II: 338; Hough 1841: 140.

34 Masson 1974 I: 287. It is not clear whether these amounts refer to Kabuli or Qandahari rupees. According to Conolly, the revenue of the Qandahar Sardars amounted to a total of 500,000 Company's rupees in 1830. (Conolly 1834 II: 106)

35 Lal 1977: 195; Leech 1839a: 51; Masson 1974 I: 287. Among the people asked to 'lend' large sums of money to the Qandahar Sardars were the relatives of Khuda Nazar Khan Ghilzai who decided to leave the city to avoid further requests for financial aid during the winter of 1853–54. During the same period the Sardars caught an envoy of Sa'id Muhammad Khan b. Yar Muhammad Khan, the ruler of Herat, on his way to Kabul and imprisoned him in the hope of extorting a ransom of 700,000 rupees from the father of the envoy. Simultaneously they demanded an advance payment of the revenue due during the following year from their subjects. (Champagne 1981: 320; KN, Lahore 31 January 1854, For. Sec. 24 February 1854 No. 44)

36 Conolly 1834 II: 45–46, 105; Ferrier 1858: 325; *Gaz.* V: 261.

37 Elphinstone 1972 II: 249.

38 Rawlinson 1871: 829–834; ST 63.

39 Newsdiary of Hafiz Rafi' al-Din at Qandahar, 11 February 1810 (Elphinstone Collection Box 18 I, l)

40 Rawlinson 1871: 830–835. According to Conolly, the Qandahar Sardars maintained 6,000 cavalry mostly recruited from the Ghilzai confederacy. (Conolly 1834 II: 45)

41 Rawlinson 1871: 837–839.

42 O. St. John 1879: 1–2.

43 MacGregor 1871 II: 61; Rawlinson 1871: 824–838.

44 The rates collected by the Qandahar Sardars were as follows
  0.2 rupee per sheep (0.1 rupee under Ahmad Shah)
  0.6 rupee per cow or mare (0.2 rupee under Ahmad Shah)
  0.7 rupee per camel (0.3 rupee under Ahmad Shah)

45 Rawlinson 1871: 827, 835–836; QM 1 June 1857 (For. Sec. 30 April 1858 No. 42).

46 *Muhasili*; initially fixed at ten per cent of the grain revenue, subsequently lowered to six per cent.

47 *Ambardari;* became part of the Sardars' revenue in the course of time.

48 *Tafawut-i sang*; this tax was justified by the new weights instituted by the Sardars in Qandahar city, which were five per cent heavier than those employed in the countryside.

49 Among these were a 'fee to the minister' at 0.8 rupees per *tiyul qulba* and a commutation for the maintenance of ice houses at 0.7 rupees per *tiyul qulba*, both of which went directly into the coffers of the Qandahar Sardars.

50 Havelock 1840 II: 43; Rawlinson 1871: 837, 846–849.

51 Lumsden 1860: 29; MacGregor 1871 II: 61; Rawlinson 1871: 864; Yapp 1963: 300.

52 Rawlinson 1871: 841; Lumsden 1860: 29; QM 1 June 1857 (For. Sec. 30 April 1858 No. 42).

53 Leech lists Ramazan Hotak, Mulla Yunus Hotak, Aminullah Khan Farsiwan and Mulla Nazu Mishnani as the entourage of Kuhandil Khan. Rahmdil Khan relied on the assistance of Dost Muhammad Khan Jawansher, a Qizilbash, who acted as his deputy (*na᾿ib*). Two of his military commanders mentioned are Mirza Ahmad Khan Farsiwan and Suhbat Khan, an Andar Ghilzai. Mulla Rashid Barakzai acted as Mihrdil Khan's adviser. (Leech 1839a: 59–60) Contrary to his elder brothers, Mihrdil Khan entertained close links with the Qizilbash population of Qandahar. (Masson 1974 I: 285–286)

54 Ghubar 1981: 401; Gregorian 1969: 46, 74; Kakar 1979: 24. Only few non-Muhammadzai chiefs, such as Ahmad Khan Ishaqzai of Lash Juwain are mentioned in the sources as entitled to carry the title 'Sardar' during Amirs Dost Muhammad Khan's and Sher 'Ali Khan's periods. (O. St. John 1881, ST 326, 328, 330, 335, 338)

55 Gregorian 1969: 30.

56 For Amir 'Abd al-Rahman Khan's period the role of Pashtun administrators in Qataghan and Badakhshan is documented by Kushkaki 1989: 16–17, 60, 139, 259.

57 Masson 1974 I: 284.

58 Champagne 1981: 297; ST 211. In the following years, Farah was to change hands several times. In the summer of 1853, as the Qandahar Sardars were locked into a confrontation with Dost Muhammad Khan over the respective spheres of influence among the Tokhi and Hotak Ghilzais, Sa'id Muhammad Khan was able to regain possession of Farah. Yet in March 1856 Farah was to fall to the control of Dost Muhammad Khan. On March 11, 1862 Sultan Ahmad Khan (r. Herat 1857–1863) was able to conquer Farah, only to lose it again to Dost Muhammad Khan's forces on July 6 of the same year. (Champagne 1981: 320, 362, 417, 436) During the Persian siege of Herat of 1856, Lash Juwain passed to the control of the Persian government but was given up to Dost Muhammad Khan under British pressure in 1858. (Champagne 1981: 419, 423; Journal of Nawwab Faujdar Khan 30 April 1858, For. Sec. 30 July 1858 No. 15)

59 As early as 1845 Kuhandil Khan submitted a formal New Year's tribute to the Qajar king, assuring him of his loyalty. In 1853 Kuhandil Khan requested aid from the Iranian government in his confrontation with Dost Muhammad Khan. (Champagne 1981: 253) In 1854 the Persian government protested Dost Muhammad Khan's occupation of Qalat-i Ghilzai and subsequently sent funds and weapons to the Qandahar Sardars for the creation of an additional cavalry regiment. (Champagne 1981: 253, 318, 321; Newsletter by Sayyid Hisam al-Din of Kunar 2 June 1854, For. Sec. 28 July 1854 No. 17; Newsletter by Sayyid Hisam al-Din 5 July 1854, For. Sec. 25 August 1854 No. 31; JN 3 August

1854, For. Sec. 25 August 1854 No. 45; Newsletter by Sayyid Hisam al-Din, Peshawar 18 August 1854, For. Sec. 29 September 1854 No. 8; Major Coke, Kohat, 30 September 1854, For. Sec. 27 October 1854 No. 11; KN 6 September 1854, For. Sec. A. 24 November 1854 No. 14; KN 21 September, 25 October 1854, For. Sec. 26 January 1855 Nos. 77, 100; Edwardes to Temple 9 January 1855, Dost Muhammad Khan's correspondence with the Persian court, For. Sec. 23 February 1855 Nos. 29, 37–39; QN 19 December 1854, KN 8 January 1855, For. Sec. 30 March 1855 No. 11; KN 19 July 1855, For. Sec. 30 November 1855 No. 44)

60 Newsletter by Sayyid Hisam al-Din (Peshawar 18 August 1854, For. Sec. 29 September 1854 No. 8); Newsletter by Sayyid Hisam al-Din (Peshawar 9 October 1854, For. Sec. 27 October 1854 No. 13)

61 KN 18 August 1851 (For. Sec. 26 September 1851 No. 26); KN 7 September 1851 (For. Sec. 31 October 1851 No. 27); KI 21 October 1851 (For. Sec. 28 November 1851 No. 16)

62 In 1854 a British informant gave the following distribution of districts among the Qandahar Sardars: Kuhandil Khan held the Qal'a-yi Bist district; his sons Muhammad Sadiq and Muhammad 'Umar were in charge of Mahmudabad near Kushk-i Nakhud and Lash Juwain respectively. Purdil Khan's son Mir Afzal controlled 'Doaba', the tongue of land created by the confluence of the Dori-Kadanai and Arghandab rivers. Mihrdil Khan was the governor of Garmser. (Mirza Muhammad Riza to Edwardes 17 March 1854, For. Sec. 26 May 1854 No. 23). According to Faiz Muhammad, Kuhandil Khan's son Ghulam Muhyi al-Din was based in Deh Raud and Tirin. (ST 218)

63 Dupree 1980: 401–402; Reshtia 1957: 136; Reshtia 1990: 208; Temple to Braden 25–29 March 1855 (For. Sec. 29 June 1855 Nos. 53, 60)

64 Mihrdil Khan died on 17 March 1855. The dates of Kuhandil Khan's death are variously given as 12 August (KN 27 August 1855, For. Sec. 28 December 1855 No. 72) and 22 August 1855 (Nuri 1956: 13; ST 218).

65 KN 21–29 April, 6 June 1855 (For. Sec. 31 August 1855 No. 58); KN 20–27 June 1855 (For. Sec. 28 September 1855 No. 40); KN 19 July 1855 (For. Sec. 30 November 1855 No. 44); QN 13 August 1856 (L/P&S/5/229 No. 49 of 22 October 1856, p. 49)

66 Muhammad Sadiq and his brothers held the citadel (*arg*) of Qandahar. The fighting took place both inside the citadel and the city proper. In his attempt to evict Kuhandil Khan's sons from the citadel, Rahmdil Khan was supported by his sons Muhammad 'Alam Khan and Ghulam Muhammad Khan Tarzi. His allies in the city proper were his son Muhammad 'Alam Khan, the sons of Purdil Khan (Mir Afzal Khan and 'Abd al-Rasul Khan), the sons of Mihrdil Khan (Khushdil Khan, Munawwardil Khan and Sher 'Ali Khan). Sardar Ghulam Muhammad Khan b. Mir Afzal Khan lost his life in the course of the fighting. (ST 218; QN 13 August 1856, L/P&S/5/229 No. 54 of 22 October 1856, p. 48) .

67 ST 218; KN 27 August–16 September 1855 (For. Sec. 28 December 1855 No. 72)

68 KN 17 September–3 October 1855; Dost Muhammad Khan to Edwardes 22 October 1855 (For. Sec. 28 December 1855 Nos. 72, 75)

69 QN (Kohat, 26 November 1855, For. Sec. 28 December 1855 No. 80)

70 Champagne 1981: 345–346, 354–379; Harawi 1990: 56–64; Reshtia 1957: 137; Reshtia 1990: 211; ST 222–223; Stack 1975: 446–451; Sykes 1981 II: 65–67; Ghulam Haidar Khan to Edwardes 27, 29 September 1855; Edwardes to Temple 19 October 1855; KN 22–30 September 1855; Edwardes to Temple 12 December 1855 (For. Sec. 28 December 1855 Nos. 62, 69, 72, 80); Edwardes 1854.

71 Reshtia 1957: 136.
72 Edwardes to Temple 12 December 1855 (For. Sec. 28 December 1855 No. 80).
73 Reshtia 1957: 136; Reshtia 1990: 209.
74 Lumsden & Elsmie 1899: 187–188; Nuri 1956: 15–18; EQN 26 January 1856 (L/P&S/5/227 No. 16 of 22 April 1856, pp. 314–316)
75 EKN 10–24 May 1856, EQN 26 May 1856 (L/P&S/5/228 No. 28 of 17 July 1856, pp. 56–66); QN 13 August 1856 (L/P&S/5/229 No. 49 of 22 October 1856, p. 48); KN 16 May 1857 (For. Sec. 30 April 1858 No. 36) Rahmdil Khan accompanied the Amir to Kabul in September 1856 but was allowed to leave the capital and to proceed on a pilgrimage to Mecca via Qandahar and Teheran in May 1858. It is not clear whether he returned to Afghanistan prior to his death in 1859. In spring 1859 he was reported to receive an allowance from the Shah of Persia. (Bellew 1862: 414; Lumsden 1860: 5, 23; Journal of Nawwab Faujdar Khan 30 April 1858, For. S. C. 30 July 1858 No. 15; Nawwab Faujdar Khan to Edwardes 12 June 1858, For. Sec. 27 August 1858 No. 13; KN 7 March–5 April 1859, For. S. C. 27 May 1859 No. 13)
76 Jalal al-Din Khan was able to take Muhammad Sadiq, Muhammad 'Umar, Samand Khan Ishaqzai, and the Persian envoy prisoner. Even so, Muhammad Sadiq and Samand Khan were able to escape shortly afterwards. Muhammad Sadiq apparently returned to Qandahar at some later point. In early May 1857 he was accused of a plot against Ghulam Haidar Khan and was deported to Kabul, where he died during the following year. (Bellew 1862: 230–231; *Gaz.* II: 184–186; Lumsden 1860: 25; EQN 26 January 1856, L/P&S/5/227 No. 16 of 22 April 1856, p. 314; EKN 7 October 1856, Muhammad 'Umar Khan to Muhammad Sadiq October 1856, Muhammad Sadiq Khan to Mir Akhor Ahmad Khan October 1856, Jalal al-Din Khan to Ghulam Haidar Khan 18 October 1856, Ghulam Haidar Khan to Merewither 30 October 1856, Dost Muhammad Khan to John Lawrence, 14 November 1856, L/P&S/5/229 No. 64 of 22 December 1856 pp. 672–743; Ghulam Haidar to Dost Muhammad Khan n.d., L/P&S/5/230 No. 14 of 31 March 1857; QM 2 May 1857, For. Sec. 30 April 1858 No. 31)
77 Dost Muhammad Khan to Canning 14 September 1856 (L/P&S/5/229 No. 54 of 22 October 1856, p. 227–231) According to Ghulam Ahmad, the combined forces of Dost Muhammad Khan, Sher 'Ali Khan and Ghulam Haidar Khan amounted to 11,490 men. (Ghulam Ahmad 1856: 728–731)
78 Edwardes to Temple 26 August 1856 (L/P&S/5/228 No. 43 of 22 September 1856 p. 723)
79 EKN 23–31 January 1856 (L/P&S/5/227 No. 16 of 22 April 1856, pp. 300 303)
80 EKN 16 May 1856 (L/P&S/5/228 No. 28 of 17 July 1856 pp. 64–65); EKN 6 July 1856 (L/P&S/5/228 No. 43 of 22 September 1856 p. 686); EKN 31 August 1856 (L/P&S/5/229 No. 54 of 22 October 1856 p. 255)
81 Bahadur Khan Fatih Khan Khatak, quoted in Edwardes to Temple 26 August 1856 (L/P&S/5/228 No. 43 of 22 September 1856, pp. 723–724)
82 Ghani 1982: 200; Edwardes to Temple 26 August 1856 (L/P&S/5/228 No. 43 of 22 September 1856, pp. 723–724)
83 The requisitioning of grain carried out in the region south of Ghazni to answer the need of Qandahar sparked unrest among the Taraki Ghilzais. (EKN 20 December 1856–24 January 1857, L/P&S/5/230 No. 14 of 31 March 1857; QM 8 April 1857, L/P&S/5/232 No. 44 of 29 July 1857, pp. 603–604)
84 At the beginning of the crisis wheat flour was reported to be one third more expensive than in Ghazni. (Edwardes to Temple 26 August 1856, L/P&S/5/228 No. 43 of 22 September 1856, p. 725) Between May 1856 and April 1857 the

price of wheat flour rose from 2.5 Kabuli *sers* (40.8 lbs) per Kabuli rupee to 0.75 Kabuli *ser* (12.2 lbs) per Kabuli rupee. Barley, sold at 3 Kabuli *sers* (48.9 lbs) per Kabuli rupee in May 1856, reached the rate of 1 Kabuli *ser* (16.3 lbs) per Kabuli rupee in April 1857. (EKN 16 May 1856, L/P&S/5/228 No. 28 of 17 July 1856, pp. 64–65; EKN 25 April 1857, L/P&S/5/232 No. 44 of 29 July 1857 p. 634) According to Bellew, the price of wheat flour even reached the rate of 4 lbs per Indian rupee while that of barley rose to 8 lbs per Indian rupee. (Bellew 1862: 229)

85 Ghulam Haidar Khan to Dost Muhammad Khan n. d. (L/P&S/5/230 No. 14 of 31 March 1857)

86 Ghulam Haidar Khan to Dost Muhammad Khan 22 January 1857 (L/P&S/5/230 No. 18 of 22 April 1857)

87 Ghulam Haidar Khan to Dost Muhammad Khan n. d. (L/P&S/5/230 No. 18 of 22 April 1857)

88 Ghulam Haidar Khan to Dost Muhammad Khan 22 January 1857 (L/P&S/5/230 No. 18 of 22 April 1857) 'Maund' is the British rendering of the local weight unit *man*, which, like other measures, varied widely throughout Afghanistan. The Kabuli *man*, for example, consisted of 8 *sers*, or 130.4 lbs. Ghulam Haidar most likely intended the Qandahari *man* which equalled approximately 8.5 lbs. (Gregorian 1969: 404)

89 Ghulam Haidar Khan sold the grain procured from Ghazni and Sabzawar to the citizens of Qandahar at the same rate as the grain merchants, whereas his own troops received flour at special rates and only had to pay an Indian rupee for 32 pounds. (Bellew 1862: 229–230; QM 8 April 1857, L/P&S/5/232 No. 44 of 29 July 1857, p. 603)

90 QM 19 September 1857 (L/P&S/5/240 No. 77, p. 395); QM 27 November–3 December 1852 (For. S. C. 30 April 1858 No. 108)

91 QM 21 June 1857 (For. S. C. 30 April 1858 No. 50)

92 Bellew 1862: 330; Lumsden 1860: 7. In 1856 Dost Muhammad Khan described his son Muhammad Sharif as the governor of Zamindawar and Garmser. (Dost Muhammad Khan to John Lawrence 4 November 1856, L/P&S/5/229 No. 64 of 22 December 1856 p. 700)

93 Lumsden 1860: 29.

94 QM 25 July 1857 (For. Sec. 30 April 1858 No. 61); also see QM 22–28 January 1858 (For. S. C. 30 April 1858 No. 112); Bellew 1862: 283–284, 332, 383.

95 *Gaz.* V: 261–262; QM 22–28 January 1858 (For. S. C. 30 April 1858 No. 112)

96 QM 9–15 October 1857 (For. S. C. 30 April 1858 No. 93)

97 Sher 'Ali Khan to Mayo 12 June 1863 (L/P&S/5/257 No. 5 of 28 July 1863, p. 490)

98 Alder 1974: 105–110.

99 Boulger 1879: 339–340; KN 12 December 1854–14 January 1855 (For. Sec. 27 April 1855 No. 8); Edwardes to Temple 27 January 1855, Dost Muhammad Khan to Dalhousie (For. Sec. 25 May 1855 Nos. 2, 4); Temple to Braden 25–29 March 1855 (For. Sec. June 1855 Nos. 53, 56, 60); Edwardes to Temple 12 December 1855 (L/P&S/5/226 No. 3 of 22 January 1856 p. 518)

100 Alder 1975: 21–24; Boulger 1879: 341–344; Ghani 1982: 380; Valuation statement of stores supplied to Dost Muhammad Khan in 1857–58 (For. F. C. 13 May 1859 Nos. 174–175)

101 Alder 1975: 24–25; Champagne 1981: 434–450, 474.

102 Major Coke 30 September 1854, Kabul News from Sayyid Hisam al-Din (For. Sec. 27 October 1854 Nos. 11, 13); Edwardes to Temple 26 August 1856 (L/P&S/5. 228 No. 43 of 22 September 1856 pp. 721–722)

103 Alder 1975: 24; Bellew 1862: 256; Davies 1932: 4–5; Lumsden & Elsmie 1899: 174, 180, 181, 187, 211, 219–220; QM 19 June, 10–12 August 1857 (For. Sec. 30 April 1858, Nos. 50, 66 B); KD 2 August 1857 (For. Sec. 30 April 1858 No. 61); Brandreth to Edmonstone 12 August 1857 (For. Sec. 30 April 1858 No. 57); KN 18 June 1858 (For. F. C. 29 October 1858 No. 501)

104 Dost Muhammad Khan to *wakil* at Peshawar n. d. (For. Sec. 30 April 1858 No. 78); KN 27 July 1858 (For. Pol. 29 October 1858 No. 503); Edwardes to Davies 14 February 1859, Nawwab Faujdar Khan to Edwardes 24 February 1859 (For. S. C. 29 April 1859 Nos. 8, 14)

105 Fragner 1989: 92; Ghani 1982: 351; Ghani in *EIr*: 558.

106 Elphinstone 1972 II: 245; Grevemeyer 1981: 85; Husaini 1967: 29.

107 The *wizarat-i diwan-i a'la* (in charge of revenues, justice, public works) was headed by 'Alam Khan Bamizai, the *wizarat-i 'askar* (ministry of war) was under the command of Sher Muhammad Bamizai Mukhtar al-Daula, and the *wizarat-i a'zam* (interior and foreign ministry) was controlled by Rahmatullah Sadozai Mut'amid al-Daula. (Fofalzai 1958: 221–237, 243)

108 Elphinstone 1972 II; 255; Kakar 1979: 47–48; Singh 1981: 353–356. Elphinstone distinguishes two levels of sardarship. This term was used both for the Durrani nobles holding the military command on the provincial level and the chief officers of the army, here corresponding to the title *amir-i lashkar*. During Ṣhah Shuja''s reign only three Durrani leaders enjoyed the latter rank. At times certain Durrani chiefs received the title *sardar-i sardaran* and were entitled to the high command of the entire army. During Shah Zaman's reign this title was conferred on Ahmad Khan Nurzai. (Husaini 1967: 29); During Shah Mahmud's first reign, Fatih Khan Muhammadzai attained the same position. (Elphinstone 1972 II: 272)

109 Ferrier 1857: 95.

110 Elphinstone 1972 I: 229–230.

111 Masson 1974 II; 256. With the erection of central government offices, Amir 'Abd al-Rahman Khan also instituted a law that all government records were to be organized in sealed books with counted sheets. (Sultan Muhammad 1900: vi, 131; Yate 1880: 361)

112 Lal 1978 I: 231; Na'imi, Appendix in Kashmiri 1951: 242; Reshtia 1957: 156; ST 274; Sayyid Hisam al-Din (Peshawar 18 August 1854, For. Sec. 29 September 1854 No. 8)

113 Until his death in 1877 Sherdil Khan assumed a prominent position in Sher 'Ali Khan's administration. (MacGregor 1844: 879; Reshtia 1957: 155–156; ST 314, 332–336, 341; Sayyid Hisam al-Din (Peshawar 18 August 1854, For. Sec. 29 September 1854 No. 8); EKN 9 April 1857 (L/P&S/5/232 No. 44 of 29 July 1857 p. 631); Another *ishik aqasi* mentioned is Khan Gul, whose tribal affiliation is not clear. (ST 110; KI 12 June 1850, For. Sec. 28 June 1850 No. 27; EKN 21 November 1855, L/P&S/5/226 No. 9 of 22 February 1856, pp. 827–828)

114 Ghulam Muhammad Khan b. Sher Muhammad Khan b. Shah Wali Khan Bamizai had played an important role in the uprising against the British in November 1841. His granddaughter was married to Dost Muhammad Khan. His brother 'Ata Muhammad had been one of the most powerful adversaries of Dost Muhammad Khan's eldest brother Fatih Khan. (Fofalzai 1958: 234; Na'imi: Appendix in Kashmiri 1951: 243–244; Reshtia 1957: 156–158; Edwardes to Davies 2 February 1859, For. S. C. 29 April 1859 No. 2)

115 KN 3 April 1850 (For. Sec. 31 May 1850 No. 75); JN 21 February –12 March 1854 (For. Sec. 28 April 1854 No. 28); Muhammad Sadiq Khan to Mir Akhor Ahmad Khan October 1856 (L/P&S/5/229 No. 64 of 22 December 1856 pp.

740–741); Kabul Diary of Nawwab Faujdar Khan 10–14 September 1857 (For. Sec. 30 April 1858 No. 78); Journal of Nawwab Faujdar Khan 10 July 1858 (For. S. C. 27 August 1858 No. 16); KN 10 August 1858 (For. F. C. 29 October 1858 No. 503); KN 16 August 1858 (For. S. C. 26 November 1858 No. 21) The position of *amir akhorbashi* was held by members of the Ishaqzai tribe from Timur Shah's time on. (Fofalzai 1967: 381–382) During the reign of Amir Sher 'Ali Khan, Mirakhor Ahmad Khan played a steady role in the administration of Jalalabad and Herat (ST 287, 330, 333, 337; KD 24 September 1868, For. Pol. A. October 1868 No. 121; KD 4 January 1869, For Pol. A. February 1869 No. 176; KD 26–28 October 1869, For. Pol. A. November 1869 No. 152; KD 12–15 November 1869, For. Pol. A. January 1870; KD 8–11 December 1871, For. Sec. January 1872 No. 37)

116 Lumsden 1860: 8; KI 14–27 July 1852 (For. Sec. 24 September 1852 No. 115); KI 24 June–8 July 1853 (For. Sec. 30 September 1853 No. 55); KN 6 September 1854 (For. Sec. A. 24 November 1854 No. 14); KN 12 December 1854–14 January 1855 (For. Sec. 27 April 1857 No. 8); KN 1 September 1855 (For. Sec. 28 December 1855 No. 72); Edwardes to Davies 2 February 1859 (For. S. C. 29 April 1859 No. 2)

117 Reshtia 1957: 147–148; Reshtia 1990: 228; Tapper 1983: 33.

118 Newsletter by Sayyid Hisam al-Din 2 June 1854 (For. Sec. 28 July 1854 No. 17); for a similar statement see Edwardes to Temple 26 August 1856 (L/P&S/5/228 No. 43 of 22 September 1856 p. 725)

119 Reshtia 1957: 152, 155; Reshtia 1990: 235.

120 Kakar 1971: 4.

121 KI 31 December 1849 (For. Sec. 22 March 1850 No. 72); KN 5 June 1854 (For. Sec. 28 July 1854 No. 10); KN 6 September 1854 (For. Sec. A 24 November 1854 No. 14)

122 Ghubar 1981: 574.

123 Lumsden 1860: 9; KN 5 June 1854 (For. Sec. 28 July No. 10); EKN 15 December 1856 (L/P&S/5/230 No. 14 of 21 March 1857)

124 KN16 April–12 May 1858 (For. S. C. 30 July 1858 No. 26)

125 Reshtia 1957: 152; Reshtia 1990: 235.

126 Ghubar 1981: 574; also see Ghani, *EIr*, 560.

127 Bellew 1862: 200, 330; Lumsden 1860: 7–11; Lumsden & Elsmie 1899: 180; ST 210, 232; Yazdani 1991: 52–53; Dost Muhammad Khan to John Lawrence 4 November 1854 (L/P&S/5/229 No. 64 of 22 December 1856 p. 700); QM 5–10 June 1857 (For. S. C. 30 April 1858 No. 45)

128 QM 11 April 1857 (L/P&S/5/232 No. 44 of 29 July 1857 p. 614); also see QM 24 May 1857 (For. Sec. 30 April 1858 No. 39).

129 ST 200.

130 The first shipments of British muskets were distributed among the Amir's sons as follows:

Ghulam Haidar Khan	640
Muhammad A'zam Khan	407
Sher 'Ali Khan	100
Muhammad 'Ali b. Sher 'Ali	300
Muhammad Sharif Khan	100
Fatih Khan b. Muhammad Akbar	253
Wali Muhammad Khan	200
Ahmad Khan	400
Muhammad Aslam Khan	400
Muhammad Hasan	300

(QM 2 September 1857, For. Sec. 30 April 1858 No. 75; Kabul Diary of Nawwab Faujdar Khan 19 January 1858, For. Sec. 28 May 1858 No. 46)

131 QM 24 May 1857 (For. Sec. 30 April 1858 No. 39)

132 KI 12 June 1850 (For. Sec. 28 June 1850 No. 27); KI 21 October 1851 (For. Sec. 28 November 1851 No. 16)

133 Fatih Muhammad Khan and Jalal al-Din Khan inherited Ghulam Haidar Khan's estates in Kohdaman, Kabul, Logar, Ghazni, and Jalalabad, a great part of which had been in the possession of their father Sardar Muhammad Akbar Khan prior to his death in 1847. (KN 6–16 July 1858, For. F. C. 29 October 1858 Nos. 501, 503; Edwardes to Temple 13 August 1858, For. F. C. 31 October 1858 No. 254; Nawwab Faujdar Khan to Edwardes 2 December 1858, For S. C. 31 December 1858 No. 8)

134 Sultan Muhammad Khan 1900: 6.

135 Bellew 1862: 407; Lumsden 1860: 9; KN 5 June 1854 (For. Sec. 28 July 1854 No. 10); KN 27 September, 6–7 October 1854 (For. Sec. 26 January 1855 Nos. 77, 100)

136 KN 9 September 1855 (For. Sec. 28 December 1855 No. 72); EKN 15–20 December 1855 (L/P&S/5/226 No. 9 of 22 February 1856 pp. 835–837)

137 KN 17 January–11 February 1858 (For. Sec. 28 May 1858 No. 48); KN 26 April–1 May 1858 (For. S. C. 30 July 1858 No. 26); Nawwab Faujdar Khan to Edwardes 19 June 1858 (For. S. C. 27 August 1858 No. 13)

138 KN 7–8 July 1858 (For. F. C. 29 October 1858 No. 501)

139 Until his death in 1871 Fatih Muhammad Khan played a steady role in Sher 'Ali Khan's administration. (ST 274, 280–294, 305, 317, 327–328; White King 1896: 307; Ghani 1961: 36; KN 23–24 July, 10 August 1858, For. F. C. 29 October 1858 No. 503; KN 16 August 1858, For. S. C. 26 November 1858 No. 21; KN 18 March 1859, For. S. C. 27 May 1859 No. 13; KN 14 August 1859, For. S. C. 28 October 1859 No. 6; Frere to Elphinstone 24 October 1859, For. F. C. 23 December 1859 17–18); KD 22 September 1861, For. Pol. A. October 1861 No. 222; KD 8–11 September 1871, For. Sec. October 1871 No. 58)

140 Lumsden & Elsmie 1899: 138.

141 MacGregor 1871 II: 60.

142 In addition, the majority of Sher 'Ali Khan's troops consisted of Ghilzais and Wardaks. (Ghulam Ahmad 1875: 59–60)

143 ST 113.

144 Singh 1981: 358–359, 364.

145 Gupta 1941: 100–104.

146 ST 56, Fofalzai 1958: 302 In another location, Fofalzai estimates that Shah Zaman's army included 10,000 infantry during his campaign to Lahore in 1797. (Fofalzai 1958: 298) Husaini estimated Shah Zaman's infantry at 3,900 men. (possibly a typographical error? Husaini 1967: 28–30)

147 Elphinstone 1972 II: 272, 274. Elphinstone mentions 12,000 Durrani cavalry and 13,000 *ghulam khana* as the main elements in Shah Shuja''s army. His description of the Durrani cavalry makes it clear that the king had little influence on its internal organization:
'They are called out by the King's order, issued to the chief of each clan, and by him notified to the Khauns under him. They assemble the men due by their several subdivisions, and bring them to the place appointed for the rendezvous of the army, where they are mustered and registered before the king. [new paragraph] The men of each clan form a separate corps, called Dusteh, subdivided and commanded according to their descent, as in the civil

arrangement of the clan. The greater part of the Doorauness only attend the king during military operations.' (Elphinstone 1972 II: 266–267)

148 The *qara naukar* were furnished in time of war by the landowners at fixed rates. In the Kabul region, they were mostly Tajiks, and each subdivision of the province (Kohdaman, Paghman, Butkhak and Logar) had to provide 1,000 men. During Timur Shah's campaign to Bahawalpur in 1788 as many as 60,000 *qara naukars* were called out. The *iljari* were raised from the poorer segments of society, theoretically at the rate of one tenth of the population. (Elphinstone 1972 II: 268–271; M. 'Azim Baraki, Jan Muhammad in Elphinstone Collection F 88 13 Kt, pp. 124–126, 263–264)

149 Reshtia 1957: 50, 153; Reshtia 1990: 86–87, 236–237; ST 113.

150 Hamilton 1906: 310–311.

151 Harlan 1939: 13.

152 Bellew 1862: 208, 245; Gregorian 1969: 84; QM 2 May, 2 September 1857 (For. Sec. 30 April 1858 Nos. 31, 75); Edwardes to James 16 May 1858 (For. S. C. 30 April 1858 No. 75)

153 Lal 1978 I: 241; ST 113.

154 Ghani, *EIr*: 559–560; ST 200.

155 Lumsden 1860: 11; QM 4–10 September 1857 (For. Sec. 30 April 1858 No. 80)

156 Burnes 1839b: 15; Lal 1978 I: 240.

157 According to Lumsden, the Amir himself only controlled 200 *jazailchis*. The distribution among his remaining sons was as follows:

Ghulam Haidar Khan	1,000
Sher 'Ali Khan	300
Muhammad Amin	200
Muhammad Sharif	100
Muhammad Afzal Khan	400
Muhammad A'zam Khan	100
Muhammad Aslam Khan	200

(Lumsden 1860: 17; QM 4–10 September 1857, For. Sec. 30 April 1858 No. 80)

158 During Shah Shuja''s first reign, the only men mounted on horses belonging to the government were 500 *peshkhidmats*, who were personal servants of the king. (Elphinstone 1972 II: 272–273)

159 There are varying estimates of the actual strength of Dost Muhammad Khan's cavalry. In the 1830s, Burnes and Lal agreed that the Amir's cavalry numbered 12,000 men. Yet Burnes was of the opinion that only about 9,000 of them were 'highly efficient'. According to Lal, Muhammad Akbar Khan commanded 2,000 cavalry men, whereas Ghulam Haidar Khan and Muhammad Afzal controlled 1,000 and 600 horsemen respectively. (Burnes 1839b: 15; Lal 1978 I: 240) At the onset of the First Anglo-Afghan War, Hough estimated Dost Muhammad Khan's total force at 14,000, of which only 6,000 were cavalry. (Hough 1841: 140, 289) For the 'feudal' cavalry available to Shah Shuja' during the First Anglo-Afghan War, Yapp gives the figure of 5,662 horsemen in the muster rolls of Kabul, and 1,218 men at Qandahar . (Yapp 1980: 311)

160 According to Ghulam Ahmad's estimate the troops under the command of Sardars Muhammad Afzal Khan and Wali Muhammad Khan amounted to a total of 9,000 men. Lumsden's assessment of the entire force serving in Turkistan is somewhat higher, arriving at a total of 13,000 men, including five regiments of regular infantry. (QM 4 May 1857 (For. Sec. 30 April 1858 No. 31)

161 Lumsden 1860: 18; QM 6 September 1857 (For. Sec. 30 April 1858 No. 80); also see Temple to Edmonstone 4 September 1856 (L/P&S/5/228 No. 43 of 22 September 1856 p. 717)
162 'Rates of Pay in Shah Shuja''s Army' (Elphinstone Collection F88 Box 13 Ho, p. 974)
163 KD 30 August–2 September 1872 (For. Sec. October 1872 No. 54)
164 Fofalzai 1958: 304–305; Fofalzai 1967: 353; ST 56.
165 There is contradictory information on the proportion between the exemption of taxes on Durrani *tiyuls* and the cash allowance received. According to the specialist of the administration of Qandahar, Rawlinson, Ahmad Shah's settlement stipulated that the entire allowance of a Durrani horseman was 25 *tomans*, out of which 19 *tomans* were treated as a cash allowance and 6 *tomans* were accounted for by the tax exemption on the *tiyul*. (Rawlinson 1871: 827). When visiting Shah Shuja''s court in 1809, Elphinstone, by contrast, reached the conclusion that the tax exemptions on the *tiyul* lands made up the greater part of the salary of a Durrani horseman: 'The pay of the Doorraunee privates is 20 Tomans, 400 Cabul rupees, or 40 £ Sterling a year... Their teools are said to be equal to nine months' pay and they receive the balance of 5 Tomans, 100 Cabulee rupees whenever they are called on to serve.' ('Rates of Pay in Shah Shuja''s Army', Elphinstone Collection F88 Box 13 Ho, p. 972; also see Elphinstone 1972 II: 266)
166 At Shah Zaman's time the pay of the *ghulams* was ten to fifteen *tomans*, i. e. 200 to 300 Kabuli rupees, per year. (ST 56)
167 Elphinstone 1972 II: 268–269; 'Rates of Pay in Shah Shuja''s Army' (Elphinstone Collection F88 Box 13 Ho, pp. 972–976; Muhammad 'Ali Khan Ayub and Jan Muhammad in Elphinstone Collection F88 Box 13 Kt, pp. 205, 263.
168 Fofalzai 1958: 74.
169 Elphinstone 1972 II: 275–276.
170 Burnes quoted in Hough 1841: 288n.
171 Burnes 1839b: 18.
172 Lal 1978 I: 241–242; Lumsden 1860: 12, 17; QM 12 July, 28 August 1857 (For. Sec. 30 April 1858 Nos. 59, 75; Ghulam Ahmad 1856: 732) According to Burnes, the Qizilbash horsemen received 84 rupees a year during Dost Muhammad Khan's first reign. The pay of the Qizilbash leaders was fixed at 58,000 rupees annually. (Burnes 1839a: 9)
173 Bellew 1862: 354; Hough 1841: 288; Lal 1978 I: 241; Lumsden 1860: 12, 17; O. St. John 1879; KN 5 June 1854 (For. Sec. 28 July 1854 No. 10); QM 12 July 1857 (For. Sec. 30 April 1858 No. 59);)
174 Masson 1974 III: 373.
175 Lumsden 1860: 18.
176 MacGregor 1871 II: 66.
177 Burnes 1834 II: 334–335; EKN 31 January 1856 (L/P&S/5/227 No. 16 of 22 April 1856, pp. 303–306)
178 Masson 1974 II: 270–271, 372; Wylly 1912: 411.
179 Vambéry 1864: 280.
180 Ferrier quoted in MacGregor 1871 II: 66.
181 Diary of Bahadur Khan Fatih Khan Khatak 5 June 1856, commenting on the military exercises outside Qandahar organized on the occasion of '*id*. (L/P&LS/5/228 No. 33 of 21 August 1856 p. 217)
182 QM 26 April 1857 (For. Sec. 30 April 1858 No. 30)
183 QM 2 May 1857, 12 July 1857 (For. Sec. 30 April 1858 Nos. 31, 59) Even when the soldiers were paid they rarely received the entire amount due to them,

'in most instances a considerable sum being withheld by the various officials through whose hands the money passed before it reached the soldier.' (Bellew 1862: 284–285, 334)

184 Temple to Edmonstone 22 September 1856 (L/P&S/5/228 No. 43 of 22 September 1856 p. 717) For a similar statement by Sir Bartle Frere see Martineau 1895 I: 229.

185 Lumsden 1860: 16; QM 27 March–9 April 1857 (L/P&S/5/232 No. 44 of 29 July 1857); QM 4 May 1857 (For. Sec. 30 April 1858 No. 31)

186 QM 12 July 1857 (For. Sec. 30 April 1858 No. 59)

187 For examples see KI 24 June–8 July 1853 (For. Sec. 30 September 1853 No. 55); KN 26 March 1856 (L/P&S/5/227 No. 25 of 17 June 1856 pp. 805–806)

188 Fofalzai 1958: 302; Kakar 1979: 95; Sultan Muhammad Khan 1980 I: 4–5; TT 10.

189 Lumsden 1860: 15–16.

190 Gregorian 1969: 87; KD 29 June–5 July 1869 (For. Pol. A. August 1869 Nos. 17–18); KD 18–21 February 1870 (For. Pol. A. April 1870 No. 39); KD 16–19 February 1872 (For. Sec. March 1872 No. 273); KD 28–30 May, 11–13 June 1872 (For. Sec. July 1872 Nos. 104, 113)

191 Elphinstone 1972 II: 247.

192 Husaini 1967: 32; also see Ali 1848: 73–80, 188, 195; Davies 1949: 62–63; ST 38–40, 56.

193 Gankovsky 1981: 85–95; Gupta 1944: 271–279.

194 Strachey, 'Revenue and Trade', f. 130.

195 Burnes 1839b: 19; Elphinstone 1972 II: 258; Ghani 1982: 360–361; Husaini 1967: 32; Strachey, 'Revenue and Trade', fs. 138–140.

196 Husaini 1967: 30–31. Also see Fofalzai 1967: 350–351; ST 56–57.

197 Strachey, 'Revenue and Trade', fs. 77, 119. As a rule, the lords of Sind had to be compelled by military might to pay their dues. Thus Timur Shah collected six million rupees in arrears during a military campaign in 1788. In 1794 Shah Zaman raised 2.4 million rupees in the same manner. In 1805 Shah Shuja' succeeded in obtaining 2.7 million rupees in Sind. (Gankovsky 1981: 85)

198 Strachey, 'Revenue and Trade', fs. 4, 55, 75–80, 102, 107, 109.

199 Ghani 1982: 133.

200 Strachey, 'Revenue and Trade', f. 6; Muhammad 'Ali Khan Ayub, Elphinstone Collection F88 Box 13 Kt, pp. 195–196.

201 Raverty 1888: 49.

202 The higher rates of revenue were taken when the cultivators did not supply seed and cattle themselves. (*Gaz.* VI: 289–290; also see Hastings 1880)

203 Gankovsky 1981: 79; *Gaz.* VI: 290–291; 427–428; 494; Rawlinson 1871: 827; Warburton 1880: 7–8; Hastings 1880; Strachey, 'Revenue and Trade', f. 8.

204 Kakar 1979: 76.

205 Fragner 1984: 210.

206 Lambton: 'Kharadj', in *EI* (2).

207 ST 209.

208 Gankovsky 1981: 78.

209 Ferrier 1858: 323. Other sources mention a tax called *khanadudi* or *khanawari* as a special tax on the houses and shops of the non-Pashtun or non-Durrani urban population. (*Gaz.* VI: 494–495; Warburton 1880: 7; Strachey, 'Revenue and Trade', f. 126; QM 1 June 1857, For. Sec. 30 April 1858 No. 42; O. St. John 1879) According to Rawlinson, not only Durranis but also the Farsiwan of Qandahar were exempt from this tax at the time of Ahmad Shah. (Rawlinson 1871: 827). Strachey mentions a house tax called *khanashumari*

for Jalalabad, but it is not clear whether is applied solely to non Pashtuns. (Strachey, 'Revenue and Trade', f. 8)

210 Burnes 1834 II: 331; Ferrier 1858: 326; Gaz. VI: 290–292; 428; Hamilton 1906: 259; Harlan 1939: 39; Harlan 1842: 168; McChesney 1968: 14.

211 The income of the city of Qandahar on the basis of *jizya* was estimated at 10,000 rupees at the beginning of the nineteenth century. (Strachey, 'Revenue and Trade', fs. 126–127) In 1857 it amounted to 6,000 Qandahar rupees. (QM 12–18 June 1857, For. Sec. 30 April 1858 No. 48) In 1879 O. St. John estimated the total amount of *jizya* collected in Qandahar at 4,600 rupees. For the city of Kabul, Molloy estimated that the *jizya* yielded 6,000 rupees in the 1880s . (Molloy 1883d) The *jizya* rates seem to have varied through time and according to location. In 1809 Strachey mentioned that the *jizya* of Ghorband amounted to 3 rupees per person, reaching a total of 500 rupees per year. (Strachey, 'Revenue and Trade', f. 39) For the district of Jalalabad Jenkyns recorded a rate of 5 rupees per person. In the town of Jalalabad it amounted to 380 rupees together with the tax on trades (*asnaf*). (Gaz. VI: 290–292) In Laghman the rate of the *jizya* ranged from 2 to 4 shahis (one-sixth to one third of a Kabuli rupee). (Warburton 1880: 7–8; Gaz. VI: 494–495)

212 Fofalzai lists *'ushr* as one of the tax rates common during Timur Shah's reign. The other taxes mentioned are *dah yaka* (one tenth), *panj yaka* (one fifth) and *se yaka* (one third). (Fofalzai 1967: 349) For the same period, the Lohani nomads are recorded to have paid 1,000 rupees yearly in the name of *'ushr* to the royal exchequer. (Raverty 1888: 500)

213 Gankovsky 1981: 81.

214 Kakar 1979: 82.

215 Otherwise the payment of and *khums* and *'ushr* seems to have been restricted to inner-community relations among certain the Hazaras and certain Tajik groups. Shi'ite jurisprudence provides for the levying of *khums* 'on a wide variety of goods and transactions and awards the money to the Imam or in his absence to needy *sayyids*.' (Personal communication from Hamid Algar) The traditional Hazara practice of submitting *khums* to local sayyids would seem to fit this precept. (Kopecky 1982:97–98; Kopecky 1986:176–180; also see Bindemann 1987: 18) According to Kakar, the Jamshedis and Hazaras of Herat paid *'ushr* to their elders. (Kakar 1979: 271 fn 64). In Badakhshan, the Isma'ili elders enjoyed both religious and secular authority and were entitled to collect *'ushr* from their fellow Tajiks. (Kakar 1979: 60, 148; Shahrani 1984b: 150.)

216 Gaz. VI: 290–292, 495; Warburton 1880: 7; Hastings 1880; Molloy 1883d.

217 QM 1–18 June 1857 (For. Sec. 30 April 1858 Nos. 42, 48)

218 Protheroe 1879; O. St. John 1879.

219 Hastings 1880.

220 Molloy 1883d.

221 A year earlier the British official Ghulam Ahmad reached a similar result, giving the income of the Amir as 3,870,000 rupees. (MacGregor 1871 II: 65) Merewither estimated that Dost Muhammad's total revenue amounted to 4,000,000 rupees prior to the conquest of Herat. ('Note on the Position of Affairs in Afghanistan'). During Sher 'Ali Khan's reign the net receipts from Turkistan and Kabul rose to 900,000 and 1.3 million Kabuli rupees respectively. As Herat furnished no revenues and needed subsidies on top, Sher 'Ali Khan's total net revenues did not exceed 2.6 million rupees. His gross income was estimated at 13.2 million. (Lambert 1886; also see Molloy 1883b)

222 QM 11 April 1857 (L/P&S/5/232 No. 44 of 29 July 1857 p. 613); Nawwab Faujdar Khan to Edwardes 19 June 1858 (For. S. C. 27 August 1858 No. 13).

In 1877–78 Ghazni submitted a revenue of 4000 *kharwars* of grain worth 130,000 Kabuli rupees. (Lambert 1886)

223 Bellew 1862: 175; Broadfoot 1886: 354, 363; Masson 1906: 114.

224 Lal 1978 I: 232–233.

225 Including Arghanda, Charkh, Istalif, and Balaghain.

226 Including Ghorband, Bihsud, and the valleys of Turkoman and Parsa.

227 Including Kharwar, Gardez, Khost, Kharotis and Shinwaris (?).

228 *Gazetter of Afghanistan* 1912 VI: 162; KN 23–24 July 1858 (For. F. C. 29 October 1858 No. 503)

229 Strachey, 'Revenue and Trade', f. 40; British informant in Elphinstone Collection F 88 13 Kt p. 94.

230 Broadfoot 1886: 345; Canfield 1973: 97–98; Masson 1906: 114; QM 10–16 April 1857 (L/P&S/5/232 No. 44 of 29 July 1857 p. 613); Hastings 1880; Molloy 1883a.

231 Burnes 1839d: 44.

232 Jones 1976: 72; Jones 1978: 3–4; ST 198; KN, Lahore 30 November 1853 (For. Sec. 30 December 1853 No. 53); Kabul Diary of Nawwab Faujdar Khan 10–14 September 1857 (For. Sec. 30 April 1858 No. 78); QM 2–14 October 1857 (For. Sec. 30 April 1858 Nos. 92–93); KN 7 July 1858 (For. F. C. 29 October 1858 No. 501); KN 17 August 1858 (For. S. C. 26 November 1858 No. 21); KN 31 August 1858 (For. S. C. 26 November 1858 No. 21)

233 Masson 1974 II: 353.

234 Lal, by contrast, is of the opinion that the combined revenue of Bihsud and Bamiyan did not exceed 70,000 rupees. Perhaps this figure represents the net revenue collected by the king. (Lal 1978 I: 233)

235 Harlan 1939: 127. The revenues of the Hazara regions north of Qandahar were also raised in the form of slaves when the local crops did not suffice to fulfill the revenue demands of the government.

236 Molloy 1883a.

237 Masson 1974 II: 372–373.

238 For examples of this process in Ghazni, Zurmat, Logar, Kohistan, Tagau and Panjsher, please see the following sources, ST 200, KN 20 December 1849 (For. Sec. 22 March 1850 No. 70); KI 18 January 1851 (For. Sec. 28 February 1851 No. 50); KN 14 April–2 May 1851 (For. Sec. 30 May 1851 No. 56); KN 1–15 May 1851 (For. Sec. 25 July 1851 No. 53); KI 21 October 1851 (For. Sec. 28 November 1851 No. 16); KN 17 January 1855 (For. Sec. 27 April 1855 No. 16); KN 30 August 1855 (For. Sec. 28 December 1855 No. 72); EKN 17 October 1855 (L/P&S/5/226 No. 11 of 8 March 1856 p. 864); EKN 6–13 February 1856 (L/P&S/5/227 No. 16 of 22 April 1856 pp. 305–307); EKN 11–19 May (L/P&S/5/228 No. 28 of 17 July 1856 pp. 64–65; QM 26 February–4 March 1858 (For. S. C. 28 May 1858 No. 10)

239 EKN 9–20 August 1856 (L/P&S/5/229 No. 54 of 22 October 1856 pp. 250–252); EKN 4–20 September 1856 (L/P&S/5/229 No. 64 of 22 December 1856 pp. 686–691)

240 KN 29 January 1850 (For. Sec. 22 March 1850 No. 75); KN 3 April 1850 (For. Sec. 31 May 1850 No. 75)

241 After the death of the wife of his half brother Nawwab 'Abd al-Jabbar Khan, for example, the Amir ordered the confiscation of her property worth more than 600,000 rupees. (EKN 26 May 1856, L/P&S/5/228 No. 28 of 17 July 1856 p. 67) For an example of confiscations by Ghulam Haidar Khan see Bellew 1862: 258–259.

242 Hough 1841: 288.

243 Gregorian 1969: 80 fn 126.
244 In 1857 Lumsden estimated that the number of the relatives who expected some sort of financial support from the Amir ran into the hundreds. (QM 11 September 1857, For. Sec. 30 April 1858 No. 82). In 1879 O. St. John reported that the descendants of the Qandahar Sardars alone collected 290,000 rupees yearly in allowances. (O. St. John 1879)
245 KN 6 May 1854 (For. Sec. 30 June 1854 No. 19)
246 Harlan 1842: 154.
247 See, for example, Oliver 1890: 184–185.
248 Personal communication from Hamid Algar; Khalil 1960: 92–93.
249 Hyder Khan 1836: 98.
250 Elphinstone 1972 I: 249–250; Fofalzai 1958: 402; Olufsen 1904: 166.
251 Burnes 1834 I: 238.
252 Elphinstone 1972 I: 282.
253 Even so, regional variations have to be taken in account. Robinson observes that the conflict between tribal custom (*rawaj*) and *shari'at* was less pronounced among the Afghan nomads than the border tribes. He describes the *powindas* following a migratory cycle between Afghanistan and India as 'strict in the performance of religious duties' (Robinson 1978: 9, 10, 14)
254 Elphinstone 1972 II: 246; QM 21 June 1857 (For. Sec. 30 April 1858 No. 50)
255 Masson 1974 II: 255–256; Baraki in Elphinstone Collection F 88 13 Kt, p. 132.
256 Harlan 1842: 145.
257 Bellew 1862: 261–263; 281–282; Elphinstone 1972 II: 262.
258 Sa'id Khan Barakzai held this post during Dost Muhammad Khan's first reign. (Na'imi: Appendix in Kashmiri 1951: 242) For the period after the First Anglo-Afghan War, Qazi 'Abd al-Rahman Khan Khan-i 'Ulum is mentioned as the *qazi al-quzat* (supreme judge). (Reshtia 1957: 156)
259 KN 25 October 1854 (For. Sec. 26 January 1855 No. 100)
260 This was the shrine of a member of the Mujaddidi family, Shah Ghulam Husain (b. Shah Ghulam Muhammad b. Ghulam Muhammad Ma'sum b. Shaikh Muhammad Isma'il b. Shah Muhammad Sibghatullah b. Khwaja Muhammad Ma'sum b. Hazrat Mujaddid Shaikh Ahmad Sirhindi), who was a contemporary of Ahmad Shah and Timur Shah. (Fofalzai 1967: 680; Habibi 1959: 858)
261 Bellew claims that the leaders of this rebellion were killed after their arrival in Kabul. (Bellew 1862: 393–401, 411–412)
262 Ghani 1978.
263 Lal 1978 II: 308.
264 O. St. John 1879.
265 Lal 1977: 180–181; Leech 1839a: 58–60.
266 Fofalzai alternately uses the titles *mīr wāʿiz and mīr waʿz.*
267 Little is known about Mulla Ahmad Khan's activities except that he was in charge of the repair of the Jami' Masjid of Kabul and commanded a military expedition to Kashmir.
268 Sayyid Ahmad was instructed in the Sufi path by Shaikh Sa'd al-Din Sahib Ansari of Kabul (d. 1810) and held an *ijazat* from Khwaja Hasan Aqa Ji of Kohdaman. At the time of Shah Zaman he was reputed to have at least 100,000 followers in Afghanistan. (Fofalzai 1958: 274)
269 Habibi 1959: 801; Elphinstone 1972 II: 278.
270 Ghubar 1981: 548; Khalil 1960: 185–186; Reshtia 1957: 168; Reshtia 1990: 263.
271 Lumsden 1860: 26; KD 12–14 December 1871 (For. Sec. January 1872 No. 38).

272 These three were sons of Shah Ghulam Muhammad Ma'sum b. Shaikh Muhammad Isma'il b. Shah Muhammad b. Khwaja Muhammad Ma'sum b. Shaikh Ahmad Sirhindi.

273 Fofalzai 1967: 418, 677–683; Habibi 1959: 857–858.

274 Edwards 1986: 288 fn. 21.

275 Fofalzai 1967: 682–685.

276 Ahmed 1976: 14, 87–98; Edwards 1986: 281–286.

277 Gregorian 1969: 52.

278 Davies 1862: 8–9; Lal 1977: 193–194; Rathjens 1962: 215–216.

279 Conolly 1834 II: 267–268; Davies 1862: 39–46, 75; Hyder Khan 1836: 98 99; Hamilton 1906: 198; Izzet Ullah 1843: 339; Khanikoff 1845: 225–226; Lal 1977: 45–46; Lord 1839b: 133; Raverty 1888: 498; Vigne 1982: 69, 107; Political Diary of Edwardes 5–12 May 1847 (L/P&S/5/9/191 No. 39 of 8 June 1847).
Detailed reports on the trade between Afghanistan and India are to be found in Anonymous, 'On Tabular Returns of the N. W. Frontier Trade with Afghanistan', pp. 250–263, MacGregor 1873 I, 3: 12–19 (reports by Grey, Graham and Macauley), MacGregor 1871 II: 52–53 (summary of Davies 1862) and Robinson 1978: 23–29. Burton (1993: 20–31) describes the trade between Bukhara, India and Iran between 1558 and 1718. For a list of the trade items exchanged between Afghanistan and Iran at the time of Shah Zaman, see Fofalzai 1958: 343. In the nineteenth century the Afghan exports to Iran mainly consisted of wool, felt, furs and skins. (Hamilton 1906: 198)

280 Conolly 1834 II: 41, 129–133, 140, 147; Davies 1862: 41; Ferrier 1858: 320–321.

281 Ghani 1982: 333–334; Rathjens 1962: 212–213; QM 24 July 1857 (For. Sec. 30 April 1858 No. 61)

282 According to Robinson, this term derives from the Pashtu root *powal*, 'to graze flocks', 'to move from place to place in search of pasture'. (Robinson 1978: 1)

283 An alternate route to the Derajat was the Ghwayi Lari by way of Zarkani. (Raverty 1888: 497–498)

284 Broadfoot 1886: 394–395; Oliver 1890: 82–83; Raverty 1888: 497–504; Robinson 1978: 23, 25.

285 Davies 1862: 42.
All the nomad groups formed a minority within their respective tribes. Davies classifies them as follows:
1,400 Lohani men with 6,000 camels,
5,000 Nasir men with 16,000 camels,
1,800 Kharoti men with 6,000 camels,
600 Daftani men with 4,000 camels,
600 Niyazi men with 3,000 camels.
The *powinda* groups listed by Raverty (1888: 498–500) amounted to a total of 6150–6850 families:
2,000 Lohani families,
2,000–2,500 Nasir families (10,000 to 12,000 souls),
700–800 Kharoti families (3,000 to 3,500 souls) with 6,000–7,000 camels,
200 Sulaiman Khel families (800–1,000 souls),
250–300 Taraki families (900–1,200 souls),
200–250 Daftani families (700–1,000 souls) with 4,000 camels,
800 Niyazi families (3,300 souls).
During Sher 'Ali Khan's reign as many as 77,000 *powindas* were registered when entering the district of Dera Isma'il Khan. (Robinson 1978:4–5)

286 Ghani 1982: 312–313;Oliver 1890: 83–85; Raverty 1888: 488–499; Robinson 1978: 23; Vigne 1982: 53–54, 68–69.
287 The trade volume seems to have dropped by one fourth during this period. ('On Tabular Returns', p. 257)
288 Lal 1977: 45–46.
289 Vigne 1982: 70.
290 Harlan 1939: 70.
291 Lal 1977: 46.
292 'On Tabular Returns', pp. 261–262.
293 Davies gives the following trade return:
1) Exports to British India
– by way of Jalalabad £156,513
– by way of Ghazni £130,000
– by way of Bolan £ 31,870
Total £318,838 (approximately 3 million Indian rupees)
2) Imports from British India
– by way of Jalalabad £120,643
– by way of Ghazni £164,000
– by way of Bolan £ 18,892
Total £303,535
(Davies 1862: 1–2, 74–75; the data seem to have been switched around in MacGregor 1871 II: 54)
294 Ghani 1982; 312–313.
295 The four passes in question were Unai (11,000 feet), alternately the Hajigak 11,700 feet) or 'Iraq passes (13,000 (?) feet), Aqrubat (10,225 feet) and Dandan Shikan (9,000 feet). (*Gaz.* VI: 22, 147, 245, 263, 374, 421, 796)
296 In winter, when the Hajigak Pass was closed, the Shibar Pass (9,800 feet) linking the head of the Ghorband valley with Bamiyan was used as alternative route. (*Gaz.* VI: 728)
297 Davies 1862: 47: Centlivres-Demont 1976: 274; Gaz. VI: 422; Rathjens 1962: 218–219; Wood 1841: 185–186, 196–206.
298 Conolly 1834 II: 55; Ghani 1982: 22.
299 Davies 1862: 47.
300 Conolly 1834 I; 414; Broadfoot 1886: 395.
301 Elphinstone 1972 I: 381; Ghani 1982: 180–181.
302 Gerard 1833: 1; Warburton 1900: 261.
303 Burton 1993: 8–9; Davies 1862: 46–47; Hyder Khan 1836: 106; Lord 1839b: 123.
304 Burnaby 1877: 447.
305 Ghani 1982: 22; Kakar 1979: 202; Lal 1977: 193.
306 Davies 1862: Appendix XXIII.
307 Burnes 1839b: 20; Ferrier 1858: 325–326; Lal 1977: 194–195; Protheroe 1879. The entire duties levied between Karachi and Herat amounted to 28%, as the value of the merchandise was estimated on the basis of its local value rather than that of its point of origin. (O. St. John 1879)
308 Lal 1978 I: 235–236.
309 MacGregor 1873 I, 2: 130.
310 Lord 1839b: 124–125.
311 Masson 1974 II: 200.
312 Ferrier 1971: 275.
313 Lal 1977: 192–193; Vambéry 1864: 260–261.
314 Masson 1974 II: 187.

315 Burnes 1839b: 20.
316 Centlivres 1976b: 127; Grötzbach 1972: 53–54; Masson 1974 II: 270.
317 Burnes 1839b: 20; Conolly 1834 II: 271–272; Lal 1977: 193; 'On Tabular Returns', p. 251–252.
318 Bindemann 1987: 18; Harlan 1939: 131–133.
319 Centlivres 1976b: 126–127; Grevemeyer 1982: 105–106; Wood 1841: 210.
320 Broadfoot 1886: 389; Conolly 1834 II; 64; Davies 1862: 47; Lal 1977: 49; Leech 1845a: 326–327; MacGregor 1871 II: 56.
321 Conolly 1834 II: 272.
322 Report by Burnes, For. Sec. 6 June 1833 No. 8 p. 2683.
323 Gankovsky 1981: 94.
324 Burnes 1834 II: 330; Burnes 1839b: 20.
325 Lal 1978 I: 235–236.
326 Davies 1862: 49, Appendix XXIII; Harlan 1939: 153.
327 QM 11 April 1857 (L/P&S/5/232 No. 44 of 29 July 1857 pp. 613–614)
328 QM 24 April 1857 (For. Sec. 30 April 1858 No. 30)
329 Davies 1862: Appendix XXIII.
330 KN 14 February 1859 (For. S. C. 27 May 1859 No. 3)
331 Lal 1978 I: 234–235. Also see Bellew 1862: 266–267 for Ghulam Haidar Khan's confiscations of horses from merchants passing through Qandahar. Even Dost Muhammad Khan's father-in-law, the wealthy merchant Nazir Khairullah was not exempt from the Amir's exactions prior to the First Anglo-Afghan War. (Lal 1978 I: 224)
332 Gregorian 1969: 79.
333 Lal 1978 II: 321–323.
334 Rathjens 1962: 211–212, 216.
335 Lumsden & Elsmie 1899: 139; Malleson 1879: 1; Merewither, 'Note on the Position of Affairs in Afghanistan'.

CONCLUSION

1 Gellner 1983: 440.
2 Centlivres and Centlivres-Demont 1988a: 231.

GLOSSARY

ābī irrigated land.

ᶜālim, pl. *ᶜulamāᵓ* a person learned in the religious law and its sources .

ᶜamala-yi sarkārī Dost Muhammad Khan's regular cavalry.

amir commander; during the Sadozai period: synonym of *wazīr*, military commander of 7,000 to 12,000 troops; during the Muhammadzai period: official title of head of state, shortened from *amīr al-muᵓminīn* ('commander of the faithful'); title of the Uzbek officials serving the Chingizid rulers of Bukhara; title of the Yarid rulers of Badakhshan.

angūrī tax on *raᶜīyat* gardens in the region of Qandahar.

āqsaqāl ('white beard') in Qataghan: village head (equivalent of *mūsafed*); in Badakhshan: powerful local leader in charge of several villages or a whole valley, military commander of 1,000 soldiers.

arbāb (pl. of *rabb*) village chief in Lesser Turkistan and Badakhshan; title of Mohmand and Khalil chiefs who enjoyed the right of revenue collection on behalf of the Mughal kings.

ᶜarżbegī chief petitioner at court.

ashraf al-wuzarā early Sadozai period: title of prime minister, grand vizir.

àṣnāf (pl. of *ṣinf*), artisans; classes of artisans; tax on trades.

atālīq tutor, guardian; supervisor of the administration and the military in sixteenth and seventeenth-century Turkistan.

badraga safe conduct through the territory of a Pashtun tribe, usually against payment.

bāj city customs.

barāt written assignment.

barak coarse wollen fabric.

beg chief, ruler; early nineteenth century: title of the Uzbek rulers of Tashqurghan and Qunduz; local Uzbek leader in charge of a tribal section, sometimes also called *khān.*

beglarbegī Safawid period: military governor-general of a major province.

chabūtara customs house.

chihilyak 'one in forty'; tax rate of 2½ percent levied on the merchandise of Muslim traders and livestock.

chindāwul 'rearguard', name of the living quarters assigned to the Jawansher Qizilbash by Ahmad Shah Sadozai in Kabul.

chūl desert.

daftarī revenue accountant.

ḍala one of two blocs Pashtun society tends to polarize around.

dallālī tax on auction dues.

darbār royal court.

darwesh mendicant; follower of a Sufi order.

dasta army contingent.

dihqān crop-sharing tenant; peasant.

dīwān government office or bureau; revenue accountant.

dīwānbegi Uzbek government official in the Chingizid empire; may have played a role in the supervision of appanage finances.

dīwān-i aʿlā Sadozai period: high office in charge of revenues, justice and public works.

farmān a royal decree.

fatwā a legal ruling.

faujdār local officer in the service of the Morcha Khel Mohmands.

fiqh jurisprudence.

ghāzī religious warrior.

ghulām khāna royal bodyguard under the Sadozais.

ḥākim governor.

hamsāya crop-sharing or non-crop-sharing tenant; tribal outsider of inferior social standing.

ḥujra men's house among the Pashtuns of Peshawar and vicinity.

ijāra lease.

īljārī militia (mostly footmen under the Sadozais).

iqṭā[c] service grants enjoyed by the Uzbek *amirs*; theoretically awarded on a temporary basis, they tended to become the permanent possession of certain amirid families.

īshān religious dignitary with Sufi affiliation; descendant of the Prophet.

īshīk āqāsī chamberlain, minister.

jāgīr service grant awarded by Sadozai kings; limited to lifetime unless the son of the deceased *jāgīr* holder inherited his father's rank at court.

jam[c]*bast* settlement of revenues; specifically the revenue assessment reserved for the Pashtuns since the time of Ahmad Shah Durrani; consisted of a fixed quota in cash or kind.

jam[c]*-i qalandar khān* assessment named after a revenue administrator of Ahmad Shah; synonym for *jam*[c]*bast*.

jarīb land measure: sixty paces by sixty paces.

jarībī horticultural tax.

*jazā*ᵓ*il* matchlock, a heavy rifle, resting on a forked iron prong.

*jazā*ᵓilchī Dost Muhammad Khan's infantry militia.

jihād exertion for the cause of Islam, particularly in religiously sanctioned warfare.

jirga (from Mongolian, 'circle'), council in which Pashtun elders settle disputes in accordance with *pashtūnwālī*.

jizya capitation tax paid by non-Muslims.

kārez subterranean canal for irrigation.

kashar (Pashtu, 'young') tribal members with little political standing or weight .

kats flood land.

khalīfa disciple of a Sufi *pīr* who has been granted permission to initiate novices and to guide them on the mystical path.

khāliṣa crown lands.

khān (Turkic, 'lord') chief of a Pashtun tribe or its subdivision; title of the Chingizid rulers until the eighteenth century; honorific for the local Uzbek leadership in the nineteenth century.

khānadūdī capitation tax instituted by Ahmad Shah for non-Durrani shepherds and settlers entering the Qandahar region; was not levied among local Farsiwan.

khānawārī extended capitation tax instituted by Qandahar Sardars; included Farsiwans who had become landless laborers during the Sadozai period.

khān khel the leading lineage of certain Pashtun tribes.

kharāj originally a land tax levied from non-Muslims; basic term for land tax in medieval Persia; mentioned both as land tax and poll tax in nineteenth-century Afghanistan.

kharwār a unit of weight, a donkey load.

khāssadār irregular foot soldier, royal or local militia.

khel (from Arabic *khail*, 'troop of cavalry'), Pashtun term for 'lineage'.

khilᶜat a robe of honor.

khud aspa Dost Muhammad Khan's tribal cavalry.

khums literally 'one-fifth'; according to Sunni jurisprudence, tax levied on the spoils of war against non-believers; according to Shiite jurisprudence, charitable tax levied on all profit earned in trade.

khushkāba land dependent on an uncertain supply of irrigation.

khuṭba the sermon delivered at the Friday congregational service in which the name of the current head of state was mentioned as a sign of allegiance.

kot system the revenue assessment applied to non-Pashtun cultivators in nineteenth-century Afghanistan; it implied that a fixed share of the gross produce had to be handed over to the government and fluctuated with the amount of crops harvested; the most common assessments were *se kot* ('three shares') and *chār kot* ('four shares'), on the basis of which one third or one fourth of the harvest was handed over to the government.

kotwāl chief of police.

kūcha a narrow street, a lane.

kuhna naukar Kabuli troops stationed at Balkh during the Sadozai period.

lak 100,000.

lalmī land irrigated by rain; dry farming.

madrasa a college of religious learning.

maḥall, maḥalla quarter, neighborhood; administrative division: district.

malik village headman, petty chief.

malikāna allowance given to village headmen.

māmā (Pashtu) maternal uncle.

man ('maund') unit of weight; one Kabuli *man* equalled eight *sers* or 130.4 lbs; one Qandahari *man* equalled 40 *sers* or approximately 8.5 lbs.

mashar (Pashtu) elder.

masjid mosque.

mihmāni fee or supplies levied for the maintenance of troops and officials passing through a certain area; fee levied by tribal chiefs for the supplies used by caravans travelling through their territory.

ming bāshī (Turkic term) head of a thousand men.

mīr the short form of *amīr.*

mīrākhor (from *amīr ākhor*), master of the horse or royal stables.

mīr wā ͨiẓ head preacher.

mīrzā (contraction of *amīrzāda*, 'born of an *amīr*'), a) prince; b) scribe, secretary, especially of the finance department.

mu ͨāfī category of land exempt from revenue payments.

mulk private property.

munshī writer; secretary.

munshī bāshī Sadozai rank, head secretary.

murīd disciple of a Sufi *pīr.*

mustaufī finance officer.

mustaufī al-mamālik revenue officer; finance minister.

mutawallī the chief trustee or administrator of an endowment.

nā ͻib deputy.

nāmūs Pashtun concept of honor, duty to protect the honor of one's family, lineage, clan, and even the entire Pashtun nation as well as the integrity of its land.

nang Pashtun concept of honor; usually used in the compound *nang o nāmūs.*

nasaqchī bāshī chief of the Sadozai security forces.

nauābād lands recently cultivated by new irrigation systems.

nāẓir overseer, steward.

naẕrāna 'offering'; a present in cash or kind to local chiefs or the head of state; a nominal tribute.

niṣfakāri revenue assessment at half of the produce.

oimāq Turkic term for a tribal organization.

pādshāh king; in the nineteenth century, this title was also used by local chiefs, e.g. Sardar Purdil Khan of Qandahar and the Sayyids of Kunar.

parwāna royal investiture, grant deed.

parwānachī court official responsible for delivering royal investitures.

pashtanwāla or *pashtūnwālī* the Pashtun code of ethics.

peshkhidmat personal servant of the king.

pīr religious leader, especially of Sufi orders.

piyāda infantry.

powinda (from the Pashtu root *powal*, 'to graze flocks'), Pashtun nomad trader.

qalang, qulang land tax, revenue.

qamchīn pūlu 'whip money'; fee paid to local escort of caravan in Turkistan.

qara naukar cavalry militia of the Sadozais.

qarīya village, suburb; administrative division in the vicinity of the city of Qandahar.

qaum tribe, community; may refer to solidarity groups of different sizes.

qāżī judge.

qāżī al-qużāt chief judge.

qulba 'plough', basic unit of land measurement: the portion of land which could be cultivated by one farmer with one yoke oxen and one plough.

quriltai an assembly of all the tribal leaders of the Chingizid empire.

ra^cīyat (pl. *ra^cāyā*) peasant; non-Durrani cultivator in the Qandahar region.

sākhlau local militia during Sadozai period.

s̱ālis̱āt tax rate of one third on the harvest.

sardār Sadozai period: military title held by the heads of the Durrani clans; Muhammadzai period: title of male members of the royal family.

sargalla tax on flocks imposed by Ahmad Shah on non-Durrani shepherds and settlers entering the Qandahar region; was also levied among local Farsiwan during Muhammadzai period.

sarmardī poll tax collected among Ghilzais between Kabul and Qandahar.

sāyir custom duty.

sayyid a descendant of the Prophet.

ser a unit of weight; approximately 16 lbs in Kabul, 0.21 lbs in Qandahar.

shāhīn, shāhang camel artillery.

shāhīnchī bāshī, shāhangchī bāshī Sadozai rank: commander of camel artillery.

shākh shumārī tax on livestock.

sikka coin; the striking of coins in the name of the head of state.

sipahsālār commander in chief of the armed forces.

suyūrghāl a hereditary service grant in cash and land.

ṭāʾifa tribe.

ṭālib religious student.

tankhwāh assignment on lands or order on the treasury for the payment of a stipend or salary.

tankhwāh-i rikābī allowance given to the *khāns* of the district of Ghazni for furnishing a certain number of cavalry in times of war.

tankhwāh-i wilāyatī allowance of the Pashtun *khāns*.

tappa 'hill', administrative subdivision on the basis of ethnic boundaries.

tarbūr, turbūr (Pashtu) a father's brother's son.

tarbūrwālī (Pashtu) rivalry between paternal cousins.

tiyūl a service grant of land which usually expired with death of beneficiary; in Afghanistan often used interchangeably with *jāgīr*.

tsalwe<u>sh</u>tī (Pashtu,'forty'), a sort of *powinda* militia under the command of an authoritarian *mīr* which was formed during migrations through hostile territory.

ulūs people, nation; in the Mongol context, a people given to a Chingizid prince; generally, a distinct group or tribal organization.

ʿurf customary law.

urūgh subdivision of an Uzbek tribe.

ʿushr tithe paid by Muslims on all crops in the name of public welfare.

wālī governor.

waqf religious endowment.

waẓīfa pension; allowance paid to the religious establishment.

wazīr counsellor of the state, minister

wazīr-i dākhila minister of interior.

wazīr-i khārija foreign minister.

wesh periodic reallotment of land based practiced by certain border tribes, such as the Tarklanris of Bajaur, the Yusufzais of the Swat valley, the Khwaezai Mohmands, the Utman Khel, and the Afridis.

yāghī rebel.

yāghistān Pashtun notion of their territories as a 'land of freedom and rebellion'.

zakāt 'purifying tax', giving up a portion of one's property for the general weal of the community (10 per cent on produce of land, fruit; 2½ per cent on livestock, merchandise, gold and silver).

zambūrak light swivel gun mounted on camels (synonym for *shāhīn*)

żarbkhāna mint; mint tax.

Appendix A

MAPS

Map 1 Afghanistan
Source: Lee 1996

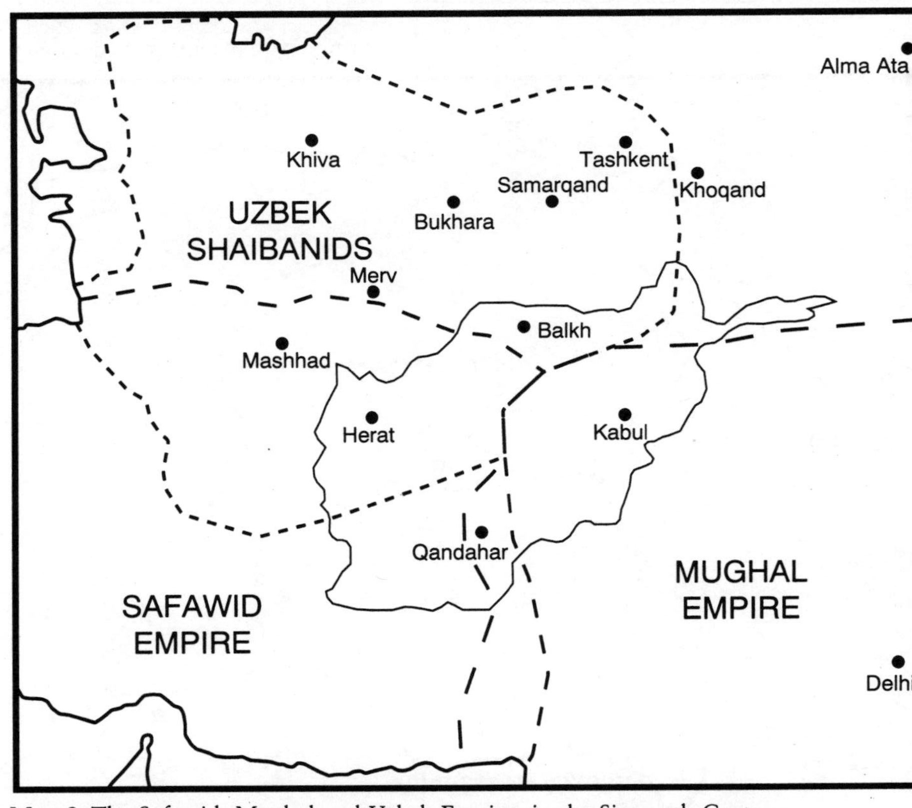

Map 2 The Safawid, Mughal and Uzbek Empires in the Sixteenth Century
Source: Olesen 1995

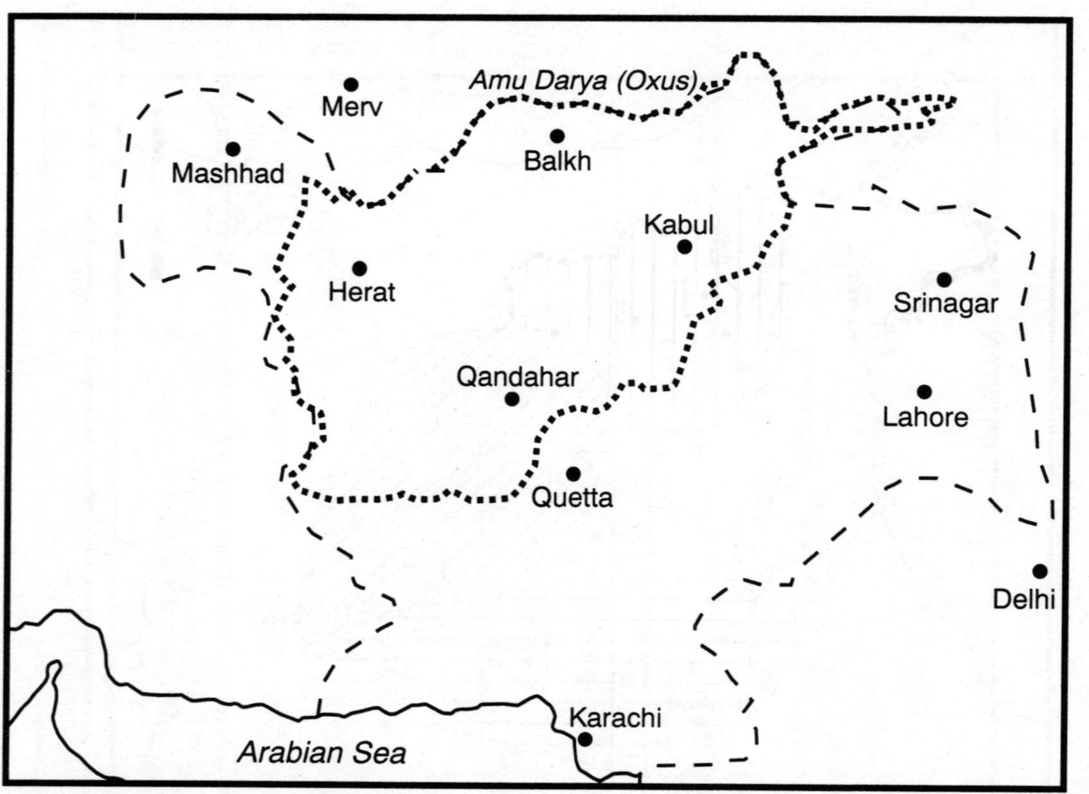

Map 3 The Empire of Ahmad Shah Durrani
Source: Olesen 1995

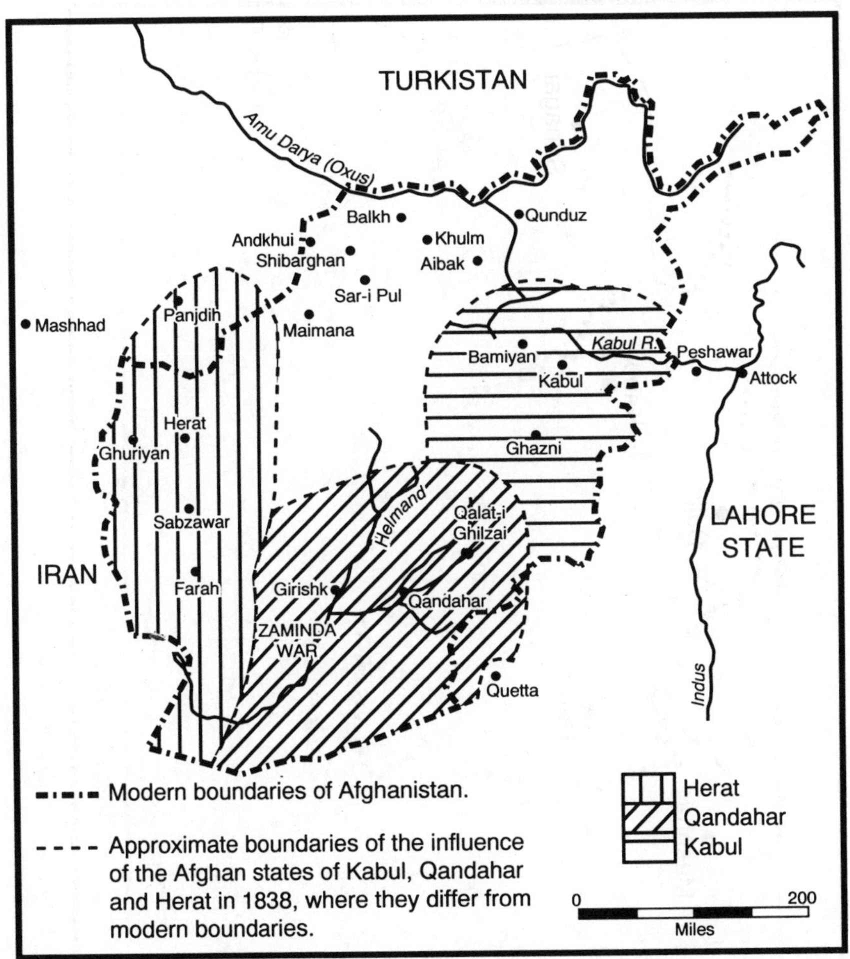

Map 4 Afghanistan prior to the First Anglo-Afghan War
Source: Yapp 1980

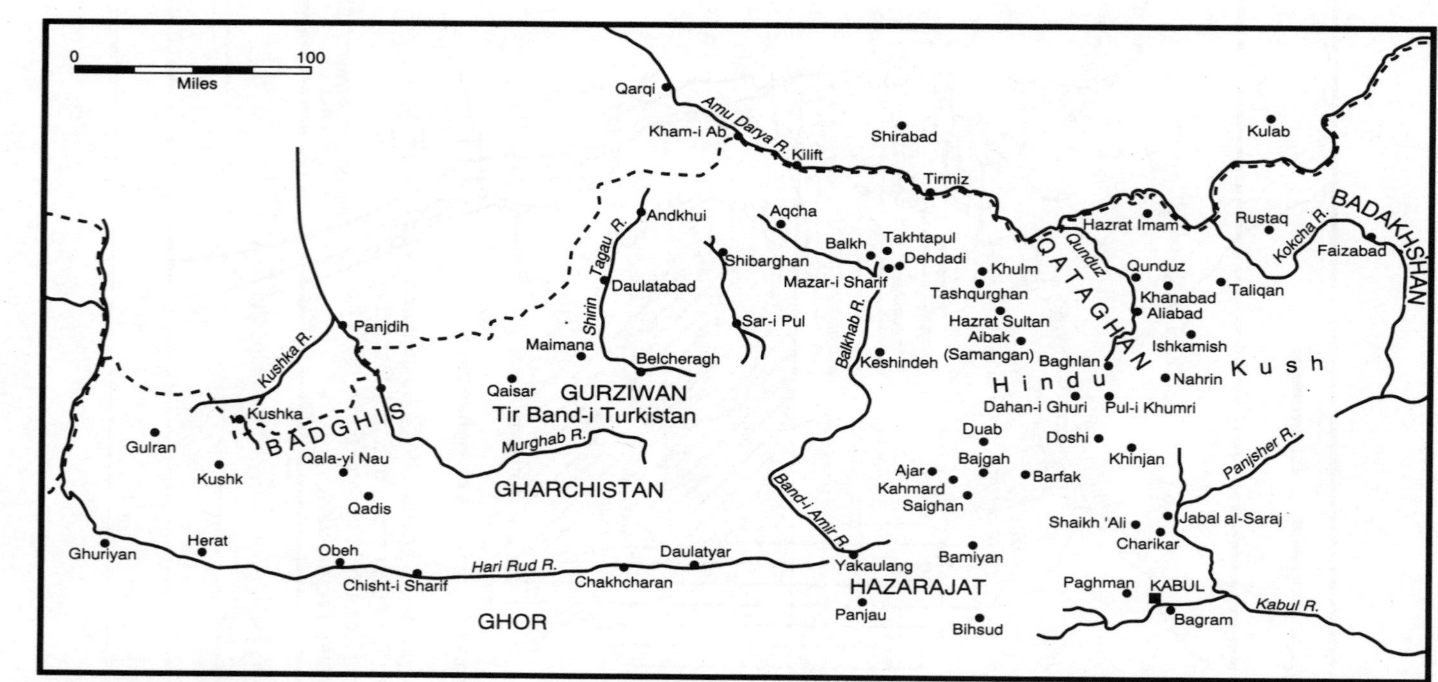

Map 5 Afghan Turkistan
Source: Lee 1996

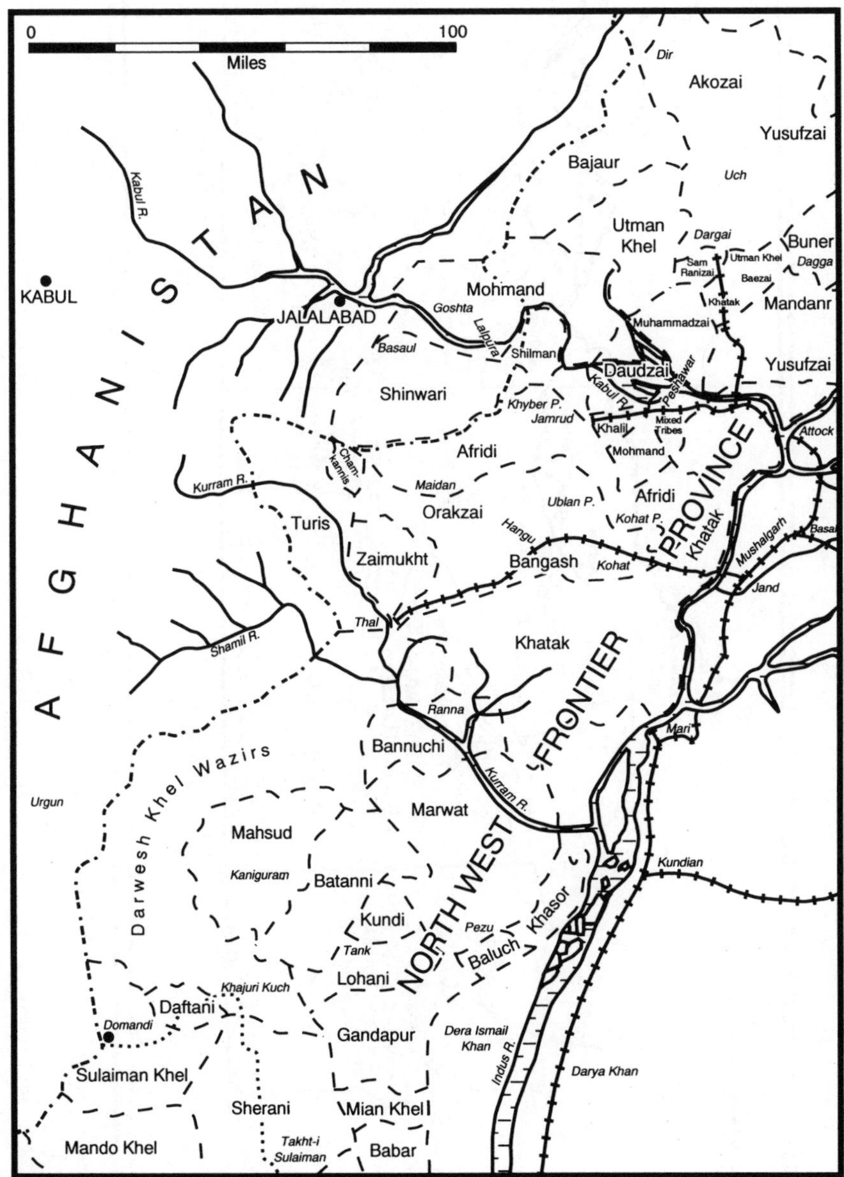

Map 6 The Border Tribes
Source: Wylly 1912

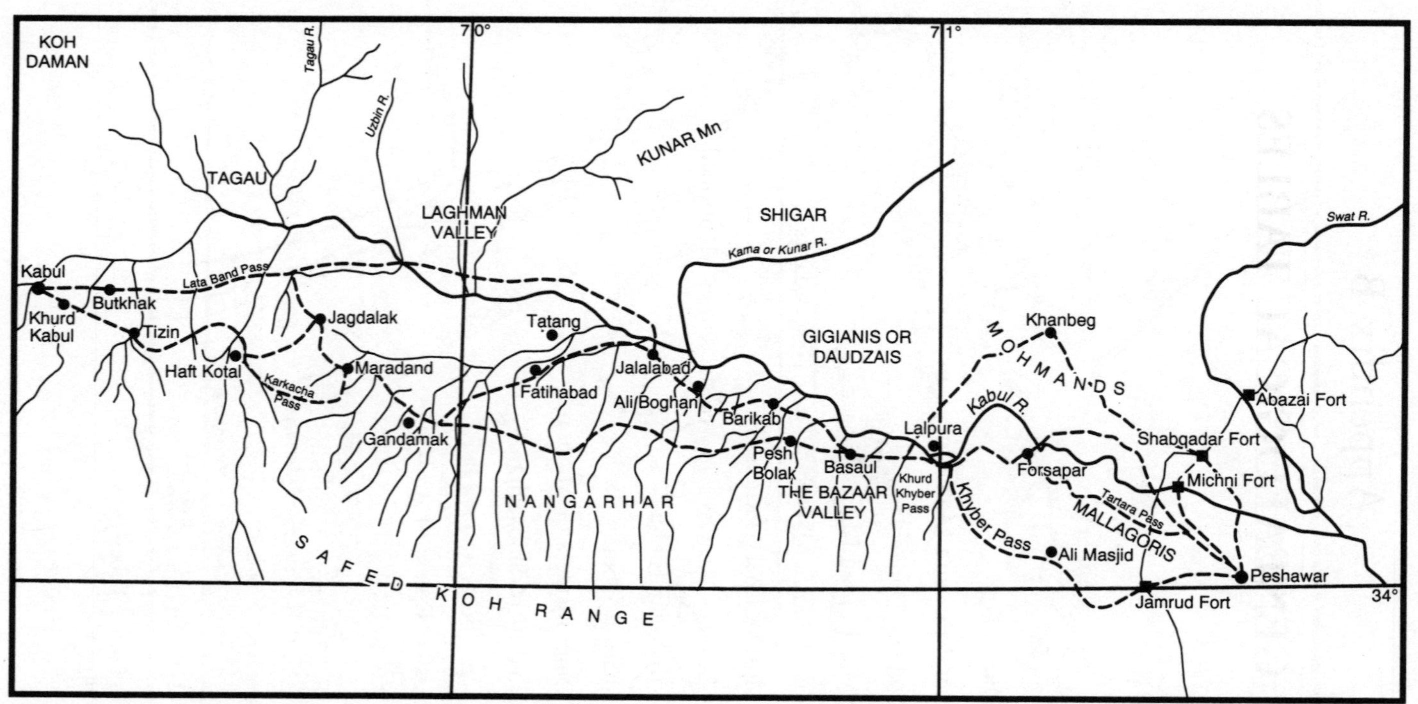

Map 7 The Trade Routes between Kabul and Peshawar
Source: Oliver 1890

Appendix B

GENEALOGICAL TABLES

1 The Durrānīs

2 The Bārakzais and Muḥammadzais

3 The Sadozai Dynasty

4 Dost Muḥammad Khān's Progeny

5 The Qandahār Sardārs and Their Descendants

6 The Morcha Khel Mohmands

7 The Ghilzais – An Overview of the Tribes Mentioned

8 The Bābakrzai Tokhis

9 The Isḥaqzai Hotaks

10 The Mingid Rulers of Maimana

11 The Ḥākims of Shibarghān

12 The Beglarbegīs of Sar-i Pul

13 The Afshār Rulers of Andkhui

Genealogical Table 1 The Durranis

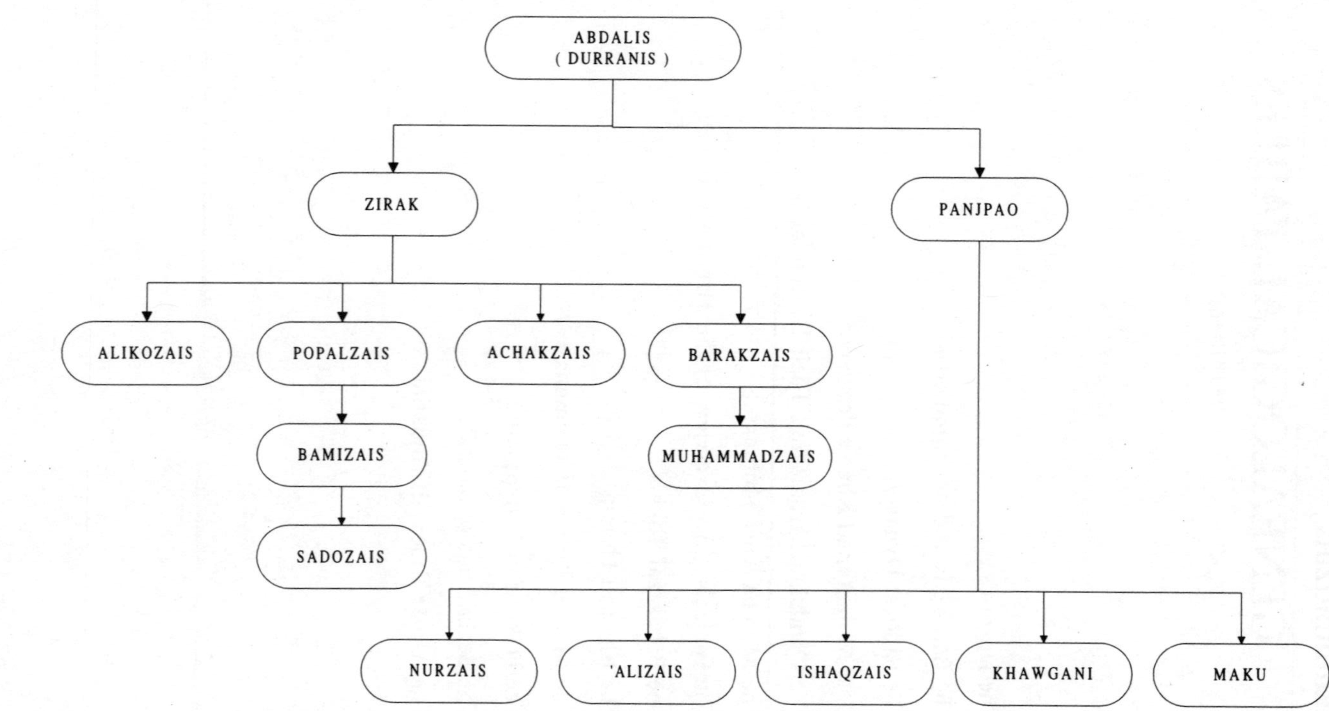

Sources: Bellew 1973: 161; Caroe 1985: 12; Elphinstone 1972 II: 96; TSu 52–60.

Genealogical Table 2 The Barakzais and Muhammadzais

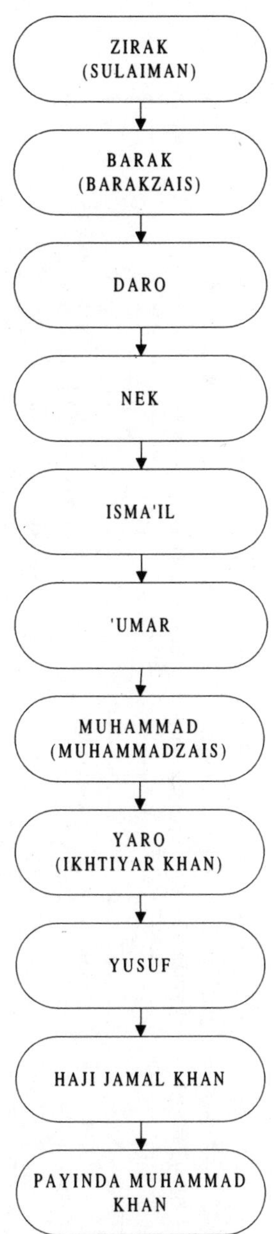

Sources: Reshtia 1957: 1; Reshtia 1990: 10–11.

Genealogical Table 3 The Sadozai Dynasty

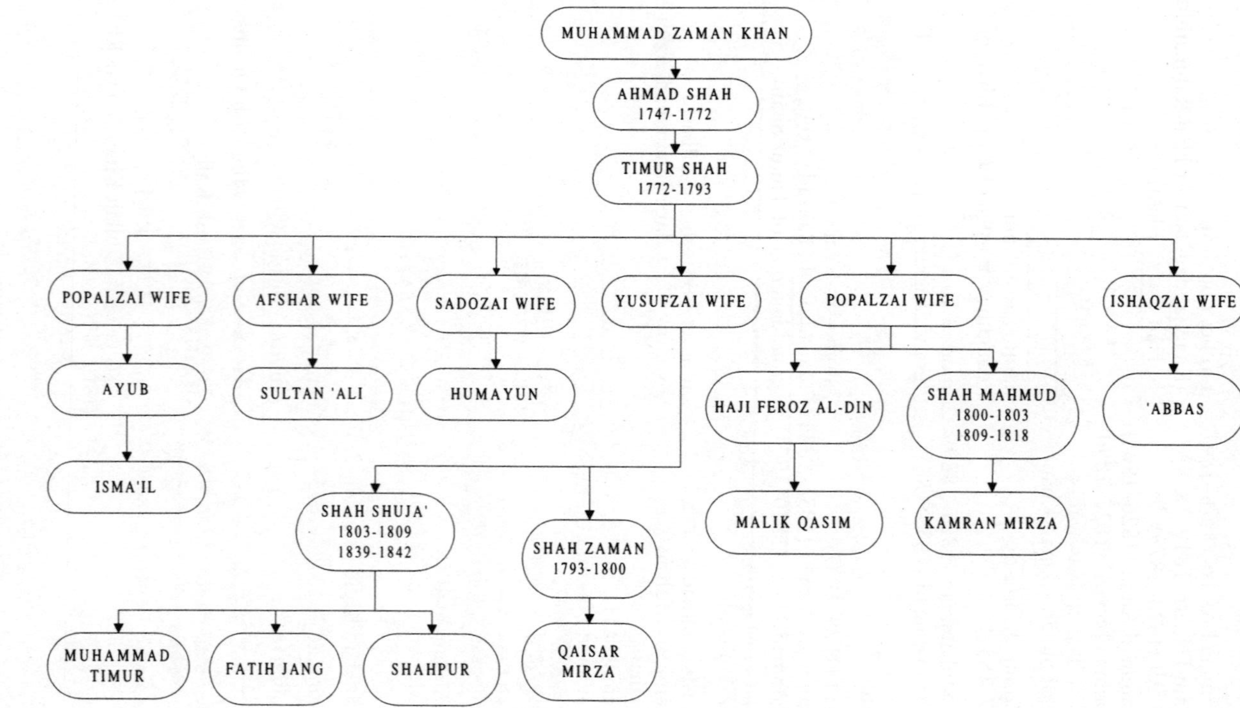

Sources: Ferrier 1858: 106; Fofalzai 1967: 24; Harawi 1990: 11, 13.

Genealogical Table 4 Dost Muḥammad Khān's Progeny*

Muḥammad Afżal (1811–1867) Muḥammad A ͨẓam (1818–1869) Shams-i Jahān	mother Bangash (daughter of Mullā Ṣādiq ͨAlī)
Muḥammad Akbar (1816–1847) Ghulām Ḥaidar (1819–1858) Sher ͨAlī (1823–1879) Muḥammad Amīn (1826–1865) Muḥammad Sharīf (1827–1890) Pādshāh Begum Nawwāb (wife of Sulṭān Aḥmad Khān)	mother Popalzai (Khadīja, daughter of Hājī Raḥmatullāh Khān b. Hājī Daryā Khān)
Muḥammad Akram (1817–1852)	mother Kohistani (daughter or sister of Baqā Khān of Parwān)
Walī Muḥammad (1825–1889) Faiż Muḥammad (1839–1867) Ḥawā Hājira	mother Turi (granddaughter of Jahāngīr Khān Tūrī)
Aḥmad (1829–1897) Muḥammad Zamān (1831–1874) Muḥammad ͨUmar (1840–1904) Ummat al-Muṣṭafā Bībī Zumurrud	mother Sadozai (daughter of Shāhzāda ͨAbbās, granddaughter of Tīmūr Shāh)
Ṣāliḥ Muḥammad Muḥammad Muḥsin Nūr Jahān Muḥammad Ḥasan (1833–1879) Muḥammad Ḥusain (1838–1871) Shāh Jahān Wafā Begum Muḥammad Aslam (1831–1871) Muḥammad Qāsim (1846–1876)	mother Jawansher Qizilbash (widow of Sardār Muḥammad ͨAẓīm Khān)
Sher Muḥammad Nek Muḥammad (1854–1882)	mother Bajauri or Ghilzai
Muḥammad Hāshim (1846–1882) Muḥammad Ṣadīq	mother Bajauri
Muḥammad Shu ͨaib (1855–1884)	mother Safi
Muḥammad Raḥīm	mother Turi or Qizilbash
Muḥammad ͨAẓīm (b.1856)	daughter of Nāẓir Mihr ͨAlī Qizilbāsh
Muḥammad Ṣādiq (1854–1872) Sarw-i Jahān	mother Siyahposh Kafir
Muḥammad Yūsuf (b. 1845)	mother Jabbar Khel Ghilzai (sister of ͨAzīzullāh Khān Jabbār Khel)

Ḥabībullāh (1851–1897) Mamlakat Sharaf Sulṭān Durr Jān Ṣāhib Sulṭān	S̱amīna, daughter of Nāẓir Khairullāh (a wealthy merchant)
Bībī Sāʾira ʿĀisha Bilqīs Muḥammad Ṣadīq Muḥammad Raḥīm	mother Qizilbash (daughter of Āqā Muḥammad Khān Qizilbāsh)
Saifullāh Khān Wakīl (1843–1866)	mother Hazara concubine
Āghā Begum Fāṭima Zainab Shāh Bānū	mother Bamizai (daughter of Tāj M. Khān b. Ghulām Muḥammad b. Sher Muḥammad b. Shāh Walī Khān Bāmīzai)
Mulk-i Jahān Badr-i Jahān	mother Hazara concubine

*The sources consulted give contradictory information on Dost Muhammad Khan's progeny and the dates of their births and deaths. Therefore, this list may contain some errors. The sources used are: Adamec 1975: 228, Tables 47, 48, 50, 51, 52, 53; Balland in *EIr* 550; Ghani 1961: 45; Lal 1978 I: 223–224; Hensman 1978: 182–183; Lumsden 1860: 6–10; Reshtia 1957: 156–158; Reshtia 1990: 243–246; ST 200, 202, 251, 288, 325, 330; SM xxv; Tate 1972: 162; Warburton 1880 Appendix II: iv; Wheeler 1979: 21; QM 19 October 1857 (For. Sec. 30 April 1858 No. 96); KD 3–5 October 1871 (For. Sec. October 1871 Nos. 402, 404); Principal Events of 1875 (For. Pol. A March 1877); KD 10–13 November 1876 (For. Sec. December 1876 No. 75).

Genealogical Table 5 The Qandahar Sardars and Their Descendants*

1. Purdil Khān (1785–1830)

Marwārīd
Sulṭān Muḥammad
ᶜAbd al-Wahīd (ᶜAbd al-Aḥad?)
Khushdil
ᶜAbd al-Rasūl
Maqṣūd
Mīr Afżal

2. Sherdil Khān (1786–1826)

Mīr Aḥmad

3. Kuhandil Khān (1793–1855)

Muḥammad Ṣadīq

Ghulām Muḥyi al-Dīn

Muḥammad ᶜUmar
Muḥammad ᶜUs̱mān

Sulṭān ᶜAlī
ᶜAbdullāh

4. Raḥmdil Khān (1796–1859)

by Ḥawā (descendant of Raḥīmdād, brother of Sardār Pāyinda Khān):

Muḥammad Aᶜẓam
Muḥammad ᶜAlam
Ghulām Muḥammad Ṭarzī
Tāj Nisāʾ
Gul Muḥammad
Ghulām Ḥaidar
Muḥammad Qulī
Muḥammad Sarwar

5. Mihrdil Khān (1797–1855)

Nūr Muḥammad
Gul Muḥammad
Sher Muḥammad

Sher ᶜAlī
Khushdil
Muḥammad Ḥusain
Tāj Muḥammad
Hājī Munawwardil

ᶜAlī Akbar
ᶜAlī Aṣghar

*Sources: Adamec 1975: Tables 73–76; Balland, EIr: 550; Ferrier 1857: 94, 479; Leech 1839: 58; O. St. John 1879, 1881; ST 218; KN 21–29 April 1855 (For. Sec. 31 August 1855 No. 58); Nawwab Faujdar Khan to Edwardes 12 June 1858 (For. Sec. 27 August 1858 No. 13).

Genealogical Table 6 The Morcha Khel Mohmands

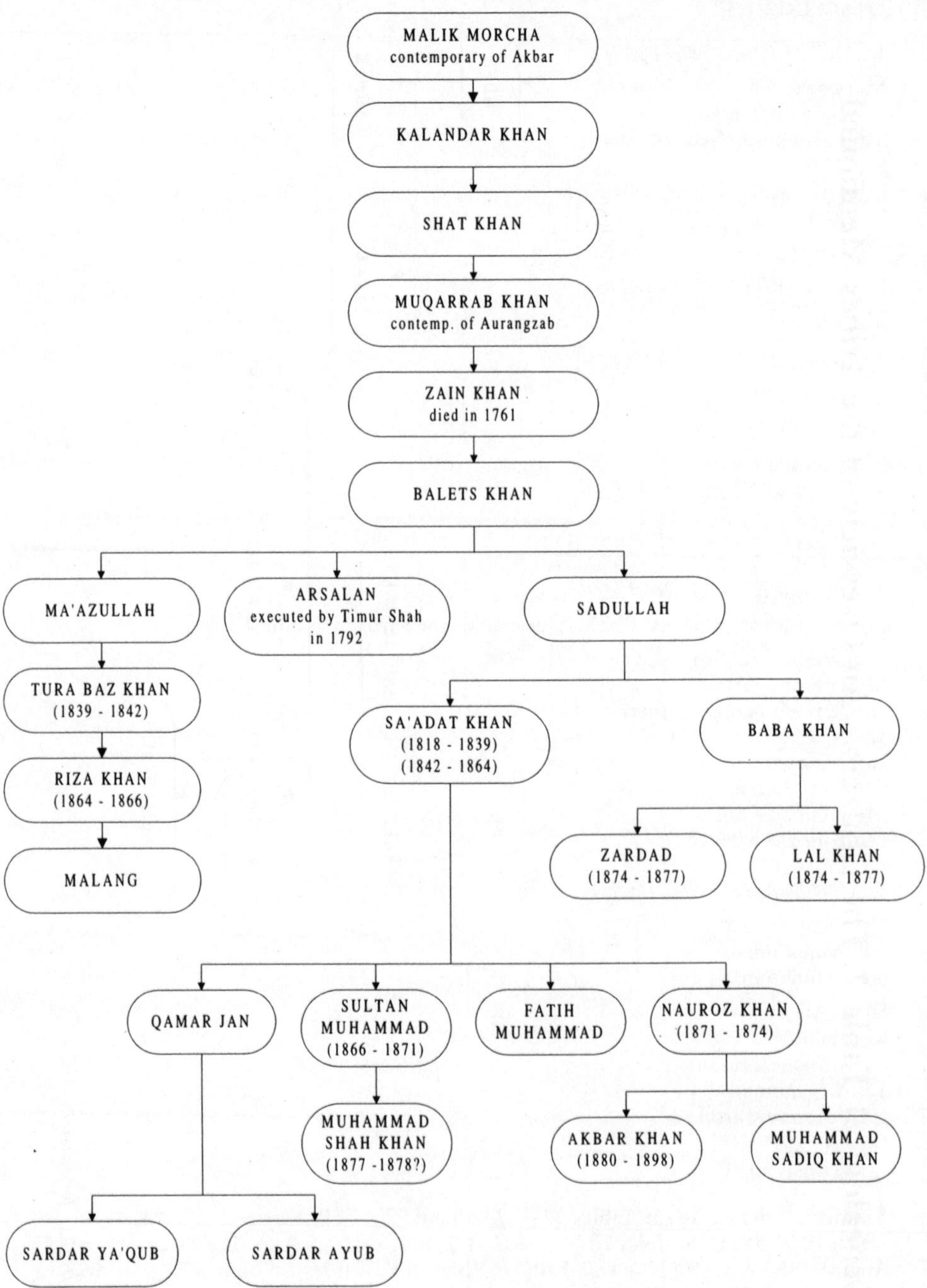

Sources: Merk 1984: 92.

Genealogical Table 7 The Ghilzais – An Overview of the Tribes Mentioned

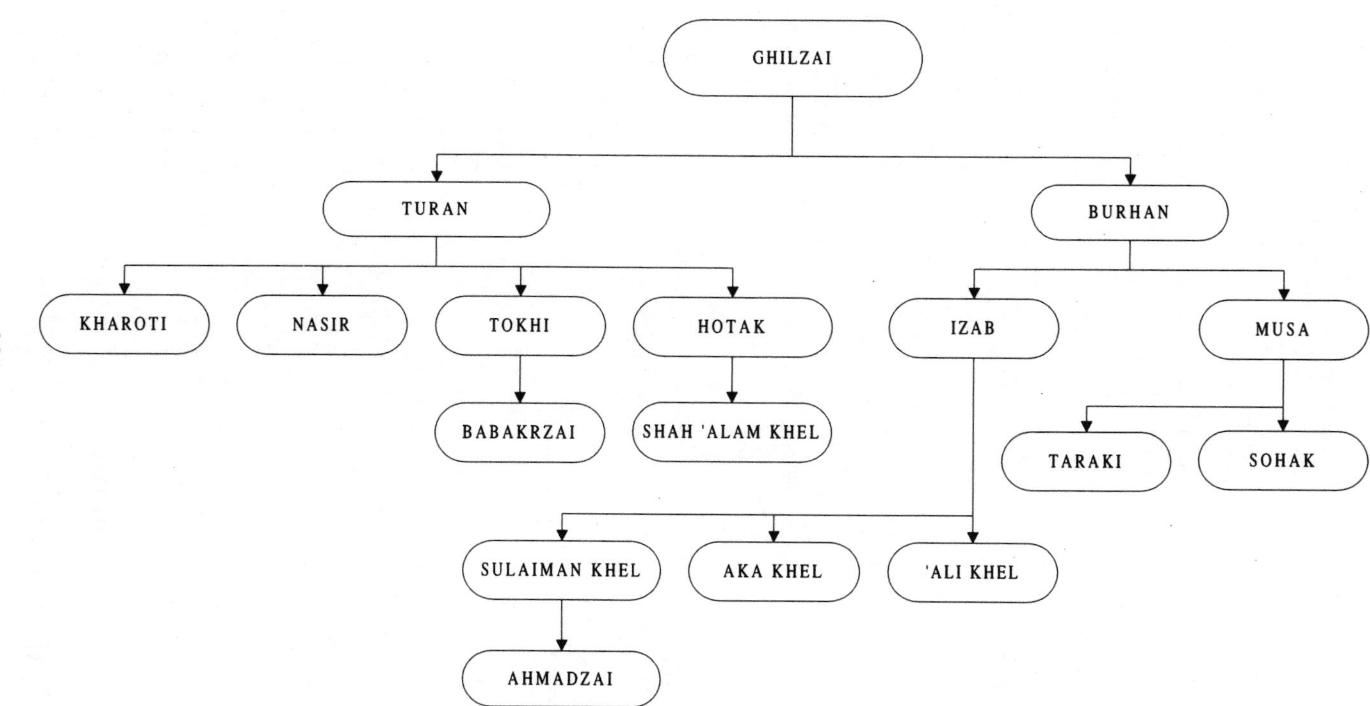

Sources: Robinson 1978.

Genealogical Table 8 The Babakrzai Tokhis

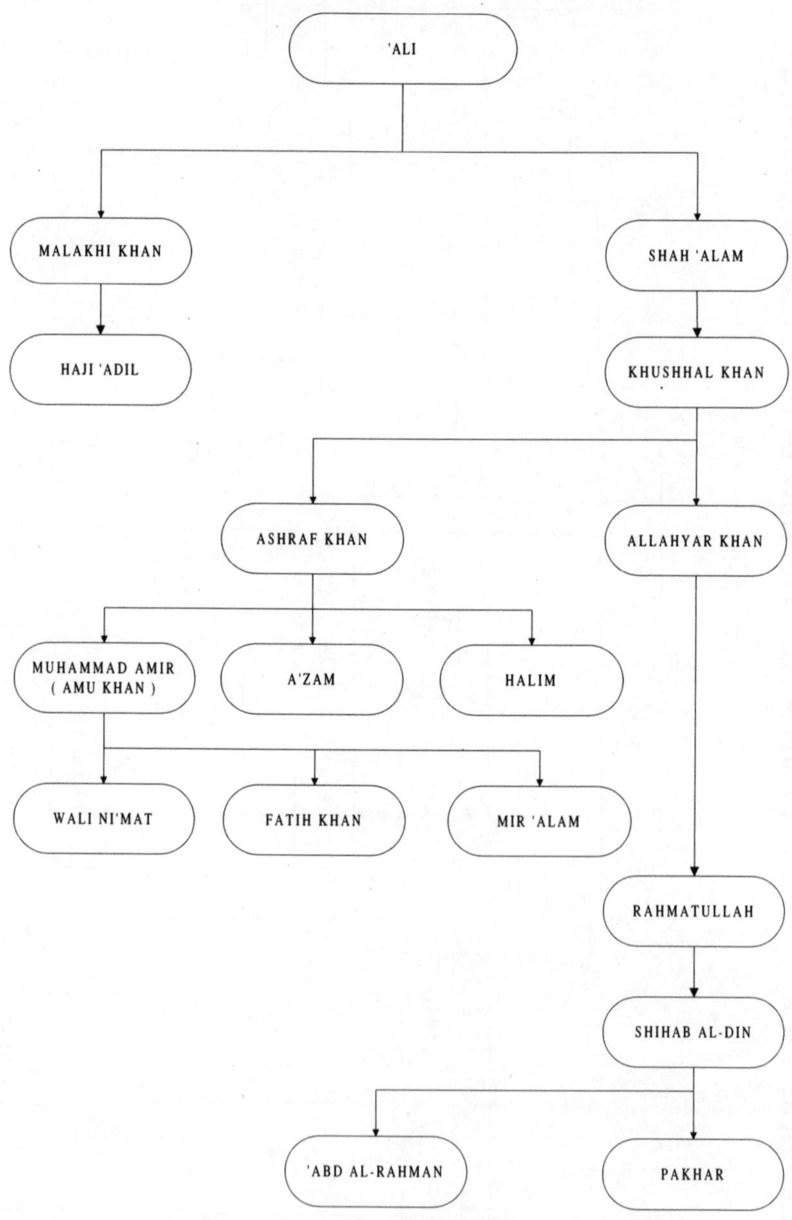

Sources: Leech 1845 a: 315–317, 319–320.

Genealogical Table 9 The Ishaqzai Hotaks

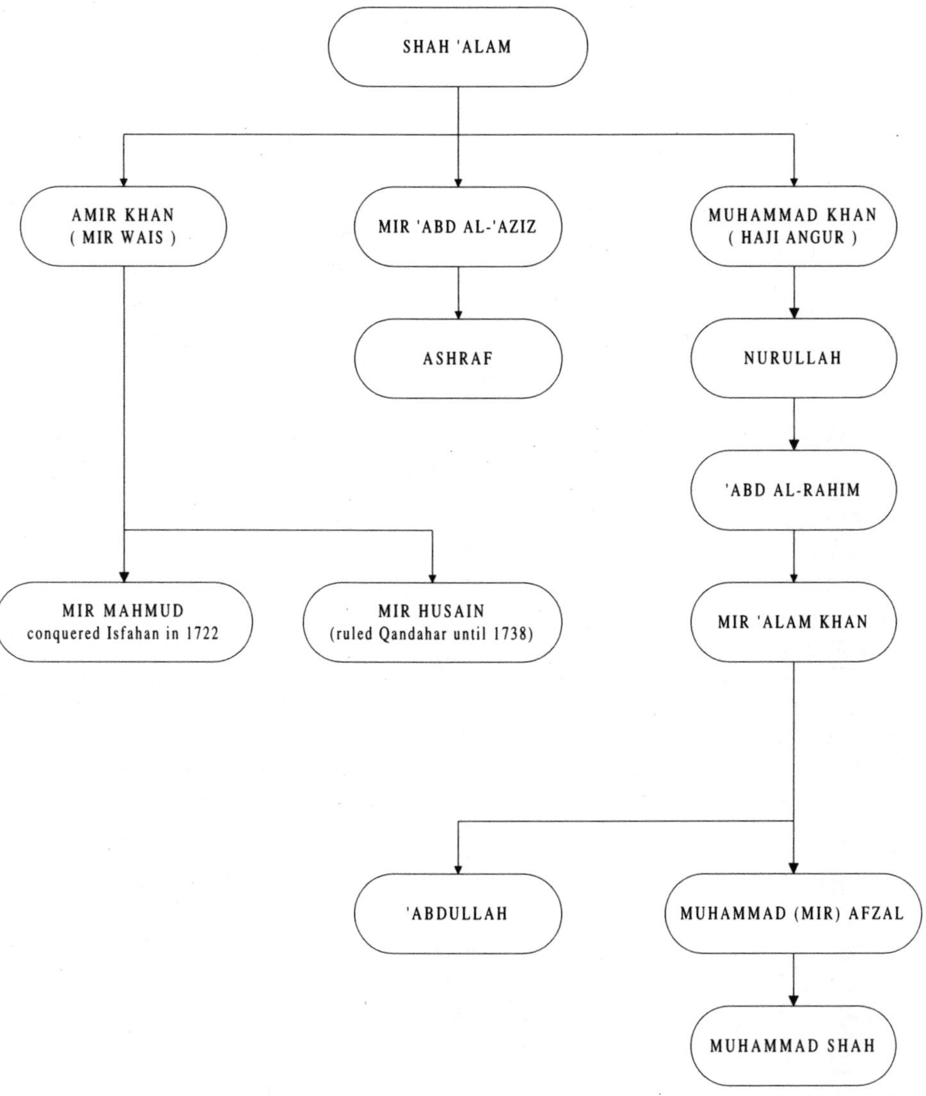

Sources: Nuri 1956: 179; Leech 1845 a: 311–322; Kakar 1971: 120, 129.

Genealogical Table 10 The Mingid Rulers of Maimana

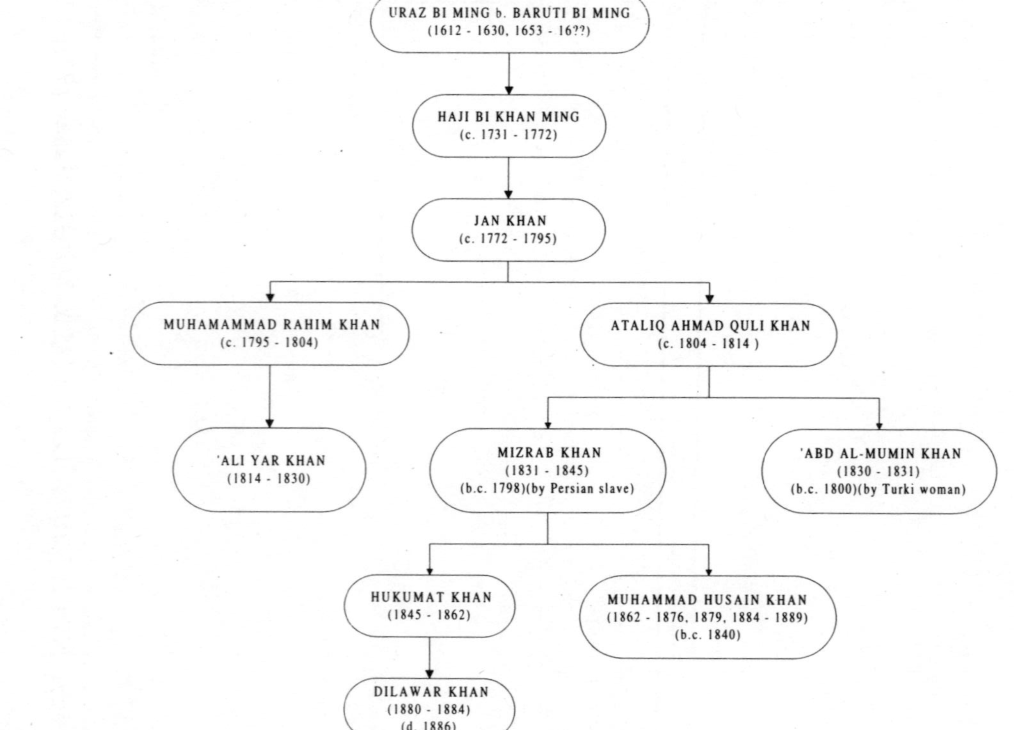

Sources: Lee 1996.

Genealogical Table 11
Hakims of Shibarghan, c. 1747–1875

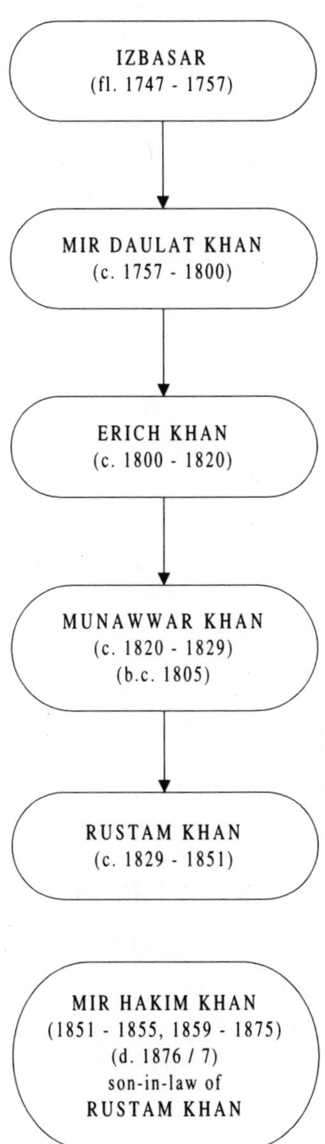

Sources: Lee 1996; Stirling 1991: 287

Genealogical Table 12 Beglarbegis of Sar-i Pul

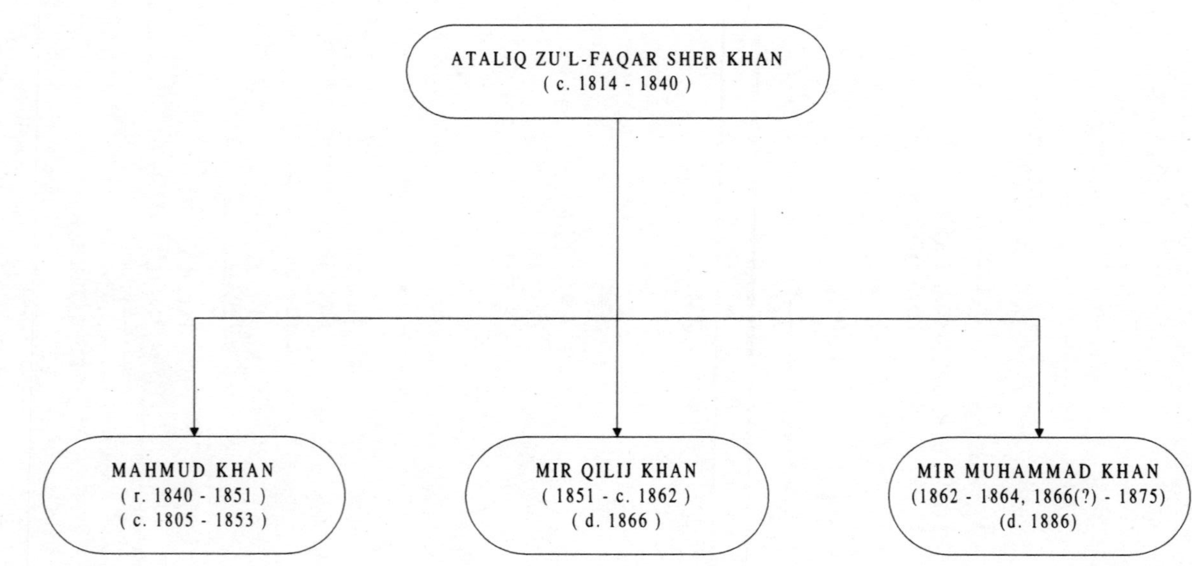

Sources: Lee 1996.

Genealogical Table 13
Afshar Rulers of Andkhui, c. 1730–1880

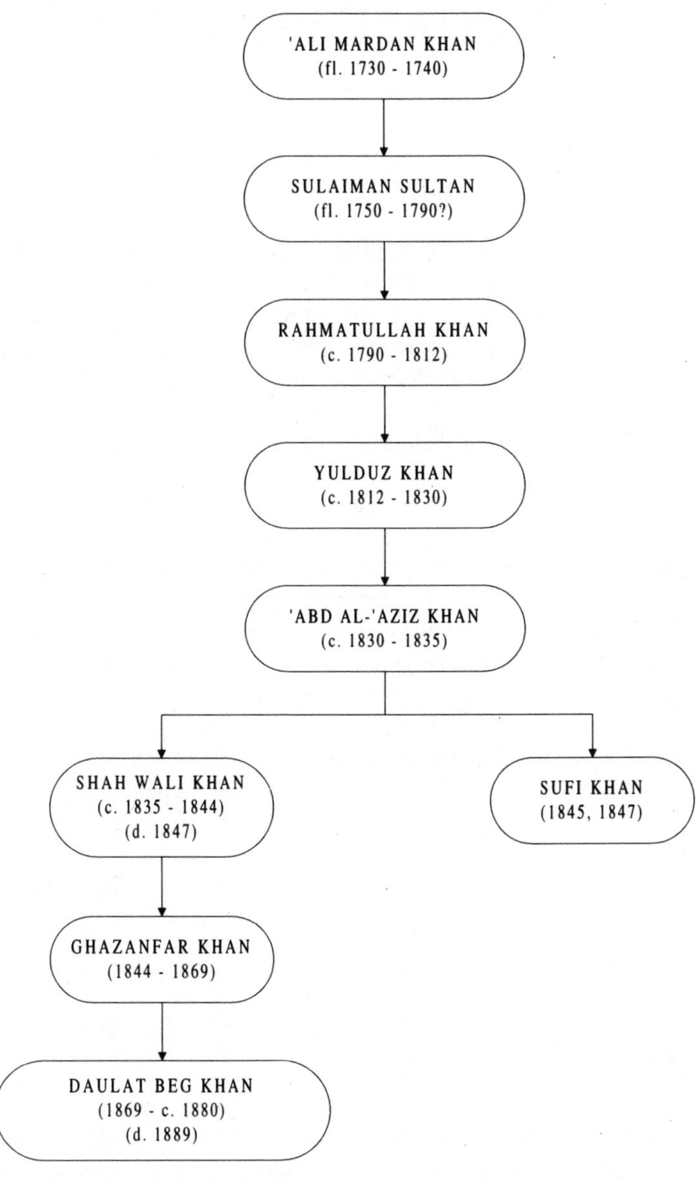

Sources: Lee 1996.

Appendix C

CURRENCIES AT THE TIME OF DOST MUHAMMAD KHAN[1]

The monetary system of nineteenth-century Afghanistan was characterized by a variety of local and foreign currencies with fluctuating exchange rates. During the reigns of Amirs Dost Muhammad Khan and Sher ᶜAli Khan gold coins were very rare. The gold coins current at Dost Muhammad Khan's time were the Bukharan *ṭilā*, the Persian *tomān* and ducats (*budqīs*) which entered the country by way of Russia. The foreign silver coins available were the Russian ruble (*som*), Bukharan *tanga*, the Persian *qirān* and the Indian rupee (*kalldār*).

During the early Muhammadzai period, rupees were struck at Kabul, Qandahar, Herat and Peshawar. Until Amir 'Abd al-Rahman Khan's time the Kabul rupee used to be 'an irregular shaped coin, hand stamped but ... made of pure silver'.[2] The *shāhī* (one-twelfth of a rupee) also was a silver coin. In 1890 the Amir established English minting machines in the capital, and the Kabuli rupee was declared the only valid currency in Afghanistan.[3] Prior to 'Abd al-Rahman Khan's time the rate of the Kabuli rupee was fairly stable, almost equalling the Indian rupee. With the addition of a percentage of copper during Amir 'Abd al-Rahman's time, its worth began to diminish. In the early twentieth century Martin reported that, 'whereas five Kabuli rupees used to be taken in exchange for four Indian, ... the exchange nowadays is two Kabuli for one Indian'.[4]

For the period of this study the following rough exchange rates are reported:

1 *ṭilā* = 7 Kabuli rupees
1 *budqī* = 6 Kabuli rupees
1 *som* = 2 Kabuli rupees and 4 *shāhīs*
1 *tanga* = 4 *shāhīs* = ⅓ Kabuli rupee
1 *qirān* = ½ Kabuli rupee.[5]

In the 1850s one Kabuli rupee was equal to 1.75 Qandahar rupees.[6] Another unit listed in the records is the *khām* ('unripe') rupee which, contrary to the *pukhta* rupee listed above, was only used in government accounts. Whereas the *pukhta* Kabuli rupee contained 12 *shāhīs*, the *khām* rupee was reckoned at 10 *shāhīs*.[7] Another fictitious unit for accounting was the *tomān*, which was worth twenty rupees *khām*.[8]

For the rupees struck during Dost Muhammad Khan's era, the following verses are recorded:

1) On the occasion of Dost Muhammad Khan's proclamation as Amir, a coin was struck with a verse composed by his prime minister Mirza 'Abd al-Sami':
Amīr Dost Muḥammad ba ᶜazm-i jang-i jihād
kamar bebast o bezad sikka nāṣirash haqq bad
'Amir Dost Muhammad, with the resolution to perform jihad,
girded his loins and struck coins; may God support him'.[9]
2) Referring to Dost Muhammad Khan as 'Lord of the Age' (*ṣāḥib zamān*), the following verse probably stems from the period prior to the First Anglo-Afghan War:
Fakhr kun ay sīm o zar az sikka-yi ṣāḥib zamān;
'Oh! silver and gold, be proud to be struck into the coin of the Lord of the Age.'[10]

The following verses were struck during Dost Muhammad Khan's second reign:

3) *Sīm o ṭilā ba shams o qamar mīdehad nawīd*
waqt-i rawāj-i sikka-yi Pāyinda Khān rasīd.
'Silver and gold give glad tidings to the sun and moon:
Payinda Khan's coin has begun to circulate.'[11]
4) In 1848 Dost Muhammad Khan issued a coin with the following verse:
Bizad zi ᶜain-i ᶜināyat-i khāliq-i akbar
Amīr Dost Muḥammad do bāra sikka bar zar.
'By the grace of the Great Creator,
Dost Muhammad has again struck coins in gold.'[12]

NOTES

1 For detailed discussions of the coins current in nineteenth-century Afghanistan, see Furdoonjee 1839: 161-164 Gregorian 1969: 401-403; Holzwarth 1990: 233-236; Kakar 1979: 215-220.
2 Martin 1907: 252.
3 The Kabuli rupee, in turn, was superseded by the *afghānī* in 1925. (Kakar 1979: 216)
4 Martin 1907: 252-253. In the 1830s and 1850s 1 Kabuli rupee was worth 0.84-0.9 Indian rupees. (Furdoonjee 1839: 160; Lal 1978 I; 236)
5 Furdoonjee 1839: 160, 162; also see Gholaum Hyder 1836: 99; Harlan 1939: 83; Izzet Ullah 1843: 332; Lambert 1886; Molloy 1883b; Sultan Muhammad 1980 I: 39; Muhammad Afzal Khan to Dost Muhammad Khan n. d. (For. Sec. 26 January 1855 No. 59); KD 15-18 October 1869 (For. Pol. A. Nov 1869 No. 150); KD 9-11 November 1869 (For. Pol. A. January 1870 No. 108); KD 24 26 October 1871 (For. Sec. December 1871 No. 273)

6 In 1857 Lumsden reported the following rates from Qandahar:
- the Indian rupee worth 16 annas,
- the Kabuli rupee worth 14 annas,
- the Qandahar rupee worth 8 annas

(QM 1 June 1857, For. S. C. 30 April 1858 No. 42; also see KD 9-10 October 1870, For. Pol. A. December 1870 No. 351)

7 Hamilton 1906: 282-283; Lal 1978 I: 236; MacGregor 1871 II: 55; Reshtia 1957: 155; Reshtia 1990: 242. This information cannot be reconciled with the following table produced by O. St. John in the 1880s, which only distinguishes *khām* and *pukhta* for the Qandahari rupee and, moreover, assumes the Kabuli rupee to contain 20 *shāhīs*:

1 Indian rupee = 24 *shāhīs*
1 Kabuli rupee = 20 *shāhīs*
1 Qandahar rupee *pukhta* = 12 *shāhīs*
1 Qandahar rupee kham = 10 *shāhīs*
1 *ʿabbāsī* = 4 *shāhīs*.
(*Gaz*. V: 230; also Rawlinson 1871: 837n)

8 MacGregor 1871 II: 55; Rates of Pay in the Durrani Army (Elphinstone Collection F 88 13 Ho, p. 972); Information from Muhammad ʻAli Ayub (Elphinstone Collection F 88 Kt, p. 205)

9 Lal 1978 I: 172; ST 127.

10 White-King 1896: 319, 326.

11 Reshtia 1957: 155; Reshtia 1990: 242; White-King 1896: 326.

12 White-King 1896: 334.

Appendix D

THE SERVICE GRANTS MADE BY AHMAD SHAH IN THE QANDAHAR REGION

Name of Tribe	*Number of qulbas granted in tiyul*	*Total of tiyul qulbas*	*Quota of horse from each tribe*	*Total of Qandahar Horse*
Durranis:				
Popalzai	965¼		806	
Alikozai	1,050½		851	
Barakzai	1,018½		907	
Alizai	661¾		819	
Nurzai	868½		1,196	
Ishaqzai	357½		635	
Khawgani	163		423	
Maku	121½		100	
		5206½		5,710
Non-Durranis:				
Tokhi	14		1,061	
Hotak	10		507	
Kakar	56		30	
Dawi	5		45	
Tirin	25		729	
Barechi	–		518	
		110		2,890
Royal attendants from all the tribes indiscriminately				3,959
Total of qulbas		5,316½		
Total of horse				12,559

Source: Rawlinson 1841: 826

Appendix E

THE POPULATION IN THE TOWNS OF AFGHAN TURKISTAN AND BADAKHSHAN AS REFLECTED BY REPORTS OF THE NINETEENTH AND EARLY TWENTIETH CENTURY

	Maimana
Stirling (1828)*	10–15,000 souls.
Burnes (1837)	1,500 houses.
Ferrier (1845)	15–18,000 in town; mostly Uzbek, small group of Farsiwan.
Vambéry (1863–64)	100,000 in state; mostly Uzbek (Ming, Atchmaili, Daz).
Faiz Bakhsh (1871)	City: Uzbeks, Tajiks, Karama Turkmens; dependencies: 12,000 Karama Turkmens.
Grodekov (1878)	2,500 souls in town.
Merk (1885–86)	4,000 families (=16,000 souls); mostly Uzbek.
Yate (1885–86)	2,500 families in city, 10,000 families in district.

	Andkhui
Stirling (1828)	8,000–12,000 souls.
Burnes (1837)	More than 1,500 houses; Afshar Turks and Arabs.
Ferrier (1845)	15,000.
Vambéry (1863–64)	2,000 houses, 3,000 tents: population 15,000, mostly Alieli Turkmens, minority of Uzbeks. Population supposedly was 50,000 in 1830s.
Faiz Bakhsh (1871)	3,000 families; Uzbeks and Sariq Turkmens.
Merk (1885–86)	550 Uzbek families, 60 Ersari Turkmen families in town.
Yate (1885–86)	1,500 families in city.
M. Aslam Khan (1886)	1830s: 12,000 families; 1886: 3,000 families; Uzbeks.
Jarring (1935)	8,000 Uzbeks; 1,000 Turkmens; 1,000 members of other ethnic groups.

Shibarghan

Ferrier (1845)	12,000 in town; mostly Uzbeks, small group of Farsiwan.
Faiz Bakhsh (1871)	2,000 families Sariq Turkmens.

Sar-i Pul

Stirling (1828)	10,000 souls.
Ferrier (1845)	18,000 in town, 70,000 in state; 2/3 Uzbek, 1/3 Sar-i Jangal Hazaras.
Grodekov (1878)	3,000 Uzbeks in town.
Gazetteer (1907)	4,000 souls.

Balkh

Elphinstone (1809)	1,000 Afghan families (*kuhna naukar*).
Burnes (1832)	2,000 in town, mostly Afghans (*kuhna naukar*).
Ferrier (1845)	Based on oral information: Population of southern Balkh consists of 3,000–4,000 souls. The citadel houses 10,000 Afghans and 5,000 Uzbeks (Qipchaq, Yabu).
Peacocke (1885–86)	600 Uzbek, Arab and Tajik families form the permanent population of the town; 'floating population' of 1,000 Pashtun, Tajik, Uzbek and Arab families.
Maitland (1885–86)	200 Tajik families in town.
Yate (1885–1886)	500 families in Balkh city; 30,000 families in district of Mazar-i Sharif: 8,000 Afghan, 14,500 Uzbek, 4,000 Turkmen, 1,500 Arab, 1,500 Tajik, 500 Hazara families.
Jarring (1935)	The whole country between Balkh and Tashqurghan is inhabited by Uzbeks.

Mazar-i Sharif

Stirling (1828)	8,000–10,000 souls
Burnes (1832)	500 houses
Ferrier (1845)	200 houses in town; thousands of Uzbek and Aimaq tents in district.
Grodekov (1878)	25,000 souls.

Tashqurghan

Elphinstone (1809)	8,000 houses.
Moorcroft (1824)	20,000 houses; mostly Tajiks and Kabulis, 'sprinkling' of Uzbeks.
Burnes (1832)	10,000 in town.
Wood (1837)	Predominantly Tajik.

Ferrier (1845)	15,000 in town, 700,000 in state; mostly Tajiks.
Faiz Bakhsh (1871)	8,000 families in city; mostly Mu-i Tanikarama Uzbeks.
Yavorski (1878)	Majority Uzbeks of the Ming tribe.
Yate (1885–86)	13,250 houses in district.
Maitland (1885–1886)	700,000 in state in 1830s.
	Qunduz
Burnes (1832)	1,500.
Lord (1837)	1,500 houses in town.
Wood (1837)	500–600 houses, fluctuating number of Uzbek nomads.
Kushkaki (1921)	15,000 souls in district.
Jarring (1935)	District: Tajiks, Uzbeks, Afghans, Hazaras, Turkmens, Arabs.
	Taliqan
Moorcroft (1824)	1,500 Tajik families, fluctuating number of Uzbek nomads.
Wood (1837)	300–400 houses.
Kushkaki (1921)	150 families.
Jarring (1935)	District: Tajiks, Uzbeks, Afghans.
	Faizabad
Wood (1837)	Destroyed by Mir Murad Beg.
TB (1907)	12,000 families.
Kuskhaki (1921)	300–400 Badakhshi houses; 600 houses Afghans and others.
	Jurm
Wood (1837)	1,500 souls
Kushkaki (1921)	300 families in town and environs.

*) The date in brackets denotes the time of visit or compilation of information.

Sources: Adamec 1979: 70, 107–108, 112, 398, 573; Burnes 1834 I: 205, 238, II: 200, 202; Burnes 1973: 225–228; Centlivres 1976b: 123–126; Elphinstone 1972 II: 184, 197–198; Faiz Buksh 1872: 12; Ferrier 1971: 197, 202, 204, 208, 209, 211, 225; Grevemeyer 1982: 159; Jarring 1939a: 74; Jarring1939b: 17–21, 49–50, 59–62; Kushkaki 1989: 63, 66, 71–72, 115, 137, 140; Lee 1985: 128; Lee 1996: 207; Lord 1839: 106; Marvin 1880: 80, 96, 110; Moorcroft 1841: 449–450, 482–483; Muhammad Aslam Khan 1886; Stirling 1991: 285–287, 301; Vambéry 1864: 238–240; Vambéry 1885: 352, 354; Vambéry 1983: 304; Wood 1841: 214, 241, 251–252, 254, 403; C. E. Yate, 'Notes', For. Sec. F No. 108 January 1888); Yate 1888: 235, 255, 339; Yavorski 1885 II: 69; Yule 1872: 454.

BIBLIOGRAPHY

UNPUBLISHED SOURCES

a) India Office Library (IOL), London

Elphinstone Collection
Masson Papers
Secret Letters and Enclosures from India 1830–1875:
L/P&S/5/8A–8B
L/P&S/5/159
L/P&S/5/190–192
L/P&S/5/226–242
L/P&S/5/257
L/P&S/5/274–277
Political and secret correspondence conducted with India after 1875:
L/P&S/7/1–5
Official memoranda:
L/P&S/18/A8–A42.

b) National Archives of India (NAI), Delhi

Proceedings of the Foreign Department:
For. A-Pol-E, For. F. C., For. P. C, For. Pol. A., For. S. C., For. Sec., For. S. S.

c) Reports and Memoranda

ABC (1886), 'Memorandum regarding the Affairs of the Char Aimak', For. Sec. F. July 1886 No. 347.

ABC (1893), 'Note on the Afghan Army' (For. Sec. F. February 1893 No. 227)

Burton, J. C. (1880), 'Report on the History and Origin of the Ghilzais', (For. Sec. F. October 1880 No. 5)

Durand, E. L. (1887), 'Report on the Hazara Tribe' (For. Sec. F. February 1887 No. 479)

Edwardes, H. (1854), 'Memorandum on the Sadozai Princes' (L/P&S/5/229 No. 54 of 22 October 1854, pp. 200–201)

Faiz Buksh (1871), 'Translation of a Report on Badakhshan, Balkh and Bokhara', Lahore: Civil Secretariat Press. (For. S. C. April 1872 No. 31 C). Partly reprinted in AQR (1894) 8 (Nos. 15–16): 172–181; 407–420; (1895) 9 (Nos. 17–20): 191–196; 434–445.

Ghulam Ahmad (1856), 'Memorandum on the Military Establishment of Dost Muhammad', KN 16 July 1856 (L/P&S/5/228 No. 43 of 22 September 1856)

Ghulam Ahmad (1875), 'Report on Kabul' (L/P&S/7/4/ Pt. I No. 19 of 7 June 1875, pp. 49–61c)

Gordon, T. E. (1875), 'Report on Sirikol, the Pamirs, and Wakhan' (L/P&S/7/4 Pt. II of 1875)

Hastings, G. E. (1880), 'Report on the Ghazni District' (For. S. S. July 1880 Nos. 201–203)

Lambert, J. (1886), 'Statement of Revenue of Afghanistan 1877–1878' (For. Sec. F September 1886 Nos. 161–166)

Lumsden, 'Memorandum Regarding the Tribes Inhabiting the Hills Bordering the Pass between Peshawar and Kohat' (For. S. C. 27 September 1850 No. 5)

Lynch, J. (1841), 'Report on the Tooran Guljies' (L/P&S/5/159 No. 53 of 8 July 1841)

'Memorandum on the Northern Borders of Afghanistan' (For. S. I. 1869 No. 71)

Merewither, 'Note on the Position of Affairs in Afghanistan, n.d., L/P&S/18 A 36)

Merk, W. (1886a), 'Diary of the March on the Return Journey from the Oxus', For. Sec. F February 1886 No. 362)

Merk, W. (1886b), 'Report on the Ersari Turkomans', For. Sec. F February 1886 No. 363.

Merk, W. (1886c), 'Report on the Taimani Tribe' (For. Sec. F August 1886 Nos. 405–409)

Michell, R. (1882), 'The Turcomans in Relation to Afghanistan and Persia' (L/P&S/ 18 C 78)

Molloy, E. (1883a), 'The Hazarajat' (For. Sec. F. August 1883 No. 316)

Molloy, E. (1883b), 'Report on Herat' (For. A-Pol-E September 1883 No. 317)

Molloy, E. (1883c), 'The Tokhi Ghilzais' (For. A-Pol-E September 1883 No. 318)

Molloy, E. (1883d), 'Kabul District' (For. A-Pol-E September 1883 No. 319)

Muhammad Aslam Khan (1886), 'Report on the District of Andkhui' (For. Sec. F. August 1886 Nos. 425–428)

Napier, G. C. (1875), Memorandum on Herat Territory (L/P&S/7/4 Pt. I No. 126 of 1875)

Nizam al-Daula (Nawwab Muhammad 'Usman Sadozai) (1855), 'Memoir of Shahzada Muhammad Yusuf', (L/P&S/5/226 No. 3 of 22 January 1856, pp. 521–523)

O. St. John, R. E. (1879), 'Report on the Revenue and Expenditure of the Provincial Government of Kandahar' (For. S. S. June 1879 Nos. 83–85)

O. St. John, R. E. (1881), 'Memorandum on the Principal Durrani Chiefs in and about Qandahar' (For. S. S. January 1881 No. 92)

Protheroe, M. (1879), 'Memorandum on the Revenue realized in Kandahar' (For. S. S. December 1879 No. 67)

Ramsay, Henry L. (1880), 'Biographical Accounts of Leading Men' (For. S. S. February 1880 Nos. 318–330; March 1880 Nos. 224–229; April 1880 Nos. 82–86)

Strachey, 'Memoir Chiefly on the Revenue and Trade of the Kingdom of Caubul,' Elphinstone Collection F 88 13 Hn, f. 136.

Yate, C. E. (1887), 'Report on the Firozkohis' (For. Sec. F. February 1887 No. 478)

Yate, C. E. (1888a), 'Notes on Afghan Turkistan' (For. Sec. F January 1888 No.108)

d) Unpublished Theses and Dissertations

Bacon, Elizabeth E. (1951a), *The Hazara Mongols of Afghanistan. A Study in Social Organization*. PhD dissertation, Berkeley.

Champagne, David Charles (1981), *The Afghan-Iranian Conflict over Herat Province and European Intervention 1796–1863: A Reinterpretation.* PhD dissertation. Austin: University of Texas.

Ghani, Ashraf (1982), *Production and Domination: Afghanistan, 1747–1901.* PhD dissertation. Columbia University.

Jones, Sarah (1976), *The Implications of Ethnic Division in Afghanistan, with Particular Reference to the Hazara Mongols.* Bachelor's thesis. Institute of Social Anthropology, Oxford University.

Reindke, Gisela (1976), *Genese, Form und Funktion afghanischer Stdte.* PhD dissertation, Freie Universität Berlin.

Stack, Shannon Caroline (1975), *Herat: a Political and Social Study.* PhD dissertation, U. C. Los Angeles.

PUBLISHED SOURCES

ᶜAbd al-Raḥmān Khān (n. d.), *Tāj al-tawārīkh, yaᶜnī sawāniḥ-i ᶜumrī-yi aᶜlāhażrat Amīr ᶜAbd al-Raḥmān Khān.* Kabul.

Abu-Lughod, Lila (1989), 'Zones of Theory in the Anthropology of the Arab World', *Annual Review of Anthropology* 18: 267–306.

Adamec, Ludwig (1972–1985), *Historical and Political Gazetteer of Afghanistan.* 6 vols. Graz: Akademische Verlags- und Druckanstalt.

Adamec, Ludwig (1975), *Who's Who of Afghanistan.* Graz: Akademische Verlags- und Druckanstalt.

Afżal Khān (1974), *Tārīkh-i muraṣṣaᶜ.* repr. Peshawar: University Book Agency.

Ahmed, Akbar S. (1976), *Millenium and Charisma among Pathans.* London: Routledge & Kegan Paul.

Ahmed, Akbar S. (1978), 'An Aspect of the Colonial Encounter in the North-West Frontier Province', *Asian Affairs* 9: 319–327.

Ahmed, Akbar S. (1980), *Pukhtun Economy and Society.* London: Routledge & Kegan Paul.

Ahmed, Akbar S. (1983), 'Tribes and States in Waziristan', in *The Conflict of Tribe and State in Iran and Afghanistan*, edited by Richard Tapper. New York: St. Martin's Press, 192–211.

Ahmed, Feroz (1984), 'Transformation of Agrarian Structure in the North-West Frontier Province of Pakistan', *Journal of Contemporary Asia* 14: 5–47.

Akiner, Shirin (1983), *Islamic Peoples of the Soviet Union.* London: Kegan Paul International.

Alder, Garry J. (1972), 'The 'Garbled' Blue Books of 1839 – Myth or Reality?', *HJ* 15 (2): 229–259.

Alder, Garry J. (1974–1975), 'The Dropped Stitch', *Afghanistan J.* 1 (4): 105–113; 2 (1): 20–27.

Alder, Garry (1985), *Beyond Bokhara: The Life of William Moorcroft.* London: Century Publishing.

Ali, Shahamat (1848), *The History of Bahawalpur.* London: James Madden.

Ali, Shahamat (1970), *The Sikhs and Afghans, in Connexion with India and Persia, Immediately before and after the Death of Ranjeet Singh.* repr. (first ed. 1883) Delhi: Punjab National Press.

Anderson, Jon (1975), 'Tribe and Community among the Ghilzai Pashtun', *Anthropos* 70: 575–601.

Anderson, Jon (1978), 'There Are No Khans Anymore: Economic Development and Social Change in Tribal Afghanistan', *Middle East Journal*, 32 (2): 167–183.

Anderson, Jon (1982), 'Cousin Marriage in Context: Constructing Social Relations in Afghanistan', *Folk* 24: 7–28.

Anderson, Jon (1983), 'Khan and Khel: Dialectics of Pakhtun Tribalism', in *The Conflict of Tribe and State in Iran and Afghanistan*, edited by Richard Tapper. New York: St. Martin's Press, pp. 119–149.

Anderson, Jon (1984), 'How Afghans Define Themselves in Relation to Islam', in *Revolutions and Rebellions in Afghanistan*, edited by Nazif Shahrani and Robert L. Canfield. Berkeley: Institute of International Studies, pp. 266–287.

Anderson, Jon (1986), 'Popular Mythologies and Subtle Theologies: The Phenomenology of Muslim Identity in Afghanistan', in *Discourse and the Social Life of Meaning*, edited by Phyllis Pease Chock and June R. Wyman. Washington, D.C., Smithsonian Institution Press, pp. 169–184.

Appadurai, Arjun (1986), 'Theory in Anthropology: Center and Periphery', *Comparative Studies in Sociology and History*. 28: 356–361.

Asad, Talal (1970), *The Kababish Arabs*. London: Hearst & Co.

Asad, Talal (1972), 'Market Model, Class Structure and Consent: A Reconsideration of Swat Political Organisation', *Man* 7 (1): 74–94.

Aslanov, Martiros (1981), 'The Popular Movement 'Roshani' and Its Reflections in the Afghan Literature of the 16th-17th Centuries. in *Afghanistan: Past and Present*. Moscow: USSR Academy of Sciences, pp. 28–44.

Astarābādī, Mīrzā Mihdī Khān (1962), *Jahāngushā-yi Nādirī*, edited by Sayyid ᶜAbdullāh Anwar. Teheran: Bahman.

Azoy, G. Whitney (1982), *Buzkashi – Game and Power in Afghanistan*. Philadelphia: University of Pennsylvania Press.

Bacon, Elizabeth E. (1951b), 'The Inquiry into the History of the Hazara Mongols of Afghanistan', *Southwestern Journal of Anthropology*, 7: 230–247.

Bacon, Elizabeth E. (1958), *Obok: A Study of Social Structure in Eurasia*. New York: Wenner-Gren Foundation for Anthropological Research.

Badakhshī, Mīrzā Sang Muḥammad and Mīrzā Afżal ᶜAlī Beg Surkh Afsar (n.d.), *Tārīkh-i Badakhshān*, edited by Manūchihr Sutūda.

Baden-Powell, B. H. (1972), *The Land Systems of British India*. 2 vols. repr. (first ed. 1892) London: Johnson Repr.

Baker, Henry D. (1915), *British India. With notes on Ceylon, Afghanistan and Tibet*. Washington: Government Printing Office.

Balland, Daniel (n.d.), 'Afghanistan–Political History', in *EIr.*

Balland, Daniel (1976), 'Passé et présent d'une politique des barrages dans la région de Ghazni', *Studia Iranica* 5: 239–253.

Balland, Daniel (1988a), 'Contribution à l'étude du changement d'identité ethnique chez les nomades d'Afghanistan', in *Le fait ethnique en Iran et en Afghanistan*, edited by Jean-Paul Digard. Paris: Editions du CNRS, pp. 139–155.

Balland, Daniel (1988b), 'Nomadic Pastoralists and Sedentary Hosts in the Central and Western Mountains, Afghanistan' in *Human Impact on Mountains*, edited by Nigel J. R. Allan. Totowa, N.J.: Rowman & Littlefield.

Barfield, Thomas J. (1978), 'The Impact of Pashtun Immigration on Nomadic Pastoralism in Northeastern Afghanistan', in *Ethnic Processes and Intergroup Relations in Contemporary Afghanistan*, edited by Jon W. Anderson and Richard F. Strand. New York: Afghanistan Council of the Asia Society, pp. 26–34.

Barfield, Thomas J. (1981), *The Central Asian Arabs of Afghanistan: Pastoral Nomadism in Transition*. Austin: University of Texas Press.

Barfield, Thomas J. (1990), 'Tribe and State Relations: the Inner Asian Perspective', in *Tribes and State Formation in the Middle East,* edited by Ph.

S. Khoury and J. Kostiner. Berkeley, Los Angeles: University of California Press, pp. 153–182.

Barfield, Thomas J. (1992), *The Perilous Frontier: Nomadic Empires and China, 221 BC to AD 1757*. Cambridge, Mass.: Blackwell.

Barry, Michael (1984), *Le royaume de l'insolence*. Paris: Flammaron.

Barth, Fredrik (1959), *Political Leadership among Swat Pathans*. London: Athlone.

Barth, Fredrik (1969), 'Pathan Identity and Its Maintenance', in *Ethnic Groups and Boundaries: The Social Organization of Culture Difference*, edited by Fredrik Barth. Boston: Little, Brown & Co.

Barthold, V. V. (1934), 'Shaibaniden', in *EI (G)* 4: 294–295.

Barthold, V. V. (1935), *12 Vorlesungen uber die Geschichte der Türken Mittelasiens*. Berlin: Deutsche Gesellschaft für Islamkunde.

Barthold, V. V. (1956–1962), *Four Studies on the History of Central Asia*. Vol. I, *A Short History of Turkistan*; Vol. II, *Ulugh-Beg*; Vol. III, *Mir 'Ali-Shir, A History of the Turkman People*. Translated from the Russian by V. Minorsky and T. Minorsky. Leiden: E. J. Brill.

Beattie, Hugh (1982), 'Kinship and Ethnicity in the Nahrin Area of Northern Afghanistan', *Afghan Studies* 3/4: 39–51.

Bechhoefer, William B. (1975), *Serai Lahori: Traditional Housing in the Old City of Kabul*. University of Maryland, School of Architecture.

Beck, Lois (1983), 'Iran and the Qashqai Tribal Confederacy', in *The Conflict of Tribe and State in Iran and Afghanistan*, edited by Richard Tapper. New York: St. Martin's Press, pp. 284–313.

Beck, Lois (1986), *The Qashqaʾi of Iran*. New Haven: Yale University Press.

Beck, Lois (1990), 'Tribes and States in Nineteenth- and Twentieth-Century Iran', in *Tribes and State Formation in the Middle East*, edited by Ph. S. Khoury and J. Kostiner. Berkeley, Los Angeles: University of California Press, pp. 185–225.

Bellew, Henry Walter (1862), *Journal of a Political Mission to Afghanistan in 1857*. London: Smith, Elder and Co.

Bellew, Henry Walter. (1880), *The Races of Afghanistan*. Calcutta: Thacker, Sprink & Co.

Bellew, Henry Walter (1901), *A Dictionary of the Pukkhto of Pukshto Language*. Lahore: M. Gulab Singh and Sons.

Bellew, Henry Walter. (1973), *An Inquiry into the Ethnography of Afghanistan*. repr. (first ed. 1891) Graz: Akademische Druck- und Verlagsanstalt.

Bendix, Reinhard (1978), *Kings or People: Power and the Mandate to Rule*. Berkeley: University of California Press.

Bilgrami, Asghar H. (1972), *Afghanistan and British India*. New Delhi: Stirling Publishers.

Bindemann, Rolf (1987), *Religion und Politik bei den schi'itischen Hazara in Afghanistan, Iran und Pakistan*. Ethnizität und Gesellschaft, Freie Universität Berlin, Occasional Papers Nr. 7. Berlin: Das Arabische Buch.

Blocqueville, Henry de Couliboeuf de (1980), *Gefangener bei den Turkomanen 1860–1861*. repr. (first ed. 1866) Nürnberg: Nomad Press.

Bonte, Pierre and Michel Izard (1991), *Dictionnaire de l'ethnologie et de l'anthropologie*. Paris: Presses Universitaires de France.

Boesen, Inger W. (1980), 'Women, Honour and Love: Some Aspects fo the Pashtu Woman's Life in Eastern Afghanistan', *Afghanistan J.* 7 (2): 50–59.

Bosworth, Clifford E. (1963), *The Ghaznavids*. Edinburgh: University Press.

Boukhary, Mir Abdoul Kerim (1876), *Histoire de l'Asie Centrale (Afghanistan, Boukhara, Khiva, Khoqand)*. Paris: Ernest Leroux.

Boulger, Demetrius Charles (1879), *England and Russia in Central Asia*. London: W. H. Allen & Co.

Brandenburg, Dietrich (1977), *Herat: Eine timuridische Hauptstadt*. Graz: Akademische Druck- und Verlagsanstalt.

Bregel, Yuri (1981), 'Nomadic and Sedentary Elements among the Turkmens', *Central Asiatic Journal* 25: 5–37.

Bregel, Yuri (n.d.), 'Bukhara', in *EIr*.

Bregel, Yuri (n.d.), 'Central Asia in the 12th-13th/18–19th Centuries', in *EIr*.

Bregel, Yuri (1991), 'Mangit', in *EI2*.

Brentjes, Burchard (1983), *Völkerschicksale am Hindukusch*. Leipzig: Koehler & Amelang.

Broadfoot, James S. (1886), 'Reports on Parts of the Ghilzi Country', *RGS Supplementary Papers* I: 341–400.

Bruinessen, Martin van (1992), *Agha, Shaikh and State: The Social and Political Structures of Kurdistan*. London: Zed Books.

Burnaby, Fred (1877), *A Ride to Khiva*. London: Cassell, Peter and Galpin.

Burnes, Alexander (1834), *Travels into Bokhara*. 3 vols. London: John Murray.

Burnes, Alexander (1839a), 'On the Persian Faction in Cabool', in Burnes et. al., *Reports and Papers*, pp. 7–13.

Burnes, Alexander (1839b), 'On the Political State of Cabool', in Burnes et. al., *Reports and Papers*, pp. 14–22.

Burnes, Alexander (1839c), 'Views and Prospects of Russia and Persia towards Candahar', in Burnes et. al., *Reports and Papers*, pp. 33–37.

Burnes, Alexander (1839d), 'On Herat, with a Sketch of the State of Affairs in the Surrounding Countries', in Burnes et. al., *Reports and Papers*, pp. 38–45.

Burnes, Alexander, Robert Leech, P. B. Lord, John Wood (1839), *Reports and Papers, Political, Geographical, and Commercial*. Calcutta.

Burnes, Alexander (1973), *Cabool*, repr. (first ed. 1842) Graz: Akademische Druck- und Verlagsanstalt.

Burton, Audrey (1993), *Bukharan Trade 1558–1718*. Papers on Inner Asia, No. 23. Bloomington: Indiana University, Research Institute for Inner Asian Studies.

Canfield, Robert L., *Hazara Integration into the Afghan Nation*. Asia Society, Afghanistan Council, Occasional Paper No. 3.

Canfield, Robert L. (1973), *Faction and Conversion in a Rural Society: Religious Alignments in the Hindu Kush. Anthropological Papers*, Museum of Anthropology, University of Michigan, No. 50. Ann Arbor: University of Michigan.

Canfield, Robert L. (1986), 'Ethnic, Regional, and Sectarian Alignments in Afghanistan', in *The State, Religion, and Ethnic Politics: Afghanistan, Iran, and Pakistan*, edited by Ali Banuazizi and Myron Weiner. Syracuse: Syracuse University Press, pp. 75–103.

Caroe, Olaf (1985), *The Pathans: 550 B.C.-A.D. 1957*, fourth edition. Karachi: Oxford University Press.

Caspani, E. and E. Cagnacci (1951), *Afghanistan: Crocevia dell' Asia*. 2nd ed. Milan: Antonio Vallardi.

Caton, Steven C. (1990), 'Anthropological Theories of Tribe and State Formation in the Middle East: Ideology and the Semiotics of Power', in *Tribes and State Formation in the Middle East,* edited by Ph. S. Khoury and J. Kostiner. Berkeley, Los Angeles: University of California Press, pp. 74–108.

Centlivres, Pierre (1972), *Un bazar d'Asie Centrale: Forme et organisation du bazar de Tashqurghan*. Wiesbaden: Ludwig Reichert.

Centlivres, Pierre (1975), 'Les Uzbeks du Qattaghan', *Afghanistan J.* 2 (1): 28–36.

Centlivres, Pierre (1976a), 'L'Histoire récente de l'Afghanistan et la configuration ethnique des provinces du nord-est', *Studia Iranica* 5: 255–267.

Centlivres, Pierre (1976b), 'Structure et évolution des bazars du nord afghan', in *Aktuelle Probleme der Regionalentwicklung und Stadtgeographie Afghanistans* edited by Erwin Grötzbach. Meisenheim am Glan: Anton Hain, pp. 119–145.

Centlivres, Pierre (1979), 'Groupes ethniques: De l'hétérogénéité d'un concept aux ambiguités de la représentation. L' exemple afghan', in *Beiträge zur Kulturgeographie des islamischen Orients*, edited by Eckhart Ehlers. Marburg/Lahn: Universität Marburg, 1979, pp. 25–37.

Centlivres, Pierre and Micheline Centlivres-Demont (1988a), *Et si on parlait de l'Afghanistan? Terrains et textes 1964–1980.* Neuchatel: Editions de l'Institut d'ethnologie.

Centlivres, Pierre and Micheline Centlivres-Demont (1988b), 'Pratiques quotidiennes et usages politiques des termes ethniques dans l'Afghanistan du Nord-Est', in *Le fait ethnique en Iran et en Afghanistan*, edited by Jean-Pierre Digard. Paris: Editions du CNRS, pp. 233–246.

Centlivres-Demont, Micheline (1976), 'Types d'occupation et relations interethniques dans le Nord-Est de l'Afghanistan', *Studia Iranica* 5: 269–277.

Chabbi, J. (n.d.), 'Abdal', in *EIr.*

Christensen, Asger (1980), 'The Pashtuns of Kunar: Tribe, Class and Community Organization', *Afghanistan J.* 7 (3): 79–92.

Conolly, Arthur (1834), *Journey to the North of India.* 2 vols. London: Richard Bentley.

Davies, Cuthbert Collin (1932), *The Problem of the North-West Frontier 1890–1908.* Cambridge: Cambridge University Press.

Davies, Cuthbert Collin (1949), *An Historical Atlas of the Indian Peninsula*, 2nd ed. Delhi: Oxford University Press.

Davies, Cuthbert Collin (1960), 'Afridi', in *EI2.*

Davies, R. H. (1862), *Report on the Trade of the Countries on the North-Western Boundary of British India.* Lahore.

DeWeese, Devin (1994), *Islamization and Native Religion in the Golden Horde.* Philadelphia: Pennsylvania State University Press.

Dickson, Martin B. (1960), 'Uzbek Dynastic Theory in the Sixteenth Century', *Trudy dvadcat' pjatogo Mezdunarodnogo kongressa vostokovedov (Moscow)* 3: 208–216.

Doerfer, Gerhard (1963–75), *Türkische und Mongolische Elemente im Neupersischen.* Wiesbaden: Franz Steiner.

Dresch, Paul (1986), 'The Significance of the Course Events Take in Segmentary Systems', *American Ethnologist* 13: 309–324.

Dresch, Paul (1988), 'Segmentation: Its Roots in Arabia and Its Flowering Elsewhere', *Cultural Anthropology* 3: 50–67.

Dubeux, M.; M. V. Valmont (1848), *Tartarie, Beloutchistan, Boutan et Nepal.* Paris: Firmin Didot Frères.

Dupree, Louis (1976), 'The First Anglo-Afghan War and the British Retreat of 1842: the Functions of History and Folklore', *East and West (IsMEO)*, New Series, 26 (3–4): 503–529.

Dupree, Louis (1980), *Afghanistan*, 3rd ed. Princeton: Princeton University Press.

Dupree, Louis (1984), 'Qizilbash', in *Muslim Peoples*, edited by Richard V. Weekes. 2nd ed. Westport, Ct.: Greenwood Press, pp. 637–642.

Dupree, Nancy H. (1975), 'Will the Sikhs Take Jalalabad?', *Afghanistan J.* 2 (2): 53–59.

Durand, Henry M. (1879), *The First Afghan War and Its Causes.* London: Longmans, Green, and Co.

Edwards, David B. (1986), 'Charismatic Leadership and Political Process in Afghanistan', *Central Asian Journal* 5 (3–4): 273–299.

Eickelman, Dale F. (1981), *The Middle East: An Anthropological Approach*. Englewood Cliffs, N. J.: Prentice Hall.

Einzmann, Harald (1977), *Religiöses Volksbrauchtum in Afghanistan: Islamische Heiligenverehrung und Wallfahrtswesen im Raum Kabul*. Wiesbaden: Franz Steiner Verlag.

Elphinstone, Mountstuart (1972), *An Account of the Kingdom of Caubul*, repr. (first ed. 1815) Karachi: Oxford University Press.

Erskine, William (1974), *A History of India*. repr. (first ed.1854) Karachi: Oxford University Press.

Evans-Pritchard, Edward E. (1949), *The Sanusi of Cyrenaica*. Oxford: Clarendon Press.

Evans-Pritchard, Edward E. (1956), *The Nuer*. Oxford: Clarendon Press.

Eyre, Vincent (1879), *The Kabul Insurrection of 1841–42*, edited by G. B. Malleson. London: W. H. Allen & Co.

Fane, Henry Edward (1842), *Five Years in India*. 2 vols. London: Henry Colburn.

Faiż Muḥammad (1912), *Sirāj al-tawārīkh*. Written in the early twentieth century. Kabul: Government Press.

Farhadi, Ravan (1978), 'Khatak', in *EI2*.

Farhang, Mīr Muḥammad Ṣadīq (1992), *Afghānistān dar panj qarn-i akhīr*. Teheran: Muʾasasa-yi Maṭbūʿātī-yi Ismāʿīlīyan.

Farrukh, Sayyid Mihdī (1991), *Kursī nishīnān-i Kābul*, edited by Muḥammad Āṣaf Fikrat. Tehran: Muʿasasa-yi puzhūhish wa muṭālaʿāt-i farhangī.

Ferdinand, Klaus (1959), *Preliminary Notes on Hazara Culture*. Historiskfilosofiske Meddelelser Udgivet af Det Kongelige Danske Videnskabernes Selskab, Bind 37, Nr. 5. Kopenhagen: Ejnar Munksgaard.

Ferdinand, Klaus (1962), 'Nomad Expansion and Commerce in Central Afghanistan', *Folk* 4: 123–159.

Ferrier, J. P. (1858), *History of the Afghans*. London: John Murray.

Ferrier, J. P. (1971), *Caravan Journeys and Wanderings in Persia, Afghanistan, Turkistan, and Beloochistan*. repr. (first ed. 1857). Westmead: Gregg International Publishers.

Fletcher, Joseph (1986), 'The Mongols: Ecological and Social Perspectives', *Harvard Journal of Asiatic Studies* 46 (1): 11–50.

Fofalzai, ʿAzīz al-Dīn Wakīlī (1958), *Durrat al-zamān fī tārīkh Shāh Zamān*. Kabul: Government Press.

Fofalzai, ʿAzīz al-Dīn Wakīlī (1967), *Tīmūr Shāh Durrānī*. 2 vols. repr. Kabul: Anjuman-i tarikh.

Fournieau, I., 'Balkh: From the Mongols to Modern Times' in *EIr*.

Fragner, Bert G. (1984), ''Rent-Capitalism' in the Light of the Economic History of Islamic Iran' in *On Social Evolution* edited by Walter Dostal. Horn-Wien: Ferdinand Berger.

Fragner, Bert G. (1986), 'Social and Internal Economic Affairs', in *The Cambridge History of Iran*, edited by Peter Jackson and Laurence Lockhart. Cambridge: Cambridge University Press, pp. 491–567.

Fragner, Bert G. (1989), 'Historische Wurzeln neuzeitlicher iranischer Identität: zur Geschichte des politischen Begriffs 'Iran' im späten Mittelalter und der Neuzeit', in *Studia Semitica Necnon Iranica* edited by Maria Macuch, Christa Müller-Kessler, Bert G. Fragner. Wiesbaden: Otto Harrassowitz.

Fraser-Tytler, W.K. (1953), *Afghanistan: A Study of Developments in Central and Southern Asia*, 2nd ed. London: Oxford University Press.

Frye, R.N. (1960), 'Balkh' in *EI2*.

Furdoonjee, Nowrozji (1839), 'Report on the Weights, Measures, and Coins of Cabool and Bokhara', in Burnes et. al., *Reports and Papers*, pp. 155–164.

Gankovsky, Yu. V. (1981), 'The Durrani Empire', in *Afghanistan: Past and Present.* Moscow: USSR Academy of Sciences, pp. 76–98.

Gankovsky, Yu. V. (1985), *A History of Afghanistan.* Moscow: Progress Publishers.

Garthwaite, Gene R. (1983a), *Khans and Shahs.* Cambridge: Cambridge University Press.

Garthwaite, Gene R. (1983b), 'Tribes, Confederations and the State: An Historical Overview of the Bakhtiari and Iran', in *The Conflict of Tribe and State in Iran and Afghanistan*, edited by Richard Tapper. New York: St. Martin's Press, pp. 314–330.

Gaube, Heinz and Eugen Wirth (1984), *Aleppo.* Wiesbaden: Ludwig Reichert Verlag.

Gazetteer of Afghanistan, Part V: *Kandahar.* (1908) 4th edition. Calcutta: Superintendent of Government Printing.

Gazetteer of Afghanistan, Part VI: *Farah.* (1908). Calcutta: Superintendent of Government Printing.

Gellner, Ernest (1969), *The Saints of the Atlas.* Chicago: The University of Chicago Press.

Gellner, Ernest (1981), *Muslim Society.* Cambridge: Cambridge University Press.

Gellner, Ernest (1983), 'The Tribal Society and Its Enemies', in *The Conflict of Tribe and State in Iran and Afghanistan*, edited by Richard Tapper. New York: St. Martin's Press, pp. 436–448.

Gerard, James G. (1833), 'Continuation of the Route of Lieutenant A. Burnes and Dr. Gerard, from Peshawar to Bokhara', *JASB* 2 (13, 15): 1–22, 143–149.

Ghani, A. (1961), 'Amir Sher Ali Khan', *Afghanistan* 16 (1): 35–56.

Ghani, Ashraf (n.d.), 'Afghanistan–Administration', in *EIr.*

Ghani, Ashraf (1976), 'A Critique of Sir Olaf Caroe', *Afghanistan* 29 (2): 18–28.

Ghani, Ashraf (1978), 'Islam and State-Building in a Tribal Society. Afghanistan: 1880–1901', *Modern Asian Studies* 12 (2): 269–284.

Ghubār, Mīr Ghulām Muḥammad (1981), *Afghānistān dar masīr-i tārīkh.* repr. (first ed. 1968) Qum: Payām-i Muhājir.

Ghulāmī, Muḥammad Ghulām Kohistānī (1957), *Jangnāma: Dar waṣf-i mujāhidāt-i Mīr Masjidī Khān Ghāzī wa sāyir-i mujāhidīn-i rashīd-i millī ᶜalaih-i mutajāwizīn.* Kabul: Maṭba ᶜa-yi Daulatī.

Glatzer, Bernt (1977), *Nomaden von Gharjistan.* Wiesbaden: Franz Steiner Verlag.

Glatzer, Bernt (1983), 'Political Organization of Pashtun Nomads and the State', in *The Conflict of Tribe and State in Iran and Afghanistan*, edited by Richard Tapper. New York: St. Martin's Press, pp. 212–232.

Gordon, T. E. (1876), *The Roof of the World.* Edinburgh: Edmonston and Douglas.

Gordon-Polonskaya, L. R. (1960), 'Survival of Gentilitial Community Organization in the Social and Economic Development of the Afghans int he XIXth Century', in *Trudy dvadcat' pjatogo Mezdunarodnogo kongressa vostokovedov (Moscow)* 2: 211–218.

Gregorian, Vartan (1969), *The Emergence of Modern Afghanistan.* Stanford: Stanford University Press.

Grevemeyer, Jan Heeren (1981), 'Im Windschatten des Widerstands: Zentralstaatsbildung und koloniale Intervention in Afghanistan', in *Traditionale Gesellschaften und europäischer Kolonialismus*, edited by Jan Heeren Grevemeyer. Frankfurt a. M.: Syndikat, pp. 82–104.

Grevemeyer, Jan-Heeren (1982), *Herrschaft, Raub und Gegenseitigkeit: Die politische Geschichte Badakhshans 1500–1883*. Wiesbaden: Otto Harrassowitz.

Grevemeyer, Jan-Heeren (1985), *Ethnizität und Nationalismus: Die afghanischen Hazaras zwischen Emanzipation, Widerstand gegen die sowjetischen Besatzer und Bürgerkrieg*. Ethnizität und Migration, Freie Universität Berlin, Forschungsgebietsschwerpunkt, Occasional Papers, Nr. 4. Berlin: Das Arabische Buch.

Grevemeyer, Jan-Heeren (1988), 'Ethnicity and National Liberation: The Afghan Hazara between Resistance and Civil War', Colloques internationaux, *Le Fait Ethnique en Iran et en Afghanistan*. Paris: Editions du CNRS: 211–218.

Grevemeyer, Jan-Heeren (1990), *Afghanistan: Sozialer Wandel und Staat im 20. Jahrhundert*. Berlin: Verlag für Wissenschaft und Bildung.

Grierson, G. A. (1919), *Linguistic Survey of India*, Vol. 8 Part II, *Specimen of the Dardic or Piracha Languages*. Calcutta: Superintendent of Government Printing.

Grötzbach, E. (1972), *Kulturgeographischer Wandel in Nordost-Afghanistan seit dem 19. Jahrhundert*. Meisenheim am Glan.

Gulzad, Zalmay (1994), *External Influences and the Development of the Afghan State in the Nineteenth Century*. New York: Peter Lang.

Gupta, Hari Ram (1941), 'Timur Shah's Army in 1793', *Journal of Indian History* 20: 100–104.

Gupta, Hari Ram (1944), *Studies in Later Mughal History of the Panjab 1707–1793*. Lahore: Minerva.

Habib, Irfan (1982), *An Atlas of the Mughal Empire*. Delhi: Oxford University Press.

Habib, Najibullah (1987), *Stadtplanung, Architektur und Baupolitik in Afghanistan*. Bochum: Studienverlag Dr. N. Brockmeyer.

Ḥabībī, ᶜAbd al-Ḥayy (1959), Appendix. In Shikārpūrī, ᶜAṭā Muḥammad, *Tāza nawā-yi maᶜārik*. Karachi: Sindhī Adabī Board.

Hahn, Helmut (1964), 'Die Stadt Kabul (Afghanistan) und ihr Umland', *Bonner Geographische Abhandlungen* 34: 5–85.

Haim, S. (1983), *Haim's One-Volume Persian-English Dictionary*. Teheran: Farhang Moaser.

Hajianpur, Mahin (1991), 'Das Timuridenreich und die Eroberung von Mawarannahr durch die Usbeken', in *Zentralasien*, edited by Gavin Hambly. *Fischer Weltgeschichte* Vol. 16. Frankfurt a. M: Fischer Bücherei Kg, pp. 162–175.

Hall, Lesley (1981), *A Brief Guide to Sources for the Study of Afghanistan in the India Office Records*. London: India Office Library and Records.

Halperin, Charles J. (1985), *Russia and the Golden Horde*. Bloomington: Indiana University Press.

Hambly, Gavin (ed.) (1991), *Zentralasien. Fischer Weltgeschichte* Vol. 16. repr. Frankfurt a. M.: Fischer Bücherei Kg.

Hamilton, Angus (1906), *Afghanistan*. London: William Heinemann.

Hamilton, Walter (1971), *Description of Hindostan*. 2 vols. repr. (first ed. 1820) New Delhi: Oriental Publishers.

Hammoudi, A. (1980), 'Segmentarity, Social Stratification, Political Power and Sainthood: Reflections on Gellner's Theses', *Economy and Society* 9: 279–303.

Harawī, Muḥammad Yūsuf Riyāżi (1990), *ᶜAin al-waqāyiᶜ*. Written in the early twentieth century, edited by Muḥammad Āṣaf Fikrat. Teheran: University Press.

Harlan, Josiah (1842), *A Memoir of India and Avghanistaun*. Philadelphia: J. Dobson.

Harlan, Josiah (1939), *Central Asia: Personal Narrative of Josiah Harlan, 1823–1841*. London: Luzac and Co.

Harrison, Selig S. (1986) 'Ethnicity and the Political Stalemate in Pakistan', in *The State, Religion, and Ethnic Politics: Afghanistan, Iran, and Pakistan*, edited by Ali Banuazizi and Myron Weiner. Syracuse: Syracuse University Press, pp. 267–298.

Havelock, Henry (1840), *Narrative of the War in Afghanistan*. 2 vols. London: Henry Colburn.

Hensman, Howard (1978), *The Afghan War of 1879–80*, repr. (first ed. 1881) Lahore: Sang-e-Meel Publications.

Holdich, T. Hungerford (1881), 'Geographical Results of the Afghan Campaign', *RGS Proceedings* 3: 278–301.

Holdich, T. Hungerford (1885), 'Afghan Boundary Commission. Geographical Notes', *RGS Proceedings* 7: 39–44, 160–166, 273–292.

Holdich, T. Hungerford (1909) *The Indian Borderland*, 1880–1900. 2nd ed. London: Methuen and Co.

Holdsworth, Mary (1959), *Turkestan in the Nineteenth Century*. Oxford: Central Asian Research Centre.

Holzwarth, Wolfgang (1980), 'Segmentation und Staatsbildung in Afghanistan: Traditionale sozio-politische Organisation in Badakhshan, Wakhan und Sheghnan', in Jan Heeren Grevemeyer (ed.), *Revolution in Iran und Afghanistan*. Frankfurt a. M.: Syndikat.

Holzwarth, Wolfgang (1990), *Vom Fürstentum zur afghanischen Provinz: Badakhshan 1880–1985*. Berlin: Support Edition.

Hough, W. (1841), *A Narrative of the March and Operations of the Army of the Indus, in the Expedition to Affghanistan in the years 1838–1839*. London: W. H. Allen & Co.

Howorth, Henry H. (1973), *History of the Mongols*, Part II: *The So-Called Tartars of Russia and Central Asia*, repr. (first ed. 1880). New York: Burt Franklin.

Ḥusainī, Imām al-Dīn (1967), 'Chand safḥa az tārīkh-i ḥusain shāhī', repr. (first ed. 1797), *Āryānā* 25 (4): 26–33.

al-Ḥusainī al-Munshī, Maḥmūd ibn Ibrāhīm (1974), *Tārīkh-i aḥmad shāhī*. Facsimile edition by Dostmurad Sayyid Muradof. Moscow: Academy of Sciences.

Hyder Khan, Gholaum (1835–1836), 'Mr. Moorcroft's Journey to Balkh and Bokhara', *Asiatic Journal* N. S. 18: 106–119, 170–182, 278–288; 19: 35–42; 95–102.

Izzet Ullah, Mir (1843), 'Travels beyond the Himalaya', *Journal of the Royal Asiatic Society of Great Britain and Ireland*. 7: 283–342.

Jackson, Keith A. (c. 1840), Views in Affghaunistaun. London: W. H. Allen & Co.

Janata, Alfred (1975), 'Beitrag zur Völkerkunde Afghanistans', *Archiv für Völkerkunde* 29: 7–36.

Janata, Alfred (1987), 'Constituents of Pashtun Ethnic Identity: The Jaji Case', *Studia Iranica* 16: 201–214.

Janata, Alfred and Reihanodin Hassas (1975), 'Ghairatman–der gute Paschtune. Exkurs über die Grundlagen des Paschtunwali', *Afghanistan J.* 3: 83–97.

Jarring, Gunnar (1939a), 'An Uzbek's View of his Native-Town and its Circumstances', *Ethnos* No. 2: 73–80.

Jarring Gunnar (1939b), *On the Distribution of Turk Tribes in Afghanistan*. Leipzig: Otto Harrassowitz.

Jawad, Nassim (1992), *Afghanistan–A Nation of Minorities*. London: Minority Rights Group.

Jettmar, Karl (1961), 'Ethnological Research in Dardistan 1958', *Proceedings of the American Philosophical Soiciety*. 105: 79–97.

Jones, Sarah (1978), 'The Hazaras and the British in the Nineteenth Century', *Afghanistan J.* 5 (1): 3–5.

Kakar, Hasan K. (1971), *Afghanistan: A Study in Internal Political Developments 1880–1896*. Lahore: Punjab Educational Press.

Kakar, Hasan K. (1973), *The Pacification of the Hazaras of Afghanistan*. Afghanistan Council, The Asia Society, Occasional Paper No. 4.

Kakar, Hasan K. (1979), *Government and Society in Afghanistan*. Austin: Universitly of Texas Press.

Kashmīrī, Ḥamīd (1951), *Akbarnāma*. Kabul: Anjuman-i tārīkh.

Kaye, John William (1857), *History of the War in Afghanistan*. 3 vols., 2nd ed. London: Richard Bentley.

Kennedy, Richard Hartley (1840), *Narrative of the Campaign of the Indus, in Sind and Kaubool, 1838–9*. 2 vols. London: Richard Bentley.

Khāfī, Ya ᶜqūb ᶜAlī (1957), *Pādshāhān-i mutaᵓakhir-i Afghānistān*. Written in 1907. 2 vols. Kabul: Daulatī Maṭba ᶜa.

Khalfin, N. A. (1958), 'The Rising of Ishaq Khan in Southern Turkestan (1888)', *Central Asian Review* 6: 253–263a.

Khalīl, Muḥammad Ibrāhīm (1960), *Mazārāt-i shahr-i Kābul*. Kabul: Anjuman-i tārīkh.

Khanikoff (1845), *Bokhara: Its Amir and Its People*. London: James Madden.

Kieffer, C. M. (n.d.), 'Abdali', in *EIr*.

Knobloch, Edgar (1981), 'Survey of Archeology and Architecture in Afghanistan', *Afghanistan J*. 8 (1): 3–20.

Kohzād, Aḥmad ᶜAlī (1955a), 'Matn-i yak ᶜahdnāma-yi qaumī ba ᶜd az qatl-i Shāh Shujā ᶜ', *Āryānā* 13 (2): 1–8.

Kohzād, Aḥmad ᶜAlī (1955b), 'Mukātaba bain-i Shāh Shujā ᶜ wa Maknātan', *Āryānā* 13 (3): 1–5.

Kohzād, Aḥmad ᶜAlī (1955c), 'Jangnama'. *Āryānā* 13 (7): 1–5.

Kohzād, Aḥmad ᶜAlī (1955–1956,1959–1961), 'Bālāhiṣār-i Kābul wa peshāmadhā-yi tārīkhī', *Āryānā* Vol 13 (1955–56) No. 9: 1–8; No. 10: 1–8; No. 11: 1–8; No. 12: 1–8; Vol. 17 (1959) Nos. 1–2: 30–43; No. 3: 8–16; No. 4; 13–20; No. 5a: 9–16; No. 5b: 13–24; No. 6: 9–16; No. 7: 25–32; ; No. 8: 9–16; No. 9: 9–16; No. 10: 5–16; No. 12: 5–16; Vol. 18 (1960) No. 1: 21–31; No. 2: 9–20; No. 3: 5–16; No. 4: 5–16; No. 6: 17–28; No. 7: 9–20; No. 8: 33–40; No. 9: 41–52; No. 10: 29–40; No. 11: 17–28; No. 12: 17–28; Vol. 19 (1961) No. 1: 17–28; No. 2: 17–28; No. 3: 17–28; No. 4: 17–28; No. 10: 29–36; No. 11: 17–24; No. 12: 29–36.

Kohzad, Ahmad Ali (1960), 'Les manuscrits relatifs a l'histoire de l'Afghanistan en XIX siecle', in *Trudy dvadcat' pjatogo Mezdunarodnogo kongressa vostokovedov (Moscow)* 2: 207–211.

Kopecky, Lucas-Michael (1982), 'The Imami Sayyed of the Hazarajat: The Maintenance of their Elite Position.', *Folk* 24: 89–110.

Kopecky, Lucas-Michael (1986), 'Die Saiyid und die imamitischen Hazara Afghanistans: Religiöse Vergemeinschaftung und Ethnogenese', in *Die ethnischen Gruppen Afghanistans*, edited by E. Orywal. Wiesbaden: Ludwig Reichert Verlag.

Kushkakī, Burhān al-Dīn (1989), *Rāhnamā-yi Qataghan wa Badakhshān*. repr. (comp. in 1922), edited by Manūchihr Sutūda. Teheran: Maihan.

Kussmaul, Friedrich (1965a), 'Badaxšan und seine Tağiken', *Tribus* 14: 11–99.

Kussmaul, Friedrich (1965b), 'Siedlung und Gehöft bei den Tağiken in den Bergländern Afghanistans', *Anthropos* 60: 487–532.

Lal, Mohan (1977), *Travel in the Punjab, Afghanistan and Turkistan to Balk, Bokhara and Herat and a Visit to Great Britain and Germany*. repr. (first ed. 1846) Calcutta: K.P. Bagchi & Co.

Lal, Mohan (1978), *Life of the Amir Dost Mohammed Khan of Kabul*. repr. (first ed. 1846) Karachi: Oxford University Press.

Lapidus, Ira M. (1990), 'Tribes and State Formation in Islamic History', in *Tribes and State Formation in the Middle East*, edited by Ph. S. Khoury and J. Kostiner. Berkeley, Los Angeles: University of California Press, pp. 25–47.

Le Coq-Berlin, A. v. (1912/1913), 'Kyzylbasch und Yäschilbasch', in *Orientalisches Archiv*, Vol. 3, edited by Hugo Grothe. Leipzig: Karl W. Hiersemann.

Lee, Jonathan L. (1987), 'The History of Maimana, N.W. Afghanistan, 1731–1893', in *Utrecht Papers on Central Asia, Proceedings of the First European Seminar on Central Asian Studies held at Utrecht, 16–18 December 1985*, Utrecht Turkological Series No. 2, edited by Mark van Damme and Hendrik Boeschoten. Utrecht.

Lee, Jonathan L. (1991), '[c]Abd al-Raḥmān Khān and the "maraẕ ul-mulūk"', *JRAS*, Series 3, 1(2): 209–242.

Lee, Jonathan L. (1996), *The 'Ancient Supremacy', Bukhara, Afghanistan, and the Battle for Balkh*, 1731–1901. Leiden: E. J. Brill.

Leech, Robert (1839a), 'Notice on the Affairs of Candahar in 1838, with a Sketch of the Preceding Dooranee History', in Burnes et. al., *Reports and Papers*, pp. 51–64.

Leech, Robert (1839b), 'Account of the Tribe of Taimanee and Their Country', in Burnes et. al., *Reports and Papers*, pp. 153–155.

Leech, Robert (1845a), 'An Account of the Early Ghiljáees', *JASB* 14: 306–328.

Leech, Robert (1845b), 'A Supplementary Account of the Hazarahs', *JASB* 14: 333–340.

Leech, Robert (1845c), 'An Account of the Early Abdalees', *JASB* 14: 445–470.

Lemercier-Quelquejay, Chantal (1991), 'Die Kasachen und Kirgisen', in *Zentralasien*, edited by Gavin Hambly. *Fischer Weltgeschichte* Vol. 16. Frankfurt a. M: Fischer Bücherei Kg, pp. 152–161.

Leyden, J. (1812), ' On the Rosheniah Sect and Its Founder Bayezid Ansari', *Asiatic Researches* 2: 363–428.

Lindholm, Charles (1980), 'Images of the Pathan: The Usefulness of Colonial Ethnography', *Archives européennes de sociologie* 21: 350–361.

Lindholm, Charles (1981), 'The Structure of Violence among the Swat Pukhtun', *Ethnology* 20: 147–156.

Lindholm, Charles (1982a), *Generosity and Jealousy*. New York: Columbia University Press.

Lindholm, Charles (1982b), 'Models of Segmentary Political Action: The Examples of Swat and Dir, NWFP, Pakistan', in *Anthropology in Pakistan: Recent Socio-Cultural and Archeological Perspectives*, edited by Stephen Pastner and Louis Flam. Cornell University Press.

Lindholm, Charles (1986), 'Kinship Structure and Political Authority: The Middle East and Central Asia', *Comparative Studies in Society and History* 28: 334–355.

Lindholm, Charles (1990), 'Validating Domination among Egalitarian Individualists: Swat, Northern Pakistan and the USA', *Social Analysis* 28: 26–37.

Lindholm, Charles and Cherry Lindholm (1988), 'Life behind the Veil', in *Ourselves among Others*, edited by Carol J. Verburg. Boston: St. Martin's Press, pp. 267–276.

Lockhart, Laurence (1938), *Nadir Shah*. London: Luzac & Co.

Lockhart, Laurence (1958), *The Fall of the Safavi Dynasty and the Afghan Occupation of Persia*. Cambridge: Cambridge University Press.

Lord, P. B. (1838), 'Some Account of a Visit to the Plain of Koh-i Daman', *JASB* 7 (1): 521–537.

Lord, P. B. (1839a), 'A Memoir of the Uzbek State of Kundooz, and the Power of its Present Ruler Mahomed Murad Beg', in Burnes et. al., *Reports and Papers*, pp. 96–124, 133–146.

Lord, P. B. (1839b), 'Prospects of Trade with Turkistan', in Burnes et. al., *Reports and Papers*, Part III, 'Commercial', pp. 122–132.

Lumsden, H. B. (1860), *The Mission to Kandahar.* Calcutta: C. B. Lewis, Baptist Mission Press.

Lumsden, Peter S. (1885), 'Countries and Tribes Bordering on the Koh-i-Baba Range', *RGS Proceedings* 5: 561–583.

Lumsden, Peter S. and George R. Elsmie (1899), *Lumsden of the Guides*. London: John Murray.

McChesney, R. D. (n.d.), 'Central Asia in the 10th–12th/16–18th Centuries', in *EIr.*

McChesney, R. D. (1968), 'The Economic Reforms of Amir Abdul Rahman Khan', *Afghanistan* 21 (3): 11–34.

McChesney, R. D. (1983), 'The Amirs of Muslim Central Asia in the XVIIth Century', *Journal of the Economic and Social History of the Orient* (Leiden) 26: 33–70.

McChesney, R. D. (1991), *Waqf in Central Asia.* Princeton, N.J.: Princeton University Press.

MacGregor, C. B. (1844), 'A Geographical Notice of the Valley of Jullalabad', *JASB*. Vol. 13, No. 2: 867–880

MacGregor, Charles M. (1871), *Central Asia*, Part II. Calcutta: Office of the Superintendent of Government Printing.

MacGregor, Charles M. (1873), *Central Asia*, Part I, Vols. I-III. Calcutta: Office of the Superintendent of Government Printing.

McMahon, A. H. and A. D. G. Ramsay (1981), *Report on the Tribes of Dir, Swat and Bajour*, repr. (first ed. 1901), edited and introduced by R. O. Christensen. Peshawar: Saeed Book Bank.

Malleson, G. B. (1879), *History of Afghanistan, from the Earliest Period to the Outbreak of the War of 1878*. London: W. H. Allen & Co.

Martin, Frank A. (1907), *Under the Absolute Amir.* London and New York: Harper and Brothers.

Martineau, John (1895), *The Life and Correspondence of Sir Bartle Frere*. 2 vols. London: John Murray.

Marvin, Charles (1880), *Colonel Grodekoff's Ride from Samarcand to Herat through Balkh and the Uzbek States of Afghan Turkestan*. London: W. H. Allen.

Marvin, Charles (1883), *The Russians at Merv and Herat*. London: W. H. Allen & Co.

Masson, Charles (1906), 'Masson's Journals', in *Selections from the Travels and Journals Preserved in the Bombay Secretariat*, edited by George W. Forrest. Bombay: Government Central Press, pp. 101–188.

Masson, Charles (1974), *Narrative of Various Journeys in Balochistan, Afghanistan and the Panjab*. 3 vols. repr. (first ed. 1842). Karachi: Oxford University Press.

Matīn-i Andkhui, Muḥammad Amīn (1993a), 'Ghażanfar Khān-i Andkhui', *Jozjānān* No. 1 (12 May 1993): 3.

Matīn-i Andkhui, Muḥammad Amīn (1993b), 'Murūrī bar nibishtahā-yi rū-yi dīwār', *Jozjānān* No. 10 (21 July 1993): 4; No. 11 (28 July 1993): 4; No. 12 (4 August 1993): 4; No. 13 (11 August 1993): 4; No. 14 (18 August 1993): 4; No. 15 (25 August 1993): 4; No. 16 (1 September 1993): 3–4; No. 17 (8 September 1993): 4; No. 18 (15 September 1993): 4; No. 19 (22 Septpember 1993): 4; No. 20 (29 September 1993): 4.

Meeker, Michael E. (1976), 'Meaning and Society in the Near East: Examples from the Black Sea Turks and the Levantine Arabs', *International Journal of Middle East Studies* 7: 243–270, 383–422.

Merk, W. R. H. (1984), *The Mohmands*, repr. (first ed. 1898). Lahore: Vanguard Books Ltd.

Miller, Charles (1977), *Khyber: British India's North West Frontier*. New York: Macmillan.

Minorsky, V. (1937), *Ḥudūd al-ᶜĀlam: 'The Regions of the World'. A Persian Geography 372 A.H. - 982 A.D.* Oxford: Oxford University Press.

Monshi, Eskandar Beg (1978), *History of Shah 'Abbas the Great*, translated by Roger M. Savory, 2 vols. Boulder: Westview Press

Montgomerie, T. G. (1872), 'A Havildar's Journey through Chitral to Faizabad in 1870', *JRGS* 42: 180–201.

Moorcroft, William and George Trebeck (1841), *Travels in the Himalayan Provinces of Hindustan and the Panjab; in Ladakh and Kashmir; in Peshawar, Kabul, Kunduz, and Bokhara*. 2 vols. London: John Murray.

Nāhiż, Muḥammad Ḥakīm (1956–1960), *Qāmūs-i jughrāfiyāʾī-yi Afghānistān*. 4 vols. Kabul: Āryānā Dāʾirat al-Ma ᶜārif.

Naushāhī, ᶜĀrif (1993), 'Risāla dar aḥwāl-i ṭāyifa-yi kāfir-i siyāhposh' *Ma ᶜārif* 10 (2): 56–72.

Nāyil, A. H. (1961), 'Riyāżi Harawī', *Āryānā* 19 (8): 27–33.

Nazarov, Khaknazar (1963), *Rawobiti Bukhoro wa Afghoniston az barpo shudani dawlati durroniho to ghaltidani amorati Bukhoro*. Dushamba.

Nāẓim, Muḥammad (1971), *The Life and Times of Sulṭān Maḥmūd of Ghazna*, 2nd ed. New Delhi: Mushiram Manoharlal.

Neamet Ullah (1976), *History of the Afghans*, translated by Bernhard Dorn, 2 vols., repr. (first ed. 1829–1836). Karachi: Indus Publications.

Nīr Harawī, Muḥammad Anwar (1964–65), 'Abdālī, Sadozai, Durrānī'. *Āryānā* 22, (11–12): 69–81.

Nīr Harawī, Muḥammad Anwar (1967), 'Tijārat-i Afghānistān dar qarn-i nūzdah', *Āryānā* 25 No. 1: 18–36; No. 2: 49–59; No. 3: 22–29.

Noelle, Christine (1995): 'The Anti-Wahhabi Reaction in Nineteenth-Century Afghanistan', *Muslim World*, 85 (1–2): 23–48.

Norris, J. (1967), *The First Afghan War: 1838–1842*. Cambridge: Cambridge University Press.

Nūrī, Nūr Muḥammad (1956), *Gulshan-i imārat*. (First printed version of manuscript originally written approximately in 1870). Kabul: Government Press.

Olesen, Asta (1995), *Islam and Politics in Afghanistan*. Richmond, Surrey: Curzon Press.

Oliver, Edward E. (1890), *Across the Border or Pathan and Biloch*. London: Chapman and Hall.

Olufson, O. (1904), *Through the Unknown Pamirs: The Second Danish Pamir Expedition 1898–1899*. London: William Heinemann.

'On Tabular Returns of the N. W. Frontier Trade with Afghanistan', *JASB*.(1841) 10 (1): 251–265.

Orywal, Erwin (1982), *Die Balūč in Afghanisch-Sīstān*. Berlin: Dietrich Reimer Verlag.

Orywal, Erwin (1986), 'Ethnische Identität–Konzept und Methode', in *Die ethnischen Gruppen Afghanistans*, edited by Erwin Orywal. Wiesbaden: Ludwig Reichert Verlag, pp. 73–86.

Ovesen, Jan (1983), 'The Construction of Ethnic Identities: The Nuristani and Pashai of Eastern Afghanistan', in *Identity: Personal and Socio-Cultural*, edited by Anita Jacobsen-Widding. Uppsala: Acta Universitatis Upsaliensis, pp. 321–333.

Pearse, Hugh (ed.) (1898), *Soldier and Traveller: Memoirs of Alexander Gardner*. Edinburgh and London: Blackwood and Sons.

Pedersen, Gorm (1994), *Afghan Nomads in Transition: A Century of Change among the Zala Khan Khel.* London: Thames & Hudson.

Peers, Edward E. (1954), *ᶜUrūj-i Bārakzai.* Kabul: Maṭba ᶜa-yi ᶜUmūmī.

Perry, John R. (1975), 'Forced Migration in Iran dring the Seventeenth and Eighteenth Centuries', *Iranian Studies* 8: 199–215.

Peters, Emrys L. (1967), 'Some Structural Aspects of the Feud among the Camel-Herding Bedouin of Cyrenaica', *Africa* 37: 261–282.

Planhol, Xavier de (1976), 'Le repeuplement de la basse valle afghane du Murghab', *Studia Iranica* 5: 279–290.

Plowden, Trevor C. (1875), *Translations of the Kalid-i Afghani, the Text Book for the Pakkhto Examination, with Notes, Historical, Geographical, Grammatical and Explanatory.* Lahore: Central Jail Press.

Poladi, Hassan (1989), *The Hazaras.* Stockton: Mughal Publishing Co.

Poullada, Leon B. (1973), *Reform and Rebellion in Afghanistan, 1919–1929.* Ithaca: Cornell University Press.

Rahimi, M. H. and M. S. Rohi (1979), *Pashto-English Dictionary.* Kabul: Academy of Sciences of Afghanistan.

Rashad, Pohandoy Abdul Shakoor (1967), 'Ashraf-Ul-Wuzara, Shah Wali Khan Bamizai', *Afghanistan* 20 (3): 35–44.

Rasuly-Paleczek, Gabriele (1993a), 'Beg, Moyzafid und Arbab: Das politische System der Chechka Usbeken und der afghanische Zentralstaat', in *Studies in Oriental Culture and History (Festschrift for Walter Dostal)* edited by Andre Gingrich, Sylvia Haas, Gabriele Paleczek, Thomas Fillitz. Frankfurt: Peter Lang, pp. 89–105.

Rasuly-Paleczek, Gabriele (1993b), 'Ethnische Identitt und Zentralstaat: Die Usbeken Nordost-Afghanistans und der afghanische Zentralstaat', in *Kultur, Identität und Macht* edited by Thomas Fillitz, Andre Gingrich, Gabriele Rasuly-Paleczek. Frankfurt: Verlag für Interkulturelle Kommunikation, pp. 73–89.

Rasuly-Paleczek, Gabriele (forthcoming), 'Kinship and Politics among the Uzbeks of Northeastern Afghanistan', *Proceedings of the ESCAS IV Conference in Bamberg*, 1991.

Rasuly-Paleczek, Gabriele (forthcoming), 'Verwandtschaft und Heirat als Mittel zur Festigung von Macht und Einfluß', *Bamberger Mittelasien Studien.*

Rathjens, Carl (1962), 'Karawanenwege und Pässe im Kulturlandschaftswandel Afghanistans seit dem 19. Jahrhundert', in *Hermannn von Wissmann Festschrift.* Tübingen: Geographisches Institut Tübingen.

Raverty, H. G. (1860a), *A Dictionary of the Pukhto or Pushto.* London: Longman, Green.

Raverty, H. G. (1860b), *The Gulshan-i Roh: Being Selections, Prose and Poetical in the Pushto, or Afghan Language.* London: Longman, Green.

Raverty, H. G. (1888), *Notes on Afghanistan and Part of Baluchistan.* London: Eyre & Spottiswoode.

Raverty, H. G. (1894), 'The Independent Afghan or Patan Tribes', *AQR* 7: 312–326.

Raverty, H. G. (1895), 'The Waziri Afghans and Their Country', *AQR* 9 (1895): 153–165.

Raverty, H. G. (1906), *A History of the Mings or Hazarahs of the Chingiz or Great Khan.* IOL Mss. London.

Rawlinson, Henry C. (1871), 'Report on the Dooranee Tribes', in MacGregor, Charles Metcalfe (1871), *Central Asia.* Vol. 2. Calcutta: Government of India Publication, pp. 823–869.

Raymond, Xavier (1848), *Afghanistan.* Paris: Firmin Didot Freres.

Reisner, Igor M. (1954), *Razvitie feodalizma i obrazovanie gosudarstva u Afgancev*. Moscow.

Reisner, Igor M. (1981), 'Specific Features of the Development of Feudalism among the Afghans', in *Afghanistan: Past and Present*. Moscow: USSR Academy of Sciences, pp.45–59.

Reshtia, Sayed Qassem (1957), *Afghānistān dar qarn-i nuzdah*. 2nd edition. Kabul: Government Press.

Reshtia, Sayed Qassem (1990), *Between Two Giants: Political History of Afghanistan in the Nineteenth Century*. (translation of *Afghānistān dar qarn-i nuzdah*) Peshawar: Afghan Jehad Works Translation Centre.

Riazul Islam (1970); *Indo-Persian Relations: A Study of the Political and Diplomatic Relations between the Mughul Empire and Iran*. Teheran: Iranian Culture Foundation.

Riżā Qulī Khān Hidāyat (1960), *Mulḥaqāt-i tārīkh-i raużat al-ṣafā-yi nāṣirī*. Vol. 10. Qum: Hikmat.

Robinson, J. A. (1978), *Notes on Nomad Tribes of Eastern Afghanistan*. repr. (first. ed. 1934). Quetta: M/S Nisa Traders.

Röhrborn, Klaus Michael (1966), *Provinzen und Zentralgewalt Persiens im 16. und 17. Jahrhundert*. Berlin: Walter de Gruyter.

Romodin, V. A. (1983), *Ocherki po istorii i istorii kulturi Afganistana*. Moscow: Nauk.

Romodin, V. A. (1985), *A History of Afghanistan*. Moscow: Progress Publishers.

Romodin, V. A. (1990), *Afganistan vo vtoroi polovine XIX-nachale XX v.* Moscow: Nauk.

Roskoschny, Hermann (1982), *Afghanistan und seine Nachbarländer*. repr. (first ed. approximately 1885). Kirchheim: Otto Spieth.

Roy, Olivier (1988), 'Ethnies et appartenances politiques en Afghanistan', in *Le fait ethnique en Iran et en Afghanistan*, edited by Jean-Pierre Digard. Paris: Editions du CNRS, pp. 201–209.

Sachau, Edward C. (1888), *Alberuni's India*, 2 vols. London: Trübner & Co.

Sahlins, Marshall D. (1961), 'The Segmentary Lineage: An Organization of Predatory Expansion', *American Anthropologist* 63: 322–345.

Sale, Lady (1985), *A Journal of the Disasters in Affghanistan, 1841–2*. repr. (first ed. in 1843). Lahore: Sang-e-Meel Publications

Salzman, Philip Carl (1978), 'Does Complementary Opposition Exist?' *American Anthropologist*. 80: 53–70.

Sarkisyanz, Emanuel (1961), *Geschichte der orientalischen Völker Rußlands bis 1917*. München.

Savory, Roger M. (1979), 'Kizilbash', in *EI2*.

Savory, Roger M. (1980), *Iran under the Safavids*. Cambridge: Cambridge University Press.

Schurmann, H. F. (1962), *The Mongols of Afghanistan*. 'S-Gravenhage: Mouton & Co.

Scott (1879), 'The Pathans of the North-West Frontier of India', *Blackwood's Edinburgh Magazine* 125: 595–610.

Shahrani, Nazif M. (1984a), 'Introduction: Marxist "Revolution" and Islamic Resistance in Afghanistan', in *Revolutions & Rebellions in Afghanistan*, edited by M. Nazif Shahrani and Robert L. Canfield. Berkeley: Institute of International Studies, pp. 3–57.

Shahrani, Nazif M. (1984b), 'Causes and Context of Responses to the Saur Revolution in Badakhshan', in *Revolutions & Rebellions in Afghanistan*, edited by M. Nazif Shahrani and Robert L. Canfield. Berkeley: Institute of International Studies, pp.139–169.

Shahrani, Nazif M. (1986a), 'State Building and Social Fragmentation in Afghanistan: A Historical Perspective', in *The State, Religion, and Ethnic Politics in Afghanistan*, Iran and Pakistan, edited by Ali Banuazizi and Myron Weiner. Syracuse: Syracuse University Press, pp. 23–74.

Shahrani, Nazif. M. (1986b), 'The Kirghiz Khans: Styles and Substance of Traditional Local Leadership in Central Asia', *Central Asian Survey* 5, No. 3/4: 255–271.

Shalinsky, Audrey (1986), 'Uzbak Ethnicity in Northern Afghanistan', in *Die ethnischen Gruppen Afghanistans*, edited by E. Orywal. Wiesbaden: Ludwig Reichert Verlag.

Shikārpūrī, ᶜAṭā Muḥammad, *Tāza nawā-yi maᶜārik*. Karachi: Sindhī Adabī Board.

Singer, André (1984), *Lords of the Khyber: The Story of the North-West Frontier.* London: Faber and Faber.

Singh, Bhagat (1990), *Maharaja Ranjit Singh and His Times*. Delhi: Sehgal Publishing Service.

Singh, Ganda (1981), *Ahmad Shah Durrani: Father of Modern Afghanistan*. repr. Lahore: Tariq Publications.

Sinha, Narendra Krishna (1951), *Ranjit Singh*. repr. Calcutta: A Mukherjiee & Co.

Skrine, Francis H. and Edward D. Ross (1899), *The Heart of Asia*. London: Methuen & Co.

Smith, W. C. (1946), 'Lower-Class Uprisings in the Mughal Empire', *Islamic Culture* 20: 21–40.

Spain, James W. (1985), *The Pathan Borderland*. repr. Karachi: Indus Publications.

Spuler, Berthold (1943), *Die Goldene Horde*. Leipzig: Otto Harrassowitz.

Steul, Willi (1980), 'Pashtunwali und Widerstand', in *Revolution in Iran und Afghanistan* edited by Kurt Greussing und Jan-Heeren Grevemeyer. Frankfurt a. M.: Syndikat.

Steul, Willi (1981), *Paschtunwali: Ein Ehrenkodex und seine rechtliche Relevanz*. Wiesbaden: Franz Steiner Verlag.

Stewart, C. E. (1881), 'The Country of the Tekke Turkomans, and the Tejend and Murghab Rivers', *RGS Proceedings* 3: 513–546.

Stirling, Edward (1991), *The Journals of Edward Stirling in Persia and Afghanistan 1828–1829*, edited by Jonathan L. Lee. Naples: Istituto Universitario Orientale.

Stocqueler, J. H. (1983), *Memorials of Affghanistan*. repr. (first ed. 1843) Peshawar: Saeed Book Bank.

Subtelny, Maria Eva (1983), 'Art and Politics in early 16th Century Central Asia', *Central Asiatic Journal* 27: 121–148.

Sulṭān Muḥammad Khān b. Musā Durrānī (1881), *Tārīkh-i sulṭānī*. Bombay: Kārkhāna-yi Muḥammadī.

Sultan Muhammad Khan (1900), *The Constitution and Laws of Afghanistan*. London: John Murray.

Sultan Muhammad Khan (ed.) (1980), *The Life of Abdur Rahman, Amir of Afghanistan*. 2 vols. repr. (first ed. 1900) Karachi: Oxford University Press.

Sykes, Percy (1981), *A History of Afghanistan*, repr. New Delhi, Manoharlal Publishers.

Szuppe, Maria (1992), *Entre Timourides, Uzbeks et Safavides*. Paris: Studia Iranica, Cahier 12.

Tanner, H. C. (1881), 'Notes on the Chugani and Neighbouring Tribes of Kafiristan', *RGS Proceedings* 3: 278–301.

Tapper, Richard (1983), 'Introduction', in *The Conflict of Tribe and State in Iran and Afghanistan*, edited by Richard Tapper. New York: St. Martin's Press, pp. 1–82.

Tapper, Richard (1990), 'Anthropologists, Historians, and Tribespeople on Tribe and State Formation in the Middle East', in *Tribes and State Formation in the Middle East*, edited by Ph. S. Khoury and J. Kostiner. Berkeley, Los Angeles: University of California Press, pp. 48–73.

Tate, G. P. (1973), *The Kingdom of Afghanistan*. repr. (first ed. 1911) Karachi: Indus Publications.

Tawakkulī, Aḥmad (1948), *Afghānistān: rawābiṭ-i siyāsī-yi Īrān wa Afghānistān*. Teheran: Chāpkhāna-yi Mihr.

Temple, R. C. (1879), 'Rough Notes on the Distribution of the Afghan Tribes about Kandahar', *JASB* Part 1 No. 3:181–185.

Teufel, F. (1884), 'Quellenstudien zur neueren Geschichte der Chanate', *Zeitschrift der Deutschen Morgenländischen Gesellschaft* 38: 235–381.

Vambéry, Arminius (1864), *Travels in Central Asia*. London: John Murray.

Vambéry, Hermann (1872), *Geschichte Bochara's oder Transoxaniens von den frühesten Zeiten bis auf die Gegenwart*. Stuttgart: J. G. Cotta'sche Buchhandlung.

Vambéry, Hermann (1885), *Das Türkenvolk in seinen ethnologischen und ethnographischen Beziehungen*. Leipzig: F. A. Brockhaus.

Vambéry, Hermann (1983), *Mohammed in Asien: Verbotene Reise nach Buchara und Samarkand 1863–1864*. repr. Stuttgart: K. Thienemanns Verlag.

Vigne, Godfrey Thomas (1982), *A Personal Narrative of a Visit to Ghuzni, Kabul, and Afghanistan*. repr. (first ed. 1840) Lahore: Sang-e-Meel Publications.

Waller, John H. (1990), *Beyond the Khyber Pass*. New York: Random House.

Warburton, Robert (1880), *Report on the District of Lughman, Chiefly in Regard to Revenue*. Simla: Government Central Branch Press.

Warburton, Robert (1900), *Eighteen Years in the Khyber: 1879–1898*. London: John Murray.

Weiers, Michael (1975), 'Die Sprache der Hazara und der Mongolen von Afghanistan in lexikostatistischer Sicht', *Afghanistan J.* 2 (3): 98–102.

Weiers, Michael (1986), 'Die Goldene Horde oder das Khanat Qyptschaq', in *Die Mongolen: Beiträge zu ihrer Geschichte und Kultur*, edited by Michael Weiers. Darmstadt: Wissenschaftliche Buchgesellschaft, pp. 345–378.

Wheeler, Talboys (1979), 'Memorandum on Afghan Turkistan', in *Historical and Political Gazetteer of Afghanistan: Mazar-i Sharif and North Central Afghanistan*, edited by Ludwig Adamec Graz: Akademische Verlags- und Druckanstalt, pp. 18–35.

White-King, L. (1896), 'History and Coinage of the Barakzai Dynasty of Afghanistan', *Numismatic Chronicle* 3rd series,16: 277–344.

Wiebe, D. (1976), 'Die räumliche Gestalt der Altstadt von Kandahar', *Afghanistan J.* 3 (4): 132–146.

Wolfe, Nancy Hatch and Ahmad Ali Kohzad (1965), *An Historical Guide to Kabul*. Kabul: The Afghan Tourist Organization.

Wood, John (1841, 1872), *A Journey to the Source of the River Oxus*. London: John Murray.

Wutt, K. (1978), 'Über Herkunft und kulturelle Merkmale einiger Pashai-Gruppen', *Afghanistan J.*, 5, 2: 43–58.

Wylly, H. C. (1912), *From the Black Mountains to Waziristan*. London: Macmillan and Co.

Yapp, Malcom E. (1962), 'Disturbances in Eastern Afghanistan, 1839–42', *BSOAS* 25 (3): 499–523.

Yapp, Malcolm E. (1963), 'Disturbances in Western Afghanistan, 1839–41', *BSOAS* 26 (2): 288–313.

Yapp, Malcolm E. (1964), 'The Revolutions of 1841–2 in Afghanistan', *BSOAS* 27: 333–381.

Yapp, Malcolm E. (1965), 'Dust Muhammad', in *EI2*.

Yapp, Malcolm E. (1980), *Strategies of British India: Britain, Iran and Afghanistan 1798–1850*. Oxford: Clarendon Press.

Yapp, Malcom E. (1983), 'Tribes and States in the Khyber, 1838–42', in *The Conflict of Tribe and State in Iran and Afghanistan*, edited by Richard Tapper. New York: St. Martin's Press, pp.150–191.

Yate, C. E. (1888b), *Northern Afghanistan, or Letters from the Afghan Boundary Commission*. London: Blackwood.

Yavorski, I. L (1885), *Journey of the Russian Embassy through Afghanistan and the Khanate of Bukhara in 1878–1879*. 2 vols. Calcutta: Superintendent of Government Printing.

Yazdānī, Ḥusain ᶜAlī (n.d.), *Puzhūhishī dar tārīkh-i hazārahā*. Teheran: Mahtāb.

Yazdānī, Ḥusain ᶜAlī (1991), *Ṣaḥnahā-yi khūnīnī az tārīkh-i tashayyuᶜ dar Afghānistān*. Mashhad: Bahrām.

Yule, H. (1872), 'Papers Connected with the Upper Oxus Regions', *JRGS* 42: 438–481.

Zimmermann, Carl (ed.) (1842), *Der Kriegsschauplatz in Innerasien*. Berlin: E. H. Schroeder.

INDEX